WILLIAM HERBERT Earl of
PEMBROOKE &c.

PORTRAIT BY SIR ANTONIO VANDYCK

A HISTORY OF

PEMBROKE COLLEGE
OXFORD

ANCIENTLY BROADGATES HALL

IN WHICH ARE INCORPORATED

SHORT HISTORICAL NOTICES OF THE MORE EMINENT MEMBER
OF THIS HOUSE

BY

DOUGLAS MACLEANE, M.A

SOMETIME FELLOW, LECTURER, AND TUTOR
FORMERLY KING CHARLES THE FIRST'S SCHOLAR; RECTOR OF OXFORD ST.

WITH ILLUSTRATIONS

Oxford
PRINTED FOR THE OXFORD HISTORICAL SOCIETY
AT THE CLARENDON PRESS
1897

'As if there were sought in Knowledge a Couch whereon to rest a
searching and restless spirit; or a Terras, for a wandering and variable
mind to walk up and down with a fair prospect; or a Tower of state, for
a proud mind to raise itself upon; or a Fort or commanding Ground,
for strife and contention; or a Shop, for profit or sale; and not a rich
Storehouse, for the glory of the Creator and the relief of Man's estate.'
(BACON, *Advancement of Learning*.)

ILLUSTRISSIMO DOMINO

ROBERTO MARCHIONI DE SÁRISBURIA

PRAENOBILIS ORDINIS PERISCELIDIS EQUITI

SERENISSIMAE BRITANNIARUM REGINAE CONSILIARIO PRINCIPALI

ACADEMIAE OXONIENSIS CANCELLARIO

COLLEGII PEMBROCHIAE VISITATORI BENIGNISSIMO

HAEC QUALIACUMQUE TEMPORIS PRAETERITI MONUMENTA

CUM PERMISSU

HUMILLIME DEDICAT

AUTHOR

'MAY this the youngest College in England have the happiness of a youngest Child, who commonly have in their Mother's love what they lack in the land of their Father.'

THOMAS FULLER, *in 1662.*

PREFACE.

————•————

IT might be impossible to do for one of the greater foundations what is here attempted for a small College, to bring
together, namely, in a single volume all that is known of its
history, and interweave therewith a kind of *Athenae*, or series
of biographical sketches, of its best remembered sons. The
domestic life of these houses of learning is usually sequestered
and uneventful. It is difficult for the historian of any particular
College 'proprie dicere' even the 'communia' of ancient
observance and picturesque tradition which are shared by
all—those incongruities between ourselves and our surroundings
which are to strangers the attractive charm of Oxford. The
chief interest then of an educational institution must always
lie in the sons whom (to use the old phrase) it has given to
serve God in Church and State. It would indeed be a task
worth doing to show on the one hand how probably every
College is linked to the successive unfolding movements of
thought, literature, and politics by some notable influence
contributed by it to the national life, and on the other hand
how each is representative of a period. Pembroke, one of the
three Stuart Colleges[1], had an old pedigree and considerable
fame before the grant of its charter by James the First, and,
either as Hall or College, records many eminent and honourable names on its roll. Of a succession of great canonists,

————
[1] Wadham 1610, Pembroke 1624, Worcester 1714.

Repyngdon, Bonner, and Story played bold parts in the prelude or drama of the Reformation. Jewell resided and taught here at a critical part of his career. Among the men of letters, of law, and of action in the spacious Tudor times were such as Heywoode, Beaumont, Peele, FitzGeffrey, Dyer, Randolph, and the Carews. Pym and Speaker Rous were leaders in the troubled days that followed. Camden, Corbet, Browne, Collier, exemplify in different ways the Stuart literature. Chief Justice Scroggs recalls the State trials of 'Popish Plot' days. Lord Chancellor Harcourt links us to the wits and tory politicians of 'great Anna's' Augustan age. In the early Georgian period there were almost contemporary at Pembroke the greatest moralist and man of letters, the greatest jurist, and the most famous preacher of the eighteenth century; and of the College days of Johnson and Whitefield, as also of Shenstone and Henderson, interesting records are preserved. Finally, an archbishop has been contributed to each of the primatial sees of Canterbury, York, and Armagh. The difficulty must be to set bounds to the human interest of a College history.

'Omnia pontus erant, deerant quoque littora ponto.'
In some cases, no doubt, the fame of an *alumnus* has to be shared with another College.

If omissions or inaccuracies in so wide a field of history and biography are noticed, the literary, limitations of a Wiltshire village may be a plea for indulgence. The author's task has been made much easier by earlier publications of the Oxford Historical Society, and by Mr. Foster's monumental work. The existence of the *Alumni Oxonienses* has rendered it unnecessary to give in every case dates of degrees and detailed biographical particulars. Other obligations I must be content gratefully to acknowledge without always naming them.

But I may express my especial gratitude to a friend of many years, GEORGE WOOD, Fellow of Pembroke, who has made rather than found time amid tutorial and bursarial duties to revise the proof-sheets of this book, and without whose vigilant help its blemishes would have been many more. I have to thank the Reverend the Master and the Fellows for giving me access to the College muniments, as well as for individual assistance.

I had designed to append a catalogue of Fellows, Scholars, Gentlemen-Commoners, Commoners, and Servitors ; but the addition of four or five thousand names would have so swollen the bulk of the volume that it has been thought undesirable. My rough materials for the purpose, collected chiefly out of the *Alumni Oxonienses*, will be deposited in the College library, as an assistance towards a *Registrum Collegii*, to be compiled, perhaps, by some future generation.

DOUGLAS MACLEANE.

Lent, 1897.

CONTENTS.

———:·———

ILLUSTRATIONS.

ADDENDA.

P. 39. Dr. William Tooker.—For a fuller account of him see Wood, *Ath. Ox.* i. 385, 386. He calls him ' an excellent Grecian and Latinist, an able divine, a person of great gravity and piety, and well read in curious and critical authors.'

P. 40. Minote Hall.—For certain gifts by Robert le Mignot to St. John's Hospital, see Wood MS. D. 11, p. 26. The references *passim* to Wood MS. D. 2 should mention pages, not folios.

P. 108, n. 1. Sir Lewis Stukeley.—It was he who seized and subsequently betrayed Ralegh. See Wood's *Ath. Ox.* i. 371.

P. 129. James Martin.—The *Eidyllia in Obitum fulgentissimi Henrici Walliae Principis duodecimi, Romaeque ruentis terroris maximi* (Oxford, 1612, small quarto, with woodcuts), was edited undoubtedly by James Martin under the name of ' Jacobus Aretius' (Ἄρης, Mars), and almost all of the thirty and more poems —besides the three Idylls in hexameter verse, called 'Amyntas,' 'Tityrus,' and ' Daphnis,' which are presumably by Martin himself—were written by Broadgates Hall men. Mr. Falconer Madan, who kindly draws my attention to this volume, possesses the Editor's copy with his list of authors' names. The Editor and writers, he remarks (*Early Oxford Press*, O. H. S., p. 80), are more disguised than usual. One of the poems is in Chaldee (Hebrew type), one in Syriac, one in Arabic, one in Turkish (these three in Roman type), and a few in Greek. The volume testifies to the learning, and I presume to the Puritan sympathies, of the Lateportenses at the close of the Hall's career. It was in 1612 very full (see page 146).

P. 141. John Milton.—This person is doubtless the same as one John Melton who gave 22s. in the year 1620 towards the enlargement of the dining hall, and who is described in Dr. Clayton's book of contributors as 'generosus, Aulae Lateportensis olim Commensalis.'

P. 238. Sir Peter Pett.—Another accomplished Bachelor of Arts from Cambridge (matr. Sidney Sussex College, 1629) was CHARLES GATACRE (Gataker, Catagree, Categorye, &c.), son of Thomas Gatacre, 'the learned presbyterian.' He took M.A. from Pembroke June 30, 1636. When Lucius Lord Viscount Falkland made his retirement at Great Tew a rural Academe, to which Sheldon, Morley, Hammond, Earle, Chillingworth, and the choicest philosophers and wits of Oxford resorted, Charles Gatacre was one of those in whose converse he took delight. Wood (*Athenae*, i. 501) thinks he was afterwards his chaplain. He became rector of Hoggeston, Bucks, in 1647, and died there November 20, 1680, aged 67. Lord Falkland's second son, Sir Henry Cary, 'so exceeding wild and extravagant that he sold his Father's incomparable Library for a Horse and a Mare,' married Rachel, daughter of the Sir Anthony Hungerford who entered Broadgates Hall in 1623. See page 233.

P. 249, line 25. Rosewell.—This is the date given in Foster. But see page 230. One HENRY ROSEWELL, who entered Broadgates in 1607, was knighted.

P. 271. Bishop Hall.—Mr. Falconer Madan has drawn my attention to two Latin poems in the *Poematum Miscellaneorum Liber Primus* (Lond. 1707, 4°) of Joseph Perkins, headed ' Ad Socios Coll. Pembro. Oxon. qui versus meos flammis mandaverunt.' Perkins, who entered Oriel in 1675, was a navy chaplain, and with difficulty supported a large family by writing flattering elegies and other verses, but was cashiered in 1697 for falsely accusing a naval officer of theft. He styled himself the 'Latin Laureate,' or, by way of exhibiting his Jacobite sympathies, the ' White Poet.' He wrote ' A Poem, in English and Latin, on the death of Thomas Kenn ' (Bristol, 4°, 1711), and was a hanger-on of the nonjurors. As such he would bear no love to the Whig Bishop of Bristol, in which town moreover he tried in vain to obtain preferment. The Bursar, however, and Mr. Joseph E. Barton, Scholar of the College, who have obligingly examined for me Perkins' poems in the Bodleian, have failed to discover the reason for the burning of his verses by the Fellows of Pembroke. The clue might have been looked for in the following portion of one of the two expostulatory epigrams :—

> ' Pieris ausa fuit vastum tentare profundum :
> Et mersa est tumidis syllaba nulla fretis.
> Sed cum Pembrokiae temeraria irrupit in aedes,
> Heu ! *Veneris* facta est victima grata *Viro.*
> O *Cravenne,* tibi flammae cessere furentes :
> Ast elegus diro jam perit igne tuus.
> Franciscum rapuit Pontus, quem jam rapit ignis :
> Conjurant fatum *bina elementa* tuum.'

The elegy, however, 'in obitum nobiliss. consultiss. fortissimique satrapae Gulielmi comitis de Craven ' (1697, 4°) and that on Sir Francis Wheeler (1697) are to all appearance harmless. Perkins ends with threatening literary vengeance on the College, much as College authorities are now threatened with the *Times :*—

> ' Fulmine disjecit scelerati tecta Tyranni
> Jupiter : et vires Musa Parentis habet.'

P. 280, n. 1. Bec Herluin tythes.—The Abbey of Bec in Normandy took its rise from Herlouin, a knight of Brionne, who had retired to this secluded vale. Attracted by his reputation for piety, Lanfranc took the cowl there, and became prior. The Abbey came to possess the Wallingford tythes, which finally were owned by Pembroke College. See page 162.

P. 288. D'Auvergne.—See *Histoire de la Maison D'Auvergne,* by Baluze, fol., 2 vols. (1708).

Pp. 304, 305. Dr. John Smyth, Master.—On his monument in the south aisle of Gloucester Cathedral it is stated that he died (aged 66) at Exeter, and is buried in the cathedral there. There are ascribed to him ' doctrina, morum comitas, religio,' and he is said to have been ' Collegio ob munificentiam carissimus.'

Pp. 341-345. I have seriously understated the number of Johnson's visits to Oxford. Dr. Birkbeck Hill points out to me that he was there in the following years :—1754, 1755, 1759, 1762, 1763, 1764, 1766, 1767, 1768, 1769, 1770, 1773, 1774, 1775 (twice), 1776, 1777, 1781, 1782, 1784 (twice). The incident described on page 343, as recalled by the father of the late Bishop of Chichester, occasions some difficulty, for Dr. Hill shows that Boswell, who left for Scotland on July 1, 1784, and did not return till after Johnson's death, cannot have been at Pembroke in November. Durnford, however, matriculated in October. He may, of course, have been staying with the Master in the preceding June, and it is more likely that he should have met Johnson thus than as an invited freshman.

P. 349. Tom Tyers.—Chalmers (*Biog. Dict.*) says that Johnson was supposed to intend Tyers by the character of Tom Restless in the *Idler*, No. 48.   Tyers died Feb. 1, 1787.

P. 383. Newcome.—There is a portrait of the Archbishop in the Master's Lodgings.

Pp. 384, n. 2, 440. I regret to record the death, since these lines were printed, of Canon Scott-Robertson and of the Rev. Henry Robinson Wadmore.

P. 396, n. 1. Dr. Adams.—A profile portrait of him is carved on his monument in the south aisle of Gloucester Cathedral.   Next to it is the monument of the Rev. THOMAS PARKER, Fellow of Pembroke, Rector of Saintbury St. Nicholas and Vicar of Churcham St. Andrew, who died December 22, 1800, aet. 47.

P. 477, line 3, add, WILLIAM FRANCIS HIGGINS, matr. Jan. 27, 1864, of Turvey House, Beds, High Sheriff of that county in 1872, who was cousin of Charles Longuet Higgins, esquire, one of Dean Burgon's 'Twelve Good Men.'— ALFRED BEAVEN BEAVEN, matr. 1864, Scholar 1865, Head Master of Preston Grammar School, 1874.

P. 504, at the bottom add
Lecturer in Mechanics.
1887. FREDERICK JOHN SMITH, M.A., F.R.S., Millard Lecturer in Trinity College.

P. 505, under *Radcliffe's Travelling Fellow*, add
1715. ROBERT WYNTLE, M.D., Warden of Merton.

ERRATA.

P. 6, line 14, *pro* 'C. Natte's' *lege* 'C. J. Nattes'.'
P. 159, n. 1, *pro* 'Rev. A. C. Bartholomew' *lege* 'Rev. C. W. M. Bartholomew.'
P. 184, lines 20, 21, *pro* 'Tesdales-Thomas' *lege* 'Tesdales—Thomas.'
P. 193, n. 1, after 'in the hands of' insert 'a member of the firm of.'
P. 233, last line but one, *pro* '1625' *lege* '1623.'
P. 235, line 31, *pro* 'Geat' *lege* 'Great.'
P. 265, line 3 from bottom, *pro* 'Ms.' *lege* 'Mr.'
P. 290, lines 9, 10, *pro* 'Sir Linton Symons' *lege* 'Sir John Lintorn Simmons.'
P. 302, n. 1. This note refers to the last line of p. 301.
P. 350, line 19, *pro* 'Taylore' *lege* 'Tayloro.'
P. 408, n. 1, *pro* '1780' *lege* '1769.'

HISTORY OF PEMBROKE COLLEGE.

CHAPTER I.

ORIGINES.

PEMBROKE COLLEGE, Oxford, is so named from that William Herbert, Earl of Pembroke, whom—if Sonnets i-cxxvi. were, as seems most probable, addressed to him—William Shakespeare calls ' Lord of my love,' ' My sun,' ' My all the world,' and ' Time's best jewel.'

' Myself almost despising
Haply I think on thee, and then my state,
Like to the lark at break of day arising
From sullen earth, sings hymns at heaven's gate.
For thy sweet love remember'd such wealth brings
That then I scorn to change my state with kings.'

Before its incorporation as a college it was called Broadgates Hall, a flourishing institution which Anthony Wood[1] and the old antiquaries boldly trace back, as a place of academic learning, to at least the Norman Conquest. In the earlier chapters of this book will be set down what is known of the history of Broadgates Hall. Pembroke College does not merely stand on its site, but carried on its existence unbroken, taking over its buildings—of which the chief one still remains—its principal, its students, and its traditions.

In the twelfth century, if not earlier, Oxford, then ' a huddled group of houses girt in with massive walls,' had for warder at its eastern and

---

[1] Wood had an affection for the metamorphosed old place, where his father was bred. Here he used to practise the violin, exercising ' his natural and insatiable genie he had to musick,' while ' William Boreman, gentleman commoner of Pembroke College, of the Isle of Wight, my companion,' played with skilled hand on the virginal. (See *Life and Times*, ed. Rev. A. Clark, Oxford Historical Society, i. 173.)

B

western gates St. Peter the Apostle, and at its northern and southern entrances St. Michael the Archangel:—

> Invigilat portâ australi boreaeque Michael;
> Exortum solem Petrus regit atque cadentem.

The church of St. Peter-in-the-East still remains, that of St. Peter-le-Bailey has moved a little from the west port, and at the Bokardo entrance to the city the very early tower of St. Michael—half military, half ecclesiastical—is yet standing. But St. Michael's at South Gate was demolished by Wolsey, to make way for his splendid quadrangle. It adjoined [1] on the east side the southern gate of Oxford, which stood about fifty yards lower down than the present entrance to Christ Church. Hutten writes in his *Antiquities of Oxford* (1625) [2] : 'There stood within these few yeares [3] an old auntient Gate of Stone . . . and there on a faier Stone were quartered the Armes of England and France in one Scutchion, the Armes of England being graven in the former and upper place and those of France in the nether, contrarie to all that I heretofore have seene. . . . On the left standeth the old and auntient Hall Broadgates, now weary of it's former name and stiled by the title of Pembroke Colledge by King James.' The south side of Pembroke College stands actually on the twelfth-century town wall. Before this wall was built, the city was protected by a *vallum* of earth, dating probably [4] from the early part of the tenth century, topped with wooden brattishes and palisading. The Castle Mount is an imposing relic of it. The ground on which the College stands is a good deal higher than Brewers Street, at the end of which, till 1834, St. Aldate's Street made a steep dip, suggesting that the original rampart coincided at this part of the city with the present mediæval wall. Probably there were always dwelling-houses between the wall and St. Aldate's churchyard.

In the angle of that churchyard there was in the middle of the thirteenth century a 'great house,' held in demesne of the priory across the road by Richard Segrym. Richard is the best-known member of a family which had been prominent in Oxford, probably before the Conquest. The name occurs thrice in the Oxford Domesday (A.D. 1086), 'Segrim' holding a mansion assessed for geld at 16*d.*, 'another Segrim' one which paid 2*s.*, and 'Segrim' 'three houses free,' paying 5*s.* 4*d.*, whereof one was waste and paid no geld. Of

---

[1] See Wood's *City of Oxford*, ed. Clark, Oxford Historical Society, i. 164, n. 5.
[2] *Elizabethan Oxford*, ed. Plummer, Oxford Historical Society, pp. 86, 89.
[3] 'In man's memory,' Wood's *City* (composed 1661-6), i. 250. It is seen in Speed's map (1610) and in Hollar's (1643); but the latter reproduces Agas.
[4] Parker, *Early History of Oxford* (Oxford Historical Society), p. 116.

721 houses then existing, 478 were waste. Of the remaining 243 only thirteen paid as much as 2*s.*, and only three as much as the half of 5*s.* 4*d.* Two of the third Segrim's houses paid this sum between them, and must therefore have been, together, the most important tenement in Oxford. They adjoined the town wall, for a ' free ' was the same as a ' mural ' house, being so called as exempted from payment of its geld on condition of the tenant keeping the wall in repair [1]. It is possible therefore that they were identical with Richard Segrym's *magna domus* [2] in the angle of St. Aldate's churchyard. Quite apart from à Wood's identification of the Segrym house with the present Pembroke College, it seems certain that one of the southern angles is meant, since there can never have been room on the north of the churchyard for a large tenement; and if so the house was near the town wall.

---

[1] Such repair consisted, before the days of solid masonry, in looking to and clearing the vallum and ditch and mending the palisade. Ibid. p. 237.

[2] There were other Segrym possessions in different parts of the town. Richard Cutrich, c. 1220-30, cries quits to Richard Segrym of all right in a property in ' Cattestrete ' (St. Frid. Charter 415, Wigram), reserving to the Lady Cristina Kepharm a rent of two shillings, and to himself and his heirs a halfpenny; for which grant Richard gave him four marks ' in Gersumam.' Richard bestowed it on the Priory, Eva, relict of Richard Cutrich, quit-claiming, c. 1250-60 (Ch. 417). Another tenement sold him by Cutrich, with a 5*s.* rent paid him by John Pady for a barber's shop and two selds in All Saints, and a messuage almost opposite All Saints Church, were given by Segrym to the canons as late as c. 1260-70 (Ch. 394), they admitting him as a brother, &c., and agreeing to perform service for him on his obit as for a canon professed and to mark his name in their martilogium. Land in ' Southbrygestrete ' outside the walls is conveyed to him, c. 1240-50, by Beatrice, daughter of Helye Winter (Ch. 229); and he, c. 1250-60, confirms the sale of the rent (3*s.* 6*d.*) by his brother Henry to the Priory (Ch. 231, 232). It is styled ' Domus Care Hospitalis S. Johannis,' and ' Domus quondam Sarte.' The Priory granted to the same Henry, c. 1250, for 6*d.* rent, the land which his father had held in St. Aldate's, and he the same year gave up all right in the land of Isward, held of the Priory by Isaac the Jew, in St. Aldate's (Ch. 291, 292). About 1230 Richard Segrym gave to St. Frideswyde's 16*d.* rent from land formerly held of him by John Halegod ' in Shidezerdestrete, ubi sunt scole legum ' (Ridehall, ' nunc Regis bedelli ' in margin), 6*d.* from a house held by the same J. H. opposite ' the gate of our Lord the King ' in St. Mary Magd. parish; 18*d.* rent and 6*d.* rent in the parish of St. Peter-in-the-East, in consideration of a rose to be paid him every St. Margaret's day (Ch. 430). He sold also for 8*s.* a rent of 12*d.* from land adjoining ' Maydenehall ' on the east (Ch. 525). This was for the Infirmary. A little later he conveyed to the Prior and Convent 5*s.* rent ' de domo I. Crompe, id est Blakehalle ' in St. Mary the Virgin's (Ch. 438), and c. 1250-1260 he gave for the office of the Chantry a 6*d.* rent in St. Edward's (Ch. 180). Another gift was of a 12*s.* 4*d.* rent in St. Aldate's inside the walls, and a 4*s.* 6*d.* rent ' in suburbio,' with three messuages (Ch. 290), Nov. 25, 1254. In 1270-71 mention is made of ' a corner seld towards the south ' in the parish of All Hallows, leased to Matilda Penny of Binsey, ' which was once Master Richard Segrim's ' (Ch. 395). Alice Segrym gave to St. John's Hospital a rent of 2*s.* from a house in St. John's Street (Wood MS. D, 2, fol. 213).

About the year 1254, then, Richard Segrym completed a series of
gifts to the prior and convent of St. Frideswyde by surrendering under
a charter of quit-claim, in perpetual alms, all that great messuage
situated in the angle of the churchyard—probably the family residence—which was sometime held by him *in dominico* of the canons,
they paying him every Christmas one halfpenny for all service, &c.
The charter recites that they receive him into their familiar fraternity,
and will, from the time of his decease, find a chaplain canon to
celebrate divine service for his soul, the souls of his parents, the soul
of Christiana Pady, and the souls of all the faithful departed, for ever.
Adam Feteplace, mayor of Oxford (1245, 1253–60), and others attest it.

Sciant presentes et futuri quod Ego Ricardus filius Ricardi Segrim
dedi concessi et quietum clamavi pro salute anime mee et animarum
omnium antecessorum et successorum meorum Deo et Ecclesiae sancte
Frid' Oxon' et Canonicis ibidem Deo servientibus illud messuagium
magnum cum omnibus pert. suis in perpetuam elemosinam quod situm
est in angulo cimiterij S. Aldati Oxon' quod de dictis Canonicis aliquando
tenui Habendum et tenendum predictum messuagium de me et heredibus
meis predictis Canonicis et successoribus suis et Ecclesie sue predicte
Reddendo inde annuatim michi et heredibus meis j obolum ad Natale
Domini pro omni servicio seculari exaccione et demanda michi et heredibus meis pertinente Et ego Ricardus Segrim et heredes mei predictum
messuagium cum pert. predicto Pr. et Can. etc contra omnes homines
Christianos et Judeos warantizabimus et defendemus imperpetuum Dicti
quoque Canonici divine pietatis intuitu pro se et successoribus suis rece-
perunt me in eorum fraternitatem familiarem in pleno Capitulo suo
unanimiter in omnibus bonis spiritualibus que in eorum Monasterio fient
imperpetuum Insuper concesserunt michi quod a tempore mortis mee
invenient j Capellanum Canonicum celebrantem specialiter divina pro
anima mea et pro animabus patris et matris mee et pro anima Xpiane
Pady et omnium fidelium defunctorum imperpetuum Et ut hec mea
donacio concessio et quieta clamacio rata imperpetuum permaneant huic
scripto sigillum meum apposui Hijs testibus Ada Feteplace tunc Majore
Oxon' et alijs [1].

In the margin of the older or Corpus Christi Cartulary is written
' De magna domo Segrim que est in dominico.' On Nov. 25, 1254,
the final concord was made of divers gifts from Richard Segrym to
the priory [2]. One of them was a rent of four shillings paid him by
Thomas de Slanfand (or Clanefend) for a tenement held of him ' in
St. Aldate's Churchyard,' for which Richard had been accustomed to

[1] Charter 288 in the St. Frideswyde Cartulary (ed. Wigram, Oxford Historical Society).
[2] Charters 289, 290.

pay the canons sixpence yearly. It was afterwards held by Matilda le Veisy or her son Thomas.

The latter gift is not clearly localized. Probably the house stood at the east end of the church, where till living memory ancient tenements remained. But the 'great house' of Segrim 'in the angle of the churchyard' is positively identified by Anthony à Wood with Broadgates Hall, now Pembroke College. 'From the said Segryms the said large tenement was called Segrym Hall, it being inhabited by Clerks in the time of the said Mr. Richard Segrym, if not before: which place... came to be called Broadgates, alias Segrym (corruptly afterward Segreve) Hall [1].' It is put very explicitly in à Wood's short treatise on Broadgates Hall inserted in his *City of Oxford* [2]; and again, under St. Aldate's Church, 'an ancient hostle or hall called in severall ages Segrim, Segrave, and Broadgates [3].' Ayliffe [4] follows Wood.

On the other hand, Wood makes another statement, at first sight inconsistent with this. Under South-west Ward he writes: 'Adjoyning South Gate were the tenements of the Segrims, burgesses of Oxon at and divers years after the Norman Conquest, and held "in dominico," as it should seem, of the Cannons of S. Frideswyde. Afterwards or about those times they were converted into hostels for people of a scholastick and religious conversation. Which continuing for that use till the decay of discipline and doctrine in our University, came to be the possession of the servants and retainers to the said Priory. At length Thomas Wolsey, that heroick and publick-spirited Cardinall, when he converted the said Priory into a College, turned also these tenements into an Hospitall . . . Behind Christ Church Hospitall before mentioned was somtimes that venerable peice of antiquity standing called Broadgates Hall, which with other halls adjoyning hath risen from that estate to a college called Pembroke College [5].' The Wolsey Hospital or Almshouse was never part of Broadgates Hall, though it is now a possession of Pembroke College. They were separated by two small properties belonging the one to Abingdon Abbey and the other to New College. Wood in a note refers to charters 71, 73, 82, and 83 [6], by which it appears that he is referring to several Segrim properties close to St. Aldate's Church, viz. Richard's 'magna domus,' his house 'in the churchyard' rented by Slanfand,

[1] Gutch's 'Wood's *Annals*,' iii. 614.

[2] *City of Oxford*, ed. Clark, i. 563 (Oxford Historical Society).   [3] Ibid. ii. 35.

[4] 'Antient and Present State of the University of Oxford' (1714).

[5] *City*, i. 193, 194.   [6] In Wigram, Nos. 262, 265, 288, and 289.

and land belonging to Segrim son of Robert, or Robilet, next a solar and cellar which were 'hard by the church,' ' in the angle, at the entry of St. Aldate's churchyard,' and which had on the south (' towards the royal way,' i. e. the way just inside the city wall) another solar[1]. I take à Wood to mean that, the 'magna domus Segrim' being represented by Broadgates Hall, the Almshouse is on the site of Richard Segrim's house 'in the churchyard' and of the house of Segrim Robertson, or of the latter only. The churchyard, there is reason to think, was once larger than it is now and may have included part of the Almshouse site, which formerly projected more to the north, almost touching the dwellings pulled down in 1834. The house at the south-east corner, within two yards of the Almshouse, is depicted in Turner's water-colour in the National Gallery, and (as seen through Tom gateway) in C. Natte's drawings, 1804. Mr. Clark marks the Almshouse site as ' Segrim's Houses.' It would seem, however, from the St. Frideswyde Cartulary that somewhere in this corner is the locality of a messuage in St. Aldate's parish demised by the Priory,

---

[1] The solar belonged to a certain Renewant, and was originally one with the solar and cellar. The latter was granted, c. 1210-20, by Henry, son of Simeon, to Warine the smith, son of Payne, the carrier of Abingdon, at a rent of 4*s.* (Charter 262). Warine soon after gave his interest to the Canons (Ch. 263); but, c. 1240-50, John Pilet gave them a rent of 8*d.* arising out of this tenement (Ch. 440). The Prior and Convent, before 1228, demised it to Henry Virun—from whom it was subsequently named—for a rent of 13*s.* 4*d.* (one silver mark), and a consideration (Ch. 264). He let it, c. 1230-40, to William Dodeman, at a rent of 10*s.*, William and his heirs to receive the water coming from the aforesaid solar (Ch. 265). At a later date it was held by Ralph le Plomer. On one side of this property was the land of Robert Chacchefravis (out of which he gave a rent of 2*s.* to St. John's Hospital), and beyond that William Lowedin's land. Next also to Robert Chachefrais' house was Walter Patyn's 'close to the churchyard '; and beyond that John de Marisco's. All these were in St. Aldate's parish (Wood, MS. D. 2, foll. 166-7). On a third side of the Virun cellar and solar Reginald the baker lived (Charter 262). It is not easy to group these properties, so as to give to each access to the street. The fixed points are the ' Via regia ' and ' the angle of the churchyard at the entry.' The rubric of Charter 262 speaks of a ' domus angularis' connected with the ' Viron & Rennenant' tenement. There may have been an entry to the churchyard at the north-east corner, but it is quite impossible to locate these properties on the north side of the church. Walter Patyn's house, hard by the churchyard, is scarcely any clue to the others. Agnes, his relict, and Joan, his daughter, granted it to Walter Haringer, who gave it to the Master and Brethren of St. John's Hospital, they paying 6*d.* yearly to the heirs of Walter Patyn, and on behalf of those heirs 16*d.* to the lord in chief, and 2*d.* to the church of St. Aldate. He also gave another messuage, once Peter the Turner's, in St. Ebbe's parish, whence the Hospital was to pay 2*s.* yearly to Benedict Kepeharme's heirs, and for him and his heirs 2*s.* to St. Abba's church, so vizt. that if the same Walter de Haringe should return safe from his pilgrimage to Jerusalem, having taken the cross, the aforesaid messuages should return to him 'soluta et quieta' for his life, and after his death should remain with the Brethren, they doing

c. 1215-25, to Henry Juvenis—who gave his name to Vine Hall—
and described as being ' at the corner as you go from our churchyard
towards St. Aldate's church on the left near the highway [1].' I take it, at
any rate, that Richard Segrym's messuage was in the south-west angle [2],

the aforesaid service to the capital lords. He also gave other lands to the Hospital
' sub sigillo viridi cum cruce.' This was in the mayoralty of Peter Torald, who
witnessed (Wood, MS. D. 2, foll. 166, 167).

It may have been thus :—

[Beef Hall Lane.]

Peter Turner ?	Marisco	Patyn [Minote]	Lowedin	Churchyard
			Cachefrais	
				Rich. Segrim

Parish boundary.

| | Reginald the baker | Virun [Broad gates] | son of Robert Segrim | Richard Segrim [Almshouse] |
| | | Renewant | | |

Via Regia.

The town wall.

In which case it was out of the son of Robert Segrym's rather than out of Richard
Segrym's house that Broadgates Hall grew. The site where I have placed Patyn's
house in the plan is described later as ' juxta cimiterium,' and belonged to St. John's
Hospital ; but was not this through Robert Mignot's gift? See page 39.

[1] Charter 269 in Mr. Wigram's edition of the Cartulary. Charter 270 is the
demise to John de Weston, about the same date, of a messuage in St. Aldate's parish
' at the corner as you go from our churchyard towards South Gate on the left.'
St. Aldate's parish is bounded by St. Aldate's Street. Wood (MS. D. 2, fol. 165)
gives a charter of quitclaim whereby Martin de Chacombe gave up to St. John's
Hospital his right in the tenement situate in St. Aldate's parish hard by the churchyard, ' virt. in the corner as you go from the said church to the hall called le
Bollehall.' It is beyond doubt that Bole Hall was to the north or north-east of
the church. In 1302 Warin Davidson gives up his right in the same. About 1240
Richard Segrym gave the Priory a tenement, rented at 4s., ' in suburbio' outside
South Gate beneath the wall, towards the Friars Minors (Charter 219). This
would be in the present Brewers Street. Walter de Oseney was afterwards the
tenant. In the map at the end of Mr. Wigram's *Cartulary* some other properties
have been localized to the south of St. Aldate's churchyard ; but dubiously.

[2] ' In angulo,' not ' in cornerio.' Since, at any rate, the fifteenth century there
has been a very large building at the south-east corner. But everything points to
the other corner. Wood had doubtless something to go upon. For ' Segrave

the site afterwards of Broadgates Hall. It was valued in 1278 at 20s.[1]

It is likely enough that when this came to be a possession of the canons of St. Frideswyde they should have made it a hostel for students. A house given them by Richard Segrym in Schidyerd Street (a rose being the rent) is found in 1278 inhabited by clerks, as Ride or Bedell Hall. To this purpose most of the conventual properties round St. Aldate's were put. Wood, however, is more or less guessing[2] when he says of the 'magna domus' that 'this hall of Broadgate was *alwaies* and while it was termed Segrim Hall possessed by schollers[3];' 'it was inhabited by Clerks in the time of the said Mr. Richard Segrim, if not before[4];' and his reasons for supposing that it 'was a place before (and perhaps after) the Norman Conquest wherein the Novices of that Priory received their first or juvenile learning[5]' are not very convincing. 'Their register, wrot in the beginning of Edward I [1272], tells us that it did of old belong to their priory and that they had time out of mind and not to be found in record a certaine quitt rent thence; which expressions, togeather with that note inserted in St. Aldate's Church making that Church to be a monastery, hath alwaies given me to suppose that it was a religious place, and where they formerly nursed up their novices[6]'. But, as a note in Gutch's edition of the *Annals* points out, 'monastery was the Saxon word for a church.' 'The word minster,' writes Mr. Parker[7], 'is often used simply in the sense of a church with a priest or priests attached.' But à Wood seizes on the name in order to build up a theory of a community of students, prepared here as in a cloister for both (he says elsewhere[8]) 'S. Frid. and *Abendon* Monasteries.' Abingdon is added on the authority of Twyne:—

'Quamobrem monasterium diceretur (nisi forte quod novitiis Abendoni-

Hall' he refers to Twyne, xxii. 254, and Charter 9 (?). See also Wood's *Life and Times*, ed. Clark, Oxford Historical Society, iv. 309, for 'Segrym Hall.'

[1] 'Itm Prior et Convent. Sce Fredeswið tenet unū ten' cū ptin q' eis dedit Ric. Segrym in ppetā. elem. sin' aliquo redditu & valz xls. p. ann.' (*Hundred Rolls*, p. 788).

[2] Mr. James Parker, M.A., writes to me: 'Wood, Ayliffe, &c., held briefs for the antiquity of the University, and every straw was seized. And, because a building was a Hall for students in the fifteenth century, therefore what was on its site was a Hall for students in the eleventh.'

[3] *City*, i. 565.　　　　[4] Gutch, iii. 614.　　　　[5] Ibid.

[6] *City*, i. 563. 'In Scripts, written in the time of King Henry I, stiled a Monastery,' Gutch, iii. 614. See the Abingdon Chronicle (Rolls Series), vol. ii. p. 174.

[7] *Early History of Oxford*, Oxford Historical Society, p. 292, n.

[8] Peshall, p. 145. At Wood's *City* (ed. Clark, Oxford Historical Society), ii. 35, n. 2, Twyne is quoted for excluding the Abingdon novices.

ensis coenobii monachis illic in academia recipiendis instituendisque de more inserviret) haud in promptu esse opinor [1].'

The two Houses presented a parson to St. Aldate's by turns. Considering the immemorial antiquity of some of our cathedral schools, there is no impossibility in Wood's theory.

Something more should be said of Richard Segrym. His name is of constant occurrence in the charters. He had a brother Henry [2], their father Richard [3], a burgher of Oxford, holding land of the Priory in St. Aldate's parish, afterwards conveyed by the canons to Henry. Richard the elder deceased before 1230 [4], and may be the same as a Segrym the Weaver mentioned c. 1220–30. His father was probably Henry Fitzsegrym, provost with John Kepeharme before 1154, and also with William Wakeman in Ralph Pady's time [5]. The Henry whose name appears as witness in 1194 may be the grandson. The next ascending progenitor is said by à Wood to have been Segrim a clerk, called Segrim the Deacon, who was living in 1138. But 'Segrimus a clerk' held land in Oxford about 1180. The former is identified by Wood with Segrim son of Robert, or Robelot, who lived near the entry of St. Aldate's churchyard [6]. But Robert's son was alive c. 1210–20. We also find an 'Alice, daughter of Segrim,' who had a son Gilbert [7]; Segrim Bywall (*juxta murum* [8]), 1129, whose house near the north gate was granted to Oseney Abbey at its foundation, the confirmation of the charter of which he witnessed with Robert and Nigell D'Oilly and Robert Bishop of Lincoln [9]; and one Peter Segrym of Yechslep (Islip), who at the Eyre of 1285 was, with thirty-seven others, presented by the jury for illegal fishing 'with Kydell and Starkell' (the former a kind of faggot). The offenders, who included the two abbots and the preceptor of Cowley, were all fined [10].

It may be asked, who was Christiana Pady, for whose soul Richard Segrym stipulated that the canons should say mass for ever? Her father, Ralph Pady [11], a burgher, had a mill in St. Edward's parish before

[1] Quoted by Bishop Tanner, *Notitia Monastica* (ed. 1744), p. 419. Dr. Ingram follows neither the Chronicle itself nor à Wood in saying that Segrym's 'distinguished mansion,' 'together with St. Aldate's Church adjoining,' is described as *monasterium*. The document says nothing about Segrym's mansion.

[2] Charters 231, 291, 292.

[3] In the Christ Church Cartulary, charter 525 (Wigram), the name appears as Roger.

[4] Charter 430.   [5] Wood MS. D. 2, foll. 367, 400.   [6] Charters 262, 263.

[7] Wood MS. D. 2, fol. 213.   [8] Parker's *Early History*, p. 274.

[9] *City*, ii. 188, 192. He had other properties.

[10] Rogers' *City Documents*, Oxford Historical Society, p. 209.

[11] Charters 162, 377. There is evidently a mistake in the date assigned to charter 117. See also Wood's *City*, ii. 174.

1180–90. With Henry son of Segrym, then provost, ' Gaufrid Padi,' Roger Brodege (or Brodgate) and others [1], c. 1170, he witnessed a grant to Oseney Abbey. With John Kepeharme he was a witness c. 1181. Christina's uncle John left her some property. His son, her cousin John, was Mayor 1227–9 and 1234, living in a house in St. Frideswyde's parish, called from him Pady House, but afterwards Ledenporch Hall, for which in 1480 the nuns of Godstow, who held it in 1192, were paying the old rent of 4s. [2] He was alive in 1262. The Lady Christina we find at the close of the twelfth century wedded to Laurence Kepeharme, who with her consent gave to Oseney Abbey some land in St. Michael's at North Gate [3], the same, probably, as the ' Segrim land' described in an Oseney rental of 1260. He died before 1228. She next was married to Jordan Rufus, Ruffy, Rasus, or le Rus [4]. On April 28, 1241, she, with her husband Jordan's assent, gave to the Priory one messuage and four selds, together with her body, which she had devoted to be buried among the canons, they agreeing that at her obit and anniversary they will do for her in the service for the dead as for a canon professed, and cause her name to be marked in the martilogium. A little later she is again a widow, and confirms to the Priory (circa 1241–50) all the lands which Jordan, her sometime husband, had with her assent demised to them, viz. those which her previous husband Laurence Kepeharme had bequeathed to the Priory, with a life-interest retained for herself [5], and also her corner messuage in All Saints'. In return the canons assign her the house in which she lives in the parish of St. Frideswyde and the full corrody daily of a canon and six silver marks yearly all her life. Before this, about 1228, Jordan and she had exchanged two properties with the Priory against certain rents [6]. Before Jordan's death, Richard Segrym had cried quits to the Priory of all his right and claim in the All Saints' messuage given them by Christina, relict of Laurence Kepeharme. One John Pady paid him (c. 1260–70) 5s. rent for several properties in All Saints' parish. In other documents his name is mixed up with Christiana's.

---

[1] Wood MS. D. 2, fol. 367. See also Charter 865.

[2] Charters 115 and 13 App.; *City*, ii. 60. Philip Pady owned the Mitre Inn temp. Henry III (*City*, i. 79). A later John Pady was provost in 1326 (Wood MS. D. 2, fol. 368). [3] Ibid. fol. 370.

[4] Mentioned in the Oseney Cartulary; Twyne, xxiii. 84.

[5] One of these was the ' domus Christinae,' afterwards Grip, Gup, or Gulp, otherwise Leberd, Hall (Charter 102; *City*, i. 169), in Richard the Second's time ' vacua placea.' Another (given, Wood says however, in the *beginning* of Henry III) was Parn Hall, afterwards Tabard, Furres, and Bear Inn, now Mr. Foster's shop in the High Street.

[6] Charter 116.

I cannot find evidence that they were akin to one another. Is it fanciful to suppose that this was a very true and faithful friend, and one who would fain once have been more than friend? The Segryms and Kepeharmes were for centuries the two leading burgher families of St. Aldate's parish, and doubtless, whether as friends or enemies, kept up a rivalry of state and dignity, the Kepeharmes having their mansion on the north[1], the Segryms on the south, of the church. Certainly they vied in their gifts to Holy Church. In Stephen's reign (1135–1154) a Kepeharme and a Segrym were aldermen or provosts of a hundred together. Laurence Kepeharme who wedded Christiana Pady, and Richard Segrym who procured her to be prayed for, were about of an age and brought into intimate connexion, witnessing deeds together more than once. Were one weaving an old tale out of guesses, it might be surmised the one had been the successful, the other the unsuccessful suitor. Christiana was buried in the priory church about 1250[2]. Richard also had an obit there[3].

[1] Benedict father of another Laurence (c. 1220–30) granted to St. Frideswyde's 'totam curiam illam que est retro domum que fuit Chiere Judee in venella (que vocatur Kepeharm Lane) que est ante domum meam.' Kepeharme Lane or Twychen seems to have been the now obscured continuation of the yard of the New Inn. Wood says it ended in Pennyfarthing (now Pembroke) Street.

[2] Wood, *City*, ii. 173. [3] Ibid. ii. 61.

NOTE ON KEPEHARME AND RUFUS.

It is not easy to make out any circumstances relating to Christiana Pady's second husband Jordan Ruffy. He was provost with Peter son of Torald in John Pady's mayoralty (Wood MS. D. 2, foll. 199, 222, 223). There are a number of persons called Rufus or le Rus or Rubeus (Redhead), as Hugh (c. 1220–30 ; another tenanted Culverd Hall, 1275), son of Stephen ; Adam son of Hugh ; Roger a fuller (c. 1210–28), William de Burgesete (c. 1220–30) ; Laurence (c. 1247), provost with Robert Minhot or Mingnote, of whom hereafter (Wood MS. D. 2, foll. 196, 214, 375),—these two witnessed an agreement in Peter Torald's mayoralty, between Richard of Dorchester and Richard son of Richard Segrym, about Elias Winter's land in 'Suthbriggestreete' (fol. 161) ;—Albert (c. 1250–60) ; Adela (c. 1260–70). A Master Adam Rufus studied under Grostête, who addressed to him, before 1210, a treatise on the nature of angels, desiring him to inquire diligently the opinions of the wise with whom he may converse. Grostête mentions him, about 1237, as ' Friar Adam Rufus of good memory,' formerly his beloved pupil and friend (*Grey Friars in Oxford*, ed. Little, Oxford Historical Society, p. 179). He is mentioned c. 1215 at Wood MS. D. 2, fol. 517. Another Franciscan, a Lector, was Richard Rufus, or le Ruys, of Cornwall, who commented on the Sentences, and was a Master, probably of Arts (ibid. fol. 142), and also B.D. He went from Oxford to Paris in 1253 to lecture, and on his return was regent-master of the Friars. Adam Marsh praised him highly, but Roger Bacon denounced in the most unsparing terms the evil influence of the erroneous subtleties which 'Ricardus Cornubiensis, famosissimus apud stultam multitudinem' had made popular. Simon le Rous was juror of Wolvercote in 1301 (*City Documents*, ed. Rogers, p. 160).

There is nothing unusual in Richard Segrym styling Christiana by her maiden name, though twice a widow. George Heriot's wife, *ex. gr.*, in 1612, had on her grave in St. Gregory's, 'Hic Alicia Primrose jacet,' though she is also called Heriot in the inscription.

Wood says of the Kepeharmes: 'People they were in their times of great repute and wealth, and bore the cheife office of magistracy of this corporation for divers yeares' (*City*, i. 199). The following stemma can be made out.

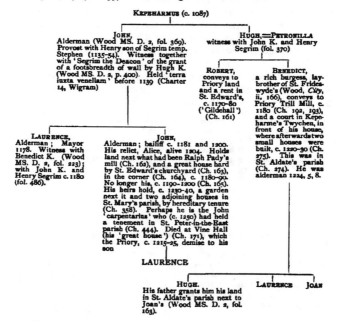

Wood gives Benedict as Laurence's father, but in a note (*City*, i. 200) says, on the evidence of Charter 171, that he was the son of John. No doubt John's son had not only an uncle but a second cousin of his name. The Laurence who married Christiana Pady deceased before 1230. But we find a Laurence Kepeharme witnessing the grant of Hart Hall to the prioress of Studley at Michaelmas 1267. (See *Registrum Collegii Exoniensis*, ed. Boase, O. H. S. p. 284).

There was a Robert (son of John), one of the jurors of St. Aldate's in 1297 (*City Documents*, ed. Rogers, Oxford Historical Society, p. 151), who had a tenement outside East Gate in 1295 (Wood MS. D. 2, fol. 367),—the name occurs a hundred years later in several deeds,—and John his son, of whom Aaron and Vives the Jews held in 1279 (*Collect.* ii. 305); alive 1318. Also a second Hugh and Petronilla. Wood certainly confuses the two couples, for he says of the earlier Petronill (*City*, i. 199) that she gave St. Frideswyde's a messuage which she had from Roger Pilet in St. Mildred's parish, whereas the grant is dated 35 Henry III (1250-1, Charter 622; see Wood MS. D. 2, fol. 527). From a Charter (621) dated c. 1240-50 it appears her husband was then dead. One John Kepeharme is described as her heir A.D. 1319 (Ch. 625; see also 194). There was a John who helped witness the conveyance of Hart Hall in 1267, together with William Kepeharme, a burgher, to whom were leased, c. 1255-60, two messuages in St. Aldate's, between the land of Roger the Spicer on the south and that of Keyna daughter of Mosse, the Jewess, on the north. He had a wife Joan, daughter of Henry Perle, and issue (Ch. 293). Of the same date also are Walter, and Robert who married Sibyll. These Kepeharmes were 'all for the most part wealthy burgesses. Whome to enumerate with their pious gifts to the Church would now perhaps seem taedious' (Wood, *City*, i. 200). Wood traces the fortunes of their house, from them called Kepeharme Hall, and of 'tenementum Kepeharme, Henxsey Hall in le Fish Street in parochia S. Aldati,' frequented afterwards by Welsh legists. It stood really in Kepeharme Lane, which was also called Hinxsey Lane, and next it in the same lane was Gloucester Hall, to the east. There was also a Kepeharme Hall for scholars next the old 'Angel' (*City*, i. 130). As for Christiana Pady's first husband, if there is no mistake in the date of Charter 102 (Wigram), Leberd or Grip Hall was conveyed to him as early as c. 1170-80. Wood however says that Laurence when a boy was 'in the year 1180, or about then, perhaps soon afterwards,' about the time that the saint's reliques were translated, miraculously restored to life at the shrine of St. Frideswyde's, after being cut by a clumsy chirurgeon for the stone (*City*, ii. 166). The name frequently occurs in the charters. Laurence and 'Xpina' convey, c. 1200-10, to Simon Rok two selds in All Saints' parish hard by St. Edward's Lane (Ch. 372). Henry Bodyn, c. 1220, conveys to Laurence, for a pound of cummin yearly, a strip of land in All Saints', next the house of Richard the man of God, the light before whose windows is not to be disturbed or minished. Laurence was to give his wife, the lady Gunnore, three ells of burnet for a cloak (Ch. 384, 385). This and divers properties in the Jewry in St. Aldate's (Ch. 261) he bequeathed to the Priory. About 1220 John of Bletchingdon ratifies the gift by Laurence of four properties in St. Mildred's, and several in St. Aldate's and St. Michael's Southgate, including the Synagogue, once Sagar Poy's. We find him (c. 1210-20) confirming to Ralph the Miller (Ralph Pady?) a conveyance of land in St. Frideswyde's parish (Ch. 110). About 1280-90 John Sowy the Goldsmith quit-claims to the Priory of all right in the properties within and without the town 'which once belonged to Laurence Kepharm.' Laurence held also of the Priory land in St. Michael's Northgate (Ch. 469), before 1190-1200. Together with his father, John Kepeharme, and Henry son of Segrym, he witnessed in 1194 the gift by Hugh de Malannay to St. John's Hospital of lands received by Hugh from John Earl of Mortain (King John). See also Charter 728.

CHAPTER II.

LEGISTS—ST. ALDATE'S CHURCH.

FROM a very early period a number of hostels for students of law, owned for the most part by religious houses, were clustered round St. Aldate's Church. The principal of these, whether called Segrym's or Broadgates Hall, was an appendage of St. Frideswyde's Priory, the original cradle of the University of Oxford. Founded as a nunnery in the eighth century, 'St. Frids' was broken up in the Danish wars, and the buildings, after some vicissitudes of occupation by regulars and seculars (the latter described by William of Malmesbury as 'clerks'), were assigned in Henry I's reign to a priory of Austin Canons ('canonists' Huber[1] calls them) placed there by Roger Bishop of Sarum. Hutten says that the place had been given by the Conqueror to the Abingdon monks, but they, perceiving it to be ruinous, gave it to Roger. In these quiet cloisters and those of Oseney Abbey, founded as an offshoot of St. Frideswyde's in 1129, we shall find the earliest Oxford schools, though neither house, Mr. Lyte remarks, ever attained great celebrity as a place of education. Here Thibaut d'Estampes taught 'secular studies' about 1118, and in 1133 Robert Pullein came from Paris and lectured in the Holy Scriptures. Another Biblical scholar was Robert of Cricklade, Prior of St. Frideswyde's. But arts and theology had a powerful rival at hand. The tradition of the famous law schools of Rome, Constantinople, and Berytus had never quite disappeared[2], and was now to be quickened into new life by an accident and by the needs of an age in

---

[1] Huber supposes they were clerks united again after the storms of the Conquest for fresh scholastic activity; and he asks, was this a regular college even before A.D. 1111?

[2] In 804 a school at York is described by Alcuin, where instruction was given not only in grammar and rhetoric, but also in law. A century earlier St. Bonitus of Auvergne is said to have been 'grammaticorum imbutus initiis, necnon Theodosii edoctus decretis.' Lanfranc, born at Pavia A.D. 1089, is described as 'ab annis puerilibus eruditus in scholis liberalium artium et legum secularium ad suae morem patriae.'

which the priesthood was no longer the only profession needing special training, and the knowledge of law, kept alive in dark ages by the clergy, was henceforth to have separate students and professors. About the year 1135 the Justinian Pandects were discovered at Amalfi. In 1149 a master from Lombardy, Vacarius, came with other civilians and a library of law books to decide the controversies between Archbishop Theobald and Bishop Henry de Blois, the pope's legate, into whose place Theobald had been put through the influence of Beket, himself a student of law at Bologna. Arriving in Oxford Vacarius introduced the study of Roman jurisprudence to crowded lecture rooms. King Stephen, jealous of Italian influences and of the supplanting of the ancient customs of Church and Realm by a foreign code, silenced him and forbade the possession of books on civil law. At Paris also it was suppressed. But the new learning was spreading rapidly over Europe, and having crossed the narrow seas was not easily expelled. In days when clerks everywhere formed one great guild, and when though there were no conveniences there was much hunger for learning, ideas ran from land to land like wildfire. To reverse Adam Smith's saying, a scholar was then of all kinds of luggage the easiest to be transported. The tendency of things moreover, both in Church and State, was towards codification and centralization. In England, Stephen's successors, especially Edward I, were attracted by the unifying and imperialist ideas of the Roman system. The Church, after the publication in 1140 of Gratian's Decretals, discovered that the civil might be made ancillary to the canon law. By the end of the twelfth century the civil law was dominant at Oxford, and Vacarius' suppressed work, the *Liber Pauperum*, had become the leading text-book of the University, giving to the students of law their name of Pauperists.

The extent to which this study had encroached on divinity and the seven liberal arts is illustrated by the history of Emo, afterwards Abbot of Bloomkap, and his brother Addo, two young Frisians, who after 'hearing and glossing' at Paris and Orleans came in 1190 to Oxford, eager to apply themselves to the 'studium commune litterarum.' This consisted of the Trivium (grammar, logic and rhetoric) and the Quadrivium (arithmetic, geometry, music, and astronomy). They were however quickly convinced that a knowledge of Roman law would be more to their advantage, or, as we should say in modern educational parlance, would pay best. Our examination statutes, like an ever-changing cloud, shift and melt and elude the clasp. But that simpler time also had its fashions and experiments, its discarded ideals and new favourites. Emo and Addo 'took up' civil law. The Mathematical Faculty has calculated that there are now four thousand different ways of achieving that degree which entitles the possessor to teach mankind as Master. These brothers had a more restricted choice of books. After hearing lectures they copied out their notes and made extracts from the *Decretum* and the *Liber Pauperum*, Addo during the former part of the night, Emo during the latter—an arrangement which, as Prof. Holland observes, had the advantage of making one truckle-bed suffice for both. Ten years earlier Daniel of Morley, in Norfolk, after studying in Paris and Toledo, returned with 'a priceless multitude of books,' but was chagrined to find Aristotle and Plato superseded by Titius and Seius, the John Doe and Richard Roe of Roman law. However, not to remain the only Grecian among Romans, he halted at Oxford to pick up the fashion-able science. Giraldus too, though he calls Oxford the place where the English clergy most excelled in clerkly lore, complains of the desertion of 'bonae litterae[1].' The haste with which the legists leapt from a rapid study of the Institutes to the Digests and the Code was also deplored by many. Roger Bacon declared that the Civil Law corrupted the study of philosophy. It was said that the Sibylline prophecy, 'venient dies, et vae illis, in quibus leges obliterabunt scientiam litterarum,' was being fulfilled. A clerk named Martin, who had himself studied law at Bologna, loudly reproved the Masters assembled in public, in that 'the Imperial laws had choked every other science;' again, the Archbishop on a public occasion blundering in his Latin, the same 'merry blade' stopped the hum that went round by crying, 'Why do ye murmur? Grammar is out of date.' The civilians were indeed the spoiled children of Alma Mater. In 1268 'the inceptors in civil law were so numerous, and attended by such a number of guests, that the academical houses or hostels were not sufficient for their accommodation, and the company filled not only these, but even the refectory, cloisters, and many apart-ments of Oseney Abbey. At which time many Italians studying at Oxford were admitted in that faculty.' 'The study of law,' writes Mr. Green, 'was the one source of promotion, whether in Church or State.' A century later the legists refused to be subjected to statutes

---

[1] Wood says that there was then a threefold division of clerks into *superseminati*, ill-grounded and superficial, *pannosi*, patchy scholars, and *massati*, 'who built an unshaken edifice upon the solid foundation of literature, as well of the divine as human law, and other faculties.' But owing to the discouragement of everything but jurisprudence the last class were 'very few and rare.'

made by 'artists' and theologists, though the claim of Bachelors of Civil Law and of the Decrees to be styled Master, and their appeal to the 'foreign court' of the Arches, were unsuccessful.

The law students were but slightly connected with the religious houses, though a knowledge of civil law had come to be an indispensable part of the training of a canonist, and 'divinity was reputed bare without it[1].' Indeed the canon law tended everywhere but in Paris, where the theologists were strong, to become an appendage thereto. Still, as Bishop Kennet observes, 'it was then customary for the Religious to have schools that bore the name of their respective order;' and belonging to the Priory, round which—as the great church of the Patroness of Oxford—a multitude of inns had grown up, were the 'Schools of St. Frideswyde' in or near Schools Street, and 'Civil Law' or 'Great Civil Law School' in St. Edward's parish. The centre of the hostels for jurists outside the west gate of the Priory was a Law School in St. Aldate's Church. It is true that the interesting

---

[1] I quote the following from Mr. Ruskin's description of Simone Memmi's frescoes in Santa Maria Novella (*Mornings in Florence.* The Strait Gate, p. 144). First of the Seven Heavenly Sciences is:—

'I. CIVIL LAW. Civil, or "of citizens," not only as distinguished from Ecclesiastical, but from *local* law. She is the universal Justice of the peaceful relations of men throughout the world, therefore holds the globe, with its *three* quarters, white, as being justly governed, in her left hand.

She is also the law of eternal *equity*, not of *erring statute*; therefore holds her sword *level* across her breast.

She is the foundation of all other divine science. To know anything whatever about God you must begin by being Just.

Dressed in red, *which in these frescoes is always a sign of power, or zeal;* but her face very calm, gentle, and beautiful. Her hair bound close, and crowned by the royal circlet of gold, with pure thirteenth-century strawberry leaf ornament.

Under her, the Emperor Justinian, in blue, with conical mitre of white and gold; the face in profile, very beautiful. The imperial staff in his right hand, the Institutes in his left.

Medallion, a figure apparently in distress, appealing for justice. (Trajan's suppliant widow?).

Technical points:—The three divisions of the globe in her hand were originally inscribed ASIA, AFRICA, EUROPE. The restorer has ingeniously changed AF into AME—RICA.

II. CHRISTIAN LAW. After the justice which rules men, comes that which rules the Church of Christ. The distinction is not between secular law and ecclesiastical authority, but between the rough equity of humanity, and the discriminate compassion of Christian discipline.

In full, straight-falling, golden robe, with white mantle over it; a church in her left hand; her right raised, with the forefinger lifted . . . Head-dress, a white veil floating into folds in the air . . .

Beneath, Pope Clement V, in red . . . Note the strict level of the book, and the vertical directness of the key.'

c

chamber afterwards used for this purpose and as a library of law books, over the south aisle, was a late Perpendicular erection. But it is most unlikely that a civil law school should be built in a parish church as late as Henry VII or Henry VIII [1], unless there had been one there before. Wood says that it was 'anciently' so used, being 'frequented by the students belonging to the Halls of Broadgate, Beef, Wolstan, Bole, Moyses, &c.[2]' The numerous legists of this quarter had no other centre of teaching. Huber says (§ 69) that even in the fifteenth century the Masters assembled their forms in the porches of houses and churches, the conventual schools alone having good lecture rooms.

The chamber in St. Aldate's is described in the churchwardens' accounts, 26 Hen. VIII, as 'yᵉ library,' being rented at '26s. 8d. p. ā.'[3] 'When the University was in a manner left desolate in the reign of K. Edw. VI. the said School went to ruin and the books were lost.' Church law-books were not likely to survive the other 'cobwebs' of mediæval knowledge swept away by the Visitors. After the foundation of Pembroke the room was again furnished with books and was used as the College library until the year 1709, the College executing the repairs, as also of the chapel below. It was taken down by a resolution of the vestry in 1842 as 'dangerous,' being then rented by Mr. P. Walsh. The loss of this picturesque feature of the church is to be deplored.

But the Broadgates students, and after them the members of Pembroke, had also the use of the aisle itself for their devotions. Probably it was shared originally by the other hostels around [4].

---

[1] It might, to judge by the prints, have been of the fifteenth century; but the unfeeling mutilation of the tops of the beautiful aisle windows by the floor points to a later date.

[2] Like Chaucer's 'Sergeant of lawe, war and wys,
    That often hadde ben atte parvys;'
or that 'parvise' where we have all been supposed to respond to the Masters of the Schools' questions.

[3] Wood MS. D. 2, fol. 67.

[4] Now that the library and school over the aisle of St. Aldate's has been destroyed, St. Mary's alone retains a similar chamber. In that church, over the old Congregation-house, a public library was begun to be built about 1320 by Bishop Cobham; but until 1409 the books were kept in the vaulted room below, locked up in chests or chained to desks. There is such a library of chained volumes over one of the aisles of Wimborne Minster, and also in All Hallows, Hereford, and in Hereford Cathedral. In St. Mary's the legists used St. Thomas's Chapel. When a great Congregation was holden, 'at the proclamation of the bedell for the faculties to receed or goe to their places, the non-Regents went in the Cancell, the Theologues in the Congregation house, the Decretists in St. Ann's Chapel, the Physitians in St. Catherin's, the Jurists in St. Thommses, and the Proctors with the Regents in Our Ladie's Chapel' (Wood's *City*, ii. 30).

In the *Oxford Sausage* there is an eighteenth-century epigram 'on Part of S. Mary's Church being converted into a law School.'

'See here—an event that no mortal suspected;
See Law and Divinity closely connected!
Which proves the old proverb, long reckon'd so odd,
That "the nearest the Church the farthest from GOD."'

The aularians having no extra-diocesan privileges, the principal of every hall and his scholars were obliged by the University statutes to repair on solemn days to their parish church for Divine Service, though sometimes they had a private oratory[1]. The appropriation of an aisle of St. Aldate's to the scholars of Broadgates may perhaps lend some colour to Wood's assertion that the budding monks who first inhabited, as he asserts, the 'ancient hostle,' performed in the adjoining Church, of which the Priory were joint-patrons, 'those usuall rites and services that were required by their rule.' Leonard Hutten says: 'In this Church there is a Chappell of newer building than it selfe, but the Founder or Builder thereof I doe not find. It is peculier and propper to Broadgates where they daily meete for the celebration of Divine Service[2].' It was the Chapel of Pembroke College till 1732, a rent being always paid of 6s. 8d.

The founder was John de Dokelynton, who also built the tower and steeple in the ninth of Edward III (1335, 6), and it was usually called by his name. Wood calls it 'Trinity Chapel and Doclinton's Chantry.' He says[3]:—

'John Doclinton or Ducklinton (he was a fishmonger, and white fishes in a red circular feild are in this chapple to this day) severall times maior of this city, desiring the health of his soule, did to the honor of the Virgin Mary and All Saints institute a perpetual chantry, 9 Edw. III, in a chappell of his own building on the south side of this church. Wherin ordaining a chapleyn to celebrate divine service for his and the soules of his wives, Sibyll and Julian, for the soules of his father and mother, and also of Henry bishop of Lyncoln, while living and when dead, setled on him and his successors for ever an annuall revenew of 5 marks issuing out of severall of his messuages in Oxon, viz., out of that that he then inhabited in Fish Street, another in St. Michael's parish at North Gate, out of two shops in the parish of All Saints, out of another tenement near Soller Hall in St. Edward's parish, and out of another in Grandpont neare Trill Milne. This gift and institution (as also the license of the king and Alexander Medbourn, the then rector of this

---

[1] The principal of Hinxsey Hall in St. Aldate's parish was licensed in 1485 'ad celebrandum in oratorio' (Wood's *City*, ed. Clark, O. H. S., i. 201).
[2] *Antiquities of Oxford (Elizabethan Oxford*, ed. Plummer, O. H. S., p. 88).
[3] *City*, ii. 37.

church, for it) was confirmed by way of inspeximus by Henry Burwash, bishop of Lyncoln, the same year 16 calends of Aprill: and afterwards paid to St. Frideswyde's Priory 6*d.* per annum, as appears by one of their rentalls of all their revenews in Oxon for the year 1517 in which this chappell is stiled Trinity Chappell.'

As a fishmonger he naturally lived near his trade in Fish (St. Aldate's) Street. Wood elsewhere says that he owned Borstall Hall (in High Street) 'in the raignes of Edward II and III¹,' which his wife Sibyll granted in 1336 to William Sedbury of Worcester; and that in his will (1348) he bequeathed Soller Hall (in Bear Lane) to his wife Alice². This then was a third consort. Chaucer speaks of a Solar Hall at Cambridge. Wood inclines to identify Docklinton's Inn in Fish Street with the Christopher².

Docklinton's name is of frequent occurrence. About 1284 the priory demised to John de Doklindon and Juliana his wife a seld, rented at 12*s.*, in the parish of All Hallows (Ch. 398). In 1303 he was bailiff with John of Beverley⁴. In 1312 he conveyed Hart Hall to Bishop Walter de Stapledon and also Arthur Hall. The former he had bought in 1301 from Elias de Herteford the younger for £20, the latter in 1308 of Agnes de Staunton⁵. In 1318 he witnessed an agreement between the Abbess of Godstow and the Rector and Scholars of Stapledon Hall, and another in 1323 between Agatha Oweyn and the same; also two grants by Elena le Boun to Thomas le Macoun in 1315, a grant of John de Ew to John de Durham on the morrow of the Conception of the Virgin 1317, and a conveyance of Nicholas Bone to Thomas and Agnes le Mason in 1322. A grant from Thomas and Agnes to Nicholas, Feb. 6, 132¾, is witnessed by him as mayor. In 1335 he bequeathed 20*s.* to each of the four Orders in Oxford. While mayor in 1327, we find him taking part in an extraordinary riot on the part of the joint commonalties of Oxford and Abingdon, in which Abingdon Abbey was sacked and pillaged of its treasures and muniments. A number of rioters were hanged, but whether Docklinton was found guilty is not clear. In the 35th of Edw. I (1307) he witnessed the lease to Balliol College of the old Synagogue, afterwards one of the numerous Broadgates Halls, almost opposite the east end of Pennyfarthing, now Pembroke, Street. In 1341 Adam de Kemerton was instituted to a chantry in St. Aldate's, no doubt Docklinton's. Richard de Lelewood left a bequest in 1349 for the repair of the Lady Chapel, and John Shawe in 1361 for St. Peter's light⁶.

Docklinton's Aisle, under part of which is a vaulted Norman crypt

---

¹ *City*, i. 129.
² *City*, i. 174. Perhaps wife is a mistake for daughter. He had a daughter Alice who owned, 1356, a hall and a shop annexed to it in St. Edward's parish (Wood MS. D. 2, fol. 58). She granted it to John de Norton.
³ *City*, i. 198.   ⁴ *Oxford City Documents*, ed. Rogers, O. H. S., p. 165.
⁵ Bodleian Charters, 287.   ⁶ Wood MS. D. 2, fol. 53.

long used as a charnel-house, was a fine specimen of Decorated
architecture at its best. When Dr. Ingram issued his *Memorials*
(1837) it was still divided from the nave by the original massive wall
pierced by three acutely pointed arches of different sizes. On opposite
sides the corbel-heads of King Edward III and his queen Philippa
remained, having once, Dr. Ingram suggests, supported the luminaries
of SS. Peter and Paul. The piscina and a niche for a small figure of
a saint existed on the south side near the place where the altar once
stood. After 1674 the east window, an elaborate specimen of pure
Decorated tracery, was somewhat obstructed by a small mortuary
chapel built by John West, Esq., lord of the manor of Hampton
Poyle[1]. In Mackenzie's print (1835) of the church, looking westward,
this chapel has a Gothic appearance. Against the west window of
Docklinton's aisle, in the companion print looking eastward, is a small
classical addition, apparently a porch, which Dr. Ingram calls 'a
modern excrescence,' but which looks like good work of Charles II's
time. The south wall of the aisle had three windows, and a west and
east window. It has in the present century been lengthened in both
directions, and the additions at both ends swept away, but the tracery
of the east window has been kept as an ornamental division between
the aisle and its continuation, after the fashion of the beautiful chapels
at Coutances. The hood-moulding of one window has the original
finials. The chamber above was lit by six square-headed double-light
Perpendicular windows, and was reached by a newel staircase at the
south-west external corner. What Dr. Ingram calls the 'disgraceful
termination' of this staircase, a double-gabled erection with a sundial
on its southern face, may have been a later addition for the storage of
books and papers. The aisle had a battlemented parapet. Round
the churchyard used to be a stone wall with a substantial gateway at
the west, and another towards the south-east. A glance at any old
picture of this, reputed the most ancient, as certainly it was the most

---

[1] On Oct. 9, 1674, his daughter Anne died in St. Aldate's parish, and was buried
in the churchyard 'on the south side close under the wall of the chancell.' A
'little chappell' was in the same month 'built over her by the fond father,'
and a monument placed to ' the truly virtuous *Mrs. Ann West*, the youngest and
dutiful Daughter of the above.' He, his wife Mary Kirke, and another daughter
were laid there. He was described as ' a Benefactor to the Church and the Poor
of the Parish.' Mr. West, who was one of Charles II's Gentlemen Pensioners,
died Jan. 8, 169⅘. Anne's shield was 'Ermine, a bend indented sable,' impaling
her mother, viz. 'parted per fess or and gules a lozeng counterchanged of the
feild : on a canton azure a lion conchant or collared and chained argent holding
a cutlas blade in his two pawes.' Wood, ii. 295. The present Master tells me
that he remembers a beautiful little chapel to the east of the aisle.

lovely of Oxford parish churches [1], and a second glance at the present uninteresting edifice, must disenchant any one with the well-meant blundering of the 'restoration' era of a generation back. If the spires of Oxford, which is incredible, are still 'dreaming,' that of St. Aldate's is an architectural *somnium aegrum.*

In the churchwardens' accounts of 26 Hen. VIII, 20*s.* appears as received for 'a tenement next y⁰ church style now called y⁰ church howse.' It adjoined a property of the prioress of Studley [2].

Besides the crypt there still remains a pure Norman arcading inside the church. 'The piety of the Norman Castellans,' writes Mr. Green, 'rebuilt nearly all the parish churches of the city.' Speed says that this church was 'founded, or restored' in 1004. The old-fashioned guide-books content themselves with saying that 'it is of antiquity beyond the reach of satisfactory investigation,' and that it was once wooden. Mr. Parker [3] dismisses as an idle tale the fabulous connexion with the probably mythical British saint Eldad, through whose means Hengist was defeated, and who caused the corpses of the 460 British barons and consuls, murdered on Salisbury plain, to be 'buried in a cimitery near adjoyning.' This saint is described by Leland as Bishop of Gloucester about A.D. 450. There is at present a St. Aldate's Church in Gloucester, mentioned first in any extant writing c. 1291. Like the one in Oxford, it is situated just inside an ancient gate of the city, on the left hand; and Mr. Parker conjectures that in both cases Aldate is really Aldgate, i. e. Old Gate, the saint's name to whom the church is dedicated having slipped out, just as St. Martin's at Quatervois is commonly called Carfax Church. The Normans, he suggests, took Aldgate, softened to Aldate, to be the name of a saint. Early in the twelfth century we find mention of 'Ecclesia S. Aldae.' Afterwards the name appears as S. Aldatus or Aldathus. The churchwardens' accounts, temp. Henry VIII, speak of 'y⁰ feast of S. Aldate,' but this need not mean more than the parish feast [4]. Wood [5] says, 'This church hath bin anciently [6] and com-

---

[1] A very pleasing water-colour by the younger Prout of Docklinton's aisle and the 'school' overhead has lately been presented to the College by Mr. Alfred Thomas Barton, M.A., Vicegerent and Senior Tutor.

[2] Wood MS. D. 2, fol. 67. The house (demolished in 1831) at the south-eastern extremity of Pembroke Street was called Church House.

[3] *Early History of Oxford,* p. 290 sq.

[4] Wood MS. D. 2, fol. 67.

[5] *City,* ii. 34.

[6] In an Exeter College computus of 1358, 'iiiid. pro vino dato Radulpho Codeford quando alloquebatur Rectorem de Seynt Holde.' *History of Exeter College,* Boase, O. H. S., p. xxi. His name was Walter de Leverton, a B.A.

monly called by the names of St. Ald's, St. Old's, St. Olave's, and now at this day St. Toll's.' The present traditional designation ' St. Old's ' is now almost peculiar to University men, the younger townspeople pronouncing ' Aldate ' as it is spelled, as they do also ' Magdalen.' In the 1773 map of Oxford by Longmate, the name is actually given as ' Aldgate,' as it also is in a guide-book which I have of 1827. Noble gives it thus in 1806. In the English version (made about the end of the fifteenth century) of the Oseney Cartulary, a charter of 1226 is signed by ' Reginald, Chapelyn of ye church of Seynte Oolde of Oxford.'

At the general taxation in 1296, the ' verus valor ' of this Church was four marks. In Henry VIII's reign it was valued at £54. In 1773 the real worth was put at £100.

The patronage of this church was given by King Charles I to Pembroke College. How at an earlier date St. Frideswyde's and Abingdon Abbey came to share the advowson is told in a curious story in the Abingdon Chronicle, ii. 174, 175[1] :—

Est in civitate Oxeneford monasterium quoddam Sancti Aldadi episcopi venerationí consecratum. Cujus omne beneficium duo clerici ex eadem villa, fratres, Robertus et Gillebertus, cum quodam Nicholao sacerdote aeque dimidiabant. Contigit autem ut, vocante Deo, praedicti duo fratres habitum monachi in hoc Abbendonensi coenobio, hujus abbatis, scilicet Ingulfi, tempore susciperent, et partem ecclesiae quae eis contingebat, cum terra et domibus infra civitatem, hereditario jure sibi pertinentibus, huic ecclesiae dono perpetuo contraderent. Quod videns Nicholaus, alterius partis ecclesiae dominus, abbatem simul et conventum convenit, postulans ut ei partem fratrum praedictorum cum sua, quamdiu viveret, tenere concederent, ita ut censum quem pars accepta exigebat (scilicet xx. solidos) annuatim persolveret. Conditionem etiam talem imposuit : ut cum habitum mutare vellet, non nisi in ecclesia ista mutaret, vel etiam si in illo habitu, quo tunc erat, vitam finiret, pars dimidia ecclesiae supradictae, quae sua erat, cum altera parte in perpetuum isto loco remaneret. Rogante etiam Nicholao, in privilegio Romano ista ecclesia posita est, quod tunc temporis renovabatur. Reversus ergo ad propria, ii. solidos per annos singulos in recognitionem pacti praenotati, extra censum consuetum, dum vixit persolvit.

Defluente vero postmodum aliquanto tempore, Nicholaus idem, subita aegritudine correptus, letali morbo se sensit detineri. Qui salutis propriae recordatus, ad fratres suos Abbendoniam nuntium transmisit, petens ut religionis habitum indueret priusquam deficeret. Qui cum mortem ejus nondum sic imminere putarent, et iccirco aliquantulum venire tardarent, Nicholaus in extasi detentus jacuit. Astantes autem Sanctae Frithes-withae canonici, jamque mortuum putantes, et idem fortasse propter

---

[1] Rev. Joseph Stephenson, ed. in Rolls Series.

lucrum suum desiderantes, nescienti habitum suum supposuerunt, sicque ad suam ecclesiam quadam vi et injuria rapuerunt. Postea tamen revocato spiritu ad se rediens, cum a Wigodo abbate Oseneiae interrogaretur, utrum ei habitus sic assumptus, aut ibi mori, placeret, respondit se amplius in quodam vili specu velle projici quam ibi detineri. Dicebat enim bono suo se ibi non posse sepeliri, ubi sepultus fidem, quam fratribus suis debuit, probaretur mentiri; se potius ad eum locum deferendum, quem seu vivus seu mortuus elegerit inhabitandum. Detentus tamen ab his qui bonis suis inhiabant, praesentis vitae finem [faciens?] inibi interceptus atque sepultus est. Partem vero ecclesiae quam Nicholai diximus esse, et jam jure nostram, negligentibus circa rerum suarum defensione[m] prolatis [praelatis?], usque hodie detinent, et perpetue detinere nituntur; nobis tamen, cum parte jam nostra, personatus dignitate reservata.

The one moiety was confirmed to Abingdon by Pope Eugenius III in 1146[1]; the other to St. Frideswyde's in 1122 (1132?) by King Henry I[2]. Ingulf (Prior 1132–58) 'ecclesiam sancti Aldadi dedit sacristae[3].' It was agreed that after the next vacancy there should be alternate presentation. King Stephen, about 1150, directed the Bishop of Lincoln not to put the prior of St. Frideswide's on trial touching the moiety of St. Aldate's and touching St. Edward's, except before himself, 'quia de propria elemosina mea sint.'

The patronage of Docklinton's chantry was at one time distinct from that of the church. For Wood[4] preserves a charter of 19 Hen. VI (1441) whereby Thomas Goldsmith and Nicholas Norton remit and release to John Fitzallen and Joan his wife, and their heirs and assigns, all their right 'in a cottage or plot also called the presteshouse in penyfarthinge streete with the advowson of Docklintons chauntry joyneing to S. Aldate's church,' as also in 'Dokelynstons yn' and in Solar hall in St. Edward's parish.

A memorial of the ancient connexion of our House with St. Aldate's Church remains in the fine alabaster tomb and recumbent effigy of John Noble, LL.B., principal of Broadgates, and official of the archdeacon of Berks. It formerly stood in Docklinton's aisle 'under the upper South window,' but has now been placed against the north wall of the chancel, one of the sides being thus concealed from view. The tomb is enriched on the south and west sides with a number of canopied niches containing angels who hold

[1] Dugdale, i. 107.
[2] The Rev. S. R. Wigram (*Cartulary of St. Frideswide's*, O. H. S., p. 10) considers that there are no sufficient grounds to doubt the genuineness and date of this charter. In the cartulary it is No. 5. Mr. Parker thinks Henry I may possibly be an error for Henry II (*Early History of Oxford*, O. H. S., pp. 292, 293).
[3] Abingdon Chronicle, ii. 291.   [4] MS. D. 2, foll. 163, 164.

shields, all blank except one. The east side shows a sculptured group, representing an aged couple kneeling—probably Noble's parents, who may have erected the monument—and their family behind.

The figure is bareheaded and vested in the gown and hood of a bachelor of Laws. The sleeves of the gown are long and pointed. The *caputium* is lined with fur, and there is a line of fur along the outer edge of the cape quite an inch wide. The tonsured head rests on a cushion. Some judicious care is needed for the inscription if it is not to become altogether illegible. It runs thus :—

> Magister Joh'es Noble in legib' bacallarius quondā principalis aule latar' portar' et offic' archd'ni Barr': et obiit secūdo die Junii Anno dnī mill'o ccccºxxij Cui' aīe ppiciet' de' Amē Nuc ipē te petim' miserere qºsque beisti Redim' p'ditos noli dāpnare redemptos.

> Miseremini mei, miseremini mei, saltem vos amici mei, quia manus dnī tetigit me[1].

The latter words, from Job (chapter xix. 21), are the prayer of a soul in purgatorial pains. Noble supplicated for D.C.L. May 14, 1510.

In the same way that this aisle was appropriated to Broadgates, the scholars of Balliol once worshipped in a part of St. Mary Magdalen Church, those of Exeter in St. Peter in the East, University College used St. Peter in the East and afterwards St. Mary's, Oriel St. Mary's, Lincoln Allhallows Church, while the parish Church of St. John Baptist is still the Chapel of Merton.

---

[1] Hearne made this inscription out incorrectly (*Collections*, ed. Doble, iii. 197). He adds :—' The Founder of Pembroke Chapell, John de Doclington, he was buried I think in yᵉ lower End of yᵉ Chapell in wᶜʰ on the Floor is a large Marble Stone with a Saxon Inscription not legible.'

CHAPTER III.

ROUND such centres as St. Aldate's the twelfth-century law-students lodged in crowded purlieus as thick as bees. At first the swarming scholars, gathered out of all nations, had found bed and board in the dwellings of the citizens and common lodging-houses. So in the *Miller's Tale* Heende Nicholas the clerk lodges with John the wright and Alisoun his young wife, the other members of the household being Gill the maiden and Robin the knave[1]. But as the University gradually took shape these lodging-houses were brought under an increasingly strict control, and became licensed hostels, inns, halls or entries, under the disciplinary jurisdiction of the Bishop of Lincoln's chancellor and his commissaries, assisted by an official called Hebdomadarius[2]. Of these receptacles there were at one time an incredible number and variety, distinguished by the name of the owner or by some fanciful designation.

Among the halls for legists on the west of the Priory none was more important or regarded in after-times as more time-honoured than Broadgates Hall at the corner of St. Aldate's churchyard. The

---

[1] 'A chambir had he in that hostillerye,
Alone withouten eny compaignye,
Full fetisly i-dight with herbes soote,

. . . .

His almagest and bookes gret and smale,
His astrylabe longyng for his art,
His augrym stoones leyen faire apart
On shelves couched at his beddes heed,
His presse i-covered with a falding reed,
And all above ther lay a gay sawtrye
On which he made a-nightes melodye,
So swetely that al the chambur rang,
And *Angelus ad Virginem* he sang.'

On the other hand the 'youngë poorë scholars two' of the Reeve's Tale dwelt in 'a great college' at Cambridge called the 'Soler Hall,' which had a warden and a manciple. The accommodation enjoyed by Hendy Nicholas was not available for all. The pest of 1448 was ascribed in part to the lying of so many scholars in one room.

[2] See Ingram's *Memorials*, St. Mary Hall, p. 16.

name was a common one. There appear to have been six, possibly seven, other halls that bore it. They were these:—

1. In the parish of St. Michael's at South Gate, probably on the right hand as one goes to Folly Bridge, conveyed 'under the name of Broadegates' by Richard Charingworth and Thomas Leye, goldsmith, to Sir Adam de Shareshull, 1362. On the authority of Olyver Smith, Wood tells us that the Brethren of the Holy Cross (Crutched Friars) had their first abode there [1], Richard de Charingworth being their Prior.

2. In St. Aldate's parish, a little south of the east end of Penny-farthing (Pembroke) Street on the opposite side. When the Jews were licensed to build synagogues the canons of St. Frideswyde exchanged it for other tenements with Copyn the Jew, of Worcester. After the Expulsion it came 'through king Edward the I his hands' to William Burnell, Dean of Wells (1291), who converted it into a hall for students, with a tenement adjoining, 'and for their better convenience turned the said Synagogue, or at least part of it, into an oratory to exercise their devotion therin.' It was now called Burnell's Inn or Synagogue. He gave it, in 1307, to Balliol College, and it was sometimes called Balliol Hall. Richard Clifford, Bishop of London, was bred in it, and afterwards endowed it, bequeathing a thousand marks to his poor scholars there. From him it was styled London College. In 1469 it appears to have the name Hospitium de le Pyke, at which date it still paid the 4*d*. rent for which Copyn the Jew had compounded long before. Among other benefactors to it was Bishop Goldwell. The religious students were Bernardines, but afterwards Benedictines. The seculars studied civil and canon law, 'having schooles neare them [2].' This Hall passed to Wolsey and was pulled down by him for the building of his new College. Wood says that it was 'called Broadyates in the 41 Edward III' [1367] [3]. So Savage in *Balliofergus* (1660); but he confuses it with the Broadgates on the other side of St. Aldate's church:—'The Synagogue whereunto did belong the entrance in at the great Port or Gate, and the sollar over it; from which great or broad Port or Gate, as it is thought, the House of the Students (now Pembrook Colledge) was call'd *Aula Lateportensis* or *Broadgates-hall*. This Synagogue and Port was given to *Stephanus de Cornubia*, Master of this House [Balliol] and the Scholars, 35 Ed. I [4].'

3. In St. Peter le Bailey parish, 'which by the name of Brodeyates was demised by Roger Burewald to Simon London in the beginning of the raigne of Henry III' (1220) [5]. In a charter of 1294 it is described as 'juxta ecclesiam S. Petri in Balliolo.'

---

[1] Gutch's *Wood, Hist. Antiq.*, and *City*, ed. Clark, i. 303, 564; ii. 490. 'On the north side of the Wheatsheafe' à Wood thinks. It was 'on Grandpond, betweene a plot of ground belonging to Einsham Abby on the north and a tenement of Thomas de Legh on the south.' The land belonged to St. Frideswyde's.

[2] *City*, i. 157-9.

[3] *City*, i. 564. Unless he is speaking of another ex-synagogue. Savage certainly is speaking of Balliol Hall. This and the other names continued till the fifteenth century (i. 158). Halls were often polyonymous.

[4] p. 27.   [5] Wood's *City*, i. 218, 564.

4. In St. Edward's parish, in Schydierd Street (Oriel Lane) —'an ancient habitation for clerks,' situated between Lumbard House (Beke's Inn) on the south and Pady House (Nun Hall) on the north.   It was also called Hunsingore's Inn, from its owner Master Richard Hunsingore, clerk, to whom the Priory gave leave, on the morrow of Holy Cross day, 1317, to raise a wall 28 feet long between a tenement of theirs called Brodegate in the corner in Schidiard Street and a tenement of his in which he had his chamber called Brodyates, adjoining it[1]. 'He, it seems, being a man of a publick spirit and excellently learned in those times, made great additions and enlargement to it for the reception of the greater number of schollers; and furthermore did his bounty only rest in that particular but also in the foundation of an oratory or chapple in this hall, for which (it seems) craving the Diocaesan's license, had it procured about the aforesaid year 1317.' Hence à Wood thinks it resembled a college than an ordinary hall. Hunsingore's chantry in St. John Baptist's Church was founded by this Richard, who was official to the Archdeacon of Oxford.   He, in 1317, 'gave severall revenews for the maintenance of a priest who should celebrate and sing divine service for his and his parents' soules. He died anno 1337, and was buried at South Newenton, of which place he was rector to the day of his death and to which he gave moneys for a preist that should celebrate there also[2].'

5. Concerning the Broadgates at the lower eastern corner of Schydierd Street, near the town wall, we know nothing, except that it belonged to the Priory. Wood does not give it in his list of halls of this name[3].

6. 'Bradyates in parochia S. Mariae,' called by Standish an 'old,' i. e. disused, hall. 'It was of old time inhabited by schollers, but (by the decay of them) by luminours, servants to them, as severall rentalls which belonged to [Oseney] Abbey tell us, stiling it thus :—"tenementum illuminatorum Brodyates cum sellario et selda in fronte." It yeilded for the most part 33*s*. 4*d*. per annum ; but in another, 5 Richard II [1381], but 26*s*. 8*d*.,' owing to the decay of the Halls[4]. It was on the site of part of Brasenose.

7. A more important one was the Broadgates on the north side of High Street in All Saints' parish, 'belonging sometimes to S. John's Hospitall within few yeares after their foundation, as appears by an inquisition 6 and 7 Edward I [1279]. This had its entrance at the wide or broad gate at the utmost house saving one of the limitts of this parish from S. Marie's and almost opposite to the Swan Inn[5]. Within the said gate hath anciently bin a larg court wherin have been divers receptacles for schollers, as also a chapple with other aedifices adjoyning, as the ruins therof did shew two yeares agoe.' Wood adds a note, 'pulled downe anno

---

[1] So Wood, *City*, i. 141, quoting Charter 156 (Wigram). But the Charter speaks only of one ' Brodezate.'   Wood, however, elsewhere (*City*, i. 564) affirms that the other was 'termed in Edward III's raigne [1327-77] Brodeyate *alias* Hunsingore Inn.' He seems nevertheless to be referring to the same charter.

[2] *City*, ii. 73.   [3] *City*, i. 564.   [4] *City*, i. 135, 565, 637.

[5] *City*, i. 81. The modern King Edward Street has been cut through the old inn-yard. See Mr. Clark's note.

1661.' Elsewhere[1] he says, 'It hath now a brod gate and was a place sometimes of venerable sanctuary for malefactors. There hath bin very ancient building, but of late hath bin pulled downe.' In illustration of its character of asylum he gives the story of John Harry, a tailor, who having stabbed a man (in 1463) 'fled for fear of loosing his life for the said fact to this place. Wherupon Mr. William Hill, one of the proctors, came to take him away and committ him to safegaurd. But upon information given to him that it was a place priviledged of old time by the Pope, and by the laying claime to the said priviledge by the Master and Covent of S. John's Hospitall, the man at length upon some small security found the benefit of the place and was dismissed. Several others I find made use of it for that purpose till the year 1530, but how long afterwards it doth not appeare.' Wood gives a list of principals. William Alburwyke, Chancellor of the University in 1324, was one of them, but before Wood's list begins.

In later times when Broadgates Hall is spoken of the one which has been incorporated as Pembroke College is always meant. Wood seems to imply that it had this name before Henry VI. It continued by the name of Segrym Hall, 'and, corruptly, Segreave *alias* Broadgates, till the raigne of Henry VI; and then altogeather called "Aula cum lata porta" or "Aula Lateportensis" because that probably the entrance therin was broader than others[2].' But elsewhere he states that this place, 'continuing by the name of Segrym Hall till about the beginning of Henry VI [1422], came to be called Broadyates (from a large entrance made into it about that time) and in writings Broadgates, *alias* Segrym (corruptly afterwards Segreve[3]) Hall[4].' If he had evidence that a wide entrance was made temp. Henry VI, he would not say that 'probably' this gave the place its name. The first principal of whom we have certain record is William Wytham, 1436; but if the Broadgates in St. Peter le Bailey parish had that designation in 1220, it seems unlikely that it would have been given for the eighth time two centuries later to a hall which already had a distinctive title. Probably all these halls received their name about the same time, like the Ledenporch, Glazen, or Chimney Halls, in a period when such peculiarities were a real distinction. We have no evidence that later, in the fifteenth and sixteenth centuries, Broadgates Hall had a noticeably wide portal[5]. In Agas's map there is shown a rather large porch. In Sir Thomas Browne's speech, however, at the

---

[1] *City,* i. 565.
[2] *City,* i. 564.
[3] 'Segrealle,' *Peshall.* 'Segrevi,' Latin edition. [4] Gutch's Wood, iii. 614.
[5] The old Broad Gate of the city of Exeter, now destroyed, looks in the pictures a very pinched entrance, just as Broad Street in Bath is one of the narrowest thoroughfares of that beautiful city.

inauguration of Pembroke College, the name is said to have been perhaps ironical. The old building was then still standing. Browne asks also 'What father or founder of this House do we recall?' In a charter of Stephen (c. 1139), mention is made of a rent of 3*s.* from land held of the Priory by Roger Brodgee, or Brodgate[1]; and it has been suggested that the hall had its name from some principal or tenant. But this would not account for the other halls of the same name, one of which *had*, we know, a wide gate. Besides, in that charter Roger is among the few that have a surname, and the surname attached to him no doubt from his residence. If so, this proves that there was a place called Broadgates as early as King Stephen.

Heywood the Epigrammatist, who was at Broadgates temp. Henry VIII, gives as one of his proverbs (No. 455) current in Oxfordshire, ' Send verdingales (farthingales) to Broadgates Hall in Oxon.' Fuller, quoting this, adds :—

'This will acquaint you with the Female Habit of former ages, used not only by the gadding *Dinahs* of that age, but by most sober *Sarahs* of the same, so cogent is a common custom. With these Verdingales the Gowns of Women beneath their Wastes were penthoused out far beyond their bodies, so that posterity will wonder to what purpose those Bucklers of Pasteboard were employed. These by degrees grew so great that their wearers could not enter (except going sidelong) at any ordinary door, which gave occasion to this proverb. But these verdingales have been discontinued this fourty years.'

In the University Register, under date Feb. 8, 157½, the official description is ' the hall commonly called "the Broadgates."'

In the Wood MS. (D. 2, fol. 224) is the record, dated 38 Edw. III (136½), of the grant of a messuage formerly belonging to William le Wylde having 'a hall called Brodeȝates in the parish of St. Ebbe on the east part.' I can only interpret this as a name for Beef Hall; in which case ' Segrym Hall' existed as ' Broadgates' as early as Edward III, and was large enough to have annexed a tenement in St. Ebbe's parish. There is also this, at fol. 472, ' Ex alio rentali : 1414 Brodyates Mr. John Baron (coll. Merton), Mr. Nic. Wytham 1425, '8 per Hibernicos 1432.'

---

[1] Charter 14 in Wigram's *St. Fridewide's Cartulary*, and see Dugdale, ii. p. 146. Wood, however, has an entry, ' Rog. Brodege (forte Brodeye ut alibi).' MS. D. 2, fol. 368. He witnessed a deed of gift to Oseney with Henry son of Segrim (then provost) and Ralph Pady. ' Bradgate' occurs thrice as a surname in the matriculation registers of the beginning of the seventeenth century. A John Broadgate, aet. 75 in 1701, was called the ' Smyrna Doctor,' being chaplain to the British factory there (Noble, i. 107). The ' Tuns' had a landlord of this name.

Originally built of timber or wattle and thatch, from the time of the great fire of 1190 all but the humblest *hospitia* were constructed, partly at least, of stone. Not a few belonged to religious houses; but the majority were originally owned by laymen, and were, after 1214, let to the clerks at rents fixed by a board of eight assessors, four being Masters and four townsmen, though even before this rents were not uncommonly fixed by a jury of Masters and citizens, called Taxers. Any building used for the reception of scholars was called *aula*, the term *domus* being usually reserved for a religious or semi-religious establishment. The University aimed at securing for its students the permanent and exclusive use of certain houses, and the proprietors of academic halls were not suffered to apply them to any other purpose than the reception of students, nor demise them without the proviso, 'in case the University had no occasion for the same.' That they might not become ruinous, the principal of each hall was to give notice to the landlord of necessary repairs, which were to be defrayed out of the rent. If the principal omitted to do so, the dilapidations fell on himself.

Unlike the Colleges, which were not originally establishments for instruction but eleemosynary houses of religion, and whose fellows, till the end of the fifteenth century, had no other duties than those of religion prescribed by the College statutes, and those of study prescribed by the University[1], and unlike the Inns, which were mere lodging-houses, Halls were distinctly teaching institutions. Either a teacher gathered scholars round him, or students associated themselves in one house and elected a head or moderator who usually was their teacher. They might migrate from hall to hall at pleasure, but could not, from the middle of the thirteenth century, be turned out. The University took steps to prevent the landlords from evicting scholars arbitrarily.

It was at this time that the idea of corporate college life—with its community of worship, organized study, and domestic order—for the training of lay Churchmen and secular clergy took shape in the House of the Scholars of Merton, the House of Balliol, and the Mickle Hall of the University in High Street. This same feeling of the desirability of discipline and domestic supervision led to the establishment of the Halls under a more settled rule. This vigorous common life was the one great difference between Oxford and Paris, intensifying corporate consciousness and bringing about the eventful influence of Oxford on the national fortunes. About the time that

[1] Huber, vol. i. § 115.

the scholars were secured from capricious turning adrift, the University forbade principals to sell their office, to hold two halls at once, and to be absent for more than a year. But it was not till 1420 that 'unattached' students were abolished, and every scholar or scholar's servant obliged to dwell in a hall governed by a responsible principal. In the first year of Henry V a statute was enacted against those 'called by the wicked name chambur-dekenys' (*camera degentes*, Wood[1]), who occupied unlicensed lodgings and were a disorderly element. These 'Irish and Welsh vagabonds' would often, 'in the habit of poor scholars, disturb the peace of the University, live under no government of principals, keep up for the most part in the day, and in the night-time go abroad to commit spoils and manslaughter, lurk about taverns and houses of ill repute, commit burglaries and the like.' Like the limitours, they were frequently licensed to beg, 'singing *Salve Regina* at rich men's doors.'

It was further, in the early fifteenth century, decreed that principals should be graduates, and should apply before the Chancellor every year for the renewal of their licence; that they should reside in their halls, keep a list of members, report disorderly conduct, and admit no student expelled from elsewhere. They took an oath to maintain discipline. The students were bound to attend lectures unless graduates. The principal was elected by his aularians; but after Leicester's chancellorship, about 1570, they were obliged to elect the person nominated by the Chancellor. When any vacancy occurred, an inventory was made of the common stock of goods and chattels pertaining to the Hall, and a cautionary deposit was given to the University by the newly admitted principal.

The principal's profits arose from tuition fees. He did not cater for the aularians. This was done by an upper servant or manciple, 'wise in buying of vitaille,' who was sometimes a scholar. These purveyors acquired so much consequence that a statute was passed forbidding any manciple to become principal of a Hall. Purveyance for twenty miles round Oxford was secured by grant of the Crown to the scholars. There was in every Hall a common table, and what each contributed to the common purse of the Hall was called 'Commons,' about eightpence to eighteenpence a week. Additional fare for private consumption could be obtained from the manciple and was called 'batells.' The rent of a single room was from 7s. 6d. to 13s. 4d. a year.

---

[1] Rather, chamber-servants—in a large house the lowest class.

CHAPTER IV.

HALLS ON THE SITE OF THE PRESENT COLLEGE.

No College stands within more natural boundaries than Pembroke College. Yet it is an almost accidental agglomeration of ancient tenements in two parishes, belonging formerly to a number of different owners. By the purchase in 1888 of the Wolsey Hospital the prócess of gradual expansion became complete. Except a minute strip of land[1] outside its western wall the College covers the whole quasi-rectangular area formed by the city wall on the south, St. Ebbe's Street on the west, Beef Lane and St. Aldate's churchyard on the north, and St. Aldate's Street on the east. The extreme length is 540 feet; the extreme breadth 130.

The academic tenements which once covered this area were as follows, beginning from the east:—'Segrim's Houses' (the Wolsey Almshouse), New College Chambers, Abingdon Chambers, Broadgates Hall, Cambey's Lodgings, Minote or St. John's Hall, the double Hall of SS. Michael and James, Beef Hall, Wyld's Entry, and Dunstan Hall. For all of these lands, except the Almshouse (which belonged to Christ Church) and Cambey's, the College paid rent till recent times.

I have already spoken of 'Segrim's Houses,' and will hereafter treat of the Almshouse upon this site. It was divided by a wedge-shaped strip of ground (averaging 17 feet broad, belonging also to the Priory, and forming part of the butt-yard) from the neighbouring New College land. Until 1866 the College leased this strip of Christ Church for a shilling yearly, collected by one of the almsmen and kept by them. In the accounts in the time of the Commonwealth, '12d. for yᵉ Almesmen in christ church Hospitall,' 'for a little ground.' In Agas's map there is something which may answer to the present double gates opening on to this slice of ground, but Dr. Ingram and

---

[1] The City are about to sell this to the College.

D

Ollier (1843) can hardly be correct in stating that the broad gates which gave the Hall its name were here ' opposite the south-east corner of St. Aldate's churchyard.' In Burghers' engraving (1700) there are on this slip a few trees (represented at the present day by two limes), and grass with formal walks, which have now disappeared. In Loggan's (1675) there are only trees and grass.

Next to this, where the Old Quadrangle now begins, stood *New College Building* or Chambers, and between them and Broadgates Hall were Abingdon Chambers. 'For the enlargement of the said Hall a certain tenement adjoining (on the east side, as it seems) was added to it, and so also was another on the east side of that which belonged to New College, and was rented by the Principal of Broadgates in the reign of Hen. VII for 6s. 8d. yearly[1].' New College Building is first found rented by a principal of Broadgates in 1498, the fourteenth year of Henry VII. In 1510 Mr. John Noble had succeeded Doctor Brian [Hygden] as tenant, paying 6s. 8d.[2], 'eo quod scholares abunde fuerint absentes per magnum tempus propter periculum infirmitatis[3].' Mr. Darbyshire and Mr. Greene, principals of Broadgates, appear as tenants in 1556 and 1564 respectively. Before Darbyshire another tenant, Dr. Gilbert, appears. 'New College hath a tenement between brodgates ō yᵉ west and yᵉ Almeshouse on yᵉ East, someties in yᵉ tenure of Dr. Gilbᵗ[4].' In the 20th of Henry VIII (1528), however, it has another name, connected perhaps with the trade which flourished close by—'Brewers tenement pulled downe by yᵉ cardinal[5].' This is the same as 'Brewer's tenement belonging to New College wᶜʰ stood iuxta eccIam Sᵗⁱ Aldati et iuxta Brodyates[6],' mentioned under 1495, and apparently identical with New College Building. If so, did Wolsey rebuild it, for there is a building next the Almshouse in Agas? Another entry in the New College bailiffs' accounts, which Wood hesitatingly assigns to the 20th of Henry VII (1504), is this : 'Will. plomer oweth lately yᵉ ten. by Brodgates[7].'

Before its annexation to Broadgates in (as it seems) 1498 there are

[1] Gutch's Wood, iii. 614. The brothers Robert and Gilbert gave to Abingdon Abbey not only their moiety of St. Aldate's advowson, but 'terram et domus infra civitatem.' These were probably the Abingdon building.

[2] Wood MS. D. 2, fol. 283.

[3] Ibid. fol. 284.   [4] Ibid. fol. 288.

[5] Ibid. fol. 284.   [6] Ibid. fol. 282.

[7] Ibid. fol. 283. In 1529 William Plummer was surety in £10 for John Harvey, late warden of the Minorites, that he would appear to answer charges laid against him. In 1537 he witnessed the will of a widow who left 'to the four ordres of fryers four nobles to singe dirige and masse at Allhallows church at the buryall and moneth mynde.' (Little's *Grey Friars*, pp. 110, n. 1, and 319.)

scholars found in it in 1495. The house was then rented by Mr. Parson Agar, 'called afterwards Dr. Akers[1].' At an earlier date the famous prelate Thomas Bekynton was principal there.

THOMAS BEKYNTON was fellow of New College, 1408–1420. While Dean of Arches he tried the heretic Taylor. He was also Prolocutor of the Lower House. As an eminent canonist he was one of three lawyers appointed to draw up articles of procedure against the Wycliffites, and— having been tutor to Henry VI—wrote a learned work in opposition to the Salique law. Bekynton was advanced to be Secretary of State, Keeper of the Privy Seal, and Bishop of Bath and Wells (1443). Together with Bishop Langton and Sir John Fastolf, he was dispatched, in 1432, as ambassador to the Court of France, to negotiate a peace, and was also a member of the great embassy sent to Calais in 1439. In 1442 Bekynton went on a fruitless embassy to Armagnac to arrange a marriage between Henry VI and one of John IV's daughters. He died Jan. 14, 146⅘, and was laid in a noble tomb built by himself. It was opened in 1850 and his skeleton found—that of a tall man with a well-formed ·skull. Bekynton's chief fame rests on his princely encouragement of men of letters and his architectural works. Besides rebuilding the palace at Wells, he erected a public conduit and fountain, the Vicars' Close, and other edifices there. His rebus—a tun and a flaming bekyn or beacon— is to be seen on the walls of Wells, of Winchester, and of Lincoln College, of which the Rector's Lodgings are due to him. He also promoted the College at Eton, where he was himself consecrated.

A rent of 20s. was paid for this land to New College from 1545 till April 16, 1866, when it was redeemed. In 1544 it was rented at 30s. 'Anno Henrici 8^{vi} 35° ad 36^{m}:—super doctorem Parre [=Apharry], principalem de Broadegates pro redditu suo hoc anno 30s.[2]'

At what date *Abingdon Chambers* came to be leased by the Principal of Broadgates we do not know, except that it must have been before the renting of the New College tenement, and before 1485, for the New College tenement is then said to be 'by Brodgates[3].' Wood says the building contained 'two or four chambers'; the area was half a rood. It was quit-rented of Christ Church, to which this Abbey property passed, for 6s. 8d.

These two tenements and Broadgates Hall adjoining seem to be represented in Agas's large map in Bodley (1578)[4] by an irregular string of unimposing houses, together with a fairly large building at about the middle of the south side of the present Old Quadrangle, and

---

[1] MS. D. 2, fol. 281. But perhaps this was John Akars, one of the 'scholars of ripe wits and abilities in Cambridge' who were among the first students of Cardinal College. (Strype, *Parker*, i. 10.)

[2] *City*, i. 607.   [3] Wood MS. D. 2, fol. 281.

[4] Ralph Agas's map however was made about 1550, though not published till 1578.

perhaps another building a little east of where the chapel now stands. The Wolsey Almshouse in Agas, Speed (1610) and Hollar (1643) is quite an imposing quadrangular pile. There are some entries in the *Oxford City Documents*, edited by the late Prof. Thorold Rogers, which refer to these localities at an earlier date. In the list of contributors to the lay subsidy or poll tax of 4 Richard II (1380-1) are these names in the south-west ward (pp. 15, 17):—

De Waltero Benham ffysshmongere et Emma Vxore eius . . xij*d.*
De Elizabetha seruiente eiusdem . . . . . . iiij*d.*
De Elena seruiente dicti Walteri . . . . . . iiij*d.*

A little lower down Joan Benham 'Spynnestere' pays 12*d.* and her servant Ellen 4*d.* On page 302, in a Town Rental of 12 Ric. II, we find, after the rent of a little tower on the east of the South Gate (the entries go westward):—

De Waltero Benham pro occupatione muri villae praedictae iuxta
    portam Australem Oxoñ . . . . ij*s.*
De eodem Waltero pro quodam turrello iuxta ostium domus suae
    ibidem . . . . xij*d.*
De eodem Waltero pro quadam venella vocata la Hamele inclusa
    iuxta caemiterium ecclesiae S. Aldati . . . . . 4*d.*

From which it appears that Walter Benham, the fishmonger, then occupied the wall just west of South Gate, and had his house there, and rented the lane called Hamel, which is now the approach to the College[1]. The 'turrellum' close to his door and rented by him must have been part of the South Gate, for there was no other bastion near.

Of *Broadgates Hall* itself the principal building still remains, viz. the refectorium, until 1847 the dining-hall of Pembroke, and now the library. The transverse portion was added in 1620. This oddly shaped room has very thick walls and one deeply splayed original window. The mullions have been altered, but the old drawings show it to have been of the fifteenth century. Broadgates continued 'for divers generations' after 1378 to be valued at 40*s.* But the priory let it to principal Noble in 1517 for 30*s.*, 'yea, for 20*s.* on the principal repairing of it,' 'which rent continuing till the dissolution of Religious houses or thereabouts (at what time there were but few scholars in the University), it fell to 13*s.* 4*d.* and so it continued till the said Hall was given to Christ Church by King Henry VIII[2].' This and the other Christ Church rent were redeemed in 1866 for £40.

[1] A hundred years before (1285), one Thomas de Benham was attached in connexion with a case of manslaughter. Robert Benham was an 'ynneholder' in the 'parish of Seynt Mary Mawdelen' in 1534. (*Oxford City Documents*, pp. 202 and 67.)

[2] Gutch, iii. 16.

Passing to the other side of Broadgates, we now come to an imposing-looking building, which fronted the churchyard on the west as far as Beef Lane. It was wider, however, than the present Master's house, and moreover stood further back, having in front of it a toft or narrow garden ground[1]. Agas and Hollar show it as a kind of oblong quadrangle, the north end having three gables. Agas seems to include this building, or these buildings, under the general designation 'Broadgates,' and, when Vertue in 1744 made Pembroke College the subject of the Oxford Almanack top, he drew the Earl of Pembroke laying at King James's feet a representation of a building closely resembling the 'quadrangle' given by Agas and intended doubtless to stand for old Broadgates Hall. The short north side of this building, or block of buildings, occupies in Agas a fifth of the whole length of Beef Hall Lane, and in Hollar a third, or even a half. A fifth is probably the right measurement. Out of the western side of the 'quadrangle' starts a fairly large building, running a little askew from Beef Hall Lane, and from the south-west corner of this juts out towards the city wall another smaller one. One other inconsiderable building is shown towards the end of the Lane. In the large open space between the Lane and the town-wall there are trees.

From Agas, of course, we do not look for scrupulous accuracy. But the buildings described above seem to answer to a row of halls for legists which we know lay between Broadgates Hall and Littlegate, now St. Ebbe's Street. These were Cambey's, Minote, SS. Michael and James, Beef, and Dunstan Halls. The first two (united in one hall from 1575, if not from 1517) are represented, I believe, by the 'quadrangle,' the double hall of SS. Michael and James by the building running out from it with a spur-like projection, Beef Hall being the more distant building standing on the Lane, and giving its name to it to this day, while Dunstan Hall had either been demolished before Elizabeth's reign, or it is the most westerly of the buildings on or near the city wall, a little distance south of Beef Hall Lane. All these came to be part of Broadgates Hall and Pembroke College. I will at the end of this volume discuss the exact position of these different buildings, some of which were standing until 1844, when the present New Quadrangle took their place.

Cambey's Lodgings, at right angles to Broadgates, is now represented

[1] This however is not clear. Wood (*City*, i. 213) represents 'Cambie's' as *behind* 'the Mr Lodg,' which he says was 'sometimes a void peice of ground.' In his diagram the words are afterwards scored through. In 1626 'Cambey's Place' was bounded on the east by the churchyard (MS. D. 2, fol. 623).

by the Master's house. In a catalogue compiled by John Rowse, who is said to have died in 1491, under the heading 'juxta ecclesiam S. Aldati' are a number of halls for legists existing in his day, but Cambey's is not one of them. They are Latiportensis, Polton, James, Michael, Beof, and Dunstan. Cambey's was either considered as practically part of Broadgates, or was not used for academical purposes; probably the latter, for the principals of Broadgates do not seem to have rented this house until 1517, at which date it belonged to a family named Cambey or Cambray—'Cambye's Lodgings, so called from one Mr. John Cambye, who held them of St. Frideswyde's Priory, an. 1517, and who also about that time did build them anew to the end that the Scholars of Broadgates might live in them [1].' He also rented the next land on the west. In no list of halls is there any that can be identified with this residence. In the St. Aldate's registers transcribed by Wood, among the burials are: 'Jan. 11, 1540, John Cambraye;' 'Jan. 18, 1545, Marg[t] Cambraye [2].'

When the Cambeys gave up their house for the use of the students of Broadgates, John Noble, already mentioned, was principal. 'Old Mr. Windsore,' à Wood tells us, called the place 'Veale Hall,' and he adds a note 'Radulph Viel [3].' There is no 'Aula Vitulina' in any of the lists of halls. Miles Windsor, born in Henry VIII's time, probably knew of a fifteenth-century occupant, Ralph Viel, and called it Veal Hall to match Beef Hall in the same lane. St. Michael's, between them, was dubbed by this humourist 'Mutton Hall [4].' Cambey's Lodgings were inhabited by clerks till 1549, when 'some difference happening

[1] So in Gutch's Wood. However in the St. Aldate's accounts of 1534 is an entry 'of a tenement lying by brodyates now in y[e] tenure of m[r]is Camby 8d. p. ā.' (Wood MS. D. 2, fol. 67).

[2] Perhaps the Ellen Camby was of this family whose brass 'on a blew flat stone' in Stanton Harcourt chancel, representing her with lifted hands, one of which holds her beads, is mentioned by Wood. The inscription, as he remarks, is noticeable at the date of 1566 :—
'Of your charity pray for the soule of Elen Camby late the wyff of John Camby, which decessed the xxiv day of June in the yere of our Lord God M[v]cLXVI. On whose soule Jesu have mercy, Amen.' (Life and Times, ed. Clark, O. H. S., i. 220.) A similar inscription close by, of 1569, asks intercession 'for the soule of Sr Henry Dodschone preist, late vycar of this church.'

[3] An industrious antiquary, but à Wood speaks slightingly of his 'vaine doting collections.' He came to Oxford in Queen Mary's reign, having been born about 1541. Windsor acted in Christ Church hall before Queen Elizabeth in 1566. He died in the year of the foundation of Pembroke and was buried in C. C. C. chapel. He lodged near St. Michael's at Southgate.

[4] One Alice Viel had a house in St. Peter le Bailey parish in the middle of the thirteenth century (Cartulary of St. Frideswyde, ed. Wigram, O. H. S., Charters 359 and 360).

between the principall of Broadgates and the owner of them, were for sometime vacant. At length the priviledges of the University being urged and produced were brought to their use againe, and annexed to the said hall of Broadgate, which continued to the last state therof.' The University forbad inns once used for academical purposes to be diverted to other uses, unless required by the owner or his family for a residence, or unless about to be let on a lease of at least ten years. At the dissolution of the monasteries, Cambey's, though still occupied by the Broadgates students, came into the hands of a layman, Thomas Owen, of Elsfield, Southants (fellow of New College 1536, B.C.L. 1544), who in the twenty-ninth of Elizabeth (1587, Nov. 7) sold it to William Tooker 'of the citie of Exon, gent.[1]' On July 22, 1596, Dr. William Tooker, then canon of Exeter and of Sarum, archdeacon of Barnstaple and chaplain to the Queen, conveyed the place to George Summaster, principal of Broadgates, who already rented the next building on the west. He, 'for the most part' rebuilt the house, and by will, dated July 1st, 12° Jacobi (1615), bequeathed it to Samuel Summaster[2] of Painsford, Devon (knighted 1616). Sir Samuel Suṁaster and Dame ffraunces his wife in 1622 sold it to Dr. Clayton, last Principal of Broadgates, and first Master of Pembroke College. Thomas Clayton, doctor in physique, with Alice his wife, conveyed it for some reason in 1625 to Mr. John Rous, of Oriel, Bodley's librarian, the friend of Milton, for £368. On April 19, 1626, 'ye said Jo. Rous sold ye said Cambies Lodgings to ye Mr fellows and scholars of pemb. coll. for 350ll,'[3] 'who repairing and making some alteration on them, were appointed to be the Lodgings of the Master.'

Next to Cambey's was an *Entry*, which *temp.* Edw. II was rented of St. John's Hospital without East Gate for 12s.:—'introitus juxta Mine Hall reddit per annum domui S. Johannis, 12s.[4]' In the list (1438) in the *Munimenta Academica* (ii. 519), 'Introitus Sancti Johannis' is given. But perhaps this was in Cat Street[5].

---

[1] William Tooker (1554–1621), Winchester fellow of New College, afterwards Dean of Lichfield, disputed in 1583 before the Polish prince. He wrote a Latin quarto, *Charisma, sive Donum Sanationis,* upholding Elizabeth's power to touch for the Evil. (Strype, *Annals,* iv. 438, 626.) He received absolution, in the Convocation of 1604, for non-comparence.

[2] Entered Broadgates Hall Oct. 23, 1607, from Devon, arm. fil., aged 16.

[3] I quote Wood MS.: 'All the tenement and garden ground having a garden of All Souls on the west known as Cambye's Place or Lodgings near Broadgates Hall.' 'Broadgates Hall, now Pembroke College,' is described as its southern boundary. But on the west was Magdalen land, not All Souls land. Perhaps Minote was looked on as an adjunct of Cambye's.

[4] Wood's *City,* i. 566.　　　　　　　　　　　　　[5] Ibid. i. 594.

Next on the west[1] was *Mine* or *Minote Hall*, belonging to the Hospital of St. John Baptist. 'It was soe called, as it should seem, from a name that owned it; of whom Robert Minhote [in a note, Robert le mignote] probably was one was provost of Oxon [with Laurence Rufus] about the 17 Henry III' (1233)[2]. Robert Minnoth witnessed among other agreements a grant of land to the Friars Preachers about 1250. His name occurs in a deed with that of Richard Segrym[3]. On folio 167 is an undated but witnessed charter by which Adam, son of Richard the vintner, grants to Robert le Mignot and his heirs all that messuage which he had of Joan, daughter of William Leggi, lying between the land which had been William's the son of Amfrid, and that which had belonged to Jordan le Jaune, 'sinser' [incenser?], in St. Aldate's parish. In another charter Robert Mingnot of Oxford grants to St. John's Hospital his land in St. Aldate's, and 14s. 6d. rent, &c. In the Hundred Rolls we read: 'Fratres Hospitalis Sancti Iohannis tenent unum tenementum quod eis dedit Robertus Myngoyth in perpetuam eleemosynam sine redditu, et valet una marca per annum.' It is placed in St. Aldate's parish (vol. ii. p. 789). In the 22nd of Edward I (1293), 'aula Minot iuxta cimiteriũ S. Ald.' paid the Brethren 20s.[4] In the 2nd of Edward III (1328) it was a house for clerks and rented by the rector of St. Aldate's at 30s.[5] In 32 Edw. III (1358) Mr. Richard Wolfe paid 26s. 8d. for it[6], and as late as 9 Ricardi II (1385) he was still the tenant[7]. It is in Simon Parret's catalogue of 1390[8]. In the 5th of Henry VI (1426) Mr. William Lawle occupied it as an academical hall[9]. In the 3rd of Henry VII (1487) Mr. Grey, vicar of Bloxham, abode 'in the hall called Minote,' paying 23s. 8d.[10] The old name, however, was giving way to one derived from the Hospital which owned the place. Thus in a rental of about 1400 the premises are described as 'tenementum Robt Minote Aula vocat. Iohannis in parochia S. Aldati[11],' and again in 1425[12]. 'Senjonyshall' in the Lay Subsidy of 1380 may be the one in Logic Lane. Standish distinguishes Myn Hall from Minote, and says he forgets what parish the latter was in[13]. He places the former on this site. Wood is not

---

[1] Though in Wood MS. D. 2, fol. 243, there is a strange remark: 'Note that Mingnot hall was in St. Tolls parish and not in St. Ebbs, and therefore I suppose it stood between yᵉ Almeshous and pembroke coll. or therabouts.'

[2] Wood's *City*, i. 521. Vide supra, p. 7.

[3] Wood MS. D. 2, foll. 161, 196, 214, 375.   [4] Ibid. fol. 232.

[5] Ibid. fol. 237. But at *City*, i. 521, the rent is put at 16s. 4d.

[6] Wood MS. D. 2, fol. 239.   [7] Ibid. fol. 240.

[8] *City*, i. 630.   [9] Wood MS. D. 2, fol. 241.

[10] Ibid. fol. 243.   [11] Ibid. fol. 469.   [12] Ibid. fol. 474.

[13] 'Tam subito meminisse non possum' (Wood's *City*, i. 636, n. 4).

quite sure if they are the same [1]. He identifies Minote or St. John's with Polton Hall. Philip Polton was principal of St. John's Hall in 1458. In Rowse's list (before 1491), Polton Hall comes between ' Latiportensis' and ' James'; Wood says, ' neare Broadgates Hall or els on the north side of the Church,' where Peshall also puts it.

PHILIP POLTON, son of Thomas and Edith, (fellow of All Souls and archdeacon of Gloucester; died Sept. 22, 1461 [2]), ' built at his owne charges the north isle adjoyning to [St. Aldate's] church, anno 1455. In which afterwards by his will, anno 1461, he instituted a chantry therin after this manner following :—

' first, that there should be a chapleine of his own presentation therunto named John Fayrwater who should for the health of his soul say mass dayly in the said chapel or isle, excepting festivall and lord's dayes on which he should celebrate in the choire of this church ;

' that the said John Fayrwater should repaire all those tenements that he should leave for the maintenance of him and his successors ;

' and lastly, after the said Fayrwater's death, the rector of this church togeather with the parishioners should have power alwaies to present another chapleine or preist whensoever the former resigned or departed this life.

' These conditions being drawed up by the founder Philip Polton, he settled severall lands and revenews on the said John Fayrwater and his successors for ever, viz., a messuage in St. Michael's parish at South Gate, two messuages in Grandpont in the same parish, and others in Abingdon, lying in Sturt Street, Boreweste Streete, Cotfettell Streete, and others in Wynyard Boningwell. Besides he gave to this church a gradual ("graduale") and a processional, and also to this his chapple a new missal, with 4 paire of preist's vestments, a silver paxill, and a large chest to containe the said utinsells and other "jocalia" belonging therunto.

' The next year after the erection of this chapple one Joane Wylmott, wife of John Wylmott of this parish, became a benefactresse to it. For she dying anno 1456 and buried here in this chapple left to her executors (her husband and Philip Polton aforesaid) her tenement joyning on the north side of the lane leading from Fish Street to Hinxsey Hall (which indeed is Keepharme Lane) in the parish of St. Aldate, as also a garden ground in St. Edward's parish on the south side of Jury Lane ; which she willed to be sold and the moneys therof to be employed for the use of this

---

[1] *City*, i. 566, and n. 5. He mentions an entry ' in an accompt of the houses of clerks in Edward the Second his raigne—" le Mine Hall de Luttlemore, 2 marcae." It was in St. Aldate's.' But Minote cannot have belonged to the nuns of Littlemore in that reign, if at all. At *City*, i. 521, he places Minote among the halls of unknown situation.

[2] On a brass in All Souls chapel: ' Hic iacet Magister Philippus Polton Baccalarius Canon., qui fuit Archidiaconus Gloucestrie, qui obiit xxii die Septembris anno Dom. millesimo cccclxi. Cuius anime propicietur Deus. Amen.' At each corner of the stone are three mullets pierced in a shield, without tinctures.

A coroner's inquest was holden in 1302 touching the death of William Bufford, who dwelt 'in parvo Balliolo in parochia S. Ebbae'—close, that is, to this Hall.

There is a mysterious 'Aula Bevana [1]' held under one principal in 1451 with James and Beef. Wood places it among the halls of an uncertain site, as well as an 'innominata iuxta Aulam Bovinam, S. Aldati [2]. Perhaps it was on the other side of the Lane. Beef Hall was given to the University by Mr. Nicholas de Tingewick, Doctor of Physic. His name, with those of the Chancellor of the University and the Warden of the House of Balliol, occurs in 1327 as witness to a deed (in the Balliol College archives) by which the Lord Nicholas de Quappelad, by the grace of God Abbot of Reading, released to the scholars of the House of Balliol £20 sterling for the soul of Adam de Poleter, burgess of Reading, for the building of St. Catherine's chapel of the said House, gave them ten silver marks for the same purpose, a glass window of the value of £10 and more, and timber, lath, &c., with the carriage of the same. In the Pembroke College Library is a valuable medical MS. called *Breviarium Bartholomei*, written by John Merfield or Marfield, a monk of St. Bartholomew's Priory in Smithfield, in the reign of Henry VI [3]. In a chapter treating of the cure of the jaundice (*ycteritia*) the writer affirms: 'Moreover lice (*pediculi*) of sheep, bruised and compounded with honey and water (*hydromel*), can cure jaundice. In consequence of which Master Nicholas Tyngewick, in his chair at Oxford, related that he rode forty miles to an old woman who had by this remedy cured an infinite number, so to speak, of persons, and that he gave her a sum of money for instructing him in that cure.' This Nicholas gave his name to Tinswick or Tingwick Hall or Inn (called *temp.* Henry III Corbett's Hall), which was repaired by Sir Peter Besills, of Abingdon, Knight, who held it of the University, and died in 1424. Later it came to All Souls College, and was destroyed to make room for their cloister. The principality had been granted to Tingewick on his own motion, 1322, in consequence of his having made it over, together with 'another tenement in St. Ebbe's parish [4],' to the Chancellor and Scholars

---

[1] '*Bevana*, annexa Bovinae, Iacobi annexa Bevanae' (*City*, i. 590). 'Annext to Bovina or Beef Hall, as is in one of our registers and an ancient catalogue of halls made in Queen Marie's raigne' (*City*, i. 513). Not in Rowse's.

[2] This can only mean that the nameless hall was in St. Aldate's, in which case it must have clung closely to the skirts of SS. Michael and James, which were just inside St. Aldate's parish.

[3] See Sixth Report of Historical MSS. Commission, p. 550. Dr. Clayton lent the folio to Twyne.   [4] Gutch, ii. 714.

of the University, on condition that they always find two Masters that
are Regents in arte dialectica, to oversee and govern the grammar
schools that he purposed to place therein. Doubtless the other tenement
was Beef Hall. The University repaired it A.D. 1352. The manciple
of 'Tyngeswycisyn' and the manciple and cook of 'Befhalle' paid
poll tax in 1380[1]. Tingewick read his lectures in the Physic School
adjoining his inn. Though medicine was his chief study, he was also
bachelor in arts and divinity, and in 1308 succeeded Ralph de Stanford
in the Sarum prebend of Major Pars Altaris. He was fellow of
Balliol till he became B.A., and in 1325 was one of the two *Magistri
extranei*, or extrinsic procurators, for seeing Devorguilla's statutes for
that college carried out. He and Friar Robert of Leicester laid down,
'in the presence of the whole community,' Fitzralph, afterwards Archbishop of Armagh, the great opponent of the Mendicants, being present,
that the statutes did not allow the members to attend any lectures
except in Arts[2].

Beef Hall was for canonists and civilians and 'in some ages inhabited by Irish clerks.' Wood surmises that several Irish bishops
were brought up here 'circa tempora Henrici VII[3].' These Irish
students were numerous enough to form one of the most important
southern 'nations,' and in the frequent street brawls *pars magna
fuerunt*. A number of Irish clerks were slain in the great fray of
St. Scholastica. By a statute of 1 Henry V (1413) it was enacted
that 'all Iryshmen and Irysh clerkes beggars be voyded out of the
realm,' except religious and (on giving security) graduates; and those
left were not to take upon them the principality of any Hall. Oxford
thereupon ceased to be 'gymnasium Hibernorum,' and the Halls for
Irish scholars, together with 'Yrysshemanstrete,' went, à Wood supposes, to decay. In 1548 (April 10) the University granted to Henry
Crosse, inferior bedell of Divinity, the house and garden called 'Byf
hawle,' with Dunstan[4]. Wood says concerning Beef Hall that it 'continued in its flourishing estate till the raigne of Henry VIII, and
then (or in the beginning of Edward VI) demised to lay persons[5].'
It was let by the University with Dunstan Hall adjoining, in 1612,
to Dionysius Edwards for 10s. 10d., the old rent. Twyne, however,

---

[1] *Oxford City Documents*, ed. Rogers, O. H. S., pp. 24, 44.
[2] *Grey Friars in Oxford*, ed. Little, O. H. S., pp. 10, 168; Gutch's Wood, iii.
73.
[3] *City*, i. 590.   [4] Wood MS. D. 2, fol. 121.
[5] *City*, i. 211. Standish, in the middle of the sixteenth century, places it among
forty-one halls 'praeter aulas iam existentes.' He adds, 'Old Halls, Beffe Hall,
Wlstan Hall.'

mentions ' Henry Milward's [1] lease of Beef Hall for forty years, dated 26 Martij, 41 Eliz. anno 1599.' Langbaine (after 1646) adds a note: ' This lease is expired and another in being.' Hutten (1626) says: ' Beefe Hall, not inhabited by anie scholars, but become the Tenement of some private person [2].'

In or close to the extreme west corner of the Lane was a small plot of ground, a ' habitation for clerks,' belonging afterwards to Magdalen, called *Wylde's Entry*. Wood says: ' All the mention of which is only (I have yet found) in the testament of one Richard Couper (1348), wherin he leaveth to Richard Seukworth, junior, a solar situated juxta Wylde's Entre ex parte australi in parochia S. Ebbae [3]. William le Wylde, who made his will March 9, 1313, and was buried in St. Ebbe's Church, had two, or possibly three, properties in this corner. One is described in 1364 as having ' a hall called Brodeǵates in the parish of St. Ebbe's' (Beef Hall?) on the east and a place formerly belonging to Robert de Kidlington on the west. A third part of it was granted in that year by Nicholas Forester to Henry de Witteney, otherwise Sclatter [4]. By his will made on St. Mark's day, 1349 (23 Edw. III), John Peggy, alderman and cordwainer, bailiff 1338, 1342, 1347, and 1348, afterwards buried in St. Frideswyde's, bequeathed to the priory, besides four ' cottagia ' in a row in St. Ebbe's parish, and his tenement with corner shop just outside St. Michael's at South Gate, and other properties, ' j tenementum quod quondam fuit Willielmi Wilde, situatum in parochia S. Ebbe, inter tenementum quod quondam fuit Willielmi Wilde ex parte una et venellam que ducit ad Ecclesiam S. Aldathi Oxon' ex parte altera [5].' He had the same month acquired this property from the executors of John de Brekhale [6]. The Wylde tenement to the south of Peggy's gift to the canons is, no doubt, the same as a cellar and solar in St. Ebbe's parish granted by Hugh le Wylde to John de Langrish and Sara his wife, situate between a tenement formerly belonging to Sir Roger de Bellofago, knight, on the south, and a tenement formerly belonging to William le Wylde on the

---

[1] He was University ' stationer' (stationarius, or virgifer, some kind of marshal) and retired through old age April 11, 1597. ' Henry Milward, stationer,' occurs as early as 1552 (*Register of the University*, ed. Clark, O. H. S., II. part I. pp. 257, 262). He was licensed to sell ale in 1596, and his widow in 1605 (p. 326).

[2] *Elizabethan Oxford*, ed. Plummer, O. H. S., p. 89.

[3] *City*, i. 210. He refers to ' liber testamentorum burgensium Oxon,' fol. 486; Twyne, xxiii. 147. Twyne gives the name William le Wylde.

[4] Wood MS. D. 2, fol. 224.

[5] *Cartulary of St. Frideswyde*, ed. Wigram, O. H. S., p. 305.

[6] Wood MS. D. 2, fol. 145.

north. John de Langrish granted it in 1350 to Henry Sclatter of Witney; and Henry de Witney, in his will made on the feast of Leonard the abbat, 1391, directed that after his wife's decease the tenement should be sold by the executors, and the money go to the repair of St. Ebbe's Church, where he was to be buried[1].

As the Wylde property on the west of ' Brode3ate's Hall in St. Ebbe's ' had Robert de Kidlington's land on the other side of it, it cannot have been actually in the corner. There would not be much need of an Entry in a corner. Couper's land, again, was close to Wylde's Entry on the north. At Wood MS. D. 2, fol. 145, mention is made of a tenement of All Souls between Wylde's tenement and Beef Hall Lane.

We have then :—

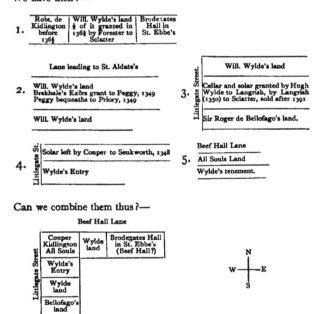

Can we combine them thus ?—

[1] Wood MS. D. 2, fol. 224. In 11 Ric. II (1387), 'Henry Wytteney, sclatter,' paid the town 7s. for a solar and cellar at Little Gate towards the Friars Preachers (*City Documents*, O. H. S., p. 302).

Subsequently we find the land divided thus :—

Beef Hall Lane

Littlegate or Milk Street	Magdalen land 'two small pieces of ground'	Beef Hall		St. James + St. Michael Halls		Minote Hall	Cambey's Lodgings	
		115 feet		(All Souls Land)		(Magdalen Land)	(Priory Land)	a toft
	Dunstan or Wolstan Hall	(University Land)	98 feet	Parish boundary			Broadgates Hall	

Slaying Lane (Brewers Street)

The Magdalen land was demised, *temp.* Elizabeth, to Henry Milward, gent. It is described in a lease of 1781 as 'two small pieces of ground on which formerly stood a tenement.' The ancient rent of 4s. and a groat acquittance was redeemed by Pembroke College, with that of Minote, Dec. 10, 1781, for £18.

It only remains to describe *Dunstan*, Wolstan or Adulstan ('Adulstan's,' Athelstan's, Atherton) Hall, situated 'on the west and south side of Beefe Hall[1],' and 'having its door or forefront butting on that street or lane that leadeth from St. Ebb's Church to Littlegate[2].' Wood says this street was for that reason more properly styled Wolstan's Hall Street. 'Adulstan' is very likely a corrupt variant of 'Wolstan.' The name Dunstan, or Dunster, remained till recent times. The land, like that of Beef Hall, was leased from the University, and measured 115 feet from east to west, and 98 feet from the Magdalen land southwards to the city wall. It was an academic hall at least as early as 1446, in which year, March 1, Robert Darry, Clerk, principal of 'Adulstane Halle, juxta Beefe Halle,' summoned one of his scholars, Roland Barrys, for non-payment of 7s. 6d., being three terms' rent of his chamber. Roland confessed, was condemned to pay within eight days, and took an oath to do so on the Gospels. It was 'allwaies till the decay of halls supplied by clerks.' Twyne (according to Wood) affirms it to have been 'given to the University by Dr. Hall,' who was principal in 1458, 1463 and 1469. He himself merely appends to the name the words, 'S. Wolstan, Rob. Wolstan.' He thinks it may be the same as a hall of uncertain site called Minard's, or Maynard's (though this may be only a variant of Minote's), 'quia non inseritur 1501.' It would seem from these last words that Dunstan had disappeared

[1] *City,* i. 211.   [2] Gutch's *Wood.*

before 1501. But à Wood says, 'Hibernici illic studuerunt et in aliis aulis proximis (1513).' Rowse gives it as a hall for legists in his day. Standish mentions 'Dunstan's' or 'Wlstan' among 'old halls' no longer existing. A hall however is described in the catalogues as not 'existens' when it had ceased to be used for academic purposes, though the building may have remained. In the Register of Congregation, April 10, 1548, 'a garden called Donstone Hawle vel Wolstone Hawle' was let with Beef Hall to Henry Crosse, who was living near University College in 1552. The two properties were finally purchased by the College from the University in 1872 for £162 6s. 4d.

It is to be noticed that all the six halls, Broadgates, Polton, James, Michael, Beef and Dunstan, are joined together by Rowse, and described as being for legists, and 'near St. Aldate's Church,' though the last two were in St. Ebbe's parish, and almost touched St. Ebbe's Church. Dunstan's was a long way from St. Aldate's. The, reason must be that these halls were connected with the civil law school in St. Aldate's Church, which however Standish speaks of a little later as no longer used for academic purposes. All of them are now part of Pembroke College.

The list given in Mr. Anstey's *Munimenta Academica* (ii. 519) is dated Sept. 9, 1438, and enumerates seventy-three Halls then existing 'pro quibus expositae sunt cautiones.' Among them are (besides a 'Brodegate') 'Latarum portarum,' 'Bovina,' and 'Sancti Jacobi.'

NOTE ON A FORMER OWNER OF THE MASTER'S HOUSE.

John Rous, through whose hands Cambey's passed in becoming part of Pembroke, was fellow of Oriel, and from 1620 till his death in 1652 Bodley's librarian. It is to him that Milton wrote, on Jan. 23, 1646, the curious Latin ode in mixed metres beginning 'Gemelle cultu simplici gaudens liber.' He is almost certainly 'our common friend Mr. R.' mentioned by Wotton in a letter to Milton, who may have become intimate with Rous when, in 1635, he incorporated as M.A. at Oxford. The occasion of the ode 'Ad Joannem Rousium' was that at Rous's request his friend had, in 1645, sent him for the Library his Prose writings and Poems, but, the latter being lost on the way, Milton sent a second copy. In this volume, on an inserted MS. sheet, supposed to be the poet's autograph, is this ode, which is addressed to the little book. The Bodleian is *sedes beatae*, whence (in Cowper's translation) 'the coarse unlettered multitude' which now censures his political writing 'shall babble far remote.' The Librarian is 'Aeternorum operum custos fidelis,' and

> 'Si quid meremur sana posteritas sciet
> Roüsio favente.'

Rous may have been a kinsman of Francis Rous, the Pembroke benefactor. His body lies in Oriel chapel. There is a three-quarters portrait of him, in a clerical dress, among the protobibliothecarii. His refusal to allow Charles I to borrow a volume from the Library, as contrary to the Statutes, is well known, and the King's kingly reply.

E

CHAPTER V.

STREETS ROUND THE COLLEGE.

St. Aldate's Street, or Grampound, which bounds the College on the east, is the cross-thoroughfare of the city of Oxford, the time-honoured road leading through the south port to the principal passage of the Thames and the country district beyond. The name Grandpont or Southbridge Street began from the Gate, and is older than the long causeway of above forty arches of stone[1] which crossed the numerous streamlets and the river. 'This street was in antient times meadow and plashy ground[2].' There were halls (Water, Parmuncer, Littlemore, Rack, Pope, St. Mary's House, and others) on either side of it. Here the Abbot of Abingdon held his court, and the Justices in Eyre the assizes[3]. The upper part of the street was once called Southgate Street or, from the fish market held in it, Fish Street[4]. Here stood Fishmongers' Hall, and the traders in fish, like John de Doclinton, had their abodes in and near the street[5]. It was on Fish Street, opposite St. Aldate's Church, that Peter Martyr's rooms in Christ Church looked, until, his windows being frequently broken and his sleep and studies disturbed by 'opprobrious Language from the R. Catholicks, as well scholars as Laicks,' he removed to the Cloisters. Between Christ Church and Pembroke, just before reaching the South gate with its chapel of the Prince Archangel, and its towers on each side, the hill grew very steep, 'as may be seen,' writes Mr. Parker, 'by the marks left of the former level both on the walls of Christ Church and the Almshouses, particularly from a blocked-up doorway in the latter.' The incline was made more gradual in 1834. This point of the road was called Tower Hill, and also Cutler's Hill[6]. Wood says in his account of the City :—

'Wee come to the place where South Gate formerly stood. The signes and tokens therof though not apparent by ruinous buildings, yet it may be discerned by a fall or discent that parts Fish Street from Grandpont, and wheron those stately towers adjoyning therto were sometimes standing[7].'

Nothing remains of the gate. But the twelfth-century wall, obliterated for some distance on the Christ Church side till it comes out again in the

---

[1] *Elizabethan Oxford*, O. H. S. p. 83. They can still be traced.
[2] *City*, i. 296, n. 3. [3] Ibid. i. 305.
[4] In Agas (1578) 'South Streate,' in Peshall's map (1773) 'Fish St.'
[5] This lingered on till the establishment of the new market.
[6] *City*, i. 296. [7] Ibid. i. 164.

Meadows, is perfect on the west side for the whole length of Pembroke College, the College standing on the wall and Brewers Street running under it. Its course may be plainly traced beyond, behind Church Street to the angle of the Castle, where some recently built houses now conceal the old masonry, and thence, more or less distinctly, by Bulwarks or Bullocks Alley, through the playground of the High School eastwards behind New Inn Hall Street to St. Michael's at North Gate. The bastions, hidden between Broad Street and Ship Street, begin again at New College, and so on to East Gate in the High Street and Merton Gardens.

The wall has not stood since Henry I without many repairings, the cost of which fell, as we have seen, upon the owners of such mural mansions as Segrym's, though exemption was pleaded when these were used for academical purposes.

'There were some schollers, I find, in King Henry III his time, when the University was thronged with students, who, having got into some of these " mansiones murales" and not suffering the mayor of the towne to levy this " muragium " of them when the king appoynted the walls to be repayred, caused the chancellor to doe it, though (as they then pleaded) they were " intalliabiles " because inhabited by clerks [1].'

Before the end of the twelfth century the wall, especially on the south side, was 'going much to ruine and the repair thereof neglected.'

'What by the continuall warr in those times, and what for want of moneys due from the murall houses, the wall I find by King Henry [III]'s time was totally ruinated. Insomuch that he, having a naturall affection or rather compassion on this place of his (sometimes) abode, (aspecially as I find, towards our churches), did by his letters patent dated at Woodstock July 10, anno regni 21 [A.D. 1237] graunt to the Mayor and burgesses, for the helpe of building their wall as alsoe for the greater security of the country hereabout, that once every weeke for three years' space [they should] receive a halfpenny of every loaded cart that brought wares to sell here; and of any cart of another county, a penny. Moreover he granted theron sumage, that is, every horse loaded with wares (except bushes, hay, or the like) a farthing,' with other tolls and assistances. 'And soe in good plight the wall did for a long time continue [2].'

After this reign, however, the wall came in parts of the south side to be levelled. In Edward II's reign (1307-1327) the walls were re-edified, and à Wood notes a contribution of the mitred abbot of Oseney for repairs in the reign of Edward III (1327-1377). But Richard II found the fortifications again badly decayed and the moat stopped up. He issued a brief, Feb. 20, 1378, for their amendment. Thereafterward till his own time à Wood 'could never know when they were all totally againe repaired : only in some places where Colledges occupied them.' Merton wall was rebuilt in the seventeenth century. Pembroke could hardly be inattentive to the masonry on which its buildings stood; but its wall is not so new. Twyne writes as though in the fifteenth century the southern defences of the city were uncared for: 'fossatum versus Merton Hall obstupatum tempore Henrici IV,' and those on the north

---

[1] *City*, i. 240.   [2] Ibid. i. 241-2.

were also neglected, though Oxford is not on that side protected by a network of streams. From the time that the effective use of cannon in sieges became recognized, the walls must have seemed of slight utility. In the siege of Oxford during the Great Rebellion the assailants came nowhere near the old town wall. Henry VIII, however, soon after his accession had enjoined the citizens to repair their walls. In Wood's time it was 'ruinated and not owning the name or shew of a wall, or else levelled with the dust,' and so he describes its condition after the Restoration at the garden end of Pembroke: 'The ruins of the wall take in their walk [the walk of Pembroke] where somtimes Dunstan Hall and part of Beef Hall [that is, the garden and appurtenances of Beef Hall] were situated.' It can, however, only have been the upper portion which was totally ruinous, as appears from the great difference of levels between the ground within the wall and that outside it. Dunstan Hall stood at about the south end of the present dining hall. The wall at that point is at present in good condition. Below the Almshouse parts of it are older.

Lying under the wall for the whole length of Pembroke College is Brewers Street or Lane, called in an Oseney rental of 1463, 'venella sub muro.' There appears to have been no moat at this part of the city [1]. Brewers Street has at different times borne the names of Lombard Lane, King Street, Pudding Lane, and Slaughter or Slaying-well Lane,

'antiently called Lumbard Lane from one Lumbard a Jew that lived or els owned land therin, leading under the south wall behind Pembroke College from Great to Little South Gate. Afterwards it was called King Street; but upon what account (whether because the King made it his private way from the south part of the towne to Beaumont) it is not now in readinesse to resolve. From that name it slipped to Slaughter or Slaying Lane because the butchers were commanded to build their slaughter houses and to kill their cattle therin. Which for severall ages they for that use employed them; but upon their overcharging Trill-Mill Streame that runneth under it on the south side with the intralls of beasts and filth, they were forbidden their use of them and removed to Lambard Land [2].'

so called it would seem from the same Jew who gave his name to Lumbard Lane. It appears that complaints from the University to Edward III, in 1339, had led to the butchers being prohibited by royal brief to kill any animal within the walls, 'but that they should select a place remote from the concourse of people and in the suburbs. Wherupon, as it should seeme, they made choice of Lumbard Lane in the south suburbs.' The nuisance, however, continued, and two centuries later 'they were at length [i.e. May 7, 1535] in King Henry VIII his raigne by the maior and comminalty commanded to remove to Lumbard Land,' and build

---

[1] 'The trench on the south side of the city also, long before the other on the north side, was stopped up and the cleansing not soe carefully praeserved because of the diversity of rivers that ran almost under the said wall.' *City*, i. 264. Mr. Clark thinks the evidence for its existence insufficient. Ibid. n. 2. So also à Wood himself, *Life and Times*, i. 97. Mr. Herbert Hurst, to whom I am much indebted in these investigations, writes: 'The signs of the fosse, as far as known, are some 20 feet south of Brewers Street, where the new Cathedral School begins.'

[2] *City*, i. 307. See also Gutch, i. 436.

their shambles 'on the voyde ground by the South [Folly] Bryge,' which bore that name[1]. 'But there neither continuing long, every Man at length killed at his oune home, soe that it was in ye Suburbs[2].' The important craft or mistery of the butchers was regulated from time to time by ordinances, given in Turner's *Ordinances of the City of Oxford*. Peshall, speaking of Lumbard's Lane (p. 256), says :—

'By forfeiture of the Jews it came into the King's hand, who conveyed it to several persons ; a mediety of it is freehold, a part belongs to the Colleges. It was afterwards called Slaying Lane from a terrible slaughter of the gownsmen, and after Pudding Lane[3].'

The Jew Lumbard carried on his business here in the reign of King John. It is curious that the only shop in this street, an old-established *mont de piété*, still exhibits the arms of Lombardy.

The name 'King Street' à Wood assigns to a date earlier than Edward III[4]. But another account makes this the designation it received after the ejection of the butchers under Henry VIII, from a family named King. In Agas's map it is called 'Kinges Street *alias* Slaying Lane.' In a will dated March 16, 1570, 'Sleying Lane also Slawter Lane.' It was also styled Slaying-well Lane from a well under the College wall. The slaughter-houses having been turned into a great brew-house, this well, in 1672, was diverted to its use[5]. The well supplied the old College kitchen with excellent water. But the conduit from Hinxey to Carfax had its first outlet here. Wood says : 'Out of that main pipe is a branch taken into Pembrook sellars : which if it should be suffered to runne, neither the Universitie nor Cittie can have any water.' (Was this interesting circumstance known to the intelligent undergraduate?) 'Pembrok College payes rent to the towne for that, I think, or else for theire building standing on the towne wall, viz. 1*s*. 5*d*. per an.[6] Of this ask Mr. Grenway[7].' For the keeping up of the wall the corporation was allowed the rents of a strip of land both outside and inside the fortification. This they came to let as building sites, 'and latterly they let out the site of the wall itself, which is now in most places rooted up and altogether removed[8].'

[1] 'Lamberds Lande,' *Coll.* II. p. 30 ; Lamberd's Lay, *City*, i. 306.
[2] *City*, i. 480 ; and Wood MS. in *Collectanea*, II. p. 17. Yet by 1556 the new shambles in Slaughter Lane were in working order, for the Town Council imposed in that year a rent of 23*s*. a year on each of the butchers' shops in it (*Collectanea*, II. ed. Burrows, O. H. S., p. 31).
[3] In a deed of Edward VI's (?) time 'Sleying lane, also called Podding lane' (Wood MS. D. 2, fol. 343). Perhaps 18 Edw. IV.
[4] King's Street by the New Schools is also part of the Via Regia. Is the name merely a translation?
[5] 'Slaying Well stopped mense Aug. 1672 ; and the water is conveyed to a brewhouse adjoyning.' *City*, i. 308, n. 4. See pp. 439, 576, 7.
[6] *City*, i. 577.
[7] 'Francis Greenway, milliner, Mayor of Oxon, 1670' (Wood's *Life and Times*, ed. Clark, O. H. S., ii. 310). He was 'of Allhallowes parish.'
[8] *City*, i. 243, n.

In this lane was 'the Stone House,' 'behind and southward from Pembroke Coll.,' in which, during the reign of the Saints, consumptive Jack Glendall, 'the witty Terrae-filius,' afterwards fellow of Brasenose, in whose company Anthony à Wood[1] delighted, acted plays and mimicries with other scholars 'by stealth[2].' Wood records 'Mountjoy Blount, earl of Newport, gentleman of the bedchamber to his Majestie, died of a violent fit of the stone in the larg free-stone house in Slaying Lane in St. Aldate's parish, M., 12 Feb. 166⅘.'[3] He was buried in the Cathedral. Oliver Smith, the antiquary, was brought up in this street. 'Oliver Smith the yonger, son of Thomas Smith of Slaying Lane, sometimes alderman and Mayor of Oxon, died at his house in Grandpoole on Th., the 14 of March 166⅘; and was the next day buried in St. Aldate's church by his ancestors, aet. 43 or therabouts, much in debt and impaired in his estate. He married . . . daughter of [Robert] Bohun, recorder of Oxon.'[4] The brewery which gave its later name to the lane was existing till this century, being known latterly as Micklem's Brewery.

From South Gate, à Wood writes :—

'The wall had its cours where King's Stret *alias* Slaying Lane now is, and on which part of Christ Church Hospitall and the south side of Pembrok College is built. Then, going on,' under the ruined wall, 'at length wee come to a gate called antiently Luttel Gate, since Little South Gate otherwise Water Gate; soe called from a common ford at Preacher's Bridg neare adjoyning and necessary for the inhabitants therabouts to water cattle.'

Little Gate adjoined the extreme south-west corner of the College[5].

'This gate, though it was called "Little," yet it was passable for a cart, and had another small doore adjoyning for foot-passengers; both which was the rode that leaded from the city to the Black and Grey Friers. And though it was not soe larg and beautifull as South Gate, yet it was built after that mode (excepting the fortresses); and had a larg chamber over it and two below adjoyning to it. Which upper chamber was, in King Edward the II's time and a great while before, inhabited by schollers, as I have seen from severall of the chamberlains' accompts of this city, viz. in a rentall of the 17 yeare of Edward the II [1323], where I find these words :—"item de scolaribus ad parvam portam pro solario, 13s. 4d."; and in another of the 19 yeare of the said King thus :—"memorandum quod Petrus de Ewe, socius Thomae le ironmonger, recepit 8s. de principali de camera ad

---

[1] *Life and Times,* i. 336.

[2] 'They would not suffer any . . . scholars to act in privat but what they did by stelth—yet at Act times they would permit dancing the rope, drolles, or monstrous sights to be seen.' *Life and Times,* i. 299. For Glendall and his acting see *Life and Times,* i. 266, 322, 336.

[3] *Life and Times,* ii. 72.   [4] Ibid. ii. 103.

[5] Wood does not seem quite clear about the conduit. He says, 'arriving first at the bridge and water called Preacher's Bridge without Little South Gate cumeth up Lumbard Lane on the south side of Pembroke College, then turning up at the east end of that lane commeth up Fish Street to Carfox' (*City,* i. 62). But in a note he says, 'the pipe comes under the river by Ballow ham and up through Little Gate and turnes up through Beef Hall Lane and from thence through a narrow passage into Penyfarthing Street, and thence up to Carfax' (p. 63 n.). See also *City,* i. 447, 448 (where a diagram is given).

parvam portam versus Fratres Praedicatores." ' The principal's name was Nicholas
Daniel. 'This I did cheifly take occasion to insert becaus the reader may conclude that the University was well filled with scollers at that time, when such
a chamber [*Note*. Did not Roger Bacon take the hight of stars her?] and that on
a common rode and place of continuall disturbance was inhabited by them and
they under a particular governor. From hence alsoe wee cannot think less of what
is delivered by historians that about thes times, or a little before, Oxford contained
thirty thousand students. But of these obscure places for schollers I have many
others that would seeme more uncouth to the reader, if he knew them.'

Skelton (1823) gives a print of Little Gate with the window of the solar
over it, in ruins and covered with ivy. It was taken down about 1790.
Joined to it on the east was perhaps Gamache (Gamage) Hall[1].

St. Ebbe's Church, close to this Gate, terminates the site of the College
at the north-west corner. Before the Domesday Survey the monks of
Eynsham had built it in honour of St. Aebba, daughter of Ethelfrith king
of Northumbria and sister of St. Oswald, who died A.D. 683, or possibly
in honour of the abbess of Coldingham of the same name in the ninth
century. The only other dedications to St. Aebba that are known are Shels-
well, Oxfordshire (now destroyed), and Ebbchester in Durham[2]. It was
given by Remigius, Bishop of Dorchester, in 1091 to the Church of the
most Glorious Mother of God at Stowe with 'Egnesham' Abbey, being
then described as 'quaedam ecclesiola S. Ebbae in urbe Oxenefordensi
consita.' The site of the church belonged before the Conquest to the
Earls of Cornwall, one of whom, Aethelmar the Fat, founded Eynsham
Abbey and gave the monks this ground—'curiam suam in Oxonia in qua
ecclesia S. Ebbae sita erat[3].' Skelton has a fine engraving of this church
before it was rebuilt in 1814. Besides the tower, only a Norman portal,
built against the south side, remains to testify that there was once here
a beautiful and very ancient building. Part of the Early English tower
fell down on Sept. 1, 1648, killing one Richard Ely. Wood enumerates
the chantries, obits, and lights which once existed. There was naturally
a close connexion with the Minorites whose convent adjoined the churchyard. Thus, in 1526, Richard Leke, 'late Bruer of Oxford, beying of hole
and perfite mynde and sike of body,' bequeaths his soul

'to almighty god to our blissed lady saint marye and to all the holy company of
hevyn, my body to be buried w'in the graye ffreres in Oxford before the awter
where the first masse is daily vsed to be saide . . . Item I will that my body be first
brought to the Church of saint Ebbe, and there dirige and masse to be songe for me.
Item I bequeth to two hundred prestes two hundred grotes to say dirige and masse
at saint Ebbys and at the gray freres with other parish churches the day of my
burying,' &c.[4]

St. Ebbe's was in former times vulgarly called St. Tabb's. Just south
of the churchyard was, it would seem, John de Grey of Rotherfield's

---

[1] See *City*, i. 518.
[2] Beda, *Hist. Eccl.* iv. cap. 19. See Mr. Parker's *Early History of Oxford*,
O. H. S., p. 295 n.
[3] *City*, ii. 53, 54.
[4] *Grey Friars in Oxford*, O.H.S., p. 318.

house which he bestowed on the Friars Minors in 1337, 'lying next their habitation on the east' within the town[1].

St. Ebbe's Street, which forms the western boundary of the College, went once, from the many dairymen who traded there, by the name of Milk Street, and also of Littlegate or Little Southgate Street. In the map in Peshall (1777) it is 'South Street.' There is some question how far these names extended northwards and southwards[2]. The road just outside the city is still called Littlegate. The present Pembroke Street has only been so styled in the present reign, having borne till then the name 'Pennyfarthing Street.' Hearne has preserved a note of à Wood's, 'Penyfarthing Streete within these 40 yeares call'd Crow Street[3].' Perhaps there was a 'Crow' inn here. There was in High Street a 'Split Crow[4].' Wood says, what is no doubt correct, that it assumed the name 'Penifarthing Street' from the wealthy family of the Penyverthinges[5], of whom 'Willelmus Pinneferdþing' was provost of Oxford with William de Winton in 1238[6]. At the Eyre of 1285, inquest was held on the body of Nicholas Penyfader, found at Osney slain by Henry of Arderne[7]. The murderer fled and was outlawed. In some records of the reigns of Henry VI and VII the street is called, à Wood says, Pynkeferthing Street[8]. There is a Pennyfarthing Street in Salisbury, connected by an idle tradition with a strike of the workmen engaged on the great Spire for five, in lieu of four, farthings *per diem*; and à Wood mentions a Penyfarthing Lane in Cambridge, 'which Londinensis saith that it was soe called from poore people inhabiting therin.' The present Master tells me that the name was changed to Pembroke Street early in this century by the influence of a physician, a Dr. Ireland, who lived in it, and whose patients pretended to think that his fee was $1\frac{1}{2}d$. In this street were a number of academic halls: Bull or Bole Hall 'on the north side of this street and almost opposite to the place where now stands a fair house built of freestone and brick.' It was 'given by a Jew to

---

[1] *Grey Friars in Oxford*, ed. Little, O. H. S., p. 305.

[2] See *City*, i. 206, 308.   [3] Ibid. 577.

[4] *Life and Times*, ii. 102, and *City*, i. 63, n. 1.

[5] Mr. C. W. Bardsley in his work on 'English Surnames' has the following instances of similar additions: 'The Wills and Inventories furnish a "Thomas Fourpence," the Hundred Rolls a "John Fivepeni," the Cal. Rot. Originalium a "Thomas Sexpenne," the Yorkshire Wills and Inventories a "John Ninepennies," and the Hundred Rolls a "Fulco Twelpence." "James Fyppound (Five pound)" is mentioned in "Materials for a History of Henry VII." So early as 1342 we find "John Twenti-mark" to have been rector of Risingham, while "William Hunderpound" was Mayor of Lynn Regis in 1417.' He mentions the equivalent Norman-French 'Grace and Joseph Centlivri.' 'Thomas Thousandpound,' the last of this class, appears in the Wardrobe Accounts (Edward I). I may add a quotation from the *Fortunes of Nigel:* 'It is an ancient and honourable stock, the Monypennies,' said Sir Mungo Malagrowther; 'the only loss is there are sae few of the name.' There was a 'Sir Tripennye' at Broadgates in 1572.

[6] *Cartulary of St. Frideswyde*, ed. Wigram, O. H. S., Charter 436.

[7] *Oxford City Documents*, ed. Rogers, O. H. S., p. 198.

[8] *City*, i. 195.

Merton College' (earlier than 1327), and was for legists. There is a list of principals in *City*, i. 600[1]. Near it, a little further west, was Moyses Hall, from Moyses or Mossey a Jew. From him it came to the Jew Lumbard, and after passing through divers hands was conveyed by Thomas, son of Philip de Wormenhalle, in 1330, to Adam de Brome, being then situated between a tenement of Oseney on the west and an Abingdon property on the east. Finally, it came through various owners, in 1362, to Oriel. Another neighbouring hostel for lawyers was Eagle Hall, mentioned by Rowse. Further west, in St. Ebbe's parish, was Little Bedell Hall : ' whether not soe called from William Stokes, bedell.' ' Mr. John Bergeveny gave caution for the hall commonly called Little Bedyll Hall situated in Pennyvirthin Street on the vigil of S. Mathew 1461.' It was rented from the nuns of Studley. In the same part of the street was St. Paul's (vulgarly Powle) Hall, the principal of which paid 33*s.* rent to Oseney Abbey in 1446. It stood ' on the east side of the Nag's Head,' and was for legists. It seems also to have been called Hattermonger House. Grove or Greve Hall, 'neare Little Bedell Hall,' was also in St. Ebbe's. Mr. Clark, however, following Wood, seems to place it in his map, at the end of *City*, vol. i., on the St. Aldate's side of the boundary, next to Moyses, on the south side of the street, just west of the entry from Pembroke Street to the College. There is a list of principals in *City*, i. 592, 606. It belonged to Oseney. John Greve was yeoman bedell of divinity. Another owner was Walter Bolle, from whom it seems to have been also styled ' Bole Hall.' Perhaps Black Hall in St. Ebbe's was also in Pennyfarthing Street.

The ale-house opposite the ancient entry from the street to the College, which bears the name of Leden, or Ledenporch, Hall, is an old building, but I do not know what authority there is for its present name. The ' porch ' is a recent addition or revival.

The houses on the south side of Pembroke Street, abutting on the churchyard, stand, doubtless, within consecrated ground, as did formerly ' a parcell of houses standing at the east end of St. Aldate's Church,' and, it would seem, on part of the present St. Aldate's Street, which were cleared away 1831-4. They belonged to the feoffees of St. Aldate's Charities, and are shown in a number of old prints. As for the former,

'Part of Penifarthing Street on the south side therof and soe far as a little entrance leading thence to Pembroke College was also anciently another parcell of the said churchyard ; but, by the increas of severall chantry preists belonging to the church of S. Aldate, was built upon as it should seem for their use[2].'

---

[1] An inquest was held Feb. 6, 1297, on John Metescharp, who died in the house of Ralph ' le Cyrgien' in St. Aldate's parish from an arrow wound inflicted by Michael manciple of the clerks dwelling at la Bolehalle in that parish. Michael with John de Skurf an English, and Madoc a Welsh clerk went through the streets about curfew with swords bows and arrows assaulting all they met. Hue being raised, J. M. went out to keep the peace of our lord the king, whereupon the manciple shot him. He and the others then fled, leaving no goods (*Oxford City Documents*, ed. Rogers, O. H. S., p. 150).

[2] Wood's *City*, i. 194.

In à Wood's diagram the house just to the west of this entrance is marked as the Priest's House. This old building (which, with the two houses next it, belongs now to the College) is said to have once been occupied by Charles I.

In Pennyfarthing Street lived, till his death in 1644, Brian Twyne, to whose antiquarian collections à Wood owed so much. Here, in 1648, William Percy, third son of the eighth Earl of Northumberland, 'died an aged bachelaur, after he had lived a melancholy and retired life many yeares. He was buried in the cathedrall of Ch. Church[1].' The street often resounded with 'the best base voice in England,' that of James Quin (1621–59), M.A., senior student of Christ Church (son of Walter Quin of Dublin), who, in Oct. 1659,

'died in a crazed condition in his bedmaker's house in Penyfarthing Street, and was buried in the cathedral of Ch. Ch. A[nthony] W[ood] had some acquaintance with him and hath several times heard him sing with great admiration. His voice was a bass, and he had a great command of it. Twas very strong and exceeding trouling, but he wanted skill, and could scarce sing in consort. He had been turn'd out of his student's place by the Visitors; but being well acquainted with some great men of those times that loved musick, they introduced him into the company of Oliver Cromwel the protector, who loved a good voice and instrumentall musick well. He heard him sing with great delight, liquor'd him with sack, and in conclusion said: "Mr. Quin you have done very well, what shall I doe for you?" To which Quin made answer with great complements, of which he had command with a great grace, that "his Highness would be pleased to restore him to his Student's place"; which he did accordingly, and so kept it to his dying day[2].'

In Agas's map, Pennyfarthing Street is the name given also to the continuation of the street past St. Ebbe's Church, now Church Street. But the usual name was Freren or Friar's Street.

NOTE: A JEWS' QUARTER.

We have seen that several of the halls in this street once had Jewish owners. Oxford had one of the wealthiest of English Jewries, a source of much trade to the citizens. 'About the year 1075 the Jews in great numbers began to settle in Oxford, and chiefly in the parishes of S. Martin, S. Edward, and S. Aldate; the two last of which were afterwards called the Great and Little Jewries. In one of them they erected a synagogue or school, and expounded the opinions of the Rabbins to the Academians. Several of their houses were inhabited by Clerks.' Fuller says that in Henry the Third's reign 'Oxford flourished with a multitude of

---

[1] *Life and Times*, i. 145.
[2] *Life and Times*, i. 287, and Gutch's *Colleges and Halls*, p. 511. Wood, however, says that the Independents used to 'love and encourage instrumental musick; but did not care for vocall, because that was used in church by the prelaticall partie.' *Life and Times*, i. 298.

students, the king conferring large favours upon them, and this among the rest that no Jews living at Oxford should receive of scholars above twopence a week interest for the loan of twenty shillings, that is eight shillings and eightpence for the interest of a pound in the year.' In 1244 a riotous mob of students attacked the Jews' houses. In 1268, during a solemn Holy Thursday procession in honour of St. Frideswyde, a Hebrew zealot tore the Cross from the proctor's hands and trampled it under foot. The Jews were condemned to make for the University a heavy silver crucifix, to be carried in procession, and to erect a marble cross on the spot—as it seems nearly opposite Pembroke College—where the profanity had been committed. It was finally placed in an open plot by Merton chapel. Neither the Church however nor the Town had power over them; they were Crown chattels without civic rights. Edward I finally banished the Jews. Wood says, 'The suddenness of their dismission obliged them for present subsistence to sell their moveable goods of all kinds, among which were large quantities of Rabbinical books. The monks in various parts availed themselves of the distribution of these treasures. At Oxford great multitudes of them fell into the hands of Roger Bacon, or were bought by his brethren, the Franciscan friars, of that University.' So also Green. Professor Neubauer, however, thinks the Jews had little in the way of books or science to impart [1]. The principal Jewries were along Blue Boar Lane. Professor Thorold Rogers however considered that, Oxford having wide privileges of asylum, a dwindling Jewish settlement continued to exist even after the Expulsion till 1840 or thereabouts. 'Finally the remaining relics were scattered, when a calamitous fire occurred in their quarter, then called Penny-farthing Street, a name since altered by a stupid and ignorant local board to Pembroke Street [2].' A number of Hebrew documents were in a house in St. Ebbe's Street destroyed by fire on Feb. 27, 1844. The Jews returned under Cromwell, and in 1650 one Jacob opened a coffee-house in Oxford.

[1] ' Notes on the Jews in Oxford' in *Collectanea*, II. pp. 287, 8.

[2] *Athenaeum*, Sept. 3, 1887, p. 311.

CHAPTER VI.

OF the splendid conventual houses in the south and west quarters of Oxford, only St. Frideswyde's, the church of the Austin canons, now stands. But the students of Broadgates looked down from the City wall on the gardens and buildings of two great monasteries. One of these was the Dominican house of the Black or Preaching Friars, who in 1221 had settled in the Great Jewry, for neighbourhood to the Schools and with a view to Jewish conversions. It is said the Mad Parliament met within their walls. But, in 1259, they moved to a site just south of the present Pembroke College, 'an obscure place without the walls and farre from the company of disciples, schollers, and auditors[1].' At the end of Brewers Street is the Black Drummer public-house, and lower down, mixed up with Commercial Road and Gas Street, are Friars Street and Blackfriars Road. Preachers' Bridge, over Trill Mill stream, is obliterated; but beyond are Friars' Wharf and Preachers' Pool. This quarter is reached from St. Aldate's Street by Speedwell Street, which at one time was called Preachers' Entry and led to Blackfriars' Gate. All this is Dominican ground[2]. The convent and church, dedicated to St. Nicholas, stood on an islet in the midst, given to the Friars Preachers by Henry III. There were schools in which lectures on philosophy and theology were given, and the public acts or dissertations on theses of divinity took place in the church or chapter-house. One of the priors, Simon de Bovil, was Chancellor of the University. Among the teachers were such as Robert Fisacre, Robert Kilwarby, Cardinal and Archbishop of Canterbury, Walter Joyce, Primate of All Ireland, and his brother, Cardinal Thomas Joyce. The Black Friars obtained respect 'with the Grandies of the Universitie,' 'by reason of their learned parts in philosophy and divinity,' and with the citizens and clergy 'because of their simple and saint-like carriage.' Their library was 'large and full of books,' and among them were many famous canonists.

'Being very skilful in the Canon Law they did erecte a large Schoole wherin they openly read and discussed many points of the Canon Law before the University, and was commonly called "Schola Juris Canonici" Canon Law Schoole, or only Canon Schoole[3].'

[1] *City*, ii. 330.   [2] See Goldie, *A Bygone Oxford*, p. 14.
[3] *City*, ii. 327.

This was in their first quarters; but beside the Trill Mill stream also, 'having procured power from the University,' they erected a school, ' where the disputations called the Vespers as also the Bachelours' Determinations were in severall ages amongst themselves performed[1].' Because of their reputation as canonists they received powers from Boniface VIII to 'review and correct' all writings treating of the Canon Law, before publication[2]. In the great Church of the Black Friars, a stone's throw from Pembroke, was interred the famous Piers or Peter de Gaveston after his beheadal.

' At the first arrivall of his body here [in Oxford] the comonalty of Oxon togeather with these Fryers meet it at the town's end, and accompanied it to this place with great solemnity; and had severall masses for the health of his soule performed by them[3].'

After three years, however, the favourite's body was removed, and

' by the king himselfe and many of the bishops and clergy (the nobles then absenting themselves) attended from thence to Kinges Langley in Hertfordshire, where with all ceremonies pompe and signes of honour was reburied in the church of the Preaching Fryers there[4].'

In 1224, three years after their arrival in Oxford, the Dominicans welcomed there a band of Franciscan or Grey Friars. The new-comers rented a house from Robert le Mercer at the west extremity of what is now Pembroke College, that is between St. Ebbe's and Littlegate, but presently moved just outside the wall 'about a stone's cast from their first hired house,' to 'the place where Muliner's [i.e. Richard le Miller's] house stood.' Here they were joined by many graduates and persons of good birth belonging to the University. Starting from very humble beginnings, the monastery grew and gathered gifts. To them as to the Black Friars King Henry gave, in 1245, an eyot of five acres[5], across the Trill Mill stream, where they made a pleasaunce. The king, wearied with State cares, came often from his palace at Beaumont to find repose among the Grey Brothers. In this retired spot, a little south and west of St. Ebbe's, sprang up a school of learning famous through Europe; for the Friars, in order to screen their novices from the temptations and turbulence of the public schools, brought in teachers from without; and among these or among the students were such as Grostête or Grouthead (the Doctor Mirabilis), Adam Marsh or de Marisco (the Doctor Illustris), Roger Bacon, Duns Scotus, Nicholas de Lyra, William Occham, Peter Philardo (the Doctor Refulgens, afterwards Pope Alexander V), Friar Bungay, John Peckham, afterwards Lord Primate, together with others of 'the greatest clerks in Christendome.' It was Grostête who turned the Grey Friars from speculative to legal studies.

' Though he never smelt of an academy or scarse tasted of humane learning, yet he constrained these his brethren to the studying and reading of the decretalls[6],'

[1] *City*, ii. 330.   [2] Ibid. ii. 336.   [3] Ibid. ii. 339.
[4] Ibid. ii. 322.
[5] 'Now belonging to Sir William Moorton, Kt., Judge of the King's Bench.' Ibid. ii. 361.   [6] Ibid. ii. 362.

'laying aside their sophisms,'—about the being of GOD and the like.
The Friary possessed two notable libraries, erected, it is said, by Grostête
and enriched by a number of Hebrew Bibles bought by Adam Marsh at
the time of the Expulsion.   In later times the Oxford Franciscans forgot
their learning, neglected their library, 'once the choicest of any of this
nation,' and allowed their books to be 'tore in peices or else condemned
to eternall silence [1],' giving some excuse to those under Henry VIII, who
called them a gang of lazy and fat-headed friars.   Antony à Wood cries,

'I professe, so often as I think of the great dammage posterity doth suffer
by the destruction of these "recondita" I am readie to burst out with greif [2].'

In the Conventual Church, 316 feet in length and 180 feet wide, with
twelve side chapels richly wrought, many noble persons were laid to rest
shrouded in the coarse frock of the Grey Friars; in particular Beatrice
de Falkeston queen of Richard 'King of the Romaines and Almaine,'
brother of Henry III.   She, dying

'on the vigills of St. Luke the Evangelist anno 1275,' was laid before the high
altar, where afterwards was placed the heart of her husband [3], 'sub sumptuosa et
mirandi operis pyramide.'   'Great comfort people did take if upon their death
bed they were assured their bodyes would be buried here [4].'

Here also was buried, in 1292, the greatest light of mediæval thought,
Brother Roger Bacon.   Wood thinks that his study was here and not at
Folly Bridge.

'It hath bin delivered to me from eminent persons of this University and to them
formerly by others of the same, both well seen in astronomy and antiquityes, that
Roger Bacon, a Franciscan fryer of Oxon, knowne to be a great astronomer, did
sometimes use in the night season to ascend this place invironed with waters and
there to take the altitude and distance of starrs, and make use of it for his owne convenience in that respect, it being very necessary, situated for its vicinity to his
covent, by conveying himself through a backway over Trillmill into Grandpont [5].'

He adds, however, in a note, 'But I believe all this was at Little Gate.'
His tomb-stone, à Wood had heard, was dug up at the end of the sixteenth
century.   There was left at Little Gate in the historian's time 'a little old
decrepit building,' of which the lower windows touched the ground,
'which, while wee were freshmen, tradition told us 'twas Roger Bacon's
and Thomas Bongei's study [6].'   One of the three gates of the Convent was
just opposite Beef Lane.

Always the scholars of Broadgates and the neighbouring halls upon
the City wall looked out on these stately houses of religious learning, and
heard the bell ringing to prayers, or watched the Brothers walking in
their peaceful garth or among their fields and orchards, and the sound of
prayer and praise was at certain hours carried to their ears.   No wonder
if some among them felt a longing to put on the black or gray cowl.   The
Franciscans had the name of enticing them from their studies.   In their

[1] *City*, ii. 383.   [2] Ibid. ii. 380.   [3] Ibid. ii. 384.
[4] Ibid. ii. 409.   [5] Ibid. i. 425.   [6] Ibid. ii. 411.

cloister 'was trained up yong lads to be fitted for their covent. And in this they did soe transgress in cogging away yong novices from their severall halls in the University[1]' that a statute was made to prevent it, and 'it was agreed they should not take any to their profession under the age of eighteen.' But this was annulled in 1366, six years later. In 1352, Fitzralph, Archbishop of Armagh, in his Defence of Curates or Apology against the Friars, preached before the Pope at Avignon, gave instances of young boys being got away from their studies.

From the windows of Pembroke College one gazes down upon a wilderness of dingy brick boxes, mixed with public houses and gas works, where once, in grove and arbour and cloister, scholastic theses of realism and nominalism were debated by the sons of St. Dominick and St. Francis beneath the towers of their majestic fanes[2]. From below, in lieu of 'solemn psalm and silver litany,' arise the shrieks of the corybantic religionists, who issuing from their adjacent barrack go nightly about the wall of our Jericho.

A few yards from St. Ebbe's Church the unlovely street brings you to a squalid square, till lately surrounding a few shrubs and vegetables. Its name shows it to be the once nightingale-haunted paradise of the Grey Friars, given them by the Lady Agnes, 'uxor Guydonis'; and here stood anciently the churches of St. Bennett and St. Budoc, guarding the West Gate of the city. Paradise was divided formerly by a rivulet, which also encompassed it in part :—

'A large plott of ground partly inclosed with the said rivelet and wheron was soe pleasant a grove of trees divided into severall walks ambits and recesses, as also a garden (and orchard adjoyning)[3].'

Wood, speaking of his own time, says, 'the place now is far from pleasure'; but in 1744 Salmon, in his *Present State of the Universities,* describes 'a pleasant Garden which goes by the name of *Paradise,* in which are Camomile and grass walks planted with evergreens and all manner of Fruit Trees and Flowers.' Thirty years later it supplied the Pembroke tables with cucumbers.

The 'city pound at Paradice' was taken down in 1781. Hereby flowed and flows (though now for the most part underground)

'the little streame called Trill from the trull or mill theron, which commeth from the Weyr streame under the quondam habitation of the Grey Fryers; then under Preachers' Bridge; and soe on the south side of the houses in Lumbard Lane, where, parting into two, one part runneth under Trill-Myll-bow and soe on the east side of Grandpont, and the other on the west side by the place where som-times the Preaching Fryerys stood. Which stream is very advantagious (especially formerly when kept deep and cleer) for [brewers, dyers, tanners, and laundresses]; and better would it be if greater care were taken against the rubbish often cast into it, and the houses of easement over it, which renders the water very unwholsome and unfit to be used by brewers as now it is[4].'

[1] *City,* ii. 397.
[2] Savonarola taught his scholars under a rose-tree in the convent garden of St. Mark's, in 1490.   [3] *City,* ii. 410.   [4] Ibid. i. 398.

Twyne remarks 'Ropy ale brewed from these rivers[1].' Trill passes 'by Bishop Howson's house,' the well-known timbered house just below the College, built by Bishop King, last Abbot of Oseney, about 1548[2], and passes under St. Aldate's Street about seventy yards south of the Almshouse. In the thirteenth century deeds it is 'aqua extra portam australem.' Trill Mill was 'owned antiently by the Kepeharmes of Oxon, of whome Benedict Kepeharme being one gave it to S. Frideswyde's Priory, circ. an. 1180[3].' A series of charters refer to this mill, which was 'upon South bridge outside South Gate' (Wigram, 8-23, 191-198). The Bow, originally of wood, belonged to the Priory. The Franciscans had a 'water-milne' by this stream to grind their corn. It wound its way among the 'groves and privat meanders and recesses' beneath 'faire structures,' of which even in à Wood's time every vestige had disappeared[4].

'Methinks it cannot otherwise be but a bewailment to divers persons especially to such that have a respect for venerable antiquity to see such places that have been so much renowned among men, to have their names buried in their ashes, and their very ruines suffer the death of a sepulcher and dye twice because they want a monument that they lived. But 'tis no great marvaile, seeing that

Mors etiam saxis nominibusque venit[5].'

The isle of the Preaching Friars was in his day

'a peice of ground desolate and naked, and yeilding nothing not so much as one stone to give testimony to the world that soe famous a place as the college of the Dominicans of Oxon was there once standing ... Had their bin but the pittance of a monument left of each place from which wee retaine something of memory of our auncestors, wee should not have bin soe much at a losse as with Tully to seek the sepulcher of Archimedes at Syracusa which was by the inhabitants therof utterly forgotten[6].'

A few small ruins were left of

'the college sometimes of the learned Franciscans. Which at this time scarce acknowledgeth a large and venerable structure to have bin once extant there and containing in severall centuries the learnedest heroes of our nation[7].'

The chief entrance had been just below Little South Gate, on the west side. The site of the monastery was mostly inhabited by tanners. And so in Peshall's time.

The sites of the Black and Grey Friars were, in 1544, sold by Henry VIII, with other monastic lands, to private speculators for £1,094 3s. 2d., and

---

[1] *City,* i. 399, n. 4.

[2] The front was rebuilt in 1628. John Howson was Bishop of Oxford 1619-1627. Ibid. i. 415, n. 2.

[3] Ibid. i. 405.

[4] The stream however was as dirty as in a later age. In 1293 the use of the 'corrupt water' of Trill Mill stream was forbidden by royal edict to the bakers and brewers, as obnoxious to health. *Collectanea,* II. 27. For its course see *Early History of Oxford,* p. 299, n. 4; and *City,* i. 415, n. 3.

[5] *City,* ii. 389.   [6] Ibid. i. 309.   [7] Ibid. i. 310.

quickly axes and hammers were at work. 'The trees were soon cut down, all the greens trod under foot, the church thrown down, and the stones, with the images and monuments of the greatest value, scattered about[1].' The 'pleasant groves and gardens,' the 'private meanders and recesses'—but it is a thrice-told tale. Johnson, viewing the decaying ruins of Oseney and Rewley, was so filled with indignation that for at least half an hour he could find no words. There were no ruins of the great buildings of the Dominicans and Franciscans for him to gaze upon, for wreck and pillage had left not one stone upon another. Their memory lives only in the names of a few miserable purlieus and dreary modern streets.

What were the sins of that age that its beauty and honour could deserve the fate that has befallen them? The words of Mr. Froude are well known :—

'The heavenly graces had once descended on the monastic orders, making them ministers of mercy, patterns of celestial life, breathing witnesses of the power of the Spirit in renewing and sanctifying the heart. And then it was that art and wealth poured out their treasures to raise fitting tabernacles for the dwelling of so divine a soul. Alike in the village and in the city, amongst the unadorned walls and lowly roofs which closed in the humble dwellings of the laity, the majestic houses of the Father of mankind and of his especial servants rose up in sovereign beauty. And ever at the sacred gates sat Mercy, pouring out relief from a never failing store to the poor and the suffering; ever within the sacred aisles the voices of holy men were pealing heavenwards in intercession for the sins of mankind; and such blessed influences were thought to exhale around those mysterious precincts that even the poor outcasts of society—the debtor, the felon, and the outlaw— gathered round the walls as the sick men sought the shadow of the apostles, and lay there sheltered from the avenging hand till their sins were washed from off their souls. The abbeys of the middle ages floated through the storms of war and conquest, like the ark upon the waves of the flood, in the midst of violence remaining inviolate, through the awful reverence which surrounded them.'

Golden ideals treasured in vessels, alas! of earth and clay.

The back way from the College to Oseney and the railway stations, along the line of the City wall, past the Norman keep and the ancient Castle mill, and so into High Street St. Thomas to the ivy-clad Church of St. Thomas of Canterbury, is about the pleasantest bit left of the old town, and has many almost Dutch glimpses of water and skyline. On the right in Castle Street are some remains of White Hall, which survived the fire of 1644. Dr. Ingram gives a picture of it as it was in 1837.

[1] Dugdale, vi. c. 3. p. 1529.

F

CHAPTER VII.

SCHOLARS OF BROADGATES HALL.

No name of a Principal of Broadgates Hall is known certainly before 1436; but it had produced some eminent canonists at an earlier date. A mediæval soldier, writer, and ecclesiastic, whom Prince (*Danmonii Orientales Illustres*) assigns to this Hall [1], was NICHOLAS UPTON, author of the treatise in four books, *De Studio Militari*, printed in 1654 by Bish. He served over seas under the Earl of Salisbury, and was before Orléans when it was relieved by the Maid. Duke Humphrey, styled by Fuller 'the Mecaenas-General of goodnesse and learning,'

'observing the parts and vertues of Mr. Upton, who at that time was not meanly skilled in both the laws, perswaded him to lay aside the sword and to take up his books again and follow his studies; withal encouraging him to take upon him holy orders. . . . Returning to the University he took the degree of bachelour of the canon and civil laws, and after that he proceeded doctor therein: a sort of learning much valued in those days.'

He was made canon of Wells, 1431, being then rector of Cheadsey, which he exchanged, Oct. 12, 1434, for Stapleford, Wilts. He became prebendary of Sarum May 14, 1446, and succeeded Edward Prents as chantor. He was also prebendary of St. Paul's. Upton built one of the houses in Sarum Close for the chantors. In 1452 he went to Rome to obtain the canonization by Nicholas V of Bishop Osmund. Fuller (*Worthies of Devon*), says that in expression of his gratitude to the Duke of Gloucester he 'presented his Patron with a Book (the first of that kind) of Heraldry.' He was himself 'of an Ancient family' in the west country.

---

[1] Prince was supplied with his information by Wood, who says: 'I am almost persuaded that Nicholas de Upton was borne in Sumersetshire (at Upton so called); that also, from our registers, he was bred in the famous hostle for Civilians and Canonists called Broadgates Hall (now Pembroke College) which was a noted receptacle in his time, and other times that followed, for Somersetshire men. But of these matters I will not be confident.' (*Life and Times*, iii. 467 n.)

A still earlier student at the Hall[1] was CARDINAL REPYNGDON, Chancellor of the University in 1397, 1401, and 1402.

Philip Repyngdon, a canon regular of the Austin priory of Sta. Maria de Pratis at Leicester, and afterwards abbot, a man of 'great and notable dexterity of wit,' had shown anti-transubstantiationist leanings in a sermon at Brackley, but 'while he was Bachelaur of Divinity he appeared an humble and benign person, insomuch that he was by all accounted a good man; but when he was doctorated in the summer of [1382], he began in his first Lecture to magnify Wycleve and his doctrine, and said he would defend it "in materia morali," and for that time keep silence till the Lord would enlighten the hearts of the Clergy concerning the Sacrament of the Altar, on which he was to preach on Corpus Christi Day next[2].' Mr. Green writes: 'In an English sermon at St. Frides-wyde's[3], Nicholas Herford had asserted the truth of Wyclif's doctrines, and Archbishop Courtenay ordered the Chancellor [Robert Rugge] to silence him and his adherents on pain of being himself treated as a heretic. The Chancellor fell back on the liberties of the University, and appointed as preacher another Wycliffite, who [i.e. on Corpus Christi Day, 1382] did not hesitate to style the Lollards "holy priests," and to affirm that they were protected by John of Gaunt. Party spirit meanwhile ran high among the students; the bulk of them sided with the Lollard leaders, and the Carmelite, Peter Stokes, who had procured the Archbishop's letters, cowered panic-stricken in his chamber, while the Chancellor, protected by an escort of a hundred townsmen, listened approvingly to Repyngdon's defiance. "I dare go no further," wrote the poor friar to the Archbishop, "for fear of death"; but he soon mustered courage to descend into the schools, where Repyngdon was now maintaining that the clerical order was "better when it was but nine year old than now that it has grown to a thousand years and more."' The harangue contained incitements to the people to pillage churches. Repyngdon did not show much more courage in this defiant utterance than in his subsequent recantation, for he had close at hand a band of men 'privily weaponed under their garments.' 'There was not a little joy throughout the whole University for that sermon,' says Foxe. The scholars threatened the friars with death. Courtenay however acted with much vigour. He procured royal breves ordering the instant banishment from Oxford of all who should receive into their Houses or Inns Wyclif, Herford, Repyngdon, or Ashton, and the destruction of all Lollardite tracts on pain of forfeiture by the University of its privileges. Herford and Repyngdon, now suspended from all academical acts, appealed in vain to John of Gaunt and then to Convocation. The duke

---

[1] Wood points it out as one of the errors of Gabriel Powell's book *De Anti-christo* that Repyngdon is assigned in it to Merton College; 'whereas it appears from Record that he was of *Broadgates* Hall, now *Pembroke* College.' (*Ath. Ox.*)

[2] Gutch's *Wood*, i. 503.

[3] In Lent, Herford argued that no religious should be admitted to any degree. The sermon was in the open air at St. Frideswyde's Cross.

himself denounced them as laics, devilish people, having nothing of God in them, and both were at Canterbury declared heretical and excommunicate. A few months later the Archbishop held a Synod at St. Frideswyde's, and after much evasion Repyngdon made a formal submission. His abilities were now transferred to the other side. In an Oxford Statute of 1400 he is styled 'clericus specialissimus illustrissimi Principis D. Regis Henrici.' In 1405 he was consecrated Bishop of Lincoln, and in 1408 received from Gregory XII the cardinal's hat of SS. Nereus and Achilles, being now looked on by the Lollards as one of their severest repressors. Thorpe said to the Archbishop, 'See now how Philip Rampington pursueth Christ's people,' and Arundel answered, 'No bishoppe of this lande pursueth now more sharplie them that holde thy waie than he doth[1].' However he disregarded the order of the Council of Constance in 1415, for the exhumation and burning of his former master's bones—Lutterworth being in his diocese—and it was not till 1428 that the Swift received Wyclif's ashes. Repyngdon resigned the Lincoln bishopric in 1420. 'Vir potens et Deum timens amans veritatem et detestans avaritiam,' an Oxford Statute describes him. He was a benefactor of Cobham's Library.

In 1412 the University decreed that the name of Philip Repyntone, Bishop of Lincoln, should be remembered specially for ever in the masses, with the names of King Henry IV, Henry Prince of Wales and his brothers Thomas, John, and Humphrey, Thomas Arundel Bishop of Canterbury, Edmund Earl of March, and Master Richard Courtenay.

The espousing by Oxford of the cause of the Simple Priests lent great moment to Wycliffite teachings in the rest of England. But when Repyngdon and Herford were silenced, it was as though a seedladen plant were cut at the root. The University drooped. The religious movement had diverted attention from the schools, and now both theological speculation and philosophical interest died down. The academic population dwindled to a shrunken remnant of literary mendicants, and for more than a century Oxford languished with a feeble life, until the revival of classical learning brought back to it some of its old energy and renown. But it was never again, great and splendid as its influence has since been, to recover the lofty position which it held during the greater part of the twelfth, thirteenth, and fourteenth centuries, when it 'exerted a weight and authority in England and Europe generally, to which no existing institution furnishes the slightest parallel or analogon[2],' when it could be spoken of as the 'sun, eye, and

[1] Foxe's account of Repingdon follows Walden's *Fasciculus Zizaniorum Wiclevi.*
[2] Kirkpatrick's *The University*, p. 7.

soul' of the kingdom, or, as by Matthew of Paris in 1256, as the
' fundamental base,' second only to Paris itself, of the Western Church,
then in the highest ascendancy of spiritual and temporal dominion, of
vigorous intellect and material splendour; or, as by Grostête, as
actually 'secunda Ecclesia.' Other causes contributed to the University's decline from that pre-eminence. Knowledge, more widely
diffused, was no longer the monopoly of clerks, nor was the clerisy any
longer the only profession. The authority of the Church was waning.
The assertion of nationalism and the break up of Christendom in the
16th century caused Oxford and Cambridge to become insular
corporations, cutting them off more and more from other European
centres of learning, and dissolving the commonwealth of letters. The
New Learning gave an impulse to scholarship and speculation that
outweighed this disintegrating cause. But in the fifteenth century the
old tide was nearly run out and the new tide had not begun to come in.
Constantinople was still in the hands of the Turks, and its treasure
houses of learning locked to the world. The false dawn of Church
Reformation had died away at Oxford with the extinguishing of the
crude doctrines of which Repyngdon made himself the mouthpiece.
It was especially the case, as Huber remarks, that ' after the suppression of the Lollard Movement canon law more and more lost scientific
interest, and became a mere scholastic ritual [1].' The revival of learning
under Colet, Linacre, Grocyn and Erasmus favoured literary and physical
rather than legal studies. Early in the fifteenth century however
the jurists and medical students had a combined, independent organization, and in 1396 they had proctors of their own. Civilians now
obtained the privilege of becoming doctors in their faculty without
proceeding first in arts, and yet keeping their seats in Congregation
and Convocation. No one however to this day may ordinarily
practise in the Chancellor's Court who is not a master in arts.

The Oxford monks (who had sided with their old enemies the
beneficed parsons to put down the new intruders into parishes) aimed
at asserting for the tonsure a complete independence of the jurisdiction
of the University. In this they were not successful. At a later date,
on Sept. 30, 1530, a grey friar, 'Dompnus' Robert Beste, was
summoned before the Chancellor together with a scholar of Broadgates
Hall on grave suspicion of incontinence and disturbance of the peace,
and was temporarily committed to 'Le Bocardo [2].' The Broadgates

[1] VoL i. § 81.
[2] He was afterwards vicar of St. Martin in the Fields, and took the side of the
Reformation. See *Grey Friars in Oxford*, ed. Little, O. H. S., p. 286.

scholar was warned to keep clear of a certain Joanna, wife of William Cooper, of St. Ebbe's, who laid traps for Minorites and then defamed them. Another Broadgates clerk, Richard Roberts, sued Robert Puller a Friar Minor, about 1534, for 25*s.* due to him 'ex causa emptionis et vendicionis.'

Friar Beste was also about to be 'arrayd' by the Mayor and Commonalty, for some offence, at the Sessions; but 'Mr. Secretarie Catly' forbad them to indict any privileged person. The cause of this intervention was the indictment of felony brought against the Proctors. The Town complained to Wolsey of the Chancellor and Scholars of the University that

'they doe vse watchinge by night without any of the kinges officers, and enter into any man's house and make search in the same house and disturbe and disquiet the same persons: and also in the nighttime when men should take their rest they will Carry Carts about the stretes and beat at men's dores and balkes to their great inquietnesse.'

In particular, William Grethedde had sworn that

'the Procters with others came and puld open in the night th e doores of the sayd W. G. and came to his house where he was goeing to his bedd in his chamber which seeinge his doores broken vp came downe with a poker in his hande for his defence and asked them, what they did in his house? They sayd, knaue thou shalt knowe what, and then they struke hime and fell hime downe and tooke his purse with ij*s.* 4*d.* in it with other thinges and brought hime to prison for the which vnlawfull acts the Procter was indited.'

The Corporation also complain that 'whereas they were comaunded by the Judges for to keepe the King's waich, they were chardged that they should not waich without the Justice, the Constable, and diuers other were in theire company,' &c.[1]

This question of Watch and Ward was a constant cause of dispute between the academic and the civic 'universities.' A papal brief of 1207 had permitted the town watch to arrest a scholar under certain circumstances; but he was to be forthwith handed over to the Spiritual Court. To prevent the recurring conflicts between the burghers and the students, the Chancellor and Regent Masters, in 1252, forbade the Nations to assemble for the keeping any saint's day with solemnity, heading any band of dancers with masks and clamour in the churches or streets, or going in procession with wreaths and garlands on their heads. Watch and Ward, together with Hue and Cry, were assigned to the University by royal privilege in 1356. But in 1518 the

---

[1] *Oxford City Documents*, ed. Rogers, O. H. S., pp. 270, 282.

University surrendered its privileges into the hands of Wolsey, and for the next few years brawls between the town and the charterless gownsmen were frequent. One of the most notable of these conflicts was the fatal encounter on June 4, 1520, between the students of Broadgates Hall and the town patrol:—

1520, June 5. Coroner's Inquisition upon the Death of Hugh Todde, in an affray between the Schólars of Broadyates and the Citizens.

Inquisition indented taken in the town of Oxford in the county of Oxford, 5th day of June, 12th year of Henry VIII, before John Hedde, one of the Coroners of our lord the King, upon view of the body of Hugh Todde, there killed and found dead. [The jury] say upon their oathes that Thomas Bisley, late of Oxford, scholar; Thomas Houghton, of Oxford aforesaid, scholar; Maurice Canop, of the same town, scholar; and Thomas Wykiswey, of the same town and county, clerk, with many other malefactors and disturbers of the King's peace assembled with them armed in a warlike manner, by force and arms, viz. sticks, swords, bows and arrows, the 4th day of June, 12 Henry VIII, about the hour of 11 at night of the same day in which Hugh Todd, John Godestowe, etc., then being the Kinges wachemen, were insulted, beaten and badly wounded, so that they despaired of their lives, and the same Hugh Todd was then and there feloniusly killed and murdered against the peace of our lord the King; and upon this the said Thomas Bisley, etc., after the said felony and murder done and perpetrated the said fifth of June, took to flyght[1].

On August 1st the King's breve was issued to Thomas Englefield, Sheriff of Oxford, for an inquiry concerning the death of Todd and the arrest of the rioters.

'Inquiratur pro domino Rege si Thomas Bisley nuper de Oxon scholaris Thomas Houghton de Oxon predict' in Com' predict' scholaris Mauritius Cannope de eisdem villa et Com' scholaris et Thomas Wyckyswey nuper de eisdem villa et Com' clericus aggregatis sibi quam pluribus aliis malefactoribus et pacis domini Regis perturbatoribus ... modo guerino araiat' et armat' vi et armis viz baculis gladiis arcubus et sagittis 4° die Junii anno regni regis Henr' 8ⁱ 12° circa horā xjᵃᵐ in nocte ejusdem diei in quosdam Hugonem Todde, Johannem Godstowe et alios ad tunc existen' yᵉ kynges watchmen riotose insultum fecerunt et ipsos Hugonem Todde et Johannem Godstowe ac alios pʳdict' ad tunc et ibidem verberaverunt vulneraverunt et male tractaverunt sic quod de vita sua desperabant ac eundem Hugonem Todde ad tunc et ibidem inventum riotose et felonice interfecerunt et murdraverunt contra pacem Domini Regis[2].'

It seems that the offenders had been banished by the University on June 16, together with John Wayat, a civilian.

The relations of Town and Gown were easy at Oxford as compared with Paris, where, if a riotous student were slain, the Provost-Marshal

---

[1] Twyne, xxiii.   [2] Ibid. v. 199.

or other Magistrate risked perpetual imprisonment, and, if he hanged
one or two to make an example, was liable to be compelled some
weeks later to take down the corpses from the gallows with his own
hands and kiss their lips. But even at Oxford a citizen's life was
cheap, as appears by the sequel :—

15$\frac{20}{21}$, Jan. 17.   Inquest on Hugh Todde.

'Thomas Wynknyslay [*alias* Whem], scholar of canon law, who was
banished when the scholars of Brodeyates fought against the townsmen
because he did not appear before the Chancellor, petitioned that he might
return to this University, which was granted upon these terms, that he
pay to the University 6*s*. 8*d*., for the reparation of the staff of the inferior
bedel of arts, xx*d*., and say three masses for the good estate of the said
regents, and for the soul of the defunct in that fight [1].'

The question between the Dogberries and the 'bull-dogs' of that age
was still unsettled in Laud's time. See Gutch's Wood's *Annals*, ii.
422, n.

The clerks of this quarter seem always to have been quarrelsome,
to judge by a murderous assault made in St. Aldate's churchyard,
Jan. 27, 1306, on three unoffending citizens [2]. The legists were
especially prominent when brawls were afoot. On May 4, 1449,
certain scholars of 'the hall commonly called Brodeyates in the parish
of St. Aldate' entered with force and arms, during the night, the
house of Richard Wyntryngham, a butcher, and assaulted him. Their
names were Master Haywode, John Foxe, John Man, William Dicson,
Thomas Blakeman, William Layberne, and — Hewode [3].

Three years before this the scholars of 'Lata Porta' were at
variance with those of Pauline Hall. John Scelott and John Snawdone
on behalf of the principal and fellows of the former, and Richard Pede
and Thomas Ashfeld on behalf of the principal and fellows of the
latter, arbitrated and composed the quarrel. The principals were to
entreat reconciliation either of other on behalf of their respective
parties. Owyn Lloyde, principal of Pauline, was to say to the
principal of Broadgates that if he had done him or his any wrong he
humbly asks pardon. Further Sir John Olney, presbyter, and Owyn
were to exchange the kiss of peace, and take a corporal oath, touching
the Holy Gospels, that they will maintain brotherly love, and bind
themselves thereto under their hand by a bond of 100 shillings, the
bond to be lodged with the Chancellor. And all the fellows were to

[1] Twyne, xxiv. 406.   *Oxford City Records.*
[2] *Oxford City Documents*, ed. Rogers, O. H. S., p. 177.
[3] Anstey's *Munimenta*, p. 590.

keep the peace. One, David Philipe, who was alleged to have struck John Olney, was to kneel, and ask and receive pardon. This 'laudum sive arbitrium' was declared, July 7, 1446, in St. Frideswyde's church, by the altar of the saint, in the presence of the parties, who confirmed the same [1].

In 1503 a more than usually deadly pest emptied the hostels and inns, so that of fifty-five halls only thirty-three were inhabited, and that slenderly.

[1] *Munimenta*, pp. 552-4. In 1451 Owyn-y-floide was Principal of Edmund Hall (p. 621).

CHAPTER VIII.

WHILE Broadgates Hall (now comprising at least New College and Abingdon Chambers, Broadgates itself, Cambey's and Mine) was extending its borders to right and left, the long-gathering storm of ecclesiastical reformation broke over the land, shaking especially the Universities. The unendowed Halls were affected by the course of events even more than the Colleges, since the confiscation of the monastic revenues deprived the poorer clerks of their exhibitions and means of support, and the University was 'almost destitute of scholars.' At the beginning of Elizabeth's reign only nine Halls, the number of the Muses, were left, viz. Alban, Broadgates, Hart, Gloucester, White, New Inn, Edmund, St. Mary, and Magdalen. Three of these are mentioned by Nicholas Robinson[1] as still devoted to legal studies—

> Candida, *Lata*, Nova, studiis civilibus apta,
> *Porta* patet Musis, Justiniane, tuis.

The times were not favourable to the Civil Law. Not only were men's minds engrossed with theological speculation, but the tide was flowing strongly away from Roman, and towards a national jurisprudence. The spirit of the Reformation was Germanic and northern. Moreover the lawyers were being drawn more and more to London, where their practice lay, and the establishment of Inns of Court was inevitable, constituting (Huber remarks[2]) a third University, Oxford and Cambridge retaining little more than the power of conferring degrees in law, for which a mechanical exercise sufficed. So scarce were civilians becoming even before the Reformation that the Kings

---

[1] *Queen Elizabeth in Oxford*, 1566. Wood however, under date 1551, says that 'the present Halls' (those i. e. that were halls in his day), 'especially those of Edmund and New Inn, were void of Students' (Gutch, ii. 110).

[2] *English Universities*, i. § 81.

sought permission from the Pope for ecclesiastics to study the Civil Law, that they might have counsellors. There was, it is true, a strongly Cæsarean feeling in Henry VIII and his son. The jurists having been encouraged to exclude the 'artists' from the Convocation which met on April 8, 1530, to consider the Divorce, the King next forbade the granting by Oxford of degrees in Canon Law, but endowed a Civil Law Professorship, with a salary of £40, together with chairs of Theology, Greek, Hebrew, and Medicine. Edward VI's Letters Patents of 1549 recite that 'it hath been shewn us that the study of the Civil Law is almost extinct. We therefore impose care and solicitude on you ut quibus poteritis viis et modis illud excitetis et amplificetis.' The king prescribed that the Law Reader should lecture on the Pandects, the Code, or the Ecclesiastical Laws of the Realm. He seems to have purposed to gather all the civilians into one College[1], the physicians into another. During Elizabeth's reign the Universities, so violently handled, were gathering anew their scattered force. Whereas in 1551, of 1015 names on the Oxford buttery books, 'the greater part were absent and had taken their last farewell,' the students now began to return. The Schools of Arts were no longer used by laundresses to dry their clothes in. The Puritan idea that the old exercises were ridiculous and degrees anti-Christian was weakened, and the 'barbarous insolencies upon treasures of good letters' stopped. But the graduates in jurisprudence were still few. Nevertheless Broadgates Hall was presided over by a succession of able lawyers, some of whom were men of eminence in an eminent age. It did more perhaps than any English institution to keep the Law of Nations alive. When in 1603 the dissolution of the faculty was feared, the Chancellor declared that 'this Academy possesses four heads or ornaments, upon which as its firmest foundations the whole structure of the University has been placed, that is the faculties of Theology, Jurisprudence, Medicine, and Artes Humaniores; of which if one were taken away the fall of the whole edifice would ensue.' And James I gave the University the right to elect two burgesses who should be grave and learned men professing the Civil Law.

The first Principal of note was Wolsey's friend, BRIAN HIGDEN (1505–1508), B.C.L. 1500, LL.D. 1506, May 28[2].

---

[1] Doctors' Commons, incorporated in 1768 as 'the College of Doctors of Law exercent in the Ecclesiastical and Admiralty Courts,' was founded by Dr. Hervie, Dean of Arches, in 1568. It was demolished in 1894. Trinity Hall was founded chiefly for civilians. There is said to have been a college for professors of civil and canon law in London as early as the eighth century!

[2] See *Registrum Univ.* vol. i. ed. Boase, O. H. S., p. 290.

On giving up his principality he became parson successively of Buchenhall (1508), of Kirkby (1511), and of Nettleton (1513). In 1508 Higden was preferred to a stall at Lincoln, becoming sub-dean in 1511. In 1515 he was made archdeacon of the West Riding of York, the next year (June 20) canon of York, with the prebend of Ulleskelf—where Leland says he built 'a pleasant house'—and a week later Dean of York. He was also canon of St. Paul's. He may have owed his preferments in part to his having been on the council of Henry VII's natural son, the Duke of Richmond; but he appears to have been a man of striking ability. In 1526, Dean Higden was a Commissioner with Ralph Fane, Earl of Westmoreland, for the signing a treaty of peace with the King of Scots, which they effected with great quickness and success. The next year we find him writing to Wolsey complaining of the transference of ecclesiastical causes from his court to London. After the Cardinal's fall, however, he continued on a friendly footing with Cromwell. As he grew old his intellects seem to have given way. Colyns, treasurer of York, writes to Cromwell, Jan. 12, 153⅘, that the Dean was 'a crasytt.' There was some design of pensioning him off, but he died in his office on June 5, 1539, and was buried in the south cross aisle of the Minster. The brass and epitaph have disappeared. He presented the church with a fine cope. He is styled by Wood a 'Benefactor to Learning,' and a fellowship at Brasenose was founded by him. In 1508 his name appears as a 'judex ad inquirendum de pace' between Allhallows Church and St. Martin's[1]. Brian's brother, John Higden, was President of Magdalen and the first Dean of King Henry the Eighth's College.

RICHARD ARCHE, or ARCHER, LL.B., Principal 1526, was vicar of Ramsbury, 1518, and of Avebury, 1520. He supplicated for D.C.L., Jan. 18, 153⅘, but was not then admitted.

Richard Wolman dying at that time, Cromwell succeeded him in the deanery of Windsor, and Arche stepped into his prebendal stall. At the same time the King made him one of his chaplains. He was vicar of Hanney, near Wantage, 1543, and rector of Clewer, 1554. In that year he became canon of Sarum, having already, on Innocents' Day, 1551, succeeded Matthew Wootton as treasurer there.

On the walls of a cell in the Beauchamp Tower are rudely cut the words: '1570: IHON-STORE . DOCTOR.' They were carved during his last imprisonment by JOHN STORY, who has been diversely regarded as 'a harmless old man,' and as the worst, next to Bonner, of the persecutors of the reformed beliefs. Strype says that he was at Broadgates with Bonner, but the dates refute this. Story was first at Henxey Hall in St. Aldate's parish, whence he proceeded D.C.L. July 29, 1538 (B.C.L. May 8, 1531). In 1537 he was elected

[1] *Reg. Univ.* vol. i. p. 296.

Principal of Broadgates, being 'a most noted Civilian and Canonist of his time.' When Henry VIII's Commissioners established the Civil Law Lecture, Story, who already, it appears, had some kind of salary from the King, was appointed chief Moderator. 'Afterwards performing excellent service at the Siege of *Bologne* in *Picardie*, in the administration of the Civil Law under the *Lord-Marshall* there, the King, in consideration thereof, did renew his former grant of the said Lecture in form of Letters Patent for the term of life of the said *John*, in the Year 1546 or thereabouts, joyning with him for his ease Mr. *Rob. Weston*, Fellow of *All Souls* College,' and afterwards Principal of Broadgates.

He was also an advocate of Doctors' Commons. The Puritan historians accuse him of very irregular conduct while at Oxford. At Mary's accession his patent was renewed, but Story resigned the Regius Professor's chair to Aubrey, and became Chancellor of the dioceses of London and Oxford, and dean of the Arches. He sate in Parliament for Hindon, 1547-52, for East Grinstead, 1553, for Bramber, 1554, for Ludgershall, 1554, 1555, for Downton, 1558. In Edward's first Parliament Story, speaking against the Prayer Book, boldly cited the text 'Woe to thee, O land, when thy king is a child' (Eccl. x. 16). He then retired into Flanders till Mary's accession. Story was Queen's Proctor at the trial of Archbishop Cranmer in St. Mary's, being 'a furious zealot for the religion of Boner' (Coote). At the trial of Philpots he said: 'I tell thee that there hath never yet been any one burnt but I have spoken with him and have been a cause of his despatch.' *Philpots*: 'You have the more to answer for, master doctor, as you shall find in another world.' Philpots avowed however that Joan Bocher had deserved her burning, 'because she stood against one of the manifest articles of the faith, contrary to the Scriptures.' Story was employed to restore the roods and images. He made a bold and passionate speech, openly in Parliament, against the princess Elizabeth, affirming the folly of lopping branches from the tree of Heresy when the root was suffered to remain. He could hardly hope at her accession to escape the axe and cord, if once trapped. Thrown into hold he broke out and escaped overseas to Antwerp, 'where he continued a most bloody persecutor, still raging against God's saints with fire and sword. Insomuch as he, growing to be familiar and right dear to the Duke of Alva, received special commission from him to search the ships for goods forfeited and for English books' (Foxe). For this office he was recommended by his knowledge of civil law. The hatred with which he was held by his countrymen rested less on religious grounds, it has been thought, than on commercial resentment. 'At length being invited under hand to search the Ship of one *Parker*, an English Man, went unwarily therein: Whereupon *Parker* causing the hatches to be shut when *Storie* was searching under deck, he hoised sail and brought him Prisoner into *England* about the beginning of *Decemb.* 1570. So that being clap'd up close Prisoner within the *Tower of London* did undergo several examinations[1].' He repeatedly refused the oath of the Supremacy, and declined even to plead, audaciously declaring himself no subject of the Queen's. He would only say, 'I wish for my part that I had done more than I did.' He was accused of treasonable correspondence with the Nevilles and Nortons. After being prayed for and animated in his faith by John Fekenham, Abbot of Westminster, a fellow-prisoner, the old man was drawn on a hurdle to Tyburn, June 1, 1571. The scene on the scaffold, after he had delivered a 'grave and becoming' address, was one of revolting and indescribable horror. After death, his head was set on London bridge and his quarters on four gates of the City. He had wished to be buried within the Grey Friars of Louvain, to which convent he had left '20 florens' for his funeral exequies. He had been a lay brother of that order and a signal benefactor. Together with More, Fisher, and others of that bloody time, John Story has been beatified by the papal see. Strype describes him as 'worse than Boner. Yet notwithstanding Story is made a saint at Rome, and his martyrdom printed and set up in the English College there[2].' He was the son of Nicholas and Joan Story.

Several other Principals were persons of eminence. One, THOMAS YONGE, became Archbishop of York and Lord President of the North. Wood writes :—

'Thomas Yong a learned Civilian, Son of *John* [son of Brian] *Yong* of *Pembrokshire* by *Elianor* his Wife, was born in that County, became a Student in the Univ. of *Oxon* (in *Broadgates* hall as it seems) about the year 1528 [B.A. 1529, M.A. 1534], where applying his muse to the study of the Civil Law took a degree in that faculty nine years after [1538], being then in sacred Orders.' D.C.L. 1565. He held various Welsh preferments. 'In 1542 he was made principal of the said hall, and soon after Chantor and Canon of *S. Davids*; where, being much scandalized at the unworthy actions[3] of *Rob. Ferrar* Bishop of that place, did, with others, draw up articles against him; which being proved before the Kings Commissioners, the said Bishop was imprison'd in the time of K. *Ed.* 6. In the reign of Q. *Mary*, *Th. Yong* fled from the nation for religion sake, and remained in Germany[4] in an obscure condition during her time. But when Q. *Elizabeth* came to the Crown, and *H. Morgan*, another accuser of *Rob. Ferrar* had been depriv'd of his Bishoprick of S. *Davids*, the said *Yong* was design'd to succeed him.' He was Spital preacher in 1557, was consecrated in January, 1559, but a year later by Parker's advice was

[1] *Ath.* i. 132.

[2] *Annals*, I. (ii) 297.

[3] Strype (*Annals*, I. (i) 370) blames Yonge, though he 'was charactered to be a virtuous and godly man.' Farrar would not visit his cathedral. He suffered by burning under Mary.

[4] He was one of six who had the courage to avow reformed opinions in the first Convocation of Mary's reign. The place of his exile was Wesel. Scory and about a hundred others shared it. These refugees did not scruple the use of the Common Prayer.

'translated to *York*, and about the same time was made President of the Queens Council in the north parts of *England.*' He was also President of the Marches of Wales. ' In Feb. 1564 he was actually created Doctor of the Civil Law, and dying [at Sheffield] on the 26 *June*, in fifteen hundred sixty and eight, was buried at the east end of the Choire of his Cath. Ch. at *York.* Over his grave was soon after laid a marble stone, with this Epitaph on it. *Thomas Yongus nuper Eboracensis Archiepiscopus, Civilis Juris Doctor peritissimus, quem propter gravitatem, summum ingenium, eximiam prudentiam, excellentemq; rerum politicarum scientiam, illustrissima Regina septentrionalibus hujus regni partibus Praesidem constituit, quo magistratu quinq; annos perfunctus est. Sedit Archiepiscopus annos septem et sex menses. Obiit Vicesimo sexto die mensis Junii, an.* 1568. He had taken to Wife in his elderly years one *Jane* daughter of *Thom. Kynaston* of *Estwick* in *Shropshire*, by whom he had issue *George Yong*, afterwards a knight living in *York* 1612, for whose sake the father, being covetous of wealth, pulled down a goodly hall belonging to him as Archbishop, for the greediness of the lead (as 'tis said) that covered it. Concerning which matter there is a large story extant, related by an author [Sir John Harrington in his *Brief View of the State of the Church of England*, p. 171] who was no friend to married Bishops[1].'

ROBERT WESTON, of Weeford, Staffordshire, was Principal from 1546 to 1549, Fellow of All Souls, 1536, B.C.L. Feb. 17, 153⅞, D.C.L. July 28, 1556,—a considerable interval. He was the only doctor admitted in Civil Law that year, and, there being too few resident D.C.L.'s to do so, Thomas Darbyshere, afterwards Principal, inceptor in Civil Law, was admitted to depone for him[2]. In 1556 he was an advocate of Doctors' Commons. Before this, while Principal of Broadgates, being then Chancellor of Exeter (Gutch's Wood, ii. 856), Weston was appointed Deputy Regius Professor of Civil Law for Story.

In Mary's reign he was made Dean of Arches, and sate in Parliament for Exeter, 1553, and after her death for Lichfield, 1558–9 (being then LL.D.). Dean of Wells, 1570. Elizabeth made him one of the Lords Justices for Ireland, and from 1567 to his death Weston was Lord High Chancellor of Ireland, being 'eminent in that place,' and Dean of St. Patrick's. He appears however never to have been in Holy Orders. It is stated on his noble monument in St. Patrick's that ' he was so learned, judicious, and upright in the Court of Judicature, all the time that he was Lord Chancellour, that no Order or Decree that he made was ever

---

[1] *Athenae*, i. 595. For papers relating to this lady's inheritance from her husband, see Strype, *Annals*, I. (ii) 300. Yonge took little or no part in the vestments controversy. But there was a conspiracy to take his life in 1565.

[2] *Reg. Univ.* ed. Clark, O. H. S., II. i. 117; and Gutch, ii. 133.

questioned or reversed.' He died May 20, 1573. There is a bronze bust of him at All Souls. On the monument in Christ Church of his only son, Dr. John Weston—who 'forum pro suggesto mutavit ut animas Christo lucrifaceret,' being ' Ciceroniana eloquentia praeclarus '—Robert Weston is described as ' Hyberniae quondam Cancellarius, et Elizabethae Reginae praecharissimus ; qui rebelles ibi perfidos non tam potentia quam sanctitate domuit.' He bore Ermine, a martlet gules ; on a chief azure five bezants. John Weston's wife, Ann, died in Christ Church in 1663, aged a hundred.

Jewel told Martyr, ' I can do nothing without Randolph.' This principal played a great part in state affairs under Elizabeth. Sɪʀ Thomas Randolph, son of Avery Randolph or Randall, was born at Baddlesmere, Kent, in 1523. After being taught by George Buchanan, he was chosen one of the first Students of Christ Church; B.C.L. 1547. In 1549 he succeeded Weston at Broadgates, but the accession of Mary in 1553 made his 'existence' there, though shared with Jewel, a ' wretchedness,' and he retired to France.

With Elizabeth Randolph was in high favour, and was singled out for various important embassies—thrice to the Scots Queen, seven times to James VI—carrying out Cecil's policy. An adverse writer describes him as 'of a dark, intriguing spirit, full of cunning and void of conscience.' Prof. Froude, however, paints a plain, blunt, stout-hearted Englishman, one who after a famous interview with Darnley 'turned on his heel "without reverence or farewell."' He needed something more than address to execute, disguised as a merchant, the secret conveyance of the Earl of Arran from his hostage-captivity at Chastelherault to Switzerland and thence to Scotland. Randolph (in Jewel's Letters called Pamphilus[1]) promoted Arran's courtship of Elizabeth, for whom Henry VIII had intended him. This was in 1560. In the northern kingdom he urged Mary to wed Leicester, and to conform to presbyterianism. She would not, she replied, 'make merchandize of her conscience.' At one time he suffered imprisonment in Edinburgh ; at another a harquebus was shot in at his window. He was finally outed from the realm in February, 1566. It is from Randolph's correspondence with Cecil, with Bedford, with the Council of State, and with Elizabeth, that we have the clearest picture of the unhappy reign of the Queen of Scots, and the most circumstantial account of Rizzio's murder[2]. In the Lansdowne, Cotton, and Scots MSS. are numberless papers drawn up by him. Randolph was also on several occasions Elizabeth's trusted envoy[3] to the courts of

---

[1] ' Pamphilus the presiding angel and companion of our friend Crito ' (Arran). ' Your guest Crito and his friend Pamphilus are not idle. The saucy youth came to Athens and won the good graces of Glycerium ' (Elizabeth).

[2] ' He was not slayne in the quenes presence as was saide, but going down the stayres oute of the chamber of presence.'

[3] In an appendix to the life of Mede (p. 76) the writer says : ' Queen Elizabeth gave a strict charge and command to both the Chancellors of both Universities

Russia and France. The Russia Company was established in consequence of a commercial treaty brought about by his diplomacy. On that embassy his secretary was Turbervile the poet. In 1571, while ambassador at the Court of Scotland, he challenged the French envoy, Virac, who had taken liberties with Queen Elizabeth's name and Randolph's own. He did not indeed receive more tokens of favour from his sovereign than knighthood and some minor posts. But his nature was unambitious. 'At length after he had painfully spent his time in continual service of his Prince and Country, at home and abroad, he quietly surrendred up his last breath in his house at St. *Peter's* hill near to *Pauls Wharf* in *London* on the 8 of *June* in Fifteen hundred and ninety, aged 67 (leaving then behind him several Children that he had by two Wives), whereupon his body, accompanied by one or two Heralds of armes, was buried 6 of *July* following in the Church of St. *Peter.*' One of his wives was sister to Sir Francis Walsingham.

In the 1583 edition of Jewel's *Treatise of the Sacraments* are these verses prefixed:—

'Ornatissimo viro Thomae Randolph armigero serenissimo ad Scotos legato integerrimo.

Quis te junxit amor docto, Randolphe, Juello,
  Oxonia, exilium, musa, laborque notant.
Et quod ad exequias defuncti ducere plectrum
  Triste, Buchananos Patriciosque facis:
(Quis tibi gratus erit pro tali munere ?) certe
  Auctior hoc studio gratia facta tua est.
Nec nihil ex illo referes. Sacra signa Redemptor,
  Essent ut fidei tessera fida, dedit.
Haec tuus exposuit sancte, tibi dedico: ne sit
  Tam rarae et fidei tessera nulla piae.

    Tuae dignitatis studiosus Johan. Garbrandus.'

Jewel's papers were all left to Garbrand.

Besides his troubles from without in Mary's reign, Randolph's principalship of Broadgates had not been undisturbed, under Edward VI, from within. On June 9, 1550, Thomas Darbishire and ten other 'scholares' of the Hall appeared before the Vice-Chancellor with a statement of their complaints against their Principal, Mr. Thomas Randoll. One of three 'scholares' who had presented him six months before to the Vice-Chancellor on his election was

to bring her a just true and impartial account of all the eminent and hopeful students (that were graduates) in each University. . . . The use she made of it was that if she had an Ambassador to send abroad then she of herself would nominate such a man of such an House to be his Chaplain, and another of another House to be his Secretary, etc. When she had any places to dispose of fit for persons of an academical education, she would herself consign such persons as she judged to be *pares negotiis.*'

G

William Tyndale. Wood[1] evidently supposes this to have been the famous translator of the Scriptures; who however was strangled in 1536. Of course it is possible that, as a Canon of Cardinal College, he may have had, while it was being built, his chamber in Broadgates. But I know no evidence for this.

GEORGE SUMMASTER[2] while Principal (1575–1619) added to the accommodation for his students. At his death these numbered seven Masters, ten Bachelors, and sixteen Commoners. To this Principal was dedicated the first edition of Hooker's two Sermons on St. Jude by Henry Jackson of C. C. C., the original editor, under Spenser, of Hooker's remains, and the 'polisher' and arranger of the disputable Book VIII, 'a me plane vitae restitutum. Tulit alter honores.' The two Sermons are dedicated thus :—

'To the Worshipful M. GEORGE SUMMASTER, Principal of Broad-Gates Hall, in Oxford, HENRY JACKSON wisheth all happiness—Sir, Your kind acceptance of a former[3] testification of that respect I owe you, hath made me venture to shew the world these godly sermons under your name.' The dedication defends Latimer's 'King of Clubs' sermon against the railing of Parsons and concludes, 'You shall read nothing here but what I persuade myself you have long practised in the constant course of your life. It remaineth only that you accept of these labours tendered to you by him who wisheth you the long joys of this world and the eternal of that which is to come.—Oxon, from Corpus Christi college, this 13 of January, 1613 (1614).'

The penultimate Principal of Broadgates was the eminent jurist DR. JOHN[4] BUDDEN, who disputed in 1605 in Civil Law before James I, and of whom Wood gives the following account :—

'Son of *Joh. Budden* of *Canford* in *Dorsetshire*, was born in that County, entered into *Merton* coll. in Mich. Term, 1582 [Dec. 14, plebeii

---

[1] *City,* i. 563, n. 2.

[2] Of the family of Somaster, of Widecombe in Devon, eight descents are described in the Visitation of 1620. The co-heiresses of the elder branch married Trefry and Kent. Thomas, a younger brother of George Somaster (Fellow of All Souls, 1578), was archdeacon of Cornwall, and continued the main line. The representative of this branch married a co-heiress of Arundell of Trerice, and was of Painsford in Ashsprington (which had belonged to the Somasters since Henry VII) in 1620. John Somaster, esqre., the last of this branch, died at Stokenham in 1681. Arms : Arg. a castle triple-towered, within an orle of fleur de lis, sa. Crest, a portcullis, arg. (*Lysons,* ccxvi).

[3] I do not know what this was. Jackson had in 1612 printed at the University Press the Sermon on Justification, and probably some smaller treatises of Hooker, and also Wyclif's *Wicket.* But none of these is dedicated to Summaster. Izaak Walton's *Life of Hooker* was dedicated to a benefactor of this College, Bishop Morley, under whose roof it was written.

[4] Godwin calls him 'William': see Hearne, ed. Doble, O. H. S., ii. 245.

filius], aged 16, admitted Scholar of *Trinity* coll. 30 of May following, took the degree of Bach. of Arts [Oct. 19, 1586], and soon after [June 27, 1589] was translated to *Glouc.* hall, for the sake, and at the request, of Mr. *Tho. Allen,* where being mostly taken up with the study of the Civil Law, yet he took the degree of M. of Arts, as a Member thereof. [He responded in Comitiis, July 14, 1595.] At length he was made Philosophy Reader of *Magd.* coll., proceeded in the Civil Law 1602, made Principal of *New* Inn 1609[1], the Kings Professor of the Civil Law soon after [1611], and Principal of *Broadgates* hall [April 10, 1611]. He was a person of great Eloquence, an excellent Rhetorician, Philosopher, and a most noted Civilian.' He was also eminent in 'astronomy and geometry.' 'This Dr. *Budden* died in *Broadgates* hall on the eleventh of *June* in sixteen hundred and twenty. From which place his body being carried to the Divinity School, *Rich. Gardiner* of *Ch. Ch.* the Deputy-Orator delivered an eloquent Speech in praise of him, before the Doctors, Masters, and Scholars of the University. Which being done, the body was conveyed thence to St. *Aldate's* Church near to the hall of *Broadgates,* and there in the Chancel was interred on the 14 of the same month.'

He wrote in Latin a rhetorical Life of Waynflete (1602), and a Life of Archbishop Morton (1607); translated into Latin Sir Thos. Bodley's Statutes of the Publick Library, and Sir Thos. Smith's *Commonwealth of England*; and did out of French into English *A Discourse for Parents' Honour and Authority over their Children,* written by Peter Frodius, a renowned French civilian.

Of Canonists who were not Principals, the most famous name is EDMUND BONNER, 'the Spunge of Blood.' Wood adopts the tale that he 'was the natural son of *George Savage,* Priest, Parson of *Davenham* in *Cheshire,* natural son of Sir *Joh. Savage* of *Clifton* in the said County, Knight of the *Garter,* and one of the counsel to K. *Hen.* 7.' His mother, Elizabeth Frodsham, was, it was said, married after his birth to Edmund Bonner, a Worcestershire sawyer. 'So,' says Strype, 'I have read in some good MSS.'

'Yet to do him and history as much right as things will bear, I shall relate what the late honourable baron Lechmere hath asserted to me. . . . He was as certainly legitimately begotten as himself or any other: that he was born at Hanly of one Bonner, an honest poor man, in a house called *Bonner's place* to this day, a little cottage of about five pounds a year. . . . He added that there was an extraordinary friendship between Bonner and his great grandfather. . . . And that he had been told by some of their family that Bonner shewed this kindness to this

[1] For an account of this election without electors, see *Reg. Univ.* ed. Clark, O. H. S., II. i. 289.

gentleman out of gratitude, his father or some of the relations putting him out to school, and giving him his education [1].'

Fuller however affirms that Bonner

'enjoyed a great temporall estate left him by his Father . . . a Priest richly beneficed and landed in Cheshire [2].' 'In 1512 or thereabouts he became a Student of *Broadgates* Hall (now *Pembroke* Coll.), being then a noted nursery for Civilians and Canonists. Soon after, having made a sufficient progress in Philosophy and the Laws, he was on the 12 June admitted Bach. of the Canon, and on the 13 of July following, an. 1519, Bach. of the Civil Law. About that time he entered into Holy Orders and performed many matters relating to his faculty in the Dioc. of *Worcester*. In 1525 he was licensed to proceed in the Civil Law, and about that time obtained the Rectories of *Ripple, Bledon, Dereham, Cheswick*, and *Cherriburton* (in *Yorks.*) [3].' In 1529 he was Wolsey's chaplain and commissary for the faculties, acting as intermediary in important transactions between the Cardinal on the one side and the King and Gardiner on the other, and he was with Wolsey when he was arrested for high treason. After the cardinal's death however his eminence as a canonist and also his dexterity in the management of affairs brought him into the good graces of King Henry, who made him his chaplain. Like Gardiner and others who afterwards joined the party of reaction, Bonner was at this time willing to help cut the papal comb. He was in much favour with Cromwell, was Master of the Faculties under Cranmer, and a promoter of the Divorce, though assigned as counsel to the much wronged Queen.

> 'You have here, Lady,
> (And of your choice) these reverend fathers, men
> Of singular integrity and learning,
> Yea, the elect of the land, who are assembled
> To plead your cause.'

Bonner was made prebendary of St. Paul's and archdeacon of Leicester, became in 1538 elect of Hereford and in 1539 bishop of London. Before this he had been employed as ambassador to the King of Denmark, the King of France, the Emperor of Germany, and the Pope, to whose court he had been sent in 1523 (though but a stripling) to protest against the King of England being cited to Rome; while in 1533 he had conveyed to Clement Henry's appeal to a General Council. In these embassies he was adroit, plain-spoken, and overbearing. Professor Froude describes Bonner as a rough, coarse, vulgar Englishman, with a downright honesty and a broad, not ungenial humour. Coote says, that he resembled Henry VIII in his rough and boisterous character. The courteous Francis I was so provoked by his audacity that he told him that if it had not been for love of his master he would have ordered him a hundred

---

[1] *Annals*, II. (ii.) 300.

[2] *Worthies*. Were this so, would Bishop Ridley have treated 'My Mother Bonner' with so much respect—ill requited by her son!

[3] Wood's *Athenae*, i. 125.

strokes of a halberd, and Pope Clement VII wished he could throw him
into a cauldron of boiling lead. In promoting the printing of the Great
Bible Bonner showed much zeal, and set up six copies in the crypt of
St. Paul's. Fuller says : 'All this time *Bonner* was not *Bonner*, being as
yet meek, merciful, and a great Cromwellite.' Thomas Cromwell had
that mark of the meek where it is written of them 'possidebunt terram.'
Meekness was not in Bonner, a man not greedy of parks and messuages.
Alarmed like others at the lengths to which innovation was running, he
threw himself, under Edward VI, into opposition, was committed to the
Fleet and deprived. At Mary's accession he was made President of
the Convocation in Cranmer's room. The part he took in the relentless
repression of the new doctrines has made Bonner's name to be, to this
day, more execrated than any other in English history. Yet, after
allowing for the present fashion with historians of reversing traditional
judgments, it is satisfactory to members of this House to find not merely
Maitland but such writers as Gairdner saying much to exculpate his
memory. Doubtless an iron-nerved lawyer, in an age accustomed to
blood and pain. But Bonner had a rough good-nature and some feeling :
'naturally a good-humoured and merciful man,' Mr. Green says. 'Not
only not unkind, but long-suffering, considerate, and generous' is Canon
Dixon's judgment. He interposed on Ann Askew's behalf. The invective
of the writers on the other side did not disturb Bonner's temper. Bale,
for instance, called him 'a very fearce furious angell of the bottomlesse
pytt,' and 'that execrable Anti-christ.' Another writes to him, 'Oh!
thou bloudy Boner and most filthy bastard born; oh! thou most cruel
tyrant of Sodoma and proud painted prelate of Gomorra. Thou art
become the common slaughter slave to all thy fellow bitesheeps [bishops].'
He was 'Ignivomus Bonerus.' Though Coote says that 'interest was his
chief religion,' when Elizabeth succeeded Bonner refused to take the
oath of the supremacy and was again deprived and committed to the
Marshalsea, in which prison he 'continued in a cheerful and contented
condition till the time of his death ; which therefore made those that did
not care for him say that he was like *Dionysius* the Tyrant of *Syracuse*,
who, being cruel and peremptory in prosperity, was both patient and
pleasant in adversity. . . . He gave way to fate in the aforesaid Prison
5 *Sept.* in Fifteen hundred sixty and nine, and was at midnight buried
near to the bodies of other Prisoners in the Cemitery belonging to
St. *Georges* Church in *Southwark*, in which parish the *Marshalsea* is
situated ':—too mild a fate, says Coote, for this monster of barbarity.
Fuller says : 'He was buried, saith Bishop *Godwin*, in *Barking* Churchyard, among the theeves and murderers, being surely a mistake in the
Printer, Allhallows Barking being on the other side of the *Thames*,
nothing relating to the *Marshalsea*. . . . But so long as *Bonner* is dead
let him choose his own grave.' He was a round, corpulent man, and
Foxe's picture of him in the Book of Martyrs may be supposed a good
likeness, since, when one showed it to him to vex him, 'he merrily laugh'd
and said, "A vengeance on the fool, how could he get my picture drawn so
right ?"' Harington tells us that 'he was so hated that men would say

of any ill-favoured fat fellow in the street, "That was Bonner."[1] Fuller says: 'He had *Sesqui-Corpus*, a *Body and Halfe*, and towards his old age he was overgrown with fat.' This was ascribed to gluttony.

An adverse biographer describes him as 'a great master of the Canon Law, being excelled in that faculty by very few of his time.' Coote observes that he did not disgrace Broadgate Hall by want of learning. Tonstal speaks of his excellent gifts and virtues. Wood says, 'He had caused formerly two of his Nephews (Sons of one of his Sisters) to be educated in *Broadgates* Hall, one of which was named *Will. Darbyshire*, who by his Uncles favour became Prebendary of St. *Pauls* Cathedral, and, dying in *Broadgates*, was buried in St. *Aldates* Church adjoyning, 3. July 1552. The other was *Tho. Darbyshire*, who proceeded Doctor of Laws, as a member of *Broadgates*, in 1555.' Strype, of course, says they were Bonner's sons[1].

It was in Oxford that the memorable sitting of Bonner in judgment upon Cranmer, who had once sate in judgment upon him, took place. By accusing of heresy the first non-royal English subject, the Queen and Bonner thought to strike awe into the semi-Zwinglian party. On St. Valentine's day, 1555, Bonner, under a commission from the Pope, degraded the Archbishop, putting on him a threadbare yeoman bedell's gown and a poor townsman's cap, in which he returned to prison.

One of the nephews of Bonner, mentioned above, THOMAS DARBY-SHIRE, became Principal of Broadgates in 1556. His abilities and zeal for the papal cause advanced him to a stall in St. Paul's, the archdeaconry of Essex, and the Chancellorship of the London diocese. In the last capacity he helped his uncle, whose chaplain he was, to deal with the persons accused of heresy.

'In the beginning of Qu. *Elizabeth*, being deprived of his Spiritualities, he went beyond the Seas, and at length entered himself into the Society of *Jesus*, and became a noted person among the Rom. Catholicks. He had great skill in the Scriptures, and was profound in Divinity: he catechized also many years publickly at Paris in the Latin Tongue, with great concourse and approbation of the most learned of that City. Whether he wrot anything I find not as yet, only that he died in a good old Age at *Pont à* Mousson in *Loraine*, an. 1604 (2 Jac. I)[2].

He was half a century later quoted as a chief authority for the Nag's Head fable[3].

[1] *Eccl. Mem.* vol. iii. (I.) p. 173.　　　　[2] *Athenae*, i. 712.

[3] Strype, *Life of Parker*, i. 118.

Another near relative of Bishop Bonner's, said to be his baseborn brother, GEORGE WYMYSLEY (Wemsley, in the Cheshire *Visitation* Winslow), became Principal of Broadgates 1532, B.C.L. 1533. He was canon of St. Paul's 1542, archdeacon of London 1543, vicar of Castleton 1546, rector of Tarporley 1553, archdeacon of Middlesex 1554, rector of Uppingham 1554, canon of Chester 1554-6.

A Cromwellian agent was SIR JOHN TREGONWELL, 'sometimes of *Broadgates*, afterwards Principal of *Vine* hall'—'dear to Erasmus.' D.C.L. 1552. Wolsey admitted him as an inmate into his family. As an experienced canonist he was employed in Cranmer's embassy about the Divorce, and also as King's Proctor in the cause itself[1]. Wood says that for his diligent service Henry VIII knighted him, but it was at Mary's coronation that he was dubbed Knight of the Carpet[2]. Tregonwell sate on a committee appointed by Convocation to investigate Henry's marriage with Anne of Cleves. He officially witnessed Cranmer's consecration. In 1536 he was a Privy Councillor with Cromwell, in 1539 a Master in Chancery. In that year the mitred Benedictine abbey of Milton, Dorsetshire, was surrendered, and conferred by Henry with other rich demesnes on the successful lawyer, whom we find serving as sheriff of Dorset and Somerset in 1554. In that year he was placed on the Commission of the Great Seal. He was also chief Admiralty Judge, and Chancellor of Bath and Wells. In Mary's reign he came out as a zealous papist, and while Nowell, as a prebendary of Westminster, was unseated by the House of Commons, Tregonwell, who also held a stall there, was suffered to remain a member of Parliament. He was then representing Scarborough. The Queen allowed him to have thirty retainers. He presided in the commission for the restitution of Bonner, and was present at Bishop Hooper's trial. Dying in 1565 he was interred in Milton abbey church under an altar tomb of grey marble. The place has changed hands many times since then, the doom of sacrilege taking the form there of no heir being ever born to it. Curiously enough the local tradition connects the rightful ownership with the Tregonwells rather than the Benedictines :—

> 'No heir to Milton shall there be,
> Till there come back the old Tre.'

A portrait of Sir John, ascribed to Holbein, is at Cranborne Lodge,

---

[1] Burgo, an Italian Minorite, for his forwardness in unqueening the injured Catherine, was stoned by the women of Oxford, thirty of whom were committed to the Bokardo lock-up. (*Athenæ*, i. 667.)

[2] *Athenæ*, i. 666. But see Strype's *Memorials*, III. ii. 181.

Dorset, where the daughter of the last of this name, Mrs. Mary Harkness, now lives.   There is more about Tregonwell in Dom Gasquet's *English Monasteries.*

SIR JAMES DYER's Reports are well known to lawyers.   The son of Richard Dyer, of Wincanton, Esquire, he was born about 1512 at Roundhill, Somerset, where the family had been long established. Tradition says that he was at sixteen years a commoner of Broadgates. Leaving Oxford about 1530,

'without the honor of a Degree, he went to the *Middle Temple* [to the Strand Inn], where making great proficiency in the Municipal Laws, was after he had continued for some time in the Degree of Barrester elected Autumn, or Summer, Reader of that house 6. *Ed.* 6., and about the same time was by writ called to the Degree of Serjeant at Law.   In the Reigne of Qu. *Marie* he was made a Justice of the *Common pleas* (being about that time a Knight and Recorder of *Cambridge*) and in the beginning of Qu. *Elizabeth* Lord Chief Justice of that Court. . . . At length this great Lawyer, having arrived to a good old age, paid his last debt to nature at *Stowton* in *Huntingdonshire* (where he had purchased an estate) on the 24. *March* in Fifteen hundred eighty and one, whereupon his body was buried in the Parish Church of *Much Stowton* in the said County near to that of his Wife, on the 9 day of *Apr.* 1582.   His said Wife was named *Margaret* dau. of Sir *Maurice Abarrow* of *Hampshire,* Knight, Widow of Sir *Tho. Eliot* of *Carleton* in *Cambridgeshire.*'   He left no issue, and the estate went to his nephews, whose posterity were at a later date baronets in Somerset.   The Sir Thomas Elyot mentioned is the author of the celebrated '*Boke of the Governour.*'   The handsome monument placed over Dyer's ashes in Great Stoughton Church still exists.   Wood does not record that Dyer was elected Knight of the Shire in 1547 for Cambridgeshire, and again in 1553[1], in which short-lived parliament he was Speaker of the Lower House.   'On Thursday Iº Martii was chosen to be Speaker first nominate by Mr. Treasurer of the King's House, the Right Worshipful Mr. James Dyer, one of the King's Majestie's servients[2] at the Law, and set in the chair.'   As Capital Justiciar he took part in several famous political trials, enjoying a high reputation among the men of that time for incorruptible integrity, learning, and acumen.   The justices of Warwickshire complained of him to the Privy Council, because he had forced them to give her rights to a poor widow.   Dyer's *Reports*[3], written in

[1] 'Elegerunt Edwardum North militem et Jacobum Dyer S'vientem ad legem milites gladiis cinctos.'

[2] Lord Campbell, overlooking this entry, denies that Dyer was then serjeant.

[3] 'Les REPORTS des divers matters et Resolutions des Reverend Judges et Sages del LEY touchant et concernant mults principal points occurrent estre debate entre eux: en le several Regnes de les tres-hault et excellent Princes, le Roys Hen. VIII et Edw. VI and le Roignes Mar. et Eliz.   Collect et Report per très-reverend Judge Sr JAQUES DYER chivaler: Jades Chief Justice del Common Banke en le temps du Roigne Elisabeth.'

law-French, have been said by a modern writer to be models of lucidity. In a long poetical lament in which, 'moaved with the passion of a common sorrow,' he sang 'the pretious vertues which governed the good Lord Dyer,' Whetstone describes him as—

> 'Settled to heare, but very slowe to speake.
> The deapth of Lawe he searcht with painfull toyle,
> Not cunning quirks, the simple man to spoyle.'

Again :—

> 'For publique good when care had cloid his minde,
> The only joye, for to repose his spright,
> Was musique sweet, which show'd him wel inclin'd :
> For he that dooth in musique much delight
> A conscience hath disposed to most right :
> The reason is, her sounde within our eare,
> A sympathie of heaven we think we heare.'

In an epitaph on him it is said :—

> 'Et semper bonus ille bonis fuit; ergo bonorum
> Sunt illi demum pectora sarcophagus.'

Sir Edward Coke, to whom Great Stoughton passed, describes the *Reports* as 'the summary and fruitful observations of that famous and most reverend judge and sage of the law, Sir James Dyer.' Camden speaks of his fellow collegian thus :—

'Jacobus Dierus, in communi placitorum tribunali justiciarius primarius, qui animo semper placido et sereno omnes judicis aequissimi partes implevit et juris nostri prudentiam commentariis illustravit.'

Without time-serving, he appears to have enjoyed the favour and respect of successive Tudor sovereigns.

The Rev. C. A. Mayo, M.A., author of *Bibliotheca Dorsetiensis*, a collateral descendant, has at Long Burton vicarage, near Sherborne, the only authentic painting of Dyer. Another portrait, taken at an earlier age, was burnt in the fire which destroyed the Wincanton Town Hall in 1877. Like Mr. Mayo's fine picture, which has in the corner Dyer's arms (or, a chief indented gu.[1]), it represented him in his robes and collar of SS. He has a long, thin, and very striking face, with sharp aquiline nose and dark piercing eyes. He has no direct descendants, but a grand-nephew, George Dyer, was living in 1623 at Heytesbury, Wilts, being then aged thirty-four. An interesting memoir of Chief Justice Dyer has appeared in the *Proceedings of the Somerset Archaeological Society*, from the pen of Mr. W. A. Jones, F.G.S. (vol. xvi. 1870).

Strype records, as a 'strange and rare' event, the restoration by Dyer to the Church of the impropriation of Staple-Grove-*juxta*-Taunton, in 1575[2].

---

[1] But on an old engraving of Dyer by Drapentier the coat is sa. 3 goats arg., and the Hunts Visitation of 1613 shows these arms to have been granted to Sir James Deyer by Dethick, Garter King.

[2] *Annals*, II. i. 579.

THOMAS OWEN, born at Condover, Salop, the son of Richard, a Shrewsbury merchant of old descent, was ' for some time conversant among the Muses either in *Broadgates* Hall or in *Ch. Church.* From thence (having first taken a degree in Arts, as it seems [B.A. April 17, 1559]) he retired to *Lincoln's* Inn, where by his unwearied industry, advanced by a good natural genie and judgment, he became a noted Councellour and much resorted to for his advice. In 25. *Elizab.* dom. 1583. he was elected Lent-Reader of that house [Treasurer 1589-1598], in 1590 he was by Writ called to the degree of Serjeant at Law, and about that time [1594] made the Queen's Serjeant, and at length one of the Justices of the *Common Pleas* [1594], which last place he executed for 5 years with great integrity, equity, and prudence. He was a learned man, and a great lover of learning and those that professed it. He dying 21. *Decemb.* in fifteen hundred ninety and eight, was buried on the S. side of the Choire[1] of St. *Peter's* Church in *Westminster.* Over his grave was soon after erected a noble monument of Alabaster, Marble, and divers coloured stones, adorned with Arms, and gilt with Gold, with his Image in scarlet robes lying thereon which remains to this day. He left behind him a Son named *Roger,* who was a Knight, and [Camden writes] *for his manifold learning, a right Worthy Son of so Good a Father.* This Sir *Roger*[2], who had been a great Friend to the Clergy, by vindicating them when aspersed in open Parliament, 11 *Jac.* 1. dyed in a distracted condition to their great reluctancy, 29. *May,* being *Holy Thursday,* in 1617.' Nothing is extant of Thomas Owen's but his Reports in the *Common Pleas.*

[1] West of the transept, next the bust of Pasquale da Paoli. The inscription is as follows:—

DEO TRINO ET VNI SACRUM.

Secundum Christi Redemptoris adventû sub hoc tumulo expectat *Thomas Owen,* Arm. filius Richardi Owen ex Maria altera filia et haerede Thomae Oteley de comitatu Salopiae arm. Qui ab adolescentia studiis juris municipalis Angliae innutritus ita industria ingenio et judicio claruit ut primum electus fuerit Dñae Reginae Elizab. serviens ad legem inde in consessum Justiciariorum Communium placitorum co-optatus, inter quos cum quinq; annos singulari integritatis aequitatis et prudentiae laude sedisset, et ex Sara uxore charissima filia et una haeredum Humfredi Baskerville quinq; filios et totidem filias suscepisset, Alicia fideli uxore secunda superstite, pie in Christo obdormivit xvi die Decemb. Año Salutis M. D. xcviii.

Rogerus Owen filius maestissimus patri optimo et charissimo officiosae pietatis et memoriae ergô hoc monumentum posuit.

Below on either side : ' Justorum animae in manu Dei sunt ' and ' Spes vermis et ego.'

Owen married twice, (1) Sarah, sister of Sir Humphrey Baskerville, (2) Alice, widow of Mr. Elks, mercer and alderman of London. She endowed a hospital at Islington for ten poor women, and a school for thirty boys, in grateful remembrance of her escape in childhood, when an arrow pierced her hat. To Bodley's library in 1606 she gave £100. The estate of Condover is still in the Owen family.

[2] He was M.P. for Shrewsbury and for Shropshire, and sheriff. Another son, Richard, was also a lawyer.

A noted Broadgates jurist was WILLIAM FLEETWOOD, natural son of Robert, of Hesketh, who, leaving Oxford without a degree,

'retired to the *Middle Temple*, where by continual industry, advanced by good natural parts, he attained to the name of an eminent Lawyer. In 5. of *Eliz.* he was elected Autumn or Summer-Reader of that house.' Some years later (1571–91) he became Recorder of London, in 1580 Serjeant at Law, and in 1592 Queen's Serjeant. 'He was a learned Man and a good Antiquary; but of a marvelous, merry, and pleasant conceit : And as touching his Learning, Justice, and Eloquence I cannot better describe them than a Poet[1] of those days hath done in certain Verses.' He left a number of legal writings. He died Feb. 28, 1598, and his body lies (à Wood believes) in the Church of Great Missenden, Bucks, where he had purchased an estate. 'He left behind him two Sons, whereof Sir *Will. Fleetwood*, Knight [M.P. for Poole and for Bucks], was one, and the other was Sir *Thomas* of the *Middle-Temple*, afterwards Attorney to Prince *Henry*. He had also divers Daughters, one whereof was married to Sir *David Foulis*, Knight and Baronet, and another to Sir *Tho. Chaloner*, Tutor to the said Prince, Son of the learned Sir *Tho. Chaloner* Knight.'

WILLIAM MARTYN (son and heir of Nicholas), was 'born and educated in Grammar learning within the City of Exeter. Where making early advances towards Academical learning, was sent to *Broadgates* hall (now *Pemb.* Coll.) an. 1579 [circa 1581, Foster], aged 17. In which place falling under the tuition of a noted Master, laid an excellent foundation in logick and philosophy.

'Afterwards going to the Inns of Court he became a Barester, and in 1605 was elected Recorder of *Exeter* in the place of *John Hele* Serjeant at Law. But his delight being much conversant in the reading of English Histories, he composed a book of the Kings of England, as I shall tell you anon. Upon the publication of which K. *James* (as 'tis said) taking some exceptions at a passage therein, either to the derogation of his family or of the Realm of *Scotland*, he was thereupon brought into some trouble, which shortned his days. . . . He was buried in the Church of S. *Petrock* in the City of *Exeter* 12 Apr. in sixteen hundred and seventeen.' Wood says that Martyn was a severe puritan. One of his books is called *Youth's Instruction* (1612), and seems to have been dedicated to his son Nicholas, then a Broadgates Student, afterwards knighted, sheriff of Devon 1639, and a member of the Long Parliament, till secluded in 1648. He died on Lady Day in 1653.

His cousin RICHARD (great-grandson of Sir William) MARTYN, born at Otterton, Devon, entered Broadgates in 1585,

'where by natural parts and some industry he proved a noted disputant. But he, leaving the said house before he was honoured with a degree,

---

[1] Tho. Newton in *Illustrium Aliquot Anglorum Encomia*, Lond. 1589, p. 121.

went to the *Middle Temple*, where, after he had continued in the state of Inner Barrester for some years, was elected a Burgess to serve in Parliament [for Barnstaple 1604, Christchurch 1604–11], was constituted Lent Reader of the said *Temple*, 13. *Jac.* 1. and upon the death of Sir *Anth. Benn* [also of Broadgates, B.A. 1587], was made Recorder of the City of *London* in *Sept.* 1618. There was no person in his time more celebrated for ingenuity than *R. Martin*, none more admired by *Selden*, Serjeant *Hoskins*, Ben. *Johnson*, etc. than he; the last of which dedicated his Comedy to him called *The Poetaster*. K. *James* was much delighted with his facetiousness, and had so great respect for him that he commended him to the Citizens of *London* to be their Recorder. He was worthily characterized by the vertuous and learned Men of his time to be *Princeps amorum* [1], *Principum amor, legum lingua, lexque dicendi, Anglorum alumnus, Praeco Virginiae ac Parens, etc. Magnae* [*sic*] *orbis os, orbis minoris corculum. Bono suorum natus, Extinctus suo, etc.* He was a plausible Linguist, and eminent for several Speeches spoken in Parliaments, for his Poems also and witty discourses.... He died to the great grief of all learned and good men, on the last day of *Octob.* in sixteen hundred and eighteen, and was buried in the Church belonging to the *Temples.* Over his grave was soon after a neat Alabaster Monument erected, with the *Effigies* of the Defunct kneeling in his Gown, with 4 verses engraved thereon, under him, made by his dear Friend Serjeant *Hoskins*. This Monument was repaired in 1683 when the Choire and Isles adjoyning, belonging to the *Temple* Church, were new wainscoted and furnished with seats [2].' Aubrey however says he died of excess of drinking. There is a scarce portrait of Martin by Simon Pass, engraved 1620. An Epistle from him to Sir Henry Wotton is in Coryat's *Crudities*, p. 237. Fuller styles him 'one of the highest Witts of our Age and his Nation.'

THOMAS SANDERSON (brother of Viscount Castleton and cousin of Bishop Sanderson), who entered in 1587, was treasurer of Lincoln's Inn 1628 and 1633. THOMAS BARKER, entered 1581, was treasurer of the Middle Temple 1623.

HENRY SWINBURNE, son of Thomas Swinburne of York, where he was born,

'spent some years in the quality of a Commoner in *Hart* hall, whence translating himself to that of *Broadgates*, took the Degree of Bach. of the Civil Law, married *Helena* daughter of *Barthelm. Lant* of *Oxon*, and at length retiring to his native place, became a Proctor in the Archbishops Court there, Commissary of the *Exchequer*, and Judge of the *Prerogative Court* at *York*. He hath written:—Brief Treatise of Testaments and

---

[1] *Athenae*, i. 374. Martyn had been '*Prince D'Amour* of the *Middle Temple* in time of *Christmas*.'

[2] It seems since the last 'restoration' of that once noble church to have vanished.

last Wills. In 7 parts. Lond. 1590 etc. Treatise of Spousals, or Matri-
monial Contracts, etc. *Lond.* 1686. qu. In which two books the author
shews himself an able Civilian and excellently well read in authors of his
Faculty. He paid his last debt to nature at *York*, and was buried in the
North Isle of the Cathedral there. Soon after was a comely Monument
fastened to the wall near to his grave, with his *Effigies* in a Civilians
Gown kneeling before a deske, with a book thereon, and these verses
under :—

> " Non Viduae caruere viris, non Patre Pupillus,
>   Dum stetit hic Patriae virque paterque suae.
> Ast quod Swinburnus viduarum scripsit in usum,
>   Longius aeterno marmore vivet opus.
> Scribere supremas hinc discat quisque tabellas,
>   Et cupiat, qui sic vixit, ut ille mori." '
>   (*Ath. Ox.* i. 386.)

The handsome gilded and painted monument, in excellent preservation,
bears several coats of arms. Dr. Tobias Swinburne, his son, was an
eminent advocate.

ROBERT HALE, father of Sir Matthew Hale, the great Chief Justice,
entered Broadgates in 1580. He retired from Lincoln's Inn through
' tenderness of conscience,' holding for immoral the barrister's duty of
making the ' worse cause appear the better.' Lord Keeper Littleton's
brothers, WILLIAM LITTLETON (1609; serjeant at law), JAMES LITTLE-
TON (B.A. 1618; a master in Chancery, chancellor of Worcester),
and JOHN LITTLETON (M.A. 1624; Master of the Temple; ejected in
1644 for being in the King's army), were, with others of the same
name, members of this House.

CHAPTER IX.

POETS AND DRAMATISTS.

ONE result of the dissolution of the Religious Houses upon the fortunes of Broadgates Hall was its transference to royal ownership. In 1522 Wolsey persuaded the priory to surrender their house and its belongings into the hands of the King, who gave it to the Archbishop himself. Clement VIII had issued a bull for the suppression of Frideswyde's on condition that Wolsey should establish in room of it a college of secular canons. In 1525, out of the priory revenues (less than £300 a year) and those of other of the smaller monasteries, was begun the 'Collegium Thomae Wolsey Cardinalis Eboracensis.' But before the foundation was actually in law completed the Cardinal fell. All the revenues he had collected passed to Henry, who in 1532 refounded Cardinal College as 'King Henry the Eighth's College,' dedicated to the praise and honour of the Holy and Undivided Trinity, the most blessed Virgin St. Mary, and the holy virgin St. Frideswyde. In 1545 however, the King, having formed an entirely new plan, required the surrender of the College once more into his hands, and finally founded the mixed cathedral and academic House known as 'the Cathedral Church of Christ in Oxford of the foundation of King Henry the Eighth.'

To this noble establishment were granted the following parts of the present Pembroke College:—'A house called the Almes House with the appurtenaunces in the p'she of saincte Aldat,' 'certene chamberes within Brodyats latlie belonginge to the late monasterye of Abendon,' and ' a parcelle of lands within Brodyats, parcelle of the possessione of the late colledge of Frideswids [1].'

Without being actually an *annexe* of the magnificent foundation across the road [2], it is probable that Broadgates was found a con-

---

[1] Dugdale's *Monasticon*, ii. p. 167.

[2] Fitzherbert (1602) says of the existing Halls: 'hae singulae a singulis fere

venient receptacle for many young men of position who could not be received at Christ Church. This appears from the number of names assigned *either* to Broadgates Hall *or* Christ Church or to both. The matriculations vary greatly from year to year. But it is noticeable that in 1583 there were as many entries (38) at Broadgates as at Christ Church and Exeter put together. In 1581, when all the numbers were much larger, there were forty-eight. At the close of the sixteenth century a new class of undergraduate was largely attracted to Oxford. Residence in a University was becoming the mark of a gentleman, and the attainment of a degree was made easier to men of birth by special statutes. Huber considers that the Elizabethan and Stuart connexion with the gentry class did the Universities no good. The young squires had little taste for learning, and the poorer scholars became a dependent race of tutors and trencher-chaplains, a class described by Bishop Hall in his second Satire. The Inns of Court were surrounded by a nebula of unpractising lawyers from Oxford and Cambridge, whose spirit and doings lent to life in London some of its boldest features, its gayest colours, its most lusty intellectual movement. On the other hand the capital influenced the academies, and lettered tastes, for which no midnight wick burned, usurped the place of paler and severer studies. Youths liberally nurtured, and more likely to play a part in the world than the old-fashioned poor scholar of the middle ages, now received the benefit of University life and training. These would especially be drawn to the Halls, for the Colleges were still chiefly eleemosynary, disciplinary, and religious. Halls have alternately served, it would seem, as the refuge of the luxurious and of the economical. The threadbare 'clerk of Oxenforde' passed away to a great extent with the Old Learning. The twenty books at the bed's head, clothed in black and red, of Aristotle and his philosophy, were by the Elizabethan student no longer always more prized than garments rich, fiddle and psaltery, nor, if money was 'of his frendes hent,' was it laid out on nothing but learning. Sir Vincentio in the *Taming of the Shrew*, beating his student son's man, Biondello, cries, 'O immortal gods! O fine villain! A silken doublet! A velvet hose! A scarlet cloak! And a copatain hat! O, I am undone! I am undone! While I play the good husband at home, my son and my servant spend all at the

collegiis pendent & ad earum exemplum se plane comparant: in eo solum dissimiles, quod hae, quam illa, legibus disciplinae laxioribus paulo liberioribusque teneantur' (Nicolai Fierberti *Oxoniensis Academiae Descriptio*, Romae. *Elizabethan Oxford*, O. H. S., p. 16).

university[1].' Even the Colleges now had young men of fortune
domiciled in them. The Halls, Fitzherbert notes, were full of them—
'divitum nobiliumque plerumque filiis, qui propriis vivunt sumptibus,
assignatae.' These affected Ovid rather than Justinian or the Stagi-
rite. At Broadgates in particular the able race of civilians was succeeded by a brilliant list of scholar-poets and statesmen, men of
action and of letters. The West-country was the quarter from
which this Hall now drew most of its students.

The catalogue of writers of the great Tudor age who were bred
at Broadgates begins somewhat earlier with JOHN HEYWOODE, 'the
old English Epigrammatist,' styled by Mr. J. A. Symonds 'a prose
Chaucer.' He was the first, says Wharton, 'to draw the Bible from
the stage, and introduce representations of familiar life and popular
manners.' Of the merry Mixed Plays or Interludes which succeeded
the older Mysteries, Miracle Plays, and dull Moralities, and in which
allegorical and real characters were combined, he was the most
noted composer. Dr. A. W. Ward calls Heywoode a lineal descendant
of the mediæval minstrels.

In his Interludes personal types superseded personified abstractions.
Though familiar on the Continent, they were the earliest of their kind in
England. 'Nothing so good of the same kind was afterwards produced.
The bridge to English comedy was thus built, and Heywoode, whose
name to Ben Jonson meant uncouth antiquity, deserves the chief credit
for its building. . . . Though his humour is bold and broad, it is wholesome and compatible with unaffected piety.' As he died about 1580,
there are but a few years between Heywoode and the consummate art of
Shakspeare. The 'Mery Play between the Pardoner and the Frere, the
Curate and Neybour Pratte,' written probably before 1521, was produced
in 1533, in the same year as 'A Play between Johan the Husband, Tyb
the Wife, and Sir Johan the Priest.' Later came 'The Four P's. A newe
and a very mery Interlude of a Palmer, a Pardoner, a Potycary, and a
Pedlar.' Strachey speaks of Heywoode's 'innocent and artless transcripts
from real life.' There is spirit and humour in his comedies, but not much
story or dramatic characterization. His longest work, or 'Parable,' is
trifling and tedious. Holinshed says of it : 'One also hath made a booke
of the *Spider and the Flie*, wherein he dealeth so profoundlie and beyond
all measure of skill, that neither he himselfe that made it nor anie one
that readeth it can reach unto the meaning thereof.' The work was three
and a half centuries too early.

Heywoode was born at North Mims, near St. Alban's. Bale
(p. 110) calls him 'civis Londinensis.' He studied at Oxford 'in that

---

[1] But Ford describes the poor student too: 'I have been fain to heel my
tutor's stockings at least seven years.'

ancient hostle called *Broadgates* in St. Aldate's Parish.   But, the crabbedness of Logick not suiting with his airie genie,

'he retired to [London], and became noted to all witty men, especially to Sir *Tho. More* (with whom he was very familiar), wrot several matters of Poetry, and was the first, some say (but I think false[1]) that wrot English plays, taking opportunity thence to make notable work with the Clergy.   He had admirable skill also in instrumental and vocal Musick. He was in much esteem with K. *H.* 8. for the mirth and quickness of his conceits, and tho he had little learning in him, yet he was by that King well rewarded[2].'   Heywoode wrote of himself to Burleigh on April 18, 1575, as an old man of seventy-eight.   He was therefore born in 1497. His '*Nature of the iiij Elements,*' probably written in 1517, alludes to the discovery of the New World by Amerigo Vespucci.   Two years earlier, in 1515, he appears in the King's Book of Payments as receiving 8*d.* a day.   In 1519 he is called a 'singer,' and in 1526 'player of the king's virginals,' receiving quarterly £6 13*s.* 4*d.*, but in 1538 his quarter shot was but 50*s.*   In that year 'Hans Holbein, Paynter' was receiving £8 10*s.* 9*d.* a quarter.   An earlier entry in 1529 shows that 'John Haywood, player at virginalles' or 'of thinstrumentes,' was granted a pension of 4*s.* yearly for life, and in 2 and 3 Edw. VI this sum is entered as paid to 'John Heiwood plaier on the Virginalles[3].'   More, his neighbour—'whom he much resembled in quickness of parts, both undervaluing their friend to their jest, and having *ingenium non edentulum sed mordax*' (says Fuller)—helped him with his Epigrams, and wrote the *Utopia* at North Mims.   He introduced his friend to the notice of the young Princess Mary, a woman of culture.   In 1538 Heywoode received 40*s.* for playing before her an interlude with his 'children'— those boy actors for whom Shakspeare had a professional dislike.   While Mary was in disgrace, he wrote his pleasing *Description of a Most Noble Ladye.*   After she came to the throne, Heywoode 'was much valued by her, often had the honor to wait on and exercise his fancy before her : which he did even to the time that she lay languishing upon her death bed.'   In his allegory already mentioned the spiders are the Zwinglians, the flies the Catholics, and Queen Mary is a maid executing with her broom (the civil sword) the commands of her Master and of her Mistress (Holy Church).   In spite of his satires on freres and pardoners, he was a convinced adherent of the old order.   Harington says that under Edward VI Heywoode narrowly escaped hanging and the 'jerke of the six-string'd whip.'   Probably he means under Henry VIII; but it was for denying the Supremacy, not the Six Articles, that Heywoode was arraigned.   He was allowed to make a public recantation at Paul's Cross on July 6, 1544.   By Edward, Puttenham states, he was 'well benefited' for the 'myrth and quicknesse of his conceits.'   The King thought that

---

[1] Palsgrave, whose play *Acolatus* was printed in 1529, is sometimes called the first dramatist.

[2] *Ath. Ox.* i. 116.   'Butter would not melt in her mouth' is first found in his Epigrams.   [3] Trevelyan Papers.

the writer of such 'harmless verses' could not be dangerous, and he was
ever a welcome guest at the board of Northumberland. But his fortunes
were brightest under Mary. At her coronation, Stow says, he sate in
St. Paul's churchyard, 'in a pageant under a vine, and made to her an
oration in Latine.' A ballad from his pen celebrated her marriage with
Philip. Before her death she gave him the lease of the Manor of Bolmer
and other lands in Yorkshire. He had enjoyed the favour of the princess
Elizabeth also; but at her accession 'he left the Nation for Religion sake
and setled at *Mechlin* in *Brabant,* which is a wonder to some, who will
allow no Religion in poets, that this Person should above all of his
Profession be a voluntary exile for it[1].' There he died, à Wood says
mistakenly, 'about 1565[2].' In his letter to Burleigh from Mechlin he
wrote, 'I have been despoiled by Spanish and German soldiers of the
little I had.' He is included in a return of Romanist fugitives of Jan. 29,
1577, at which time he owned lands in Kent and elsewhere. There is
a full length presentment of Heywoode in the *Spider and the Fly*—one of
the first printed English books with a number of cuts—in academical
gown and round cap, with dagger at his girdle. Chin and lips are close
shaved. The face has been thought melancholy, though Camden, who
dwells somewhat partially on the 'golden gift' of 'the great Epigrammatist,' speaks of his 'mad, merry wit.' He had taken part, it would
seem, in the Coventry plays, for he says of a friend,—

> 'For as goode happe wolde have it chaunce
> Thys devyll and I were of olde acquaintaunce;
> For oft in the play of *Corpus Christi*
> He hath played the devyll at Coventry.'

Fuller says, 'I may safely write of him what he pleasantly writes of
himself, that he "applied mirth more than thrift, made many mad plays
and did few good works."' . . . His *Monumenta literaria* are said to be
non tam labore condita quam lepore condita.' By his wife Eliza he had
Ellis, Jasper, and Elizabeth. The sons were Oxonians and seminary
priests. Jasper, born in 1535, was expelled from Merton, of which
College he was the last 'Christmas King,' Lord of Misrule or Rex
Fabarum, and elected fellow of All Souls. At Elizabeth's accession the
converted rake retired to St. Omer, and became a learned controversialist
in the Society of Jesus. Gregory XIII appointed him to the perilous
post of first Provincial of the Jesuits in England, which he filled with
great dignity. He was not, as Fuller states, hanged and quartered, but
was shipped out of the realm. He translated Seneca when at Oxford.

A notable Elizabethan, SIR EDWARD DYER, poet and courtier,
cousin of Judge Dyer, is claimed for Broadgates Hall.

He was born about 1540 at Sharpham Park, Fielding's birthplace,
which had been granted to his father Sir Thomas Dyer[3] by Henry VIII,

---

[1] 'It is much that one so Fancyful should be so conscientious.' *Fuller.*
[2] *Ath. Ox.* i. 117.
[3] Associated with the Bishop of Bath and Wells, Sir Hugh Paulet, and Sir John

after the hanging of Abbot Whiting of Glastonbury. Leaving Oxford without a degree he travelled abroad, and on his return was taken into the service of the Court of Elizabeth. He obtained great influence over Leicester, then Chancellor of Oxford, and was employed by the Queen in several embassies, particularly to the Low Countries in 1584 and to Denmark in 1589. On his return Dyer was knighted and made Chancellor of the Most Noble Order of the Garter. Leicester is said to have intrigued to replace Hatton by Dyer in the post of personal favourite to Elizabeth, who, however, suddenly withdrew her favour from the poet. Understanding that he was sinking to the grave under the weight of her displeasure, she relented, and gave a substantial token of friendship by estating him with large lands, though, Oldys says, Dyer would never fawn and cringe even to his royal mistress. His chiefest friend was Sir Philip Sidney. Gabriel Harvey, in a letter to Edmund Spenser, 1580, styles them 'the two very diamonds of her majesties courte for many speciall and rare qualities.' Spenser published some of Harvey's poems with a dedication 'to the right worshipfull Gentleman and famous Courtier Master Edwarde Diar, in a manner oure only Inglisshe poett.' Sidney left his books to be divided between Dyer and Sir Fulke Greville, whom he calls his worthy friends and fellow poets. Dyer wrote pastoral odes and madrigals. Puttenham in 1589 pronounced him to be 'for elegie most sweet, most solempe and of high conceit.' His most famous poem, ' My mind to me a kingdom is,' was set to music by Byrd. Dyer's later life seems to have been passed in retirement. John Davies, in the preface to the *Microcosmus*, 1603, addresses him thus :—

> ' Thou virgin knight, that dost thyself obscure
> From world's unequal eyes.'

Other poets too wrote verses to him. Aubrey says, 'he laboured much in chymistry and was esteemed by some a Rosie-Crucian, and a great devotee to Dr. John Dee and Edward Kelly.' He died in 1607, and lies in St. Mary Overy, Southwark. His verse not being collected, his fame decayed till recent times of renewal of all things.

RICHARD CAREW I will mention among historical writers. A courtier scholar, who, either before or after studying at Cambridge, is thought to have resided for a time at Broadgates Hall as a gentleman commoner, is SIR FULKE GREVILLE, Lord Brooke, companion, kinsman, and biographer of Sir Philip Sidney, patron of Overall and Egerton, fosterer of the child Davenant's budding genius, enlightened master of Jonson and Shakspeare, friend of Bruno and Bacon. Greville had a long life and a tragical death.

He was born in 1554 at Milcot in Warwickshire, of descent from the great baronial houses of Beauchamp of Powick and Willoughby de Broke (his mother was Anne daughter of Ralph Neville, Earl of Westmoreland),

St. Loo in a precept issued by Edward VI for the support of the foreign weavers brought to Glastonbury by the Duke of Somerset.

and was at school with Sidney in Shrewsbury. His studies at Cambridge
and Oxford ended, he travelled, and on his return, 'in his youth or prime,
for that is the time or never' (writes Naunton), was introduced to the
court by his Uncle Robert Greville, 'where he was esteemed a most
ingenious person, and had in favour by all such that were lovers of Arts
and Sciences.' After one or two romantic escapades and a little soldiering,
from which the kind jealousy of the Queen snatched her young scholar,
he settled down, in various lucrative offices, as one of Elizabeth's
favourites, 'which he held,' Naunton says, 'for no short term, but had
the longest lease of any, and the smoothest time without rub.' When the
envoys from the King of France came with a splendid retinue in 1581
to treat of the Queen's marriage with the Duke of Anjou, Sidney and
Greville distinguished themselves in that magnificent throng by their
brilliancy in the tourney[1] and in less dangerous pomps. In 1588,
April 11, being at Oxford in the train of his kinsman Essex, he 'among
other persons of honour and quality was actually created Master of Arts.'
In 1599 Greville was designated as rear-admiral of the fleet to be sent
against the Spaniards. During this reign he frequently sate in Parliament
for his county with Sir Thomas Lacy, a member of Broadgates. In 1603,
at the coronation of James I, he was created Knight of the Bath, and
was granted soon after the ruined Castle of Warwick, on repairing which
he spent £20,000. He was, however, not in Cecil's good graces. Cecil
being dead, Greville became Chancellor of the Exchequer, and in 1621
was created Baron Brooke of Beauchamp's Court, and made a Lord of
the Bedchamber. He was of the Privy Council to Charles I, by whose
encouragement probably he founded a history praelectorship at Cambridge.
'He was always esteemed a brave Gentleman and honourably descended,
as being sprung from the family of *Willoughby*. Lord Brook was
favoured by Qu. *Elizabeth* and such that knew he had interest in the
Muses. His life was always single, and though he lived and died a
constant Courtier of the Ladies, yet he prosecuted his studies in History
and Poetry. In which, consider him as a Gentleman of noble birth and
great Estate, he was most excellent in his time.' Southey says that
Dryden appeared to have formed his tragic style more on Lord Brooke
than on any one else. Two of Greville's tragedies, *Alaham* and *Mustapha*,
were after the ancient Greek fashion, with choruses and the like, but were
not acted. Among his works are treatises, travels, tragedies, and sonnets,
biography and contemporary history, the titles of which are given by
Wood, who proceeds: 'At length our author, neglecting to reward one
Haywood, who had spent the greatest and chiefest part of his time in
his personal service, for which he expostulated the matter with his Master,
but was sharply rebuked for it, the said *Haywood* thereupon gave him
a mortal stab on his Back[2] (they two being then only together) in the

---

[1] Peele, the Broadgates Hall poet, celebrates him in the lists:—
  'Fair man at arms, the Muse's favourite,
   Lover of learning and of chivalry,
   Sage in his saws, sound judge of poesy.'
[2] Rous (1628) says: 'Did in his privy chamber stabbe him about the brest

Bedchamber at *Brook* house in *Holbourne* near *London*, of which wound he died 30. *Sept.* in sixteen hundred twenty and eight, aged 74. Which being done, the Assassianate discerning his own condition desperate, went into another room, and lock'd the dore, murdered himself with his own Sword. On the 29 of *Oct.* following he the said Lord *Brook* was buried in a Vault, situate on the north side of the collegiat Church at *Warwick*, which formerly had been a chapter house belonging thereunto : wherein he had, in his lifetime, erected a fair Tomb, with this Epitaph thereon : *Fulke Grevil Servant to Queen Elizabeth, Counsellour to King James, and friend to Sir Philip Sidney*[1].' He was succeeded by his adopted heir, Robert Greville, the Roundhead commander slain before Lichfield by the deaf and dumb Dyott.

Greville's literary work is described by Mr. Saintsbury as 'curious,' his principal production in verse being *Poems of Monarchy*, ethical and political in character. He has been recently edited by Dr. Grosart. Two vignettes in his lines have caught modern fancy, one the description in *Caelia* of Myra,

> ' Washing the waters with her beauties white';

the other the couplet,

> ' O'er enamelled meads they went,
> Silent she, he passion rent.'

The two persons in the whole range of English literature whom Charles Lamb, according to Hazlitt, would most desire to have seen in the flesh, were Sir Thomas Browne and Sir Fulke Greville. Among other encouragements to learning, he obtained the office of Clarencieux at Arms for a Broadgates worthy, William Camden, and raised John Speed from the position of a mechanic to that of an historiographer. Bacon submitted his *Life of Henry VII* to Greville's criticism. Together with Sir Edward Dyer, he was pall-bearer at Sidney's obsequies. The three had been intimates from boyhood. Sidney writing to 'dearest Dyer' says :—

> ' Join hands and hearts, so let it be,
> Make but one mind in bodies three.
> Welcome my two to me,
> The number best beloved ;
> Within my heart you be
> In friendship unremoved.'

He wrote in the margin, 'E. D.; F. G.; P. S.'

Greville, a man 'of almost universal study,' has been called 'a mysterious, confused, and affected writer, whose ambition it is to confine in the golden

---

with a knife, but by some rib mist his aime and then stabbed him in the belly. The lord crying out he ranne into the next roome and locked the dore, and then ranne upon his own rapier against the wall; but fayling, he took the former knife that lay by his dead maister and stabbed himself therwith, and so died ere any could breake in.'

[1] *Athenæ*, i. 444, 5.

fetters of verse subjects unsuitable for the simplicity of prose.' His
reputation stands on higher ground as patron and lover of letters than
as writer.

Two uncles of 'glorious John' Dryden were at the Hall: Sir
John Dryden (Dreidon), second baronet, matr. Oct. 29, 1596, aged
fifteen years; of the Middle Temple, 1602 ; married Rebecca,
daughter of Sir Robert Bevile; Sheriff of Northants, 1635; M.P.
1640–53, 1654–55; ob. 1658 (his elder son, Sir Robert, was Sheriff
of Northants 1667, ob. 1708, aet. 76, unmarried; the other, Sir John
was M.P. for Hunts 1690 and 1699–1708), and William Dryden,
entered March 20, 160⅘, aet. 15 ; buried at Farndon in Woodford on
Christmas Eve, 1660.

Their sire, Sir Erasmus, of Canons Ashby, godson of the great Erasmus,
had a third son Erasmus Dryden (ob. 1654), father of the poet (1631–1700),
whose third son, Sir Erasmus Henry (1669–1710), inherited the title in
1708. The last was sub-prior of the Convent of the Holy Cross at
Bornheim, and attached to the mission in Northamptonshire. The
family had been convinced puritans. Sir John, the elder of the Broadgates brothers, is accused of having turned the church at Ashby into
a corn-barn. His father, Sir Erasmus, was imprisoned in old age for
refusing to pay a benevolence to Charles I; and his grandfather (who
married Sir John Cope's daughter and heiress) was a stout Calvinist,
though Erasmus was his friend. Sir John Pickering the regicide, 'Clerk
to Noll's Lord Chamberlain,' was a grandson of the first Sir Erasmus,
and one of Pickering's sons caused a mutiny in his regiment by insisting
on preaching them an over-long sermon. The poet maintained an intimacy
with the elder branch. The carefully finished Epistle beginning 'How
blest is he that leads a country life,' is addressed 'To my honoured
kinsman, John Driden, of Chesterton.' He had inherited Chesterton
from his mother—'You, like Jacob, are Rebecca's heir.'

An orb of almost the first rank in the Shakspearian galaxy was
George Peele, 'the English Ovid' (Warton), a Devonian, born
about 1558. Mr. Collier thinks his father was Stephen Peele, a
ballad-writing bookseller, two of whose productions are printed by
the Percy Society. But in the MS. Depositions in the University
Court he writes himself in 1583 (being witness in a case) as ' civitatis
Londinensis, generosus.' Together with Marlowe, Lyly, Nash,
Greene and Lodge, Peele headed the important and interesting group
of university wits. These, says Mr. Saintsbury, ' made the blank
verse live for dramatic purposes, dismissed—cultivated as they were—
the cultivation of classical models, and gave English Tragedy its
Magna Charta of freedom and submission to the restrictions of actual

life only.' Peele entered Broadgates from Christ's Hospital, aged about twelve, in March, 1571, passing thence, like many others, to Christ Church, where he was elected student in 1574. 'Going through the several forms of Logic and Philosophy he took the degrees of Arts,' viz. B.A. June 12, 1577 (the term of Hooker's magistration), and M.A. 1579. In Oxford he was 'esteemed a most noted poet.'. There he wrote the *Tale of Troy.*

Nash, even after Marlowe had made his voice heard, spoke of Peele as 'the chiefe supporter of pleasance now living, the Atlas of poetrie, and *primus verborum artifex.*' 'Unless we make allowance,' writes Campbell, 'for his antiquity, the expression will appear hyperbolical; but with that allowance we may justly cherish the memory of Peele as the oldest genuine dramatic poet of our language. His *David and Bethsabe* is the earliest fountain of pathos and harmony that can be traced in our dramatic poetry. His fancy is rich and his feeling tender. . . . There is no such sweetness of versification and imagery to be found in our blank verse anterior to Shakspeare[1].' Principal Ward speaks of Peele's 'fearlessly affected' diction. 'Scattered through his plays and pastorals are more than one lyric of imperishable charm. The growth of his powers had been stimulated by a University training, and his works abound in classical allusions.' It was his blank verse—most tantalizingly easy of all forms of metrification, but one whose delicate secret has been whispered in the ear of only two in a former age and few in ours— which especially attracted the admiration of his Oxford contemporaries. Leaving the groves of Oxford after nine years' stay, in 1581, for London, he lodged on the Bankside over against the Blackfriars Theatre, in which he was part shareholder and fellow actor with Shakspeare, as one of the Lord Chamberlain's servants. His voice, we are told, 'was more woman's than man's.' He withdrew later to the rival company of the Lord Admiral, probably piqued by the rising importance of the Warwickshire poet, his junior and not college-bred. Greene, addressing Peele, Marlowe, and Lodge, calls 'Shakscene,' 'an upstart crow beautified with our feathers'—that is, probably, historical plays, of which Peele's *Edward the First* is the earliest example. Greene and Nash were indignant that the plays of non-academic workmen were at first preferred by the managers to those of Peele. We read, however, that his tragedies and comedies had their full share of applause, and Peele was made City Poet, with the ordering of the pageants. 'He knew what belonged to the stage part as well as any in the Metropolis.' In 1583, being then five and twenty, he was manager of two Latin plays, *Dido* and *Rivales,* by Gager, presented at Oxford before the Polish prince, Albertus Alasco, among the charges of whose entertainment in an old accompt-book are these entries: 'To Mr. Peele for provision for the playes at Christchurche, xviij^{li}.' 'The Charges of a Comedie and a Tragedie and a shewe of fire worke, as appeareth by the particular bills of Mr. Vice-

[1] *Speculum of British Poets,* i. 140.

chancelor, Mr. Howson, Mr. Maxie and Mr. Peele, 86^{li}. 18s. 2d.'[1] The next year with the help of the Queen's quiristers he represented his *Arraignment of Paris,* a court-show, before Elizabeth, and was received under the patronage of the Earl of Northumberland, to whom he dedicated his *Honour of the Garter.* Peele became the friend of Drake and Norreys, whom he speeds on their way

> 'to lofty Rome
> There to deface the pride of anti-Christ,
> And pull his paper walls and popery down,
> To steel your swords on Avarice triple crown,
> And cleanse Augeas' stalls in Italy.'

After his death there was printed in 1627 a book of 'Clinches,' called the *Merrie conceited Jests of George Peele, Gent., sometime a student in Oxford; wherein is shewed the course of his life how he lived,* &c. Such a narration told in full would be a sorry tale—a fine intellect dragged down in stews and taverns till a miserable death of nameless disease closed his brief career about 1598. Greene, in his *Groatsworth of Wit,* appeals to his boon comrade, as one driven, like himself, 'to extreme shifts,' to avoid a life of vice. In January, 1595, amid sickness and want, Peele penned a supplication from 'a scholler' to Lord Burleigh. It is endorsed : 'Goorg. Peele M^r of Arts Presents the tale of Troy in 500 Verses by his Eldest daughter, necessities servaunte.' He had annexed the *Tale of Troy,* he tells us, to the *Farewell,* in the hope of rousing his countrymen to emulate the example of their glorious and renowned predecessors the Trojans. Very unlike his own 'exquisite bower,' 'seated in hearing of a hundred streams,' was the noisome garret where his wife and daughter tended his last hours. 'When or where he dyed,' writes à Wood, 'I cannot tell ; for so it is, and always hath been, that most Poets dye poor and consequently obscurely, and a hard matter it is to trace them to their graves.' 'Peele's songs,' Mr. Bullen writes, 'are as fresh as the flowers in May.' 'A rogue and a sharper, according to tradition ; but surely the author of the *Arraignment of Paris* and of the noble song in *Polyhymnia* must have been a man of gentle and chivalrous character.' 'Peele at his best,' says Mr. Morley, 'writes English into music.' His friend Nash speaks of 'his pregnant dexterity of wit and manifold varietie of inuention, wherein (me judice) he goeth a steppe beyond all that write.' A modern critic says, however, 'His work is graceful and elegant, but it has neither sinew nor majesty. . . . His was an adroit, subtle, versatile mind, without massiveness or passionate intensity.' Peele left some charming pastoral verse. Spenser perhaps alludes to him in *Colin Clout* under the name Palin. Steevens supposes that he is the George Pyeboard of *The Puritan,* by Wentworth Smith, but ascribed to Shakspeare, and acted by the children of St. Paul's. A 'peel' is a long-handled board used by bakers. Dyce thinks that *Comus* owes its idea to Peele's *Old Wives' Tale,* 'a highly imaginative

---

[1] An ordinance of 1593 forbade the acting of interludes and plays by the common players, whose resort to Oxford bred many mischiefs.

drama.' His *Bethsabe* is an example of the conjunction of Holy Scripture with dramatic show. Mr. Bullen has lately edited Peele's works.

The most probable account of his parentage is that his father was James Peele, citizen and salter of London, and clerk of Christ's Hospital, the first to introduce the Italian system of book-keeping. He published '*The Pathewaye to perfectnes in the Accomptes of Debtour and Creditour*, in manner of a dialogue, very pleasaunte and profittable for Marchauntes and all that mind to frequent the same.' The governors, on Sept. 19, 1579, bound him over 'to discharge his house of his son George,' then an M.A.

Had there not been a Shakspeare, the splendid roll of English dramatists would have been headed by that 'mysterious double personality'—

> ' Beaumont and Fletcher, those twin stars that run
> Their glorious course round Shakespere's golden sun.'
> (Colman.)

Always excepting *his* astonishing universality of range, 'such a total of work,' says Mr. Saintsbury, 'so varied in character, and so full of excellences in all its variety, has not been set to the credit of any name or names in English literature.' Yet both Beaumont and Fletcher were men of gentle lineage and sufficient means, and had no inducement to work for money. FRANCIS BEAUMONT came of a family that had been for generations eminent in the law. His grandfather was Master of the Rolls, and his father, Francis, became in 1593 a Judge of the Common Pleas. His mother was Anne, daughter of Sir George Pierrepoint of Holme-Pierrepoint, Notts. The Beaumont family had long been established at Grace Dieu in Leicestershire:—

> ' Grace Dieu, that under Charnwood stand'st alone,
> That lately brought such noble Beaumonts forth,
> Whose brave heroick Muses might aspire
> To match the anthems of the heavenly quire.'
> (T. Bancroft, 1739.)

Wordsworth also apostrophises it :—

> ' Haunt of that famous youth, full soon removed
> From earth, perhaps by Shakespere's self approved,
> Fletcher's Associate, Jonson's Friend beloved.'

Francis, third son of the judge, was, with his two brothers, John and Henry, admitted a gentleman commoner of Broadgates Hall in Lent Term, 1597. The entry is, ' 1596(7), Feb. 4. Francisc. Beaumont. Baron. fil. aetat. 12.' He was not born therefore in 1586. Wood (*Ath.* i. 447) says he was educated in Cambridge, mistaking him for his cousin Francis, Master of the Charterhouse. There is no doubt whatever that the dramatist was at Broadgates. Here he remained nearly three years. His biographers speak of his 'acquirements in classical learning.' When he left the Hall with his brothers somewhat suddenly in consequence of his father's death, and without a degree, he was entered (Nov. 3, 1600) of the Inner Temple.

But legal studies did not long detain him from the drama. The boy became one of the 'charmed circle' of the Mermaid, founded by Raleigh, where the wit combats between Jonson and Shakspere are described by Fuller as like combats between a Spanish great galleon and an English man-of-war. Jonson had a tender affection for his 'dear Companions,' John and Francis Beaumont, who also were intimate with Drayton and Chapman. *Salmacis and Hermaphroditus* was put forth in 1602 when the author was but eighteen. When he linked himself to Fletcher is not known, but their first play seems to have been acted before 1607. The next few years were crowded with magnificent effort, but his body was unequal to his spirit, and worn out, it would seem, by his strenuous mind he sank suddenly into an early grave, dying March 9, 161⅚. He had married Ursula, daughter of Henry Isley of Sundridge, by whom he had two daughters. Beaumont was buried in the Abbey Church at Westminster, at the entrance of St. Benedict's Chapel, but no inscription marks the grave, not even 'a garland on my hearse, Of the dismal Yew.' His own verses on the Tombs in Westminster Abbey are well known :—

> 'Here's an acre sown indeed,
> With the richest royall'st seed
> That the earth did e'er suck in
> Since the first man died for sin.
> Here are sands, ignoble things,
> Dropt from the ruin'd side of kings;
> Here's a world of pomp and state,
> Burned in dust, once dead by fate.'

His untimely death wrung from Jonson the fine lines beginning,—

> 'How I do love thee, Beaumont, and thy Muse.'

And Fletcher probably is the author of the elegy,—

> 'Oh, noble youth, to thy ne'er dying name,
> Oh, happy youth, to thy still growing fame,
> To thy long peace in earth this sacred knell
> Our last loves sing. Farewell, farewell, farewell!
> Go, happy soul, to thy eternal birth,
> And press his body lightly, gentle earth.'

Aubrey says, 'there was a wonderful consimility of fancy between Mr. Francis Beaumont and Mr. John Fletcher, which caused that dearness of friendship between them. I have heard Dr. John Earl, since Bishop of Sarum, say, who knew them, that his (Beaumont's) main business was to correct the super-overflowings of Mr. Fletcher's wit.

They lived together on the Bankside, not far from the Play house, both bachelors; had one bench in the house between them, which they did so admire; the same cloaths, cloke, etc., between them.' Beaumont, it is thought, had more of the elevated, sublime, and tragic genius. Dryden tells us that 'he was so accurate a judge of plays that Jonson, while he lived, submitted all his writings to his censure, and, 'tis thought, used his judgment in correcting, if not in contriving, all his plots.'

Mr. Swinburne says: 'In the Olympian circle of the gods and giants of our own race who on earth were their contemporaries and corrivals? They seem to move among the graver presences and figures of sedater fame like the two spoilt boys of heaven, lightest of foot and heart and head of all the brood of the deity.'

It has been mentioned that with Francis Beaumont two of his brothers entered Broadgates on Feb. 4, 159⅚. The eldest, SIR JOHN BEAUMONT, was aged fourteen. His name is not unknown in literature. At Oxford he applied himself to poetry as well as law.

On leaving, after three years' residence, he was entered[1] of the Middle Temple. In 1626 he was by King Charles I made a baronet. 'The former part of his life he successfully employed in Poetry, and the latter he as happily bestowed on serious and beneficial Studies. And had not death untimely cut him off in his middle age he might have proved a Patriot, being accounted at the time of his death a person of great knowledge, gravity, and worth[2].' The Duke of Buckingham introduced his poems to the King. The best known is *Bosworth Field*, to which were prefixed commendatory verses by Jonson, Drayton, and others. It is in the heroic couplet and has some animated lines. He was a man of strong religious feeling and seriousness, and inclined in King James's time to the deeper and better side of puritanism, though his chivalrous devotion made him a Cavalier and Loyalist. Like Milton's earlier puritan feeling, his was not iconoclastic. His poems *Of the Epiphany, Upon the Two Great Feasts of the Annunciation and Resurrection, The Crown of Thorns*, and other sacred verses, reach a high literary level. The last, in eight books, has been lost; one was suppressed. Sir John died in 1628, aged forty-six, and was buried at Westminster, 'in the broad aisle on the south side.' He had espoused a lady of the family of Fortescue, by whom he had seven sons and four daughters. One son, Sir John, himself a poet, fell at the siege of Gloucester on the King's side, in 1644. He 'was of such uncommon strength that it was reputed by old men who knew him that he did leap sixteen feet at one leap, and would commonly at a stand leap and jump over a high long table in the hall, light on the settle beyond the table, and raise himself up[3].' Another son, Francis,

[1] The *Dictionary of National Biography* says in Nov. 1547. What is this a misprint for?
[2] *Athenae*, i. 446.
[3] Nichols, *History of Leicestershire*.

entered the Society of Jesus. On a third, who died aged seven years, the bereaved father wrote the affecting verses 'On my dear Son Gervase Beaumont':—

> 'Can I, who have for others oft compiled
> The songs of death, forget my sweetest child,
> Which like a flower crush'd with a blast is dead,
> And ere full time hangs down his smiling head,
> Expecting with clear hope to live anew
> Among the angels, fed with heavenly dew?
>
> Dear Lord, receive my son, whose winning love
> To me was like a friendship, far above
> The course of nature, or his tender age,
> Whose looks could all my bitter griefs assuage.
> Let his pure soul—ordain'd seven years to be
> In that frail body which was part of me—
> Remain my pledge in heaven, sent to show
> How to this port at every step I go.'

Sir John Beaumont is described as 'a gentleman of great learning, gravity, and worthiness.' Drayton sang his 'much-lamented death.'

The 'history,' a popular companion poem to the chronicle play, is connected with the name of CHARLES FITZGEFFREY, 'the poet of Broadgates Hall,' whence was dated, on Nov. 17, 1596, the *Life and Death of Francis Drake*[1], 'written in lofty verse when he was Bachelaur of Arts,' and dedicated to the Queen. It gained for him from Meres, in *Wit's Commonwealth* (1598), the name of 'young Charles Fitz Jeffrey, that high towring Falcon.' Commendatory verses were prefixed by Rous, Wheare, and other College friends. His father, Alexander FitzGeffrey, was priest of Fowey. Charles 'was born of a gentile family in the county of Cornwall, became a Commoner of Broadgates Hall in 1592 [1590, *Dict. Nat. Biog.*, July 6, 1593, *Foster*], aged 17, took the degrees in Arts [B.A. Jan. 31, 159⅘, M.A. July 4, 1600], entred into the Theological Function, and at length [1603] became Rector of *S. Dominick* in his own Country, where he was esteemed a grave and learned Divine, as before he was, while resident in the University, an excellent Latine Poet[2].'

Besides his *Drake*, called by Mr. Saintsbury a remarkable poem, he printed among other sermons *The Blessed Birthday, Holy Transportations, The Curse of Corn-Hoarders*, and *Elisha his Lamentations*—at the funeral, in 1622, of the patron of his benefice, Sir Anthony Rous of Halton, in St. Dominick, father of Francis Rous (with whom and Degory

---

[1] Under whom served Edward Grenvill of Broadgates (1585). He was killed at Carthagena. Sir John Drake entered the Hall in 1607; Sir Lewis Stucley, vice-admiral of Devon, in 1589. Clyfforde of Chudleigh was another name on the books.　　　　　　　　　　[2] *Athenae*, i. 516.

Wheare FitzGeffrey took his B.A. degree); *Death's Sermon unto the Living* at the 'funerals,' in 1620, of Dame Philippa Rous, the second wife, daughter of Sir Rich. Carew, dedicated to her son '*Jo. Pym* Esq ;' and *Compassion towards Captives* (in Barbary). 'He hath also,' says à Wood, 'made *A Collection of choice Flowers and Descriptions*, as well out of his, as the works of several others, the most renowned Poets of our Nation: collected about the beginning of the raign of K. *James* I, but this, tho' I have been many years in seeking after, yet, I cannot get a sight of, it.' He died in his parsonage, and was buried under the altar, Feb. 22, 163⅘. Robert Hayman, his familiar, styles him Bachelor of Divinity. Perhaps he received this degree at Cambridge, where he incorporated in 1617. FitzGeffrey had two sons, Charles and John, at Gloucester Hall. He has an epitaph in his friend Robert Chamberlaine's *Epigrams and Epitaphs*, and John Dunbar wrote lines upon him. Davies penned an epigram 'to my deare freind Mr. C. Fitz Ieffrey.' Hayman in his *Quodlibets* styles him 'learned and witty' and 'a most excellent poet.' FitzGeffrey appears from Hayman's somewhat partial lines to have been blind of one eye :—

> 'Blind poet Homer you do equalize
> Tho' he saw more with none than most with eyes.
> Our Geoffrey Chaucer, who wrote quaintly neat,
> In verse you match, equall him in conceit.
> Featur'd you are like Homer in one eye,
> Rightly surnam'd the sonne of Geoffery.'

Dr. Grosart republished the *Poems of Charles FitzGeoffrey* in 1881.

RICHARD CORBET, prelate, jester, and poet in an age of sour precisianism, who carried on into a gloomy generation the lively, gay, and airy spirit of Ben Jonson, was born at Ewell, Surrey, his parents being Vincent and Benedicta Corbet, or Poynter[1], of Salopian descent.

After having his schooling at Westminster, he entered Broadgates April 7, 1598, aged fifteen. He was 'esteemed one of the most cele-

---

[1] Vincent was a gardener. Ben Jonson, who afterwards bandied many a joke with the son, wrote the following epitaph on the father:—

> 'Dear Vincent Corbet, who so long
> Hath wrestled with diseases strong,
> That though they did possess each limb,
> Yet he broke them ere they broke him,
> With the just canon of his life ;
> O life that knew not noise nor strife,
> But was, by sweetening so his will,
> All order and composure still ;
> His mind as pure and neatly kept
> As were his nourseries, and swept
> So of uncleanness and offence
> That never came ill odours thence.'

He bequeathed a considerable fortune to his son.

brated Wits in the University, as his Poems, Jests, Romantick fancies and exploits, which he made and perform'd *extempore*, shew'd[1].'   In 1599 he became a student of Christ Church.   In 1602, June 30, he was admitted B.A. together with Robert Burton, *alias* Democritus Junior.   On June 9, 1605, he and Burton became Masters two days before Walter Raleigh of Magdalen took B.A.

The same year he was ordained deacon.   He 'became a most quaint Preacher and therefore much followed by ingenious men.   At length being made one of the Chaplains to his Maj. K. *Jam.* I. (who highly valued him for his fine fancy and preaching) he was by his favour promoted to the Deanery of *Ch. Ch.* in *Oxon, an.* 1620[2], being then D. of D. [1617].   Senior *Student* of that house, Vicar of *Cassington* near to *Woodstock* and Prebendary of *Beminster Secunda* in the Church of *Sarum*[3].'   He was also at different times incumbent of Puttenham, of Stewkley, and of Brightwell Baldwin.   As Deputy Orator and Proctor in 1612, he pronounced a funeral oration in Latin on the death of Henry Prince of Wales : 'very oratorically speeched it in St. Maries church.' He calls the Prince in one of his poems 'the expectancy and rose of the fair State.'   To a rival anniversarist on the same subject, Dr. Daniel Price, Corbet addressed the lines :—

> 'Even so dead Hector thrice was triumph'd on
> The walls of Troy, thrice slain when fates had done,
> So did the barbarous Greekes before their hoast
> Torment his ashes and profane his ghost,
> As Henrye's vault, his peace, his sacred hearse,
> Are torne and batter'd by thine Anniverse.'

In 1613 he came into conflict with the Abbotts.   Gilchrist says: 'Preaching the Passion Sermon at Christ Church he insisted on the article of Christ's descending into hell, and therein grated upon Calvin's manifest perverting of the true sense and meaning of it ; for which (says Heylyn), he was so rattled up by the Repetitioner (Dr. Robert Abbott[4], brother of the Archbishop), that if he had not been a man of very great courage it might have made him afraid of staying in the University This, it was generally conceived, was not done without the Archbishop's setting on.'   B.D. and D.D. May 8, 1617.   To the following period belong some of the raciest and least edifying anecdotes of this strange divine.

Aubrey tells us : 'After he was doctor of divinity he sang ballads at the Crosse at *Abingdon*; on a market day he and some of his comrades

---

[1] *Ath. Ox.* i. 511.
[2] Chalmers says 1627.   [3] *Athenae*, i. 511.
[4] Wood (Gutch, ii. 315) omits the Repetitioner's name, and makes the encouragement to have proceeded from Robert Abbot.   A Repetitioner repeated the Lent sermons from memory.   So, e. g., Wood records, ' 1679, 27 Apr. Low-sunday, Rawlyns of Pembr. Coll., repeated at St. Marie's, very well.'

were at the taverne by the Crosse, which by the way was then the finest of England. The ballad singer complayned that he had no custome—he could not put off his ballads. The jolly doctor puts off his gowne, and puts on the ballad-singer's leathern jacket, and being a handsome man, and a rare full voice, he presently vended a great many and had a great audience.

'He had a good interest with great men, as you may find in his poems; and that with the then duke of *Bucks* his excellent wit ever 'twas of recommendation to him. He was made dean of *Christ Church* after Dr. *Goodwin's* death against Dr. *Fell.*

' His conversation was extreme pleasant. Dr. *Stubbins* was one of his cronies; he was a jolly fat doctor, and a very good house-keeper. As Dr. *Corbet* and he were riding in *Lob* Lane in wet weather ('tis an extraordinary deepe dirty lane) the coach fell and *Corbet* said that Dr. *S.* was up to the elbows in mud, and he was up to the elbows in *Stubbins.*

'A.D. 1628 [1629] he was made bishop of *Oxford*; and I have heard that he had an admirable grave and venerable aspect.' The anecdotes which follow, however, are mere βωμολοχία. One piece of buffoonery must be *ben*, or *mal*, *trovato* :—

'His chaplaine, Dr. *Lushington*, was a very learned and ingenious Man and they loved one another. The bishop would sometimes take the key of the wine-cellar and he and his chaplaine would lock themselves in and be merry : then first he layes down his episcopal hood, "There layes the doctor;" then he putts off his gowne, "There layes the bishop;" and then 'twas "Here's to thee *Corbet*" and "Here's to thee *Lushington*."'

It is hard to think that such clowning commended itself to the austere and fastidious king or the martinet Laud. Though we open our eyes at the description of him as 'poet and saint,' there must have been something more solid in Corbet than the vivacity of a Friar Tuck to commend him for promotion, for which he had humorously sued Charles before his accession :—

> ' For ever dear, for ever dreaded prince,
> You read some verse of mine a little since ;
> And so pronounced each word and every letter
> Your gratious reading made my verse the better.
> Since that your highness doth by gifte exceeding
> Make what you read the better for your reading,
> Let my poor Muse thus far your grace importune,
> To leave to read my verse, and read my fortune.'

When he preached as chaplain before James at Oxford, in 1621, the King had given him a ring, which occasioned the following doggrel :—

> ' The reverend dean,
> With his band starch'd clean,
> Did preach before the King ;
> A ring was his pride
> To his bandstrings tied.
> Was not this a pretty thing?

> 'The ring without doubt
> Was the thing put him out,
> And made him forget what was next.
> For every one there
> Will say, I dare swear,
> He handled it more than his text.'

In Rous's Diary are some satirical verses from Dean Corbet 'to the Gentlewomen of the Newe Dresse,' with 'the ladies and gentlewomen's answer,' in which they allude to his tying the ring round his neck.

It was Corbet's real literary merits and vigorous though rollicking muse that advanced his interest at Court. Headley says, 'Corbet appears to have been at the head of that poetical party who, by inviting Ben Jonson to come to Oxford, rescued him from the arms of a sister University who has long treated the Muses with indignity.' Jonson said that he owed his degree of Master to the favour of the University, not to his study[1]. Mr. Saintsbury, while he calls Corbet a 'poet of no small power,' thinks he had too much of the flavour of the University wit. He has, however, 'both pathetic and imaginative touches on occasion.' 'The "Exhortation to Mr. John Hammond," a ferocious satire on the Puritans, distinguishes itself from almost all precedent work of the kind by the force and directness of its attack, which almost anticipates Dryden.' Coleridge wished Corbet's poems, collected first in 1647, might be published for modern delectation, and was sure they would be popular.

His opposition, genial but forcible, to the flowing tide of iconoclasm helped to commend him to King Charles. The following lines were written by him upon the Fairford windows :—

> 'Tell me, you anti-saints, why brass
> With you is shorter lived than glass;
> And why the saints have scapt their falls
> Better from windows than from walles?'

Aubrey declares he was 'apt to abuse and a coward.' Fuller, however, says, 'he was of a courteous carriage and no destructive nature to any who offended him, counting himself plentifully repaired with a jest upon him[2].' A merry humour was a link between him and Laud, whose energy, however, and policy of Thorough were not to the mind of easy-going Corbet. In 1632 he left Oxford for Norwich, 'though in some respects,' says à Wood, 'unworthy of such an office.' In this year he was satirized with others in some Oxford verses called 'The Academicall Army of Epidemicall Arminians, to the Tune of the Soldier.' Two days after Corbet's translation Laud ascended the metropolitical throne and at once began to tighten the strings of discipline throughout the province. At Norwich Corbet, himself a new broom, but of less stiff twig, took a few gentle measures, and seems to have succeeded with a Mr. Ward of

---

[1] *Aliter* 'studies'; that is, importunity. So in *Henry VIII*, sc. 1, 'To use our utmost studies in your service.'

[2] *Worthies.*

Ipswich (who had violently resented the *Book of Sports*), as we may gather from the following letter[1].

'Salutem in Christo.

'My worthie friend

'I thank God for your conformitie and you for your acknowledgment: stand upright to the church wherein you live; be true of heart to her governours; think well of her significant ceremonyes; and be you well assured I shall never displace you of that room which I have given you in my affection; proove you a good tenant in my hart, and noe minister in my diocese hath a better landlord. Farewell! God Almightie blesse you with your whole congregation.

'From your faithful friend to serve you in Christ Jesus
'RICH. NORWICH.

'LUDHAM HALL,
the 6 of *Oct.* 1633.'

Laud was determined to effect a task in which Elizabeth and Parker had failed, and dislodge from consecrated buildings in London and Norwich the foreign Protestant congregations. Corbet's method of carrying out the Primate's injunctions is amusing.

'To the minister and elders of the French Church[2] in Norwich, these:

'Salutem in Christo.

'You have promised me from time to time to restore my stolen bell and to glaze my lettice windows. After three yeares consultation (bysides other pollution) I see nothing mended. Your discipline I know care not much for a consecrated place, and anye other roome in Norwiche that hath but bredth and length may serve your turne as well as the chappel: wherefore I say unto you, without a miracle, *Lazare prodi foras!* Depart, and hire some other place for your irregular meetings: you shall have time betwixte this and Whitsontide. And that you may not think I mean to deale with you as Felix dyd with St. Paul, that is to make you afraid, to get money, I shall keepe my word with you, which you did not with me, and as neer as I can be like you in nothinge.

'Written by me, Richard Norwich, with myne own hand, Dec. 26, anno 1634.'

Old St. Paul's standing in need of reparation, Corbet gave £400 himself and stirred up his clergy to contribute in the following letter. Wood says that he supplied some of them who were poor with money for the purpose, in order to encourage others.

'Saint Paul's church! One word in the behalf of Saint Paul; he hath spoken many in ours: he hath raised our inward temples, let us help to requite him in his outward. Should I commend Paul's to you for the age, it were worth your thought and admiration. A thousand years, though it should fall now, were a pretty climacterical. See the bigness, and your eye never yet beheld such a goodly object. It's worth the reparation, though it were but for a landmark; but, beloved, it is a church, and consecrated to God. . . . Are we not beholden

[1] Harl. MSS. No. 464, fol. 12.
[2] The Walloons at first used the quire and the Dutch the nave of the great Dominican church, now St. Andrew's Hall. Later, the latter were given a long lease of the quire, and the former were assigned the Bishop's chapel. A Dutch sermon is still preached once a year. Strype's *Parker*, ii. 77, 83, 84; iii. 185.

I

to it, every man, either to the body or the choir: for a walk or a warbling note; for a prayer or a thorough path? It hath twice suffered Martyrdom: and both by fire. Saint Paul complained of Stoning twice; his church of firing: stoning she wants indeed and a good stoning would repair her. Saint Faith holds her up, I confess. Oh that works were sainted to keep her upright! . . . I am verily persuaded were it not for the pulpit and the pews (I do not now mean the altar and the font for the two Sacraments, but for the pulpit and the stools as you call them) many churches had been down that stand. Stately pews are now become tabernacles with rings and curtains to them. There wants nothing but beds to hear the word of God on; we have casements, locks and keys, and cushions: I had almost said bolsters and pillows: and for these we love the Church.'

He lies buried at the upper end of the quire of his cathedral church. A brass plate let into the stone has the words :—

'Ricardus Corbet, Theologiae Doctor, Ecclesiae Cathedralis Christi Oxoniensis primum alumnus deinde decanus, exinde Episcopus, illinc huc translatus et hinc in caelum, Jul. 28, 1635.'

Not, let us hope, a mistranslation. 'To laugh and make others laugh,' says Sanford, 'seems to have been the business of his life.' In days of ever-deepening shadows and foreboding this was not an office unworthy of a Christian; and, if Corbet wore bells on his mitre, he lived to see, as he complains himself, his office even more out of fashion than his verse. He wrote this couplet on the birth of 'the New-Borne Prince' (afterwards Charles II) :—

> ' Thrice happy childe! whom God thy father sent
> To make him rich without a parliament.'

In his epitaph on Dr. Donne there is a good phrase about divinity being
> ' Not of the last edition but the best.'

But this 'boon and jolly blade,' of whose tavern conviviality in youth with Jonson and other dramatists there are many stories, had neither politics nor divinity, only a mirth-loving soul. Here are some lines on the Re-casting of Great Tom of Oxford :—

> ' Brave, constant spirit, none could make thee turn,
> Though hang'd drawn quarter'd, till they did thee burn.
> Yet not for this nor ten times more be sorry,
> Since thou wast martyr'd for the church's glory.
> But for thy meritorious suffering
> Thou shortly shalt to heaven in a string;
> And though we griev'd to see thee thump'd and bang'd,
> We'll all be glad, Great Tom, to see thee hanged.'

Corbet's name and, possibly, appearance are referred to in John Taylor's lines 'upon my good Lord the Bishop of Norwiche' :—

> ' Raven he was, yet was no gloomie fowle,
> Merrie at hearte though innocent of soule;
> Where'er he perkt the birds that came anighe
> Constrayned caught the humour of his eye.
> Under that shade no spights and wrongs were sped,
> Care came not nigh with his uncomlie head.'

Aubrey, we saw, describes him as 'a very handsome man.' His portrait by Jansen hangs in Christ Church hall. Corbet built himself a 'pretty house' upon Folly Bridge. By his wife, Alice, daughter of Dr. Leonard Hutten, he had two children, Vincent and Alice. To the latter, aged three, he addressed some tender lines. The former (born 1627), at school at Westminster, is described by Aubrey as 'a very handsome youth; but he is run out of all, and goes begging up and down to gentlemen.'

Corbet's zeal for the fabrick of St. Paul's was not shared by every Pembrochian. 'Mr. John Burges, upon the proposal of the collection for the re-edyfying of St. Paul's Church in London, which was tendred to him among others 3 June 1632 in Pembroke College Hall, did speak foolishly and indiscretly many insufferable words, as particularly "that Churches were not simply necessary, because God might be served by us as well in caves and dens and woods," and also that he "would rather give 10 shillings towards the pulling down of that Church to build other Churches where they want them than 5 shillings towards the repairing of it" etc.; which passages being attested to his face before his Majesty's Commissioners Ecclesiastical, was by them ordered to make a recantation at Oxford as the Vicechancellor should appoint, which being by him performed in a Convocation held 14 of March, was in a capacity to obtain that preferment which he was in seeking[1].'

[1] Gutch's *Wood*, ii. 393.

CHAPTER X.

HISTORICAL WRITERS.

An early historian who, à Wood thinks, was educated in 'the ancient hostle called *Broadgates*, wherein several of both his names and time have studied,' was Sir John Rhese, ap Rise, or Prise, 'born of a gentile and ancient family in *Wales*,' the same probably as a John Price admitted B.C.L. July 12, 1534.

Being 'encouraged in his studies by *William* Earl of *Pembroke*, he made great advances therein, especially as to the Histories and Antiquities of his own Country. In 1546[7], March 2. he, with many others, received the honor of Knighthood from the hands of *Edward* Lord Protector of *England.* About which time our Author observing the great and manifold errors which were made by *Pol. Virgil* in his *Historiae Anglicae Libri* 27, wherein many things redounded to the dishonor of the British[1] nation, he thereupon published *Fides Historiae Britannicae; Defensio Regis Arthuri.* And wrot about the Year 1553 *Historiae Britannicae Defensio.*' This was published after his death by his son Dr. Richard Prise in 1573. There are also ascribed to him by à Wood *A Description of Cambria* (1584 and 1663) and *Tractatus de Eucharistia.* He died in Mary's reign. Foster, however, says he was perhaps chancellor of St. Asaph diocese in 1559, canon 1560 (as LL.B.), M.P. for co. Brecon 1547-52, for Hereford 1553, for Ludlow 1554.

William Salesbury, of 'an ancient and gentile family in *Denbighshire*,'

after studying law at Thavies and Lincoln's Inn, 'applied his muse to the searching of Histories, especially those of his own Country.' He was 'a most exact Critick in British antiquities,' and made a Welsh-English Dictionary (1547), 'thought by the Kings Majesty very meet to be set forth to the use of his gracious Subjects in Wales.' He also published *The Laws of Howell Da* and other antiquarian works. An excursion into theology produced the 'Battery of the Pope's bottereulx, commonly called the High Aultar,' 1550.

---

[1] I. e. Welsh.

Several members of the famous Cornish family of Carew came to Broadgates. DEAN GEORGE CAREW (1500–1583) graduated from the Hall in 1522.

His grandfather, Sir Nicholas, Baron Carew, died in 1470. His father, Sir Edmund, of Mohun's Ottery, relieved Exeter when invested by Perkin Warbeck, was knighted on Bosworth field, and fell before the walls of Thérouanne in 1513. After leaving Broadgates George Carew, to cure a heart ache, travelled in foreign lands, then took Holy Orders, espoused Anne, daughter of Sir Nicholas Hervey, and was successively archdeacon of Totnes 1534, canon of Exeter 1535, canon of Wells 1545, precentor 1549 and archdeacon of Exeter 1556–9, prebendary of Chichester 1555, prebendary and also precentor of Sarum 1555–83, precentor of Bath and Wells 1560 and 1565, canon and dean of Windsor 1560, dean of Exeter 1571–83 (then being D.D.); in 1552 he was made dean of Bristol, in 1553 ejected, in 1558 restored. He resigned and was again appointed in 1581. He was also registrar of the Garter and master of the Savoy. From 1559 to 1561 he was dean of Christ Church. Mr. Foster enumerates nine minor cures of souls held by him at various times. He died June 1, 1583, and is buried in St. Giles'-in-the-Fields. It was the dean's pretty boy Peter Carew (afterwards B.A. from Exeter, 1572) who so delighted Elizabeth by his Latin oration, ending with a couple of Greek verses, that she made Cecil come in to hear the speech again, and who enacted the Lady Emilia in Edward's *Palamon and Arcyte* before her in Christ Church Hall. The child actor's sweet song after gathering flowers in the garden evoked the enthusiasm of the auditors, and the Queen rewarded him with embraces and eight gold angels. Sir Peter, knighted in Ireland, fell in battle there in early manhood. He lies under a fine monument ' in or near the Lady Mary's Chappel,' in Exeter Cathedral. The Carews of Haccombe now represent Dean Carew's line.

Sir Peter's younger brother, GEORGE EARL OF TOTNES, living longer achieved greater renown. He entered Broadgates as a gentleman commoner in, he tells us himself, 1564, having been ' borne 29 May, 1554.' He was ' taken from yᵉ Universyty ' in 1573. Wood gives 1572 as the date of matriculation, misled perhaps by a list of members of the Hall in that year, which includes two Carewes. At Oxford he ' made a good proficiency in learning, particularly in the study of antiquities,' historical and legal; but, ' being more delighted in Martial Affairs than in the solitary delights of a study,' he left without a degree, in spite of his long residence.

Young Carew went to Ireland (where an ancestor, John Carew, who fought at Cressy, had been Lord Deputy), and served as a volunteer under Sir H. Sidney against Rory Oge O'More, Earl of Desmond, and other chiefs. His services attracting royal notice, he was made Lieutenant-Governor of County Carlow and Constable of Leighlin Castle. In 1578 we find him a navy captain, but next year he was again in Ireland, being created Governor of Askettan Castle and Master of the Ordnance, a post which he held afterwards in England also. He was sworn of the Council and knighted. In 1589 the University created him M.A. Carew took part in Essex's expeditions to Cadiz, in 1596, and to the Azores in 1597. Next year, accompanied by Sir Robert Cecil, he was sent as envoy to the King of France. In 1599, his presence being indispensable in Ireland, he was made successively Treasurer at War, Lord President of Munster, and Lord Justice, his vigorous support of Mountjoy enabling that lord to put down O'Neil's rebellion. Carew now desired to return to England, his health failing and anxieties crushing him, but the Queen would not suffer him to do so. His final achievement was the defeat of the Spanish descent upon Ireland in 1601. A gallant soldier in these wars was HENRY LORD FOLLIOTT, knighted by Essex in 1599, and made Governor of Ballyshannon. He entered Broadgates in 1586 [1].

A little before her death, Elizabeth wrote thus to Carew in her own hand :—

'My faithful George,

'If ever more services of worth were performed in shorter space than you have done, we are deceived among many witnesses. ... It shall neither be unremembered nor unrewarded. And in the mean while, believe, my help nor prayers shall ever fail you.

'Your sovereign that best regards you,

'E. R.'

James on his accession treated Carew with honour, made him Governor of Guernsey, and in 1605 created him Baron Carew of Clopton. As Captain Carew he had espoused Joyce, co-heiress of William Clopton of Clopton, who resented the match so much that he proposed to disinherit his daughter, but afterwards acknowledged his mistake. Lord Carew was made vice-chamberlain and treasurer to James's queen, together with other distinctions. On the accession of Charles in 1625 he received the Earldom of Totnes. He died, full of years and honours, at the Savoy, March 27, 1629, and lies in the Clopton Chapel in Stratford-on-Avon church, with his countess, under a noble monument [2] adorned with emblems of his warlike calling, erected by Ursula Neville. It is figured in Dugdale. Wood styles Carew 'a faithful Subject, a valiant and prudent Commander, an honest Counsellour, a gentile Scholar, a lover of Antiquities, and a great Patron of learning.' His chief historical work is *Pacata Hibernia*, a record of the Irish wars (published in 1633 by his natural son, Sir Tho. Stafford). There are in the Bodleian a number of his papers, maps, and monuments relating to Ireland, and Nicholson speaks of forty-two volumes, written by Carew, on the affairs of that

---

[1] I may here mention Sir JAMES BLOUNT (entered Broadgates 1597), standard-bearer to the Lord Mountjoy, and WILLIAM FARRINGTOUN (1585), made Constable of Lancaster Castle by Elizabeth, 1599.

[2] He bore, Or, 3 lions passant, sa.; the Crest, a lion passant, sa.; the Supporters 2 antelopes gu. armed, crined, and hoofed, or.

kingdom, at Lambeth, besides others elsewhere. Lodge says, 'the account transmitted to us of the extent of his compositions and collections is nearly incredible.' Granger observes, they are 'written with the unaffected openness and sincerity of a soldier.' He left a son Peter and a daughter Anna, married to Sir Allen Apsley. The best portrait of Carew is Geldorp's, now in the National Portrait Gallery.

RICHARD CAREW (1555–1620), whose portrait by Evans appears in one edition of the *Survey*, was entered, aged eleven, as a gentleman commoner of Christ Church, but 'had his Chamber in *Broadgates* hall, much about the time that his kinsman *George Carew* (afterwards Earl of *Totnes*) and *Will. Camden* studied there.' Here, at the age of fourteen, he was required, as he modestly says, 'upon a wrong conceived opinion touching my sufficiency,' to dispute *extempore—impar congressus Achilli—*'with the matchless Sir Philip Sidney, in the presence of the earls of Leicester, Warwick, and other Nobility, at what time they were lodged in *Ch. Ch.* to receive entertainment from the Muses.' It is said that the dispute ended in a drawn battle, probably through the chivalry of the older combatant. After three years in Oxford and three at the Middle Temple he

'was sent with his Unkle in his Embassage unto the King of Poland.' He was afterwards sent into France 'with Sir *Hen. Nevill*, who was then Embassadour Leiger unto K. *Hen.* 4. that he might learn the French tongue.' In 1577 he wedded Juliana Arundel of Trerice. In 1586 he was pricked as high sheriff of Cornwall, and made Queen's deputy for the militia. He became in 1589 an active member of the Society of Antiquaries, established by Archbishop Parker, and helped Camden in preparing the *Britannia*. Ben Jonson classes him with Cotton and Selden, and Dunbar, in two Latin epigrams, extols his attainments, styling him 'another Livie, another Maro, another Papinian.' Spelman speaks of his 'ingenium splendidum, bellarumque intentionum faecundissimum.' FitzGeffrey wrote an epigram upon him. Carew's *Historical Survey of Cornwall*, 1602, 'still remains one of the most entertaining works in the English language. In its pages may be discerned the character of an English gentleman in the brightest age of our national history, interesting himself in the pursuits of all around him, and skilled in the pastimes of every class[1].' His *Epistle Concerning the Excellencies of the English Tongue*, 1605, is interesting for its mention of Shakespeare in a comparison of English and foreign writers. He died Nov. 6, 1620, 'as he was at his private prayers in his Study (his daily practice) at fower in the afternoon,' and was buried in East Anthony Church among his ancestors. Camden wrote his epitaph. A splendid monument was placed over his ashes. He is styled by Wood 'a religious and ingenious Man, learned, eloquent, liberal, stout, honest and well skill'd in several

[1] *Dict. of Nat. Biog.*

Languages, as also among his neighbours the greatest Husband and most excellent manager of Bees in Cornwall.' From Hymettus also he gathered honey, his earliest work being a rendering of Tasso's *Godfrey of Bologne.* Carew's *Letters to Sir Thomas Roe* are published by the Camden Society. His son was Sir Richard Carew.

Among the Oxford Writers à Wood also mentions a Thomas Carew of the same family, educated either at Exeter or Broadgates, who took holy orders and dedicated some sermons to his kinsman the President of Munster in 1605.

A *Survey of Cornwall* was also written by TRISTRAM (not Thomas) RISDON (whose father was treasurer of the Inner Temple and recorder of Totnes), a Devon antiquary and a Broadgates man. He was buried at Winscot, 1640.

WILLIAM CAMDEN, 'historicus ille plane immortalis,' 'the Varro, the Strabo, and the Pausanias of Great Britain,' born in the Old Bailey May 2, 1551, was the son of Sampson Camden of Lichfield, a member of the Guild of Painter-Stainers, and Elizabeth, daughter of Giles Curwen, of Poulton Hall, Lancashire, of an ancient Cumberland family. From Christ's Hospital he passed to St. Paul's School, and thence in 1566 to Magdalen as a servitor; but, being disappointed of a demy's place, he was invited by Dr. Thomas Thornton (who maintained him thenceforward), tutor to Sir Philip Sidney, to enter Broadgates Hall, where a number of distinguished men were then studying. Wheare, in his funeral oration over Camden, says that after studying logic at Magdalen,

'Mox transit ad antiquissimam Aularum Lateportensem, ubi per duos annos et dimidium constanter haesit ... sub ductu et disciplinatu viri etiam tunc temporis praeclari nominis et nunc admodum reverendi Tho. Thornton S. Th. Doct. et multa jam annorum lustra cathedralis illius Ecclesiae Vigorniensis, Regalisque hujus nostrae Aedis Christi Prae-bendarij. Nec minus pietati studuit hic noster quam liberioribus scientijs, cujus luculenta quaedam adhuc exstant vestigia apud *Latepor-tenses,* nempe benedictiones sive precatiunculae mensales[1], quas ipse juvenis Latine primum meditatus est, et ad hunc usq; diem a servientibus quotidie solenniter recitantur. Eodem tempore aderant, una ejusdem Aulae Commensales Camdenoq; nostro perquam amici et familiares (ex ipsiusmet ore accepi quod refero), honoratissimus nunc Dominus Baro *Carewus,* serenissimo nostro Regi *Jacobo* ab interioribus Consilijs, prae-nobiles etiam *Johannes Packingtonius, Stephanus Powlus, Edwardus Luceius,* omnes postea Equites Aurati, aliiq; plures notae praestantioris viri . . . quod ego in honorem charissime nutricis mee lubens repeto,

---

[1] Only one is extant—the grace after meat. In Hearne's time there was but one. 'Mr. Camden, when he was a very young man of Broad-Gate Hall, now Pembroke College, made the Latin Grace which they use to this day.' (*Collections,* ed. Doble, O. H. S., iii. 90.)

adeoq; gratulor tibi, veneranda Lateportensis, de hoc tuo Alumno prae multis alijs; mihimet ipsi quoq; haud parum gratulor quod iisdem tuis uberibus quibus ille (ô si pari effectu et profectu dedisset Deus!), cum ad hanc Academiam recens accederem, lactari contigit. . . . Ab Aula *Lat.* ad *Regale* Aedis Christi Collegium transijt dicam? an raptus est? plane ita. Nam venerabilis Thorntonus ductor ejus et doctor tanto cum amore prosecutus est, ut suum totum et magis peculiari modo voluerit [1].'

Camden stood for a fellowship at All Souls, but was disappointed through the efforts, it is said, of the papists, he having already, at the age of twenty, made enemies by religious controversy. He suppli-cated in June, 1570, for his bachelor's degree, 'having spent four years in the University in Logicals,' and again in March, 1573. It was granted, but he failed to complete it by determination. Meanwhile he had followed Dr. Thornton, promoted in 1568 to a canonry, to Christ Church, but left Oxford in 1573 for London, where he devoted himself to antiquarian studies, to which he had at Oxford given all his spare time, being encouraged by his fellow students, Richard and George Carew and Philip Sidney. He became usher at Westminster School, but was not prevented from travelling over the greater part of England, amassing with immense labour an incredible store of materials—'umbraticus vir et pulvere scholastico obsitus' (Smith). His *Britannia* (1586), dedicated to Burleigh, was received with universal applause. In June, 1588, we find him supplicating Con-vocation, as already B.A., 'that, whereas from the time he had taken the degree of bachelor he had spent sixteen years in the study of philosophy and the liberal arts, he might read three solemn lectures, and so be allowed to proceed.' However, it appears he did not do so. When he attended Sir Thomas Bodley's obsequies in 1613, his fame was so great that the University offered him the degree of Master, but he refused the tardy honour. His Greek Grammar (1597) was used till recently at Westminster, of which he became head master in 1593, one of his many eminent pupils being Ben Jonson, whom Camden afterwards took away from bricklaying and sent round the world with Sir Walter Raleigh's son. In 1597 he was made Richmond Herald and Clarencieux king of arms. The year before he had compiled a book on the churches and chapels of Oxford, now unhappily lost, but his fame is associated with greater researches. After the Powder Plot Camden was chosen by the King to be one of a learned college projected (in the Jacobean love of controversy)

[1] '*Camdeni Insignia.* Parentatio Historica facta in Schola Historica per De-goreum Whear, Historiarum Praelectorem.' Published 1628.

at Chelsea, to publish argumentative works against the papal pretensions; but the scheme fell through, and Dean Sutcliffe's splendid
endowment reverted to his heirs. In 1622 Camden carried out a
long-cherished plan of endowing a 'Reader of Histories' at Oxford
with the valuable rents of Bexley Manor, Kent, which he had bought
from Sir Henry Spelman. He declined knighthood, and his last
years were spent in retirement at Chiselhurst, where he died
November 9, 1623. He was buried with much state ten days later
in the south transept of Westminster Abbey Church. A monument
of white marble above his grave represents him half length, the left
hand resting on his *Britannia*. It was defaced in 1646, but repaired
at the cost of the University. This inscription is on it :—

> Qui fide antiqua et opera assidua
> Britannicam antiquitatem
> indagavit,
> simplicitatem innatam honestis
> studiis excoluit,
> animi solertiam candore illustravit,
> Gulielmus Camdenus ab Eliza-
> betha R. ad Regis Armorum
> (Clarentii titulo) dignitatem
> evocatus
> HÍc spe certa resurgendi in
> Xto s. e.
> Q.
> obiit anº. Dñi. 1623: 9 Novembris
> Aetatis suae 74.   [He was not quite 73.]

Next him rests Casaubon. Camden was of a gentle, happy disposition, of
middle height, ruddy-complexioned. The picture by Gheerardts in the
Bodleian was originally placed by Wheare, the first praelector, under
the History Reader's pew, 'inclosed in shuttings.' The National Portrait
Gallery has one, and there was one in Painters' Hall. Camden's name
is inscribed by the University on its roll of Benefactors. His house at
Chiselhurst passed to the Westons, from them to Harry Spencer, Esq.,
who sold it to Charles Pratt, whose barony of Camden, created in 1765,
took thence its name. Recently it was the home of the exiled Emperor
and Empress of the French. Among many Oxford verses on Camden's
decease were :—

'Nuncius Chronogrammaticus de obitu V. C. Guil. Camdeni Clarentij ad Th.
Cl[ayton] Reg. Prof. in Med. Aulae Lat. P.

> 'Latarum Praeses Forium dignissime, quali
> Me nuper arbitraris aegritudine
> Mactum dum propero Camdenum visere, alumnum
> Vestrae inclytum Aulae olim,' &c.

'Chronogramma by Georg. Stinton, Art. Mag. Lateport.

> 'CaMDenVs pIVs seneX obIIt.'

Latin and Greek epigrams were composed by Dr. Clayton, John Pember, A.M., Nath. White, gen., Fr. Chaloner, gen., Thos. Browne, gen., Steph. Plummer, A.B., Thos. Wilcox, A.B., all of Broadgates, and a great many others.

The SIR JOHN PAKINGTON (1549–1625), Knight of the Bath and Privy Councillor, Camden's friend at Broadgates, was son of Sir Thomas, of Aylesbury. He was remarkable for wit, beauty, and strength. Elizabeth delighted in her 'lusty Pakington.'

Beggared by his splendour and generosity[1], he espoused in 1598 a rich widow, Dorothy Barnham (whose daughter was wife to Lord Verulam), and in 1603 entertained the new King with great magnificence at Aylesbury. Dame Dorothy, 'a little violent lady,' got Sir John clapped into prison in 1617; but Bacon, who heard the matter, decided against his mother-in-law. There is a portrait of Pakington at Westwood Park. He took B.A. Dec. 13, 1569, and was then entered of Lincoln's Inn.

Sir R. Naunton in *Fragmenta Regalia* (1630) says :—

'Sir *John Packington* was a Gentleman of no mean family, and of form and feature no way despisable; for he was a brave Gentleman, and a very fine Courtier; and for the time he stayed there (which was not lasting) very high in [the Queen's] grace; but he came in, and went out, and through disassiduity drew the Curtain between himself and the light of her grace; and then death overwhelmed the remnant, and utterly deprived him of recovery: And they say of him, that had he brought lesse to the Court than he did, he might have carried away more than he brought; for he had a time on it; but an ill husband of opportunity.'

Of Camden's other fellow-students at the Hall, SIR STEPHEN POWEL, or POLE, was of an Essex stock: B.A. 1569; M.A. 1572; incorporated at Cambridge 1571. SIR EDWARD LUCY was brother of Shakespeare's Squire Lucy of Charlcote. There was a bachelor at Broadgates named Lucye in 1572, no doubt the same[2].

DEGORY (DIAGORAS) WHEARE, born at Jacobstow in Cornwall, 'retired to the habitation of the Muses called *Broadgates* Hall,' aged 19, July 6, 1593; B.A. 1597; M.A. 1600; elected fellow of Exeter 1602, where he resided six years. After travelling beyond the seas in the acquirement of learning, he returned to England, where 'he was entertained by the Lord *Chandois*, and by him respected and exhibited to.' After his patron's death he took up his residence in Gloucester Hall, where he contracted an intimacy with the antiquary and 'soul

[1] His subsidy valuation was the highest of the Worcestershire justices in 1587, except that of Sir John Littleton. Freake, bishop of Wigorn, describes him to the Lord Treasurer as 'a good, wise gentleman.'

[2] Mr. Clark thinks he may be Timothy Lusie, B.A. April 26, 1567, probably overlooking Sir Edward. Timothy was 'lowzie Lucy's' youngest brother.

and sun of all the Mathematicians of his time,' Thomas Allen, the reputed magician, at whose instance Camden, in 1622, appointed Wheare first professor of the history chair founded by him, in preference to Brian Twyne. Wheare's *Method of reading histories* was still in use at Cambridge in 1700. Clerk of the Market 1617. He became Principal of Gloucester Hall (1626–47), which his abilities raised from absolute ἐρημία ἀνδρῶν to its highest point of prosperity, and of which he completed the then chapel and other buildings. Wheare died in 1647, and was buried in Exeter Chapel under the eagle, his study in books and manuscript collections passing to Francis Rous. ' He was esteemed by some a learned and gentile man, and by others a Calvinist.' He had been Pym's tutor at Broadgates, and through him Rous entered there. *Charisteria*, 1628, is dedicated to Pym.

For his son's sake I here mention Thomas Wood, born at Islington January 29, 158⅞. He entered Broadgates June 20, 1600, but migrated to Corpus Christi, where he had obtained a clerk's place ; B.A. 1604. While still an undergraduate he led to the altar one Margaret Wood, whom his son calls ' an antient and rich maid,' with part of whose portion, and £500 left him by his parents, he bought land at Tetsworth, Oxon, which he for a time cultivated. In 1608 he bought for a residence Postmasters Hall, opposite to Merton, and in 1616 purchased the lease of the Flower de Luce Inn, near Carfax. On March 10, 161⅔, he graduated in Civil Law from Broadgates, and afterwards obtained some legal practice. As he was exempted from the jurisdiction of Clarencieux king of arms, it has been thought that he held some college office. But there is no proof of this.

After the decease, in 1621, of his wife, who left him her entire fortune, Thomas Wood tried his fate in a new direction and took *secundis nuptiis* the Mary Pettie [1] whom as a child, many years before, he had dandled in his arms and promised some day to wed, now a wealthy young lady. She bore him six sons, of whom Anthony, the fourth, was born Dec. 17, 1632. He saw the light in Postmasters or Portionists Hall, and grew up native to every stone and every memory of the Oxford for whose history his affectionate industry was to do so much. In October, 1630, Thomas Wood refused to accept knighthood and paid the fine. In 1636 he took little Anthony to see the ' glorious train ' which escorted the King down St. Aldate's Street to Christ Church gate, a sight which the boy never forgot. In 1642 Oxford became a centre of military affairs, two of his lads ran off to go soldiering for the King, and Thomas Wood himself

---

[1] Several of the Petties were buried in St. Aldate's church.

had to shoulder a musket in the University train bands. His affairs suffered through the war; he had to give up Postmasters Hall for a residence for the Master of the Rolls, Lord Culpepper, and the family plate went to the royal mint at New Inn Hall, including Anthony's christening mugs. Thomas Wood died Jan. 19, 164⅜, and is buried in Merton ante-chapel. He was 'a fat and corpulent man.'

MORGAN GODWYN, a native of Anglesea, son of Bishop Francis Godwyn (whose memory, says à Wood, 'cannot but be precious in succeeding ages for his indefatigable travel in collecting the succession of all the Bishops of *England* and *Wales*'), and grandson of Dr. Thomas Godwyn, Bishop of Bath and Wells, migrated from Christ Church to Pembroke, whence he took B.C.L. July 6, 1627.

He afterwards incorporated at Dublin. He was master of Newland Free School, canon of Hereford, and was made by his father archdeacon of Salop 1631, rector of English Bicknor 1639, and of Lydney 1641. In December, 1645, the Assembly of Divines reported that 'he hath wholly deserted the same, and betaken himself to the forces against the Parliament.' He is said to have died in 1645 (i.e. before Lady Day, 1646). He is the translator of Bishop Godwyn's *Annales Rerum Anglicarum*.

FATHER BAKER, ecclesiastical historian, I have put among the divines.

CHAPTER XI.

DIVINES.

An important part of the career of Bishop John Jewell connects him with Broadgates.   When the President of Corpus Christi boasted that his foundation alone had kept its treasury and ornaments entire, he received the reply, 'You have done so indeed; but you have wilfully lost one Jewell and great treasure far more precious than any of them.'   Fuller says [1] :—

'On his refusal to be present at mass and other popish solemnities, he was driven out of the College and retired himself to Broadgates-Hall, where he continued for a time in great danger. . . . As for Mr. Jewel he continued some weeks in Broadgates-Hall, whither his scholars [2] repaired unto him, whom he constantly instructed in learning and religion. . . . He had not lived long in Broadgates Hall, when by the violence of the popish inquisitors being assaulted, on a sudden, to subscribe, he took a pen in his hand and, smiling, said, "Have you a mind to see how well I can write?" and thereupon underwrit their opinions. Thus the most orient Jewel on earth hath some flaws therein.'

The Principal of Broadgates, Randolph, was a friend of Jewell's, and he continued to lecture there, but no longer publicly.   In Lawrence Humphrey's *Joannis Juelli Angli Vita* (p. 77) he tells us:—

'Ex hoc Collegio detrusus Iuellus primum exulavit quasi in Aula Lateportĕsi, in qua privatim more suo quosdam instituit, et multos sane auditores velut Magnes attraxit : nam ut alii complures assectabantur, sic Discipuli, praeceptore fugato, amplius in Collegio manendum sibi non existimabant . . . Aequo diutius Oxoniae haerens, novis legatis haereticae pravitatis Inquisitoribus derepente superveniĕtibus, consensum in fide Romana ab omnibus subito et severe exigentibus, ac contra recu-

---

[1] *Church History*, viii. 10–15.
[2] Among others Roger Prynne and Edward Anne. The latter had been whipt in the hall of Corpus for writing doggerel against the Mass, a lash for every verse. He afterwards became a fellow of All Souls. As Jewell by papists, so Hooker was driven from Corpus by puritans.

santes dira fulmina Papaliter ejaculantibus, tandem in arctū angustumq; conclusus: Quid, inquit, subridens, An me quoq; scribere necesse est? et meam manum videre volupe est? et cordi vobis est periculum facere quam eleganter sciam pingere litteras? Ita praefatus, invita et properante manu nomen scripsit, et Chirographo suo visus est certa Papisticae doctrinae capita hoc modo comprobare. Sic, proh dolor, Petrus in aula Pōtificis aliquanto lōgius et plus satis se ad ignĕ calefaciens Christū negavit' (p. 84).

The place where the subscription took place was St. Mary's. Fuller speaks of Jewell's residence at Broadgates as extending over 'some weeks,' but after a visit to London he returned to Oxford, and there 'lingered and waited.' It was soon after Mary's accession, in July, 1553, that he migrated to Broadgates. On Jan. 24, 155$\frac{3}{4}$ ('Pridie Pauli'), Jewell dates a letter to Parkhurst, 'E Latis Portis, ubi exul aetatem[1] ago, et Randolphus mecum una, misere uterque, sed melius fortasse quam illi volebant quibus hoc molestum est quod vivimus.' In April, 1554, Jewell acted as notary to Cranmer and Ridley in their Oxford disputation. His recantation probably took place in October. After his flight from Broadgates, he reached Frankfurt, March 13, 155$\frac{4}{5}$. The account given in the Life prefixed to the 1611 edition of Jewell's *Works* is as follows:—

'After his expulsion hee staied himselfe a while at *Brodegates* Hall, where fame of his learning drew many scholars unto him.' The University however chose him 'in this shipwracke of his estate to be her Oratour. In whose name he curiously penned a gratulatory letter to *Queene Mary*,' whose promise not altogether to change the Religion 'stayed *Jewel* so long in *Oxford* till the Inquisition caught him.... Howbeit, this subscribing, as it much obscured the glorie of his persecutions, so it nothing procured his safetie; because his familiar conversing with *Peter Martyr* was euidence enough against him; and *D. Martial* Deane of Christs Church had certainly caught him in a snare laied for him, had he not by the speciall providence of God gone that verie night when hee was sought for a wrong way to London, and so escaped their hands.... I would most willingly have laid my finger upon this foule scarre, but the truth of love must not prejudice love of truth.... *Jewel* almost assoone as he came to *Frankford* made an excellent sermon, and in the end of it openly confessed his fall in these words: It was my abject and cowardly minde and faint heart that made my weake hand to commit this wickednesse. Which when he had brought forth with a gale of sighs from the bottome of the anguish of his soule, and had made humble supplication for pardon, first to Almighty God, whom he had offended, and afterwards to the Church, which he had scandalized; no man was found in that great Congregation who was not prickt with compunction and wounded

---

[1] 'Aestatem' in the Parker Society's edition of Jewell's Works.

with compassion; or who embraced him not even after that sermon as a most deare brother, nay, as an Angell of God.'

Among others who fled overseas in Mary's first year was RICHARD TREMAYNE, a Devonian (B.A. from Broadgates 1548). He was a noted preacher and had just been chosen fellow of Exeter. On Elizabeth's accession he became archdeacon of Chichester, and sate in the Convocation that established the Articles, being then canon and treasurer of Exeter cathedral. In 1565 he is described as of Broadgates Hall. He married Joan, daughter of Sir Peter Courtenay, and died in November, 1584.

The last Bishop on whom Parker laid hands (April 17, 1575) was WILLIAM BLETHYN, whom he had recommended to the Queen, as a Welshman and well qualified, for the long vacant see of Llandaff[1]. The archbishop dispensed him to hold the archdeaconry of Brecknock and other preferments, not exceeding £108 in worth, with his meagre bishoprick. Dying October, 1590, he was buried in the chancel of Matherne church, Monmouthshire, where the prelates of Llandaff had a seat. Blethyn had studied civil law 'in New Inn or Broadgates Hall, or in both.' B.C.L. Nov. 14, 1562. He was presented to the vicarage of Brampford Speke, Devon, in 1564, and to the parsonage of Twing, Yorkshire, in 1565.

Another Welshman, BISHOP JOHN PHILLIPS (1555–1633), who gave the Manxmen the Bible and Prayer-book in their own tongue, was first at St. Mary Hall, whence he took B.A. 1579; M.A. 1584; but this last degree he completed from Broadgates at an Act celebrated July 10, 1584.

After being preferred to several cures in Yorkshire, he became archdeacon of Man 1587 and of Cleveland 1601, and chaplain to Henry, Earl of Derby, King of Man. He succeeded Lloyd as bishop there 1605[2], retaining most of his preferments *in commendam*, the income of the see being not more than £140. The same year saw him rector of Hawarden. Phillips lived among his flock and was an exemplary Father in God. He obliged the clergy to preach, made parish registers obligatory, reduced to writing the orally transmitted canons of the island, and by 1610 had finished the *Mannish Book of Common Prayer*. It was not popular with the clergy, who were accustomed to extemporize. The governor too, John Ireland, was a puritan, and thwarted the bishop's endeavours to revive decency of worship. One of the latter's first acts was to commit to prison one who had disobeyed his warning that 'no man should irreverently lean or rest on the Communion Table.' He now complained that Ireland had 'placed a layman in the chaplain's place to read service to the garrison in scandalous manner, vizt. in his doblett and hose, and

---

[1] Strype, *Life of Matthew, Archbishop of Canterbury*, ii. 421 ; *Ath. Ox.*
[2] Wood however says 'about 1614,' and is uncertain who was Lloyd's successor.

sometime in his livery coat.' Also that 'the Bishop being the cheef competent spirituall judge . . . Mr. Lievtennante will take all appeales to himself and sendeth forth his prohibition.' He 'threateneth to fine any that will call me Lord Bishop.' The governor had also taken on him to issue dispensations to eat flesh in Lent. Phillips had to give up the project of printing his translation, and it remained while he lived in MS. Governor Chaloner (1658) averred that the bishop devoted twenty-nine years' labour to a rendering of the Holy Scriptures into Manx; he himself gave to 'Sir' Hugh Cannell, vicar of Kirk Michael, £14 addition to his stipend for that he had been 'assistant to the late reverend father in God John Phillipps, Bishopp of this isle, in translatinge of the Bible.' So à Wood states that 'the said *Joh. Philipps* translated the Bible into the *Manks* tongue.' But it is lost, and even Bishop Wilson knew nothing of it. The Manx Prayer Book has lately been reprinted. Prof. Rhŷs testifies to the rapid extinction of this interesting tongue under the present educational system. Bishop Phillips died Aug. 7, 1633, and was buried in St. German's Cathedral. The site is unknown.

The following are mentioned by Wood among ' Oxford Writers ':—

Dr. JOHN MILWARDE [1], matric. Nov. 23, 1581, at Christ Church; M.A. from Broadgates, June 22, 1584. He was chaplain to James I, and author of *Jacob's Great Day of Trouble and Deliverance*, preached at St. Paul's Cross, 1607, 'upon his Maj. deliverance from Gowries treasons.'—JOHN HUDSON, M.A. 1575, canon of Chichester, with other preferments : author of a *Sermon at Paul's Cross*, 1584.—WILLIAM CLARKSON, 'Student in Physick,' M.D. 1590, Fellow of the College of Physicians 1592.—SIMON PRESSE, matric. April 28, 1580, B.A. March 18, 1582, vicar of Down Ampney, rector of Egginton, author of a *Sermon concerning the Right Use of Things Indifferent.*—HANNIBAL GAMON, matric. Oct. 12, 1599, M.A. 1606, minister of St. Mawgan, Cornwall, 1619, and one of the Assembly of Divines 1643.—THOMAS PRIOR, matric. Jan. 20, 160⅔, M.A. 1611, canon of Gloucester. Died 1632.—JAMES MARTIN, M.A. 1611, a German ; wrote against Baronius. — JOHN FLAVELL, matric. Oct. 11, 1583, aet. fourteen, M.A. 1591, B. and D.D. 1616, rector of Tallaton, Devon, and a dignitary.—HENRY WELSTEDE, matric. Nov. 14, 1606, M.A. 1613, who held several cures. He wrote the *Cure of a Hard Heart.*—BENJAMIN COX, anabaptist and covenanter, B.A. 1613.—RICHARD GARDINER, matric. Oct. 28, 1604, M.A. 1611, rector of Croft 1618, licensed to practise medicine 1621.—JOHN GUMBLEDON, matric. June 18, 1618, as bateller, M.A. 1624, B.D. 1632, parliamentarian, chaplain to Robert Earl of Leycester, and preacher at Longworth, Berks, rector of Coyty and other cures in Glamorganshire.— SAMUEL EATON, who matric. April 16, 1602, aged seventeen, may be the same, à Wood thinks, as a Puritan of that name, who, being suspended in 1631, emigrated to Holland and thence to New England ; but,

[1] A John Milward entered Pembroke in 1671 ; perhaps buried in Westminster Abbey.

returning, took the Covenant and 'became a most pestilent leading Person in the trade of Faction in Cheshire and Lancashire.' Having 'feathered his Neast' in one or two cures, he was ejected at the Restoration, 'yet he carried on the trade of Conventicling in private, and was thereupon brought several times into trouble and imprison'd.' He died at Manchester in 1664, aged, Calamy says, sixty-eight. We are probably dealing therefore with two kinsmen, both sons of a Cheshire clergyman. (See Foster's *Alumni*.)

Of the seminary clergy who risked their necks in Elizabeth's reign, one was SABIN CHAMBERS, a Leicestershire man (matr. June 13, 1580, M.A. 1583), who when at Oxford 'had the vogue of a good disputant.'

Being dissatisfied with the Reformed teaching he entered the Society of Jesus, in Paris, in 1588, aged about thirty. Afterwards he had a chair of Divinity in the University of Doll, 'and at length was sent into the Mission of *England*, to labour in the Harvest there.' The only work of his known to à Wood was *The Garden of the Virgin Mary*, St. Omer, 1619. He died in March 163⅘.

A more remarkable man was 'the most holy and seraphical father,' DAVID (in religion AUGUSTINE) BAKER, nephew to Dr. David Lewes, Admiralty judge. Born Dec. 9, 1575 [1], he passed from Christ's Hospital to Broadgates Hall, of which he became a commoner March 28, 1590.

Leaving without a degree, he pursued his legal studies at the Inner (not Middle) Temple (1597), and was thought qualified to be made Recorder of Abergavenny. At Oxford and in London he had followed loose courses and professed atheism. 'Led away by sin, he gave up all practices of religion. "Yet there remained in him a natural modesty whereby he was restrained from a scandalous impudence in sin." ' A marvellous escape from drowning, while at Abergavenny, turned the course of his life, and filled him with horror of the past. Some Romanist books of devotion which greatly moved him led Baker to join the renewed congregation of Benedictines in London, and in 1605 he went to Italy to take the habit. Returning home he found his father, William Baker, steward to Lord Abergavenny, on his deathbed, and received him into the communion of Rome. His transparent devotion of life and great powers of intellect gave him much influence among English Romanists, passing as he did from one house to another, usually in the disguise of a lawyer. Some time after King Charles' accession Baker became spiritual director of the English Benedictine nuns at Cambray, employing his time in making collections for an ecclesiastical history of England, in which work

---

[1] Wood MS. B. 4, however, is 'An account of the life of the venerable father Augustin Baker, monk of the English congregation of S. Benedict, who died in England upon the 9th of Aug. anno Domini 1641, aetatis suae 63: his happy soul rest in peace. Amen.' He was sixty-six.

he had been assisted by Camden, Cotton, Spelman, Selden and Bishop Godwyn. He published a learned history of the order of St. Benedict, on which Serenus de Cressy based his Church History and Reyner his *Apostolatus Benedictinorum in Anglia*, and a large number of ascetical and contemplative treatises, from which the *Sancta Sophia* of de Cressy was extracted[1]. He is described as a master of the spiritual life. 'He was esteemed the most devout austere and religious person of his order. He was also an excellent common lawyer.' His works are preserved at Cambray. Baker, unlike Napier—hanged and quartered in the Castle yard in 1610—and other Oxford seminarists, died an ordinary death of the plague, Aug. 9, 1641, in Gray's Inn Lane, and is buried in St. Andrew's, Holborn.

An exile under Elizabeth was THOMAS CLARKE, a Warwickshire man, who entered Broadgates Oct. 11, 1583, aged seventeen ; B.A. Feb. 23, 158$\frac{4}{5}$. He became a seminary priest of the college at Rheims, but afterwards recanted his opinions in a sermon at Paul's Cross, July 1, 1593. He was presented to the rectory of Kinwarton in his own county in 1606.

CHRISTOPHER PHIPPE, who was an M.A. of the Hall at his death in 1621 (aged twenty-nine), changed his religious allegiance and became Divinity reader among the English seculars at Doway. Buried in St. Aldate's.

EDWARD GRANT, 'the most noted Latinist and Grecian of his time,' resided for several years at Broadgates or Christ Church ; B.A. 1572, M.A. (from Exeter) 1572.

He was appointed Master of his old school of Westminster, Camden being his usher; canon of Westminster 1577, B.D. 1579. 'A most noted Latin poet' and 'well skilled in all kinds of humane literature.' He edited Roger Ascham and wrote his life, also a Greek Grammar. Grant died in 1601, and is buried in the Abbey Church. He was at various times prebendary of Ely, vicar of South Benfleet, rector of Barnet, rector of Toppersham, and elsewhere.

EDWARD PHILIPPS entered in 1574, took the degrees in Arts (M.A. 1583) and became a preacher at Southwark, where he was much esteemed

---

[1] '*Sancta Sophia*, or Directions for the Prayer of Contemplation, &c., Extracted out of more than XL Treatises written by the late Ven. Father F. Augustine Baker, A Monke of the English Congregation of the Holy Order of St. Benedict : And Methodically digested by the Reverend Father Serenus Cressy of the same Order and Congregation, and printed at the Charges of his Convent of S. Gregorie, in Doway' : 2 vols. Doway, 1657, 8vo.—with a fine engraving of Baker in his religious habit prefixed. A new edition was published at London in 1876. The *Life and Spirit of Father Baker* by James Norbert Sweeney, D.D., was printed at London in 1861. Nine folio volumes of ascetical treatises perished in the pillage of the convent at Cambray, and two books on the Laws of England were destroyed in the English Revolution of 1688. Four of the six volumes of historical collections, long thought to be lost, have been found in the Jesus College library.

as a painful expounder of God's Word by a large auditory of Puritan tastes. Judge Henry Yelverton, after Philipps' death, published 'Two and thirty godly and learned Sermons' 1605, which he had taken with his own pen from the preacher's mouth. Philipps lies in St. Mary Overie Church.

Wood gives an account of WALTER WYLSHMAN, 'a Cornish man born, educated in *Exeter* coll. took the degrees in Arts, stood as a member of Broadgates hall in an Act celebrated 1594, to compleat it, being about that time [1606, Foster] Minister of *Dartmouth*, and much resorted to for his frequent and practical way of Preaching.' The only work of his mentioned is *The Sincere Preacher*. He died 1636, and lies in St. Saviour's, Dartmouth. During his incumbency the beautiful painted stone pulpit was put up.

ISAAC COLFE, fourth son of Amandus, 'of Calais,' one of the Canterbury Huguenots, entered July 23, 1579, aged twenty; B.A. Feb. 17, 15$\frac{78}{80}$, M.A. July 4, 1582. He was vicar of Stone and of Brookland, Kent; master of Kingsbridge Hospital in Canterbury 1596, canon 1596; died July 15, 1597, and is buried in the chapter-house. He printed several treatises of divinity. His eldest brother, Richard, student of Christ Church and vicar of Cumnor, &c., was canon and sub-dean of Canterbury. Richard's three sons, Abraham, Isaac, and Jacob, 'ministers of the Word of God,' gave twenty-three MSS. to the Bodleian in memory of him.

In 1579, with a view to expelling the remains of popery, catechetical lectures were instituted in Oxford by the dominant party. Readers however being scarce, especially in the Halls, certain foreign exiles were appointed. To Broadgates was assigned the Pastor Dominus DE LA BENSERIS [1] from Caen University, whither however he was recalled the next year. At that date several Switzers were studying at the Hall.

WOLPHGANG MUSCAL, from Berne, who entered July 20, 1578, aged twenty-two, was grandson of Wolphgang Musculus, the Swiss Reformer, who became Divinity Professor at Berne in 1549, and died 1563. Lawrence Humphrey, Jewell's biographer, befriended the young man at Oxford, and wrote several letters about him to his father, Abraham Musculus. He says, under date March 3, 157$\frac{8}{9}$: [2]—

'Immanuel. Your son has left us and has staid some months in London. . . . He was very dear to me, both for the sake of your honoured and venerable father, and for yours, and also for his own. . . . It somewhat distresses me that your son has left us so soon, and that I was not able to be of so much service to him as I wished. He had however a great desire to see the University of Cambridge and other parts of

---

[1] Gutch, ii. 198.   [2] See *Zurich Letters* (Parker Society).

England, with a view to returning with more learning, though not with more money.'

Wolphgang's compatriots at Broadgates, entered the same day, were JOHANN RODOLPH AB ULMIS (Ulmerus, Ulmius) and JOHANN HULDRIK À VACHNAN ('Tigurini'), concerning whom Humphrey wrote to Rudolph Gualter, who was anxious about his young friends. They were amiable and studious. Humphrey was embarrassed, however, about their means of support. Those members of the University from whom help might have been looked for were themselves in want and dependent upon others. The Bishop of Winton had given something to Rudolph :—

'He has lately returned to us from Devonshire where the Earl [of Bedford] is now residing, not indeed overburdened with money, but yet in some measure provided with it and presented with a salary. I have placed both the young men in Broadgate Hall, as we call it, not far from Christchurch, where John's father was most liberally and kindly entertained in King Edward's time.'

The writer begs Gualter to aid them by his patronage, and secure the speedy payment of their promised stipend. Francis, Earl of Bedford, wrote to Humphrey, Feb. 28, 1579, of his interest in Ulmer, from whose honourable principles and devotion to learning he hoped much for the benefit of God's Church. Cole, President of C. C. C., also interested himself in 'Ulmer's son.' John ab Ulmis, the Reformer, had come to Oxford under the patronage of Suffolk and of Dorset, March 2, 1549, and, after studying at 'the King's College,' been made Fellow of St. John's. His brother John Conrad, if not himself, was a member of 'Broad Yates' in 1551 and 1552. Conrad had been commended by Gualter to Martyr's care. Writing to Wolfius an account of a day's work, he says,—

'At four we read privately, in a certain hall in which we live, the rules of Law, which I hear and learn by rote, as I do the Institutes. After supper the time is spent in various discourse ; for either sitting in our chamber, or walking up and down some part of the college, we exercise ourselves in dialectical questions.'

The following is a pleasing picture of a saintly young scholar. NATHANIEL POWNOLL, a Kentish man, was entered a bateller of Broadgates Hall in 1599 (Oct. 19), aged fifteen, becoming two years later a student of Christ Church.

'Running with wonderful diligence through all the forms of Philosophy, he took the degree of M. of Arts, *an.* 1607 [June 18] . . . He lived constantly in the University 10 years, in which time he learned eight Languages, watched often, daily exercised, always studied, insomuch that he made an end of himself in an over fervent desire to benefit others. And tho he had, out of himself, sweat all his Oyl for his Lamp, and had laid the Sun a-bed by his labours, yet he never durst adventure to do that, after all these studies done and ended, which our young Novices, doing nothing, count nothing to do; but still thought himself as unfit, as he knew all men were unworthy of so high an Honour, as to be the Angels of God. And since in him so great examples of piety, knowledge, industry and unaffected modesty are long since fallen asleep, there is no other way left but to commend the titles of his Monuments to posterity, which are these :—

'The young Divines Apology for his continuance in the University—Meditations on the Sacred Calling of the Ministry—Comment or Meditation on the first seven Penitential Psalms of David—His daily Sacrifice. . . . He died in the prime of his years, to the great grief of those who knew well his piety and admirable parts, about the year sixteen hundred and ten, but where buried, unless in the Cath. of *Ch. Ch.*, I know not[1].' Hearne[2] gives the Epitaph of the ingenious, pious and learned Mr. Nath. Pownoll, 'from his Book in the Bodl. Library, 8° A. 28. Th. BS. being written before it by one of his near Relations.'

Epitaphium.

Flos iuvenum, decus Oxonij, spes summa parentum,
Te tegit ante diem (matre parante) lapis.
Hoc satis est cineri. Reliqua immortalia Caelo
Condit amorque hominum, condit amorque Dei.

Dr. Thomas Lushington, Sir Thomas Browne's tutor at Broadgates, 'a famous scholar of his time,' and the occasion of some theological controversy, the son of Ingram and Agnes Lushington, of Sandwich, entered March 13, 160⅘, aged seventeen, and remained, off and on, studying divinity, till after the conversion of the Hall into a College, when he followed Bishop Corbet to Norfolk as chaplain, and obtained through him, besides various preferments, Corbet's vacated prebendal stall at Sarum (1631), and the place of chaplain to Prince Charles.

'When the grand rebellion broke out he lost his spiritualities and lived obscurely in several places, publishing there divers books to gain money for his maintenance. At length upon the return of K. *Ch.* 2, in 1660, he was restored to his spiritualities and had offers made him of great dignities in the Church, but being then aged and infirm he chose rather to keep what he had with quietness than to be a Dean with riches. He was esteemed a right reverend and learned Theologist, yet in many matters imprudent and too much inclined to the opinions of *Socinus*[3].' A sermon at St. Mary's in 1624 on St. Matt. xxviii. 13, in which he was thought to reflect on the impending war with Spain on account of the breaking off of the Spanish match, was called in question before Dr. Pearce the Vice-Chancellor, and he had to preach a recantation sermon the next Sunday on

---

[1] *Ath. Ox.* i. 312.   [2] *Collections,* ed. Doble, O. H. S. iii. 81.
[3] *Athenae,* ii. 171.

Acts ii. 1. Otherwise he would have been brought before Parliament. Other passages in the offending discourse were considered to deal lightly with the sacred mystery of the Resurrection. 'The truth is this our Preacher was a Person more ingenious than prudent, and more apt on most occasions to display his fancy than to proceed upon solemn reason. If not, he would not in his said Sermon have discanted on the whole life of our Saviour purposely to render him and his Attendants, Men and Women, objects of scorn and aversion as if they had been a pack of dissolute vagabonds and cheats. But the best of it was that tho he then assumed the Person of a Jewish Pharisee and Persecutor of Christ, yet presently after, changing his stile, as became a Disciple of Christ, he with such admirable dexterity (as 'tis said) answered all the Cavillations and Invectives before made, that the loudly repeated applause of his Hearers hindred him a good space from proceeding in his Sermon[1].' A commentary on the *Hebrews* by a continental Socinian was translated by Lushington in 1646, under the initials ' G. M.,' and denounced in 1655 by Richard Porter, B.D. of Cambridge, prebendary of Norwich, who describes it in his *God Incarnate* as 'written by a nameless D. of D. who now resides in this County but formerly in *Broadgates* Hall (for so it was then called) wherein he hath vented such blasphemies against *Jesus Christ* as (without special revocation and repentance) will in the end bring both him and all his seduced Sectaries, to that woful *Broad gate* of which mention is made Matth. 7. 13. *Lata est porta quae ducit ad perditionem.* . . . It is to be feared that the pernicious Doctrines therein contained have many Abetters and Favourers in these dangerous times ; albeit his Commentary is the first of all the Serpents nest that dared to peep out and appear in our English Print.' Lushington was one of the earlier Latitudinarians inside the Church of England, a movement which accompanied and followed the Catholic reaction. His influence on Browne was probably considerable. He also translated Crellius' *Galatians,* and wrote a Latin treatise, not published, on the theology of Proclus, as well as a Logic and other philosophical works. He died at Sittingbourne in great retiredness at Christmas, 1661, and was buried in the south chancel aisle. His monument (destroyed by fire in 1762), of alabaster and marble, showed him half-length in his doctor's gown and holding a book. Beneath was an inscription beginning 'Siste viator, raro calcabis doctos simul et mansuetos cineres,' and under it piles of books. On the stone covering his actual grave he was said to have been a member both of Lincoln and of Pembroke Colleges[2]. Aubrey (*Letters,* ii. 293) calls him 'a very learned and ingeniose man.'

In John Rous's diary (Oct. 6, 1629) he records :—

' I was at Mondeford courte, where asking Mr. Tayler what newes, he

---

[1] *Athenae,* i. 172 ; Gutch, ii. 353.
[2] *Ath. Ox.* i. 173. See Gutch, ii. p. 335. In Halsted's *Kent* it is said : ' The S.E. chancel belonged to the Chilton Estate ; there are many gravestones of the family of Lushington in it.' The Rev. W. Bell, vicar of Sittingbourne tells me that he can find none, but that there are several at Rodmersham.

tould me that Mr. Barret had there showen a sermon unprinted, lately preached at Whitehall before the King, upon Mat. 28. 13, saying, "Say ye his disciples came by night and stole him away" by Dr. Lushington, Oxfordiens. I asked the drifte of it; he tould me "witte." I asked what was remarkeable; he said, first the beginning, "What newes." Every man askes what newes; the Puritan talkes of Bethlehem Gabor[1], etc. Besides this, the doctor fell belike to personate the chiefe priests and elders, in a florishing description of our Saviour and his apostles, as imposters, etc. (a wicked witte), and then comes to demande why the soldiers should say it, etc. "Because," saith he (yet he mistooke his marke, see verse 14) "the soldiers were audacious and durst doe anything. In those times (said he) the soldiers did depose and chuse Emperors, yet the time had beene when the priests did this. But now peasants will doe all, by prerogative of parliament," etc.'

In 1634, 'Dr. L. at Norwich, after his sermon to the trayners, gave out these verses :

> " Skill, Number, Courage cannot prosper us
> Without our posie, Nisi Dominus.
> The strongest cities have been ominous
> To theire own keepers, Nisi Dominus.
> And every stone to the towne and us
> May prove a bullet, Nisi Dominus.
> The gunne or sticke may make a piteous
> And bloody muster, Nisi Dominus.
> Since power and skill in armes be governed thus,
> We dare say nothing, Nisi Dominus."'

Walker (*Sufferings of the Clergy*) says of Lushington : ' He was indeed a learned man, but I wish I could honestly omit him, for his translating the *Socinian* Comment on the *Hebrews* plainly shows that he was infected with that *Heresie*; and his *Sermon* on the *Resurrection* (lately Reprinted in a Collection of other Prophane Pieces, under the title of the *Phœnix*) shews him, I doubt, to be something worse.'

With Lushington Sir Nicholas Bacon of Gillingham, Sir Charles Le Gros of Crostwich, and Sir Justinian Lewyn had a share in persuading Browne to go to Norwich. Wilkins thinks that all these were contemporaries at Broadgates. Certainly Lewyn was there. He was made Doctor of Law in 1637, and became Judge-martial of the army under Thomas, Earl of Arundel, in the Scottish expedition of 1639, and afterwards a Master in Chancery and a knight. He was a nephew to Sir Justinian Lewyn, Dean of the Arches, who died 1598. Sir Charles Le Gros (son of Sir Thomas; knighted in 1603) was father of the Thomas Le Gros to whom Browne dedicated his ' Urn Burial.'

[1] Waivode of Transylvania.

CHAPTER XII.

HIGH POLITICS.

PETER SMART, a man of considerable attainments, regarded by the Puritans as 'the Protomartyr of these latter days of Persecution,' ' a Minister's son of Warwickshire, was educated in the College School at Westminster, became a batler of *Broadgates* Hall, 1588, aged nineteen years, and in the same year was elected *Student of Christ Church*, where he was esteemed about that time a tolerable Latin Poet.'

'Afterwards taking the degrees in Arts, he entered into orders, became Chaplain to Dr. *W. James*, Bishop of *Durham*, who not only confer'd upon him a Prebendship in that Church [1609–1629], but also the Parsonage of *Bouden*[1], and was the chief instrument of promoting him to be one of his Majesties High Commissioners in the Province of *York*. But this person being puritannically given, took occasion in 1628 to preach against certain matters, which he took to be popish Innovations[2], brought into the Church of *Durham* by Mr. *John Cosin* and his Confederates, as Copes, Tapers, Crucifixes, bowing to the Altar, praying towards the East, turning the Communion Table of Wood, standing in the middle of the Choire, into an Altar-stone railed in at the East end thereof, etc. But this his Sermon[3] or Sermons, preached several times to the people, being esteemed seditious, he was questioned . . . in the *High Commission Court* at *York*[4], where for his said seditious Sermon or Sermons and his refusal

[1] Boldon. He was non-resident. Smart was also Master of Durham grammar school.

[2] Everything before Bishop Neile had been ruinous and filthy. The 'copes embroidered with idols, used a long time at Mass and May-games,' had been suffered to be taken from the Cathedral and used by boys in their sports.

[3] 'The Vanitie and downefall of Superstitious Popish Ceremonies; or, a Sermon preached in the Cathedrall Church of Durham by one Peter Smart, a Præbend there, July 27, 1628. Contayning not onely an historicall relation of all those popish ceremonies and practises which Mr. Iohn Cosens hath lately brought into the said Cathedrall Church, but likewise a punctuall confutation of them; especially of erecting altars and cringing to them (a practise much in use of late) and of praying towards the East—Psal. 4. 2, Phil. 3. 18, 19.—Printed at Edenborough in Scotland 1628 By the Heyres of Robert Charteris.'

[4] See 'The Acts of the High Commission at Durham' (Surtees), App. 198. The trial was adjourned to York. While it was dragging on Smart indicted

to be conformable to the Ceremonies of the Church, he was deprived of his Prebendship and Parsonage, degraded from his Ministry, fined 500*l.*

Cosin at the Durham Assizes. Sir James Whitelocke quashed the indictment, but it was renewed the next year (1629) before Sir Henry Yelverton, who, in a colloquy with the prebendaries the day before the Assizes were opened, assured them that he considered Smart's discourse to be 'a very good and *an honest* sermon.' One of them said, 'that in that sermon *singeing of service* was condemned for a superstitious ceremonie and an idle vanitie; but he hoped his lordship did not think soe.' The judge answered, 'that he thought so too, and that truely for his parte he never liked of our singeing of the service; and he gave this reason for his dislike, because he could never understand a word of it when the organs plaied, and this he repeated often.' One of the company told him 'that they were bound by the statutes of that Church to perform ther service in the Choir in this manner, *cum cantu scilicet et jubilatione.*' '*Cum jubilatione,*' said Judge Yelverton, 'that is, with whistling. And for my part, said he, I never liked of your whistling of service. One of the prebendaries hereupon desired him, saying, Good my lord, doe not call it whistling, for it is a word of disgrace. The judge replied upon him short again, and said, Sir, I know what I say. I call it whistling.... He said, moreover, that he had been alwaise accounted a Puritane, and he thanked God for it; and that soe he would die. One of the company told him, that he imagined one of Mr. Smart's indictments would be for standing up at the Nicene Creed, which notwithstanding the Bishop, as *ordinarius loci,* had appointed to be done. To this he said, That the Bishop could not do it, and that they must stand only at the Apostles Creede.' However the judge's legal instincts afterwards came to the top, and he told Smart the indictment could not be grounded on any direct law, and forbade the Clerk of the Crown to file it. When Cosin was impeached in 1611 he related that after the rising of the Court Judge Yelverton had called Mr. Smart, and caused him to take defendant by the hand and promise peace and unity with him. In a subsequent interview with the prebendaries he went so far as to insist that Smart's 'courses against Mr. Cosen & the Church were truly unchristian. That through Mr. Cosin's sides he strooke deepe into all the Cathedrall Churches in England. That he found Mr. Cosin of a better temper and disposition than Mr. Smart by farr. That he *wondered at his refusal* to stand at the Nicene Creed, *the Bishop having counselled it,* whose counsells were commandes to him.' Terms of peace might have been arranged, but the prosecution of Smart had now been removed from Durham to York and Lambeth. In this year Smart issued his *Treatise on Altars,* which formed the groundwork of the future accusations against Cosin. Of course the principal matter was the fixing the Holy Table altar-wise against the east wall, the result being that 'the minister *cannot* stand at the north side, there being neither side toward the north.' The usual Laudian reply to this very pertinent objection was the questionable one that north side meant or might mean north end; since when, as the duellists in Hamlet their rapiers, the disputants have exchanged arguments. Smart's other points were such as the 'glorious Copes embroidered with images,' a 'precious golden pall to cover the altar, having upon it the false story of the Assumption of our Lady,' the gilded and painted altar of stone with its crucifix and tapers and other *ornamenta,* the making 'profound legs' and curtsies towards the altar, and going from it backwards, the organs, and horrible profanation of the Lord's Supper and also of the Sacrament of Baptism with 'an *hideous noise* of musick.' In Mr. Parker's *Introduction to the Revisions of the Book of Common Prayer* the charges of Peter Smart occupy considerable space. They influenced the subse-

and imprisoned many years. At length when the *Long* Parliament began, he, upon petition and complaint, was freed from his Prison in the *Kings-bench* (where he had continued above eleven years), was restored to all he had lost, had reparations made for his losses and became a witness against Archbishop Laud.' Smart on his release in 1640 was the principal promoter of the impeachment of Maynwaring and Cosin. He died in 1642, the severity of his long imprisonment having impaired his constitution. His poems in Latin and English were called, à Wood says, in auction catalogues *Old Smart's Verses.* Neal says he was a person of grave and reverend aspect.

A notable Parliamentarian who, Wood thinks, had his name on the books of Broadgates—'a receptacle mostly in the Reign of K. *Jam. I.* for *Dorsetshire* men'—was CLEMENT WALKER, author of the *History of Independency*, written (says Warburton) 'in a rambling way, and with a vindictive presbyterian spirit, full of bitterness; but it gives an admirable idea of the character of the times, parties, and persons.'

Leaving Oxford without a degree, he played the part of royalist country-gentleman in Somerset, his declamations against the Puritans expressing, à Wood considers, his real mind. 'Before the Civil War commenc'd, he was made Usher of the *Exchequer*, but when the Presbyterians were like to carry all before, he closed with them, was elected one of the Burgesses for the City of *Wells*, and became a zealous Covenantier, and was Advocate to that Congregation of Murderers that adjudged *Rob. Yeomans* and *George Bowcher* Citizens of *Bristow* to death, *having had* (as 'tis said) *his hands stayned with his own Wives blood before he dipped them so deep in those Martyrs.*' He and Prynne were 'inseparable Brethren.' Walker took a prominent part against the Independents. He attacked Fairfax 'for his folly to be led by the nose by *O. Cromwell*,' and Cromwell for his 'devilish hypocrisy.' Cromwell put him in the Tower, where he died in 1651, being buried in Allhallows, Barking.

'The greatest Member of Parliament that ever lived,' JOHN PYM, entered as a gentleman-commoner, May 18, 1599, aged fifteen[1]. At Broadgates he displayed an unpuritanic joy in the Muses, his fellow-student FitzGeffrey styling him, in 1601, ' Phoebi deliciae, lepos puelli.' Wheare was his tutor. Leaving, as it seems, without a degree, he was entered of the Middle Temple in 1602.

A clerkship in the Exchequer was obtained for Pym, and the foundation of his great acquaintance with finance was thus laid. In 162¼ he was chosen for Calne, and in the next few years was second only to Eliot as

quent ritual controversy and the final revision of the Prayer Book in 1661; e. g. the present rubric prescribes that the Nicene Creed shall be said *or sung*, and that standing.

[1] He was the orphaned heir of Alexander Pim. When he was six years old his mother married Sir Anthony Rous, father of Speaker Rous, the Pembroke benefactor. FitzGeffrey describes her as 'no Lyonnesse in her House,' ' making her

a leader of opposition. Pym's persistency in urging the strict execution of the penal laws against papists cemented his popularity, and in 1626 the impeachment of Buckingham was confided mainly to his hands, in 1628 that of Maynwaring. The scabbard was now thrown away on both sides, and Pym had twice seen the inside of a prison. There is a tale that he, Cromwell, and Hampden were prevented in 1638 from embarking for America. He was certainly a patentee of Connecticut and Providence. When however he had brought about Strafford's condemnation, the Queen contrived that Pym should be offered the Chancellorship of the Exchequer, the Earl of Bedford engaging that Strafford's head should not fall. But Bedford died, and, Pym being supposed now to meditate the daring step of impeaching the Queen herself, Charles resolved to openly arrest him with four others, in the face of Parliament. The charge was treasonable correspondence with the Scots rebels. The miscarriage of this design raised the west country gentleman to the height of influence out of doors, as his abilities had already made him master of the House of Commons. He had been one of the 'twal kings' for whom James I ordered 'twal chairs' to be set, and the royalists lampooned him as 'King Pym.' He has been called 'the English counterpart of Mirabeau,' without the profligacy. The Grand Remonstrance was drawn up by him, and carried by his eloquence. He was not only the orator of his party, but its soul and centre. Though by temperament a legalist, Pym now discarded all legality—'a master of revolution,' Mr. Goldwin Smith calls him. He refused to discountenance the rabbling of the Bishops in the precincts of St. Stephen's[1], urged Parliament to seize the forces of the Crown and the machinery of government, secured the presbyterians by placing the re-modelling of the Church in the hands of the Assembly of Divines—himself (though an Episcopalian) taking the Covenant—and swept on the nation and parliament into irretrievable war. Being excepted, with a few others, from the King's proclamation of pardon, Pym committed his followers beyond recall by the impeachment of Henrietta Maria. 'No man,' says the royalist historian, 'had more to answer for the Miseries of the Kingdom, or had his Hand or Head deeper in their contrivances.' He was 'the most popular Man, and the most able to do hurt, that hath lived at any time.' 'His parts,' Clarendon continues, 'were rather acquired by industry than supply'd by Nature or adorned by Art. . . . He had a very comely and grave way of expressing himself, with great volubility of words, natural and proper; and understood the Temper and Affections of the Kingdom as well as any Man; and had observ'd the errors and mistakes in Government, and knew well how to make them appear greater than they were.' To organize the revolting forces

Closet as an Apothecaries shop for the poore Neighbours in time of their sicknes.' Brymore House, near Bridgewater, the ancient seat of the Pyms, belongs now to the Earls of Radnor, descended from John Pym's sister Mary, wife of Sir Thos. Hales of Bekesbourne. Neal, I know not why, styles Pym 'a Cornish gentleman.'

[1] 'God forbid the House of Commons should proceed in any way to dishearten the people to obtain their just desires in such a way.'

and keep the war supplied with money was Pym's achievement. When the King was winning, Pym was the rallying point of puritanism. He was himself at the head of the ordnance. But he died early in the struggle, Dec. 8, 1644, his death, 'the discourse of all tongues,' being ascribed by his enemies to the loathsome *morbus pediculosus*, or ' Herodian visitation.' He was ' buried with wonderful Pomp and Magnificence in that place where the Bones of our English Kings and Princes are committed to their rest.' The spot was ' the void space or passage as you go to the chapel of K. *Henry* 7,' by the entrance of St. John Baptist's chapel. In 1660 his remains were removed, and thrown into a pit on the north side of the Abbey church. He was a man of portly form, which a maid of honour said was that of an ox, and a forehead so high that scribblers compared it to a shuttle.

Pym's contribution to the enlargement of the buildings in 1620 shows that he kept up some connexion with Broadgates. A little junior to him there were FRANCIS, ARTHUR, WILLIAM, and JOHN STRODE, the cousins of Pym's fellow ' parliament-driver,' who lay next him in the Abbey, and JOHN STRODE, Sir William's younger brother. The last is said by Prince to have been ' a great favourite of the nobility and gentry, who spent much of his time about London, and was counted the best bowler [1] in all England.' ' The grandfather of all these was Sir William Strode, of Newnham, Devon, their grand-mother Elizabeth Courtenay of Powderham Castle. Arthur Strode's brass in St. Aldate's church still remains. Others of the family were at Broadgates. A number of the Devonshire Heles also entered *temp.* Elizabeth and James. One, SAMPSON HELE, sate for Plympton 1614, and for Tavistock (where Pym succeeded him) 1624. In May, 1613, one JOHN MILTON (but in the *supplicat* Thomas), of Broadgates, described as 'generosus nuper ab exteris nationibus reversus,' was studying in the Bodleian. His name follows that of Isaac Casaubon. Prof. Masson tells me, however, that he cannot connect with certainty this Milton with the poet's family, who were yeomen, not leisured gentlemen.

Mention should here be made of a famous controversy of which Broadgates Hall was originally the centre. At the close of James I's shambling reign everything seemed prepared for an Armageddon between the principles of Authority and Liberty, and the fray of contending theories naturally began at Oxford :—

> Chronica si penses, Cum pugnant Oxonienses,
> Post paucos menses Volat ira per Angligenenses.

[1] i. e. player of the royal game of bowls. *Danmonii Illustres.*

Beaumont is much out of favour with Hazlitt for the lines in the *Maid's Tragedy* idealizing non-resistance, though Dryden blames him for making Evadne the minister of vengeance on the royal criminal. Amintor exclaims:—

> 'In that sacred word
> "The King" there lies a terror. What frail man
> Dares lift his hand against it? Let the gods
> Speak to him when they please; till when let us
> Suffer and wait.'

And Shakespeare's *Richard II* almost turned the scale in 1688. James I, however, had helped the revolted Hollanders, and his conscience was uneasy. He referred the question of his consistency to the Convocations of clergy. The churchmen in reply laid down the principle of passive obedience to all settled authority, whatever its origin[1]. But for Pharaoh's consent the Israelites might not have quitted Egypt. The University followed with a like pronouncement. Puritanism, however, was still strong in Oxford. The following narrative[2] of events in 1623-25 is in Wood, MS. D. 18, fol. 44:—

'The Relation of Mr. William Knights case as it is related by Dr. Clayton of P. C. who had it from his own mouth.

'Dr. [Thomas] Clayton of Broadgates hall having out of respect to his house procured the priviledge of a Lent term at St. Peter's to be preach't by one of his own house pitch't upon one Mr. William Knight of the same Hall (an ingenious man, as he had before approued himself in a Sermon at St. Marye's, and a witty coppy of verses before Barton Holiday's translation of Persius) to performe that seruice, who accordingly did it taking his text out of y[e] xix ch. of the 1st of Kings, & y[e] latter part of the 9th v.[3]; the words are, what doe'st thou here Elijah, upon w[ch] subject

[1] 'If any man shall affirm either that subjects, when they shake off the yoke of obedience to their sovereigns and set up a form of government among themselves, do not therein very wickedly, or that it is lawful for bordering kings to invade their neighbours, or that any such new forms of government, begun by rebellion and after thoroughly settled, the authority of them is not of GOD, he doth greatly err.' James, who reigned by hereditary right, and whose aid lent to the Dutch Protestants was thus disallowed, was much dissatisfied with this resolution by the spiritualty.

[2] Written Oct. 13, 1688, by Dr. John Bateman, President of the College of Physicians, from the mouth of Dr. Richard Clayton, Master of University College, sometime of Broadgates.

[3] Romans xiii. 1, Wood thinks. The gist, Heylin says (*Life of Laud*, pt. i. lib. 2), was 'that the inferiour Magistrat had a lawfull power to order and correct the King if he did amiss,' the preacher quoting Trajan's speech to the captain of his guard, 'Accipe hunc gladium; quem pro me, si bene imperavero, distringes, sin minus, contra me.'

taking occasion to speake of the persecutions of the Prophet, and the meanes he used to prevent and avoyd them, he proceeded also to state this Question, viz. whether subjects se defendendo in case of Religion might take up armes against theyre Soveraigne, wch he resolved in the Affirmative; for this tenent after Sermon he was sent for and Questioned by the then Vicechancello^r & the now Bishop of Bath & Wells Dr. Peir's, & required by him to deliuer up his notes, wth an Account of the Contriver's or Abetto^rs of his sermon (for some such he would not be pswaded but that there were and those of the Grandees) & withall to whom he had showed his sermon before he preach't it; to all wch he returned this that in this Ten^t. he had followed Paræus then professo^r at Heidelberg in his Commentaryes upon ye 13th to ye Romans [1] & to name his best Autho^r the King's Majestye's practice, who then at that very time was sending releif to the Rochellers then in Armes ag^st theyre naturall L^d and King; And for such as had before seen his Sermon he knew of none but one Mr Herbert of ye same house Minister of Radley, and one Mr Code a young Master of theyre hall [2], upon wch Answer both he, and Herbert wth Code, were committed to prison by the then Vicechancellor, who presently sent news of this seditious sermon abetted, as he informed, by severall grave Diuines, to ye Court [3], upon wch Knight was sent for out of his prison here at Oxon, and committed upon a slight examinacõn by ye Ld Keeper Williams to ye Gate-house, Herbert and Code remaining Prisoners here behind; and order was sent down that all studyes should be search't for Paræus' his Commentary at Oxoñ & Cambridge & burn't here at Oxford, at Cambridge, & at Paul's Crosse, wch was accordingly executed very vigorously (every schollar being sent for into ye Publick Hall, & ye keys of theyre studyes [4] demanded & theyre studyes search't while they stayd there) about six or seven weeks after it happened that Dr Prideaux' his Month being come he accordingly waited at Court, and there being mett by ye Prince, after Charles ye 1st, D^r, saye's the Prince, you haue strange doing's at Oxford, seditious sermons preach't and these contriued by Graue Diuines there, to wch Dr Prideaux replyed I confesse to yor highnesse that a hott headed young fellow preach't a seditious sermon there, but for yor grave Diuines, I cannot imagine whom yor highnesse means, Oh, sayes ye Prince, one Herbert & one Code, Herbert & Code! sayes ye D^r does y^r highnesse call those graue Diuines, why, Herbert is a poore Countrey-Vicar of 30^l p. Annum; & for Code he is a young, debauched Master of Arts and his ffather, who is now high sheriff of Cornwall is now upon disinheriting him; Say ye so, sayes ye Prince is this truth & presently fell of to other

---

[1] Published in 1617. David Waengler (Græcized to Paræus) was first a Lutheran and then a leading Sacramentary; 1548-1622.

[2] John Herbert, M.A. before 1619. John Code, matr. Nov. 10, 1615.

[3] Note 'to Dr. Laud B. of S. Davids.' In Laud's *Diary*, Apr. 16, 1622, is this: 'I was with his Majesty and the Prince's Highness to give notice of Letters I received of a Treasonable Sermon Preached in Oxon Sunday Ap. 14 by one Mr. *Knight* of *Broadgates*.'

[4] i.e. libraries.

discourse, and presently after Herbert & Code were released[1], but Knight still continued in y* Gatehouse. About two yeare's after it happened that my L^d of Oxford (who wth my L^ds of Southampton, & Essex had been sent ouer to y* relief of y* Netherlands) returning out of y* Low-Countryes had a Contest with y* Duke of Buckingham, upon wch he was committed to y* Tower & severall of his ffriends and officers to y* Gatehouse, and among y* rest one of his Captaines was lodged in y* prison in y* next roome to Knight's and hearing one walk up and down frequently in y^t roome asked who was there & what he was, to wch Knight replyed y^t he was a poore schollar & made his case known to him, with wch ioyned wth theyre often following discourses y* Captaine moved promised Knight y^t if ever he was released he would remember his fellow prisoner Knight, wch happening very shortly after upon a re-conciliation between y* Earle and y* Duke he was mindfull of his promise & obliged the Earle to sue to y* Ld Keeper William's for his enlarge-ment wch y* Earle accordingly did & promised that he should trouble them no more in England but goe his Chaplain with him into y* Nether-lands ; to wch y* Ld Keeper easyly & readyly condiscended being much troubled[2] y^t Knight should lye so long in Prison, whom they imagin'd had been released long before & had quite forgotten, & accordingly sent for Knight & giuing him many faire words clad him in a new suit of Clothe's & furnish't him wth 20^t for his pockett, and had him before y* King where he made his submission, & after went with my L^d of Oxford as his L^p Chaplain oversea where, his body not able to beare so suddain a chang of Aire and Dyett after so close an imprisonment he shortly after dyed.

'Mr Herbert of Radley y* person before mentioned as a Cosufferer wth Code upon Knight's Account dyed y* 13th of this Instant Octob^r, & Dr Clayton preached his funerall sermon[3].'

In consequence of Knight's discourse, described by the Privy Council as 'a wicked sermon by one Knight, an unadvised young man,' the Vice-Chancellor was commanded to assemble the Heads, 'and put them in mind of the Direction sent thither some few years since by his Majesty, that those who design'd to make Divinity their Profession should chiefly apply themselves to the Studies of the Holy Scriptures, of the Councils, Fathers and ancient Schoolmen ; but as for the Moderns, whether *Jesuits* or *Puritans*, they should wholly decline reading their Works,' that thereby (said James) 'they may bee the better enabled only to preach CHRIST crucified, which ought to be the end of their Studies.' The Bishops, assembled in London, condemned Knight's proposition as 'contrary to the Holy Scriptures,

---

[1] The Vice-Chancellor however was first to satisfy himself as to the inclinations of opinion previously noted in them.

[2] Rather, Wood elsewhere suggests, to spite his rival Laud.

[3] 1688. Dr. Richard Clayton. See Wood's *Life and Times*, ii. 125.

the Sense of the antient Fathers, and utterly repugnant to the Doctrine and Constitution of the Church of *England*.' The Oxford Doctors and Masters decreed 'that by the Doctrine of the Holy Scriptures it is in no Case lawful for subjects to make use of Force against their Prince.' All graduates were to take their corporal oath to condemn Paraeus' theses[1]. 'And that Calvin's doctrines might not revive here: An order was made at the same Convocation that the King's directions above-mentioned for the regulating of their Studies should be hung up in the College Chapels and other publick Places. And from this time Calvin's authority began to decline in the University. He was not now consulted as their Oracle.'

The Oxford Parliament of 1664 enacted that it is not lawful, on any pretence whatsoever, to take up arms against the King; and the University again in 1683 published a decree inculcating Non-Resistance, while condemning the *Leviathan*. This decree was burned by order of the House of Lords in 1709, but was reprinted in 1710 in answer to Hoadly's *Original of Government.*

Some Broadgates men who sate in Jacobean parliaments were WILLIAM CARNSEWE, Fellow of All Souls (Camelford, 1597, 1601); ROBERT SANDERSON, Viscount Castleton's brother (? West Looe, 1588); SIR PHILIP KIGHLEY (Evesham, 1604); CHARLES THYNNE (New Lymington, 1614; Westbury, 1628); his brother, SIR HENRY, entered the same day; their father was Sir John Thynne of Longleat; JOHN TREFUSIS (Truro, 1621). JOHN PERROT, son of Sir John Perrot, Lord Deputy of Ireland, was brother of Sir James, an opposition leader under James I.

---

[1] The first proposition censured was this: 'That it is lawful for Bishops and Pastors with the Consent of the Church, to deliver wicked and unjust Magistrates to *Satan*.' Three others asserted that when a Chief Magistrate forces his subjects upon blasphemy or manifest idolatry, or 'commits an open Rape, as it were, upon Privilege and Property,' he is to be treated like a highwayman, 'in the Character of one that goes on the Road' (Salmon).

CHAPTER XIII.

FOUNDATION OF PEMBROKE COLLEGE.

BETWEEN 1605 and 1612 a surprising increase in the numbers at Broadgates is observable. In 1605 it comes last but two with forty members. The census taken in the vacation of 1612 shows it seventh of twenty-four with a hundred and thirty-one members[1]. Yet the numbers matriculating had rather fallen off. In those eight years seventeen entered as 'armigeri filius,' twenty-six as 'generosi filius,' one as 'militis filius,' one as 'mercatoris filius' (he paid fees as a gentleman), eleven as 'clerici filius,' and thirty-three as 'plebeii filius.' The designation of clerical parentage is always noticeable, 'Verbi ministri filius' in Elizabeth's reign passes into 'clerici' under James, that into 'sacerdotis' under Charles I, reverting to 'ministri' in the Commonwealth time and till 1676. Thenceforward 'clerici' was used.

In 1619 Summaster's long principality ended and Budden's short one followed. Dr. Thomas Clayton succeeded in 1620. He at once took in hand the expansion of the buildings. The College possesses a duodecimo, presented in 1795 by Sir Hugh Palliser, containing a list of subscribers. The first page is headed Σὺν Θεῷ; on the next is this: 'We whose names here follow in this booke, in our love to learning, the University, and particularly to Broadgates Hall in Oxford, wᶜʰ needeth enlargement of the Hall for meeting at Commons, Disputations, &c., as also some lodgings for Students, do contribute as followeth— July 15, 1620. Thos. Clayton, Principall, xxˡⁱ to be paid presently towards the providing of materialls. Who promiseth his best care for the disposing of all to the best use of the house, and account to the Contributors of the employment of all the money which shall come by their love and bounty. Thomas Clayton, Principall.' The other

---

[1] Wood's *Life and Times*, O. H. S., iv. 151. The larger bodies were Queen's (267), Magdalen (246), Christ Church (240), Brasenose (227), Exeter (206), and Magdalen Hall (161). The total membership of the University was, in 1605, 2254, and in 1612, 2930.

names, forty-eight in number, include 'the right honorable my Lady Viscountesse' [Lucy] Doncaster (wife of James Hay Lord Doncaster, afterwards Earl of Carlisle) 'five peices' (£5 10*s.*); 'Sr William Spencer, Knight of the Bathe to Prince Charles, sonne and Heire of the Right Honorable Lord Spencer,' 44*s.*; Lady Penelope Spencer, 44*s.*; Sir Richard Anderson, of Pendley, Herts (whose son Robert entered the College in 1625), 44*s.*; the noble Lady Mary Anderson, 22*s.*; Sir Thomas Wrothe, 'sometymes Scholler to the Principall,' 40*s.* (he was a Rumper, and on the commission for the trial of the King, but did not act); Mr. Robert Nedham, 'of Shavington, in the countye of Salope,' 22*s.* (his son Robert, third Viscount Kilmorey, entered the College in 1625); Mrs. Margaret Washington, 11*s.*; Richard Astley, Warden of All Souls, 33*s.* Most of the entries are autograph, followed by the signatures. The most interesting is, ' Aprilis 27°, 1623°, Johannes Pym, Armiger, de Brimore in comitat Somerset, quondam Aulae Lateportensis Commensalis, donavit 44*s.* Jo : Pym.' Out of these moneys the transverse portion of the old dining-hall, which is shaped like a rather crooked T, was added. The plan of erecting new chambers for students was swallowed up in a larger transformation. What I find it difficult to explain is the language used by the orators at the inauguration of Pembroke College in 1624. They speak of 'nostras utroque cornu nutantes jam diu fortunas.' Some Principals took Halls merely to provide themselves with a house, and encouraged leakage of students[1]. But in Clayton's first year the entries rose from three to twenty-nine. He attracted to the Hall men of intellect like Browne, and men of family like Sir Anthony Hungerforde. Both these came up in 1623.

The incorporation and endowment of the ' oldest of the Halls ' as a new College, in the year 1624, is a somewhat curious story.

---

[1] The Rev. Andrew Clark writes to me : ' Clayton seems to have been a man of substance, and had his professorship and, I suppose, his practice. If he wished to empty the Hall, so that he should have no trouble, he could have done much in four years. See what Wood says about St. Alban Hall (*Life*, i. 402 ; ii. 19, 264), and Gloucester Hall (ii. 398 ; iii. 1). Of course Clayton as a Head of a College with endowment became a very different person, and was no doubt much pleased to push Pembroke on. I have in my mind a general statement by Wood that the decay of the Halls was due to the practice of appointing to the Headship of them Professors, who turned the Hall into a house for their families. A Hall, owing to the absence of persons attached to it by endowment, had a very precarious existence. If the resident M.A.'s moved, their servitors, who made up the undergraduate element, would have to move also. See an exodus from St. Alban Hall, Wood's *Life*, ii. 468.'

THOMAS TESDALE, or Tisdale[1], a fortnight before his decease at Glympton, near Woodstock, made a testament, dated May 31, 1610[2], bequeathing the splendid sum of five thousand pounds to purchase lands, &c., for maintaining seven Fellows and six Scholars to be elected out of Roysse's Free Grammar School in Abingdon into Balliol or some other College in Oxford.

In 1627 there was penned (and left in MS.) by Francis Little, of Abingdon, a connexion of Tesdale's wife, '*A Monument of Christian Munificence*, or an Account of the Brotherhood of the Holy Cross and of the Hospital of Christ in Abingdon.' The Master and Governors of the Hospital caused it to be printed in 1871[3]. It gives the fullest account of this bountiful merchant.

'THOMAS TEASDALE, of Glympton, in the county of Oxon, Gent., was born at Stanford Dingley, in the county of Berks. His father, whose name was also Thomas Teasdale, came from that village to this town & dwelt at Fitz-Harris' farm[4] in good account and reputation. He was chosen Governor of this Hospital A.D. 1554, in the first and second year of King Phillip and Queene Marie, & in December, 1556, he died. After his death the said Thomas Teasdale, his son, was brought up by his uncle, Richard Teasdale, of Abingdon, Sadler, and when the free school here was founded by John Royse, citizen and Mercer of London,

---

[1] The name is also spelt Teasdale, Teasdell, Teasedale, Tisdale, Tesdall, Teisdall, Teysdale, Tisedale, &c.

[2] So Gutch's Wood, iii. 616. But Little (vide infra) dates the will Feb. 28, 1609 [1610]. It is not at Somerset House.

[3] Edited by C. D. Cobham, D.C.L., crown 8vo. 'Mr. Frances Littell, allast Brooker, was buried the xth of Janewary, 1630,' in St. Nicholas. He was for thirty-eight years a Governor and twice Master of Christ's Hospital. I find the name Francis Little as Governor, 1585-1610, and Master, 1596-7; but perhaps this was his father. One Francis Lyttle, from Berks, entered Christ Church Feb. 14, 161¼. The *Monument* was clearly known to Wood.

[4] The official pedigree (vide infra) makes Fitzharris Farm to be situated at Stanford. Wood falls into the same error. In the Oxford *City Records* (ed. Turner, p. 331) is this entry: 'Abyngdon. 1569, Nov. 25. M^d that at this Counsell was left in the kepyng of Mr Mayors chyst, wch lyeth w^thin the kepynge of the fyve Key Kepers chest, on blacke boxe, sealed, in the wch boxe ther ys one lease made by the Maior, Baylyffs, and Burgesses of the borrowgh of Abyngdon, of on ferm called Fytts Harrys unto Edmund Benet and John Tysdale, wch lease, wth a byll of one Edmund Benet and Richard Benott for the name of John Tysdale, is made wth thre hands and seales unto the said byll, to shew for what use and order ye said lease ys left in the custody and kepyng of the Mayor and fyve Key Kepars, and delivered at this present Counsell.' In 1666 Fitzharris was in the occupation of Joan Badcock, widow, who still held it in 1681. In 1666 the corporation of Abingdon borrowed £200 on it and another farm 'for the use of his Majestie.' The farm and house are now parted. The latter, the home of Tesdale's childhood, is close to the town, and is a gentleman's residence in a small park.

in the year 1563, he was the first scholar that was chosen and admitted by the founder into the school, being then about sixteen years of age. Afterwards, when he came to man's estate, he married in Abingdon & traded in the making of malt, then a very gainful course there; whereby in short time and by God's assistance & his own diligence, he got great store of wealth & substance, and grew as fast in credit & estimation in the town among his neighbours. For in the year of our Lord 1569, the one and twentieth of his own age, he was chosen one of the common council of the town, & in the year 1571 he was elected one of the bayliffs of this borough, & again elected one of the bayliffs in 1574. In the year 1577 he was chosen a Governor of this Hospital, & 1579 the Master thereof; 1580 a principal burgess of this borough, & 1581 he was elected Mayor thereof; but by reason he had a little before left the town, & was departed from thence with his family, he was freed from serving that office by the payment of a fine to the Corporation. And liking better of a country life, he dwelt the most part of his time at Glympton aforesaid, at which place & many others, in divers shires & countries, he traded in sowing & making of woad (used by dyers) & was held to be the greatest dealer therein that was in the whole realm; whereby, and by tillage for corn and by grazing of cattle, he attained to a great estate. Then first to testify & declare unto the world his thankfulness to God who so abundantly blessed his labours, he maintained at his own charge a lecture every Sunday in his Parish Church of Glympton, where he dwelt, giving twenty pounds yearly to the Preacher, whom he always desired to be of special note and of the best account in the University of Oxford. He was always a lover of God's Word and a great favourer of the preachers & professors thereof, & still prospered accordingly. He was a bountiful Housekeeper & gave much alms and relief to the poor, to whom his purse was ever open & his hand never shut; & having no child living on whom to bestow his wealth, he gave in his lifetime many liberal portions to the marriage of divers of his kindred, & to some of them stocks of money to trade withal, that while he yet lived he might be an eye-witness of their honest endeavours & frugal courses. And by his last will & testament—dated at Glimpton aforesaid the last day of February, in the year of the world's salvation One Thousand Six Hundred & Nine, he gave many large and liberal legacies to all those that were of his name & consanguinity. Besides he gave unto Maud his wife two thousand pounds, to divide & bestow amongst her own kindred. He likewise gave portions to all his household servants, to recompense their true and faithful service, something also to his familiar friends & old acquaintance. But his gifts and legacies to pious & charitable uses surmounteth all. And first he gave unto divers towns & villages that were near his dwelling ten pounds apiece, & to some places more remote other sums of money to succour & relieve the poor and needy people of those places, & appointed that all men women and children that came to his funeral for relief should have, every one of them, sixpence a-piece in money. He gave thirty pounds to the poor of Stanford Dingley where he was born, & thirty pounds to the poor of Abingdon where he was bred. Further more he gave to this Hospital, for the perpetual maintenance of an Usher in the free School at Abingdon, all his Glebe lands & tythes in Upton [1], in Warwickshire, worth above sixteen pounds a-year. Besides all this he gave unto the most Reverend Father in God George, then Lord Bishop of London, now Archbishop of Caunterburie, Sir John Bennett, Knight, Doctour of Civill Lawes, & to Henry Airay, Doctour of Divinity, then Provost of Queenes Colledge in Oxford, as unto feoffees & devisees in trust, five thousand pounds for the purchase of lands for the perpetual maintenance of seven fellowes & six scholars, to be from time to time chosen out of the free school in Abingdon & placed in Balioll college in Oxford, if the Master & Fellowes thereof would entertain that company with those provisions, & upon such conditions as were ordained by his will, or else the said gift was to be conferred by the said devisees upon some other college that would accordingly accept the same. The election of which scholars from the said free school is to be made up of poor men's children born at Abingdon, and brought up in the said School, & next after six of the poorest of his own kindred, which are first to be chosen.

'Master William Bennetts poor scholars [2], are next, by his will, to be preferred. The electors are the Master & the two senior fellows of the college wherein they shall be placed, the Master & the two senior Governors of this Hospital, and the master of the free school, to have a voice also in the said election. The said Thomas Teasdale by his will hath also ordained that all those seven fellows of his foundation, after a convenient time that they have studied & proceeded in the arts, shall every one of them successfully apply their studies unto Divinity & profess the same in preaching, otherwise after a time, limited by his will, they are to be removed from their places, declaring, or at least intimating thereby, his care for the preaching & teaching of God's Holy Word, that men's souls may be saved, & God may be glorified. The rest of his estate unbequeathed he gave unto the aforesaid Maud his wife, as a token of his love & affection towards her, & farther to shew also his trust & confidence in her, he made her his sole executrix of all his will; & so having set his worldly estate in order, it was not long after he fell grievously sick, & feeling death approaching, he drew his comfort out of Holy meditations, & in the end gave place unto nature; and at Glympton aforesaid he died, the thirteenth day of June, in the year of salvation one thousand six hundred & ten and of his own age threescore & three, the climacterical year of his life, & was buried at the place of his decease.

'Mawde Teasdale, wife to the forementioned Thomas Teasdale, was also a benefactor to this hospital, who was born at Henley-upon-Thames

---

[1] This glebe was parcel of the rectory of Ratley. The lands, &c., were let at a rent of £14. They were vested in the same trustees as the £5,000.

[2] See afterwards. Bennet directed Tesdale to see that after six years' schooling in the Free School they should either be apprenticed at the cost of the charity, or, 'if any of them should prove fit to make scholars,' they should receive liberal assistance towards their expenses at the University.

in the County of Oxford, the daughter of Reinhold Stone, of that town, Gent. Her parents always lived in good fortune & reputation. First she was married to Edward Little, then of Oxford, and afterwards of Abingdon, whose widow she was when the aforesaid Thomas Teasdale married her[1], and after his death she was a widow until she died, which was six years & six dayes after her husband's decease. This good Christian gentlewoman & grave matron, when sickness came & put her in mind of her mortality, she deferred not to address Herself to her last will, wherein she gave sundry portions of monies to divers pious & charitable uses, some to the poor of several parishes that were near unto her, & one hundred pounds to provide means to maintain two sermons yearly for ever, to be preached in the parish church of Henlie where she was born, one upon Christmas day & one upon Easter day ; & towards the relief of fourteen poor women of the said town of Henlie, a penny a-piece, to be given in bread in the said parish church every Sunday for ever. Moreover she gave this said town of Henley three hundred pounds, to be lent unto fifteen young tradesmen, twenty pounds apiece, for six years together, & afterwards to six other in like manner for ever. Also she gave two hundred pounds to be bestowed in St. Marie's church in Oxford, for the building of strong and sufficient galleries in the same church, whereby all people might stand the more conveniently to hear the Word of God, to his Glory & their own comfort ; but especially at the time of the solemnity of the Act, at which time multitudes of strangers do usually resort. Furthermore she gave unto this Hospital fifty pounds, to be employed towards the relief of twelve poor widows of this town, to every of them a penny loaf of bread every Sunday in St. Helen's Church for ever ; & having no child living to enjoy her wealth she gave the rest of her great estates unto her kindred & her near allies, & made two executors, to whom she gave one hundred pounds apiece to see her will faithfully performed & justly executed. And having thus disposed of her worldly wealth, & received in Christian manner fit consolation for her soul's health, death, in execution of the Almighty's sentence, was ready to discharge her soul of the prison of her flesh, which she joyfully rendered to her Redeemer & left the world upon Wednesday, the nineteenth day of June, in the year of man's happiness 1616, & of her own age threescore & eleven, & lieth buried by her husband in the parish church of Glympton aforesaid.

'The five thousand pounds before mentioned, which was given by Thomas Teasdale for the benefit of seven fellows & six scholars, to be maintained in Oxford as aforesaid, was by the provident care & prudence of the most Reverend Archbishop of Caunterburie, at length obtained, & by his means disbursed & settled upon lands & rents, which he had also endeavoured to confer on Baliol Colledge in Oxford, according to the will of the donor ; but the Master & fellows thereof refused to accept the same upon those conditions which were prescribed by the said Thomas Teasdale's will; wherefore the said Archbishop, very desirous to perform the

---

[1] She was then but twenty-two ; Tesdale was twenty. They seem to have had three children, who died young.

trust reposed in him, & willing to help forward so good a work as was intended, hath settled the said lands upon Pembrooke Colledge in Oxford, lately founded in the said University, chiefly for that purpose, by King James, his letters patent, dated the nine & twentieth day of June Anno Domini 1624, attributing & describing the foundation thereof to be done at the costs & charges of the said Thomas Teasdale & one Richard Wightwicke, to consist of one Master, ten fellows, and ten scholars, with the priveleges liberties & immunities granted by the said letters patent : of which number of fellows and Scholars, the aforesaid Thomas Teasdale is founder of seven Fellows & six scholars & the said Richard Wightwicke is founder of three fellows & four scholars, who have all liberal allowance appointed to their places. This colledge is placed upon Broadgates Hall in Oxford & the name of the Hall extinguished & abolished in the foundation of the said College, by the consent & aprobation of the Right Honorable William, Earle of Pembroke, Lord Chamberlaine of the King's Household, & Chancellor of the said University & with the allowance & good liking of Thomas Clayton, Doctor of Physic, late Principal of the said Hall, & now Master of the College.

'The Mayor, Bayliffs & Burgesses of Abingdon, out of their pious & charitable disposition to so good & godly a work, did begin, & to their great costs & charges followed, the suit for the founding of the said college, wherein they considered also the public benefit that would thereby come & accrue unto the whole town by preferring of the poor town-born children from the school unto the college ; which school the mayor bayliffs & burgesses do gladly advance, for that they are patrons of it ; for which charitable deed of theirs, in procuring the said college, they do worthily deserve to be accounted among the benefactors of this Hospital ; for by the prosperity of the school & benefit of the college, in breeding & bringing up of poor men's children, the Hospital may happily be freed from future charges ; & besides the Master & the two senior Governors of the Hospital have an interest in the College, by being electors of Thomas Teasdale's scholars out of the school into the college ; in which respect the aforesaid Richard Wightwicke, for giving the like power & prerogative to the said Master & Governors in choosing three of his scholars may also justly challenge a place amongst the benefactors of the said Hospital.'

This account is by no means complete or impartial as regards the transformation of Broadgates Hall into Pembroke College and the circumstances of its endowment. We know from *Balliofergus* that Balliol College regarded itself as tricked in the matter. The governing body cannot have actually refused Tesdale's conditions, seeing that they acquired Caesar's Buildings for chambers for the new fellows and scholars. Wood, who through his father had means of information, says that 'several articles of agreement were made between the Mayor, Bailiffs and Burghers of Abendon and the Master and

Scholars[1]' of Balliol, and Savage gives the terms of these 'condescensions.' The negotiations however, for some reason, were not completed thirteen years after Tesdale's decease, when the thoughts of the citizens were suddenly turned in a new and more ambitious direction. About 1623 RICHARD WIGHTWICK, B.D., rector of East Ilsley, Berks, formerly of Balliol, offered to augment Tesdale's foundation. 'It fell then under consideration,' says Fuller in the *Worthies*, 'that it was a pity so great a bounty, substantial enough to stand of itself, should be adjected to a former foundation (some intentions there were to have made it an addition to Baliol College), whereupon a new College (formerly called Broadgates Hall in Oxford) was erected therewith by the name of Pembroke College.' Nutt (*Magna Britannia*) says, 'The Feoffees and the Corporation of Abingdon made suit to the King through the Earl of Pembroke.' They prayed that 'within Broadgates Hall and on the site, circuit, and precinct thereof the King would constitute a College, consisting of a Master, Fellows and Scholars,' with power of holding land. Little, who must have known all the circumstances, evidently wishes to clear the Corporation from blame; and it is possible that there was some hitch in the arrangement with Balliol. But I have not been able to ascertain the evidence for the following statement in Blundell's *Brief Memorial of Abingdon School* (1863): 'As at this time the pressing necessities of Baliol had just been relieved by advances made to its master and scholars by the trustees of Blundell's grammar school at Tiverton, on conditions somewhat similar to those proposed by Teasdale, they declined an overture which, if accepted, would have practically divided their fellowships between Abingdon and Tiverton.' The feoffees in whom Tesdale's benefaction was vested at the time were Sir Nicholas Kempe, Knt., and William Baker, Esq. The Mayor of Abingdon in 1622 was Richard Curtyn, and in 1623 Richard Checkyn, both connected with the Tesdale family, and in 1624 Tesdale's kinsman, Christopher Tesdale—unlikely men to disregard the intentions of the founder. Wood[2] says that the aid of Parliament was invoked, but I find nothing in the Statutes at Large.

The inscription placed on Tesdale's monument by his relict describes him as 'lyberally beneficial to Balliol Colledge,' and the last entry in the continuation (1613) by Howes of Stowe's Chronicle says simply that he 'gave 5000*l*. to maintain seven fellows and six scholars, to be placed in Bailyoll Colledge.'

[1] Gutch, iii. 616.　　　　[2] Gutch, iii. 619.

The Rev. A. B. Valpy, M.A., rector of Stanford Dingley (grandson of Dr. Valpy of Reading), has furnished me with the following from the very early registers of that parish: '1547. Thomas Teysdall was baptized yᵉ 13th of October 1547.' The Norman font remains. Another extract relates perhaps to his mother's brother: 'John Knapp and Jane Myler weare married yᵉ 24th day of November 1559.' What is known respecting Tesdale's progenitors and kindred may be seen in the pedigree[1] at the end of this chapter. His father was thrice married, and Thomas was the elder child of the second wife, Joan Knapp. The first wife, Cecilia Hyde, died of the pest, in 1545, with five of her six children. The survivor, Elizabeth, became the ancestress of Lords Arlington and Ossulston, of Sir James Whitelocke, and of the Dukes of Grafton. When his father died the co-Founder was nine years old. We learn some further particulars of his youth from the testament, dated October 31, 1556, of the elder Thomas, who is buried in St. Helen's, Abingdon.

After the usual pious commendations and a few small charitable bequests, including one to the church of Allhallows in Wallingford, the testator bequeathed to his son Thomas all his right, title, interest, and term of years in the 'personnage' of Allhallows, Wallingford, as well as a sum of £100, to be his on his twenty-first birthday; 'and yf it shall pleas God to calle hym out of this worlde before he shall come and accomplishe the age of xxj years then my will and mynde is that the sayd some of c li. shall be payd and delyvered to my daught' Elizabeth Benett or her children at the discreation of my overseers if she shall chaunce to dye before the saide Thomas.' The will goes on:

---

[1] I have compiled this from the wills at Somerset House, from Little's *Monument*, and from the very full Tesdale pedigrees collected by Robert Dale, Blanch Lion, in 1695, and preserved at the College of Arms. W. A. Lindsay, Esq., Windsor Herald, has courteously allowed me full access to these records. Dale has written the following at the head of the principal pedigree:—' The Preamble beginning thus. Immediately after the Death of Thomas Tisdale late of Glimpton, gent., who by will gave maintenance for 13 Scholars in Oxford, viz. 6 of his kindred and 7 others, it was thought expedient by the Ancient'st of his kindred, Christopher Tisdale and others, for the avoiding of Controversies which might arise about Electing his kinsmen to the said Places, that his pedigree should be made known as far as it mought be, and also his Kindred which he seemeth to intend by his last will, wherein he hath (as it were) marked out every person, or at least every Family, of his kindred with a Legacie given to him or them in the name of a kinsman or kinsmen. By the Testimony of Christopher Tisdale his kinsman, who was at the decease of the said Thomas about 68 years of age and was son of John Tisdale (which was Uncle to the said Thomas), the first Tisdale that was born in the County of Berks, who died a man of great age about the 36th year of his said son Christopher's age. This Christopher upon the Report of his said Father and his own knowledge did declare,' &c.

'Item I wille that my brother Richard Tesdall and William Hopkyns shall have the custody and kepeing of my said sonne Thomas . . . untill the saide Thomas shall come to and be of the age of xxj yeres . . . and bringe hym up in lerning, and when he shall sufficientlye be lerned and of age to be a prentice thenne they shall cause him to be bound prentice' at London, the Wallingford rents meanwhile being used for his benefit. In case of his death before twenty-one, the aforesaid parsonage and lease were to pass to Thomas Bennett. The lease of Fitzharris farm is left to his wife Agnes Tesdall, who is to 'have the oversight and be tutor' of their youngest son John, during his 'noneage.' To his brother John Tesdall the testator left £4, to his brother Richard £6 13s. 4d., and to his sister Elizabeth Tringe or Dringe £4. The widow was residuary legatee. The next generation are found filling the chief civic chairs of Abingdon, governors also and Masters of the Hospital of Christ's Poor. Thomas Tesdale the younger was kept by his uncle's side, and never, as far as can be learned, apprenticed in London. Fuller however relates that he was clothier to the royal army and at one time an attendant at Court. His wife had been one of Elizabeth's maids of honour. In the borough records of Abingdon the various Tesdales of the time are always described as 'gentleman.' Some were maltsters. On Nov. 18, 1585, 'Anthonye Teysdale,' with others using that trade, was ordered to 'bring into the Marckett everye Marckett daye three bushells of maulte, upon paine of a fine of 3s. 4d.' The same 'Anthony Teisdall, gent.' was elected Mayor in 1597 and 1599, but objected to serve a second year, alleging that the 'execucon of his said office' had been 'very chargeable unto him.' The excuse was allowed. In 1603 he was made a 'veiwer of mounds and bounds'; in 1588 and 1607 Master of Christ's Hospital. He died in 1610. This Anthony was a first cousin of our Thomas. Anthony's son, Thomas, was elected Recorder October 2, 1628, being succeeded in 1632 by Bulstrode Whitelock[1]. Thomas Tesdale the co-Founder had some trouble about his civic duties. In 1579 there is an entry in the Chamberlain's Accompts : 'Item, paid to Mr.. Halle- well yat he payd to Mr. Ploden for councell about th' eleckcyon of Mr. Tesdall xxs.' Seven years afterwards, in the Corporation Minutes, '27 Septbris 28 Elizabethae':—

---

[1] Afterwards Speaker, one of Cromwell's lords, and President of the Council of State. This notable man was Recorder of Oxford in 1649 (and High Steward), but I find no mention in any life of him that he held this office at Abingdon, as the Corporation papers show is the case. He married Tesdale's grandniece, Rebecca Bennet.

'The causes that Thomas Teysdall gent dothe alledge to the Mayor Baylyffs and Burgesses to be reasonable causes whie he shoulde not take upon hym to be Mayor of this yere next following to which he was elected unto the first of September last and desirethe theie maye be allowed accordingly . . .

First   This I saie that a four years agon being elected to the s^d office I fulfilled the s^d charter and to my charge paide the fine   Also that my dwelling and mansion howse is nyne or tenne myles hence at Kydlington where my busynes is so greate at this tyme that my absence thence may torne me to suche losses that it is hard to recover again Also that I have in this Boroghe neither howse, furnyture for a howse, provision or any thing towards the same acordingly.'

An order allowing these causes, ' with others secretly known,' and discharging the fine, is signed by the Mayor, Paul Orpwood, and others. But on Jan. 12, 32 Eliz.,—

' It is ordered by the Comen Councell of the s^d Borough That yf Richard Quelche and Thomas Teysdall gents do not come to the Mayor for the tyme being before the firste daye of Maye next comyng or [show] lawfull cause whie theie or either of them do exempte themselves oute of the towne or not companying with the Mayor for to geve there good advises for the Government of the said Boroughe That then he which shall not come and shewe cause and the cause allowed lawfull by the Mayor Baylyffs and Principall burgesses or the more parte of them That then he or theie not comyng as aforesaid shalbe disfranchised of his principall burgessheppe.'

Kidlington, where Tesdale had in 1586 his ' dwelling and mansion house,' is but a short distance from Glympton, to which he must before long have removed. The expansion of the wool trade, and consequent conversion of small yeoman holdings into large sheep grazings, was having economic results which at the end of Elizabeth's reign were loudly deplored. He lived at Ludwell Manor [1], which is actually in Wootton parish. This is a typical Oxfordshire stone village climbing picturesquely the hill on which stands the pretty Late Decorated Church. Two or three miles away, half a mile beyond Glympton Church, is Ludwell Farm or Manor House, now the property of Sir George Dashwood, Bart., in a somewhat lonely position on high ground—a haunt, as seen on a summer's evening, of ancient peace, with its old fish-ponds and fifteenth-century windows. In the interior is a remarkable chimney-piece. The family no doubt

---

[1] The tenant still pays a yearly rent-charge of 6s. 8d., which is given to the poor, and is supposed to be Maud Tesdale's gift. The house was lately for sale.

went down to Glympton for service, and on his monument and in
the foundation charter Tesdale is said to have belonged to that
parish. Glympton is a sequestered village set with rich pastures and
noble forest trees. Between the parsonage and the church lies one
of the oldest and smallest deer parks in England, through which runs
the little Glyme. This a few miles on fills the lake at Blenheim. The
abbot and monks of Kenilworth were once the owners and patrons
here. The Church of the Blessed Virgin Mary stands in a leafy
enclosure surrounded by old-fashioned gravestones, and consists of
nave and chancel, with west tower and south porch. The architecture
generally is of the Late Decorated and Perpendicular period, but there
is a very wide Transition Norman chancel-arch, and a fine Norman
font, rescued not long ago from base purposes. Some remains of an
old west porch, with the dog-tooth, are built into the tower, which is
a plain ivy-clad erection without parapet or pinnacle. The ravages
of restoration have destroyed much of the beauty of Glympton, as of
most ancient churches. The hammerbeams of the nave roof however have been preserved, and the carving of the old pews introduced
into the new. Nor has the north wall with the Tesdale tomb been
interfered with. On the chancel-arch is inscribed DEDICACIO HVIVS
TEMPLI IDUS MARTII : the year is obliterated.

The alabaster monument of Tesdale and his wife, erected to him in
her lifetime, is very fine. The figures kneel face to face at a faldstool, on large red cushions—grave and buxom presentments. Both
wear large ruffs, and the man a coif or skull-cap and a municipal
gown. This and the lady's dress are uncoloured; otherwise the
whole monument is elaborately painted and gilt. It has been re-
touched recently. Between the two arches, the soffits of which are
richly coffered, Tesdale's arms are impaled with his wife's[1]. The
monument is surmounted by a large shield blazoned with Tesdale's
arms with a great teazle for the crest. Some delicate ornamentation
of red roses and golden lilies runs about the tomb. On the rear
wall are two tablets, the one inscribed :—

EN QUO TANDEM.

Huc ubi Nestoreos implerunt stamina soles
Humana in foveam dejicit ossa ligo.
Indistincta patet calvaria, nec minus urget
Ora super regis quam super ora gregis.

[1] Party per fess, or and gules; in chief three bars sable ; in base three fleurs de
lis of the 1st ; for Little.

The other,

DISCE MORI.

Maxima nosse mori vitae est sapientia; vivit
Qui moritur; si vis vivere disce mori.
Vita prior mortem, sed mors tibi vita secunda
Vitam quae vita est non moritura dabit.

Two tablets under the gilded claws which support the monument bear the mottoes 'Terrena vide Caelestia crede,' and 'Pietas in fine coronat.' The principal inscription is as follows :—

(Auspice Christo).

Here lyeth the Body of MAUD TESDALE yᵉ Relict of THOMAS TESDALE of this Parish of Glympton Eᵉᵠ wᶜʰ said Maud left this vale of misery and finish'd her days of mortality in yᵉ true Faith and fear of yᵉ Lord Jesus wᵗʰ singular patience, peace of Conscience, and contentment, yᵉ 19 day of June An. Sal: 1616. Whose true and sincere love unto Religion, whose Charitable devotion towards yᵉ Poor, whose respective Care and kindness to sundry bordering Towns Sᵗ. Marys Church in yᵉ Famous University of OXON Henly upon Thames where she was born and hath shew'd her bounty Most liberaly ABINGDON where she sometimes liv'd and hath left a Perpetual remembrance of her love GLYMPTON Charlbury and Ascott in all wᶜʰ places she hath lovingly anointed Christ JESUS in his poor meᵐbers shall forever testify and declare.

Her never dying faith and loyalty to her above mention'd most Religious and worthy Husband (so far as mortality could provide to stretch yᵉ same) this Monument erected purposly by her own command and charge upon her death bed to propagate his memory rather than her own may and doth fully wittness and convince.

Sic sic coelestis qui lux es singula lustrans,
Vivere da nobis, da bene, Christe, mori.

On the faldstool is a round tablet with the words :—

Hoc Fundatoris
sui Monumentum
pene collapsum instaurarunt
Magister et Socii
Coll. Pembrochian.
Oxon. A.D. 1704.

On Nov. 2, 1871, the College voted £10 to repair the tomb, a fire having slightly damaged it early in that year.

On the floor is a large black marble slab with a brass plate representing Tesdale standing, it would seem, on an ale cask, in allusion to his earlier trade as maltster, and thus inscribed :—

Here lyeth, expecting a joyfull resurrection, the body of
Thomas Tesdale, esquier, a man in the judgement of all

Men that knew him in the whole course of his life
Religious towards God, sober & honest in his conversation,
Just and upright in his dealings amongste men, bountifull
In hospitality, lyberally beneficial to Balliol Colledge
In Oxford, the free school at Abington in Berks, ·
Charitable to the poore, lovinge and kinde to his wife,
As also to his and her kindred; who was borne at Stanforde
Deanlye in the county of Berks, and there baptized
The xiiith day of October, 1547, and when he had lived almost
LXIII yeres, deceased at Glympton 13 June, 1610.
Maude Tesdale, his sorrowfull wife and sole executor,
In testimony of her true faythful love toward him,
Erected this small memorial of him.

There are no Tesdale entries in the Glympton registers, which date from 1667 only [1].

Of Bennet's Poor Scholars Little gives this account (pp. 63–4):—

'WILLIAM BENNET, of Fulham in the County of Middlesex, Gent, was the next benefactor to the Hospital, & the best of any before him in the Greatness of his gifts since the Hospital was founded. He was born at Clapcott, near Wallingford, in the county of Berks, & was brought up in his youth by his uncle, Master Thomas Teasdale, at the free school at Abingdon. The said William Bennett out of a thankful commemoration to the place of his education, gave in trust to the said Thomas Teasdale, two messuages & three Yard lands & a half lying in Broad Blunsdon & Widdill in the county of Wiltshire, to the end that the said Thomas Teasdale should convey & assure the same unto the Master & Governors of the Hospital of Christ of Abingdon, for the perpetual relief & benefit of six poor children, born in the town of Abingdon, to be bred in the said schools six years together, & to be farther ordered in such manner & form as should seem best to the said Thomas, who conveyed the said land accordingly, and ordered as followeth. That the said six scholars should be chosen from time to time by the Master & Governors of this Hospital, & should wear livery gowns [2] & be called Master William Bennett's poor scholars. . . . He died and was buried at Fulham aforesaid upon Friday the nineteenth day of February in the year of Christ's incarnation one thousand six hundred & eight.

'Ralph Bennet of Chaleigh, in the County of Berks, gentleman, the eldest brother of William Bennet aforesaid, having by law a right & interest in the third part of the said land, out of his own charitable disposition relinquished his title, & gave all his interest in the land to the said Hospital. . . .'

SIR JOHN BENNET, one of the trustees of Tesdale's benefaction, is

[1] I am indebted to the Rector, the Rev. A. C. Bartholomew, M.A., for much courteous help afforded me on visiting his parish.
[2] Until this century Bennet's Scholars wore a dress very similar to that still worn at the greater Christ's Hospital, in the Greyfriars, London.

mistakenly described in the *Dictionary of National Biography* (following à Wood) as his grandson, whereas he was his nephew in the modern sense of 'nephew.' This eminent civilian, the grandfather of Lords Arlington and Ossulston, was at Christ Church (Junior Proctor 1585), and was made D.C.L. in 1589, afterwards becoming Vicar-general in spirituals to the Archbishop of York, prebendary of Langtoft, and Chancellor. In 1599 he was a member of the Council of the North. In 1597 he was elected for Ripon, in 1601 for York, and again in 1604 for Ripon. He spoke in Parliament in favour of a bill giving to justices summary powers over persons not attending church on the Lord's day, and also argued against monopolies, making Raleigh blush by an adroit reference to monopolies in cards. In 1603 before the Coronation he was knighted. He now became Dean of the Arches, Chancellor to the Queen-Consort, and in 1617 was sent on a special mission to Brussels to procure the punishment of the author and printer of a pasquinade satirizing James and his Court, called *Corona Regis.* He found in Flanders a third wife, a 'large' woman, who was too much for him. Bennet sate on the Commissions of 1620 to put in force the laws of Elizabeth against heretics. In 1621, on Williams' advice, together with a greater man, Lord Bacon, he was impeached for 'divers exorbitant oppressions and bribery' and sale of privileges, and was sentenced to pay the enormous fine of £20,000, together with imprisonment. He died in indigence and obscurity, though it would seem that the sentence had been remitted; for Bacon writes thus to King James: 'Your Majesty hath pardoned the like to sir John Bennett, between whose case and mine (not being partial to myself but speaking out of the general opinion) there was as much difference, I will not say as between black and white, but as between black and grey or ash-coloured.' The King declared that the lawyers 'were so nursed in corruption that they could not leave it off.' Bennet does not appear to have misused any part of the Tesdale money, 'which money, deposited in so careful hands, was advantageously expended,' says Fuller. He was also Bodley's executor. When in 1611 the idea was agitated of completing Bodley's Library by the erection of a quadrangular pile to form the Schools of the University, Bodley wrote as follows to Dr. Singleton the Vice-Chancellor :—

'It may please you to be informed, that where it hath been long desired by the University that God would raise them up an instrument, by whose creddit and care they might be provided of better built Scholes, for their publick professions, than those ruinous Little Roomes with which their turnes, at this present, are with much inconvenience and undecencie served: I have of late upon occasion conferred about it with Sir Jo. BENNETT[1], who, like a true affected sonne to his auncient Mother, hath opened his minde thus farre unto me, that if he thought he should finde sufficient contributors to a worke of that expense, and the assistance of frendes to joyne their helping hand to his, he would not only very willingly undergoe the collection of every man's benevolence, but withall take upon him to see the building itself to be duly performed. . . . I am strong of opinion that, in case the University (having that prevailing power which they may always hold with him in all their occasions) will vouchsafe to take notice of as from one of his forward inclination, to imbrace that imployment, and will in wryting unto him use such hopeful tearmes of speeding as may well befitt a mother to presume upon her childe, he will not only not stagger in condescending to their suite, but set it on foot with such alacritie as they shall soon be advertised that he hath gotten the possession of a rich contribution. For he hath great store of frendes of eminent calling, and he is furnished with meanes to compasse many more, which, in regard of his integritie and abilitie to answer whatsoever he receiveth, will be easily induced to part for such a purpose with liberal sums of money. And that there may be no question of good successe to their desires, I should deem it very requisite that they would also addresse their letters of intreaty to my L. Grace of Canterburie, to my L. their Chauncellor, and to my L. B. of London, that their Lordships would be pleased to take for their motive the true information which I have delivered of Sir *John Bennett's* prone affection, and thereupon proceede to exhort and incite him to undertake the business out of hand.'

The University wrote to Bennet, who replied in a Latin letter promising his best endeavours. His own contribution would be at least a tenth of the entire charge. The day after Bodley's funeral (March 29, 1613) the first stone of the Schools was laid, to the accompaniment of 'musick with voices and other instruments,' by the Vice-Chancellor and Sir John Bennet, who ' offered liberally thereon.' Besides the moneys bequeathed by Bodley, the building absorbed about £4,500 in contributions. Bennet was returned as burgess for the University in 1614 and 1620, but 'removed from sitting.' He died Feb. 15, 1627, and is buried in the Greyfriars Church in Newgate Street, London.

DR. HENRY AYRAY, another Tesdale trustee, was Provost of Queen's from 1599. His puritanical views had got him into trouble at the end of Elizabeth's reign. As Vice-Chancellor, in 1606, he in turn convented a rising B.D. of St. John's, William Laud, for a sermon preached in St. Mary's. His brass in Queen's College Chapel

[1] John Day says, ' The great renowne of the Name of Oxford hath raised up three Worthies, I meane a Bodley, a Bennet, and a Wadham.' (Day's *Dyall,* 1614.)

M

described him as succeeding Bishop Robinson there 'as Elisha Elias,' and he was represented as kneeling with a scroll issuing from his mouth inscribed 'Te sequar.' He died Oct. 10, 1616, aged fifty-seven—'Vivere desiit semper victurus.' His father was William Ayray, favourite servant of Bernard Gilpin, 'the Apostle of the North.'

One of the purchases of realty made out of the Tesdale moneys is of interest, viz. the rectorial tithes, whereof Tesdale held the lease, of Wallingford Allhallows and St. Mary the More. These had been bestowed on the famous abbey of Bec in Normandy by Milo Crispin.

'Wigod of Wallengford held the mannor of Wallengford in King Harold's time and afterward in the dayes of King William I. He had by his wife a certaine daughter whome he gave in marriage to Robert D'oyly. This Robert begat of her a daughter named Mawd who was his heire. Miles Crispin espoused her and had with her the honour aforesaid of Wallengford. After the decease of Miles, King Henry I bestowed the aforesaid Mawd upon Brent Fitz-Court, who both betook themselves to a religious life, and King Henry II seised the honour into his hand [1].'

From the abbey the tithes passed into the hands of Pole and then of Wolsey. Early in the present century the Master and Fellows of Pembroke, desiring certain information about the tithes, entered into a Latin correspondence with the Abbot and monks of Bec, who transmitted an extract from their chancellery relating thereto. The Wallingford tithe amounted to £284 10s. Tesdale's trustees also purchased the Allhallows glebe, the site of the glebehouse, and the freehold of the churchyard. On May 3, 1616, they bought from Thomas Baskervill, for £3,800, Can or Calne Court in the parish of Lydiard Tregooze, Wilts, lately tenanted by Sir Thomas Wroughton, Knt., deceased. £800 remained in their hands.

The date of Tesdale's will is very close to that of the laying of the foundation-stone of Wadham College on July 31, 1610, and to the issue to Thomas Sutton, on June 22, 1611, of letters patents for founding his hospital and free school of Charterhouse. The monastic revenues were all gone. The kings had no money. There was, however, beginning a revival of private benefaction. In the same year, 1610, George Palyn, citizen and girdler of London, gave a large sum to the two Universities.

Little gives the following account of the other co-Founder (p. 71):

---

[1] Wood's *City*, O. H. S., i. 278. The whole was sold, Nov. 29, 1616, by David Bennet to Thomas Freeman for £950.

'RICHARD WIGHTWICK was born at Donnington in the parish of Lilshall, in the county of Salope, & descended from worshipful ancestors, their house yet remaining, called Wightwicke Hall, not far from Wollerhampton in the said county of Salope. He was brought up in learning in Balliol Colledge, Oxford, in which university he profited & proceeded Bachelor in Divinity; & afterward was chaplain to the Right Honorable Henry Lord Norrice of Ricott[1]; and in process of time was preferred to the vicarage of Hampstead Norris and to the parsonage of East Ilsley in the county of Berks, where he now dwelleth. He hath all his time lived a single life, & is a man very prudent, provident, & circumspect in all his actions, diligent & painful in his calling & profession, & just in all his dealings in worldly affairs, & by good desert in his vocation and ministry hath attained to his ecclesiastical promotions. And, moreover, by God's blessing & his own industry, hath also compassed & gotten a fair temporal estate; out of which, he hath now, upon a fit opportunity, supplied with his wealth what was wanting unto Thomas Teasdal's bounty, to make perfect the body of the new-erected College with a convenient & complete company. He hath seen almost fourscore years & yet liveth in perfect health. The form of this college existeth yet in the old building of the aforesaid hall, & therefore it were to be wished, that such as God hath enabled would set their helping hands to the new building therof, in some fairer fashion, & so deserve to be remembered & commended amongst these honorable benefactors to that famous university.'

The family of Wightwick derive their name from the little town of Whitwick, near Ashby-de-la-Zouch, a seat of the hosiery manufacture. In Domesday for Staffordshire Westewic is spoken of as a member of the lordship of Tettenhall Regis. Upon an eminence on the Bridgenorth Road between Tetenhall and Perton still stands the old family mansion. The place belonged to the Wightwicks from King John's time till 1827, when it was sold, together with five other Staffordshire properties. One of these was Dunstall or Tunstall, a fine moated house near Wolverhampton. After the Wars of the Roses a younger son, Thomas, settled at Lilleshall, in Shropshire. He died in 1565; his wife, Elizabeth Moseley, in 1580. They had, it seems, four children,

---

[1] He was the son of Sir Henry Norreys (beheaded May 14, 1536, 'in the cause of *Queen Anne Bullen*') by Mary, daughter of Thomas Fiennes, Lord Dacre of the South. Through his wife Margaret, co-heiress of John Lord Williams of Thame, he acquired the manor of Rycote, Oxon, where he was knighted in 1566, 'being then aged 30 or upwards.' Knight of the shire for Berks and for Oxon; ambassador to France, 1572; Baron Norris of Rycote, 1572. His sire having been attainted, he had an act of restoration of blood 1576. Created M.A. at Oxford April 11, 1588, He died July 1, 1601, and is buried at Rycote, but has a monument in Westminster Abbey. 'He was father (though himself of a meek and mild disposition) to the Martiall brood of the *Norrices*' (Fuller).

Richard, Thomas, William, and Jane[1].   The first of these was the co-Founder of Pembroke.

Richard Wyghtwicke, born about the end of Henry VIII's reign, graduated B.A. from Balliol, July 2, 1580, when he was about thirty-two; M.A. July 4, 1583; B.D. May 31, 1593. Two years later he was presented to the rectory of Albury, Oxon, and in 1607 to that of East Ilsley, Berks. So says Mr. Foster. Little, his contemporary and neighbour, does not mention the Albury preferment. Albury, four miles from Thame, is a tiny parish in the gift of the Earl of Abingdon. Its church is 'a neat modern structure.' Hampstead Norris is a perpetual curacy, now presented to by the Marquess of Downshire. The portrait of Wightwick in Pembroke hall may be by the same hand as that of Tesdale, but it is clearly of the earlier seventeenth century, and not a fancy picture. In Wood's *Historia* (1674) the heads of the co-Founders are given.

NOTE A.

WIGHTWICK'S HOME.

Ilsley is the Hildeslei of Domesday and the Ildesleye of the Valor Ecclesiasticus. Hildes-hlawe is mentioned in Eadred's Grant of 955, the derivation being *Hild* goddess of war, and *hlawe* a hill, or *hild* a battle, and *laeg* a field, for this is one of several places to which the great battle of Ashdown is assigned. The Ridgeway, the old Roman street from Wantage to Silchester, the British Grim's Dyke, and Icknield Street, all pass through Ilsley. At West Ilsley Marco Antonio de Dominis, Archbishop of Spalatro and Primate of Dalmatia[2], was rector in the reign of Charles I; after him Calybute Downing; and King Charles visited there, in 1644, another rector, Goodman, Bishop of Gloucester, who also

---

[1] Among the Lichfield wills Mrs. Mary Grace Wightwick, of Canterbury, tells me she has found that of Thomas Wightwick, dated 1565, containing mention of his son 'Rygard.' The testament of Elizabeth, the widow, appoints as executors 'Richard Wyghtwicke, Wyllyam Wyghtwicke and Jane Wyghtwicke, my children.'

[2] Shortly before this unsatisfactory conformist, who had been much honoured by the University, and by the King preferred to the Deanery of Windsor and sacerdotal rectory of the Savoy, two Carmelite friars, Giulio Cesare Vanini and Giovanni Maria, had endeavoured to obtain preferment from James I, but failing reverted to the papal allegiance, were imprisoned, but escaped from England. Vanini was finally burnt as a heretic at Toulouse. De Dominis also fell between two stools, and died in a Roman prison.

trimmed. (He dedicated a sermon to Cromwell and ended a Romanist.)
The adjoining East or Market Ilsley had formerly the largest sheep fairs,
next to Smithfield, in the kingdom, and in comparatively recent times as
many as eighty thousand sheep have been penned there on the Wednesday
in Easter week.

> 'Ilsley, remote amidst the Berkshire downs,
> Claims these distinctions o'er her sister towns—
> Far-famed for sheep and wool, though not for spinners,
> For sportsmen, doctors, publicans and sinners.'

The allusion in the third line is to a successful resistance to the introduction of the spinning wheel. At an agricultural meeting here some
fleeces shorn in the early morning were sent to Newbury, there manu-
factured into cloth, the coat made of which was returned to East Ilsley
the same day and worn by the chairman that evening at dinner. There
are four racing stables in the parish, in one of which Eclipse was trained
as a yearling, and probably foaled. The 'Butcher' Duke of Cumberland
occupied here a fine house for racing purposes called Keat's Gore. It
was taken down in 1764 except the stables, which George IV later tried to
purchase. The place was in early times one of considerable size, and
there lingers a tradition that, besides a nunnery, there were eight churches
in it. In Domesday it is one of six towns in the county mentioned as
having a priest. The manor was held in 1087 by Geoffrey de Mandeville,
afterwards by the baronial family of Somery, and from the early thirteenth
century by the St. Amands. Almaric de St. Amand had here, *temp.*
Henry III, a gallows and assize of bread and ale (*furcas et assisas panis
et cerevisiae*). In the fifteenth century the manor passed to Gerard de
Braybrooke, and after him to the family of Babington. Then, in 1605, it
came to a local sheepmaster called Hildesley, enriched by the rising
trade, of the same family as Bishop Hilsley who succeeded Fisher at
Rochester; from the Hildesleys in 1650 to the Moores of Fawley; from
them to the Allens of Compton; from them to the Heads of Hodcott; the
present manorial owner is Lord Wantage. The interesting old manor-
house is now a farmhouse.

The parsonage of East Ilsley was given by King John in 1199 to the
Knights Hospitallers of St. John of Jerusalem, who presented for nearly
three centuries. In Wightwick's time the patrons seem to have been the
family of Barnes; one of them, Joseph Barnes, succeeded him in 1630 as
rector. He was ejected by the Parliament in 1654, and 'his leg broken by
a brutal kick from one of the Commissioners.' Afterwards the advowson
belonged to the Kennets. In Pope Nicolas' Valuation the benefice is set
down at fifteen marks, with a pension of 6s. to the priest of Abingdon,
and in Henry's VIII's Valor at £22 13s. 4d. The Church of Our Lady
stands strikingly on the top of the hill on whose slope the village is built.
It is 'a plain church of any date.' After 1199 it was restored, and a south
aisle added, and about 1250 the chancel was restored or rebuilt in the
Early English style, with foliated lancet windows. The arches on one
side of the nave are Transitional. The eastern window is a single lancet

with foliated head, and a circle a little above it. There are traces of
a stair to the rood-loft, and the rood-beam remains embedded in a repul-
sive arch. This, with an extremely ugly north nave aisle, in which the
old Perpendicular windows are inserted, dates from 1845. The fine
Norman font was for some time buried beneath the Jacobean pulpit, in
which probably Wightwick preached. The seventeenth-century oak
seats, bearing the Hildesley arms, have been unfortunately removed.
There is a monument to William Hildesley, dated 1596, and an interesting but mutilated brass (post-Reformation) to his wife Margaret Stonor,
placed by their youngest daughter, a nun. The Hildesleys stuck to the
papal side for several generations, and these monuments in the parish
church are therefore of much interest. The royal arms are those of
Charles II. This church has a low battlemented Early Perpendicular
tower. An inscription on the inside says that it was rebuilt in 1625,
during Wightwick's incumbency; but the mediæval character of the
tower is not impaired. It was re-stuccoed in 1883, when the south aisle
was restored. The nave and aisle roofs are ancient. Of the five bells,
the tenor, weighing nearly a ton, is inscribed 'Richard Wightwick gave
this Bell, 1625'; he gave also an interesting clock, which struck on the
tenor, but had no face. It is said to have been wrought by the village
blacksmith, and bore the date 1627. This was superseded in 1885 by
a fine modern clock which displays as well as sounds the hours. Who
in Wightwick's simple days required to know the time within sixty
minutes[1]?

The older registers were destroyed in the Rebellion. But of those
which date from 1653 the very first entry is the marriage of a Richard
Wightwicke to Mary Westall, and the name, spelt with an 'e' at the end,
is of frequent occurrence down to the middle of the eighteenth century.
Rector Richard was a celibate; but in his will, besides a Richard
Wightwicke of Albrighton, Salop, he mentions 'Richard, son of Thomas
Wightwick, my kinsman,' and a cousin Samuel, as well as kinsmen of
other names, who having no residence specified were doubtless of East
Ilsley. The co-Founder of Pembroke then belongs to a family which had
struck root at Ilsley. It is impossible to say how he came to be presented
to the rectory. His body lies in the chancel, the spot unmarked by any
stone. As appears by his will, he left a small charity to the poor of the
parish, which has vanished. Perhaps it was recorded on an old table of
charities, the last fragments of which the present incumbent, the Rev.
T. R. Terry, F.R.A.S.,[2] remembers to have seen.

Ilsley lies pleasantly among the lonely downs, its position marked for
many a mile by a solitary three-sailed windmill. It contains one or two
handsome houses of the Queen Anne period, and the Swan Inn was

[1] In 1633 a person writing from Barnstaple to London could get an answer
in eleven days, three of which were allowed as a reasonable interval for the
meditating and composing of the answer. This was deemed quite a dashing
return of post. *Felicia saecula!*
[2] Sometime Fellow and Bursar of Magdalen. I am indebted to Mr. Terry for
much kind assistance. Magdalen College are the patrons since 1829.

probably there in Wightwick's time. The old rectory was destroyed thirty or forty years ago. The rectors had ceased to live in it, but it was sometimes used for a curate. The present population is 519. In 1841 it was 733.

A grandson of Richard's first cousin Humphrey, George Wightwick, acted as curate at East Ilsley in the last year of Richard's life. He is said to have brought all his family with him from Patshull, Salop, in that year. Richard's kinsman, Walter Wightwick, was buried at Ilsley in 1622.

NOTE B.

WILLS OF THE CO-FOUNDERS.

That parte of MR. THOMAS TISDALE his last Will and Testament which concerns the College.

'Item Whereas God hath blessed me in my worldly state with increase of substance, I being minded and resolved to dedicate some good part thereof together also with some of my kindred in more especial manner to his glory and service of the church, do therefore give and bequeath unto the reverend Father in God George Abbott, Doctor of Divinity, now Bishoppe of London, Sir John Bennet Knight, and Henry Ayry, D^r of Divinity, the sum of five thousand pounds of lawful English mony, to be payd by mine executors within convenient tyme after my decease, upon special trust and confidence in them reposed, and to the intent and purpose that they shall as soone after the receipt of the said summe as conveniently they can disburse the same in and for the purchase of some lands, tenements, and hereditaments in Fee simple of the yearly value of two hundred and fifty pounds at the least, holden in free and common soccage, and of cleere and undoubted title not subject to any incumbrance, or doubt of eviction, as they easily may gett, at twenty yeares purchase or under; the yearly rents, revenues, and proffitte of which lands and tenements my will is shall be imployed and disposed to and for the maintenance and sustentation of thirteene Schollers in Balliol Colledge in the University of Oxford, if there they may be conveniently placed and entertained according to the purpose of this my will; and if not, then in University Colledge in Oxford, if there they may be so placed and entertained; and if not, then in some such other Colledge within the University, as my said devisees and trusty friends shall think and finde fitt for that purpose[1]; And my will is that sixe of the sayd Schollers shall perpetually be of my

[1] The Patent of Foundation, reciting Tesdale's will, merely says, 'in some College within our University to be elected.'

kindred, and of the poorer sorte of them, And the other seven of the poorer sort of such as are or shall be borne in Abingdon, and as poor Schollers of Mr. William Bennett my kinsman deceased, brought up in the school there, if amonge them fitt choyce may be made; else of others of the said Schoole and there brought up, being capable apt and likely in some good measure to prove Schollers, if such can there be found; and that sixe of those thirteene shall be called poore Schollers or Abingdonians, whereof two being of my kindred shall be of such as are brought up and instructed in the said Schoole of Abingdon, if such there can be found, and shall have the yearly mayntenance of fifteene pounds by the year to each of them; and the other foure twelve pounds by year to each of them, and the other seaven shall have yearly each of them five and twenty pounds for their maintenance, whereof those foure which are to be of my kindred my will is shall be taken out of the said Schoole of Abingdon if there such may be found answerable to my intent, if not, then out of any other Schoole in England.   And my will is that election of such Schollers (to be taken into the sayd Colledge) shall be made by the Master, Head, or Governor for the tyme being of such Colledge in which they shall be placed and the two senior fellowes of the same Colledge and by the Mastcr and two senior Governors of the hospital of Christ in Abingdon for the time being, and by the Schoolemaster of the said Schoole for the time being; and that from tyme to tyme after the first election, in case any of those to whom the greater and more liberal maintenance is allowed happen to dye or to be remooved, that then one of the sixe poore Schollers or Abingdonians shall be chosen and taken into his place and roome; and if he so dying or removed shall be one of the foure of my kindred, then one of those two poore Schollers of my kindred to be taken into his roome; and if not, then one of the others; and that those thirteene Schollers shall be tyed to perfourme such exercises of learning, and be subject to such censures and punishments, as well for default and neglect therein as for not comming to prayers, and for all and every other defaulte and misdemeanors as other fellowes and Schollers of the said Colledge are and be.   And that they shall within one yeere or sooner after they shall be of sufficient time and continuance in the University proceede Masters of Arts and enter into the ministry within three years or sooner after their being Masters of Arts.   And in case any of them shall have and obtayne any Benefice with cure of soules, then my will and meaning is, that within six months after his being admitted and instituted to the said Benefice, he shall relinquish his place and maintenance in the Colledge, and an other shall be chosen in his place.   And to the end my sayd thirteene Schollers may be more fully and perfectly incorporated in the body of such Colledges, and in other points not by me mentioned nor contrary to the purpose of this my will be ordered ruled and governed by and according to the statutes of the same, and be capable of Lectures and other offices, as other fellowes and Schollers of and in the said Colledge are, my will and desire is that the said 6 poore Schollers or Abingdonians may be received and admitted to be Schollers of the said Colledge, and the other seaven to be fellowes of the same.   And if that so may be

effected, that then my said devisees do in such sorte as may stand with
the performance of this my will, or the substance and effecte thereof,
conveye and assure to the said Colledge by their true and right names of
incorporation, the said lands, Tenements, and Hereditaments so to be
purchased, license of Mortmaine to receive the same being first had and
obtained. And to the intent the said Colledge nor the members thereof
may no way receive losse hindrance or detriment by this admission to
their body and participation with them I further will in recompence of
such participation, the said Colledge do injoy and receive of the annuall
proffitte of the premisses yearly thirty and six pounds, the same to be
taken out of the said yearley allowance of five and twenty pounds by
yeare appoynted to each of the seaven of the said Schollers, so as each
of them so accepted into fellowshippe shall have only twenty pounds by
yeare, ten pounds of the said thirty and sixe pounds to the Master or
head of the said Colledge for the increase of his maintenance. And the
sixe and twenty pounds residue to and for the body of the same Colledge;
and if neede be building rooms and chambers in the said Colledge for the
said fellowes and Schollers my will is that the placeing of the said seaven
to whom larger allowance is appointed as aforesaid, to be forborne untill
with the same yearly allowance such rooms and chambers may be there
built. And that in the meane time, only the sixe poore Schollers be
chosen and placed, out of whom after building of the sayd roomes and
defraying of the charge thereof, five of the said seaven may be supplied.
And to the intent that all questions, doubts, debates, and controversies
touching the election, ordering, placing, and displacing of thirteene
Schollers and Fellowes, and other the operation of this my will touching
them and their revenues to their maintenance designed, may be with ease
and without great charge composed and decided, my will mind and desire
is that the Vice Chancellor of the University of Oxon for the tyme being,
the Provost of Queenes Colledge for the tyme being, and the President of
Corpus Christi Colledge for the tyme being, or any two of them agreeing
together, shall and may arbitrate, adjudge, and decide the same, unlesse
that some matter of great moment and difficulty arise, whereof they
cannot well agree and determine, which I will and desire may in such
case be referred to the decision of the Bishoppe of London for the tyme
being. And in case necessity shall require an Act of Parliament to be
made for the full and perfect settling, establishing, and ordering of the
premisses touching the said Schollers according to mine intent and meaning hereby declared, my will is that the charge thereof be saved and
reserved out of the sayd greater yearly maintenance to and for the seaven
appointed as for and touching the building is before limited.'

RICHARD WIGHTWICK'S Will was enrolled in the Prerogative Court
of Canterbury.

' In the name of God Amen.

' I Richard Wightwicke of East Ilsley in the countie of Berks Clerke
being weake in bodie but of good and perfect memory Doe make this my

last will and testament in manner and forme followinge ffirst I commend
my soul to God through the intercession of Christ Jesus hopeinge and
stedfastly beleeving to have all my sinnes pdoned through the merritts of
my blessed Saviour and I will that my bodie bee decently buried in the
Chauncell of the pish church of Ilesley where now I am Rector Item
touchinge the disposinge of my outward estate wch it hath pleased god
to blesse me withall ffirst I give and bequeath to the poore of the towne
of Ilesley three pounds to bee paid unto them wthin two moneths after
my decease Item I give and bequeath unto the parish of
Hamsteed Norris three pounds to bee paid unto them wthin two moneths
after my decease Item I give and bequeath unto my kinsman Edward
Meare all that my house and lands with Thapptennce wch I bought
of Lawrence Hide lyinge in Cheevely in the Countie of Berks To have
and to hold to him y° said Edward and heires for ever Item I give and
bequeath unto the M^r ffellowes and schollers of Pembroke Colledge in
Oxon (of wch Colledge I am a Cofounder) one afiuity or rent charge of
ten pounds per Annum issuing out of the lands of Thomas Hinde which
annuity I entended when I bought it and accordingly doe now bequeath
it unto the said Mr Fellowes and schollers and theire successo^{rs} for ever
to the use and benefitt of the said M^r and his successo^{rs} And I will that
this shalbe in discharge of my promise wch I made to them of giving
them two hundred pounds for the purchasinge of tenne pounds per annum
and my meaninge is and accordingly I doe will that the two hundred
pounds wch the tenants were to paye for the purchaseinge of the said ten
pounds per annum bee paid to my executors towards the payment of my
debts otherwise if the M^r ffellowes and schollers will not accept of this
ten pounds per annum (as I hope they must and will) then I give and
bequeath the said rent charge or annuity of tenn pounds issuinge out of
the lands aforesaid to Samuell Wightwicke Esqr for ever towards the
payments of my debts and satisfyinge of my legacies Item I give and
bequeath unto Richard Wightwick the sonne of Thomas Wightwick my
kinsman fortie pounds Item I give and bequeath unto Richard Meare
and William Meare the sonnes of Jeffery Meare deceased each of them
Twentie pounds apeese Item I give and bequeath unto Edward Meare
Robert Meare and Richard Meare the sonnes of Richard Meare my
kinsman each of them twentie pounds apeece Item I give unto Richard
Wightwicke the sonne of Francis Wightwicke of Albrighton in the
Countie of Salop Twentie pounds Item I give and bequeath unto Isabell
Wightwicke the wife of Henry Smith five pounds and to her two children
fortie shillings apeece wch severall legacies I will shalbe paid unto them
wthin one yeare after my decease And if any of them die before the
legacies bee paid unto them then my will is that the legacies of such of
them soe dyinge shalbee equallie devided amongst the brothers and sisters
of the child soe dyinge Item I give and bequeathe unto Richard Prise
sonne of Mr Prise of fframebrough ten pounds to bee paid wthin one
yeare Item I give and bequeath unto the children of Katherin Meare
the wife of John Smith fifteene pounds to bee devided amongst her
children and for the faithfull performance of this my will I make my

aforesaid loveinge Cosen Samuell Wightwicke Execut[or] of this my last Will and Testament revokeing all other and former wills hopeinge that he will carefullie see this my last Will performed and observed according to my appointment In witness whereof I have hereunto sett my hand and seale the eleaventh day of January Anno Dni one thousand six hundred twenty nine—Richard Wightwicke—sealed subscribed and published in the presence of John Price[1] Samuell Whichcote Thomas Wightwicke.'

Proved 3rd }
Feby 1629 }

[1] From Price of Framborough the present Master is directly descended. The Smiths were a West Ilsley family. Shortly after Wightwick's decease the College bought the lease of the Clapcot tithes in the parish of Allhallows, Wallingford. For the reversion of these it paid in 1873 £663 to the Ecclesiastical Commissioners.

PYM'S SIGNATURE (*see page* 147).

PEDIGREE A.

THE TESDALE FAMILY IN CENTURIES XVI AND XVII.

JOHN TESDALE ' of the North.'

A son, died in Northants, not far from Daventry, leaving issue.

John, took the surname of Cliffe on entering religion; *bur.* April 28, 1540, being there; Prior of the late dissolved Monastery of Abingdon, as by the Register of St. Nicholas in Abingdon appeareth.

Thomas, brought from the north by his brother John, who placed him in the parsonage of Hanney, Berks, and afterwards settled him in Fitzharris farm in Sandford nth Stanford Deanley; styled 'Old Thomas.' = 1. 1500, Elizabeth Sharpe of Hanney.

Elizabeth, *b.* 1517. = 1541, Thomas *Dyringe.*
    Thomas, *b.* 1542. Jasper, *b.* 1544.

Margery, *b.* 1511. = — *Maidsins* of London.

Richard (1509-97), sadler of Abingdon; bred up the co-Founder.

Richard, *ob.* 1602, sadler; Governor of Christ's Hospital 1583; Master 1590. = Mary Meadows Chickin ¹ (= (2) Rich. Curtin, Mayor 1622, 1626.)

Elizabeth, *ob.* 1658 = Rich. *Dews* of Harwell, esq., High Sheriff of Berks.

Fourteen children.

Jone, *bur.* Nov. 8, 1549, at Stanford. Ann.

Thomas, 'of Fitzharris in Sandford Deanley,' 1507-56. = (1), 1534, Cecilia Hyde of Culham (died of the plague 1545).

Elizabeth, *b.* 1535. = Richard *Bonsal.* See Pedigree B.

Thomas, *b.* 1537. John, *b.* 1539. Margery, *b.* 1541. Francis, *b.* 1543. William, *b.* 1545. All five died of the plague, 1545.

Ann Molins (3). See Pedigree B.

(T. T.) Joan, dau. of (2) Wm. Knapp of Harcourt, Berks.

THOMAS (1547-1610). = June 10, 1567, Maud Stone (1545-1616).

A daughter.

John (c. 1505-78), born at Hanney; held an office in Abingdon Abbey; called 'Old John' in the Interrogatories. = Joan, dau. of Richard Prince of Nuneham Courtnay.

See next page.

¹ Sister, I think, of Richard Cheekyn, Mayor 1613, 1623, and 1631. By her will (Dec. 17, 1644) she devised her house in West St. Helen's Street for a dole of bread to twelve poor men and twelve poor women on the Sabbath of each week.

PEDIGREE A (*continued*).

DESCENDANTS OF THOMAS TESDALE'S UNCLE, JOHN TESDALE.

JOHN TESDALE (c. 1505-78).

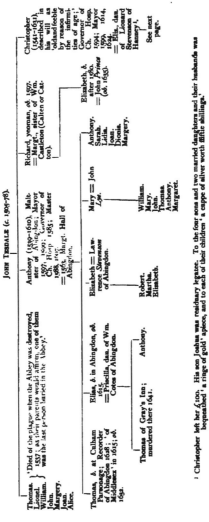

Thomas. } 'Died of the plague when the Abbey was destroyed,
Lionel. } 1537; as their parents would affirm, one of them
John.   } was the last person buried in the 'Abbey.'
Margery.
Joan.
Alice.

Anthony (1539-1610). Maltster of Abingdon; Mayor
1597, 1609; Governor of
Ch. Hosp. 1585; Master
1588, 1607.
= 1562, Margt. Hall of
Abingdon.

Richard, yeoman, *ob.* 1597.
= Margt., sister of Wm.
Castleton (Calten or Cat-
ton).

Christopher
(1541-1631),
described in
his will as
'old and feeble
by reason of
the infirmi-
ties of age';
Governor of
Ch. Hosp.
1594; Mayor
1599, 1614,
1624.
= Eliz., dau.
of Lionard
Stevenson of
Hanney[1].

See next
page.

Elizabeth, *b.*
after 1560.
= John *Prince*
(*ob.* 1635).

Anthony.
Sarah.
Lidia.
Joan.
Dionisia.
Margery.

Thomas, *b.* at Culham
Parsonage; Recorder
of Abingdon 1628; 'of
Middlesex' in 1615; *ob.*
1692.

Elias, *b.* in Abingdon, *ob.*
1615.
= Priscilla, dau. of Wm.
Cotes of Abingdon.

Elizabeth = Law-
rence Stevenson
of Abingdon.

Mary = John
Lye.

Thomas of Gray's Inn;
murdered there 1641.

Anthony.

Robert.
Martha.
Elizabeth.

William.
Mary.
John.
Thomas.
Anthony.
Margaret.

[1] Christopher left her £100. His son Joshua was residuary legatee. To the four sons and two married daughters and their husbands was
bequeathed 'a ringe of gold' apiece, and to each of their children 'a cuppe of silver worth fiftie shillings.'

PEDIGREE A (continued).

DESCENDANTS OF THOMAS TESDALE'S COUSIN, CHRISTOPHER TESDALE.

CHRISTOPHER TESDALE (1541–1631).

John (1581–1670), b. at Calham Parsonage; Mayor 1648. = Eliz. Kent of Abingdon.

Martha, b. 1578 at Calham: ob. coelebs. Benjamin, b. 1583 at Abingdon, Mayor 1637, Twice married. Ann, b. at Abingdon 1585; ob. coel. Frances, b. at Abingdon 1598.

Christopher, b. in Abingdon 1591; Original Fellow; Canon of Chichester and of Wells; Member of Assembly of Divines.

Elizabeth, b. at Abingdon 1591. = (1) Dr. Thomas Godwyn, Original Fellow; bur. at Brightwell. = (2) Jonathan Nunne.

Marmaduke (1649–87), Fellow 1671.

Joshua (1595–1643), b. in Abingdon; surgeon or bonesetter[1] there; Mayor 1642. = Jane ——

John, b. at Abingdon 1616; Fellow of Pembroke (?1632); Chaplain to K. Charles I.; Member of Assembly of Divines: ob. coelebs after 1695.

Thomas, mercer, of Oxford Thrice married.

Christopher, died young. Elizabeth = Fras. Payne, Mayor of Abingdon. Catherine = Edw. Brooks. Martha = Anth. Hearne. Frances = Philip Lockton. Dorothy = William Elliker, R. of Frilsham, Berks.

John, living 1695. Thomas. Elizabeth = Isaac Coil of Salisbury: ob. 1673.

Christopher (1641–1675). Fellow 1668; Rector of Hurstbourne Tarrant. = Susanna Bunny (1652–92).

Richard, mercer, of Oxford: ob. 1670.

Benjamin, upholster, of London. = Sarah, dau. of Thomas Penniman of Yorks.

Elizabeth, unmar. 1695.

Christopher, surgeon, of Abingdon. = Lydia, dau. of Jasper Bottlemaker, mercer, of Faringdon.

Joshua, living 1695; = Jane, dau. of Wm. Dickinson, of Fittsharris Farm.

Thomas, joyner, of London: ob. c. 1680.

Christopher, b. 1672; Fellow 1690. Elizabeth, ob. coelebs. Susannah = Wm. Sly of Newbury.

Frances, b. 1639, in 1695 'an old maiden.' Hannah, twice married. Elizabeth = Geo. Eaton, of Abingdon.

Richard, silkman, of London. ? Expelled from Roysse's School 1671. = Elizabeth Gray, s. p.

Joseph, b. 1665; mercer, of Abingdon. = Mary Spencer of Oxford.

Jasper, unmar. in 1695. ? Expelled from Roysse's school 1671.

Christopher = Mary, dau. of John Meaks.

Joshua, William, Jane, Mary.

? Thomas, in 1695 a soldier in Flanders = Frances Green of Abingdon.

Elizabeth, unmar. in 1695.

John, b. 1660, mercer, of Abingdon. = Jane, dau. of Mark Alder of Drayton.

John.

---

[1] One Mr. Thomas Tisdale intervened on behalf of the Oxford townsmen's rights in a dispute with the proctors, Aug. 1677 (Wood's *Life and Times*, ii. 383).

PEDIGREE B.

BENNET-TESDALE DESCENTS.

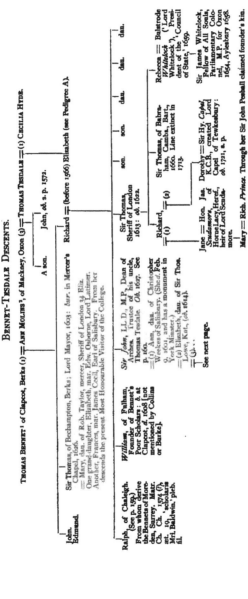

THOMAS BENNET[1] of Clapcot, Berks (1) = ANN MOLINS[2], of Mackney, Oxon (3) = THOMAS TESDALE[3] = (1) CECILIA HYDE.

John, ob. s. p. 1572.

A son.

Richard = (before 1566) Elizabeth (see Pedigree A).

John. Edmund.

Sir Thomas, of Beckhampton, Berks; Lord Mayor, 1603: bur. in Mercer's Chapel, 1626. Mary, dau. of Rob. Taylor, mercer, Sheriff of London 34 Eliz. One grand-daughter, Elizabeth, mar. Edw. Osborne, Lord Latimer. Another, Frances, mar. James Cecil, Earl of Salisbury. From her descends the present Most Honourable Visitor of the College.

William, of Fulham, Founder of Bennet's Poor Scholars: *d.* 1608 [not mentioned by Collins or Burke].

Ralph, of Claeigh. (See p. 159.) From whom derive the Bennets of Morden, Surrey. Matr. Ch. Ch. 1574 (?), æt. 19, 'scholaris fil.' Mr[s]. Baldwin. 'pleb. fil.

Sir *John*, LL.D., M.P., Dean of Arches. Trustee of his uncle, Thomas Tesdale. *Ob.* 1627. See p. 160. —(1) Ann, dau. of Christopher Weekes of Salisbury. (She *d.* Feb. 9, 1614, and has a monument in York Minster.) —(2) Elizabeth, dau. of Sir Thos. Lowe, Knt., (*ob.* 1614).

See next page.

Sir Thomas, Sheriff of London 1613: *ob.* 1622.

Richard, ‖ (1) ‖ (2)

Jane = Hon. Jas. *Scudamore*, of Hornelacy, Heref., heir of Lord Scudamore.

Sir Thomas, of Babraham, Cambs., Bart., 1660. Line extinct in 1713.

Dorothy = Sir Hy. *Capel*, K.C.B., created Lord Capel of Tewkesbury: *ob.* 1721, s. p.

Mary = Rich. *Prince*. Through her Sir John Pettall claimed founder's kin.

son. son. son. dau. dau. dau.

Rebecca = Bulstrode *Whitelock* ('Lord Whitelock'), President of the Council of State,' 1659.

Sir James Whitelock, Fellow of All Souls, Parliamentary Colonel, M.P. for Oxon 1664, Aylesbury 1658.

dau.

[1] In Wallingford Allhallows Church, now pulled down, was an inscription: 'This is the monument of Thomas Bennet, of Clapcot, Esqre., who had issue Thomas Bennet, Citizen and Alderman of London, his third sonne, who gave twenty pounds yearly for ever to fifteen poor people of the town of Wallingford.' John Bennet was one of the gentlemen of the county in 1433. [2] Tesdale's widow, however, was named Agnes. See p. 155. He can hardly have had a fourth wife. Adam Molins, dean of Sarum, founded the school and chantry at Oxyngham, Berks.

PEDIGREE B (*continued*).

SIR JOHN BENNET, M.P., LL.D. = (1) Ann Weekes.

Elizabeth = (1616) - *Gregorie*, Esq.

other issue.

Arthur, *ob.* 1692.

Anne, *ob.* 1693.

John, *ob.* 1773.

Grey, *b.* 1704.

Sir Thomas, of Babraham, born at York 1592, Fellow of All Souls 1611, D.C.L. 1661, Knighted 1661, Master in Chancery 1645-?).
= (1) Charlotte, dau. of Wm Harrison of London (*ob.* 1658).
= (2) Thomasine, dau. and co-heir of Geo. Dethick, Esq., son of Sir W. Dethick, Garter King.

Sir Henry, K.G. (1620 1685). Student of Christ Church 1696. Created Viscount Thetford and Earl of Arlington 1665. Member of the Cabal; Secretary of State; Lord Chamberlain = Isabella, dau. of Lewis de Nassau, Lord of Beverweert and Count of Nassau.

Isabella = Henry Fitzroy, first Duke of *Grafton*, natural son of King Charles II.

Charles Duke of Grafton, Earl of Arlington.

Sir John, of Dawley (Arlington), (1589-1696), Matr. Christ Church 1605 (of Wilts); knighted at Theobalds 1616. = Dorothy, dau. of Sir John Crofts, of Saxham, Suffolk, Knt. (*ob.* 1659).

Henry, 'a little crooked, despicable, fellow' (*L.* 4 *T.* ii. 304), *ob.* 1686.

Sir John Bennet, K.C.B., *b.* 1618 ('Knight Benet?), created *Baron Ossulston* 1682: *ob.* 1695. Benefactor.
= (1) Elizabeth, widow of Edm. Sheffield, second Earl of Mulgrave, and dau. of Lionel Cranfield, Earl of Middlesex. No issue.
= (2) Bridget, dau. of John Howe, Esq., of Langnor, Notts, sister of Scroop, Ld. Viscount Howe (*ob.* 1703).

Dorothy, *ob.* 1694.

Arabella = John, Lord *Burleigh*, *ob.* 1697.

John, *ob.* 1773.

Charles, second baron, created Earl of Tankerville 1714 = in 1695, Lady Mary Grey, only dau. and heiress of Forde, Lord Grey of Werk, Visc. Grey of Glendale, and fifth Earl of Tankerville, at whose death that viscounty and earldom expired, till the latter was revived in the person of his son-in-law. (She died 1710.)

Bridget, *b.* 1696 = John, first Earl of *Portsmouth*.

Sir Charles, Earl of Tankerville, K.T., *b.* 1697.

Annabel, *b.* 1698 = (1721), Lord Wm. *Paulet*, second son of Charles, first Duke of Bolton.

Mary, *b.* 1701 = (1720) Wm. *Willmer*, Esq., M.P., of Sywell, Notts.

Henry, *b.* 1702.

Grey, *b.* 1704.

The present Earl, Charles Augustus Bennet, P.C., is the sixth in this line. He bears, as a second crest, for Bennet, out of a mural coronet, or, a lion's head, gu., charged on the neck with a bezant. In right of descent from Edward I the Earl of Tankerville is entitled to quarter the royal arms of Edmund Plantagenet.

PEDIGREE C¹.

DESCENTS OF RICHARD WIGHTWICK, CO-FOUNDER.

Of those whose names are marked thus * the College possesses portraits.

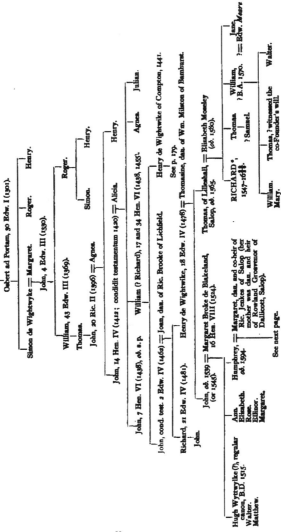

WILLIAM DE WIGHTWICK.

Julian.

Osbert ad Portam, 30 Edw. I (1301).

Simon de Wightwyke = Margaret.   Roger.   Henry.

John, 4 Edw. III (1330).

William, 43 Edw. III (1369).

Thomas.

Roger.   Simon.   Henry.

John, 20 Ric. II (1396) = Agnes.

John, 14 Hen. IV (1412; condidit testamentum 1420) = Alicia.   Henry.

John, 7 Hen. VI (1428), ob. s.p.   William (? Richard), 17 and 34 Hen. VI (1438, 1455).   Agnes.   Julian.

Henry de Wightwike of Compton, 1441. See p. 179.

John, cond. test. 2 Edw. IV (1462) = Joan, dau. of Ric. Brooke of Lichfield.

Henry de Wightwike, 18 Edw. IV (1478) = Thomasine, dau. of Wm. Milston of Barnhurst.

Richard, 21 Edw. IV (1481).
John.

Thomas, of Lilleshall, = Elizabeth Moseley
Salop, ob. 1565.   (ob. 1560).

John, ob. 1559 = Margaret Broke de Blakeland,
(or 1545)   16 Hen. VIII (1524).

Humphrey, = Margaret, dau. and co-heir of
ob. 1594.   Ric. Jenks of Salop (her
              mother was dau. and heir
              of Rowland Grosvenor of
              Dallicot, Salop).
See next page.

RICHARD*,
1547-1618.

Thomas.   William,   Jane,
?Samuel.   ?B.A. 1570. = Edw. Mears

Thomas, ? witnessed the
co-Founder's will.

William.   Walter.
Mary.

Ann.
Elizabeth.
Rose.
Ellinor.
Margaret.

Hugh Wyttwylke (?), regular
canon, B.D. 1515.
Walter.
Matthew.

¹ The earlier part of this pedigree follows Erdeswicke's MS. *History of Staffordshire*, written about 1595. Shaw's *Staffordshire* and Jones's *History of Tettenhall* vary from it in some points.

PEDIGREE C (continued).

DESCENT OF FRANCIS WIGHTWICK[1] OF WOMBRIDGE, AND OF STUBBS, HUSBAND OF MRS. DOROTHEA[1] WIGHTWICK, FROM THE CO-FOUNDER'S COUSIN HUMPHREY.

HUMPHREY WIGHTWICK (ob. 1594).

George, of Clifford's Joyce = John *Granger*. Margaret = Francis *Tomkis*. John, 1540-96; of Clifford's Inn; Inn, ob. 1612. *bur.* at Wolverhampton = (?) 1575, Alice Okden.

George, b. 1578, curate at E. Ilsley, 1630.

Waler, 1583-1622, *bur.* at E. Ilsley.

Francis, *bur.* at Tettenhall, 1616; grant of Arms, 1612 = Margaret Moreton of Engleton.

Samuel, b. 1602 (? 1592) of Berks; Prothonotary of King's Bench; exor. of co-Founder; = (2) Abigail Wright, of Brookset, Essex.

Francis, b. 1576 at Pattingham, Staffs.; of Albrighton, Salop.

Richard (see co-Founder's will).

John, ? of Wolverhampton, adm. of Emmanuel Coll., Camb., Apr. 4, 1646; intruded Fellow of St. John's, Oxford, 1651-62; = Jane Pritchard.

Peter. Samuel. Humphrey = Lettice Vernon. George. Mary. Abigail = (1) Sir H. *Williams*, bart.; = (2) Sir T. *Lane*, knt.

Seven children.

Abigail. Dorothy.

Alexander, 1587-1648, of = (1) Anne, dau. and Wightwick; matr. Oriel, coheir of 1604; student of Inner John Hant, Temple; compounded for of Shrews-knighthood; *bur.* at Tet-bury. tenhall.

(2) Alice Lane, of Bentley Hall.

John = Mary, dau. of Ric. James, of Shrewsbury.

Francis = Thomasine, dau. and coheir of John Dennis, of Weymouth, merchant.

Mary = James, son of Sir James *Beverley*.

James, of Lawrence Waltham, Berks, esqre. = Mary Radge[*].

Thomas, York Herald 1717. Francis. Martha.

William, of Albrighton, Salop; = Catherine Lattyge.

FRANCIS, 1711-83, of Wombridge.

Sarah = Ric. *Bruce Fyrdde*. Samuel, *ob.* coelebs, 1684.

Margaret = Edw. *Jordon*, of Prior's Leigh, Salop.

Francis of Wightwick and Tunstall, Staffs., 1616-92. Matr. Pembroke, Oct. 10, 1634. Of Inner Temple, 1646; = Elia. dau. of Ric. Pyott, esqre., High Sheriff of Staff.

Jane, *ob.* coel.

Richard, b. 1655 = Martha (? Elizabeth) dau. of Thos. Willet, of Fulham.

William = (1) Sir

Elizabeth = John Adams.

Humphrey, Fellow 1673. *William* (Johnson's tutor).

Elizabeth, A 1652 = Roland Fryer (? Thomas, Staffs. 1694-1703), Univ. Coll. 1692. Left issue.

Thomas = Ann Tristram. Great-grandparents of Stubbs Wightwick[*], of Great Bloxwich, J.P., D.L. (ob. 1828). = DOROTHEA, 3rd dau. of Ric. Fryer, esqre., M.P., of the Wergs, Staffs. The main Wightwick line ended with him.

William Adams[*], Master.

Dr. *William Adams*[*], Master.

Elizabeth, Anne. Granada.

Francis, 1683-1724; Bencher of Middle Temple; = Elizabeth, dau. of James Hancox, of Worvil, Salop; clerk (she died 1726).

William, of Albrighton, Salop; = Elizabeth Fryer (? Thomas, Staffs. ...

Hancox[*], *ob.* coelebs, 1731.

Rev. *John*, matr. Pemb. 1729; ?Fellow, 1731. Left issue.

Francis, *ob.* 1715. Elizabeth, *ob.* 1726. James, *ob.* 1740.

¹ *Vide infra*, among Benefactors.   ¹ Aunt to Jane Lane, who saved King Charles II after Worcester fight.

PEDIGREE C (continued).

COLLATERAL BRANCH OF THE WIGHTWICK FAMILY.

HENRY DE WIGHTWICK, 1441.

Thomas Whitwick.

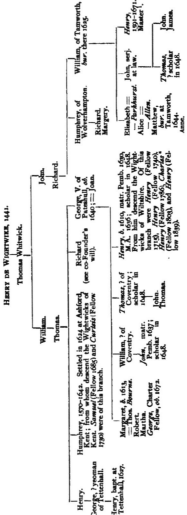

¹ To 'my sonne Henrye Wightwicke' were left by his father 'my best gowne, my best satten suits of apparell, my cloake, my saddle, and all my bookes.'

CHAPTER XIV.

NATALITIA AND STATUTES.

THE Letters Patents and the Charter of Mortmain, dated on the festival of St. Peter the Apostle (June 29), 1624, were read in the common hall on August 5, and at the same time the new Master, Fellows, and Scholars were formally admitted. There was present a large and distinguished company, including the Vice-Chancellor, Dr. Prideaux, Robert Lord Dormer, afterwards Earl of Carnarvon, and William Dormer his brother[1], Sir Francis Godolphin[2], knight, Sir John Smith, knight, Dr. Daniel Featley[3] (Archbishop Abbot's chaplain), the Proctors, a great number of other Masters, and the Mayor, Recorder, and principal Burgesses of Abingdon. The co-Founder, Richard Wightwick, was, it seems, not present. He lived at no great distance, at East Ilsley, but was advanced in years.

[1] Both entered Exeter this year. Lord Carnarvon fell at Newbury in 1643, being lieutenant-general of the King's forces. Sir Fleetwood Dormer, a cousin, entered Pembroke in 1634. He settled in Virginia.

[2] He entered Exeter June 25, 1624. Sidney Earl of Godolphin, Lord High Treasurer, was his third son.

[3] Or Fairclough (Fertlow), son of the cook of Magdalen and C. C. C. He was fellow of Corpus. While chaplain to the embassy at Paris he had much learned controversy with the doctors of the Sorbonne. His rectory at Acton was occupied in 1642 by the Roundheads, who taking him 'to be a Papist, or at least that he had a Pope in his belly, they drank and eat up his Provision, burnt down a Barn of his full of Corn, and two Stables, the loss amounting to 211*l.*, and at the same time did not only greatly profane the Church there by their beastly actions, but also burnt the rails, pull'd down the Font, broke the windows and I know not what' (*Athenae*, ii. 37). They also sought him in the Church to murder him. Featly was however placed in the Assembly of Divines, but, excepting to the Covenant, was judged by the Commons 'to be a Spye and a betrayer of the Parliaments cause, was seised upon, committed Prisoner to the Lord *Petre's* house, and his Rectories taken away.' He was allowed, however, to go to Chelsea College, of which he was Provost, to die. Though a Calvinist, his character and polemical abilities are highly extolled by Wood. 'He was of small stature, yet he had a great soul and had all learning compacted in him. He was most seriously and soundly pious and devout.' See *Life and Times*, ii. 244, n. 3.

When he made his will, four and a half years later, he was 'weak in body.'

Having recited the terms of the Tesdale benefaction, the Patent (as quoted in Wood MS.) proceeds :—

'And wheras also Richard Wightwike doth intent to name and elect certaine other fellowes and scholars from yᵉ said schoole into some certaine coll. in yᵉ universitie for yᵉ maintenance of whom he doth indeavour to settle lands and tenements for their maintenance, and there-upon yᵉ Major Ballives and Burgesses of Abingdon supplicated yᵉ King yᵗ he (Will: E. of pembr. chanc. of yᵉ universitie granting his consent) would grant yᵗ within broadgates hall in yᵉ university of Oxon he would constitute a Colledge consisting of Mʳ fellowes and scholars and yᵗ he would grant to yᵉ sᵈ Mʳ and fellowes yᵗ they might be made capable to receive lands tenements and hereditaments, the King ordaines and con-stitutes yᵗ within yᵉ said hall of Brodgates be one perpetuall coll of divinity civil and common law arts medicine and other good arts and yᵗ it shᵈ consist of one Mʳ 10 fellowes and 10 graduat or non-graduate scholars. And yᵉ King further grants yᵗ it shᵈ be a body politick known by yᵉ name of *the Master Fellows and Scholars of the foundation of King James at the cost and charges of Thomas Tesdale and Richard Wightwicke.* The King assigns nominates and constitutes Thomas Clayton M.D. yᵉ first and modern Mʳ of yᵉ said coll.'

A Grant of Arms accompanied the instrument of foundation. Burke gives them thus: Per pale azure and gules, three lions rampant, two and one, argent (for Herbert). A chief per pale, or and argent, charged on the dexter side with a rose gules and on the sinister side with a thistle vert (for King James). This is incorrect, as a glance at the actual grant in the muniment-room shows. The chief should be argent and or, as they are blazoned over the door of the Library. But the error, reproduced in Burgon's *Arms of the Colleges* and on the New Schools, is almost as old as the foundation of Pembroke. The University being exempt from the wholesome jurisdiction of the Heralds' College [1], it is stated that only two or three of the colleges have a correct shield.

---

[1] Somerset and Bluemantle appeared in 1634 'in their rich coates,' but the University disallowed their commission. 'Moreover there was sent to the vice-chancellor a table of all the College arms blasoned in their proper collours and mettalls set forth by authoritie by Jo. Scott; and that the Colledges could not shewe the heraldes any other armes than them there sett forth, and so it would be needlesse for them to enquyre any further about it' (*Life and Times,* iv. 52). Wood records of the year 1670, 'Sir Edw. Bish came to visit.' The boat clubs are the leading offenders against heraldic laws, especially the law which forbids the placing of a colour upon a colour, but only on a metal. At Pembroke for a short time the Eight actually bore a *white* rose on a crimson cap, as though York and Lancaster had never fought! The College colours are cerise and white.

Wightwick's arms are, Azure, on a chevron argent, between three pheons or, as many crosses patée gules.

Tesdale's are, Argent, a chevron, vert, between three teasells proper. Wood mistakes these for leaves or pineapples, vert [1]. Dean Burgon (who, however, is wrong in his suggestion that the thistle in the College coat should be a teazle [2]) saw that they must be a cant on Tesdale's name. Dale the herald describes the arms rightly. The teazles, however, were assumed by the Berkshire family without a grant from Heralds' College. The original blazon was Sable, three pheons argent.

The first oration was delivered by 'THOMAS BROWNE, Studiosus non Graduatus Commensalis Collegii,' afterwards famous as the author of the *Religio Medici*. He addresses his auditors for the last time by the old name of 'Lateportenses.' They wonder, no doubt, whether he has risen to speak 'in invidiam Pembrochianorum an in gratiam.' But they have not met to pour forth lamentations over the grave of the Hall. 'En Aulam vestram vagam & ἀδέσποτον (quem enim hujus domûs patrem aut fundatorem recolimus?) in tutelam recepit Mecaenas nobilissimus,' who is about to make of a Hall of brick a College of marble, which no envy, *or only passing envy*, shall look upon. He insists on the continuity of Hall and College : 'Eadem jura omnia, idem Magister et Principalis, eaedem aedes, nisi quod nobiliores, *Lateportensis Pembrochiensis* et vice versâ *Pembrochiensis Lateportensis*, Tros Tyriusque hoc tantum discrimine, quod nos prius titulo nescio quo forte Ironico appellatos jam vere magnificum nomen insigniet.'

The second oration was delivered by JOHN LEE, B.A., one of the new scholars, extremely flowery, and packed with elaborate mytho-

---

[1] Gutch, iii. 627.
[2] 'The arms of Tesdale, the unintentional founder of a new College, are not used by the Society. The bearings are those of the Earl of Pembroke, with an augmentation granted by James I of a chief of the badges of England and Scotland. That the latter may have been considered particularly happy in view of the fact that the arms of Tesdale contain a thistle or "teazle" as their principal charge is probable. It has been said that the original grant to the College placed the rose of England upon an *argent* field, and the thistle of Scotland upon *or*, in order to equalize as far as possible the honours due to the two countries, and probably also as a delicate compliment to King James. It is to be observed that the portraits of the co-Founder in the hall, dating from 1624, have the arms of the College as they are now borne' (Notes on the Heraldry of the Colleges, by Mr. Percival Landon, in *Archaeologia Oxoniensis*, part iv, 1894). The last statement is an error. Tesdale's and Wightwick's portraits have a correct shield.

logical allusions, as befitted a Bachelor. ' Gallum debemus candido serenissimi Claytonis Aesculapio cujus unius beneficio, velut gustato Glauci gramine, nostri in his aedibus revixit Tisdallus.' Jealousy may croak till she burst. Some day (without waiting for the Greek kalends), a splendid pile, rivalling all others, will rise for the Muses. The Lord Archbishop is called 'fiduciarius Tisdalli haeres, qui nostras utroque cornu nutantes jamdiu fortunas grato tibicine suffulcire dignatus est.'

MATTHIAS TURNER, M.A., Prelector of Physic and Philosophy, delivered the third oration. To the members of Broadgates the change is not in truth 'exilium intra eadem maenia.' He deprecates tragic lamentation over the extinction of the ancient hall, whose youth, like that of Aeson, was to be gloriously renewed. Turner had been at Balliol (M.A. 1622, B.D. 1632, being then rector of Dynedor). He was 'an excellent Philosopher, had great skill in the Oriental Languages, and wrot (as he himself professes) all his Sermons which he preached, in Greek[1].' Viscount Sligo, ambassador to France, made him his chaplain.

DR. CLAYTON, the new Master, in the last oration, refers to the somewhat embarrassing position in which the new foundation stood, and earnestly declares that he had not in any way sought the honour which had come to him. He prays God's blessing on the College.

A royal commission had been issued to George, Archbishop of Canterbury, William Earl of Pembroke, the Vice-Chancellor for the time being, Sir John Bennet, Sir Eubule Thelwall, the Master for the time being, Walter Dayrell, Esq., recorder of Abingdon, and Richard Wightwick, clerk, or any four of them, to make and constitute wholesome statutes for the good government of the House. Bennet, Thelwall, and Dayrell were lawyers. The connexion of the first of these with Tesdale has been already mentioned.

SIR EUBULE THELWALL had three years before procured from King James a new charter empowering commissioners to frame a perfect body of statutes for Jesus College, of which he had just become Principal, and which he was in 1624 building and embellishing. There is, however, no noticeable resemblance between these statutes,

---

[1] *Athenae*, i. 843. It will be remembered that Queen Elizabeth herself was a fluent Grecian. The Puritans built more on Greek than on Latin. 'Philosophy disputations in Lent time; frequent in the Greek tongue' (*L. and T.* i. 300). This was under the Commonwealth. Turner died in 1656.

which are puritan in tone, and the ones made for Pembroke. Thelwall was a Master in Chancery, and Master of the Alienation Office.

WALTER DAYRELL, a kinsman of the famous 'Wild Darrel,' came of the family seated since the twelfth century at Lillingston Dayrell, Bucks[1], of which county his father, Paul, was high sheriff in 1563 and 1580. Of Walter's brothers, one, Sir Thomas, married Margery, daughter of Bishop Horne[2]; another, William, was fellow of Magdalen, 1576; a third, Paul, was Master of Christ's Hospital, Abingdon, in 1601. Walter himself entered St. Mary Hall March 27, 1579, aged fifteen; of Gray's Inn, 1598, and of Staple Inn; bencher and autumn reader, 1616. In 1604 the Abingdonians chose him 'to be of counsell with this Corporation'; Recorder 1609; Governor of Christ's Hospital from 1603. He died on St. Peter's day[3], 1628, leaving three sons and three daughters. Of these Thomas was ejected from a fellowship at All Souls in 1648, and Walter from a student's place in Christ Church. He was afterwards canon and archdeacon of Winchester. Mary was wedded to Dr. John Morris, Professor of Hebrew, and Alice to Serjeant ('Old Charles') Holloway. A nephew, Anthony Dayrell of Lillingston, entered Pembroke in 1639. Dayrell was succeeded as Recorder, Oct. 2, 1628, by one of the Tesdales-Thomas.

Prideaux was Vice-Chancellor in 1624. While he was still in office a body of statutes was drawn up and signed by him and five other Royal Commissioners. Wood was not aware of this. He says, 'Three years afterwards were statutes made, to the end that the members thereof might be well governed, and within the space of one year following were subscribed, sealed[4], and published.' Accepted Frewen, afterwards Archbishop, being then Vice-Chancellor. The 1628 statutes, however, were only a modification of those of 1624. The latter are on vellum and are signed by 'G. Cant: [Abbot]. Pembroke.

[1] In Sir Ralph Verney's will (1528) 'my cowzen Paule Darrell, Deputye and under-sherif,' is mentioned. This was Walter's grandfather (ob. 1566). A remoter ancestor, Sir John, gave Littlecote to his third son, Sir George, who fought in the Wars of the Roses, and was great-grandfather of Queen Jane Seymour. Sir Edward ('Wild') Darrel was his son.
[2] Bishop Horne, in 1579, bequeathed 'to Paul Dayrell my nephew' (i. e. grandson), 'my best bason and ewer' (Strype, Annals, II. (ii.) 377, 8).
[3] Hearne says 'June 21.' 'A Monument in St. Nicholas Churche in Abbingdon in the North Wall of the Chancell to the Memory of Walter Dairell, Esqr., Recorder of Abbingdon, who died June 21, 1628, Aet. 63' (Collectanea, ed. Doble, O. H. S., iii. 393). The inscription is worth reading.
[4] 'There are no seals on any of the copies; they were 'chirographis commissionariorum signati.'

Jo. Prideaux vicecañ: Oxon. Jo: Benet. Eub. Thelwall. Tho: Clayton Collegii Pembroch: Magister.' Walter Dayrell was dead in 1628, but not in 1624; and Wightwick also does not sign. It seems his plans were not yet matured. The later statutes vary most from the earlier in regard to his fellows and scholars. His name is affixed to all the five extant copies of the statutes as finally settled. The signatures are 'G. Cant. Pembroke. Richard Wightwicke. Ac. Frewen, Vicecanc. Oxon. Eubul Thelwell. Tho. Clayton, Coll. Pembrok. Magister.' Sir John Bennet was dead. It is observable that the 1624 edition draws no line of separation between the two foundations, the same rules being made for both, and the fellows ' of the College' acting as electors to both. Some of the 1624 provisions were avowedly temporary [1].

STATUTES.

The statutes open with the invocation of the Most Holy and Undivided Trinity. The desire of the commissioners is to constitute a House ' piam, literatam, studiosam, in Dei gloriam, bonum Ecclesiae et reipublicae '; and, forasmuch as they know that ' except the Lord build the house their labour is but lost that build it,' they begin with ordinances respecting divine service ' in the College Chapel or other convenient place to be assigned by the Master and the majority of the Fellows.' Morning prayers are to be held between five and six o'clock, but out of term at seven o'clock, to be attended by all fellows, scholars, commoners, and servitors resident in College. There is a fine of twopence for absence without good cause, of a penny for coming in after the Psalms or going out without leave, but below the age of eighteen offenders may be punished either by the rod [2] or by a fine. There is to be a commemoration of founders and benefactors, and a giving of thanks for them in the public prayers, it would seem daily.

---

[1] The Oxford University Commissioners, one of them the Master of the College, reported in 1852 (p. 247) that ' a charter was obtained in 1629 from King James I.' James had then been dead four years.

[2] So at Cambridge at this date, ' Escholiers audessus de 18 ans non chastiez ou fustigez, mais mulctes par amendes pecuniaires' (MS. note-book of Eli Brevint, minister of Sercq, c. 1620). In 1617 our University decreed whipping for junior offenders, and in 1623 the wearing of boots with a gown was to be similarly corrected. The rod was in force after the Restoration (see Wood's *Life and Times*, ii. 140); but I believe the Pembroke statutes are the last occasion of it being prescribed at Oxford. (See *Collectanea*, ed. Prof. Burrows, O. H. S., ii. 429, 430.)

There is no direction whether the services are to be in Latin or in English. The present Act of Uniformity, which expects that College services will be in Latin, dates from 1662 only. Attendance at University sermons is prescribed; to the sermons in Latin, or 'ad clerum,' and the service at the beginning of term, and other public solemnities, all the members of the College, properly habited, are to accompany the Master or Vicegerent. Maintainers of heresies and of opinions not approved by the Church of England are to be fined 6*d.* for the first offence, 2*s.* 6*d.* for the second, suspended from all emoluments, except their chamber, for the third, and, if the error is not renounced within three months, expelled. Profane swearing is to be punished by a fine of 12*d.*, or, if the offender is under the age of eighteen, by corporal correction. Grace is to be said in Latin before and after meat, and about the middle of dinner and supper a chapter or convenient portion of Holy Scripture is to be read aloud in Latin [1]. All are to sit modestly, becomingly, with their caps [2] on their heads, according to their condition, reverently and silently during this reading. The meals are to be 'in accordance with the statutes of the realm, and the ordinances of the Church of England'—i. e. as regards feast and fast days.

The statutes speak next of the different members of the society, which is to be constituted as a. well-ordered Family in the due subordination and mutual helpfulness of its different parts.   The office of the Master, as of a good father, will be to shew himself a pattern of honest conversation, of wisdom, of toil and study, that the whole family may have a mirror after which to fashion itself. A pious, honourable, and prudent Paterfamilias can do much for the advantage and splendour of the household; and the commissioners, solicitous that the Master shall not fall short of this ideal, ordain that he shall be a man of sound religion, attached to the faith of the Church of England, circumspect and discreet, studious, of at least thirty years, a doctor in theology, medicine, or civil law, or a Master in Arts, or a Bachelor in one of the superior faculties, a present or sometime fellow. If, however, a suitable fellow or former fellow cannot be

[1] Archbishop Bancroft, as Chancellor, issued an injunction in 1608 for the familiar employment of Latin in colleges, 'whereof there is now so much use both in studies and common conversation.' One of Laud's reforms was to insist on the speaking of Latin at meals.

[2] The cap is part of the proper vesture of a clerk *inter divina.* In 1659 'the gentlemen commoners of the University of Oxon petitioned to sit with their caps on their heads as the Masters and Bachelors did,' viz. in church. See *Life and Times*, i. 290.

found, then the electors may go outside for a Master, who however is first to be sought in Balliol, and next in University College, in honour and memory of Thomas Tesdale, Esq., and of the Most Reverend George, now Archbishop of Canterbury, his first trustee, 'qui propensissime fuere affecti erga dicta Collegia.' His salary is to be £20 out of the Tesdale rents and £10 from those of Wightwick, besides all emoluments arising from room-rents, admissions, presentations to degrees, and other accustomed dues which the Principal of Broadgates Hall had hitherto received. The Fellows are the *filii-familias*, and must be 'probi, pii, prudentes, qui patri subsidio esse possint in bene administranda familia.' They are to be at least seventeen years old, graduates, scholars within the three years preceding, celibate, of good report, sufficient in learning, needy, not given to drunkenness, sloth, or brawling. Next come the Scholars, who are to be deemed the sons of the Master and Fellows, and so the grandchildren of the Founders (the figure is a little confused)—'Amor paternus non descendit in filios solum sed in nepotes etiam.' A statute follows regarding the duties of the College servants, those mentioned being the obsonator, the promus, the coquus, the faber, the lignarius, the lapidarius, the hortulanus, the tonsor, and the janitor. The tonsor, or College barber [1], remained till quite recent memory, his name appearing on the buttery books. But there are now no perukes to dress for hall. All fees paid to servants in the Broadgates days were to be continued. After the *famuli* come regulations concerning the 'commensales *seu* comminarii.' Their presence is encouraged as it had been nowhere else so markedly. Living at their own charges in College, the Commoners are to be regarded as 'guests and strangers,' who, as in every well-ordered household, should be courteously welcomed and kindly treated. They are to be assigned rooms and enjoy all the commodities of the common College life [2]. Their payments are to be those usually made by commoners at Broadgates. They are to be under the same rules of discipline as fellows and scholars. All members of the College, including servants, are at admission to swear on the Holy Gospels to observe the statutes and not to reveal College secrets; but scholars and commoners under the age of fifteen are to make a promise only, and not an oath. In

---

[1] The Oxford Guild of Barbers, incorporated in 1348, was dissolved not long ago. This craft maintained of old 'a light before Our Lady in Our Ladye's Chapel.' (*City*, ii. 62.)

[2] In 1851 of seventy-three undergraduates seventy were commoners. Most of the Scholars' places were filled by graduates, or were vacant.

case of candidature for the proctorship or any like University office, that candidate is to be preferred on whom the Master and the major part of the M.A.'s shall have agreed.

The rules of discipline, *in domo togata pacata qualem cupimus*, are of the usual kind. Carrying arms, except when starting from, or having lately returned to, Oxford, is to be punished with expulsion. For contumelious language, a senior is to be fined, a junior to be flogged. Violence accompanied by bloodshed incurs a fine of 6*s.* 8*d.*; without bloodshed, of half that sum. Any one, whether fellow or other, sleeping out without leave is to be fined at least 12*d.* Revealing the secrets of the College is to be punished with a mulct of 2*s.* 6*d.* Dissolute habits and associates, and also forbidden games, are the subject of other rules, and there is one against appeals to outside courts of law. Subordination to those in authority, reverence and uncovering the head before superiors, mutual courtesy and concord between all, are inculcated. As regards studies, 'In familia bene ordinata neminem decet esse otiosum.' The following scholastic exercises, forming a very complete course of study, and having no reference to any University Schools, are ordained: (1) *A Catechetical lecture,* 'delivering the sum and foundation of the Christian religion,' to be read ' singulis diebus Sabbati seu Saturni ' in full term, at 10 a.m. All B.A.'s and non-graduates are bound to attend; those of a higher grade are invited to do so. The praelector is to receive 6*d.* a term from every fellow, scholar, or commoner. (2) *A Natural Philosophy lecture,* at 9 a.m. on Mondays, Wednesdays, and Fridays, the auditors to be all non-graduates in the higher class. The praelector is to moderate their disputations on Mondays, Tuesdays, Wednesdays, and Fridays. He will receive 13*s.* 8*d.* in each of the four terms. (3) *A Logic lecture,* at 6 a.m., immediately after mattins on Mondays, Wednesdays, and Fridays, to be attended by non-graduates of the lower class. The praelector will act as their moderator, and receive 13*s.* 4*d.* a term. (4) *A Rhetoric lecture,* at 9 a.m. on Tuesdays and Fridays, the auditors being all non-graduate scholars, commoners, and servitors in College; the reader to receive 10*s.* a term. (5) *A lecture in the Greek tongue,* at 2 p.m. on Tuesdays and Fridays, the salary of the lecturer being 10*s.* a term. All non-graduates imbued with Greek are to attend. The various praelectors are to be appointed by the Master at the beginning of Michaelmas term, and he is to pay·their salaries out of the room-rents received by him. It is also ordained that there shall be *Theological disputations* every other Thursday in term at 4 p.m., at which all M.A.'s who have completed the first year of their regency are to respond and expone, the Master or the Praelector Catechisticus moderating and receiving from the disputants 4*s.* a term. *Disputations in Philosophy* are to take place every Saturday at 4 p.m., the respondents being all Bachelors of Arts, and the moderator the Junior Dean, with the same reward. All non-graduate scholars and commoners are to *declaim publicly* in hall on Saturdays after common prayers, and all graduates to exhibit their *themes* or exercises; and then they are to submit themselves for correction at the hand of the Master, Vicegerent or Deans, for all offences against the statutes, absence from prayers, and other excesses. An exception is made in favour of 'commensales magistrorum et baccalaureorum' (fellow-commoners). Servitors, whether scholars or batellers, are ordered to declaim every Thursday just before or after dinner. All non-graduates shall live under some graduate tutor, as arranged by the Master, except the 'commoners of B.A.'s and M.A.'s,' who are to enjoy their own freedom in their studies and the scholastic exercises of the College. Every one, before receiving the grace for his degree, is to *appose or respond* publicly in hall in some problem to be approved by the Master. On the day that he is presented, he is to give a public dinner in hall, or pay 20*s.* for the use of the College. B.A.'s seeking the grace for M.A. are to respond in some thesis, or deliver to the Master a commentary on some portion of Aristotle. They too are to feast the College at an expense not exceeding 40*s.* In 1852 there were three tutors, but no other lecturers.

The remaining statutes relate to the offices of the Master's Vicegerent, of the two Censors or Deans, and of the two Bursars; to lands and rents; to payment of batells and dues; to sanitary matters; to the two chests, one for muniments, the other for valuable plate and for money; and to the College seal. There is a statute about expulsions, including the extreme case of the removal of a Master, which actually occurred within forty years; another ordinance is about dress, since 'vestis et tegit corpus et detegit saepe animum'— the apparel oft proclaims the man. Long hair is forbidden, and no one is to be seen in Oxford wearing cloak or high boots (pallio aut ocreis [1] indutus). A member of the College absent on affairs of Church or State, if it be with consent of the Master and the Fellows of his foundation, is to receive his salary [2]. If any is sick or in

---

[1] 'Would you think it possible that the wise founders of an English university should forbid us to wear boots?' (Southey, Letter to Grosvenor Bedford, Esq., Jan. 16, 1793.)

[2] A similar provision for leave to travel abroad existed at Exeter, Merton, and Wadham.

affliction, the whole Family is to succour and care for him, joying with them that rejoice, and weeping with them that weep; and if the misfortune be of a material nature, the other members of his own foundation are to provide for him with Christian affection out of their revenues. A final ordinance provides for the appointment of a Visitor, to be to the College 'anchora in arduis,' viz. the High Chancellor of the University, 'as well in honour of the present most noble High Chancellor, the most honoured Lord, William Herbert, Earl of Pembroke, who has imparted to the College a name, privileges, and many favours, as also in right and equity; for that the most illustrious Chancellors of the University are Visitors of all Halls, and among them of Broadgates Hall [1].' It speaks of Pembroke's 'love to letters and lettered men, the patronage of whom the University in general, and this College in especial, commends to his protecting care.' (Tesdale's will however designated the Bishop of London for the time being as the decider of disputes.) With the consent of the Visitor the College might make additional statutes.

It will be observed that, doubtless on Clayton's account, the Master was not bound, like the fellows, to Holy Orders or celibacy. The modern statutes require him to be a person capable in law of holding the Gloucester canonry. Except Christ Church, Pembroke is therefore the only society which is now obliged to have a clerical Head. Savage says that Clayton was 'a good Divine; and this his skill he did seasonably exercise towards his Patients.'

The regulations made by the Commissioners respecting the Tesdale fellowships and scholarships followed in the main the directions of his will. Of his seven fellows, four were to be of his kinship [2], and all

---

[1] These great officials were originally the Bishop of Lincoln's chancellors resident at Oxford, which was in the Lincoln diocese. The Chancellor had ecclesiastical jurisdiction and granted licence to teach. He was not in the beginning, like the Parisian Rector, a creature of the University. In course of time, however, he came to be elected—a change very unwelcome to the town. In the Wars of the Roses the Universities sought the protection of some powerful noble as their Chancellor. The Stuart attention to academical affairs added importance to the office, a deputy or vice-chancellor performing the ordinary duties, which rule has obtained ever since. Pembroke College has in this way been brought into connexion with a number of eminent statesmen, whose decisions on disputed points are interwoven into the law of the College. In 1657 the Presbyterians endeavoured to upset the parliamentary Visitation, and brought in a bill fixing the office of Visitor of the several societies in some distinguished non-resident. The Earls of Pembroke were to be perpetual Visitors of Jesus and of Pembroke Colleges (Gutch, *Annals*, ii. 676–680).

[2] Founders had always provided for their own blood. 'Forasmuch as I have, under God's eye, converted the inheritance of my lands in fee, which by the

seven were to be taken from among the scholars, having been educated in Abingdon Free School, of at least seventeen years, graduates in Arts (this was not required for the Wightwick foundation), sufficient in learning, of good report and conversation, celibate and in need of support, their private income not exceeding £40 ; to be elected by the Master and the Fellows of the Tesdale foundation [College, 1624], the Master having the casting vote. All were to be students of theology, to proceed M.A. as soon as possible, and within three years of magistration to be admitted to the priesthood. A benefice with cure of souls outside Oxford [1624, inside as well], to vacate the fellowship. Of his scholars, two were to be of his poorer kindred, educated at Abingdon by preference, but, if there were none such there, then at some other school. The other four were to be chosen from the poorer natives of Abingdon, brought up as Bennet Scholars ; but, if none were found fit, then from others in the same school, if any be found there apt and meet. The election was to take place at the school at the annual visitation, viz. on the Monday[1] next following the first Lord's Day after August 1 ; the electors being the Master of the College (to whom a double vote was given), the two senior Tesdale fellows [fellows of the College, 1624], the Master and two senior governors of the Hospital of Christ's Poor in Abingdon, and Roysse's schoolmaster. In case of an equality of votes, the decision was to rest with the Vice-Chancellor, the President of Corpus, and the Provost of Queen's. The limits of age were thirteen and nineteen—in 1624 eighteen. The stipends were fixed at £20 for the fellows, £15 for the two scholars of founder's kin, and £12 for the other four, the Master receiving £20 out of the Tesdale rents instead of £10. In 1852 four Tesdale fellows were receiving £154 each, and four non-kin scholars £28 each and rooms. Three kin fellowships and two kin scholarships were vacant for lack of competent candidates to fill them.

For the Wightwick foundation the original statutes were in 1628 considerably modified. Whereas in the earlier statutes only one

---

custom of the realm was due to my heirs or kinsmen, for the purposes of this charity, I will and enact that if any young children of my kin need support in consequence of the death or poverty of their parents,' &c. Walter de Merton's Statutes, 1274 (*Memorials of Merton College*, by Hon. G. C. Brodrick, O. H. S., p. 339). In 1647 the Craven Scholarships were to benefit Lord Craven's poor kindred.

[1] Not Tuesday, as in Nutt's *Magna Britannia*. Archbishop Laud, in 1634, decreed that in default of competent scholars from Abingdon, the College might elect out of any school in Berkshire.

of the three fellows was to be of his kindred, and all three to have been educated at Abingdon, in the later constitutions two were to be of his kindred or name, with no restriction as to place of birth or education. In 1624 the kin fellow was to study theology, proceed M.A., and be ordained priest; one of the others was obliged to the study of medicine, and to graduate in that faculty; the third was to study Civil Law, and take the B.C.L. degree. But in 1628 all three were to apply themselves to divinity and take holy orders, proceeding to B.D. within twenty years. Was this due to the new King's policy? Instead of being elected by the fellows of the College, there was to be promotion by seniority from among the scholars, founder's kin or Abingdonian, the only qualifications mentioned being celibacy and poverty, for an income of more than £10 vacated the place. In 1624 the rule had been the same as for Tesdale's fellows. A cure of souls, whether inside or outside Oxford, vacated a Wightwick fellowship. Of the four Wightwick scholars, it had been ordained that two should be of his kindred, out of Abingdon School, or, if none found there, from some other; two from the poorer boys at the school, 'or some other School,' being apt and meet. The later statutes say that two shall be of Wightwick's name or kindred, wherever born or educated, and two from the free grammar-school at Abingdon. Vacancies were now to be filled not by the Master and two senior fellows electing, but in the case of the Abingdon scholars in the same way as those of Tesdale, while in the other case whoever should be first presented by one of the two founder's kin fellows to the Master and two of the senior fellows was to be elected. The limit of age was raised from eighteen to nineteen. Scholars as well as fellows were now to make divinity their profession. The stipend of fellows was fixed in both editions at £20, and of scholars at £10. To the Master £10 a year was assigned. In 1852 the Master was receiving (besides his canonry) £860, Wightwick fellows £95 and £74, and the scholars £28 or £30.

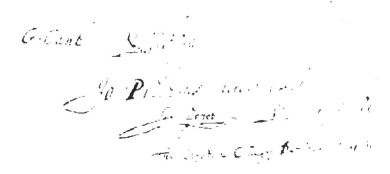

SIGNATURES TO STATUTES OF 1924

SIGNATURES TO STATUTES OF 1628

CHAPTER XV.

WIGHTWICK'S benefaction was at the date of the Patent of Foundation still in intention. By an indenture dated June 1, 1625, he
granted to his nephew Samuel Wightwick a lease for ninety-nine years
of his manors and estates at Marlstone, Thatcham, Bucklebury, and
Bowdones, all in Berkshire [1]; and subsequently, on August 1, 1628,
granted a further lease of the same properties for a term of 400
years, to commence at the expiration of the former lease, subject to
a yearly payment of £70. To another nephew, Walter Wightwick,
he gave like leases, for the same terms, of his property called
Quarrels, in the parish of Appleton, Berks, subject to a reserved rent
of £30. On August 13, 1628, after decreeing that each of his
fellows should receive from his rents £20 yearly, and each scholar £10,
he ordained that the rent-holders should pay £500 for the building
of chambers in the new College and for the stipend of the Master,
ex fundatione sua, viz. £300 for the years 1625, 1626, 1627, at the
Michaelmas next coming, another £100 in 1628, O.S. (one moiety on
September 29, and the other on March 24), and in 1629 two further
instalments of £50 each. The salary of the Master *ex fundatione sua*
was to be £10 a year. 'Quae omnia, Deo volente, perficientur intra
tempus praedictum, viz. intra vicesimum quintum diem Martii anno
1630; adeo ut omnes Socii et Scholares meae fundationis percipient
stipendia et pensiones suas in vel a vicesimo quinto die Martii 1630,
et postea in perpetuum.' Six weeks later, on Sept. 30, 1628, Wightwick enfeoffed all the lands, whose leases he had granted to his
nephews, to Pembroke College, granting it the reserved rents of £70
and £30. These the College still receives. The actual properties,
now greatly increased in value, will not come into its possession for
another 230 years. The statutes provide for a *pro rata* reduction
of stipends in case of diminution in the income of the foundation.
In his will, made Jan. 11, 16$\frac{38}{39}$, a few days before his death,

---

[1] The Marlstone property (625 acres) is now in the hands of Messrs. Huntley
and Palmer.

Wightwick asks the College to accept an annuity of £10 issuing out of the lands of Thomas Hinde, 'for the use and benefitt of the Master and his successo^{rs},' in lieu of £200 which he had promised for the purchasing of a like annuity.

Wightwick's benefaction, though now of inconsiderable value, seemed to those nearer his time to be a very large one. Fuller says : ' What the yearly value of his living was I know not, and have cause to believe it not very great : however one would conjecture his Benefice a Bishoprick by his bounty to *Pembroke Colledge.* . . . When he departed this life is to me unknown.' More modern gifts by those of his name and kindred to the College have largely augmented its usefulness. Richard Wightwick's other possessions appear to have been small, since in his last testament he disposes of but £200 personalty and one piece of realty. He therein speaks of himself as ' co-Founder,' and he can scarcely be denied the title, considering that but for his bounty, which was no mere deathbed bequest, but an actual bestowal during his lifetime of £100 of income, Pembroke College would not have been founded.

Like most other founders he retained, or was given, the right of nominating the first persons who were to profit by it. ' Quos omnes,' the statutes provide, ' durante vita naturali, quales quando et quomodo sibi videbitur, licebit sibi ad arbitrium eligere et amovere ; nec eorum aliquis post mortem suam sub praetextu defectus aetatis gradus aut literarum amovebitur.' In the Patent of June 29, 1624, the first Tesdale and Wightwick fellows and scholars are named. On Dec. 6, 1632, there is an injunction of Bishop [1] Laud, as Visitor, allowing one fellow and three scholars, of Wightwick's kin and nominated by him, they being at the date of the injunction twelve years old and at school, to receive their full pensions, albeit non-resident, until their seventeenth year, if meanwhile they remain 'in ludo literario, ut instructiores ad bonarum artium studia ad Collegium accedant,' for the reason that 'fundator consanguineis suis ejus aetatis in Socios et Scholares nominatis in eo indulsisse videatur ' ; but it was not to be a precedent for the future. Wightwick died in January, 16$\frac{32}{33}$. The fellow and scholars mentioned in the injunction must therefore have been but four years old, if they were of those first appointed in 1624, and in any case of tender age when nominated. The Bishop decrees a deduction of 3*s.* for each week of absence in the case of other fellows, and 1*s.* 6*d.* in the case of other scholars (four days' residence sufficing to the week) ; but Henry and George

---

[1] It is signed ' Guil. Londin.,' but a later decree, ' W. Cant.'

Wightwicke are to enjoy their fellowships undiminished, Master Wightwicke their founder appearing to have dispensed them. These two fellows are mentioned in one of the statutes as kin and original fellows of the founder, and as being, by his desire, dispensed from the rule depriving of his place any fellow or scholar who marries, or has an income of above £10 by the year, or holds a benefice with cure of souls. It is decreed that Henry Wightwicke shall enjoy his fellowship for five years from admission in any case, while George shall be fellow and have seniority in College according to admission, 'etsi gradum academicum non suscepit.' Henry, afterwards Master, was in 1624 thirty-four years of age. George was, it is said, son of George Wightwicke, vicar of Patshull. Both were distant cousins.

The original fellows and scholars of the double foundation, as named and constituted in the royal patent, were:—

Fellows—Thomas Godwyn, Robertus Payne, Christoferus Tesdale, Nicholaus Coxeter, Carolus Sagar, Thomas Westley, Henricus Wightwicke, Johannes Price, Willielmus Liford, Willielmus Griffith.

Scholars—Johannes Lee, Willielmus Reade, Franciscus Dringe, Ricardus Allein, Johannes Bowles, Johannes Grace, Thomas Millington, Humfridus Gwyn, Ricardus Kirfoote, Georgius Griffith.

There is no George Wightwick in this list. But at the end of the 1624 statutes, after declaring that the surviving Founder is to have the right during his life of appointing and removing his fellows and fixing their stipends, the commissioners ordain that all the titular fellows and scholars nominated in the Foundation Charter shall resign all their right and title in the said places within a month after being admonished by the Master in writing so to do; if they fail to resign, their places to be *ipso facto* vacant; but five existing scholars are excepted from this compulsory retirement, viz. Lee, Dring, Read, Allen, and Bowles. In the room of the remaining five scholars and ten fellows others are to be elected as soon as provision shall have been made 'de necessariis structuris Collegii et impensis circa statum Collegii stabiliendum expendendis.' We have seen that the Wightwick stipends did not begin to be paid till 1630. As regards Tesdale's beneficiaries, his will directs that the seven fellows, if chambers have to be built for their reception, are not to be placed till out of their allowance the cost be defrayed, 'and that in the meane time only the sixe poor Schollers be chosen and placed.' It appears from *Balliofergus* that there was found at Balliol 'a present receptacle for the said six scholars, which were there received and settled accordingly, receiving their Exhibitions by the hand of our Bursars,

Dring, Lee, Crabtree, Allen, Bowles, and Read: whereof Crabtree[1] dyed of a stab with a Knife given him by the unlucky hand of a Freshman of three weeks' standing.' None of the six matriculated till at least eleven years after Tesdale's decease.

In the Articles of Agreement originally made between the Mayor, Bailiffs, and Burgesses of Abingdon and the Master and Scholars of Balliol College, it had been arranged that the rents should remain in the chamber of the town of Abingdon until such time as there be raised a competent sum to erect buildings uniform to the said College, the College allowing ground for the said buildings, and meanwhile providing a convenient lodging for the seven fellows and six scholars. But the fellows, it seems, were not appointed, no place being found for them. Balliol College, however, received £300 out of Tesdale's money, which, with the addition of £40 or thereabouts, was expended in acquiring the rooms known as Caesar's Lodgings, nearly opposite the east end of St. Mary Magdalen Church.

Balliol had acted rashly in spending money before the negotiations with Abingdon were ratified. They were to take effect 'if so be it shall seem good to the Lord Archbishop of Canterbury his Grace.' It would seem that when the Abingdonians showed themselves bent on a new College Abbot refused to ratify the agreement. The King's wish to be a Founder may have had something to do with this; or Wightwick, who, says Ayliffe, 'had long since thought of endowing this charity,' may have made a point of the Broadgates Hall plan. Wood however says[2], 'Mr. Wightwick had intentions to found Fellowships and Scholarships in some Colleges.' There can have been no prejudice against Balliol, since Wightwick was of that College, Abbot's brother Robert was at the time Master, and the Archbishop's own connexion with it, as alumnus and Visitor, was what had turned the designs of his friend Tesdale in that direction. But at any rate the agreement fell to the ground, and Balliol College found itself with Caesar's Buildings on its hands. Dr. Henry Savage, Master of Balliol, whose *Balliofergus*[3] (1668, but written in 1661) contains an account of the inauguration of Pembroke called *Natalitia Collegii Pembrochiani*, shows a not unnatural resentment. 'This rejeton had no sooner

[1] John Crabtre, B.A. from Balliol, Oct. 16, 1623.
[2] *Colleges and Halls*, p. 616.
[3] Hearne says: 'Ibi mendae innumerae comparent, prout nobis indicavit Antonius Woodius. Savagius nempe hoc opus invita Minerva suscepit. Quin et Woodius ipse saepius cespitavit' (*Collections*, ed. Doble, O. H. S., ii. 271). Savage was helped by à Wood (see *Life and Times*, ed. Clarke, O. H. S., ii. 136). He died 1672, aged sixty-eight.

taken root than the Master and his company called the Master and Society of our Colledge into Chancery for the restitution of the aforesaid £300.' Wood says: 'The Fellows for the most part inclining to demur, and the rather because that Coventry, then Lord Keeper, sometime of Balliol College, had promised them a gracious hearing, it was in the end (for he was not faithful to them) referred to George Archbishop of Canterbury, sometime of the said College also, who, knowing very well that the Society was not able at that time to repay the said sum, bade the fellows go home, be obedient to their Governour, and JEHOVAH JIREH, i.e. GOD shall provide for them. Whereupon he paid £50 of the said £300 presently, and for the other £250 the College gave bond to be paid yearly by several sums till the full was satisfied. The which sums as they grew due did the lord Archbishop pay.' By the original agreement the Master of Balliol was to have received £20 yearly from Tesdale's donation. The Archbishop in his award decreed to him as compensation Caesar's Buildings with their garden. The sense of injustice however rankled long. Savage says bitterly, ' 'Tis hard to judge whether has had the more malignant aspect upon our College, viz., The Thievish glance of Mercuries Eye or the Fiery looks of Mars.' He complains that the citizens of Abingdon had no regard at all to the condescensions of Balliol College, which could not have been greater without manifest injury to the ancient foundation. 'The place the Abingdonians pitch'd on was Broadgates hall, where that they might take such footing as that nothing might be able to remove them they made the Earl of Pembroke the Godfather of this new Christened Hall, King James the Founder of it, but (ad onera et costagia) at the cost and charges of Tisdale and Whitwick, allowing these only the priviledge of Foster Fathers.'

Under the Laudian cycle fixed in 1629 Pembroke was to have a proctor once in the twenty-three years.

ROYSSE'S SCHOOL AT ABINGDON.

The Free School of the Blessed Trinity, within the borough of Abingdon, has had such a close connexion with Pembroke College, which it claims as a daughter, that a brief account must be given of it. The monks of Abingdon, who had had the schooling of Archbishop Aelfric, of the Royal Clerk Henry I., of Geoffrey of Monmouth, and legend even says of Constantine the Great, were turned adrift in 1538, and an educational vacuum resulted. To provide for the humanities

in his native town John Roysse [1], citizen and mercer of London, by
indenture of Jan. 31, 1563, gave to the mayor, bailiffs and burgesses
the sum of £50 to provide a schoolhouse, and on Feb. 23 two
tenements in Birchin Lane, producing 20 marks yearly, for the
maintenance of a schoolmaster. The corporation covenanted that
before the Feast of the Annunciation of our Blessed Lady the Virgin
next coming they would provide one meet convenient schoolhouse able
to receive three score and thirteen [2] scholars, and also cause the said
schoolhouse to be assured to some body politic for ever for the use
of a free school. Roysse intended to disinherit a profligate son
Thomas, though 'for God's sake especially and for his good mother's
sake, which was my wife,' he provided for his son's eldest child, John.
The residue of his fortune, save for some minor charitable bequests,
he gave for the endowment of his Grammar School, directing that, as
it was founded in the sixty-third year of the century and of his own
age, there should be in it for ever three and sixty free scholars. As
it chanced, Tesdale, who founded the ushership (abolished in 1868),
died at the age of sixty-three, the grand climacteric. The number is
no longer observed. Indeed, less than a hundred years ago the free
scholars had dwindled to zero. But every day, now, as of old, the
school bell tolls sixty-three times. The school was built under the
wing of the ruin of the old abbey, hard by whose great gateway,
opposite St. Nicholas' church, still stands the humbler school gate,
embattled and bearing the founder's arms. The Earl of Abingdon
spent £100 in 1811 in restoring it. Inside a little courtyard is the
old schoolroom, over whose little square porch is the invitation
Ingredere ut proficias. A tablet on the wall sets forth that ' Johannes
Royssius hanc Scholam instituit Anno Dom. 1563.' The interior is
now dismantled, and used by a volunteer corps. The eagle lectern,
the old pictures, and the clock inscribed *Pereunt et imputantur* are
in the new home. But the decaying panelling and forms, the old
floor, the master's and usher's seats with the iron clasp that held the
corporation mace on Visitation days, and a pretty little curving gallery
with gilt balusters, these still remain, The gallery bears on its front
the words ἐὰν ᾖς φιλομαθὴς ἔσῃ πολυμαθής.

Among the Ordinances made by the founder, breathing the quaint
and pious spirit of the time, was the following: ' The scholemaster

---

[1] The computus ' Johannis Royse de Civitate Oxon Wollen draper,' under
date 27° Elizabethae, is given in *Oxford City Documents*, O. H. S., p. 117.

[2] The Master was allowed ten pupils of his own. The others paid 1*d*. A
' libera schola ' is an uncontrolled, not a gratuitous, school.

shall thryse in the daie hear with a loud voice the children say thes prayers following[1]: that is to saie, in the morning upon their knees the Pater Noster, Ave Maria, and the Crede; and at the end thereof shall saye Upon our founder John Roysse and all Christian people the Blessed Trynytye have mercy; and at 11 of the clock when they go to dinner, upon their knees, *Deus in nomine tuo salvum me fac* c^t., and at the ende therof shall saye Upon our founder John Roysse and all Christian people the Blessed Trynytye have mercy; and at night at the breakinge upp of the schole shall saye upon their knees *De profundis* c^t., with the suffrages, c^t., and at the end therof shall say Uppon our founder John Roysse and all Christian people the Blessed Trynytye have mercy.'

On the Sunday after his decease a preacher was to be provided at St. Helen's, who in some part of his sermon was to say, 'For John Roysse's soul, late citizen and mercer of London, and all Christian people, the Blessed Trinity have mercy'; and this to be done yearly for ever. The preacher was to receive 6*s.* 8*d.*, the mayor and burgesses 20*s.* for 'a potation or drinking,' and afterwards bread, drink, and cheese were to be distributed, at a cost of 12*s.*, among the poor, who were in return to pray for his soul. The same supplication was to be offered by twelve old widows, 'women or men,' to whom every Sunday at his tomb in St. Helen's 'twelve pence in white bread, being good, sweet, and seasonable' was to be dispensed. Four and twenty pensioners were further to kneel round his tomb every Sunday to receive alms. Of these religious observances only the potation remains. They are noticeable as being of post-Reformation date[2]. The prayers for his soul which the founder so anxiously enjoined on his children have fallen into disuse, but every Founder's Day his tomb is reverently visited and adorned with red roses. By his will in 1568 he left £5 for a tomb to be erected 'near unto the quior door'; the top stone, whence the dole was to be distributed, he ordered should be the great stone from the arbour of his London garden. It bears his arms, a rampant griffin carrying on his shoulder a red rose.

---

[1] In the borough records is a curious entry of Sept. 6, 1671, recording the expulsion by order of the corporation of Richard, Jasper, and another Tesdale, with other scholars of Roysse's School, for refusing attendance, in accordance with the Founder's statutes, at divine service, albeit admonished by the Visitors and the common council. I have not found the name Tesdale in the records after this.

[2] Such phrases as the following (from the testament of Henry Mylton, Nov. 25, 1558) are common in Elizabethan wills: 'I bequethe my soul to GOD, to Our Lady Saint Mary, and to all the Holy Company of Heaven.'

Besides Tesdale and Wightwick Abingdon School has had several generous benefactors. Its many eminent sons witness to the utility of their bounty. Pope is said to have been one of these, but not with certainty. Degory Wheare, Thomas Godwyn, John Lemprière, Philip Morant, Richard Graves, Sir William Boxall, R.A., Sir Thomas Smith (James I's Latin secretary), Lord Chief Justice Holt, Sir Edward Turnor, Speaker and Lord Chief Baron, Lord Wenman, Archbishop Newcome, Lord James Beauclerk, Bishop of Hereford, were educated at the school. It has given seven Masters to Pembroke (Dr. Langley, Dr. Radcliffe, Dr. Brickenden, Dr. Adams, Dr. Sergrove, Dr. Smith, and Dr. G. W. Hall), and four Heads to other societies, viz. W. Walker, D.C.L., to St. John's, John Clarke, D.D., to Oriel, John Viscount Tracy, D.D., to All Souls, and James Gerard, D.D., to Wadham. Roysse ordained that the children of poor men [1] and fatherless children of widows should be preferred, if apt for learning ; but the Corporation were ' not to refuse any honest man, gentleman, or rich man's sonne or others in the said town or elsewhere that be willing to have them taught in the said schole.' As usual in eleemosynary foundations, reforms and the spirit of the age have deprived the poor of much that was intended for them ; and the Royal Commission of 1819 elicited the fact that Bennet's Poor Scholars seldom, if ever, in spite of Bennet's and Tesdale's wills, offered themselves for election to Pembroke scholarships. However, they have continued down to the present time, whereas Roysse's sixty-three children by Dr. Lemprière's time (1799–1809) had vanished, though in 1766 they existed in full numbers, besides forty boarders in the Master's house. The boarders went on, but the Day Boys grew fewer and fewer. The explanation given to the Commission was that few of the inhabitants of Abingdon wished a learned education for their sons. They had not, it would seem, appreciated the Classical Dictionary. The boarders on the other hand were usually placed at the school with a view to the Pembroke scholarships, to which they were considered eligible after a short residence. They were a source of income to the Ludimagister, and more of a credit to the College as regards attainments than the ordinary Abingdon tradesman's son. Any pupil coming within a twelvemonth of an expected election was required to pay the Master twenty guineas. The

---

[1] Hearne records (1712), 'The Town of Abbingdon was pitch'd about 20 Years agoe. It cost above a thousand Pounds. All the Charges were defray'd by one Person who had been educated in the Free-Schoole. He was of mean Extract' (*Collections*, ed. Doble, O. II. S., iii. 394).

usher taught humanity to Bennet's Poor Scholars exclusively. These arrangements the commissioners considered a departure from the intention of the foundation. At present the re-constituted school is flourishing in point of numbers under the Rev. Thomas Layng.

In the year 1870 the school was moved into new buildings just outside the town. They lack as yet a chapel. There was a small water-colour of the old schoolhouse made by Samuel Smith, one of Dr. Lemprière's pupils, in 1793, and copied by another, Augustine Gratton, in 1844.

Along one side of St. Helen's churchyard, near the bank of the Isis, lies, behind its fragrant limes, the long, low, cloistered Hospital of the Poor of Christ (founded by Edward VI in the home of the Fraternity of the Holy Cross), one of the most beautiful of the monuments of mediæval piety and munificence. In the small panelled hall, lit by the blazoned glass of a large oriel, among other interesting portraits, is the best picture of Tesdale, and next it the presentment of 'Mawd Teasdale,' his wife, painted in 1612, in her sixty-seventh year. She is in widow's weeds and holds a small book of devotion. The inscription on the former is, "Hanc Thomae Teasdale Armigeri Effigiem d.d. Joannes Stevenson Hypodidascalus, 1763.' There is also a portrait of Roysse. The property of his school has always been vested in the governors of Christ's Hospital, who employ the considerable wealth of that foundation for public-spirited purposes. It may be hoped that they will not suffer the old schoolhouse to fall into decay.

NOTE A.

CAESAR'S LODGINGS.

MR. CLARK writes (Wood, *City of Oxford*, i. 634, *n.*): 'The building called " Cesar's Lodgings " or (more shortly) " Cesar," was a tumble-down house opposite the place where the Martyrs' Memorial now stands. The current modern tradition ascribes the origin of its name to its having been the residence of Sir Julius Caesar (1558–1636). Wood however says it was so called from the residence there of Henry Caesar, afterwards dean of Ely, Sir Julius' brother. This building was not taken down till some years after 1840. Having got the name "Cesar," an opposite stack of buildings was naturally called "Pompey." Pompey was pulled down shortly after 1830.' Chalmers says it was 'an area on the north-west consisting of several detached lodgings.' Wood says that

Julius and Henry were the sons of '*Caesar Dalmarius* of the city of *Trevignie* in *Italy*, doctor of Physick and Physician to Qu. *Mary* and Qu. *Elizabeth*, Son of *Pet. Maria Dalmarius* of the said City Doctor of Laws, but descended from those of his name living at *Frejus* or *Cividad del Friuli* in the confines of *Italy*[1]' As regards Sir Julius, ' In the beginning of 1581 he was created Doctor of [Civil] Law in the University of *Paris* and had Letters testimonial for it, under the Seal of that University, dated 22 Apr. 1581, wherein he is stiled *Julius Caesar alias Dalmarius, Dioc. London in Anglia, filius excellentissimi in Art. & Med. Doctoris Caesaris Dalmarii, in Universitate Paris*, etc. This Julius Caesar, who was also Doctor of the Canon Law, was afterwards Master of the *Requests*, Judge of the *Admiralty*, in the time of Qu. *Elizabeth*, a Knight, Chancellour and under-Treasurer of the *Exchecquer*, Master of the *Rolls*, and Privy Counsellour to K. *James*, and K. *Ch. I.* He gave way to fate at the *Rolls* in Chancery lane, 16. April, 1636, and was buried in the Chancel of *Great St. Ellen's* Church in *Bishopsgate-Street* in *London*, near to the grave of his father before mention'd, *Caesar Dalmare* or *Athelmer*, who was buried there in 1569[2]' He sate in parliament for Westminster, Middlesex, Reigate, Bletchingley, New Windsor, and Malden. He was connected by marriage with Bacon, who died in his arms. His sons, Sir Charles, Sir John, Julius, Robert, and Thomas, were all men who played a leading part.

Lloyd (*State Worthies*) describes Sir Julius as 'a person of prodigious bounty to all of worth or want, so that he might seem to be Almoner-general of the Nation. . . . The story is well known of a gentleman who once borrowing his Coach (which was as well known to poor people as any Hospital in England) was so rendezvous'd about with Beggars in *London* that it cost him all the money in his purse to satisfie their importunity ; so that he might have hired twenty Coaches on the same terms.' He bore Gules, three roses arg., on a chief of the 1st so many roses of the 2nd, 'embleming the fragrancy of the Memory he hath left behind him.'

In the eighteenth century Caesar's Buildings were threatened with demolition. In a poem recited in the Sheldonian on July 8, 1773, at the installation of Lord North, decrying changes that were taking place, the author says :—

> ' Ignoscant Baliolenses
> Si verum fatear. Quanquam nitidissima surgat
> Fisheri moles, mihi sit cum Caesare semper
> Pompeiove locus; veteri gratoque recessu
> Et studiis apto. Sed ni malus auguror, ipse
> Cum Pompeio una Caesar mox concidet. Unam
> Haec aetas utrique feret malesana ruinam.'

---

[1] *Athenae*, i. 738.   [2] Ibid. i. 753.

NOTE B.

CHARTER FELLOWS AND SCHOLARS.

THE first of the original fellows was THOMAS GODWYN, already known as a learned writer. He entered Magdalen Hall, May 7, 1602, aged fifteen (second son of Anthony, of Wookey, Somerset, pleb.) ; demy of Magdalen 1604-10 ; B.A. 1607 ; M.A. 1609. He was then chosen Chief Master of Roysse's School, which he brought into a flourishing condition. He printed 'for the vse of Abingdon Schoole' a *Florilegium Phrasicon* (1613? or 1614), and also in 1613, published at Oxford, his *Romanae Historiae Anthologia.* Finding the pedant's profession too laborious for his strength, he left Abingdon in 1616 to become chaplain to Bishop Montague. In that year Godwyn proceeded B.D., and dedicated to his patron *Synopsis Antiquitatum Hebraicarum* (Oxford, 4to, three books). While at Abingdon he espoused Philippa Tesdale, whom I cannot trace, and afterwards Elizabeth Tesdale. Wood thinks he was in 1624 still master of Abingdon School. His *Moses and Aaron*, put forth the next year, attracted a good deal of learned notice and went through many editions. Bishop Montague in 1626 presented him to Brightwell, Berks, where he died March 20, 164⅜, and is buried in the chancel. His wife survived him. An Arminian work of Godwyn's—*Three Arguments to prove Election upon Foresight of Faith*—embroiled him in a warm controversy with Dr. William Twiss of Newbury. According to Samuel Clarke, 'Dr. T. promptly whipped the old schoolmaster.' Godwyn had taken D.D. Nov. 18, 1637.

ROBERT PAYNE (matr. Christ Church, July 5, 1611, aged fifteen ; B.A. July 4, 1614 ; M.A. July 4, 1617) was the second Charter fellow. He came from Abingdon. He was canon of Christ Church 1638-48 ; created D.D. Nov. 1, 1642. Dr. Payne seems to have been sequestered in 1646 from the rectory of Tormarton by the Westminster Assembly, because 'he hath deserted the Cure for the space of three years past, and resided in yᵉ garrison of Oxon.'

CHRISTOPHER TESDALE was at first at New College (matr. Feb. 22, 161⅘, aged nineteen ; B.A. Oct. 29, 1614 ; M.A. June 10, 1618). In 1626 he was made canon of Chichester, and in 1628 preferred to a stall at Wells; parson of Rollstone, Wilts, 1633 ; of Hurstbourne Tarrant, Hants, 1638 ; of Everleigh, Wilts, 1646. He sate in the Westminster Assembly, with his cousin John Tesdale, and preached before the House of Commons a fast sermon—'Jerusalem, or a Vision of Peace'—Aug. 28, 1644. His son and grandson were fellows.

NICHOLAS COXETER was also an Abingdonian. He had been a member of Broadgates (matr. Nov. 10, 1615, aged eighteen ; B.A. from Magdalen Hall 1619 ; M.A. 1622). In 1625 he became vicar of Dunstew, Oxon.

CHARLES SAGAR was probably the son of Charles Sagar, parson of South Morton (ob. 1602), and himself rector there, dying 1637.

THOMAS WESTLEY entered Christ Church June 2, 1617, aged nineteen (of London, gent.); B.A. 1617; M.A. 1620. In 1625 he was preferred to Marcham, Berks; in 1634 to Wells St. Cuthbert; and in 1635 to East Brent. At the Restoration he was made canon of Wells.

WILLIAM LYFORD, son of William Lyford, rector of Peasemore (ob. 1632), entered Magdalen Hall April 28, 1615, aged seventeen; demy of Magdalen 1617–20; B.A. 1618; fellow of Magdalen 1620–33; M.A. 1621 (incorporated at Cambridge 1623); B.D. 1631. He succeeded his father at Peasemore (1632–7); vicar of Sherborne, 1632. He sate in the Westminster Assembly. Died Oct. 3, 1653. There were Lyfords at Stanford Deanly, and William was doubtless a Tesdale fellow.

HENRY WIGHTWICKE was afterwards Master; *vide infra.*

JOHN PRICE was on the Wightwick foundation. Probably B.A. from Magdalen July 7, 1627.

WILLIAM GRIFFITH was a member of Broadgates (matr. Nov. 10, 1621, aged eighteen; of com. Gloucester, gent.). He proceeded B.C.L. March 17, 162⅘.

SCHOLARS.

JOHN LEE, son of John, of a good Abingdon family, entered Balliol as a Tesdale scholar Oct. 11, 1622, aged nineteen; B.A. Oct. 19, 1622. At Pembroke, 'as at Balliol, he was an indefatigable Student and of proficiency answerable. He wrote an enterlude, but never acted or published, and hath a Lat. Speech in print[1].' M.A. July 2, 1625. The speech is that delivered at the inauguration of the College. He died shortly after. 'It may be said of all the other five together compared to him,' writes Savage of the Tesdale scholars, 'as was answered of *Mercuries* Picture in the fable compared to *Jupiter's* and *Juno's*, viz. That he that would buy these two, should have the third into the bargain.'

WILLIAM READE was also an Abingdonian, and placed at Balliol (matr. Oct. 26, 1621, aged seventeen; B.A. Oct. 16, 1623).

FRANCIS DRINGE took B.A. from Balliol Feb. 6, 162⅘; M.A. from Pembroke, July 6, 1626. Kin to Tesdale.

RICHARD ALLEN, from Abingdon, plebeii filius, entered Balliol July 16, 1621; B.A. June 10, 1624. He was afterwards fellow of Pembroke; M.A. April 17, 1627. Allen was beneficed near Ewelme. He wrote *An Antidote against Heresie; or a Preservative for Protestants against the Poyson of Papists, Anabaptists,* etc., Lond. 1648, dedicated to his uncles, Sir Thomas Gainsford, Knt., and Humphry Huddleston, Esq.

JOHN BOWLES took B.A. from Balliol June 22, 1626. He became a fellow of Pembroke; M.A. 1629; created B.D. 1642. For his warfare with the Parliamentary Commissioners *vide infra.*

JOHN GRACE.

THOMAS MILLINGTON, son of Walter, of Hopton Castle, Salop, pleb. Matr. June 15, 1627.

HUMPHREY GWYNNE.

[1] *Ath. Ox.* i. 851.

RICHARD KIRFOOTE.

GEORGE GRIFFITH, afterwards Bishop of St. Asaph, entered Christ Church, as a Westminster student, Nov. 12, 1619; B.A. June 26, 1623; M.A. May 9, 1626; B.D. Oct. 23, 1632; licensed to preach 1633; D.D. Nov. 4, 1634. He was the third son of Robert Griffith, of Carreylwyd, gent., and was born at Llanfaethlu, Anglesey, Sept. 30, 1601. He was distinguished as a college tutor and as a preacher. He became chaplain to Bishop Owen, who made him Canon and Archdeacon of St. Asaph (1632), and rector of Newtown, Llanfechain, Llandrinio, and Llanymyrach. In the Convocation of 1640 he urged the need of a new edition of Bishop Morgan's Welsh Bible, himself afterwards undertaking a translation of the revised Common Prayer of 1661 into the British tongue. He described himself as an 'episcopal presbyterian'; and in a public disputation with Vavasour Powel, in 1652, argued that 'mixt ways' were better than separation. Dr. Griffith had much controversy with the Itinerants. 'Keeping up the Offices and Ceremonies' of the Church he was deprived of 'most or all of his Spiritualities,' and 'therefore rewarded after his Majesties Restauration.' By Sheldon's influence he was nominated to St. Asaph, and consecrated Oct. 28, 1660, with four others. The see, however, had very meagre revenues. Griffith took some part in the Savoy Conference, 'speaking but once or twice a few words calmly.' Lloyd affirms that the new form of Adult Baptism was composed by him. Certainly he was one of three prelates charged with the task. In his diocese he restored order and cared for sacred fabricks. He died Nov. 28, 1666. The short inscription on his tomb in his cathedral church ends, 'Qui plura desiderat, facile investiget.'

The last four of these scholars were named on the Wightwick foundation.

CHAPTER XVI.

KING, CHANCELLOR, AND PRIMATE.

THE charter granted to the College designated it as 'of the foundation of KING JAMES[1].' Kings, at any rate in more recent centuries,
have not usually been able to give more than their favour and name to
any institution; or if, like Henry VIII, they have bestowed more, it
has been taken from Peter to enrich Paul. If James I gave Pembroke
nothing but his patronage, Charles I presented it with a substantial
endowment, and his Grand-daughter augmented the income of the
Mastership with a canonry.

There is perhaps some disinclination to claim the shrewdest of
Sophomores as Founder, as there is at Christ Church disinclination to
own the greatest and most erudite of Robbers. But James I's many
unkingly qualities have created a disposition to do him less than
justice as an acute patron of letters, who attracted many learned men
to England. When he visited Oxford he came, Mr. Goldwin Smith
remarks, to 'a seat of learning where he felt supreme, and, to do him
justice, was not unqualified to shine[2].' Southey quotes Burton:
'When he went into the Bodleian he broke out into that noble speech:
"If I were not a king I would be an University man; et si unquam
mihi in fatis sit ut captivus ducar, si mihi daretur optio, hoc cuperem
carcere concludi, his catenis illigari, cum hisce captivis concatenatis
aetatem agere." ' He would have been pleased to know that, though the
chains of that priceless captivity have long been struck off the books,
a fellow[3] of his own College succeeded in defeating the conversion
of the Bodleian into a lending library. At the Hampton Court Conference the king excelled both sides not only in good temper but in

[1] In a document of 1636, 'of the foundation of James late king, in the charge
and custody of Thomas Teasdell and Richard Whitwick.'

[2] Christopher Trevelyan reports to his father that the King showed great learning
in his disputing and moderating: 'who always graced the University exceedingly'
(Trevelyan Papers). 'He was not more pleasant at no time since he came into
England.'

[3] The late Professor Chandler.

learning. It was to James that Shakespeare paid the fine compliment,

' Knowledge makes a king most like his Maker';

and he wrote with his own royal hand a letter to the playwright. If the splendid panegyric at the end of *Henry the Eighth* is flattery, to have been flattered by Shakespeare is glory enough. This prince was a considerable benefactor of the library of St. Andrews. For the Bodleian he procured the valuable right to a copy of every book issued. He loved to connect himself with the universities of his kingdoms and concern himself with their minutest affairs. He visited Oxford within two years of his accession. He confirmed it and Cambridge in their privileges, and gave them their representation in Parliament and patronage of Romanist livings. James augmented thè Regius professorship of Divinity, and the chairs of Law and Physic. This set an example, and in his reign Saville founded two Mathematical lectures, Camden a History chair, Sedley one in Natural Philosophy, Dr. White one in Moral Philosophy, Tomlins an Anatomy lecture; the Physic Garden was inaugurated, and the noble structure of the Schools built. Besides the two new Oxford foundations, Harvard was endowed by a Cambridge man not long after James's accession. His wish, therefore, to be considered the founder of a new College at Oxford was not an unmeaning whim, but one of many proofs of an enlightened enthusiasm for the promotion of the arts and knowledges.

Over the south entrance of Wilton church, now destroyed, under the many-quartered arms of Herbert, was the following inscription, as given by Sir Richard Hoare [1]:—

' Be it remembered, that at the 8th day of April 1589 [1580?], on Friday, before 12 of the clock at night of the same day, was born William Lord Herbert of Cardiffe, first child of the Noble Henry Herbert, Erle of Pembroke, by his most dere wyfe Mary, daughter of the Right Hon[ble] Sir Henry Sidney, Knight of the most noble order, &c. and the Lady Mary [2], daughter to the famous John Duke of Northumberland, and was Xt'ned the 28th day of the same month, in the mannour of Wilton. The Godmother, y[e] mighty and most excellent Princess Elizabeth, by the grace of God Queene of England, by her deputye the most virtuous Lady Anne Countice of Warwick; and the Godfathers were the Noble and famous Erle Ambrose, Erle of Warwick, and Robert Erle of Lycester, both great uncles to the infant by the mother's side, Warwick in person, and Lycester by his deputye Philip Sydney, Esq., uncle, by the mother's side, to the fore-

---

[1] *History of Wiltshire*, Hundred of Branch and Dole, p. 143.
[2] The Countess Mary was that ' Subject of all verse, Sidney's sister, Pembroke's mother,' of whom Jonson sings, and to whom the *Arcadia* was dedicated.

named young Lord Herbert of Cardiff, whom the Almighty and most precious God blesse, with his mother above-named, with prosperous life in all happiness, in the name of God. *Amen.*'

The petition of the burgesses of Abingdon to King James had been presented by the Chancellor of the University, WILLIAM HERBERT, third EARL OF PEMBROKE, the most eminent of a family, Welsh in origin, in which that title had been twice revived, viz. by Edward IV and by Henry VIII. It was resolved to name the College after him. Aubrey styles him ' the greatest Maecenas to learned men of any peer of his time or since.' He and his brother Philip, the Puritan libertine, are the ' incomparable pair of brethren' to whom Shakespeare's first folio was dedicated by the editors in 1623. Mr. Gardiner calls him 'the Hamlet of Charles's Court.' In his 'Observations on the Life of William, Earl of Pembroke,' Fuller says :—

' He was an ancient gentleman of good repute, and therefor well esteemed ; a proper person well set, and of graceful deportment, and therefor well beloved of King James and queen Anne ; his inclination was as generous as his extraction, and manners ancient as his family. One of his ancestors is renowned, for that he would condescend to deliver his embassies in no language but Welsh ; he is commended for that he would comply with no customs in his converse but the old English— though his contemporaries make that his defect rather than his ornament, proceeding from his want of travel rather than his observance of antiquity : he having had only (saith the historian) the breeding of England, which gave him a conceited dislike of foreign men their manners and mode, or of such English as professed much advantage thereby ; so that the Scots and he were ever separate ; and therefore he was the only old courtier that kept close to the commonalty and they to him, though never suspected by either of his sovereigns ; not because he was not over-furnished with abilities (as that pen insinuates) to be *more* than loyal, but because he had too much integrity to be less.

' Being munificent and childless, the University of Oxford hoped to be his executor, and Pembroke Colledge his heir—Pembroke Colledge, I say, called so not only in respect to, but also in expectation from him, then chancellor of the university ; and probably had not our noble Lord died suddenly soon after (according as a fortune teller had informed him, whom he laughed at that very night he departed, being his birth-night), this colledge might have received more than a bare name from him. " He was (saith one of his own time [1]) the very picture and Viva Effigies of nobility ; his person rather majestick than elegant ; his presence, whether quiet or in motion, full of stately gravity ; his mind generous and purely heroick ; often stout but never disloyal ; so vehement an opponent of the Spaniard as, when that match fell under consideration, he would some-

---

[1] Anthony Wood, *Athenae,* i. 795.

times rouze to the trepidation of king James, yet kept in favour still; for
that king knew plain dealing as a jewel in all men, so was in a privy-
councellor an ornamental duty. . . . The same true-heartedness commended him to king Charles, with whom he kept a most admirable
correspondence, and yet stood the firm confident of the commonalty;
and that not by a sneaking cunning but by an erect and generous
prudence, such as rendered him as unsuspected of ambition on the one
side as of faction on the other, being generally beloved and regarded[1]." '

The story of his death on April 8, 1630, is thus referred to by
Clarendon :—

At a meeting 'of some Persons of Quality, of relation or dependence
upon the said Earl of Pembroke (Sir Charles Morgan, Dr. Feild Bishop
of St. David's, and Dr. Chafin the Earl's chaplain) at Supper one of them
drank a health to the Lord Steward ; upon which another of them said
that he believ'd his Lord was at that time very Merry, for he had now
outliv'd the day which his Tutor Sandford[2] had prognosticated upon his
Nativity he would not outlive; but he had done it now, for that was his
Birth-day, which had compleated his age to fifty years. The next morning, by the time they came to Colebrook, they met with the news of his
Death.'

He died at Baynard's Castle, his house in London. Aubrey says
that he ' intended to prove a great benefactor' to the College. ' He was
master,' says Clarendon, ' of a great Fortune . . . but all serv'd not
his Expence, which was only limited by his great mind and occasions
to use it nobly. . . . He was rather regarded and esteem'd by King
James than lov'd and favour'd. . . . As his Conversation was most with
men of the most pregnant parts and understanding, so towards any
such who needed support or encouragement, though unknown, if fairly
recommended to him, he was very liberal.' Every New Year's day
Jonson received £20 from Pembroke to buy books. Inigo Jones
visited Italy at his charges. Massinger was trained up at Wilton and
supported by the Earl at St. Alban Hall. He was the friend of Donne.
Chapman, Davison, and others dedicated grateful poems to him.
Bacon thanked him for ' the moderation and affection his lordship
shewed in my business,' and solicited his future favour ' for the
furtherance of my private life and fortune.' Across the ocean the
Virginians spoke of the Pembroke River, now the Rappahannock, and
part of the Bermudas was named after the powerful and princely
noble. He died leaving no child to inherit, and the young College
that bore his name may have hoped to be regarded as his issue.

---

[1] *State Worthies*, ii. 230.

[2] Similar predictions were made by Ellinor Davies, and by Thomas Allen of
Gloucester Hall (*Athenae*, i. 866). Wood there says he died April 10th.

> 'O that you were yourself! But, love, you are
> No longer yours than you yourself here live.
> Against this coming end you should prepare,
> And your sweet semblance to another give.'

If so, such expectations were shattered by his sudden and intestate death. The year before he had purchased the famous Baroccio library of 250 Greek MSS. brought from Venice by a London stationer, and 'by the Perswasion of Archbishop Laud' presented it to the University. It was thought to be 'the most valuable Collection that ever came into England.' He gave it 'remembering the obligation he had to his Mother the University, first for breeding him, after for the honour they did in making him their Chancellor.' He was elected January 29, 1617. 'Following Laud's direction,' says Prof. Margoliouth, Pembroke was both a benefactor and reformer of the University. His escutcheon is over the south gateway of the Schools.

There is a brass statue of this earl, designed by Rubens and carried out by Lesœur, in the Bodleian Gallery, once at Wilton, and a full-length painting by Vandyck—in a black dress with George and Garter, holding his white wand of office. In this and in the fine portraits at Wilton by Vandyck and Mytens he is seen not in 'the lovely April of his prime,' or in that first melancholy beauty of 'a woman's face with Nature's own hand painted,' the 'seemly raiment' of the poet's heart—

> 'The flowers I noted, yet I none could see
> But sweet or colour it had stolen from thee'—

but he appears in the early autumn of noble manhood a little before his untimely death, not yet 'crush'd and o'erworn' by decay's 'injurious hand,' or dimmed by 'age's steepy night,' and 'wreckful siege of battering days.'

> 'Time, carve not with thy hours my love's fair brow,
> Nor draw no lines there with thine antique pen.'

William Herbert lies with his mother, with Sidney, and others of his house, in Salisbury Cathedral, in front of the present high altar; but no 'marble herse' marks the spot.

> 'Your monument shall be my gentle verse,
> Which eyes yet not created shall o'er read;
> And tongues to be your being shall rehearse,
> When all the breathers of this world are dead.'

> 'O Muse, it lies in thee
> To make him much outlive a gilded tomb,
> And to be praised of ages yet to be.'

It is related that, when his body was opened for embalming, he lifted his hand, 'affording a presumption that he died of apoplexy.' 'A singular lover of learning and of the professours thereof,' says Wood. 'Himself learned, and endowed to admiration with a poetical genie, as by those amorous and not inelegant Aires and Poems of his composition doth evidently appear; some of which had musical Notes set to them, by *Hen. Lawes* and *Nich. Laneare.*' Pembroke's poems, mingled with verses by Raleigh, Dyer, Carew, and others, were edited in 1660 by Donne, and reprinted in 1817. They are graceful but not sinewy. Clarendon, in a fine study of his character, of which he does not conceal some darker features, styles this nobleman 'the most universally loved and esteemed of any man of that age.'

There is an older Foundation of the same name at Cambridge—which claimed in Wood's time to be the oldest in the land—Ridley's 'own dear College,' called from the number of its prelate sons 'collegium episcopale,' and by Elizabeth apostrophized as 'domus antiqua et religiosa.' Spenser, Gray, and Pitt were there. Pembroke Hall, which has dropped that honourable style for the commonplace 'College,' was founded in the fourteenth century by Mary, widow of Aylmer de Valencia, Earl of Pembroke, and was long called 'the Hall or House of Valence Mary.' These earls of Pembroke were unconnected with the later family which bore and bears that title.

Tesdale's noble bequest had been suggested by DR. GEORGE ABBOT (1562–1633), then Bishop of London—'ad hanc munificentiam,' wrote Clayton to him on the morrow of the inauguration of Pembroke College, 'per Te edoctus, animatus Tisdallus.' 'Patronus noster colendissimus,' he styles him. Abbot had been Fellow of Balliol (1583) and Master of University (1597). The deanery of Winchester, which Elizabeth gave him in 1599, had connected him with New College. As principal trustee under Tesdale's will he could have secured the £5,000 for one of these societies. His promotion of the Pembroke project may have been actuated by the wish to please the King. The statement in the *Dictionary of National Biography* that the archbishop 'contributed largely to the new foundation of Pembroke' must not be understood of pecuniary benefaction [1], nor was he in sufficient favour

---

[1] Abbot gave £100 to the Balliol Library, £100 to University, and £150 to the Schools building. He founded the hospital for decayed tradesmen at Guildford (where his father had been a clothworker), and built a conduit at Canterbury. Heylin however asserts that 'marks of his benefactions we find none in places of his breeding and preferment.' Onslow says, 'he was eminent for piety and a care for the poor, and his hospitality fully answered the injunction King James laid on him, which was to carry his house nobly, and live like an archbishop.'

at Court in 1624 to do much for its fortunes.   Yet he stood in a very
fatherly relation to the new College.   'Paucis habeto gratitudinem
Tuorum Pembrochiensium,' writes the Master, 'rationem redditam
actorum in natalibus Collegii hujus nuperi, in honorem & solatium
Tuum, qui benefacta Tui Tisdalli non male locata laetabere.'   The
Primate is humbly prayed to number the members of the College,
bereaved of their Founder, his friend, among his sons.   As Tesdale's
beneficiaries they were committed to his guardianship.   While Vice-
Chancellor, Abbot had endeavoured to check the rising Laudian
movement, and Clarendon remarks that he was 'totally ignorant of
the true constitution of the Church of England[1].'   But he did not
impress any puritan character on the newly founded College.   Wood
says that the archbishop ' was a learned man and had his erudition all
of the old stamp.'   'King James,' remarks Speaker Onslow, 'had too
much affectation that way to prefer any one to such a station who had
not borne the reputation of a scholar.   His parts seem to have been
strong and masterly, his preaching grave and eloquent, and his style
equal to any of that time.'   Clarendon ambiguously observes, ' He
had been master of one of the poorest colleges in Oxford, and had
learning sufficient for that province.'   Abbot's best known work is
his *Exposition of Jonah*, delivered between 1594 and 1599 in
St. Mary's early on Thursday mornings, ' sometimes before daybreak.'
But his chief glory must be his part in the sacred and deathless
English of the Four Gospels.   He seems to have been an honest but
tactless ruler, who had the art of making enemies and shooting at
the wrong quarry.   ' According to his desire his body was buried in
the Chappel of *our Lady* within *Trinity* Church in *Guildford*.   Over
his grave was soon after built a sumptuous Altar, or Table-monument,
with his proportion in his *Pontificalia* lying thereon, supported by six
pillars of the Dorick order, of black Marble, standing on six pedestals
of piled books with a large inscription.'

---

[1] ' He considered the Christian religion no otherwise than as it abhorred or
reviled popery.'   Clarendon speaks of his morose manners and sour aspect.   Wood,
who however praises his piety and gravity, remarks that 'he, having never been
Rector or Vicar of a parish, and so consequently was in a manner ignorant of the
trouble that attended the ministers of God's word, was the cause (as some think)
why he was harsh to them, and why he shew'd more respect to a Cloak than
a Cassock' (*Athenae*, i. 499).   His services however in restoring apostolic
discipline in Scotland, while in attendance on the Earl of Dunbar, had caused
James to nominate him to the see of Lichfield and Coventry.   He strongly dis-
approved his brother Robert's second marriage just after his consecration as
bishop.

CHAPTER XVII.

MASTERSHIPS OF CLAYTON AND LANGLEY.

THE last Principal of Broadgates and first Master of Pembroke was a man of considerable mark, DR. THOMAS CLAYTON, Regius Professor of Medicine. The previous century had been one of much advance in physical studies. In 1524 Thomas Lynacre had endowed two lectures in that science, hitherto in monkish hands. Edward VI consolidated the two lectureships in one, and a royal endowment was added to the chair by James I, who in 1617 annexed to it the Mastership of Ewelme Hospital. Dr. Clayton, who had been made King's Professor of Physick March 9, 1611, was the first to hold the Ewelme preferment, when it fell vacant in 1628. In 1623, shortly after Harvey's great discovery of the circulation of the blood, Mr. Richard Tomlyns, of Westminster, endowed a praelectorship in Anatomy, and the first reader nominated by him[1] was Dr. Clayton, who delivered his inaugural lecture March 12, 1624. Clayton was also Musick Professor in Gresham College, 1607-11. He had originally[2] been a member of Balliol (matr. Oct. 15, 1591, aged sixteen; B.A. Oct. 17, 1594), but took M.A. from Gloucester Hall (where he had pupils) March 31, 1599. In 1605 he disputed in Natural Philosophy before the King. He was licensed to practise medicine in 1610; M.B. and M.D. from Balliol June 20, 1611. On June 14, 1620, in his capacity of Professor of Medicine, he was nominated by the Earl of Pembroke to succeed Budden as Principal of Broadgates. What part Clayton took in bringing about the transformation from Hall to College we can only surmise. It has

---

[1] The Regius Professor of Physick was always to be the Reader. The salary of £25 was enlarged in 1638. ' The chief office of the Reader is every Springtime, immediately after the Assizes are ended, to procure an intire and Sound body of one of the Malefactors then condemn'd or hang'd; or, if that cannot be done, to get an intire and sound Body of some other Person; which being thus procur'd he is oblig'd to have it prepar'd and cut up by some Skillful Surgeon' (Hearne, ii. 379). He was to lecture four times on the corpse and have it decently buried, 'for which he is to allow fourty shillings.' Every term he must 'read publickly upon the Bones' thrice.

[2] Gutch in a note (p. 617) says he was first at Gloucester Hall. Clayton had his schooling at Newcastle-on-Tyne.

already been mentioned that he built the upper end of the refectory. He saw a large part of the quadrangle erected. 'The limits of the College being too small,' he acquired, in 1626, for £350 Cambey's for a Master's residence; in 1629 the lease of Summaster's (Minote Hall) was conveyed to the College by Richard Evans, barber and innholder; that of the All Souls tenement[1] by Thomas Ray of New Woodstock; that of Wylde's Entry and that of Dunstan Hall by John Glover of New Woodstock; and finally (for £120) the lease of Beef Hall by Evans, Ray, and Glover. The dismantled Library over Docklinton's aisle 'for some years before the Grand Rebellion broke out partly employed for chambers'; in Clayton's Mastership this desecration was put an end to, and the room was 'furnished and repaired by several Benefactors.' He himself gave £20 'for the setting up of four pews or repositories, besides several books as well printed as written.' 'William Gardiner of Linton, sometime of the University, gave most of, if not all, his Study of books. Sir Robert Hanson[2] of London, knight, and Dr. John Wall, sometime[3] Rector of St. Aldate's church, did give divers others.' Francis Rous 'did intend to give his whole Study, but being dissuaded to the contrary gave only his own works and some few others.'

Clayton was one of Laud's Delegates for reforming the University in 1633. In 1647, just before his death, he was placed on the Delegacy for resisting the parliamentary Visitation and the imposition of the Covenant. He died July 10, 1647, and was buried on the morrow in St. Aldate's, where two of his daughters and a son-in-law also lie. By his wife[4], daughter of his predecessor in the Chair of Medicine, Dr. Bartholomew Warner (1558–1619), he had three sons, Sir Thomas, William, and James (of whom the first two were at the

[1] So Gutch's Wood, *Colleges and Halls*, p. 623. But rather on Oct. 28, 1634.

[2] Lord Mayor 1672–3; born 1608. His great-grand-daughter, Elizabeth Wayte, of Dauntsey, was married to 'Mr. HARRY WHITWICK' (fellow of Pembroke, rector of Ashley, near Malmesbury), at Broad Somerford, Wilts, Dec. 9, 1715. Their mourning rings are in the possession of a descendant, Miss Theresa Pitt, of Malmesbury. The portraits of Sir Thomas and Lady Hanson, dated 1638, belong to Mrs. Sarah Wightwick, of Codford St. Peter, Wilts. A son, BERKELEY, entered Pembroke Aug. 6, 1662; buried in the Temple church, Nov. 9, 1679.

[3] 1617. Canon of Christ Church 1632; of Sarum 1644; vicar of Chalgrove 1637. He was also chaplain to Philip Lord Stanhope. His sermons, *Alae Seraphicae*, were partly preached in St. Aldate's. He gave £2,040 to Oxford City for charitable uses. (See *Athenae*, ii. 259.) He was 'a quaint Preacher.' Archbishop Williams said he 'was the best read in the Fathers of any he ever knew.'

[4] One of his sisters-in-law was married to John Speed, M.D., son of 'the Chronologer'; another to William Taylor, M.D.; a third to Anthony Clopton, S.T.P., rector of Stanford Dingley, Wood's godfather.

College and physicians), and four daughters, Bridget, Jane, Susanna, and Elizabeth[1]. Clayton bore—Argent, an owl; a chief indented, sable.

Under Dr. Clayton were fostered, in an inquiring age of faëry and imaginative Baconianism, the medical studies of that last of the great nurslings of Broadgates and first of the eminent sons of Pembroke, SIR THOMAS BROWNE—most strange and fascinating of our prose writers, 'the cardinal example,' according to Mr. Saintsbury, 'of the thought and manner of his time,' 'uniting in an extraordinary degree' (says another writer) 'fantastic speculation with scientific research, exquisite imaginative subtlety with patient common sense, unquestioning faith with calculating accuracy of thought, childlike reverence with minute questioning of strange mysteries, and blending many contradictory elements into harmony through the sweetness of a spirit of meditative gentleness.' His father, Thomas Browne, of worshipful Cheshire descent, had settled in London as a mercer, and died, leaving £9,000. The widow gave her hand to Sir Thomas Dutton, and left her boy to the care of rapacious guardians. A family group by Dobson, which is, or was, at Devonshire House, represents him in childhood. He was sent, however, to Winchester, and on December 5, 1623, entered Broadgates, aged eighteen. Mr. Foster (*Alumni*) says that he was a fellow of Pembroke; I do not know on what evidence. One of the treasures of the College library is the MS. of the *Religio Medici*, presented in 1783 by the Rev. T. Wrigley, M.A. A letter to Dugdale on receipt of the second volume of the *Monasticon*, dated 'Sept. xi [1661] Norwich,' was given in 1895 by Dr. G. Birkbeck Hill. It was in the Dawson-Turner Collection till 1859. Browne took B.A. Jan. 31, 1624; M.A. June 11, 1629, having, on July 10, 1637, incorporated D.Med. from Leyden (Padua, *Foster*).

After practising medicine for a time round Oxford, he was induced by Dr. Lushington, his college tutor, then rector of Burnham Westgate, to settle at Norwich, where he was much resorted to for his skill. He is also described as sometime of Shipden Hall, Yorks. In 1641, though he held woman to be 'but the rib or crooked part of man,' and had wished the race of men might be propagated like trees, he espoused Dorothy Mileham, who bore him twelve children. The following year *Religio Medici*, written in 1634, was surreptitiously given by a friend to the world, and in a Latin version excited attention throughout Europe by

[1] Elizabeth Clayton = John Milbourne, of Alleston, Glouc., gent. One of her sons, Thomas, was fellow of Merton; ob. 1676, aet. 23; the other, Clayton, represented Monmouth in Queen Anne's reign. Dr. Clayton's sister, Mrs. Elizabeth Lee, collected donations in 1620 from merchants living on London Bridge for the 'new hall' of Broadgates. His brother James was also a donor.

its paradoxical orthodoxy, its curious learning, its rich and lofty sentiment.   Guy Patin writes from Paris in 1645, 'On faict icy grand état du
livre intitulé *Religio Medici*.'   The recondite erudition displayed in these
musings of 'a philosopher most inward to nature' would be more widely
appreciated than the stately and strange charm of Browne's style.   Kenelm
Digby admired the book, and feared for his own literary pre-eminence.
Salmasius said, however, that it 'contained many exorbitant conceptions
in religion, and probably would find but frowning entertainment, especially
among the ministers.'   Buddaeus enrols Browne among English atheists.
The *Religio* was indexed at Rome.   On the other hand he was accused
of Romanism.   The book has been called 'a *tour de force* of intellectual
agility; an attempt to combine daring scepticism with implicit faith in
revelation.'   His questionings indeed are those of an inquisitive child.
'There is nothing,' he says, 'more acceptable unto the ingenious World
than this noble Eluctation of Truth; wherein against the tenacity of
Prejudice and Prescription this Century now prevaileth[1].'   Browne
represents the double reaction, conservative and latitudinarian, against
Calvinism.   The Quakers, because of his mysticism, hoped he would join
them.   He says of himself: 'I am naturally inclined to that which mis-
guided zeal terms superstition, my common conversation I do acknowledge
austere, my behaviour full of rigour, sometimes not without morosity;
yet at my devotion I love to use the civility of my knee hat and hand,
with all those outward and sensible motions which may expresse or
promote my invisible devotion.   I should cut off my arme rather than
violate a Church window, than deface or demolish the memory of a Saint
or Martyr.   At the sight of a Crosse or Crucifix I can. dispence with my
hat, but not with the thought or memory of my Saviour.   I cannot laugh
at the fruitlesse journey of Pilgrims or contemne the miserable condition
of Friars, for, though misplaced circumstances, there is something in it of
devotion.   I could never hear the *Ave Marie* Bell without an oration
[prayer]. . . . At a solemne procession I have wept abundantly, while my
consorts, blind with opposition and prejudice, have fallen into an accesse
of scorne and laughter.   There are, questionlesse, both in Greek, Roman,
and African Churches, solemnities and ceremonies whereof the wiser
zeales do make a Christian use, and stand condemned by us, not as evill
in themselves, but as allurances and baits of superstition to those vulgar
heads that look asquint on the face of truth, and those unstable judgements that cannot consist in the narrow point and centre of justice,
without a reele or stagger to the circumference.'

He speaks of himself as 'sworn subject to the faith of the Church
of England':—

'It is an unjust scandall of our adversaries, and grosse error in our
selves, to compute the Nativity of our Religion from *Henry* the eight,
who though he rejected the Pope refused not the faith of *Rome*, and
effected no more than what his own Predecessors desired and assaied
in ages past.   It is as uncharitable a point in us to fall upon those

[1] *Christian Morals*, ii. § 5 (p. 189).

popular scurrilities and opprobrious scoffes of the Bishop of *Rome*, to whom as to a temporall Prince we owe the duty of a good language. I confesse there is cause of passion between us; by his sentence I stand excommunicated. Heretick is the best langue he affords me; yet can no eare witnesse I ever returned to him the name of Antichrist, man of sin, or whore of *Babylon*. It is the method of charity to suffer without reaction.' 'I am of that reformed new-cast Religion, wherein I dislike nothing but the name; of the same beliefe that our Saviour taught, the Apostles disseminated, the Martyrs confirmed, but by the sinister ends of Princes, the ambition and avarice of Prelates, and the fatall corruption of times so decaied, impaired, and fallen from its native beauty that it required the carefull and charitable hand of the times to restore it to its primitive integrity. . . . Yet have I not shaken hands with those desperate Resolvers, who had rather venture at large their decaied bottome than bring her in to be new trimd in the dock . . . as to stand in diameter and swords point with them. We have reformed from them, not against them; for, omitting those improperations and termes of scurrility betwixt us which only difference our affections and not our cause, there is betwixt us one common name and appellation, one faith and necessary body of principles common to us both; and therefore I am not scrupulous to converse and live with them, to enter their Churches in defect of ours; and either pray with them or for them.'

But together with this Laudianism there is something of the school of Hales and Chillingworth in our author. Browne was a student of Dante. He was of course an alchemist and an astrologer. In 1664 he was chosen *socius honorarius* of the College of Physicians, and when Charles II visited Norwich in 1671 he was knighted. Though a royalist, Browne had taken no part in the literary controversies of the Rebellion. His daughter Anne married Edward Fairfax, grandson to Thomas Lord Viscount Fairfax. The uneventful tenor of his life has caused speculation as to the meaning to be attached to his own account of it: 'For my life, it is a miracle of thirty years, which to relate were not a history but a piece of poetry, and would sound to common ears like a fable.' Perhaps he means that every life is a string of mysteries.

Johnson, who was unlikely to appreciate the Rabelaisian fancy of this great and learned knight, or the quaint humour which could contrive a dialogue between twins before birth as to their future prospects in this world, writes somewhat slightingly of Browne, and criticizes even his racy Latinisms, which had, Boswell says, influenced his own diction. Lamb, in his charming way, is a direct imitator, and he was among Coleridge's first favourites. 'Rich in various knowledge, exuberant in conception and conceits, contemplative, imaginative, often truly great and magnificent in his style and diction. . . . Whatever happens to be his subject he metamorphoses all nature into it. He seems like no other writer, and his vast and solitary abstractions, stamped with his peculiar style, like the hieroglyphic characters of the East, carry the imagination back into the primaeval ages of the world and forward into the depths of eternity.' A later critic says that the last chapter of *Urn Burial* is 'a solemn homily on death and immortality unsurpassed in literature for sustained majesty of eloquence.' The *Garden of Cyprus, or the Quincunxial Lozenge* is the most fantastical of Browne's writings. A very delightful one is his *Pseudodoxia Epidemica, or Inquiry into Vulgar Errours*, published amid the clash of arms in 1646. Johnson observes justly: 'He fell into an age in which our language began to lose the stability which it had obtained in the time of Elizabeth, and was considered by every writer as a subject on which he might try his plastick skill by moulding it according to his own fancy.' He has, Prof. Spalding observes, 'all the distinctive characteristics of the last age of the Old English period in a state of extravagant exaggeration.' I give another specimen of his manner from *Urn Burial*:—

'Time hath endless rarities . . . and a large part of the Earth is still in the Urn unto us. . . . . Egyptian ingenuity was more unsatisfied, contriving their bodies in sweet consistencies, to attend the return of their Souls. But all was vanity, feeding the wind, and folly. The Egyptian mummies which Cambyses or time hath spared avarice now consumeth. Mummy is become merchandize, Misraim cures wounds, and Pharaoh is sold for balsams.'

Browne died on his seventy-seventh birthday, Oct. 19, 1682, after eating too plentifully, Stukeley says, of a venison feast, and was buried in the great church of St. Peter Mancroft. A monument placed by his relict on a pillar south of the sanctuary, at the foot of which he lies, or lay, states him to have been 'Schola primum Wintoniensi, postea in Coll. Pembr. apud Oxonienses bonis literis haud leviter imbutus.' Dame Dorothy died in 1685. The skeleton was accidentally exposed in 1840, and his skull was 'knaved out of its grave' by the sexton, and found its way into the Norwich Hospital museum, with a portion of the beard. His hair was 'profuse and perfect and of a fine auburn colour,' but this doubtless was a periwig. The skull, on which Dr. Charles Williams of Norwich, a learned Brownian, has written a pamphlet, was toothless, dolichocephalic, the forehead remarkably low and depressed, the back deep and capacious. In 1893 the vicar of St. Peter Mancroft (Rev. W. PELHAM BURN, a Pembroke man) was requested by the vestry to beg the hospital to repair the sacrilege by restoring Browne's remains, but without result. 'Who,' he asks himself, 'knows the fate of his bones, or how often he is to be buried? Who hath the oracle of his ashes, or whither they are to be scattered?' Browne's three-quarter presentment in the Bodleian used to hang in the Anatomy School. An oil painting was presented to St. Peter's church by Dr. EDW. HOWMAN[1], a Pembrochian, who in 1739 was living in the Brownes' house at Norwich. It hangs in the board-room of the hospital. His friend Whitefoot tells us: 'his complexion and hair was answerable to his name; his stature was moderate, and a habit of body neither fat nor lean, but εὔσαρκος. . . . He was always cheerful, but rarely merry. . . . His modesty was visible in a natural habitual blush.' The College of Physicians has a half-length portrait. Lord Erskine was a direct descendant of Sir Thomas.

[1] Ob. 1753. His monument is in St. Stephen's church at Norwich. Edward Browne sold the house in 1685 to Dr. Roger Howman, his father.

Another pupil of Dr. Clayton's was Dr. George Joliffe, who migrated from Wadham to Pembroke 1638; M.A. 1643; incorporated at Cambridge 1650; M.D. from Clare Hall 1652. His anatomy lectures in the College of Physicians, about 1653, got him 'a great name.' 'He made some discovery of that fourth sort of Vessels plainly differing from veins, arteries, and nerves, now called Lympheducts[1].' Joliffe, who served as lieutenant under Lord Hopton, was buried in St. James', Garlickhithe, 1655. An eminent man in the same art whom Clayton had attracted to Broadgates was Dr. Edward Dawson, Anthony Wood's godfather, originally at Cambridge and afterwards (1620) of Lincoln College; M.D. 1633; Fellow of the College of Physicians 1634. He, like Joliffe, died young, Dec. 16, 1635. Clayton and Dawson took the leading part in the inauguration on July 25, 1622, of the Physick Garden[2]. In a Latin Epistle printed with John Day's *Concio ad Clerum*, Clayton's care for souls as well as bodies is spoken of. Day styles him 'Oxoniensium medicorum decus.' A testimony from a foreigner is contained in the dedication by Dr. James Primerose of his *Academia Monspeliensis*, 'clarissimo viro et amico singulari Thomae Clayton.' Savage styles him 'a good Linguist, to whom great Avicenne might speak and be understood without an Interpreter.'

Dr. Clayton was fortunate in securing for the new College the services of Dr. Thomas Jackson of C. C. C., afterwards President of that society, Dean of Peterborough, and Chaplain to King Charles I— 'not more noteworthy,' Walton says, 'for his learning than for his strict and pious life, testified by his abundant love and meekness and

---

[1] *Athenae*, ii. 100.

[2] Described by Mons. Sorbière in 1664 as 'small, ill-kept, and more like an orchard than a garden.' This however and the Apothecaries' Garden at Chelsea were the earliest public gardens in England. A garden attached to a University was formed at Pisa in 1545, and at Padua still earlier. With a gift of £250 from Henry Earl of Danby to buy a piece of ground for 'a nursery of phisicall simples,' Oxford University purchased in 1621 the Jews' cemetery. 'Afterwards much soil being conveyed hither for the raising of the ground, the day for the laying the first stone therof was designed. Which being come, viz. S. Jeamses day, 1622 [1621, *Life and Times*, iv. 149], the Vice-chancellor, Dr Peirce, about 2 of the clock in the afternoone togeather with the proctors and most of the doctors of the University solemnized it with great ceremony. For in the first place Mr. . . . Dawson, a phisitian of Broadgates, speak there an elegant oration; then Dr. Clayton, the King's Professor of Phisick, another; and last of all the Vice-chancellor; with the offering severall sums of money according to the antient fashion. Afterwards the said Earl proceeded in building of it, and enclosing it with a very faire wall of freestone, and in the front therof next to East Bridge Street a comly gatehouse. Then caused to be planted therin divers simples for the advancement of the faculty of phisick' (Wood's *City*, i. 291).

charity to all men.' Wood styles him ' the ornament of the University
in his time.' Bishop Horne speaks of Jackson as ' a magazine of
theological knowledge, everywhere penned with great elegance and
dignity, so that his style is a pattern of perfection.' He was logician,
mathematician, philologist, orientalist, and much more, but all his
attainments were ' as Drudges and Day-labourers to Theology.' His
biographer, Vaughan, records that Dr. Jackson ' read a lecture of
divinity in [his] college every Sunday morning, and another day
of the week at Pembroke College (then newly erected) by the instance
of the Master and Fellows there.'   As however he went to his
northern preferment in 1625[1], he cannot have done this for any
length of time, unless he resumed his lecture on his return to Oxford
in 1630.   Jackson was much esteemed by the King and by Laud,
and his profound patristic studies weaned him from Puritanism—
' transported beyond himselfe,' writes Prynne, ' with metaphysicall
contemplations, to his owne infamy and his renowned Mother's
shame, I meane the famous University of Oxford, who grieves for his
defection, from whose duggs he never suckt his poisonous doctrines.'

Dr. Clayton was followed in his chairs[2] by his son, Dr., afterwards
Sir, Thomas Clayton, Fellow of Pembroke, who had submitted to
the Visitation, and taken the Engagement—a ' poore-spirited fellow,'
says Wood.   At the Restoration he made himself useful to the
winning side, and partly owing to his absence from Oxford on
' public employments' the Act of June, 1660, was omitted.   He was
placed now himself on a commission to visit the University.   Through
the solicitations at Lambeth of his brother-in-law, Sir Charles Cotterel,
Master of the Ceremonies, Clayton was made, in 1661, Warden of
Merton.   His forcible entry on his office is a well-known episode.

' All seniors that had known what Thomas Clayton had been, did look
upon him as the most impudent fellow in nature to adventure upon such
a place, that had been held by eminent persons.   They knew him well
to have been a most impudent and rude fellow.   They knew him to have
been the very lol-poop of the University, the common subject of every
lampoon that was made, and a fellow of little or no religion, only for
forme-sake.   They knew also that he had been a most lascivious person.

---

[1] Dr. Fowler's *Memorials of Corpus Christi College*, p. 186. He vacated his fellowship Jan. 3, 162⅘, and was dispensed to hold Newcastle with Winston May 12, 1625.
[2] Matters were not quite smooth, though Clayton had ' cringed to the men of
the intervall.'   On June 12, 1649, Rous and the London Committee ordered ' That
the Visitors of the Universitie of Oxon doe represent the whole state of the businesse
concerning the place of Physicke Professor.'   On July 11 the Visitors ordered
' That Dr. Clayton be required to give a full accompt touchinge this businesse,
imediately on his retourne to Oxon.'

. . . The fellows of Merton Coll. did usually say, in the hearing of A. W., that as the College was dissolv'd in the time of the grand rebellion, so 'twas no matter to them if it was dissolv'd againe, rather than Tom Clayton should be warden thereof.'

Dame Bridget's pride and frivolity made her even more odious than her husband. Women in College had been hitherto looked upon as 'a scandall and an abomination [1].' Everything had to be altered for her, while for Sir Thomas, a man of great stature, the wicket gate had to be made higher, and a bedstead large as King Og's to be bought for £40 out of the College bag. Clayton was Regius Professor till 1665, but had resigned the Anatomy Chair in favour of his deputy, Sir William Petty, in 1650. He can hardly have been fit for the post, since, ' being possest of a timorous and effeminate humour, he could never endure the sight of a mangled or bloody body.' Though, or because, he had 'sided with all parties,' the University chose him its burgess in the Restoration Parliament. Pepys mentions meeting Clayton at the Swedish Agent's. ' Much extraordinary noble discourse of foreign princes.' He died Oct. 4, 1693, at his country seat, The Vach, near Chalfont, bought by him from the king's brother, and formerly the place of Fleetwood the regicide [2]. He was buried with his lady [3] in ' a little vault of bricks ' under the tower of Merton.

It is curious that in the next century also Pembroke supplied Merton with a quarrelsome physician for Warden, DR. ROBERT WYNTLE, an 'excellent scholar,' and one of the two first Radcliffe Travelling Fellows. He was chosen fellow of Merton at the 'Golden Election' of 1705. In Elizabeth's reign, JAMES GERVASE, D.C.L. (Proctor 1555), after being Principal of Broadgates, returned to Merton as Warden, and held office in an atmosphere of discord.

A later Regius Professor of Medicine (1729) was DR. WILLIAM BEAUVOIR, a Guernsey man, Fellow of Pembroke 1704.

SIEGE AND VISITATION.

The Rebellion broke out in August, 1642. On September 1 the University was notified by the King that he had sent a troop of

[1] In 1561 ' the quen['s] grace has commondyd that all cathedralles and coleges and studyans places that they shuld putt ther wyffes from them owt of the serkutt of evere colege ' (*Diary* of Henry Machyn). ~

[2] One of this family, HARVEY FLEETWOOD, son of Sir William Fleetwood (comptroller of Woodstock Park, and cupbearer to James I and Charles I), took B.A. from Pembroke in 1674.

[3] By her he had James and Bridget. The former (matr. at Merton 1666, aet. 15) wedded Elizabeth, daughter of Sir Richard Howe, Knt., who died in childbed in Merton College, April 9, 1661, and is buried in the chapel.

horse for its defence, and a council of twenty-eight was appointed, on which Pembroke was represented by JOHN BOWLES, M.A. On October 29 Charles, defeated at Edgehill, entered Oxford. The following January the King's first request for plate was sent to the Colleges and Halls. It has to be remembered that the King was fighting the cause of Oxford at least as much as Oxford was defending his. Wood expressly says, 'All sent, except New Inn.' Mr. Clark thinks this beyond doubt. But in the list preserved in the Tanner MSS. only twelve Colleges are named. The others were probably a little behind-hand in responding. Pembroke has silver going back to 1655, but nothing earlier. Aubrey says that William Earl of Pembroke gave the College a great piece of plate. It is unlikely that this should have been lost, and no doubt it went with whatever else the young society possessed to the mint at New Inn Hall[1]. The King's letter is preserved in the College archives. When a money contribution was being raised, the College collected £8 17s.—almost as much as any other. In April, 1643, a list of scholars able and willing to serve the King was prepared.

On 'die Sabbati 13° Jan. 1643' (1644), the war now drawing nearer, an order was issued for fortifying, victualling, and cleansing the city. Edward Heath was ordered to visit St. Aldate's, Pembroke, and New Inn Hall, and to call to him for assistance the constables, churchwardens, and any other persons he should think fit. The College was to supply sixty persons to work at the fortifications, to be called together by beat of drum. Defaulters were to pay one shilling per diem. The Heads of Merton, Brasenose, Lincoln, and Pembroke were 'quickened' by orders from London, early in 1645, to supervise the 'training of the scholars in martial discipline[2].'

In a return of all strangers within the city, Pembroke was shown to contain seventy-nine men, twenty-three women, and five children. While the King was in Oxford, the Secretary of State, Sir Edward Nicholas, had his lodging in the College, to which posts galloped up constantly, bringing stirring news. His second son, Edward, married Bridget, daughter of Sir Thomas Clayton.

[1] Pembroke College, Cambridge, has an 'Anathema Cup,' given by Dr. Layton, Bishop of Winton, and inscribed *Qui alienaverit anathema sit*, which accordingly was not given to King Charles. Pyxes and other sacramental vessels were, it would seem, respected. But no great sanctity would be felt to attach to Lord Pembroke's gift. The Rev. Henry Nowell Barton (scholar 1840–4, fellow 1844–9) tells me that he heard, but heard only, that a quantity of plate was found, when the new buildings were being erected, in an old privy. The silver was supposed to have been hidden in the Rebellion.

[2] Clarendon State Papers, i. 255.

On Midsummer Day, 1646, the city was surrendered, the royal army marching out with drums beating and colours flying. The victors were accompanied by their chaplains, who took possession of the pulpits. In September six (originally seven) ministers arrived from the Parliament 'to draw off from their loyal Principles and orthodox Religion the Scholars and inhabitants': 'their names— Cornish and Langley, two fooles; Reynolds and Harrys, two knaves; Cheynell and rabbi Wilkinson, two madmen.' The second, HENRY LANGLEY, M.A. (son of Thomas Langley, an Abingdon shoemaker), had been at Pembroke[1], of which he was afterwards the *de facto* Master. These preachers were sent to prepare the way for a parliamentary Visitation. In spite of Wood's description of them—'their prayers and sermons were very tedious; they made wry mouths, squint eyes, and scru'd faces, quite altering them from what God and Nature had made them. They ·had antick behaviours, squeaking voices and puling tones, fit rather for Stage players and country Beggars to use than such that were to speak the Oracles of God'— or possibly because of these qualities, they seem to have had a good deal of success. 'Those of the Gown that could not brook such persons did either leave the University or abscond in their respective houses till they could know their doom by the approaching Visitation.' But great numbers flocked to the Thursday conferences at the 'Scruple Shop,' near the Saracen's Head, where doubting brethren had hard cases of conscience resolved, as well as to the Sunday exercises. Langley was one of the rising hopes of the New Model. In *Oxonii Lacrymae*, 1649, he is described as 'one Langley, a *Novice*, run so giddy in his wheels that he usually stuffs his *Pulpit-peece* with rare *hyperbolicall Non-Sence*.' The Presbyterians, however, were not likely to have everything their own way, and the Six were extremely embarrassed by an Independent regimental chaplain, Erbury, sometime of Brasenose, who not only held rival meetings but interrupted theirs. A conference was arranged for November 12, at which Erbury, the 'champion of the Seekers,' backed by a carpenter-captain, a shoemaker-colonel, and a crowd of preaching troopers, was triumphant over the ministers, whom he challenged to say whence they had their call. 'At which the Doctors were unresolved what to answer, for if they should say from the Bishops they feared to displease the people, to whom they had often preached that they were antichristian, and

---

[1] He entered Nov. 6, 1629, with his cousin WILLIAM LANGLEY, afterwards preferred by the Assembly of Divines.

yet they could not deny it, they having been all episcopally ordained[1].'
Langley in especial is described as reduced to muteness, though ''twas
thought he reserved his resolutions for the other sex.'   A month later
Erbury undertook to prove that the fulness of the Godhead dwelt
bodily in himself and the other saints in the same measure as it dwelt
in Christ on earth.   On this point the ministers had another disputation with him in St. Mary's, but finding they could make no head
against this blasphemous fanatic they complained of him to Fairfax.
Erbury disappeared, but Langley and his fellows had already, in
Wood's phrase, let Hell loose, and pulpit and rostrum rang with the
profane harangues of illiterate buff-jackets.   The young scholars, idle
and debauched through soldiering, were scattered.   The seniors were
soon to be displaced.   Scarcely the face of a University remained
amid that wreck of honour and learning—the Schools deserted, the
Colleges ruinous, their treasure-chests empty and libraries pillaged.

Within a week of the surrender of Oxford the parliamentary
Committee for the University, presided over by FRANCIS ROUS, of
whom more will be said among the Pembroke benefactors, ordered
that no person be admitted into any mastership, governorship,
fellowship, scholarship, or other preferment.   This was directly in
contravention of the treaty for the surrender of the garrison.   On
July 10, 1647, Clayton, Master of Pembroke, died, and three days
later the fellows proceeded in all haste to elect HENRY WIGHTWICK, one
of the original fellows.   At the end of August, however, came a parliamentary ordinance.   In the Journals of the House of Lords, 1647
(23 Car. I), die Jovis, 26° die Augusti, is this entry:—

'Whereas Thomas Clayton, Doctor of Physic, and Master of Pembrook
Colledge, Oxon, is lately deceased ; and whereas the said College is not
yet visited, according to an Ordinance of Parliament, whereby the Fellows
are not yet so constituted as that it is fit for them to execute such a Trust
as to make Choice of a new Master; and whereas we have perfect Assurance of the Sufficiency, Abilities, and good Affection to the Parliament,
that are well known to be in Mr. *Henry Langley*, of that College, and
One of the Seven Preaching Ministers sent by the Parliament to that
University, whereby he is rendered very fit for the Government of that
College: It is therefore ORDERED and Ordained, by the Lords and
Commons in this present Parliament assembled, That the said Mr.
Henry Langley be Master, and that the said Mr. *Henry Langley* from
the Day of the Date of these Presents is Master of *Pembrook Colledge* in
Oxford, in the room of the said Dr. *Clayton* deceased ; and that he is
therefore to enjoy all Salaries, Lodgings, Benefits and Emoluments of what

[1] Gutch, *Annals*, ii. 499.

Sort or Nature soever, that do or ought to accrue thereby, to all Intents and Purposes, in as full and ample Manner as the said Dr. *Clayton* did or ought to have enjoyed the same, by virtue of the said Place; and all Fellows, Scholars, Commoners, and all Manner of Students, Officers and Servants, belonging to the said College, are to give full Obedience and Conformity hereunto, as they, or any of them, will answer their Neglect to the Parliament.'

By Michaelmas everything was ready for the Visitation to begin. On Sept. 30 all Heads were summoned to send in their books, and delegates were nominated for each College and Hall to inquire into the behaviour of its members. Langley and SAMUEL BRUEN (incorporated July, 1647, from St. Andrews; afterwards put into a fellowship at Brasenose; Proctor 1655) were appointed for Pembroke. On October 6, the Heads (except Dr. Fell, the Vice-Chancellor) appeared without their books to demand sight of the Visitors' commission. On the 7th the first blood was drawn. Wightwick came before the Visitors, and gave in the following answer, ' whereby,' says Walker, ' he won that Honour of being the first Person that dropp'd in this Noble Conflict ':—

' I do here appear according to Summons; I have seen your Commission and examined it. I find his Majesties name in it, the date of the year of his Reign, and a great Seal annexed unto it; but whether this Commission were granted and issued by his Majesties royal assent I desire to know; and I desire leave to repair to his Majestie to that end, and rather because if it were not granted and issued with his Majesties knowledge and assent I cannot with a safe conscience submit to it, nor without breach of oath made to my Sovereign, and breach of oaths made to the University, and breach of oaths made to my College.

' Et sic habetis animi mei sententiam.

'HENRY WIGHTWICKE.'

Accordingly next day there was fastened up in the Hall of Pembroke, ' An Order to all the Members of Pembroke College for their personall appearance in their Colledge Hall ':—

' We the Visitors of this University doe require you and every of you to appear in your Colledge Hall to-morrow morning, between the hours of 7 and 8, to hear our Order read concerning the Maistership of your Colledge. As you will answere the contrary.'

On Oct. 9 (Sat.) the Visitors ' thrust out Mr. Whightwicke from his Headship by virtue of an Instrument stuck up in the Common Hall, by Tipping [1], one of the Visitors, and [John] Langley the Mandatary.' The following was the ' Order of the Establishing Mr. Langley Maister of Pembroke Colledge ':—

[1] William (' Eternity ') Tipping.

Q

'We, the Visitors authorized by severall Ordinances of Parliament and a speciall Commission under the great Seale of England for regulation and reformation of this Universitie of Oxon, Haveing this day taken into serious consideration the business between Mr. Hen. Langley and Mr. Hen: Whitwicke concerning the Maistership of Pembroke Colledge in the same Universitie, doe find that the sayd Mr. Langley by Ordinance of Parliament dated the 26th of August 1647 was ordained Maister of the sayd Colledge and that the pretended election of the sayd Mr. Whitwicke was made after severall Inhibitions from the Parliament duely executed to the contrary. Wee therefor after a full and serious consideracion had of the premises doe hereby declare that the pretended election of Mr. Whitwicke being unduely made as afore said is voyd, and that the sayd Mr. Whitwicke is no Maister of the sayd Colledge : And that Mr. Langley is rightly constituted and appoynted Maister of the same Colledge according to the sayd Ordinance. In pursuance wherefor We doe by these presents require the Fellowes, Schollers, Commoners, and all Officers and Servants belonging to the sayd Colledge to give full obedience and conformitie to the sayd Mr. Langley as Maister of the sayd Colledge according to the severall Statutes and Customes. As they will answere the contrary.'

On May 9, 1648, Langley was appointed by the new proctors one of twenty delegates ' to answer and act in all things pertaining to the publique good of the University.'

The fortunes of Pembroke during the Visitation did not differ from those of the other Colleges. It was not likely to be protected by its proper Visitor, Laud's successor, the Roundhead Earl of Pembroke.

In Barlow's ' *Pegasus* or the Flying Horse from Oxford : Bringing the Proceedings of the *Visitours* and other *Bedlamites* there [1],' there is an account of the Earl's state entry on April 11, 1648. ' There was a Gentleman prepared to make a speech in the high-street at Christ church gate over against Pembroke Colledge, where all the well-affected Schollers who could not get horses stood in their gownes ready to entertaine their Chancellour with cheerfull acclamations, but a fierce shower hindred that solemnitie. . . . The Speech intended between Christ Church and Pembroke was to this effect. My Lord . . . You are welcome to us, the Genius of the place salutes you Chancellour, the severest Muses smooth their brow, and all the Graces begin to smile : Muses and Graces cry, Welcome *Pembroke*: hearke how your Colledge sounds : the Schollers learne of the buildings to Eccho forth your praises and welcome. Hearke how it rings againe. Thrice welcome Noble Chancellour, welcome *Pembroke*.'

---

[1] ' Printed at *Montgomery*, heretofore called *Oxford*,' 1648.

The mockery was to lie in the silent walls. ' The long-Legg'd peece of impertinency which they miscall *Chancellor* ' was succeeded by Oliver (1653), and he by 'the titmouse Prince called' Richard Cromwell[1], but there is no record of any personal intervention on their part in the affairs of the College. The more presbyterianly inclined members of the College no doubt looked for special favours from the Earl, and when he went to the Schools the day after his entry to be admitted to office, the graduates who accompanied him were 'chiefly of Pembroke College, Magd. Hall and New Inn, who were now expectants[2].' In the subsequent convocation seventeen Masters were created from those two halls and four from Pembroke, ' most of which had lately come from Cambridge and entred themselves in those Houses in hopes of preferment[3].' The next day (April 15), a paper was stuck on the gates of all Colleges and Halls prohibiting the use of the Common Prayer and establishing the Directory. The next step of the Visitors was to summon the members of each House and require their formal submission. On May 5, Wood says, ' appeared 19 Members of Pembroke Coll. all which did positively submit except Franc. Brickenden Bac. of Arts,' who desired time to give in his answer. In the Visitors' Register, under date May 5, 1648, there is an entry :—

'This day Sr. Brickenden[4] of Pembrooke Colledge, Batchelor of Arts, was suspended from the profitts of his place (for behaveing himself contemptuously towards the Vice-gerent of the said Colledge) untill he gave satisfaction for his offence.'

On May 15 he was declared expelled. Besides Henry Wightwick,

---

[1] ' Durante tyrannide Parliamentariâ Philippo comite Pembrochiae, Olivario et Riccardo Cromwelliis Cancellariorum nomine sese hic venditantibus' (Decree of the Restoration Convocation). [2] Gutch, ii. 564.

[3] Walker (*Sufferings of the Clergy*) writes : ' A Rabble from Cambridge came to their Assistance [i. e. of the Visitors], without which perhaps they could scarce have found enough to have filled up these Wide and Ghastly Breaches they made in the severall Houses.' He says they were Presbyterians or Independent Novices who had flocked to Cambridge after it had been reformed into confusion. Wood, describing the chamber frolics and closet tippling of the Saints, adds : ' Nay, such that had come from Cambridg and had gotten fellowships would be more free of entertainment than any, and instead of a cup of college beare and a stir'd machet which use to be the antient way of entertaining in a College at 3 or 4 in the afternoon, they would entertain with tarts, custards, cheescaks, or any other junkets that were in season ; and that fashion continued among the generalitie till the restauration' (*Life and Times*, i. 298). They did not then, in private, 'blaspheme custard through the nose.' The ' Cambridge bachelaurs' also brought in a new cut of gowns (ibid. i. 300).

[4] He was afterwards Fellow and M.A. ' Mr. Francis Briggenden' died Jan. 14, 1664, aged forty, and is buried in St. Aldate's (ibid. ii. 70).

the extruded Master, there were four others of the name of Wightwick in residence. One of them, George, answered, ' We submitt.' Three other fellows, Peter Jersey, William Brage, and Paul Darand, replied, ' I doe submitt.' Four bachelors (one being Peter Pett) made the same answer, and nine undergraduates. Samuel Bruen answered, ' I humbly submitt to the power of Parliament restinge in the Visitors, wittnesse my hand.' In all twenty-two seem to have given their submission. George Wightwick was made B.D. that year ' ex regis gratia.'

On May 24, 1648, the following questions were proposed ' to Mr. Boulds, of Pembrooke Colledge ':—

1. Doe you submitt to the authoritie of Parliament in this Visitation ?
2. Doe you submitt to the present Government of this Universitie by the Chancellor, Vice-Chancellor, and Proctors established by the imediate authoritie of both Houses of Parliament ?
3. Doe you submitt to Mr. Langley as Master of Pembrooke Colledge ?
4. Doe you observe the Directory in all the publique exercises of religion in your parish ?

The Answere of Mr. Boulds.

I cannot submitt to this Visitation, but only to the power of his Majestie in generall and of our lawfull Visitor in particular, which is according to our Statutes unto which I am sworne, besides I doe not hear of any satisfactory Answere given to the Reasons of this Universitie.

As concerninge the Directory I did use it, and was inforced upon my conscience to use againe the Book of Common Prayer, or els I had lost the major part of my parish.

To the 2d. I, John Boulds, doe referre myselfe to the Answere of the Universitie.

On May 26 it was

' Ordered that Mr. John Bowles, Fellow of Pembrooke Colledge, be hereby suspended from all power and priviledge of a Fellow or Member of Pembrooke Colledge. And from all and singular the profitts and emoluments of his Fellowshipp.'

On June 29 he was, with others of other Colleges, expelled the University. But three years later, on Feb. 4, 1651, the Visitors say :—

' Being informed that the said Mr. Boules is againe retourned to Oxon, to the parish of St. Giles, and takes upon him the cure as formerly ; we therefore hereby require and command the said Mr. Boules to desist from officiating as pastor or minister of the said parish, and to depart from the University as he will answer the contrary at his perill.'

On July 12, 1648, a further summons was put out to all who had not yet appeared and answered. On July 14 William Collier, the butler,

and Thomas Turner, the cook of Pembroke, replied : 'I referre myselfe
to the Master and Fellowes, and will submitt as farre as it concernes
mee in my place.' John Kingsley made answer : 'I humbly conceive
that I manifested my submission by waiting on the Worshipfull Mr.
Langley, as present Master of Pembrooke Colledge, to whom I shall
for the future as formerly acknowledge myselfe servant, being Member
of the said Colledge.' These three answers were taken as negative.
The following were reported to Rous's committee of Lords and
Commons as not appearing, and were expelled :—

PEMBROOKE COLLEDGE.

Mr. [Henry] Whitweeke, the pretended Master.
Mr. [Henry] Whiteweeke ⎫
Mr. [John] Darby   ⎬ Socii.
Mr. [Thomas] Carey   ⎭
Mr. [Thomas] Whitewicke ⎫
Mr. [Thomas] Daffy   ⎪
Ds. [Thomas] Whitweake   ⎬ Schollers.
Ds. [Henry] Wyatt   ⎪
Ds. [Francis] Brickendine⎪
Ds. [Silas] Blisset   ⎭
[Richard] Dew
[Robert] Paine.

As well as Collier, Turner, and Kingsley. These places had to be
filled. Walker, in his *Sufferings of the Clergy*, says : 'By February
11th, 1649, the Visitors had chosen into this College at Five several
Elections Fourteen *Fellows and Scholars* : Which may serve to give
some Light into the Number of those they had ejected from it. The
list and dates are in the Visitors' Register [1].

The Names of such as are chosen into Colledges.
PEMBROOKE COLLEDGE.

Aug. 11, 1648. Sʳ [Nathaniel] Lane ⎫ Fell:
                Sʳ [Joshua] Tompkins ⎭
                Rob. Steele   ⎫ Schol:
                [Philip] Potter   ⎭
Oct. 10.   Jo: Hoy, Fell: [a Cambridge B.A.]
           Paul D'Arand [M.A. 1648; afterwards Minister of the
              French church at Southampton]. Ob. 1669.
           Jo: Powell [a Cambridge M.A.; afterwards Fellow of
              Merton].
           Pet: Jersey [appointed Aug. 13, 1649; one of the
              assistants to the Delegates; proctor 1642; rector of

---

[1] Camden Society, ed. Burrows, p. 176.

St. Peter's, Jersey, 1662, and of St. Andrew's, Guernsey, 1663].

Oct. 16.   [Thomas] Roswell, Schol:

[Nathaniel] Brownesword [matric. Nov. 27, 1650; B.A. 1652. It was ordered, April 11, 1654, 'Whereas Nathaniel Brownesword, Bachelor of Arts, was elected into a voyd Scholarship in Pembrooke Colledge, Oxon, and hath absented himselfe from the Colledge for the space of two years last past: the Visitors of the University of Oxon doe hereby require the said Nath: Brownesword to repair to the said Colledge within the space of one moneth from the date hereof; otherwise his Scholarship aforesaid shall be disposed of to another person'].

Jan. 4, 1649.   Fouke, Schol:
Potter, Fell:

Feb. 11, 1649.   Robert Parr, Schol:

April 22, 1650.   John Hall, Schol: [afterwards Master].

July 24, 1650.   Hall, Fell:

Oct. 1, 1656.   Jo: Huntbache, Schol:

On Sept. 25, 1648, 'at a meetinge of the Visitors' it was

'Ordered: That all the allowances and dues of the persons undernamed, not haveinge appeared, or submitted to the authority of Parliament in the Visitation, be suspended, and detayned from them untill further Order: And the Master, Bursers, and other Officers of the said Colledge are required to take notice hereof, and to forbeare the payment of such allowances or dues to them accordingly:

Mr. Henry Whightwicke	
Mr. William [?] Darby	Fellowes of Pembrooke Colledge.
Mr. Tho: Cary	
Mr. Tho: Whightwicke, Jun:	
Mr. Hen: Wyatt: Ba: Art:	
Mr. Fran: Brickendine	Scholl: of Pembrooke Colledge.'
Mr. Rich: Dew	
Mr. Robert Payne	

However, Henry Wightwick, jun., submitted.

Oct. 2, 1648. 'Ordered: That Mr. Henry Whightwicke of Pembrooke Colledge procuringe his submission (to the authoritie of Parliament in this present Visitation) attested by good and sufficient witnesses in the countrie where he now lives, Ordered to be accepted of and approved.'

Not however till Feb. 19, 164⅞, was it

'Ordered: That the Suspension of Mr. Henry Whitwicke be taken of (his Submission being receaved), and that hee shall receave his stypends and dues belonginge to his place in Pembrooke Colledge, both the arrears

due to him for tyme past, and the profitts thereof for future tyme, as fully
as if noe Suspension had beene made.'

Henry Wightwick, the lawful Master, and others held out.
Among 'Persons removed from their places' on the above Oct. 2,
1648, are :—

'Tho: Carey: for his Non-appearance and his enjoyment [of] a benefice
contrary to the Statute of that Colledge.
Mr. Darby: for his contempt.
Mr. Henry Whitwick, Sen: for his high contempt.'

On the following Jan. 4 it was

'Ordered: That all proceedings in Mr. Wyatt's case of Pembroke
Colledge be stayed till the Maister of the Colledge be acquainted with it
and his Answeare received: And that Mr. Wyatt shall have allowance
of Battles in the Colledge till the matter be determynd.'

The next day,

'Ordered: That the suspension of Sr Wyatt, Schollar of Pembrooke
Colledge, be taken off: And that hee be left to the Maister and Fellowes
of the House to be admitted Fellow into the Abbingeton place (lately voyd
by the death of Mr. Steede), accordinge to the Statutes of the House,
unlesse cause be shewed to the contrary within this month: and in the
meane tyme hee is to enjoy the profitts of his Schollar's place.'

The Visitors put DANIEL HARFORD and WILLIAM HANN, who had
become members of Pembroke, into fellowships at All Souls and New
College respectively.

The College soon subsided into obedience under the resolute rule
of Langley. It had suffered greatly, Professor Burrows remarks, in
the war, 'in which its members had engaged with more than usual
ardour on the king's side,' furnishing fifty officers to the royal army.
Whereas the annual average of matriculations up to 1644 had been
fourteen, from 1644 to 1650 only two names were entered. Naturally
the College was greatly exhausted. In 1650, however, there were
twenty-two matriculations, and again in 1651, a number exceeded by
six Colleges only. There were then 169 students. Twelve years
later the average entries had sunk to six annually.

By the statutes of Pembroke, as of some other Houses, on
Saturdays after prayers the juniors were to declaim publicly and the
graduates to exhibit themes. This rule was abrogated from April 18,
1651, in order that all might prepare themselves for the Lord's Day.
After the battle of Worcester the Visitors ordered all scripture
histories or figures painted, carved, or in glass, of our Lord, our Lady,
and the saints to be defaced, crosses to be destroyed, and the King's

arms removed. Even the tables of the Ten Commandments were sometimes wrecked by ignorant hands among the 'monuments of superstition.' Doubtless Docklinton's aisle shared the general fate[1]. In 1653 a further clearance was made of all tutors not certified to be 'godly,' and candidates for fellowships and chaplaincies had to bring testimonials to that effect. After their own fashion the Visitors seemed to have striven to promote religious learning. Sermons were their specific for everything. On November 24, 1653, the Heads and Governours of every College were ordered to render an accompt what preaching or divinity exercises take place therein. When the Visitors met on Nov. 14, 1657, 'it was certified by the Master and Fellows of Pembroke College, who doe at present, in their turnes, uphould preaching every Lord's Day, doe intend to maintaine that exercise untill they receive an Order from the Visitors, requiring all Masters of Arts in the College to join with them.' It was ordered that all Masters in this, as in other Colleges, should perform and continue the exercise of preaching once a week on the Lord's Day, beginning at seven o'clock in the forenoon, in their respective courses.

In July, 1650, William Collier, the College butler, supposed to be expelled, took a prominent part in a plot 'of the remaining cavaliers to seize on the garrison, Visitors, and all the armes they could find, to the end that they might joyne them selves to others that had plotted in the same manner in other parliament garrisons, to relieve the distressed cavaliers that were besieged in Colchester. The plot was discovered by one or more of them when they were in their cups, which made every one shift for themselves as well as they could[2].' Hearne writes to Thomas Rawlinson, Dec. 20, 1717 :—

'As to your querie at Num. 33 of *Rustica Descriptio Visitationis fanaticae Oxon.*, Mr. Collier (commonly called honest Will. Collier) was strangely tortured in New College, where he was imprisoned and condemned to be hanged, but freed after he was up the ladder. . . . The foresaid Will. Collier, who was a right Cavalier, (and therefore made yeoman beadle[3], Dr. Peter Mew, and others, having a true value for his loyalty, which made Dr. Peter Mew always use him as a familiar, as well before as after he was made bishop; I say this Will. Collier) being a hard drinker[4] had a room at the tavern which was always called Will. Collier's

---

[1] In every window were Docklinton's arms, and in the window above Noble's tomb ' was the Proportion of a Man kneeling, with Four Children behind him ; and by it was written *Will. Noble* ' (Peshall, p. 149). Among other coats of arms in the church was that of Bishop Beckington.

[2] Wood's *Life and Times*, i. 146.   [3] Of Law ; elected Dec. 18, 1666.

[4] Wood says of Wyat's election to be Public Orator, March 26, 1679 : ' Wyot,

room, and often old Collier's room, which nobody whatsoever was to use but himself and such as came to him. Here he constantly sat when the business of the University was over, unless he was obliged to go to some other place, and would drink and be very merry. There are many stories going about this honest old Cavalier.'

Wood says that it was another of the conspirators who actually mounted the ladder at the Catherine Wheel, near St. Mary Magdalene's. Collier was shut up in one of the chaplains' chambers under New College hall, and there tortured by placing a lighted match to his hands tied behind his back, in order to wring from him the names of the persons privy to the plot; but he managed to 'escape through the window and over the high embattled wall adjoining, and so saved the hangman a labour.' He died Nov. 9, 1692, 'in his house in Pennyverthing Street [1].'

The third Visitation, begun in 1654, was finally ended by the King's return, and the waking of Oxford and England from their long sick dream. On June 4, 1660, it was 'ordered by the Lords in Parliament assembled that the Chancellors of both Universities shall take care that the several Colleges in the said Universities shall be governed according to their respective Statutes. And that such persons who have been unjustly put out of their Headships, Fellowships, or other Offices may be restored according to the said Statutes of the Universities and Founders of Colleges therein.'

Among clergy dispossessed of their benefices during the Rebellion were such as Dr. GEORGE GILLINGHAME, chaplain to Charles I and canon of Windsor; WILLIAM DOWDESWELL, rector of Brinkworth and canon of Worcester, sequestered from Streynsham and Croome d'Abitot; ROBERT JOYNER, from Chew Magna; PETER ALLEN, from Tollesbury; WILLIAM PARGITER, from Carlton; WILLIAM LANE, from Aveton Gifford; EDWARD MOOREY, from a Magdalen chaplaincy; JOHN EEDES, from Honiton [2].

Mention has been made of Sir ANTHONY HUNGERFORD (half-brother of Sir Edward, the parliamentary commander), who entered May 9, 1625, aet. 15. He sate for Malmesbury in the Long Parliament until disabled in 1644. He was then heavily fined for

---

a bib and smoking companion; a keeper of inferior company (. . . Collier and others in St. Ebbs parish).' *Life and Times*, ii. 446.

[1] Rather Beef Hall Lane. His wife, Katherine Lane, was buried in St. Aldate's, March 26, 1672; his mother Ursula, 'wife of Will. Collier the elder,' Feb. 20, 1665. He and Turner the cook seem to have been partisans of Sir Thomas Clayton's (ibid. i. 385).

[2] See Walker's *Sufferings of the Clergy*, ii. 237.

delinquency, though he had not borne arms for the King, and thrown into the Tower. In 1648 his estates were seized. Cromwell wrote him a sympathetic letter in 1652[1]. The next year he succeeded to Farleigh Castle. The site of the present Charing Cross Station, where the old family mansion stood, was sold by his spendthrift son Edward, and became the Hungerford Market. Sir Anthony, dying in 1657, was buried in Black Bourton church.

Langley, who on April 12, 1648, had been placed by Lord Pembroke and the Visitors into the stall at Christ Church from which Morley, afterwards Bishop of Winton., had been thrust, retired from Oxford at the Restoration to his house at Tubney 'in Bagley Wood,' where he took 'sojourners (fanaticks' sons), taught them logic and philosophy, and admitted them to degrees[2].' He 'oftentimes preached in Conventicles at Abendon[3].' Metford of C. C. C. says he was looked on as insipid and dull both in preaching and conversation, and 'tedious even when shortest[4],' and that he made his hearers smile by his affected sighings. He may have had some learning, however. In 1648 he had been placed on a committee, with Cornish and Button, to examine all candidates for fellowships and scholarships[5]. After the putting forth of the Declaration of Toleration in March, 1671, Langley, together with John Troughton, Henry Cornish, B.D., and Thomas Gilbert, B.D., was 'appointed by the principal heads of the Brethren to carry on the work of preaching within the City of *Oxon.* The place where they held their meetings was in *Thamestreet* without the north gate, in a house which had been built by *Tom Pun,* alias *Tho. Aires[6].'* 'Fanaticks brisk in Oxon. . . . Constant preachers in Broken hayes were Dr. Hen Langley' and the others[7]. Dying in September, 1679, he was buried in St. Helen's at Abingdon. Langley was originally a quirister of Magdalen (1627, aged 16); he matriculated from Pembroke Nov. 6, 1629; Fellow 1635; B.A. 1632; M.A. 1635; B.D. 1648; D.D. 1649. He was by a parliamentary order of June 20, 1643, made rector of St. Mary Newington. 'A judicious solid Divine,' says Calamy, 'not valu'd in the University according to his Worth.'

In a pamphlet put forth after the Restoration, called *The Lords' loud call to England,* by Henry Jeffy, a Fifth Monarchy man, instances are

[1] See Carlyle's *Cromwell,* p. 216.
[2] Wood's *Life and Times,* ii. 1.   [3] *Athenae,* ii. 771.
[4] Dr. Fowler's *History of Corpus,* O. H. S., p. 207.
[5] Of seven names of persons examined on March 15, 1648, one is 'John Ouseley, Pembr: 1 yeare, mediocriter.'
[6] *Athenae,* ii. 511.   [7] *Life and Times,* ii. 244.

given of judgements that had befallen members of the University who had re-introduced the Prayer-Book, and other anti-Puritans. One is that of 'a Scholar of Pembroke College, who said he came purposely to Town to see Dr. Langley outed, and then he would give a plate to the College. He was invited to dinner by a Scholar and never went out of the room more, but died there [1].' Wood comments on this story:

'The Scholar's name was William Grosvenour, the only Son, as I have heard, of Grosvenour of Brand in Shropshire, and one of the grand-children of Sir Rich. Grosvenour of Cheshire; but that he should say such words that the Relator reports, I could never understand of any person but this. He had before taken a great journey which, with the excessive heat of the weather, had put him into an indisposition of body, and being invited into a Fellow's Chamber in Oriel Coll. [John Whyte-hall] to whom he had brought commendations from his Relations, found himself much worse than before, so that his fever increasing and con-tinuing more and more violent upon him for 10 days space, died the 28 July [1660], and was buried in the Chancel of St. Mary's Church [2].'

A somewhat noted Puritan was presented to St. Aldate's during the Commonwealth, no doubt by Langley, viz., Henry Hickman, the antagonist of Heylin and Durell, and author of *Apologia pro Ministris in Anglia (vulgo) Nonconformistis.*

Royalist Officers.

Wood (MS. F. 28, fol. 24) gives the following [3]—the only list made for any College:—

'The names of such psons of Pembroke Coll. in Oxon who were officers in the army of K. Ch. I against the rebellious Parliament.

WILL. SCROGGS—Captaine of a foot company—afterwards Ld. Ch. Just. of Engl. & a Kt.

JOH. BENNET, a capt. afterwards a kt & a benefactor to Pemb. Coll. new buildings.

Sr EDM. BRAY of Geat Barrington, com. Gloc. Capt. of horse [4].

Mr. THO. TREGUNWELL, collonel of a Reg. of Horse.

Mr. FLEETWOOD DORMER, a Cornet undr ye Earl of Caernarvan.

Mr. EUSEB. DORMER—a Lieutenāt [5].

---

[1] Gutch, ii. 705.

[2] 'Beares the garbes for his armes' (*Life and Times*, i. 325). Grosvenor of Eaton bears Az. a garb or. William Grosvenor matr. June 15, 1657; student of Gray's Inn, 1656.

[3] Printed in H. W. Chandler's 'Court Rolls of Great Cressingham.' I have collated Professor Chandler's list with the original.

[4] Captain Edm. Bray matr. B.N.C. 1627; ob. Nov. 30, 1642; monument at Fyfield.

[5] Son of Sir Fleetwood, and brother of last named. Did not pay his fees for M.A. and was degraded, Oct. 23, 1637 (Wood). Originally at Magdalen Hall.

Mr. THO. SAVAGE a Capt. of Foot[1].

Mr. MORDĂT WASHINGTON, a cornet.

Mr. HEN. HEYTY a Leivt-coll. at Worcester—afterwards a Col.—livinge now 1682 at Minster Lovell com. Oxoñ.

Mr. JO. PEACOCK, capt. of Foot—after yᵉ kings returne he was made a major, Leivt. Coll. & at length Coll. Lives now in yᵉ parish of Comnore, Berks.

ANTH. BRAY Leivtenät.

OLIVER PLEYDELL, Capt. of Foot.

CONWAY WHITTERN Capt. of foot[2].

WILL. JAMES, Capt. . . . . . .

JOH. WATERWORTH, a sea-capt.[3]

JAMES GUNTER, capt.

WALT WINTER, Leivt.[4]

GEORG. RUMSEY, Leivt.

HEN. MORGAN, Cornet.

GILES BOURN, Cornet of Dragoons[5].

ROG. CLERK, Leivt. to yᵉ Lᵈ Hoptons regim.[6]

WILL. CLERK, chaplayne to yᵉ Lᵈ Hoptons regim.[7]

THO. GREENVILL, an officer unᵈ Sir Bevill Greenvill[8].

WILL.
HUᵖH. } MAYO, Leivtenants unᵈ the Lᵈ Hopton.

WILL. SANDYS, Capt. unᵈ the Lᵈ Hopton[9].

CHARLES BARTER—an officer.

THO. MARTIN, off.

JOH. BIRCH, Leivt. of Foot.

JOH. BRAY Leivt. of Foot.

EDM. WELSH.

WILL. ANNE, Leivt. (Tho. Anne rather q.)[10].

WILL. HILL capt.

WILL. NORREYS cornet in yᵉ Lᵈ Hoptons reg.

JOH. BOWER[11].

---

[1] Matr. 1638. Of Elmley Castle, High Sheriff of Worcestershire.

[2] Matr. 1636; see page 253.

[3] Matr. 1639; of Lincoln's Inn, 1641.

[4] Orig. at Jesus College; matr. 1637.

[5] Matr. 1635; a kinsman, I think, of Bishop Gilbert Bourn.

[6] Orig. at Trinity College; matr. 1634.

[7] Orig. at Christ Church; matr. 1633. 'I do not yet here yᵗ he was an officer' (Wood).

[8] Or Greenfields. Matr. 1635; preacher, it seems, to the Hon. Society of Lincoln's Inn; rector of Combe St. Nicholas; canon of Exeter 1662. Sir Bevil was slain in Lansdown fight.

[9] Matr. 1623. Son of Sir Samuel Sandys, brother of Sir Edwyn. He was M.P. for Evesham 1640 (expelled 1641) and 1661.

[10] Thos. Anne matr. 1634; vicar of Erchfont, Wilts, 1662.

[11] Orig. at Trinity College; matr. 1631.

ROB. CHAßLAYNE an ensigne in y⁰ life-guard¹.
GEORG. JOLLIFF, Leivtenant unđ y⁰ Lđ Hopton.
WILL. QUARTERMAN . . . afterwards M.D. & the king's physit.
⎰ FRANC. WEST ye cook—a cornet of horse.
{ JOH. SKINGRESLEY ye manciple, a Leivtenant of Foot.
⎱ WILL. COLLIER y⁰ butler—a Leivt.—(from whŏe I had this Cat.).
JOH. ALLEN, Ensigne.
JOH. BRAGG, Ensigne.
JOH. BOAT, M.A. Leivt.
ROB. DUKE.
JOHN COMBES capt. of Dragoons.
TH. TWYNE Leivt.
WILL. CLAYTON, capt.—afterwards major to Collon. Legg².
GEORGE BRETT.
EDW. PALÃ capt.'

Wood adds, ' If pemb. coll wᶜʰ is the least coll in Oxoñ did yeild so many officer's to serve his maj. wᵗ did then the other colleges doe? ' He speaks, however, of but twenty officers from Christ Church out of the hundred Students, not reckoning the Commoners. Wood does not mention Sir THOMAS LITTLETON, knight and baronet, M.P. for Worcestershire 1621–40, colonel of the county horse and foot, who was taken at Bewdley and imprisoned in the Tower ; B.A. from Broadgates 1614. His father, John, was convicted of high treason in 1601.

Some members of the College not hitherto mentioned, who sate in Parliaments of Charles I, were :—Sir THOMAS COTTON, Bart. (Great Marlow 1625, St. German's 1628, Hunts. 1640); HENRY BELLINGHAM (Chichester 1628); THOMAS PRESTWOOD (Totnes 1628); EDMOND ROCHE (County Cork 1639); Sir WILLIAM SARSFIELDE (Cork City 1634); ROGER KIRKHAM (Old Sarum 1646); Sir NICHOLAS MARTYN, sheriff of Devon 1639 (Devon 1646); EDMOND FOWELL (Tavistock 1646, 1659; Devon 1656; Plymouth 1660). In the next reign WILLIAM YORKE (Wilts 1654, Devizes 1661)—he was a bencher and buried in the Temple Church ; JOHN SILLY (Bodmin 1659); NICHOLAS DENNYS, bencher of the Inner Temple (Barnstaple 1660–78); RICHARD WILLIAMS (Radnorshire 1677, 1685; Brecknockshire 1678).

The College produced, besides Scroggs, some lawyers of note, such as Sir WILLIAM CHILDE(B.C.L. 1632), a Master in Chancery; JOHN GREENE (entered 1659), treasurer of Lincoln's Inn 1693 ; or RICHARD WALLOP

¹ Matr. 1635. His father, Peter Chamberlayne, was Physician to James I, Charles I, Charles II, and their consorts.
² Son of Dr. Clayton, the Master. Created Med. Bac. 1642.

(entered 1634), treasurer of the Middle Temple 1673, cursitor baron of the Exchequer 1696. He was buried in the Temple church. In November, 1654, Dr. Langhorne, pro-vice-chancellor, told Convocation that the faculty of law had been languishing for some years and was all but dead. Convocation therefore, as it had done half a century before, petitioned Parliament for its encouragement. 'As it is a distinct body from the Canon law wee humbly conceive it to be very sutable to the present government, and a profession of much use and public concernment.' Wood says, 'it seems the Civil Law was put down [1].' 'In Reg: Congreg. Q. a, fol. 61 a. is a Latin letter of the University to the Lord Commissioner Fiennes, dat e domo Cong[ls] 16 Kal. Jan. 1656 for his being a freind and patron to the Universitie and giving his hand for the continuing and upholding of the Civill Law, when readie to go to ruine or fall [2].' At the Restoration, on Sept. 5, 1660, Convocation drew up a petition to the King 'for the continuance and promotion of the Civill Law and its professors,' praying his Majesty to 'have respect to such persons as are fit for judicature and employment in ecclesiasticall courts, wherby such as have spent their life in that profession may enjoy some reasonable meanes and our yonger students be encouraged to endeavour the enabling of themselves in the same way.' Wood adds, 'If I am not mistaken, after the king's restauration there were severall places belonging to civil lawyers conferred on laymen, which caused this petition to be put up. No answer appears [3].'

One of the Cambridge bachelors brought to Oxford in 1647 was the noted civilian Sir PETER PETT, who must be distinguished from his father's first cousin Peter Pett, the Chief Commissioner of the Navy.

He belonged to a family of hereditary shipbuilders [4]. His grandfather, Peter Pett, was a master-shipwright at Wapping, and his father, Peter Pett, at Deptford. Sir Peter was baptized there, Oct. 31, 1630. From St. Paul's school he went to Sidney Sussex (June 28, 1645 ; B.A. March 7, 164⁴⁄₅). On July 4 he incorporated at Oxford, being a member of Pembroke College. Soon after he was made fellow of All Souls 'by the Favour of the Visitors.' Pett however was one of the royalist *virtuosi* and wits who patronized the 'coffee-house' opened by the cavalier Tillyard opposite All Souls. He, Sir Kenelm Digby and others, gave handsome entertainment in the Salutation tavern near St. Mary's to Davie Mell, 'the most eminent violinist of London,' B.C.L. 1650. When

---

[1] *Life and Times*, i. 187.   [2] Ibid. i. 210.   [3] Ibid. i. 332.
[4] In the Clarendon State Papers Sir Robert Maunsell (Aug. 3, 1620) recommends to Mr. Aylesbury Peter Pett for the building of the new pinnaces, stating that the family have had the employment since Henry VII's time.

the Royal Society was started amid much suspicion by a band of Oxford philosophers, Pett became an original Fellow. At the Restoration Charles II made him Advocate General for Ireland; in which capacity he received knighthood from Ormonde. He sate in the Irish Parliament for Askerton 1661-6. His duties in Ireland seem to have engrossed his time, for on Nov. 18, 1675, he was expelled the Royal Society for 'not performing his obligation to the Society.' Pett occupied himself with much literary work, chiefly polemical, on theology and trade. In 1693 the *Memoirs* of Arthur Earl of Anglesey and the *Genuine Remains* of Bishop Barlow were edited by him. He died April 1, 1679. He was 'Heir and Executor' to Archbishop Williams. Pett is frequently mentioned in the Diaries of Evelyn and Pepys. The picture of Dr. Harmer in the Bodleian was presented by him in 1695.

Another Fellow of the Royal Society was Dr. WILLIAM QUARTERMAN (M.D. from Pembroke 1657), physician to King Charles II. He was attached to the Navy, and engaged on the royal side. Fellow of the College of Physicians 1661 ; M.P. for New Shoreham 1662. Buried in St. Martin's in the Fields, June 11, 1667.

NOTE.

HEADS of Houses who have been members of Broadgates or Pembroke (besides Storey, Wheare, Clayton, Wyntle, Blackstone, and Durell, mentioned elsewhere) are :—

Dr. FRANCIS BEVANS. Entered Broadgates (from Caermarthenshire) 1572; fellow of All Souls 1573; B.C.L. 1579; incorporated at Cambridge 1581 ; D.C.L. 1583; Principal of New Inn Hall 1585-6; chancellor of Hereford Diocese 1587; an advocate of Doctors' Commons 1590; Member for Bishop's Castle 1593. He was Principal of Jesus College from 1586 till his death in 1602. He is buried in Hereford Cathedral.

Dr. RICHARD CLAYTON. B.A. from Broadgates 1622; fellow of University 1639; Master 1665-76; canon of Sarum 1661.

Dr. JOHN MORLEY, Rector of Lincoln 1719-1731. Having matriculated at Trinity Feb. 26, 168⅚, aged sixteen, he migrated to Pembroke; B.A. 1689; fellow of Lincoln 1689-1712; M.A. 1692; B.D. 1703; D.D. 1711. He held the rectory of Sutton from 1711. He died June 12, 1731.

Dr. JOHN CLARK, Provost of Oriel 1768-1781. Matriculated at Pembroke (from Colvel, Cambs., clerici fil.) March 18, 174⅚, aged sixteen ; B.A. 1752; fellow of Oriel 1755-68; M.A. 1756; B. and D.D. 1768; vicar of St. Mary's 1765-8; canon of Rochester and rector of Purleigh 1768. Died Nov. 21, 1781.

Dr. DRUMMOND PERCY CHASE, the present Principal of St. Mary Hall. Born at Château de Saulruit, near St. Omer, Sept. 14, 1820; entered Pembroke Feb. 15, 1838; scholar 1838; migrated to Oriel 1839; B.A. 1841 (1st class Lit. Hum.); fellow of Oriel 1842; M.A. 1844; tutor 1847-9, 1860-6; proctor 1853; B. and D.D. 1880; President of the Union Society 1842; Vice-Principal of St. Mary Hall 1848-57; Principal 1857; Select Preacher 1860; vicar of St. Mary's 1856-73 and 1876-8.

Dr. EDWARD MOORE, now Principal of St. Edmund Hall. Born at Cardiff Feb. 28, 1835; entered Pembroke May 26, 1853, from Bromsgrove School; B.A. 1859; fellow of Queen's 1858-65; M.A. 1860; tutor of St. Edmund Hall 1862; fifty-second Principal 1864; B.D. 1867; proctor 1871; D.D. 1878; President of the Union Society 1860; Select Preacher 1887. Dr. Moore had a distinguished career in the Schools, and has filled a number of responsible posts in the administration of the University. The study of Dante in England owes much to his scholarly labours.

CHAPTER XVIII.

PURITANS AND OTHERS.

THE change from young men of position studying law and the muses before entering upon life to a more plebeian and puritanical class of undergraduate coincides more or less with the conversion of the Hall into a College, but affected, it would seem, every part of the University[1].

In the room of the dispossessed Charter fellows others were appointed, but by whom is not clear. Of one of these, GEORGE HUGHES, 'the bright star of the west,' Calamy gives a large account. He was born in Southwark in 1603[2]. Having first been entered at Corpus Christi in 1619, and taken B.A. there, 'he had so general a Reputation then for his Proficiency in his Studies that Dr. Clayton being made Master of *Pembroke-College*, upon the first Erection of it, he procur'd Mr. *Hughes* to be one of the first Fellows of it. Several Persons of great Eminency afterwards were his Pupils here, as *Henry Langley*, D.D., second Master of *Pembroke*, *Tobit Garbrand*, M.D., Principal of *Gloucester-Hall*, and many others.'

He was ordained about 1628, being known in the University as a Puritan. For some time he preached in and around Oxford, and afterwards was Lecturer of Allhallows, Breadstreet, proceeding B.D. (as obliged by statute) July 10, 1633. Silenced by Laud, he had thoughts of transferring himself to New England, but was dissuaded by 'old Mr. Dod,' Lord Brooke made him his chaplain, he married a Gentlewoman of Coventry, and Lady Maynard got the Earl of Bedford to present him to Tavistock, where, by his endeavours, 'a mighty Reformation was wrought.' Thenceforward he was, Wood says, 'the most noted Presbyterian (if not Independent), of his time in *Devonshire.*' Having to flee before the King's forces from Tavistock and from Exeter,

---

[1] Lady Brilliana Harley writes in 1638 to her son at Magdalen Hall: 'I belieue that theare are but feawe nobellmen's sonne in Oxford; for now, for the most part, they send theaire sonnes into France when they are very yonge.'

[2] His mother was then fifty-two years old, and he was her firstborn. She afterwards lived to a great age.

R

Hughes was appointed vicar of St. Andrew's, Plymouth, where he 'continued in great liking among the *godly party*.' Calamy says[1], ''tis no Wonder this excellent Person should have a share with so much good Company in *Tony Wood's* ill-Nature and Slanders; that he should call in question his Degrees,' &c. He rebuts the charge of self-seeking and of fanaticism, and says that Hughes, though from 1654 an Assistant for ejecting 'scandalous' clergy and schoolmasters, did not act. He was accused, in a book called *Foxes and Firebrands*, of making one Newland, a Popish ecclesiastic, his pretended butler, and calling on him to pray and expound. Also of living in greater power and equipage than any archbishop. He certainly appears to have exercised a more than episcopal influence in the West-country, and Calamy relates how, after his ejection at the Bartholomew of 1662, Bishop Gauden's Visitation at Totnes was forsaken by the whole body of clergy, when they heard that Hughes was in the town, in order to accompany him on horseback towards his home. Wood writes: 'Exercising his function in private, that is in Conventicles, among the Brethren, contrary to the Act, he was with *Tho. Martin* conveyed into *S. Nicholas* Island near Plymouth, an. 1665, where they remained about 9 Months. In which time our author *Hughes* wrote an answer to *Joh. Serjeants* book entit. *Sure-footing*. At length his health being much impaired, as the Brethren reported, and his legs black and swoln, he was offer'd his liberty, upon condition of giving security of 1000*l.* [2000*l.* Calamy] not to live within 20 miles of *Plymouth*: Which being accordingly effected by the Brethren without his knowledge he retired to *Kingsbridge* in *Devonsh.*, found entertainment in the house of one *Daniel Elley*, a Brother, and was much frequented to the last by the fanatical party.' 'He hardly cared,' says Calamy, 'for any other Discourse but what was serious and heavenly, and had such an affecting Sense of the Cloud that was upon GOD'S Church by the Ejection of so many eminent Ministers, that he was scarce seen to indulge any Mirth after that day.' Preaching the Lord's Day before his death, he ended with the words, 'And now all my Work is done.' 'The Evening before he dy'd, he ordered his Watch to lie by him, and desir'd a Relation to observe when it was two a Clock, *for* (says he) *that is my Hour*. And accordingly just then he expir'd, An. 1667: in his 64th Year.' On the monument in Kingsbridge church 'to the fragrant ever-to-be-cherished memory of the much desired George Hughes,' he is described as 'Sacrae sensus paginae penitiores eruere, homines concione flectere, precibus Deum, mire edoctus. Qui Solis aemulum ab Oriente auspicatus cursum (ortum Londinâs), occidentale dehinc sidus diù claruit, lucem in vita spargens undique, moriens luctum : Vitaeq; (vere vitalis) curriculo in an. lxiv perducto, optima perfunctus, perpessus mala, requiem tandem invenit, animo quidem in Caelis, corpore vero in subjacente tumulo. . . . Posuit honoris et amoris ergo Thomas Crispinus Exoniensis.' This Crispin founded the Kingsbridge Grammar School. The inscription is from the pen of Hughes' son-in-

---

[1] *Athenae*, ii. 280.

law, Howe, Cromwell's chaplain. Calamy calls Hughes 'a Master in most Parts of Learning, especially a great Textuary, and Divine. . . . An acute disputant, a judicious Casuist.' One of his sermons, preached before the Commons on a fast-day, May 28, 1647, is entitled *Vae-eugae-tuba*, or '*The Wo-joy-trumpet*.' Another, *Drie-Rod blossoming*. His son Obadiah was imprisoned with him at Plymouth.

A pupil of Hughes at Pembroke (entered 1624, aged 15), was WILLIAM SEDGWICKE. At College he 'profited more in Divinity than Philosophy,' being 'instructed in Presbyterian principles by his Tutor.'

At first, as Rector of Farnham, he conformed, but in 1641 put in a curate there and attached himself as chaplain to the troops of Sir William Constable, afterwards a Regicide. After the ejection of the Loyalist clergy he became the chief preacher in the city of Ely, being commonly styled the Apostle of the Isle of Ely. Wood says : 'He was a conceited whimsical person, and one very unsetled in his opinions : sometimes he was a Presbyterian, sometimes an Independent, and at other times an Anabaptist. Sometimes he was a Prophet, and would pretend to foretel matters in the pulpit, to the great distraction of poor and ignorant people. At other times having received revelations, as he pretended, he would forewarn people of their sins in publick discourses, and upon a pretence of a vision that Doomesday was at hand, he retired to the house of Sir *Franc. Russell* in *Cambridgeshire*, and finding divers Gentlemen there at Bowles, called upon them to prepare themselves for their dissolution, telling them that he had lately received a revelation that Doomesday would be some day the next week[1].' Butler has some lines on him in *Hudibras* (part ii. canto iii. 475-8). Sidrophel, seeing the paper lanthorn at the end of the boy's kite through his telescope, says :—

> 'When stars do fall 'tis plain enough
> The day of judgment's not far off;
> As lately 'twas reveal'd to SEDGWICK
> And some of us find out by magick.'

To which an editor appends the note: 'This *Sedgwick* had many persons (and some of quality) that believed in him and prepared to keep the day of judgment with him, but were disappointed ; for which the false prophet was afterwards called by the name of *Doomsday Sedgwick*.' He was Minister of Coggeshall and of Covent Garden.

Having published *The Leaves of the tree of Life for the healing of the Nations*, the author 'went to Carisbrook Castle in the Isle of *Wight*, and desired the Governours leave to address himself to K. *Ch.* I. then a Prisoner there. Mr. *Jam. Harrington* one of the Grooms of the *Bed-chamber* being acquainted with the occasion, told his Maj. that a Minister was purposely come from *London* to discourse with him about his spiritual concerns, and was also desirous to present his Maj. with a book he had lately written for his Majesties perusal; which, as he said, if his

[1] *Athenae*, ii. 335.

Majesty would please to read, might, as he imagined, be of much advantage to him, and comfort in that his disconsolate condition. The King therefore came forth, and *Sedgwick* in decent manner gave his Maj. the book. After he had read some part thereof, he returned it to the author with this short admonition and judgment: *By what I have read in this book, I believe the author stands in some need of sleep.* These words being taken by the author in the best sense, he departed with seeming satisfaction.' 'His Heart' remarks Calamy 'was better than his Head.' He preached *An Arke against a Deluge* and other Fast and Thanksgiving Sermons before the House of Commons (Wood MS. D. 18).

One of the earliest Fellows was DR. WILLIAM STAMPE, son of Timothy Stampe, of Brewern Abbey, 'of a good family.' Walker says, he entered April 20, 1627 (1626, Wood), aged 16. He was the first presented by the College to the Rectory of St. Aldate's (1637). In 1641 he became vicar of Stepney,—

'Where he was much resorted to by persons of orthodox principles for his edifying way of preaching. But when the restless Presbyterians had brought all things into confusion, he was violently thrust out, imprison'd, plunder'd, and at length forced to get away and fly for the safety of his life. At that time *Oxford* being the chief place of refuge for men of his condition, he made shift to get there about the beginning of 1643, and his case being made known to the King then there, this Order following was written by Lord *Falkland* his Secretary to the Vice-chancellour : " The Kings Majesty taking into his Princely consideration the great Sufferings of Mr. *Will. Stampe*, who hath not only undergone a long and hard Imprisonment of 34 weeks, but also is now outed of a very good Living, and all this for preaching Loyalty and Obedience to a disaffected Congregation to the extream hazard of his life: His Majesty being willing to repair these his Sufferings, and to encourage his known Abilities (for which by special favour and grace he is sworn Chaplain to his dearest Son the Prince) hath commanded me to signifie to you, that you forthwith confer on him the degree of Doctor of Divinity, &c."[1] On the declining of the King's cause Stampe followed the Prince beyond the seas, and afterwards was made chaplain to the King's sister, the beautiful Queen of Bohemia, preaching to a congregation of English exiles at Charenton. He died of a fever at the Hague about 1653, in early middle life, and (Bishop Morley told Wood) was buried in the church of Loesdune.

Others of this time were :—

FRANCIS GOLDSMITH, grandson of Sir Francis, of Crayford, Kent, entered Pembroke from the Merchant Taylors as a Gentleman Commoner in 1629. Here he laid the foundation of legal studies, migrating later to St. John's. He annotated Grotius. Died 1655. His daughter Catherine married Sir Henry Dacres, Knight.

[1] *Athenæ*, ii. 98.

JOB ROYS, son of a scrivener and akin to the founder of Roysse's School, came from Abingdon to Pembroke in 1650, and 'soon after was, elected one of the Post masters of *Mert.* Coll. where continuing under the tuition of a severe Presbyterian became well qualified with the spirit. . . . Retiring to the great City he became a puling Levite among the Brethren, for whose sake, and at their instance, he wrote and published *The Spirits Touchstone,* Lond. 1657, which was esteemed an inconsiderable canting piece. . . . If you had set aside his practical Divinity, you would have found him a simple, shiftless, and ridiculous Person.' He died in 1663, 'being then weary of the change of the times, and the wickedness, forsooth, that followed[1].'

JOHN TOY, 'born and bred in Grammar Learning within the City of *Worcester,* became either a Servitor or a Batler of *Pembroke* Coll. in 1627 [May 23, 1628, Foster], aged 16 years.' He became chaplain to the Bishop of Hereford, and Master of the Free and later of the King's School in his native town. He wrote a poem *Worcesters Elegie and Eulogie,* Lond. 1638; *Quisquiliae poeticae tyrunculis in re metrica non inutiles;* and perhaps an Encheiridion of Greek Grammar. He died on Innocents' Day, 1663, and was buried in Worcester Cathedral, where a monument with a eulogistic inscription was erected to him. Toy was vicar of Stoke Prior.

Another Worcester man was THOMAS HALL, uncle of Bishop John Hall and son of Richard Hall, a clothier, by Elizabeth Bonner his wife. He was 'bred up to Grammar learning in the King's School there under the famous *Hen. Bright,* who perceiving him to be a youth of pregnant parts, was by his perswasion sent to *Ball.* Coll. in 1624 (aged 14): but being his chance to be put under the tuition of a careless Tutor, he was removed to *Pembroke* Coll. then newly founded, and became Pupil to Mr. *Tho. Lushington,* reputed by the generality of scholars eminent for his Philosophical learning[2].'

After B.A. (Feb. 7, 162⅘) he served the cure of King's Norton and was master of the Free School. 'Being a frequenter of the Lectures at *Bermingham* in *Warwickshire* maintained and held up by the old Puritans, they so much operated on his spirit, that he relinquished his former principles, and in many respects became an enemy to the Church of *England,* and in fine so rigid in his perswasion that he was disliked by the Brethren. . . . At the turn of the times in 1641 he shew'd himself openly a Presbyterian and complied altogether with that party, not for preferment sake but because they were against Bishops and Ceremonies. At length in 1652, having *the testimony of godly and able men,* had the degree of Bach. of Divinity confer'd upon him by the then members of the University.' He appears to have been a single and humble-minded man, 'a lover of books and learning and of a retired and obscure life.' Among other treatises he wrote *Histrio-Mastix,* 'A whip for

[1] *Athenae,* ii. 220.   [2] Ibid. 233.

Webster[1] (as 'tis conceived), the quondam Player'; *The Loathsomeness of Long Hair; Funebria Florae*—The downfal of May-games; *Reasons and Arguments* against painting spots, naked breasts, arms, &c.; *Samaria's Downfall; The Beauty of Magistracy; The Font guarded with xx arguments,* against antipædobaptism; *The Pulpit guarded with xvii arguments,* proving the sinfulness of private persons preaching without a call; *The Collier in his colours,* &c., 'wherein you have the filthy, false, heretical and blasphemous tenents of one Collier an Arrian, Arminian, Socinian, etc. The said *Tho. Collier* was a husbandman, sometime Teacher to the Church at *York* and at *Westbury.*' Hall was however, as times went, a lover of peace. Calamy says he was 'often accused, curs'd, threatened with Death, many times plundered and five times imprison'd,' during the War. Other of his works were devotional. He translated *Ovid* under the titles, *Phaeton's Folly* and *Wisdom's Conquest.* He died in deep poverty, April 13, 1665, and was buried at 'his beloved King's Norton.' He had prevailed on the parishioners to build a school there, to which in his lifetime he gave his study of books. He was a benefactor also to the library of Birmingham School. 'A very hard Student, a considerable Scholar, a well furnish'd Divine, of an holy and unblamable Life,' says Calamy.

THOMAS HUNT, also from Worcester, entered Jan. 29, 16$\frac{28}{29}$ (1628, Wood, *Ath.* ii. 547), aged seventeen; M.A. 1636 (B.A. from Wadham 1632). After teaching at Salisbury and in the Church of St. Dunstan in the East, he was preferred to the Mastership of the Free School of St. Saviour's, Southwark, where he was a successful pedant. He wrote (1661) '*Libellus Orthographicus,* or the Diligent Schoolboy's Directory, very useful for grammar-scholars, Apprentices, etc. or any that desire to be exactly perfect (especially) in the English Orthography'—an art then in some need of elucidation. Also '*Abecedarium Scholasticum* : or the Grammar Scholars Flower-garden, wherein are these following flowers : to wit Proverbs, proverbial Sayings, Sayings also on several subjects.' Dying Jan. 23, 1682, he was buried in St. Saviour's[2].

[1] John Webster, chaplain in the rebel army. His *Academiarum Examen* was also answered by Seth Ward's *Vindiciae Academiarum.*

[2] The lot of many of these collegian pedagogues is described in *The Schollers Complaint,* 1641 (Rous) :—

'All in a mellanchollike study, None but my selfe,
Me thought my muse grew muddy,
    After seaven yeeres reading, and costly breeding,
      I fell and could find no pelfe.
Into learned rags I've read my plush and satten
And now am fitte to begge in Greeke and Latine,
Instead of Aristotle I would I had a patten [patent ?].
    Alas, pore scholler, Whither wilt thou goe!

The tongues and arts I've skill in, Divine and humane;
But all 's not worth a shilling.
    When the women heare me, They will but jeere me,
      And say I am profane.

EDMUND HALL, younger brother of Thomas Hall mentioned above, entered in 1636, aged 16. Leaving without a degree, he took the Covenant and became a parliamentary captain. After the victory of the . Parliament he retired to the College, and was made fellow in 1647.

In 1649 he proceeded M.A. 'about which time he express'd himself an Enemy to *Oliver* for his diabolical proceedings and was thereupon committed to custody[1].' He had written three pamphlets called *Lingua Testium, Manus Testium,* and *Digitus Testium* to prove that Cromwell 'had slain the Witnesses, was very Antichrist, and impossible for him to raign above three years and a half.' He was released after a twelve-month on giving bail. 'About that time he became, tho a Calvinist, a conceited and affected preacher several years in these parts, kept pace with the leading men during the Interval, complemented with the times at his Majesties restauration, and endeavoured to express his loyalty, yet could not endure to be called Captain. Afterwards he became Minister of a Market Town in *Oxfordsh.* named *Chipping-Norton,* where being much frequented by the neighbourhood obtained the character, from some of a fantastical, and. from others of an edifying, preacher.' He was presented, in 1680, by Sir Edmund Bray, a royalist who had made him his chaplain, to Great Risington, and, though of elderly years, wedded 'a fair and comely wife.' 'His Sermons preached before the University of *Oxon* had in them many odd, light, and whimsical passages, altogether unbecoming the gravity of the Pulpit : And his gestures being very antick and whimmical did usually excite somewhat of laughter in the more youthful part of the auditory.' One of his works, *Lazarus's soares lick'd,* was against Dr. Lazarus Seamon who had affirmed, about

> Once I remember I preached with a weaver;
> I quoted Austin, he quoted Dod and Cleaver.
> I nothing gotte, he got a cloake and beaver.
> > Alas, pore scholler, Whither wilt thou goe?
>
> Shippes, shippes, shippes I discover, Crossing the maine;
> Shall I in them saile over,
> > Be Jew or atheist, Turke or papist,
> > > To Geneva or Amsterdam?
> Bishoprickes are voide in Scotland. Shall I thither?
> Or shall I after Finch or Windebanke, to see if either
> Want a priest to shrive them? Oh no! 'tis blustering weather,
> > Alas, pore scholler, Whither wilt thou goe?
>
> Hoe, ho, ho! I have hitt it; Peace, Goodman foole,
> Thou hast a trade will fitte it;
> > Draw the indenture, Be bound at a venture
> > > An apprentice to a free-schoole.
> Here thou art king, by William Lillies charter;
> Here thou maist whip and strip, hang, draw, and quarter,
> And committe to the redde rodde Tom, Jack, Will and Arthur.
> > I, I! 'tis thither, Thither will I goe.'

[1] *Athenae,* ii. 609.

1648, that a usurper ought to be submitted to. He printed a sermon preached at Stanton Harcourt at the funeral of the Lady Anne, mother of Lord Chancellor Harcourt (1664), with a Funeral Speech spoken at her grave. Hall died in August, 1687, and is buried at Great Risington.

The dispossession of so many preachers on St. Bartholomew's Day, 1662, was a necessary deduction, less from their nonconformity or from justice to the clergy whom they had displaced, and to the majority of their flocks to whom they refused to minister, than from the essential principles of the Church as regards ordination. The Church could not but insist that they should receive apostolic commission. Of those more honest and consistent men who could not in conscience accept this slur upon the 'call' they had already received, none draws our respect more than JOHN HUMPHREYS, of whom Calamy gives a long account. He matriculated March 22, 163⅞; M. A. 1647. When the King was at Oxford, he went thither from the parliamentary quarters; but we find him later a moderate Presbyterian, receiving from the existing powers the vicarage of Frome-Selwood.

Writing in favour of free admission to the Lord's Supper, he 'was hereupon counted a Man of the Old Stamp, and no Favourite of those Times. As he never took the Covenant, so did he never joyn in the Association with the Presbytery. He was all along for bringing in the King: And one Day openly alluded to that Text of the Prophet, *I will overturn, overturn, overturn, until he come whose right it is, and I will give it him.* Hereupon a Warrant was sent for him from *Okey,* for a seditious Person. But his Danger blew over when the King return'd and Episcopacy came in with him. Some at Court were willing to remember him for preferment.' The King having said in his Declaration that the Bishop should call in some rural presbyters to help him in examining and laying on of hands, the Bishop of Bath and Wells invited Humphreys on an occasion of the kind. He told the Bishop frankly that he had received orders from a classis of Presbyters, and thought that sufficient; but after some friendly conference, indenting only for some little variation in the formula and that he should not be put upon any subscription, after two days he complied and was ordained deacon and priest. Humphreys had already written in favour of the lawfulness of re-ordination 'in order to the securing of ministerial usefulness,' and an Irish prelate told Dr. Williams that 'he converted all *Ireland* (excepting two *Scotts*) with that book.' But when he considered it now in his own case, he remembered not only that the Councils and Fathers condemned re-ordination as sacrilegious, but that the circumstances of his yielding had been such as to cast doubt on his former ordination, especially as he had submitted to be made deacon. 'His Soul was hereupon wounded, diseased, oppressed.' Not content with a public profession of his 'penitent Grief and Sorrow,' in which he did 'retract, revoke, renounce and reject' his re-ordination, he went in much distress to the Bishop's Registrar, and, before witnesses, tore his paper of Deacon's Orders and threw it into the fire. He yet reserved the evidence of his priestly character, not knowing but it might serve him in the exercise of his function; but, when the Act of Uniformity made it clear that he could not continue to minister without accepting the Prayer Book, he took 'an honest Man' as witness into his chamber, tore his Priest's Orders also, threw one part into the flames, and wrapped up the other part in a letter to the Bishop, 'that you may see unto what a pass the Trouble of a Man's Mind some Times may bring him, to get his Peace again when he hath forgone it; which the Lord of his Mercy make use of to your Honour for Caution and Tenderness towards others.' During Charles II's reign he wrote a vast number of pacificatory pamphlets; for one paper of counsel to Parliament he was committed to the Gate-house, and one, *The Sacramental Test*, was voted to be burnt. At the Revolution he addressed to the Convention a breviate, *Advice before it be too late.* He died about 1719, having almost fulfilled the expectation that he would be 'the longest Liver of all the Ejected.' Nathan Denton survived him. When Calamy pressed him for an autobiography he replied that he 'desired no more than to go to his Grave with a Sprig of Rosemary.' In all his life of ninety-nine years 'this good man,' says Calamy, 'has never been able to be of the rising side.' Perhaps THOMAS HUMPHRIES of Pembroke, the 'blockhead,' whom Hearne (iii. 458) asserts to have preached a stolen sermon before the University on the Divine Authority of the New Testament, was his son.

THOMAS ROSEWELL, of an old Somerset stock, entered Dec. 9, 1650. B.A. July 6, 1651.

Being presented by Lady Hungerford to Rhode, he was there 'Solemnly Ordained by Mr *Strickland* (whose Daughter he Married) and others,' in July, 1654. In 1658 he moved to Sutton Mandeville, Wilts, whence he was ejected after the Restoration. But his interest belongs to a later date. After ministering privately for ten years at Rotherhithe, he was arrested, Sept. 23, 1684, by the warrant of Chief Justice Jeffries, for High Treason and committed to the Gate-house. In the trial at the King's Bench bar, Nov. 18, it was alleged that in a sermon on Sept. 14 Rosewell had said 'that the People made a flocking to our said Sovereign Lord the King, upon pretence of healing the King's Evil, which he could not do'; but that they ought rather to resort to himself and other Traiterous persons, for that 'we are Priests and Prophets, that by our Prayers can heal the Dolours and Griefs of the People. We have had Two wicked Kings (meaning the most Serene *Charles* the First, late King of *England* and our said Sovereign Lord the King that now is) who have permitted Popery to enter in under their Noses, whom we can resemble to no other Person, but to the most wicked *Jeroboam.*' If his hearers would stand to their principles, he did not fear but they would overcome their enemies, as in former times, 'with Ram's Horns, broken Platters, and a Stone in a Sling.' Three women swore to these words, who, Calamy says, were afterwards pilloried for perjury. In spite of a good defence, the prisoner

was convicted and sentenced, but 'Sir *John Talbot*, who was present at
the Tryal, was pleas'd, of his own accord, to represent the Passages of
it, with his Opinion, to King *Charles*; who gave Direction to the Lord
Chief Justice *Jeffreys*, that he should have Council assign'd him, to plead
to the Insufficiency of the Indictement, in Arrest of Judgment. Accordingly on *Nov.* 27, Mr *Wallop*, Mr *Pollexfen*, and Mr *Thomas Bampfield*
Argu'd upon the Case, and the Court took time till the next Term to
consider of Judgment: And King *Charles* in the meantime granted him
a Pardon, which he pleaded some few days after that King's Death, and
was discharg'd. He outliv'd his Tryal Seven Years; and dy'd *Feb.* 14,
169⅘, and was Interr'd at *Bunhill*. His Funeral Sermon was preach'd
by Mr *Matthew Head*.' Rosewell's *Life* was published by his daughter,
1718.

THOMAS RISELEY, made fellow by the Visitors in 1654 (matric.
Dec. 9, 1650; B.A. 1652; M.A. 1655), resigned or was ejected at
the Restoration. Calamy says,—

'There is some Account of him in a Preface prefix'd by Mr *Howe* to
a Treatise of his, intituled, *the Cursed Family*, 8vo. 1700. In the University he pass'd his time as a Recluse; and after his Ejectment, he liv'd as
obscurely in the Country, as he did before in *Oxon*. He rather aim'd
at acquiring solid useful Knowledge, and Learning, than Fame: and was
contented rather to shine to himself, than the World. His little Book of
the *Curse* belonging to Prayerless Families, shews him to have been a
valuable Man.' A MS. note in my copy of Calamy adds: 'A large
account of his *Life* is publish'd by Mr Charles Owen who preach'd his
Fun^ll Serm^n 1716.' Riseley was born near Warrington, Aug. 27, 1630.

Calamy also gives particulars of the following:—

GEORGE TROSSE (son of Henry Trosse, Esquire, counsellor at law),
born at Exeter, entered Aug. 6, 1658, aged twenty-seven. His tutor was
Thomas Cheseman, the Nonconformist. He became 'Pastor of a considerable Congregation in *Exon*,' where he suffered a six months' imprisonment in South Gate.

WILLIAM REEVES, B.A., after his ejection from Resbury, Bucks,
'preach'd no where Statedly but here and there Occasionally, and pretty
much at *Abingdon*. He was once much Troubled on occasion of a
Charge of Treasonable Words, sworn upon him in a Sermon he preach'd
on *Psal.* 2. 1. But upon a Tryal he was Acquitted. He dy'd *An.* 1683.'

WILLIAM CROSSE (matr. July 25, 1655, born at Frinkford, Oxon), was
'ordain'd by the Presbytery at *Nottingham* and call'd to *Attenborough*,'
and to Beeston, Notts. 'After his Ejectment he liv'd at *Loughborough*,
where he preach'd when the Law allow'd him. He dy'd Pastor of a
numerous Congregation in *Derby* in 1698. He was a good practical
Preacher; and exemplary in his Conversation. The Seventh Sermon in
the Collection of Farewel Sermons of the Country Ministers (upon 1 *Sam.*
30. 6.), is his.'

JOHN LANGSTON went from the Free School at Worcester to Pembroke as a servitor in 1655, and spent some years there. He was thrust into the benefice of Ash Church, but made way for the old incumbent on the King's return. ' Retiring to London he taught a private grammar school near Spitalfields, was disturbed, and went into Ireland as chaplain to Captain Blackwell, returning to his school again in 1663. Here he wrote his *Lusus Poeticus Latino-Anglicanus in usum Scholarum* (1675), and his *Poeseos Graecae Medulla* (1679). He at length accepted an invitation from a dissenting congregation at Ipswich. He met with a great deal of violent usage there, and was forced to publish a Vindication to prove that he was not a Jesuit. 'He shew'd great sweetness of Spirit towards his own People, and towards People of different Perswasions, untill he fell asleep on *Jan.* 12, 170⅔. *Ætat.* 64.'

THOMAS CHESEMAN, the blind tutor and preacher, was ejected from East Garston, Berks. 'No sooner did he step into this World than he trod upon the Thorns of a very sharp Affliction, being depriv'd of his Eye-sight by the Small Pox before he was four Years Old. He was bred in the School at *Tunbridge*, and went thence to *Pembroke* College *Oxon*; where he continu'd till he was Master of Arts [July 9, 1656], and had among others Mr *Timothy Hall* (whom K. *James* made a Bishop) for his Pupil. When he was ejected by the Act, he came up to *London* and Preach'd frequently in the Churches here, and was never apprehended. He afterwards returned into the Country, and Preach'd in his own House at *Market-Ilsley*, to such as would venture to hear him; And he continu'd it, till a Writ *de Excommunicato capiendo* came out against him; by virtue of which he was a Prisoner in *Reading* for 15 Weeks, but he was Releas'd by an Order of King and Council procur'd for him by some Friends in *London*. After King *Charles's* Indulgence he Preach'd openly; and held the Exercise of his Ministry to a good Old Age. He was a good Scholar and useful Preacher.'

Other 'ejected or silenced ministers' mentioned by Calamy in *Baxter's Life and Times* were :—

FRANCIS MENCE (entered 1660), who suffered, however, chiefly at the hands of fellow sectaries. In 1694 he published '*Vindiciae Foederis* with some seasonable Reflections upon various unsound and Cruel Passages taken forth of two Furious Books of Mr. *H. Collins* printed against Infant's Baptism. By *Fran. Mence*, some time of *Pembroke* College in *Oxford*, now an unworthy Pastor of a Church of Christ in *Wapping* near *London.*'—THOMAS WALROND (1633), ejected from Woolfardisworthy;— 'a very learned Man. He quitted a considerable Place, and incurr'd the Displeasure of his Family, which was much to his Damage.'—JAMES RAWSON (B.A. 1618), 'a Conformist in the Time of King *Charles* I; but counted the Terms of Conformity too rigorous after the Restauration.' He had been put by the Earl of Northumberland into the rectory of Haselbury Bryant. Rawson wrote a quarto on Election and Reprobation, dated 1658.—JAMES PERRY (1641), dispossessed of Micklemarsh, Hants. 'His Living was worth 300*l. per Annum.* He was a very popular

Preacher, and continu'd the Exercise of his Ministry at Odiham in this County *gratis*, 'till Sickness disabled him.'—THOMAS KENTISH (1651), ejected from Overton ; 'a very serious, useful, friendly, candid Person.' He 'came to *London*, and was Pastor of a Society that met for Divine Worship in *Cannon Street*.'—JOHN MALDEN (1638), ejected from Newport. He was 'a Man of great Learning, an excellent Hebrician, one of exemplary piety, and a solid Preacher. As he liv'd, so he dy'd, very low in his own Eyes.'—EDWARD WARRE (1650), dispossessed of Cheddon, Somerset, but 'preached in private in the Parish after he was Ejected.'—RICHARD SARGENT (1640), removed from Stone, Worcester-shire ; 'a Man of extraordinary Prudence, Humility, Sincerity, Self-denial, Patience, and Blamelessness of Life.'—To these may be added HENRY COXE, ejected from Bishopstoke, Hants, and NATHANIEL WHITE (1623) from Market Lavington, Wilts.

We have a very different kind of person from the foregoing in the famous SIR WILLIAM SCROGGS, born at Deddington, Oxon, at the end of James I's reign. `His father William was affirmed by Dugdale (to whom Scroggs had refused to pay the usual fees of knighthood) to have been 'a one ey'd Butcher near Smithfield Bars, and his Mother a big fat Woman with a red face, like an Alewife[1] ;' also that the father was 'a very ill-humour'd man' and would never pay his tithes. He gave his son however a good education, and sent him, aged 16, to Oriel (matr. May 17, 1639). Thence he migrated to Pembroke, ' where, being put under the tuition of a noted Tutor, he became Master of a good Latine stile and a considerable Disputant.' B.A. Jan. 23, 16$\frac{4}{5}$. 'Soon after, tho the Civil War broke forth, and the University emptied thereupon of the greatest part of its Scholars, yet he continued there, bore arms for his Majesty, and had so much time allowed him, that he proceeded Master of Arts in 1643.'

' About that time he being designed for a Divine, his Father procured for him the reversion of a good Parsonage; but so it was that he being engaged in that honorable, tho unfortunate, expedition of *Kent, Essex,* and *Colchester*, an. 1648, wherein, as I have been credibly informed, he was a Captain of a Foot Company, he was thereby disingaged from enjoying it ' (*Athenae*, ii. 565). He had been entered of Gray's Inn, however, in Feb. 1640, but, owing to the turmoil of the State, was not called till June 1653. As a lawyer, a 'bold front, a handsome person, an easy allocution and a ready wit' (*Foss*), enabled him to push his way quickly. Wood however says that his fluency as a speaker was spoiled for listening to by ' some stops and hesitancy.' He was 'a person of very excellent and nimble parts,' but of debauched morals. Soon after the Restoration he was knighted, and chosen counsel for the Corporation of London. But in April 1665 he made petition alleging that it being his duty to walk

---

•   [1] So in the Tom Tickle-foot and Justice Clodpate lampoons.

before the Lord Mayor on certain days of solemnity, but being unable to do so from wounds sustained in the late King's cause, he had been therefore suspended from his place, and praying redress. In April, 1668, he was assigned as counsel for Sir W. Penn, and the next year was bencher of Gray's Inn and King's Serjeant. Roger North says that Chief Justice Hale detested Scroggs and refused him his serjeant's privilege when arrested under warrant for assault and battery. Lord Danby was his chief patron, through whom he was made a Judge of Common Pleas, Oct. 23, 1676, and on May 31, 1678, Lord Chief Justice. As a judge he showed himself able, but ignorant, arrogant, and brutal. In his conduct of the State trials arising out of the ' Popish Plot,' he thought he was gaining the favour of the Court by riding the Protestant horse, browbeating the prisoners, and backing Oates and Bedlow. One day however, says North, ' the Lord Chief Justice came from Windsor with a Lord of the Council (Chief Justice *North*) in his coach, and among other discourse *Scroggs* asked that Lord if the Lord *Shaftesbury* (who was then Lord President of the Council) had really that interest with the King as he seemed to have. No, replied that Lord, no more than your footman hath with you. This sank into the man, and quite altered the ferment, so as that from that time he was a new man[1].' Luttrell asserts his conversion to have been due to Portuguese gold. Being now on the unpopular side, Scroggs (nicknamed ' the Mouth') was indicted by Oates and Bedlow for encouraging popery, and for profanity, drunkenness and corruption ; but at the hearing before the King and Council in January, 1600, he triumphantly beat down and outreviled his accusers. In the next parliament the Commons impeached him (Jan. 1681) for getting rid of a presentment in the King's Bench against the Duke of York for absenting himself from Church, and for issuing illegal warrants ; but the Upper House refused to concur. When a new parliament met at Oxford the following March, the attack was renewed ; Scroggs pleaded Not Guilty, and that parliament also was dissolved. But the King thought it prudent to remove him, granting him a pension of £1,500, and a patent of King's Counsel to his son Sir William (1652-1695, treasurer of Gray's Inn 1686-8). Scroggs retired to his estate at Weald Hall near Burntwood, Essex, where he died Oct. 25, 1683, and was buried in Southweald Church. Wood speaks of his ' courage and greatness of spirit,' and ascribes his change of front to patriotism ' when he saw this Popish Plot to be made a shooing-horn to draw on others.' One of his daughters was married to Lord Chief Justice Wright, the other to a son of Lord Hatton.

Some members of the College mentioned by Wood among the Writers, or as otherwise noted, about this time, are :—

CONWAY WHITTERNE, created Med. Bac. Dec. 20, 1642, when the King after the battle of Edgehill retired to Oxford, and declared his pleasure that there should be a creation (sometimes called the Caroline Creation) in all faculties of such as had done him service in that fight. Whitterne was at

---

[1] *Examen*, 568.

one time Captain of a Company of Foot. He also fought for Charles II at
Worcester. Rector of Kingham (1676) and Daylesford (1680).—WILLIAM
NORREYS, afterwards a Cornet in the Lord Hopton's army, was made
B.A. in the same creation.—WILLIAM DOWDESWELL, perhaps the canon
of Chichester of that name, 'accounted a learned man among those of his
Society,' was created M.A. at the same time, as one of those who 'had
retired to the King at *Oxon* to avoid the barbarities of the Presbyterians.'
At the Restoration he received a prebend at Worcester.—JOHN WYBERD
(entered 163$, *aet.* 24), a mathematician, who left England when the
troubles began, travelled in Germany, and was made Doctor of Physick
(being styled 'Trinobans Anglus') at Franaker in West Friesland, whence
he incorporated at Oxford in 1654. He wrote '*Tetagmenometria,* or
the Geometry of Regulars practically proposed,' Lond. 1650.—PHILIP
MARINELL, a Channel Island fellow (matr. 1653), translated (1660) from
the French *The Hinge of Faith and Religion,* written by Ludovicus
Capel, professor of Divinity at Samur. He was buried in St. Aldate's
churchyard, near the south door.—PAUL LATHOM (matr. 1654); created
M.A. 1661 at the Clarendonian Creation; prebendary of Sarum and
a writer.—Dr. ANDREW DOMINICK, 'originally of *Trin.* Coll. where he
had in a manner been drawn off from his Religion to that of *Rome* but
reclaimed by the endeavours of Dr. *Christoph. Wren,* afterwards Dean of
Windsore.' Created D.D. in 1661, when Lord Clarendon the Chancellor
visited Oxford, being then beneficed in Wilts. He published among other
things *Dies Nefastus* (1662).—In the same Creation SAMUEL COTTON, and
LAWRENCE HUNGERFORD vicar of Hambledon, were made Doctors of
Divinity.—Wood does not mention Dr. ELISHA COYSH (matr. 1650),
fellow of the College of Physicians 1673 (buried in St. Mary Aldermary
1685).—Dean SAMUEL CROSSMAN, author of 'Jerusalem on high' and
other 'Sacred Poems,' is assigned by Professor Palgrave in his *Treasury*
to this House, but appears to have been bred at Pembroke Hall in
Cambridge.

CHAPTER XIX.

CLAYTON's *de jure* successor in the mastership, HENRY WIGHTWICK, had in his salad days set the University by the ears. At the end of 1613[1]

'a spirit of sedition possessed certain of the Regent Masters against the Vicechanc. and doctors. The chief and only matter that excited them to it was their sitting like boys bareheaded in the Convocation House, at the usual assemblies there, which was not, as 'twas thought, so fit, that the Professors of the Faculty of Arts (on which the University was founded) should, all things considered, do it. The most forward person among them, named Henry Wightwicke, of Gloucester Hall, having had an intimation of a Statute which enabled them to be covered with their caps, and discovering also something in the large west window of Saint Mary's Church, where pictures of Regents and Non-Regents were sitting covered in assemblies before the Chancellor, clapt on his cap, and spared not to excite his brethren to vindicate that custom, now in a manner forgotten ; and having got over one of the Regents to be more zealous in the matter than himself, procured the hands of most, if not all, of them to be set to a Petition (in order to be sent to the Chancellor of the University[2]), for the effecting and bringing about the matter. But the Vicechancellor, Dr Singleton, having had timely notice of the design, sends a full relation of the matter to the Chancellor; whereupon answer was returned that he should deal therein as he should think fit. Wightwicke therefore being called into question for endeavouring to subvert the Honour and Government of the University, whereby he ran himself into perjury (he having before taken an Oath to keep and maintain the Rites, Customs, and Privileges of the University) was banished; and his party, who had proved false to him, severely checkt by the Chancellor.

'At length Wightwick's friends laying open to him the danger that he

---

[1] Gutch, *Annals*, ii. 317.

[2] Thomas, Lord Ellesmere. A little earlier, in 1591, Dr. James the Vice-Chancellor, an anti-puritan, pronounced John Vicars, a regent-master of Broadgates, deprived for a year of the liberties of the University for brawling in Congregation (Gutch's *Wood*, ii. 247).

would run himself into, if he should not seek restauration and submit, did, after his peevish and rash humour had been much courted to it, put up a Petition (subscribed in his behalf by the Bishop of London[1] and Sir John Bennett) to the Chancellor of the University, for his restauration, which being with much ado granted, but with this condition, that he make an humble recantation in the Convocation, sent to his Vicechancellor what should be done in the matter, and among other things thus. "For the manner of his submission and recognition which he is to make, I will not take upon me to direct, but leave yt wholy to your wisdomes, as well for manner as for the matter; only thus much generally will I intimate unto you that the affront and offence committed by Whittwicke in the Congregation House by his late insolent carriage there, was verie great and notorious, and that offence afterwards seconded and redoubled by another, as ill or worse than the former, in his seditious practizing and procuring a multitude of handes, thereby thinking to justifie and maintain his former errors, and his proud and insolent disobedience and contempt. I hold yt therefore very requisite that his submission and recognition, both of the one fault and of the other, should be as publique, and as humble, as possible with conveniencye may bee. Which being thus openly done, as I hope yt will bee a good example to others, to deter them from committing the like offences hereafter, so I do also wishe this his punishment may be only ad correctionem et non ad destructionem." '

He made his submission on the morrow of St. John Baptist's Day, 1614, in the middle of the chancel of St. Mary's. In it he says, after acknowledging that he had put on his cap,

'Scitote quaeso praeterea, me supradictum Henricum a sententia domini Vicecancellarii ad venerabilem Domum Congregationis provocasse, quod nec licitum nec honestum esse in causa perturbationis pacis facile concedo. Scitote denique me solum manus Academicorum egregie merentium Theologiae Baccalaureorum et in Artibus Magistrorum in hac corona astantium Collegiatim et Aulatim cursitando rescripto apponendas curasse.'

He writes himself both 'Whitwicke' and 'Wightwicke.' The submission was followed by his restoration. Wood adds:—

'This person could never be convinced when he became Master of Pembroke College, 46 years after this time, that he made any submission at all, but carried the business on and effected it against all the University: as to his young acquaintance that came often to visit him and he them (for he delighted in boyish company) he would after a pedantical way boast, supposing perhaps, that having been so many years before acted, no person could remember it: but record will rise up and justify matters, when names and families are quite extirpated and forgotten among men.'

[1] Abbott. These names seem a link between Tesdale and the Wightwick family.

In 1620, six years after Wightwick's rebuff, Prideaux being Vice-Chancellor, the Regent Masters, including Gilbert Sheldon, Peter Heylin, Robert Newlyn, and many others, renewed their claim to be covered, and the Chancellor, Lord Pembroke, recommended Convocation to allow it, 'it being no where seen that those that are admitted Judges are required to sit bare-headed.' It was accordingly agreed that all Masters might wear square caps, any one bringing in his hat to lose his suffrage. Before half a century had elapsed however the privilege was disused, the masters finding it troublesome to bring their caps and preferring to sit bare-headed. By an ordinance of June 1, 1621, undergraduates were to stand uncovered before masters.

Dr. Ingram considers Henry Wightwick's reply to the parliamentary Visitors only equalled by Hough's stand against James II. His career had not a very edifying sequel. He was advanced in life when restored to the Mastership in 1660. On the Epiphany (Sunday) 1661, 'Mr. *Whighwick*, Mr. of *Pemb*. Coll. *Oxon*, preached at S. Maries on this text, Master, what shall I doe yt I might inherit eternall life? Where he, striving too much yt his voice might be heard, fell in sownn. This I took notice of here, in case the phanaticks may take advantage of it hereafter, to publish it as a speciall judgment of God, as they did on some occasions last Aug. Mr. Whitwicke, as I was told, eat not a bit from Saturday noon before, neither took rest that night, and besides he is an old man[1].' On Dec. 21, 1664, he was removed from his place as Master by an order from the Earl of Clarendon read in the College hall. 'Mr. Whitwick's place pronounced void by the Chancellour for severall misdeameanours. This man had been absent from the Universitie many yeares and had forgot an Universitie life and the decorum belonging to a governour. Testy, peevish and silly. Drinks with yong Mrs. and Bachelors. Visit ... Ewre of C. C. Coll.[2], a fat drunken Bachelor, and hath been discovered at his chamber in a morning smoaking and drinking. His preaching at St. Marie's ridiculous. His person ridiculous, like a monkey rather than a Christian[3].' There was a bibbing Rector at Exeter College after the Restoration, for whom Wood makes a similar excuse, that he had in his long exile and 'extreme misery' unlearnt the habits of a scholar and divine; and the restored President of Corpus, Dr. Newlyn, seems

---

[1] Wood's *Life and Times*, i. 379.
[2] Probably Henry Ewer, matr. 1662.
[3] *Life and Times*, ii. 25.

S

also to have been demoralized by adversity. Wightwick was rather high-handed and autocratic, as the following appeal against his enforcement of the Statutes seems to show. The appellant is a different Henry Wyat from the intruded fellow of that name.

'To the Right Honorᵇˡᵉ Edward Earle of Clarendon Lord high Chancelоʳ of England Chancelʳ of yᵉ University of Oxon & by yᵉ Statute of Pemb. Coll. their peculiar Visitor

'The humble petičon of HENRY WYATT Dʳ in physick & fellow of Pemb. Coll.¹

'Humbly sheweth

'That yoʳ peticonʳ was contiñally persecuted & threatned expulsion in yᵉ time of Dʳ Langlys Mʳship for adhering to yᵉ King but is now actually expeld by Mʳ Wightwick yᵉ present Mʳ upon pretence of a certain clause in yᵉ statutes wᶜʰ obliges those of yᵉ foundation to be ordaind Ministers wᵗʰin 4 yeares after they are. mʳˢ of Arts whereas all yᵗ time there was noe episcopall and lawfull ordination to be had & since to be ordained will not fulfill yᵉ statute and therefore upon a full debate it was ordred² by yᵉ Visitors appointed by his Maᵗʸ for regulating the Univʳsity that yoʳ peticonʳ should be restord to his fellowship & yᵉ profitts thereof and had time granted till Michaelmas next to resolve whether he would enter into Orders or not But yᵉ Mʳ in a peremptory Contempt of yᵉ said Order hath in yoʳ peticonʳˢ absence proceeded notwithstanding to a full expulsion & admitted another into his place & not only done this but many other rash and imprudent Acts against yᵉ Consent of all yᵉ fellows to yᵉ great prejudice & almost ruine of yᵉ whole society

'Yoʳ peticonʳ therefore most humbly prayeth (forasmuch as he is a kinsman to yᵉ Founder & hath been alwaies faithfull to his Maᵗʸ & a great sufferer both att home & abroad & hath as yett no other preferment) that yoʳ Honʳ would be pleasd to restore him to his fellowshippe & yᵉ profits thereof that he may have yᵉ same favour wᶜʰ others injoy & a longer time granted him before he be compeld to take Orders the statutes allowing a yeare of grace even to those who have other certaine preferment.

'And yoʳ peticonʳ shall ever pray etc'

'Oxford Sept. 23, 1661

'This Petition having been delivered to Me so late before my going out of Town that I have not time to send for the Master of Pembroke Coll: I desire Mʳ Vicechanceller to examine the Business & to see if He can, by calling both Parties before him, settle it; If not to make a speciall Report of it to Me.   'Clarendon C.'

¹ Tanner MSS. 338, fol. 405.   ² Viz. on April 9, 1661.

Minutes of the Hebdomadal Board.

'Upon reading y⁰ Pembroke Coll. Statute touchinge y⁰ tyme for fellowes to be invested into holy orders, forasmuch as Mʳ Henry Whitwick Master of y⁰ said coll: did upon his owne power, without y⁰ consent of y⁰ fellowes of the said Coll: or application to the Visitor then beeing pronounce Dʳ Henry Wyat fellowe of the said Coll: Non Socius and did consequently expell him his said fellowᴾᴾ the Board Upon due debate and consideraċon of the matter did revoke and null y⁰ said Act of Mʳ Henry Whitwick as to the expulsion of the said Dʳ Henry Wyatt And did decree him to be restored and did then restore him to his said fellowᴾ and all the rights and profites thereunto belonging with the arreares from the time he was pronounced Non Socius to the present, And did give farther tyme to the said Doctor Henry Wyat to enter into holy orders for satisfaċon of the said statute till Michaelmas next.'

Dr. Wyatt afterwards applies for further extension of time and urges,

'The Statute does not say I shall be expell'd if not in Orders but only thus: Omnes obligabuntur ad studium theologiae et erunt Presbyteri intra 4tuor annos a suscepto gradu Magistri. And I believe in some cases this may alsoe be dispensed wᵗʰ, as in case of Travell wᶜʰ is allowed by y⁰ Statute; It is not to be imagin'd yᵗ a man should take Orders whilst he is in y⁰ Catholique Countries. Add to this if a man be employed in any publique service either in y⁰ Church or State a dispensaċon is allowable by Statute, as I am and can procure y⁰ King's hand for it, as well as Mʳ Williamson of Queens Coll: has done in y⁰ like case. I should like wise be readie to thinke yᵗ if y⁰ ffounder were now living (whose kinsman I am and therefore might expect as much if not more favour than any other) yᵗ he would not presse y⁰ statute so rigorously against mee, especially in such times when men were not only driven from their prefermᵗˢ but their professions alsoe, wᶜʰ I was compelld to do for my present mayntenance at y⁰ time. And my being a Phisitian now does not prevent me from taking Orders, wᶜʰ for ought I know I may doe (if prefermᵗ falls for mee) y⁰ next publique Ordinaċon.'

Dr. Wyatt had been made Doctor of Physic at the special Restoration creation in all faculties 'of such that had suffer'd for his Majesties Cause, and had been ejected from the University by the Visitors appointed by Parliament.' He met with a tragic fate, May 3, 1664, near Tangier, whither he had gone in the capacity of physician with the Earl of Teviot, at the hands of the Moors.

Wightwick became rector of Kingerby, Lincolnshire, and died and was buried there in June, 1671.

In place of the fallen Wightwick, JOHN HALL was chosen Master on New Year's Eve, 1664—'bred in the Interval; a presbyterian;

clownish, covetuous, and quarrelsome among the fellowes; some good preachers bred under him.' He was presented soon after to St. Aldate's, where he drew large congregations 'of the precise people and scholars of the University by his edifying way of preaching.' This prelate was born in 1633 at Bromsgrove, where his father, John Hall (1599–1657; son of Richard Hall, clothier), was vicar. He entered Merchant Taylors' School in June, 1644, and four years later went to Wadham. On April 22, 1650, having submitted to the Visitors, he was put by them into a Scholar's place at Pembroke, where his uncle Edmund was his tutor. B.A. 1551; M.A. 1653; B.D. 1666; D.D. 1669. He received presbyterian ordination in 1655 [1], but must have been re-ordained after the Restoration. In the College books his signature appears, Aug. 15, 1660, as praelector Graecus. 'Recd. then of Dr. Langley for reading yᵉ Greek Lecture three termes ending with Easter term last past, yᵉ suṁe of thirty shillings, I say rec. By me Jo: Hall.' Langley was still acting as Master. In 1658 Hall had moderated the philosophy form, receiving 13s. 8d. for one quarter. To conciliate the Puritans, the King made Hall his chaplain. In 1676, May 24th, he was chosen Margaret Professor of Divinity, though, Wood says [2], 'Mr. Rowson was cried up to be the man.' Next, 'Grows proud; forsakes by degrees his old companions, viz. — Walker, and — Stone;' probably Obadiah Walker and William Stone, principal of New Inn Hall, both suspected papists. In 1678, 'Dr. Hall of Pembroke (presbyterian) preached sharply and bitterly against the papists on 5th Nov. at St. Marie's. Quaere whether Dr. Hall was originally appointed to preach. The same night the pope, in the shape of an old man, was burnt at a fier at Edmund Hall . . . (his belly being full of crackers) [3].' This was after the Plot. Wood states that on December 23, Dr. Hall treated him very rudely and tried to pick a quarrel about religion. 'A malepert presbyterian since this

---

[1] In the Visitors' Register, July 17, 1655, is 'The Testimoniall of John Hall, Master of Arts, of Pembrooke Colledg :—Wee whose names are underwritten, by our knowledg of John Hall, Master of Arts of Pembrooke Colledge, doe hereby testifie to all persons whom it may concerne that we judg him godly studious and for his standing in the University of good proficiency in learning.
        'Ra. Fenton   Sam. Bruen
        Hen. Hoy   Jo. Spilsbury
        Edm. Hall   Phil. Potter.'
John Spilsbury (ejected from Bromsgrove Vicarage in 1662) married Bishop Hall's sister, and their son John, nonconforming Minister of Kidderminster, was Hall's heir. Fenton was of All Souls. The rest were of Pembroke.

[2] *Life and Times*, ii. 346.

[3] Ibid. ii. 422.

plot, nothing of malepertness before[1].' When Stephen Golledge, the
' Protestant Joiner,' was to be drawn and quartered by John Ketch
before Oxford Castle, Aug. 31, 1681, 'Dr. John Hall, Master of
Pembroke Coll. and Dr. George Reynell of C.C.C. had several times
prayed with him[2].' Prideaux writes to John Ellis, Sept. 22, of this
year, ' Somebody hath lately scattered about the town a Catalogue of
Whigs, or those which he thinks soe, in every Colledge, which hath
put us into some disorder, several very honest men being inserted
among them with ill characters which doe not belong to them. . . .
Dr. Bathurst and Dr. Hall are the two that begin y[e] list.' On
July 16, 1683, however it was ordered by the Hebdomadal Board
that Dr. Hall, as Margaret Professor, with Jane the Regius Professor
and the three senior Doctors of Divinity, should ' consider of
those principles and grounds which did encourage, produce, and carry
on the damnable association designe and conspiracy against the life
of his sacred majestie, his royal brother, and the being of the government established in church and state ; and with all possible speed
deliver in Latin to the vice-chancellor what they have resolved upon.'
Several condemned articles were on July 21 read in Convocation,
' taken from severall rebellious and seditious authours,' and the books
burnt in the Schools quadrangle, the scholars of all degrees and
qualities who surrounded the fire giving ' severall hums ' while they
were burning. Dr. Hall with others had an audience of the King
three days later to present an address from the University congratu-
lating the King and the Duke on their delivery from the Protestant
Plot. In April 1685 he had so far redeemed his character from the
charge of whiggery that, with Dr. Mill, he was chosen by the clergy of
the diocese of Oxford to be clerk of the Convocation for the parliament about to begin. ' This John Hall is to preach the Coronation
sermon at St. Marie's and takes all occasions (being a Presbyterian)
to shew himself loyall[3].' But the sermon, which was preached in
English on St. George's day, the day of James II's Coronation, did not
give satisfaction. In it he persuaded the auditors ' not to hearken in
the least after popery,' and to ' pray for the King that God would open
his eyes to see the right.' Wood calls it a ' lukewarm, trimming

[1] *Life and Times*, ii. 428.
[2] Ibid. ii. 553. The plot against the King's life was to have been carried out at
Oxford. Burnet doubts the plot. Golledge, he says, suffered with great constancy
and with appearance of devotion. His last words were to Mr. Crosthwaite,
' Pray, Sir, my service to Dr. *Hall* and Dr. *Reynell*, and thank them for all their
kindnesses to me.'
[3] Ibid. iii. 137.

sermon.' When it ended there was a great bonfire at the door of
St. Mary's, and the day was celebrated 'with great solemnity [1].'

After the Revolution, Hall was one of those chosen to fill the
places of the non-juring prelates, succeeding Dr. Ironside, who had
been translated to Hereford, in the see of Bristol. He was consecrated Aug. 30, 1691, in St. Mary-le-Bow Church by Tillotson
with four assistants, and Burnet preached the sermon [2]. When
Tillotson died, Nov. 20, 1694, Hall (according to Tanner) was,
together with Trelawny of Exeter, proposed by William to his Council
for the Primacy. The Latitudinarians favoured Hall and their opponents Trelawny; so that William at last pitched upon Dr. Tenison [3].
There were not many Whigs of eminence to choose among; but, if
he really was thought *capax summi imperii*, Hall cannot have been
the clown that Wood, who had the fortune to write his enemies' lives,
represents him to have been.

Noble (who calls him Joseph) speaks of Hall as 'a faithful and
munificent head of a college.' Wood's charge of 'quarrelsomeness
among the fellows' seems to relate to the disputes referred to in the
following correspondence [4], not yet printed, except the last letter. The
favour of the Master with the new Government did not make the
fellows, probably, more loyal to him. On the other hand the Visitor
was bound to stand by Hall against high-church disaffection.

'A defence of the procedure of the ffellows of Pem. Coll, together wth
their petition humbly presented to the High & Noble Prince, his Grace
the Duke of Ormond, their honrd Visitour.

'Tho' the grievances we lye under, are such as must of themselves
very sensibly affect us, yet this is the most unsupportable aggravation
of all afflictions to Us, y^t they s^d occasion this frequent trouble to yor
Grace And now specially after a com̃ission granted for inquiry into
the causes of our complaints We are extreamly concerned least any
further application to yor Grace may possibly make us liable to be
censur'd as importunate & litigious men. We were so apprehensive of
this danger, & carefull of avoyding yor Grace's ill opinion on this
occasion, that we could probably have been perswaded quietly to have

---

[1] Under date July 1688, Wood mentions an odd circumstance of an Irishman
named Connor, who made a hermitage in Bagley wood 'for devotion and reading
sake, continuing much in abstinence from beare, ale, or meates. Carried home at
the desire of Dr. Hall, because then many people flock'd to him.' *Life and Times*,
iii. 273.

[2] Burnet says that the fifteen bishops named by William in 1689–90 'were
generally looked on as the learnedest, the wisest, and the best men that were in the
Church' (*History*).

[3] *Life and Times*, iii. 474.

[4] Wood MS. F. 28, foll. 242–5, and Carte MSS., foll. 689 sq.

resign'd up our own privileges if they had not been so interwoven wth ye rights of yor Grace y^t we could not have the happiness of being ye only sufferers.'

The Master had made allegations against one of the Wightwick Fellows, HENRY WOOD[1], 'as to his plentifull fortune and bad manners.' The petitioners point out that the Commission did not pretend that these charges were made out. It was not the case that they had set up Mr. Wood in opposition to the Master. 'And indeed our former compliance wth his orders had been so great and extraordinary, that it can hardly be imagin'd we would now seek an unjustifiable occasion of disobeying him.' His Grace had further to decide on the Master's claim, grounded on a private statute which they had never seen, to a necessary voice, equivalent to a negative voice, in elections to Fellowships on Lord Ossulston's foundation. This was 'a new and hidden law,' 'directly repugnant to our ffundamental statutes.' Under those statutes elections must take place *statim*, and therefore need not await the return of the Master, if absent. The petition goes on:—

'We cannot [but] be very apprehensive of ye Ld Ossulstone's interposition in this affair, because we have no reason to think y^t yor Grace will consent to any forrain visitatoriall power, wch will be strangly derogatory to ye rights of yor Grace. We have all imaginable respect for ye Ld Ossulston, but can pay him no more than w^t is consistent with our duty to our Visitour and to ye Founders. We purchased not his Fellowships wth the loss of y^r jurisdiction. The contract made between his Lordship and this College hath been religiously observ'd, but as one party never had nor desir'd a liberty of Retrenching the conditions of it, so ought not the other to claime a Right of augmenting them.'

They ask for a new Commission to consist partly of Fellows and Heads of Colleges:—

'For since we understand from Mr Vice-Chancellour y^t many busy & ill men have censur'd the Coṁissioners justice in this affair, We who have been & still are very carefull in preserving ye credit of yor Grace's Coṁissioners, do humbly desire That such Visitours may be appointed as even those ill mens jealousies cañot possibly charge wth any suspicion of partiality.'

Among other matters for which they are humble suitors to the Visitor is this:—

'That since ye Statutes of ye Coll. are allow'd by the Coṁ. to direct such an alteration in ye Burser's proffits as the Fellows desire yor Grace would be pleased to take away a grievance of so antient a date, the

---

[1] Chaplain of Magdalen, 1690-3; Rector of Aldridge, Staffs., 1693; Canon of Lichfield, 1700-18; Vicar of Wellington, Salop, 1709.

redress of w^oh even from ye time of our Founders hath been happily reserv'd for yor Grace.'

They beg that, Mr. Thomas Horne's [1] neglect not appearing to the Duke's Commission, his pupils may be restored to him, and that Mr. Foxall be reinstated in the College. For Dr. Hall having 'commanded the Vicegerents and Mr. Coxeters Pupils to leave their Tutours,' as well as Mr. Horne's, he 'expell'd a Young Gentleman of this house, Mr. John ffoxall [2] for not leaving his Tutour on that command, tho he hath yet been able to charge him with noe other contumacy to the Master than a due Obedience to his Mothers and Guardians appointment, and a just respect to his Tutour.' These pupils Dr. Hall had 'assign'd to that very Person, his late Servitour, whom the ffellows had allmost unanimously rejected.' They further allege that the Master had twice within a year been proved guilty of neglect in the administration of the Holy Sacrament, and their accusation of him in this particular was therefore neither frivolous nor groundless. The Manciple also had confessed to preaching in conventicles and 'did not at any time resort to the prayers of the Church of England.' The Statutes command the yearly visitation of the College lands. This had not been done. They require the keys of the College chest to be reposed in other hands during the Master's absence. He had taken them away. Lastly, they had accused the Master of rendering no account of moneys deposited with him. They pray that 'yor Grace would give such orders for ye removall of these grievances as you in yor prudence shall think fitt.'

The Duke apparently called on Dr. Hall to answer these allegations before a new Commission.

'To his Grace the Duke of Ormond Chancellor of ye University of Oxford & Visitor of Pembroke Colledg.

'May it please y^r Grace

'Not long since upon a Complaint of the Vice-gerent & fellows of Pembroke Colledg you were pleased to give us a letter to be sent to our Master to signifie the complaints made against him and to demand an answer from him to the said complaints; but after the strictest enquiry that we can make after Our Master we cannot find him, that we may deliver y^r Graces letter to him; we have sent a messenger at least a hundred miles after him, & he c^d get no intelligence either where he was or when he w^d be at the Colledge. Our request therefore to y^r Grace is y^t considering the greivances wch we at present ly under, you w^ld be

---

[1] Matr. 1679, from Stratford-on-Avon; M.A. 1685; Chaplain of St. Mary Overie, Southwark, and buried there within the altar rails 1728.

[2] Son of Matthew of Wolverhampton. Probably a Wightwick scholar.

pleased to issue forth a citation that Our Master & Fellows may appear before y^r Grace, or any other persons w^m ye Lordship shall think fit to depute, so y^t our Case may be heard & our grevances adjusted, before y^r Lordships conserns may call you out of this kingdom. We wish y^r Grace all health & happiness & remain

> 'Y^r Graces most humble Servants
> Y^e Fellows of Pembroke Colledg.

(Signed) ' Henry Wood deputed by them.'

Endorsed : ' Address of y^e Fellows of Pembrok: Colledg:

March 9th $\frac{8\,8}{8\,9}$ '

From one of the Fellows to the Duke's secretary :—

' Honrd S^r

'Upon y^e gratefull remembrance of y^e service you did us in o^r business, & y^e freedom you were pleas'd to permit us of writing to you, I presume to give you y^e trouble of y^e following relation.

' O^r M^{str} having deny'd himself w^n o^r messenger came (as we are since inform'd) to ye place where he was, and after a long absence on y^t occasion, arriv'd here on friday night : we were several times to wait upon him & could not get admittance ; at length we sent to acquaint him y^t we had business of moment & must speak wth him, but would not detain him two minutes ; y^n he sent to us to know w^t it was, we sent him word y^t it was from o^r visit^r, & we must deliver it o^{r}selves : he return'd us y^s answer, if it was so, we might send it by his man, for he was not at leisure, neither should be y^t day : wch was yesterday. Notwithstanding his emergent occasions, ye same day in ye afternoon o^r vice-gerent surpriz'd him as he was coming out of his lodgings & deliver'd him ye L^r. I suppose by ye time Mr. Wood has waited upon you, by these proceedings, its more than probable y^t ye M^{str} designs to put off ye business till ye Duke is gone, & y^n to tyrannize ; therefore 'tis ye humble request of ye whole Society y^t you would use y^r interest with my Ld Duke y^t there may be a speedy citation both for him and us ; for if any persons should be deputed we suppose they will be Heads of houses wch most people here do look upon as parties, insomuch y^t ye statutes of some Coll^e provide against y^m. We are satisfied, s^r, y^t 'tis in y^r power to free us from ye yoke, and we have no reason to doubt of y^r good will

> 'I am S^r
> 'Y^r most obliged humble Servt
> 'Tho. Horne

' Pemb: Coll: Mar: 9.'

Addressed : ' To Mr. Gascoin at the Duke of Ormond's in St. James's Square, London.'

Endorsed : ' Pembroke Colledge. Ms. Horne. Rec^d. 11th March.'

From the Dean of Christ Church to the Duke's secretary :—

' My Lord Duke commanded me yesterday to send you the five names following of those prsons whome his Grace designes to inquire into the affair of Pombrook College, viz.

'Dr. Jonathan Edwards Vice chancellor
'Dr. Henry Aldrich Dean of Christchurch
'Dr. William Jane Canon of Christchurch
'Dr. John Hough President of Magdalene
'Dr. John Rudston Fellow of S^t. Johns which lasts ye D^r of Law; all the rest Doctors of Divinity.

'Or any three of them, the Vice chancellor being one.

'I am S^r
'Your very humble Servant
'H. Aldrich.

'Bow street April 2. 1690.

'For Henry Gascoin Esq. at his Grace the Duke of Ormond's house in S^t. James's Square.'

Endorsed: 'Dean of C^h Church Rec^d. 5 Apr. 90.'

From Mr. Horne to the Duke's Secretary :—

'Honrd S^r

'Pardon me if I am further troublesome to you: We are very desirous to know w^n we may expect my Ld Duke's determination of o^r affair, & a line or two to y^t purpose would be extremely obligeing. The M^{str} is very severe upon us, & takes all advantages to starve us out of ye Coll: he put another of my Pupills out of ye house but last week only for being absent prayers, tho' ye young man had not been well for two or three days together: & we expect he will expell ye rest of ye pupills if ye case be not taken notice of. The University has a quite different notion of o^r business from w^t some people talk in London. W^t we chiefly insist on viz: ye case of ye Election, manciple, & Pupills are thought highly reasonable on o^r side: ye last of these ye Comm^{rs} acknowledge to be so, since o^r ffellowships are so small: and some of y^m promis'd to represent it, tho' we do not find it in their Report. I am very well satisfied y^t tis in y^r power S^r to do us no small kindness we shall be very gratefull, & as will ye whole society so shall I more especially acknowledge my self S^r

'Y^r most obliged hum: Servt
'Tho: Horne

'Pemb Coll May 18

'To Mr Gascoigne Secretary to his Grace the Duke of Ormond in S^t. James's Square London'

Endorsed: 'Mr Horne of Pembrok Colledge Rec^d 23rd of May 1690'

From the Visitor to the College [1] :—

'To Dr. Hall Master and to the Fellowes of Pembroke College

'Whereas We have lately received a Complaint from the Fellows of Pembroke College in Oxford and appointed Commissioners to heare and make Report of the difference between the Master and the Fellowes of the said College, After due Consideration of the whole matter, We have

---

[1] College Register.

thought fitt for securing the future quiett of the College, to determine as followes.

'1. That upon any Vacancy of Fellowship or Scholarship of my Lord Ossulston's Foundation an Election shall be made within three Months at farthest.

'2. That in all Elections into the said Foundation noe person shall be reputed duely elected without the consent of the Master.

'3. That upon disagreement between the Master and Fellowes concerning such Election the sole Right of Nomination to such Fellowship or Scholarship shall be in the Founder during his lifetime, and after his Death, in the Vicechancellor of the University of Oxford, the Dean of Christ Church, and President of Magdalen College for the time being, or any Two of them; And in case either the Dean of Christ Church or the President of Magdalen College happen to be Vicechancellor, then the Vicechancellor shall have but one Vote, and to supply that defect, the King's Professor of Divinity shall be added to the Number.

'4. That whereas the Master and Fellows have some years since agreed upon a Rule to be observed about administring the holy Communion, We do strictly require that Rule to be carefully observed for the future by the Society, whether the Master be present or not.

'5. That whereas there are good grounds of Suspition of the Manciple's disaffection to the Service of the Church, We do strictly require the Master in the presence of the Fellowes to admonish the Manciple, carefully and regularly to attend at the beginning of Divine Service, and frequently to receive the holy Communion, so as not to administer any further occasion of Suspition which he hath hitherto lain under.

'6. We declare that We are fully satisfyed with the Master's Integrity and Care of ye College Concerns, and the Injustice of the Fellowes suggestion to the Contrary, and do require the Fellowes to repair this Injury by a dutifull behaviour for the future; and We do desire the Master that forgetting what is past he will treat the Fellowes with the same Kindnesse and tendernesse as he should have done if this difference had never happened.

'Lastly We do strictly require these our Injunctions to be entred in the College Register that they may be punctually observed for the future. Given under my hand and Seale the 2^d Day of June 1690.

'ORMONDE.' *L. S.*

'Concordat cum Originali factâ debitâ Collatione per Me

Ben: Cooper Notarium pubcum.'

Things did not go altogether smoothly, in Dr. Hall's Mastership, with Abingdon. On February 15, 16$\frac{8}{9}$, it was ordered by the Corporation,

'That Mr Recorder (togeither with Mr Hawe) be desired to goe to the Master of Pembroke Colledge in Oxen and treate with him concerning the not performing of the will of Thomas Tesdale, Esq., as to soe much of the same will as doth concerne the Scholars of Mr Tesdale's foundacion, and that the Chamberlen doe waite on Mr Recorder with his fee of xx*s*. And it is further ordered that, in case the said Master doe not give them an answere to their satisfaccion, that then (for redresse therein) they waite on the Visitours appointed by the same will.'

The following also are among the Borough Records, which it is to be hoped the citizens will cause to be printed :—

'23° Novembris, 1671 [James Curten, Mayor].

' Forasmuch as wee were this day informed by Dr. Hall, Master of Pembrooke Colledge in Oxon, that a greate parte of the revenewes of the Fellowes and Scholers of the said Colledge, of the gift of Mr Thomas Tesdale, is withheld by the Deane and Prebendes of Windsor, to the great impoverishing of the said Fellowes and Scholers, who have desired our assistance in their just defence of the said suite, wee, therefore, conceiveing ourselves obliged, as Trustees of the said Mr Tesdale's will, doe order that the summe of twenty poundes be paid to the handes of the said Dr. Hall, to be by him layd out towardes the prosecucion of the said suite for recovery of the same revenewes soe withheld, as aforesaid, before the first day of the next Hillary terme.'

' ij° Maii, 1673 [John Claxon, Mayor].

' This day ordered that Mr Jonathan Hawe be, and is appointed, by this Corporacion, to attende his Grace the Duke of Ormond, Visitor of Pembrooke College in Oxon, and exhibite a complaint against Dr. Hall, Master of the same Colledge, for refuseing to admitt into the same Colledge, Richard Mayott, Master of Arts, into the Fellowshipp of William Barnes, clarke, nowe vacant, and that the said Mr Hawe doe then use his endeavour to obteyne from His Grace a commission for visiting the said Colledge.'

' xxij° Aprilis, 1674 [Simon Hawkins, Mayor].

' Ordered that Mr James Curten, th' elder[1], and Mr Hawe doe goe to London the next terme in the busines of Pembrooke Colledge and Mr Wrigglysworth his gifte.'

' xix° Maii 1674 [Simon Hawkins, Mayor].

' Ordered that Mr Jonathan Hawe, Mr John Payne, Mr Robert Blackaller, and Mr Richard West, or any three or two of them, doe attende the Commissioners who are authorized by his grace the Duke of

---

[1] Fined 5*s*. in 1649 for refusing the mayoralty and committed to gaol till he should pay it. His father (?) Richard, whose portrait is at Christ's Hospital, of which he was the ' pious Benefactour,' married Tesdale's sister-in-law. Richard's epitaph in St. Helen's is worth printing :—

<blockquote>
' Our CURTAINE in this lower Press
Rests folded up in Naturs Dress.
His dust p-fumes his Vrne, and He
This Towne with Liberalitie.'
</blockquote>

Among other charitable bequests in his will (June 20, 1641) was a dole to be taken from a table near his tomb.

Ormond to visite Pembrooke College in Oxon, and that five pounds be delivered by the Chamberlen to Mr John Payne ; to be by him layd out in the prosecucion of this matter at the discrecion of the persons above-named.'

Dr. Hall did not resign his place of Master on being raised to the Episcopate, and resided at the College, where, as we shall see, he procured the building of an imposing Master's House. As Margaret Professor he enjoyed a stall, annexed to that lecture by Charles I, in Worcester Cathedral. Wood notes, Jan. 169½, ' Mr. [Thomas] Sikes told me that Dr. Hall, bishop of Bristow, suffers 8 yong scholars to his college, not to weare gownes, and Thomas Gilbert, a noncon-formist Independent, to read to them[1].' Hall, though then a Bishop, was assailed by the Terrae Filius of 1703. He is styled by Messrs. Abbey and Overton the last of the Puritan bishops, that is of the covenanting and pre-Evangelical school. It was ' ominous of a coming period of inactivity that he should have been contemplated by many as a proper person to succeed Tenison in the Primacy.' Had William nominated Hall to the archiepiscopal throne, the disaffection of the priesthood of the Church of England to the government would probably have broken out in some overt resistance. Noble says he was ' a scholar and a pious divine, but known more in than out of Oxford.' He suffered his episcopal duties to lie neglected while he lived the life of an academic recluse. He deceased Feb. 4, 16⅞⅝. His picture, engraved in 1796 by Trotter, is in the Master's Lodging. ' This Bishop Hall,' says Calamy,

' Was one of eminent piety, but not much esteemed by the young wits of the University. He catechized at St. Toll's[2], near his College, every

---

[1] *Life and Times,* iii. 379; also iii. 442. ' Old Father Thomas Gilbert ' (buried July, 1694, in the chancel of St. Aldate's) was ' An ancient divine who then lived privately in Oxford ' (Calamy). Ejected from his many preferments he had retired at the Restoration to St. Ebbe's parish, preaching privately in conventicles. Wood, whom however he supplied with information and good jests (*Life and Times,* ii. 244), calls him ' epitaph-maker to the Nonconformists.' ' 1681. Whit-son-ale at Halywell was Tom Gilbert's picture preaching in a tub set up: " done by ten loyall harts and sound heads of that parish "—'twas very like ' (Ibid. ii. 541). But he testifies to his ' singular merit,' for which he was ' commonly called *The Bishop of Shropshire* ' (Peshall, p. 148). Calamy describes Gilbert as an ' excellent Scholar, of extraordinary Acuteness and Conciseness of Style, and a most Scholas-tical Head. He had all the Schoolmen at his Fingers-Ends.' He ' statedly attended the preaching of Dr. Hall, Bishop of Bristol (of whom he was a great admirer, and who, he used to say, preached like Dr. Preston, the famous Puritan), one part of the Lord's Day, as he did on Mr. Oldfield, at the Meeting, the other. Some few of the Dissenters in Oxford used to do so too.'

[2] Bishop Hall has a monument, with gilt mitre and two coats of arms, in St. Aldate's Church. The inscription records that he ' having been Minister of this

Lord's day evening, and I sometimes heard him. *He could bring all the Catechism of the Westminster Assembly out of the Catechism of the Church of England.* I never heard Mr Gilbert applaud anyone more than this bishop ; a letter of whose, to Mr Risley the Nonconformist, which I have inserted in my *Account of the ejected Ministers,* plainly shows him to have been of an excellent spirit [1].'

Evelyn heard Dr. Hall, on July 11, 1669, preach the Act Sermon at St. Mary's 'in an honest practical discourse against Atheisme [2],' and Hearne mentions a sermon of his before the University, in 1706, without discommendation. Indeed, while describing him as ' a thorough pac'd Calvinist, a defender of the Republican Doctrines, a stout and vigorous advocate for the Presbyterians, Dissenters, &c., an admirer of whining, cringing Parasites, and a strenuous Persecutor of truly honest Men, as occasion offer'd itself,' Hearne goes so far as to say that he 'was a learn'd Divine, a good Preacher, and his Lectures, while Professor, were look'd upon by the best Judges as excellent in their kind [3].' The grim old Tory's wrath however was excited by the epitaph to be put on the south chancel wall at Bromsgrove to Bishop Hall's memory [4] : —

' Whoever made this long, tedious Inscription, 'tis certain 'twas contriv'd on purpose to gain Proselytes to the Whiggish Party, of wch the Bp. was a great Admirer & Favourer, & 'twas to none but Men of Rebellious Principles that he bestow'd his Charity. Let them be what they would if they were Men of that Stamp they should be sure to meet with Encouragement from him. What else made him foster & advance one Slooper, & one Haynes, & some others that had no Learning, & were hardly endued with common sense ? but they are known to be of the Antimonarchical, Pharisaical Strain, & can cant themselves into the good Esteem of any of the Calvinistical Brethren. What made him at the same time discourage & depress all ingenious honest Men that were for Fidelity to their rightfull Sovereign, and Enemies to Presbyterians and other Sectarists ? 'Tis well the Compiler of this Epitaph has said nothing of the B^{p's} Loyalty, he being one of the Rebell B^{ps} & (had he been endued with all the other Virtues attributed to him in it) this would have been

parish near forty-three years, did in his Life time purchase an Estate with One Hundred Pounds. The income whereof is to be laid out in Buying of Cloaths for Poor Men and Poor Women of this Parish (who do not receive Alms) yearly for ever. And who gave 200^{li} toward Buying of a Parsonage House.'

[1] *Life,* i. 271 sq.   [2] *Diary,* p. 342.

[3] *Collections,* ed. Doble, O. H. S., ii. 343.

[4] Ascribed to William Adams, student of Christ Church. It records the zeal with which he drove back ' ingruentes Romae et Socini errores,' his carelessness of dignities, his unwearied fidelity to his duties, and charity to the poor. The Bishop bequeathed £800 for the poor of Bromsgrove and £70 annually to purchase Bibles for distribution in the diocese.

sufficient to blacken his Character, & to render his Name odious among all Men of true Integrity & Probity, such as strictly & firmly adhere to the Doctrines of Passive Obedience & Non-Resistance[1].'

A different portraiture from Hearne's is given by Dunton[2]. 'He has attain'd to great Eminency of Learning and Moderation, and is an Ornament to the Church of England. His Charity to those that are in Want, and his Bounty to all Learned Men that are put to wrestle with Difficulties, are so very extraordinary, and so many do partake of them, that I need not enlarge in his Character; for 'tis acknowledg'd by all that the whole Business of his Life is to feed that Flock over which the Holy Ghost has made him Overseer.' He fed it however at a distance.

In the Book of Benefactors, on splendidly illuminated vellum, given by the Bishop to the College, it is said of him that he raised it 'ab humili conditione ad florentissimam qua nunc viget.'

---

[1] *Collections*, iii. 50.   [2] *Life and Errors*, 1705, p. 445.

CHAPTER XX.

SEVENTEENTH-CENTURY BUILDINGS AND ACCOMPTS.

THE speeches made at the inauguration of the College anticipated a great transformation of the old buildings, which were unimposing and 'vetustate collapsura.' The various descriptions of Broadgates as ' old,' ' ancient,' ' the oldest of all halls,' ' a venerable piece of antiquity,' took some colour, no doubt, from the appearance of the place. Accordingly ' divers of the buildings, especially those of Broadgates Hall that lay southward, next to Slaying Lane, being pulled down,' part of the ' monies of Tesdale and Wightwick and divers Benefactors ' was at once employed in beginning a stone quadrangle. In Agas's map the top of the town-wall is seen rising above the level of the ground, as it does still beyond the Chapel ; but this was now built into the masonry of the quadrangle. The south and west sides were quickly raised, and also a portion of the east side. Fuller notes under 1626, ' an old Hall turned into a new College was this yeare finished.' The forefront of Broadgates was however repaired, and left standing ; troublous times came ; and it was not till 1670, in Dr. Hall's Mastership, that the quadrangle was continued and the east side finished. In 1673 the irregular line of tenements facing St. Aldate's was half pulled down and its place taken by a ' fair fabrick of freestone.' The remainder of the north front as far as the common gate was built by Michaelmas, 1691 ; the gate tower in 1694. This work is more Palladian in character than that of 1626, which had stringcourses running between and over the windows. The later windows have heavy sills, but no hood-moulds, and are differently arranged ; the dormers show alternately pointed and round heads ; there is a single heavy stringcourse running horizontally between the ground floor and first floor. The tower has Italian pediments and an open balustrade. It may be noticed in Burghers' print that originally the south ground-floor rooms had steps leading up to them. This is no longer so, the level of the quadrangle, which then as now was gravelled, having since risen.

Sir J. Peshall notes: ' In digging the vault of Pembroke College great Numbers of human Skeletons were [found?] interred, some 16 Feet deep, many with their Feet inverted to the South.' This looks like pre-Christian sepulture; but probably the bones had been disturbed before. The vault is just inside the gateway on the right. It seems very probable that the churchyard originally extended beyond its present limits [1].

It has been said that the building of the College north front was begun in 1673 and finished by 1691, except the tower, added three years later. In 1675 Loggan published his print of Pembroke College, showing a *completed* quadrangle exactly as Burghers (1700) represents it when actually built—even to the position of the chimneys —except in one remarkable particular: he has put the tower in the *middle* of the frontage, and it is of Gothic rather than classical design. It is beyond question that such a tower never existed. It may have been in contemplation to place one there, though the gateway would more naturally face, as it had always done, the entry from Penny-farthing Street, for the roadway in front of the College was then a mere lane between walls. It is said that in 1830, during the alterations, the foundations of such a tower were found. But it is quite impossible that, if built in 1675, it can have changed its position and character by 1694. Loggan cannot even have had before him the design of so Gothic a tower, though he must have drawn from the projected plan in other respects. Perhaps the tower was postponed for lack of funds.

The Lodgings, rebuilt in 1596 by principal Summaster, were acquired, repaired, and somewhat altered by the College immediately after its foundation. Loggan just shows the front in perspective, as it would seem an Elizabethan dwelling of lath, timber, and plaister, with dormers and overhanging upper storey. When the College front was completed, Bishop Hall, the Master, desired for his own residence a stone edifice more in keeping with the rest of the frontage, and by Michaelmas, 1695, the outside of a new Master's House was built, with a slight encroachment on Beef Hall Lane [2]. The building was deservedly admired. Ayliffe (1714) says: 'There are erected for the use of the Master very large, elegant, and convenient Lodgings, and, if the

---

[1] Additions to Wood, p. 29. Like Wordsworth's Oxfordshire churchyard :—
  'Where holy ground begins, unhallowed ends,
  Is marked by no distinguishable line.'
[2] In 1695, from the Annunciation of the blessed Lady St. Mary the Virgin, the Corporation leased to the College a piece of void ground, thirty feet long, four feet broad at the western end and one foot at the eastern, at a peppercorn rent.

whole College had been made suitable hereunto, it would be one of the neatest colleges in the University.' The expense of this erection was borne chiefly by Bishop Hall himself. A few years earlier, in 1689, the President of Corpus had built himself a house in the classical style. The whole expenditure on building from 1670 to 1699 amounted to £2,261 1s. 4d., towards which the College contributed £400 from the common chest, and from other sources of revenue, such as degree fees, nearly £200 more. There was some further expense after 1699. Among earlier contributors are the names of Mr. James Hoare, jun.[1], Comptroller of the Mint, a gentleman-commoner (£100); Sir John Bennet—to whom Loggan's print is dedicated: 'Collegii Patrono et Benefactori'—(£200); 'Mr. Jno. Morris of A. ffriers' (£50, and a later legacy of £50); Geo. Low, esq. (a legacy of £58 10s.). In 1693 'My Lord Ossulstone' gives another £50. I also find Mr. Thomas ffoley, gentleman-commoner, son of Speaker Foley and Member (1691–1737) for Weobley, Hereford, and Stafford (£50); Mr. George Townsend (£278 2s.): this was the surplus part of the rents bequeathed by that benefactor, who died in 1683; Sir Thomas Street, one of the Barons of the Exchequer, 'by the marriage of his lady of the kindred of Mr. Wightwick' (£20); Sir Thomas Clayton (£10); and among other minor donors a Wightwick and several Wightwick fellows. Many give £10, or ten 'guineanos aureos,' 'instead of a plate[2].' Among the names is that of the manciple, Mr. William Suthwell (£20).

The new Master's Lodgings, sixty feet in length, instead of the sloping roof and attics of the College front, had a third storey and gables, six on each side and one at the end. The east side had seventeen windows, of equal size and regularly placed, the lower ones surmounted by hoodmoulds, those in the top storey by alternate segmental and angular pediments. At the north end were three windows. A triple stringcourse ran round the building. The door had a coved hood with shell ornament in the soffit. Salmon[3] describes the house as 'a handsome modern Edifice,' and says it 'has the Appearance of a gentleman's House as much as any Thing in Town.' Burghers, as

---

[1] Howard in Gutch. *William* Howard, son of Edward, Earl of Carlisle (entered Pembroke 1693), was M.P. for Carlisle and for Northumberland; buried in Westminster Abbey July 24, 1701, *vide infra* p. 367. The Book of Benefactors says that Mr. James Hoar 'primus donavit.' He also gave a large silver-gilt cup with cover.

[2] Gentlemen-commoners presented a piece of plate on admission or at leaving. Mr. Foley, e. g., gave a large goblet 'Japanice caelatum.'

[3] *Antient and Present State of the Universities,* 1744. An odd gift by a scholar (Nathaniel Gower, M.A.) was 'sex aeneas seras Magistri Hospitio affigendas.'

soon as the College was finished, was commissioned to make a drawing of the entire building. His extremely fine plate, of which a reduced
facsimile is presented at the end of this volume, besides a general
view of the Quadrangle, the old 'Refectorium,' the gardens,
'Summaster's Building' and the Master's House, with a ground
sketch of Docklinton's aisle, gives separate drawings of the two
latter, viz. 'Magistri Hospitium' and 'Capella Collegii,' and of the
Library, with its 'Ascensus Helicus.' The Library has a single gable,
on the face of which is a sundial. On a displayed shield, having the
College arms below and Bishop Hall's above, is a dedication to
the latter—'Revd⁰. in Christo Patri ac Dno. Domino JOHANNI HALL
EPISCOPO BRISTOLIENSI, Collegii Pembrochiani Magistro et Instaura-
tori, hanc ejusdem delineationem jure debitam D.D. C.Q. Michael
Burghers.' His receipt is extant : 'Apr. 18, 1700. Recd. then of yᵉ
Right Reverend yᵉ Master of Pembroke College yᵉ sum of twelve
pounds three shillings for drawing and engraving Pemb: Coll: and for
yᵉ copper plate. I say recᵈ. by me, Michael Burghers, £12 3s. 0d.'
In all 475 'Cuts of yᵉ College' were printed. The last 125 cost 27s.

In 1709, Bishop Hall having bequeathed all his books[1], an ugly
room was built over the hall, destroying the lantern[2], and the chamber
above Docklinton's aisle was finally disused. The new apartment,
which is not shown in the prints of 1733 and 1744, was the College
Library till 1847, and is now a lecture room. Among Hall's books is
a Nuremburg Chronicle inscribed by Whitgift's hand—'hunc librum
habui ex dono a magistro Pynson impressore[3]—Aprilis, mccccclxxxviii,
Londini,'—and a volume of scholia on Aristotle has the autograph 'Is.
Casaubonus.' Besides other mediæval MSS., given probably by
Dr. Clayton, is a small twelfth-century Bede and a fourteenth-century
Sententiae. The finely illuminated *Breviarium Bartholomei*, mentioned
above on page 44, of which there is a very inferior copy in the Harleian
collection, is full of information as to usages and manners in the
fourteenth century, as well as recondite medical lore. Quite recently,
by the gift of Mrs. Sophia Evans, wife of the late Master, the College
has acquired the unique Aristotelian and philosophical library of an
illustrious and affectionately deplored member of the College, HENRY

[1] Dr. G. W. Hall, however, told Croker, 'Certainly not all, and those which
we have are not all marked by him.' A good many have the Bishop's fine
bookplate.
[2] Shown by Loggan and Burghers. 'The antient manner of building was to
set hearths in the midst of rooms for chimneys, which vented the smoke at a
louver in the top.' Carew, *Survey of Cornwall.*
[3] Richard Pynson was one of Caxton's assistants.

CHANDLER, Waynflete Professor of Moral and Metaphysical Philosophy. The Johnson papers and some remains of Shenstone and of Blackstone are a valued possession. The Historical Manuscripts Commission also mentions the Logbook of Nelson's *Victory*, a small duodecimo, ending June 30, 1805, four months before Trafalgar. On the first leaf is written ' Thomas Atkinson, Master of H.M. Ship the *Victory.*' It was bought a few years later in London, in a lot of books, by Dr. G. W. Hall, Master of the College.

The eighteenth-century chapel and modern architectural changes will be mentioned later. In 1760 a fire occurred in College : ' Paid for fire engines £3 3*s.*' ' Mending the Bucketts, 13*s.*' ' Workmen at the fire for Bread and Cheese, £1 18*s.*' But not much damage was done.

GARDENS.

Except the tiny strip along the wall, reserved part for the Master and part for the Fellows, the pleasant triple paradise of the College has vanished, represented now only by the forbidden turf of the New Court. In that old garden Gilbert White, who paid a short yearly visit to Oxford, studied the habits of the Channel Island *lacertae.* He writes, Feb. 28, 1769, to Thos. Pennant, Esq. :—

' Dear Sir,—It is not improbable that the Guernsey lizard and our green lizards may be specifically the same ; all that I know is that, when some years ago many Guernsey lizards were turned loose in Pembroke College garden in the University of Oxford, they lived a great while, and seemed to enjoy themselves very well, but never bred. Whether this circumstance will prove anything either way I shall not pretend to say.'

In Agas's map scattered trees are dotted between Beef Hall Lane and the town wall. Gardening did not reach its highest refinement till the end of the seventeenth century, when Dutch and French fashions in the topiary art followed one another with rapidity. Yet continuity is the chiefest beauty of so personal and living a haunt of memories as a garden. Loggan—*temp.* Charles II—shows three elaborated enclosures. In the westernmost, always appropriated to the Fellows, are trellised and arched galleries, clipt shrubs, formal beds or ' knottes,' a bowling-green, and, traced on the ground, a large dial. Part of this garden on the north is walled off. The second, called in 1651, when the wall was built, the Master's garden, has long plots bordered with low shrubs, a square of grass with trees, and in the south-west corner a ball court [1]. Both these gardens were in St. Ebbe's parish. The third, called in 1697 the Commoners' garden, is exquisitely adorned with mounts, arbours, and alleys—' an out-of-door room' duly furnished. The grotesque head (like the ones in front of the Sheldonian) which is now in the garden stood in the centre. In Burghers' engraving, five and twenty years later, the gardens are laid out quite differently and more simply with broad spaces of grass, in which grow the arbor vitae and dwarf trees. A rank of larger trees along ' Southgate-wall ' had disappeared, with all the bowers and walks, and the dial. A new feature was a raised terrace [2] in the Fellows' garden, at the west end of which stood a pagoda, or summer common-room [3]. Urns carrying flowering shrubs are ranged all along on the low rampart, and in the easternmost garden. In 1733 *Oxonia Depicta* again shows a changed fashion. The pretty urns are gone, but cut walls of yew and formal quincunces re-appear in the enclosure of the Fellows. The middle garden is all sward, the common garden has become the new ' Chapel court,' and is a mere space of grass, or perhaps gravel (it was weeded in 1758), traversed by a path. (Williams' Map of Oxford is far from accurate, and gives the College two regular quadrangles.) The Almanack top of 1744, by Vertue [4], exhibits the Master's garden laid out geometrically in turf ambulacra and shrubs. The upper part of this almanack represents King James handing the charter to Pembroke, who kneels, holding his wand of office, at the foot of the throne. Behind stand Tesdale and Wightwick. To the right is Bishop Hall, showing the design for the new Lodgings to Lord Ossulston, who is in armour, with the riband of the Bath. A cherub points to the ground-plan on the floor. A group on the other side represents benefactors, viz. Rous, Townsend, Boulter (?), Dame Holford and Mrs. Stafford. In a framed picture Charles I is seen presenting to a female (the College ?) a chart of the Channel Isles and a model of St. Aldate's, Bishop Morley standing by. In another Queen Anne hands to Lord Chancellor Harcourt the deed

[1] Nine or ten academians are walking or playing ball in the Master's garden in Burghers' picture.

[2] Two years before, in 1698, the citizens leased to the College, for 50s., a strip of ground along Slaughter Lane, 44 feet in length, 4 feet 7 inches broad, extending from the west corner of the College wall to the Ball Court of the said College. Was this the actual top of the city wall ?

[3] This is more architectural looking in the later prints. In 1752 £18 was paid for 'building the Common Room wall.'

[4] George Vertue designed the Almanacks from 1723–1751, who ' instead of insipid emblems introduced views of publick buildings and historick events' (*Lord Orford*).

for conferring the stall at Gloucester, of which a picture is shown. The design was printed partly on silk handkerchiefs, one of which is now before me. Skelton in 1823 revived Vertue's print, but credits the Master's garden with an imposing bower on a terrace at the south end, and omits the ball-court. A large mulberry-tree in the Fellows' garden was called Shenstone's Tree. The small tables in the Common Room were made from this when it was cut down. A sketch of the tree is now before me. The pleasant row of limes which show above the battlemented wall on the south side of the quadrangle was planted in the first year of Dr. Evans' Mastership (1864).

COMMONWEALTH AND RESTORATION ACCOMPTS.

The following extracts from a book of Bursars' accounts for the time of the Commonwealth and the latter part of the seventeenth century seem worth recording :—

1650. Janu^r. 21. P^d. to M^r. Austin for an order of the Visitors
    against horses and longe haire [1] . . . . . 2s. 6d.
1651. For the colledg chappel, a Noble.
    For the use of M^r. Hall[2] towards his Art Supper . 1l. 5s. od.
    P^d. to M^r. Lane for pistolls holsters and other things, wth
        expences in riding the Coll horse . . . 1l. 9s. 6d.
    To the Collectours of St. Ebbs parish for ye two coll. gardens 6s.
    Oct. 17. P^d. to M^r. Langley the Beadle ye proportion of
        Pem. Coll Layd by ye delegatie of the universitie for
        Anastasius Comenius . . . . 8s.
1652. P^d. to M^r. Loveday for the Coll horse standing there 3l. os. od.
    Jan. 1. Rec. of D^r. Langley Mast^r. of Pemb. Coll. the sume
        of eight pounds five shills. in full sattisfaction for all coales
        served in for the use of the Coll. from the beginging of the
        world to the date hereof. In witness hereof I have put my
        marke   Hen Kibble his — marke
1653. Feb. 3. Given to ye wayts[3] . . . . 2s. 6d.

[1] See Gutch, ii. 625. 'On May 7, 1650, the Visitors ordained, that all the Scholars of this Universitie doe in their haire and habite conforme themselves to the Statutes of the same in that behalfe, forbearinge all excesse and vanitie, in powdering their haire, wearing knots of ribands, walking in boots and spures and bote-hose-tops: And the severall Heads of Colledges and Halls are desired to take spetiall and speedy care to see this Order put in execution in their respective Houses.'
[2] Afterwards Master.
[3] So that Candlemas carol-singing was not yet suppressed in Oxford. Wood says, however, 'saying prayers at folks' doors for alms, stopped by the fanaticks' (see *Life and Times*, ii. 212), and (Gutch, *Annals*, May 1, 1648) 'This day spent in zealous persecuting the young people that followed May-Games, by breaking of

Payd more then yᵉ gathering in yᵉ hall for Glascow in
Scotland . . . . 10*s*. o*d*.
For pitching and ordering yᵉ rubbish and one and twenty
load of gravell to cover yᵉ colledg walk next to yᵉ churchyᵈ.
wall yᵉ sum of . . . . 2*l*. 13*s* o*d*.
Wall in yᵉ Coṁoners garden broken downe . . . 13*s*. o*d*.
Dec. 3. For three orders frō yᵉ visitours to pemb Coll. 4*s*. 6*d*.
1654. Payd to goodman Ranckelyn the smith for chynning
[chaining] the books in the Library[1] . . . 1*l*. 8*s*. o*d*.
Raysing the Colledg wall where yᵉ colledg stable was . 13*s*. o*d*.
Goodman Edwards for pishing [pitching] the Lane towards
Mr. Martyns and mending yᵉ range in yᵉ kichin 1*l*. 9*s*. 6*d*.
Proportion for a horse till they [the College] sent in a horse.
This tax was set by yᵉ university . . . . . 12*s*. 11*d*.
A year's sacrᵗ. wine . . . . 13*s*. 8*d*.
For mending yᵉ pipes and conveying yᵉ water to pembrooke
Colledg [see page 53] wᶜʰ is payd every yeare . 1*l*. 0*s*. o*d*.
Sʳ Risley a schollar for moderating in yᵉ philosophy forme
for half a yeare . . . . 27sh. and a groat.
1655. Payd to yᵉ sadler Thomas Reiveby by man John for a fore-
pectorall, a payre of holsters and a Bridle for John Brooks
when hee did service in yᵉ Vniversity troope for pemb. 4*s*. 6*d*.
℞. of Dr. Langley for yᵉ Bayliffs yᵗ carried Slade to prison 3*l*. 0*s*. o*d*.
Mending the colledg plate . . . . . . 8*s*. o*d*.
Feb. 22. For a wheelebarrow & pitching the lane by Mr.
Martines . . . . 9*s*. o*d*.
Paid to paul Isaiah a converted Jew sent down by his Highnes
to yᵉ University of Oxford five sh. wᶜʰ was pemb. coll.
proportion of £20 given by yᵉ university.
1656. Recᵈ of the Master for a Sword for the College in the time
when the coll. found a horse at the time of Salesberi. By
me Henry Wyatt seaven shills.
For two Hungarians yᵉ sum of five shillings when yᵉ vice-
chauncelor sent Thomas his man to yᵉ colledg for something.
1657. May 23. Yᵉ proportion of Pemb. Coll. of ye thirty pounds
chardgd upon yᵉ colledges for yᵉ officers belonging to yᵉ
visitation . . . . 7*s*. 10*d*.

Garlands and taking away Fiddles from Musicians; dispersing Morice Dancers,
and by not suffering a green bough to be worn in a hat or stuck up at any door.'
By 1661 'carolling in publick halls and Christmas sports' had vanished.

[1] So, in 1646, Adams the smith was paid his bill 'for swivells for the Library
bookes' in the Bodleian. When Selden's books were sent to the Bodleian in 1659,
£25 10*s*. was paid for new chains. The removal of chains from books did not
take place generally till the latter half of the eighteenth century. In the *Foreigner's
Companion through the Universities* (1748) the inconvenience of chaining is
noticed. At King's College, Cambridge, in 1777 a man was paid £1 7*s*. for nine
days' work in removing the chains. At Eton the removal was effected half a
century earlier. There were chains at Wadham till 1761, at Brasenose till 1780.
At Merton they still remain. See Blades' *Books in Chains*.

Whiting the Coll. hall . . . . 10s. 0d.

Apr. 24.   Coales supplied to Coll. for ½ year . . 17l. 10s. 0d.

(The coquus is paid £8 15 0 a quarter.)

M^r. Seymour still keeps all Beckhallowin [1] tythes in his hand, having payd nothing to nobody as yet. Of this hee promiseth to give an account.

Slatting Somersett building [2] . . . . . 2l. 6s. 10d.

1658.   July 8.   B. of ye M^r. of ye colledg by deputy Fleetwood Trumpeter for sounding to ye colledg as to all others . 5s. 0d.

Dec. 21.   For ye Almesmen in christ church Hospitall . 12d.

Gravelling Coll. quadrangle, 19 loade of gravell . . 19s. 0d.

5 days work . . . . 5s. 0d.

Pitching in ye lane on ye back side of ye colledg, and gravelling . . . . 9s. 6d.

Mending wall in ye fellows garden . . . . . 5s. 0d.

Mar. 12.   B. of D^r. Langley the sum of five sh. ye Pemb. Coll. proportion of twenty pounds wch ye university at a Delegacy did agree to give to pet Samuell a converted Jew Balsamides a distressed Græcian and Jacq. Fourre a converted Catholiq; . . . . 5s. 0d.

1660.   May 7.   For weeding ye Quadrangle ag^t. Mr. Southworth's [3] buriall . . . . 1s. 6d.

Payd goodwiffe forrest for washing Coll. linen for ye Quarter ending midsum last past . . . . . . 8s. 0d.

1673.   Rec^d for three Kilderkins of Double Beer layd in for ye Beavers of ye workmen [4] . . . . . 18s. 10½d.

Dec. 3.   Gathered by ye manciple for freshmen's gawdies [5] 18l. 2s. 0d.

1694.   Pitching before the College gate . . . . 3l. 2s. 0d.

1695.   Pulling down and bringing up part of the found^n. of the Hall wall [6] . . . . 3l. 9s. 0d.

1696.   Pitching before the College from Alms House to further corner of the Lodgings, and a little ashlar wall at the corner of the Alms House . . . . . 14l. 12s. 0d.

1697.   A Perpend. Wall before the Lodgings . . . 8l. 8s. 11d.

Two Mound walls to the Cockyard . . . 9l. 0s. 0d.

Levelling and pitching do. and the passage y^t goes down to the commoners' garden . . . . . 1l. 19s. 0d.

[1] Bec Herluin. The name Herlewyne occurs in and before the thirteenth century in Oxford. The family of Harlewin of Ascerton in Sidmouth was not extinct in the seventeenth. Arms, az. three apples arg. a file in chief. Evelyn enters in his *Diary*, Oct. 31, 1648, 'I went to see my manor of Preston Beckhelvyn and the Cliffhouse.'

[2] i. e. Summaster's, originally Minote Hall.

[3] Edward Soothworth, matr. July 20, 1654; B.A. Feb. 12, 165⅘. The custom is still observed at funerals of making the circuit of the Old Quadrangle.

[4] Engaged in building the College front. 'Beavers,' i. e. drink (buvoir).

[5] These are explained in the chapter relating to Johnson. Vide infra.

[6] Adjoining the Lodgings, then being built.

It appears from these accounts that at the time of the Commonwealth a Tesdale scholar's place was still worth in money £3 or £3 15s. a quarter, from which 'full quarteridge' were subtracted 'decrements,' viz. dues and everything not included in his allowances, about 11s. 6d. to 14s. 6d. One fellow's 'battles and decrements' were £1 6s. 6d. the half year; those of another (George Wightwick) £1 17s. 6d. The Latin Lecturer received £2 a year, the Praelector Graecus the same. The Bursar £1. I confess that the entry under 1655, 'mending the colledg plate,' throws suspicion on the completeness of the society's surrender of its silver to King Charles.

The Historical MSS. Commission mentions an entry, under date July 11, [16]72, which I cannot find:—

'Recd. then of Mr. Frampton 11s. 10d. for the maintenance of the workmen and the marshall of the beggars. I say recd. by me 60l. 11s. 6d.'

The bedell, workmaster, or marshall of the beggars had nothing to do with the Christ Church almsmen, as suggested in the Commission's Report (vi. p. 549); see Wood's *Life and Times,* i. 466; iii. 63; iv. 79.

CHAPTER XXI.

CHANNEL ISLAND FOUNDATIONS.

AMONG the earlier benefactors of the College was KING CHARLES
THE FIRST, who came to the throne the year after its foundation.
It owed to him—for the possession is now gone—the advowson of
St. Aldate's and its connexion, still maintained, with the Channel
Islands, whence came to it the energetic ruler who alienated the
St. Aldate's patronage. King Charles desired to divest the Crown
of Church property. At the beginning of the war he made a
peculiarly solemn vow to that effect. In 1634, by the advice of the
new Primate, he had given back to the poor clergy of the Church of
Ireland all the impropriations then remaining in the Sovereign. It
was in pursuance of this policy that, in 1636[1], he 'of his pure
affection' bestowed the patronage of St. Aldate's on the adjacent
College, so lately founded by his father, and sprung out of the loins
of the two religious houses to which the advowson had belonged. In
1642 the King wrote to the Vice-Chancellor of 'our perpetuall care
and protection of such nurseries of learning.' No doubt Laud, the
Visitor of the College, and ever on the alert to promote the interests
of learning, counselled the restitution—an unselfish act, considering the
anxiety of himself and of his Master to modify the complexion of the
Church by suitable appointments and the likelihood that Pembroke
would still feel the influence of Abbot, who died in 1633.

Another object which the King and Laud had at heart was the
improvement of the state of learning among the Channel Island

---

[1] It was in this year that the King and Queen visited Oxford 'with no applause,'
the scholars standing sullen and uttering no Vivat Rex! When he came to Christ
Church the Dean and Canons conducted him with all the lords into the noble
priory, now cathedral, church of St. Frideswyde; but, 'before he entered, he knelt
down at the large South door, where lifting up his hands and eyes, with his long
left lock (according to the then mode) shelving over his shoulder, did his private
devotions to his Maker.' (Gutch, *Annals*, ii. 408.) Charles declared in 1641,
'I would rather feed upon bread and water, than invade or take away any part of
the Church patrimony.'

clergy, and the recovery to Anglicanism of the oldest domain of the English Crown. In 1563, the year of the foundation of Abingdon School, Elizabeth had endowed a College in Guernsey on the ruins and out of the property of a convent of Cordeliers, and for a time this served the needs of Jersey also. The famous Saravia, Hooker's friend and confessor, was the first master, Isaac Basire the Orientalist the second or third. In 1598, however, the Presbyterian 'Colloque' of Jersey proposed to unite the two schools of that island into a college for the instruction of youth in laudable arts, and Laurens Baudains endowed it with certain wheat rents. The Queen granted letters of mortmain, which however were not made patent, though the ' Collége d'Élisabeth ' is mentioned in 1604 as already founded. In December, 1610, the Colloquy complained that the College remained neglected and that the revenues thereof were diverted from the founder's purpose, to the great scandal of the entire isle. James I accordingly, in 1611, ordered the incorporation of thirteen Governors to use Baudains' benefaction and any others for the maintenance of scholars to be trained up in 'learning and in the studie of divinity' at the English Universities. Thirty Jersey quarters of wheat however would not go far towards this end. Among the Orders in Council of 1618 is one 'concerning the petition delivered to the Commissioners [Conway and Bird] by Sir Philipp de Carteret, Seigneur of St. Owen and some other Justices in the name of the three Estates.' . . . ' Whereas they further petition that his Majestie would be pleased to graunte unto them some places in such of those Colledges as are in his Majesties guifte for the maintenance at the Universities of such poore Schollers as shall be recommended by the three Estates of that Island,' it was ordered that this request be granted.

No opportunity occurred in James I's reign for carrying out the promise. Meanwhile natives destined for the ministry were frequently sent at the charges of the States of the two Islands to Saumur—sometimes however to Cambridge. Thus, in 1627, Thomas Guille was allowed £200 tournois for three years to study at Saumur[1]. In Jersey, the Anglican worship was revived in 1619, but ' the religion '

---

[1] The livre tournois of twenty sols is one-fourteenth of the pound sterling. I am indebted to the Rev. G. E. Lee, M.A., the learned Rector of St. Pierre Port, Guernsey (and brother of a well-known Pembrochian, Mr. Austin Lee, C.B., of H. B. M. Embassy at Paris), for a perusal of the documents on which the above narrative is based. Even after the foundation of the King Charles Fellowships and Morley Scholarships, the States sometimes supported ordinands at College. Thus, from 1722-41, Thomas Williams, ' étudiant à Oxford,' was allowed £400 tournois a year.

had still a strong hold on the ministers. Guernsey, whither the Prince de Condé had retired, expelled, in 1593, all natives who did not conform to the Geneva Platform [1], and only accepted the Prayer Book at last, in 1662, at the pike's point, the ministers resigning their cures rather than be re-ordained. When, in 1630, King Charles proposed to abolish the Calvinistic discipline, Lord Danby represented that there was nothing to put in place of it—'There being many old ministers in Guernsey, if they die, we shall not know whence to supply them with others; for out of France they will not come to us, and here we can find few or none.'

Two years later, however, there fell to the Crown by escheat, through lack of heirs, properties belonging to Sir Miles Hobart, alderman of London [2], viz., seven messuages and two gardens in Lad Lane in the parish of St. Lawrence in the Old Jewry [3], holden in free burgage of the City of London at a rent of £45 10s.; also a moiety of a cottage, now Whittington Farm, at Meidenham (Medmenham), Bucks, 'being 123 acres, 52 acres of Medows, 53 of pasture, and 205 of woods.' With this windfall the King purposed to redeem his Father's promise, hoping to wean the clergy of the Norman archipelago from Calvinism by bringing them to Oxford. With the Hobart properties, to be held 'by fealty in free and common socage,' the King founded three *Fellowships*, at Exeter, Jesus College, and Pembroke respectively, for natives of Guernsey and Jersey, Sir Anthony Rous [4], Mr. Oliver Ridge and Margaret his wife, co-heir of Miles with Sir Anthony, forgoing their pretended rights ('pretensum jus suum in eisdem).' It was signified to be 'his M^{ties} intention that within convenient tyme the sayd Fellowes or Scholars shall return to the sayd severall Ilands upon fitt Promocions to them offered there.' The letters patents, addressed 'to the Maister, Fellowes and Scholars of Pembrooke Colledge,' and dated June 1636, declare:—

[1] Richard Girard was flogged in 1573 for upholding the mass. The Anglican worship was retained in Castle Cornet, whither English residents were ferried over. The deanery was in abeyance for a hundred years; as recently as 1755 the Dean was obliged to have recourse to the civil power to enforce the reading of the Litany in a parish church. Till quite lately the surplice was not used at all in certain parishes.

[2] M.P. for Marlow, 1628-9. Imprisoned for locking the door of the House of Commons. Died at Marlow July 4, 1632.

[3] In Gresham Street; now occupied by the firm of Pickford. This property has become valuable.

[4] Not Francis Rous's father, who died 1622. The great-grandfather of Rous the diarist was Sir Anthony of Dennington, Suffolk, Treasurer of the Chamber to Henry VIII. He died in 1547.

'Sciatis quod nos pietate et pio zelo erga Deum moti veramque cognicionem et cultum divini ejus nominis et sacrosancti Christi Evangelii propagacionem intime affectantes necnon ex propenso animo et favore nostro in bonas literas Religioni observandae promovendae et per tota Regna et territoria nostra propagandae de gratia nostra concessimus,' &c.[1]

The King named the first Fellows; afterwards the Dean (not the baillif) and jurats of either island were to nominate. In 1857, at which date the Pembroke Fellow was receiving £154 a year, the three Fellowships were converted into six *Scholarships* of not less than £50 (now £80) yearly, the senior Scholar in each College having rooms also.

The first post-Reformation Dean of Guernsey was of Pembroke. JOHN DE SAUSMAREZ was made Canon of Windsor in 1671, and created D.D. (June 7) by virtue of letters from the Chancellor: ' Mr. Joh. Saumers, Dean of Guernsey, is a person that hath done his Majesty and the Church very good and acceptable Service, particularly in his prudent and successful endeavours in bringing the misled Subjects of that Island to be conformable to the Liturgy of the Church of England, during the space of ten years,' &c. He was given other English preferments. Ob. 1697. The third Dean, JOHN BONAMY (entered Pembroke in 1685), was Fellow of Exeter. NICHOLAS CAREY, entered 1789, was Dean 1832–58.

The portrait of Charles I which is now in the Hall, hung, before the eighteenth century, in the *quondam* Civil Law School. Pointer (*Oxoniensis Academia*) says, 'In the Library (which is over the Chapel adjoining to St. Aldate's, *alias* St. Old's, vulgarly called St. Tole's Church, as St. Ebb's is call'd St. Tabb's Church), besides Books, is a very fine Picture of the Royal Martyr King Charles I, Benefactor to this College.' It is a half-length; the King wears his George. It appears to be contemporary, and to have interest; but the arm is out of drawing.

Charles I's policy was continued after the Restoration by GEORGE MORLEY, Bishop of Winton, to which diocese the Islands had been transferred from Coutances[2]. He founded at Pembroke *five Scholar-*

---

[1] See Heylin's *Laud,* p. 336, and Laud's *History of his Chancellorship,* v. 140. The indenture quadripartite received the University seal, 'in assimulatione parvâ,' July 2, 1636.

[2] King John first procured their annexation to the province of Canterbury, placing them under the Bishop of Exeter; but this arrangement lasted only a short time. At the request of Henry VII Pope Alexander VI again joined the Islands to the Church of England, first to Sarum in 1496, and then to Winchester in 1499. The Bishop of Coutances ignored this transference, and exerted jurisdiction in

ships, of £10 with chambers, three for Jersey and two for Guernsey. Bishop Morley's benefaction was in part an after-thought. In 1674, Charles II signified to Corpus Christi College[1] his express will and pleasure that one of their Hampshire Scholarships should be appropriated to natives of the Channel Isles, under the mistaken idea that there were three scholarships confined to Hants. The King's letter was reinforced by one from Morley as Visitor and as Bishop of Winchester. The County and College however resisted the plan and it was not carried out. Morley thereupon himself made provision for the purpose. Dean Prideaux writes to John Ellis, on July 28, 1674 :—

> 'The fellows with contempt rejected his letters which he wrot to them, whereby he enjoined them to transfer on of those two places, which the founder entail'd on Hampshire, on Jersey and Garnsey; but he beeing now informed that it is not within the limits of his or the colledge's power to alter a clause which is inserted in their charter, or deprive a county of their right which will not tamely be parted with, the gentlemen thereof beeing resolved to commence a law sute if any such thing should be enacted, he hath wholely omitted the mention thereof by his Commissioners, and excuseing his attempt to others by alledgeing he was compeld thereto by the Kings command on the instigation of Sir George Carteret. But, however, that he may come off with credit, it is talked that he himself will make provision for those places by some new settlement of his own on some colledge or other in the University ; but I suppose it will be hard for him to find one that will receive his donation except Pembroke, the fittest colledge in town for brutes.'

Prideaux spares no one. Exeter he calls a place of ' drinking and duncery.' Pembroke, in spite of its Master, was a high-church College. After the Revolution the Jacobitism of the University disgusted Prideaux, who, in 1691, professed 'an unconquerable aversion to the place.' Aldrich in turn styles him 'an unaccurate, muddy-headed man.' Morley's action was creditable, though his relations with Corpus present him in an overbearing light. He was certainly liberal with his purse. Besides five exhibitions at Pembroke, he gave £2,200 to Christ Church, £1,800 in all to St. Paul's Cathedral, spent at least £10,000 in repairing Farnham Castle after its occupation by Cromwell, and £4,000 for the purchase of Winchester House, besides repairing the palace at Winchester, and he bequeathed £1,000 for the augmentation of some small vicarages. His Winchester benefactions have been computed at £40,000.

Guernsey and Jersey till 1568, when Dean After refused obedience till the Bishop had sworn allegiance to the Queen of England. Elizabeth then declared the Islands to belong to Winchester.

[1] See Dr. Fowler's *History of Corpus Christi College*, 1893, p. 247.

George Morley (1597–1684) took a considerable part in the politics of his day. Though nominated on the Assembly of Divines he gave a year's income of his canonry at Christ Church for the prosecution of the royal cause, and persuaded the University to make a firm stand against the parliamentary visitation. He negotiated the surrender of the Oxford garrison, and, as one of the King's chaplains, assisted in effecting the treaty of Newport. Refusing to give his *parole* not to appear openly against the parliament, he was stripped of his preferments, and during the Interregnum ministered to the exiled King and his adherents at Antwerp, Breda, and the Hague. He helped to smooth the task of Restoration, being not unacceptable to the Calvinist party. In 1660 he was made Dean of Christ Church, and then Bishop of Worcester, and two years later succeeded Duppa at Winchester. Morley was a principal manager at the Savoy Conference, and, according to Baxter, was the ablest speaker of all the prelates. He is described by Burnet as 'a pious and charitable man, of a very exemplary life, but extreme passionate and very obstinate.' Morley was the intimate friend of Clarendon (who calls him 'the best man alive'), Hammond, Sanderson, Chillingworth, Sheldon, and Waller, whose poems he corrected, and who said that 'from him he learned to love the ancient poets.' He was the patron of Izaak Walton, and Ken was his chaplain. Burnet says that he 'had been first known to the world as a friend of the Lord *Falkland's*; and that was enough to raise a man's character.' Morley died in 1684 in his eighty-seventh year. He laid one of the foundation stones of the Sheldonian Theatre in 1664, offering on it gold and silver. There are paintings of Morley at Farnham, Charterhouse, Oriel, Christ Church, and Pembroke. In the last only is he represented in the robes of Prelate of the Garter. His character for fearlessness and for asceticism (he ate but one meal a day), and also for irascibility, can be detected in it. Burnet says he was 'of eminent parts in all polite learning, of great wit, readiness and subtlety in disputation, and of remarkable temper and prudence in conversation.' Morley's known wit made Waller call him 'one of Jonson's sons.'

The following are the main heads of the indenture of foundation for these scholarships. It is dated May 4, 1678 :—

1. George Morley, Bishop of Winchester, founds five Scholarships at Oxford for the islands of Jersey and Guernsey. 2. This he does for the encouragement of virtue, education, and the advancement and propagation of true religion in the said islands forming part of his diocese, and with the intention of animating the said scholars to qualify themselves and be advanced to the rank of fellows. 3. The sum vested in the Dean of Christ Church and in Pembroke College for the purpose is 68 pounds, 11 shillings and 9 pence sterling. 4. The Dean and Chapter shall receive annually £60 sterling ; the remainder being otherwise disposed. 5. Five scholars of the College of Pembroke, natives of the isles of Guernsey and Jersey, shall receive each ten pounds sterling out of his donation, and the said Scholars shall be called Bishop Morley's Scholars. 6. There shall be paid to the principal of the College 40*s.* yearly for the apartment of each

scholar. 7. The revenue of vacant scholarships shall be applied to the use of the said College of Pembroke. 8. The Dean, Baillif, and Jurats of either Island to nominate. 9. The scholars are not to retain the appointment more than five years, nor after having obtained a living, or any other emolument ; they must be resident in College, except the last year, that they may have liberty to travel in France for their improvement in that language. 11. But they shall solemnly promise to return to the Islands to serve the public as preachers, schoolmasters, or otherwise [1]. 12. At the age of 21, each scholar shall solemnly bind himself before the Dean & Baillif in a penalty of £200 to fulfil his engagement. Such as refuse shall not be admitted. 13. Such as have obtained the age of 21 and refuse to ratify their promise shall be deprived of their appointment.

The £68 11s. 9d. arose from property in the forest of Chute, and was to be collected by the housekeeper for the time being of Wolvesley Palace. £8 11s. 9d. was to be retained by the housekeeper. In 1857, the five Exhibitions were consolidated into one. Any surplus on the King Charles foundation from suspended Scholarships or otherwise was to be applied to the augmentation of the Morley Scholarship, which was to be considered as incorporated. Bishop Morley's Scholar now receives £80 and rooms. The £60 collected by the Wolvesley housekeeper is now paid direct to Pembroke College. On this foundation [2] was—

EDWARD D'AUVERGNE, the military historian, son of Philip D'Auvergne, who claimed descent from a cadet of the house of the last reigning Duke of Bouillon. He took M.A. in 1686, and became rector of St. Brelade's, Jersey, and chaplain to the Scots Guards, in which capacity he went through the campaigns, of which he is the chronicler, in Flanders and the Netherlands. He went with William himself to Holland. William made him his chaplain and gave him the rectory of Great Hallingbury, Essex. He was married in Westminster Abbey, 1704, to Suzanne Sabenone, and in 1729 espoused Esther, daughter of Philip Le Geyt, Lieutenant Bailli of Jersey. A son of his only son Philip went down in the *Royal George* in 1782. D'Auvergne died at his parsonage Dec. 2, 1737, aged 77. Insignia and relics of the ducal house are preserved by comparatively humble families of this name in Guernsey and Jersey.

---

[1] They were relieved of this engagement in 1857; at that time, by the deduction of 18d. for each week of non-residence, the value of the exhibitions was reduced to about £7 a year, with rooms worth £5 or £6 yearly.

[2] The first Morley scholars at Pembroke were, John Ahier, Charles (son of Philip) Dumaresq, Edward Dauverne, ex insula Caesariensi, admissi Sep^bris 25°, 1678; Thomas Picott, ex insula Sarniensi, adm. Oct. 8°.

On Dec. 11, 1678, Charles II addressed the following order to the baillifs, deans, and jurats of the Islands [1] :—

'Trusty & well beloved, we greet you well. Whereas our royal father of happy memory, for the encouragement of learning in our islands of Guernsey & Jersey, did found & endow three fellowships in our University of Oxford to be from time to time supplied by persons born in our said islands, & upon all vacancies to be nominated by you, the bailiffs deans & jurats of the said islands under such rules & limitations as by his charter of foundation it doth more at large appear, & whereas the present Lord B[p] of Winchester, for the aforesaid end and purpose, hath lately founded and endowed five Scholarships in the said University to be from time to time in like manner supplied by the nomination of you. . . . For the rendering both foundations subservient to his designed end, our will & pleasure is that, on the nomination of fellows into places w[h] shall be hereafter vacant, such shall be preferred as have been formerly nominated to their respective scholarships & have by their good carriage & improvement in learning fitted themselves for the employments w[h] belong to fellows in their respective societies.' . . .

In 1857 the right of nomination was cheerfully relinquished by the deans, baillifs, and jurats, of the Islands. The King Charles and Morley foundations were henceforth to be open to all natives of the two bailiwicks of Guernsey and Jersey, and to others, not natives, who should have been educated for two years past at Elizabeth College, Guernsey, or Victoria College, Jersey. These institutions had not previously been recognized. The former, after almost suffering extinction through the disinclination of the natives to a classical education, was re-chartered by George IV, in 1825, at the instance of Sir John Colborne, afterwards Lord Seaton [2], Lieutenant-Governor of Guernsey. Victoria College was founded largely through the exertions of Dr. Jeune. The education is modelled on that of English public schools, the sons of English residents form the majority of the pupils, and the masters are of necessity chiefly brought from England. The islands, sundered bits of Normandy, where the old French tongue and customs linger as a pathetic survival, have been Anglicized and Anglicanized more than enough. But the intention of King Charles and Bishop Morley, that Oxford-bred divines should return home to serve the meagre island cures, is now defeated [3]. I believe that not

---

[1] Duncan's *History of Guernsey*, p. 345.

[2] Of Waterloo fame. Jeune was tutor to his sons while he was Governor of Canada. Jeune was succeeded by the Rev. Robert Jones, who entered Pembroke in 1824. I have heard from him the authentic account of the famous charge of the 52nd Foot, which Lord Seaton told him on his death-bed.

[3] Even before 1857 the Charles I Fellows frequently remained laymen, or accepted English preferments. Falle, the learned historian (whose son Philip

one of the present clergy in the four Isles has been on either of the foundations. From another point of view it has been doubted by Mr. F. Brock Tupper, in his *History of Guernsey*, ' whether they have really benefited these islands, as from their commencement they have been a source of intrigue, partiality, and litigation.' Nevertheless the Channel Island foundations did their work. Among eminent men in recent times who have been educated in the Islands may be named the present Vice-Chancellor (Dr. Magrath), Archdeacon Denison, Mr. Walter Wren, Sir Peter Renouf, Field Marshal Sir Linton Symons, and Bishop Corfe.

Lequesne (*History of Jersey*, p. 176) observes :—

'·Owing to the vague wording of the grant, there has occasionally been a disagreement between the Islands, as to the right of nomination to [the King Charles] fellowships. To obviate this difficulty, the rule laid down in 1804 by the late Duke of Portland, Chancellor of the University of Oxford, was, " that the Island which had simultaneously enjoyed two fellowships should next enjoy but one, without any reference to the number of individuals who might have been elected fellows." It prevented the possibility of one Island enjoying the three fellowships at once. " Thus," adds the Rev. Ed. Durell, " from 1790 to 1820 Jersey enjoyed two fellowships and had but two fellows elected ; whereas Guernsey had but one, the Pembroke College Fellowship, into which about half a dozen Guernsey men were successively elected." In the reign of King Charles II, Bishop Morley, " taking into his serious consideration that the inhabitants of these Islands have not the advantages and encouragement for the education of their children, which on their behalf are desirable, and which others of his Majesty's subjects do enjoy, founded five scholarships in Pembroke College. . . . They have been productive of the singular advantage of having brought forward many individuals who have done honour to the island by their learning, their virtue, and their talents. Among these are the names of Drs. Brevint, John and David Durell, Dumaresq, Bandinel, and John and Edward Dupré." '

Deans Brevint and Durell however were not at Pembroke. The former (M.A. at Saumur) was the first King Charles Fellow at Jesus College. His son (?), DANIEL BREVINT, entered Pembroke in 1655. Two Pembroke DUPRÉS, Edward and Michael, like D'Auvergne, were Jersey rectors and military chaplains. Michael and John Dupré went from Pembroke to Exeter fellowships.

entered Pembroke 1709), complains of this 'abuse, and contradiction to the will of the Royal Founder.' For this foundation consult the Rev. C. W. Boase's *Exeter College*, O. H. S., p. cxiv. *n*, and p. cxxi.

CHAPTER XXII.

OTHER BENEFACTIONS.

It will be convenient to add here a list of the other benefactors of the College :—

The first of those, after the Founders, who ' gave us wherewith to scholay' was JULIANA, wife of Alexander, STAFFORD, of High Holborn, gentleman, who, by her will, dated Feb. 6, 162$\frac{2}{3}$, devised lands in the parish of Harlew, Essex, in trust for a yearly payment of £5 to each of four poor Scholars of St. Katherine Hall in Cambridge, and the same to either of *two poor Scholars* of Pembroke College, in Oxford, all of whom were to study divinity and carry themselves soberly and religiously; to be nominated respectively by the Master of Katherine Hall and the Chief Governor of Pembroke College ; the Scholarships to be held during residence and until M.A. This fund is now amalgamated with Mr. Oades' benefaction for poor Scholars of the College.

Three Scholarships were founded by a member of the College, of whom some account must be given—FRANCIS ROUS, called in his day ' Lord Rous.' Wood gives the following account of him in the *Athenae* (ii. 147):—

' Francis Rous, a younger son of Sir *Anth. Rous* Knight, by *Elizab:* his first wife daugh: of *Tho: Southcote* Gent. was born at *Halton* [otherwise Lanrake] in *Cornwall*, and at 12 years of age became a Commoner of *Broadgates* Hall, *an.* 1591 [1], where continuing under a constant and severe discipline, took the degree of Bach: of Arts ; which degree being compleated by *Determination*, he went afterwards, as it seems, to the Inns of Court, tho some there be that would needs persuade me that he took holy orders, and became Minister of *Saltash* in his own Country [2]. Howsoever it is, sure I am, that he being esteemed a man of parts and to be solely devoted to the puritanical Party, he was elected by the men of *Truro* in his own Country to serve in Parliaments held in the latter end

---

[1] He entered with his elder brothers, Richard and Robert, July 6, 1593. Noble says, B.A. 1591.

[2] This was another Francis Rous, father of the author of *Archaeologiae Atticae.* Saltash is near Halton.

of K. *James*, and in the Reign of K. *Ch:* I. In 1640 also he was elected again for that Corporation to serve in that unhappy Parliament which began at *Westminster* 3 *Nov*, wherein, seeing how violently the Members thereof proceeded, he put in for one, and shew'd himself with great zeal an Enemy to the Bishops' Prerogative, and what not, to gain the Populacy, a Name, and some hopes of Wealth which was dear unto him. In 1643 he forwarded and took the *Covenant*, was chosen one of the *Assembly of Divines* and for the Zeal he had for the *holy cause*, he was by authority of Parliament made Provost of *Eaton* Coll: near *Windsore* the same year [1643–1658] in the place of *Dr Rich: Steuart* who then followed, and adhered to, his sacred Majesty. In the said Parliament he afterwards shew'd himself so active, that he eagerly helped to change the Government into a Commonwealth, and to destroy the negative voice in the King and Lords. In 1653 he was by the Authority of *Ol. Cromwell* nominated a Member of the *Little Parliament* that began to sit at *Westm:* 4 *July*, and was thereupon elected the Speaker, but with a collateral Vote that he should continue in the Chair no longer than for a month, and in *Decemb.* the same year he was nominated one of *Olivers* Council. But when the good things came to be done, which were solemnly declared for, (for the not doing of which the *Long* Parliament was dissolved) *He as an old bottle, being not fit to leave that new wine, without putting it to the question, he left the Chair, and went with his Fellow old bottles to Whitehall, to surrender their Power to General Cromwell, which he, as Speaker, and they by signing a Parchment or Paper, pretended to do.* The colourable foundation for this Apostasie, upon the monarchical foundation, being thus laid, and the General himself (as Protector) seated thereon, he became one of his Council, and trusted with many matters, as being appointed in the latter end of the same year the first and prime Tryer or Approver of publick Preachers[1] and the year after a Commissioner for the County of *Cornwall*, for the Ejection of such whom they then called scandalous and ignorant Ministers and Schoolmasters. Afterwards he sate in the following Parliaments under *Oliver*, and being an aged and venerable man, was accounted worthy to be taken out of the H. of Commons, to have a negative voice in *the other house*, that is House of Lords, over all that should question him for what he had done, and over all the people of the Land besides, tho he would not suffer it in the King and Lords. This person who was usually stiled by the Loyal Party the *old illiterate Jew of Eaton* and another *Proteus*, hath divers things (especially of Divinity) extant, wherein much enthusiastical Canting is used . . . Our Author *Rous* gave way to fate at *Acton* near *London* on the seventh day of *January* in sixteen hundred fifty and eight, and was buried in *Eaton* Coll: Church, near to the entrance of that Chappel joyning thereunto, formerly built by *Rog: Lupton*, Provost of the said College. Soon

---

[1] The 'Inquisitio Anglicana' (as it was called) of the Triers ousted such clergy as were unable to show what work of grace had been wrought in their souls, and declare the day and hour of their call by the Spirit. One poor man was kept thus under examination for seven weeks. One of Rous's coadjutors in this sifting process was the loose-lived mountebank, Hugh Peters.

after were hanged up, over his grave, a Standard, Pennon, &c. and other Ensigns relating to Barons, containing in them the arms of the several matches of his Family. All which continuing there till 1661 were then pulled down with scorn by the loyal Provost and Fellows, and thrown aside as tokens and badges of damn'd baseness and rebellion. Those of his Party did declare openly to the World at his death that "he needed no monument besides his own printed works and the memorials of his last will, to convey his name to posterity. And that the other works of his life, were works of charity, wherein he was most exemplary, as the poor in many parts would after the loss of him tell you," &c. The Poet of *Broadgates* called *Ch. Fitz Geffry* did celebrate his memory while he was of that house, and after his death *Pembroke* College did the like for his benefaction to the members thereof.'

' Mr Rous, Esqu. of Essex' is mentioned in John Rous's Diary as answering in 1626 Montagu's *Appello Caesarem.* Neal also calls him 'Esquire,' and on his picture at Pembroke, which shows him, aged 77, in gown and broad band, he is styled ' armiger.' A certain number of laymen sate with the Westminster Divines[1]. Soon after obtaining the provosty of Eton, Rous, who appears not to have proceeded beyond B.A., nearly lost it by the operation of the Self-denying Ordinance ; but an exception was made by the Commons in his favour. Clement Walker, reckoning the preferment bestowed by the Godly among the Independents, says ' Mr Rouse hath *Eaton* college worth 800*l.* per annum, and a lease of that college worth 600*l.* per. ann.' He substituted the Directory for the Common Prayer for the scholars' use. M^r. Lyte gives his ' Rules for the Schollers.' The old trees in the Playing Fields are said to be of Rous's planting. He enjoyed an opinion, Clarendon says, of some knowledge in the Latin and Greek tongues, but was ' of a very mean understanding.' Chalmers remarks, ' Lord Clarendon and his contemporaries undervalue his abilities, which certainly did not appear to much advantage in parliament, where his speeches were rude, vulgar and enthusiastic, both in style and sentiment, yet perhaps none the worse adapted to the understanding of his hearers.' Rous represented not only Truro but Tregony, Devonshire, and Cornwall. He certainly played a directing part in the events of that stormy time. In Revolutions it is commonly second-rate men who come to the front. Rous meditated modelling the Commonwealth after the pattern of the Jewish theocracy, and only when he found an assembly of ignorant and vulgar men unequal to this task did he propose to Barebone's Parliament to resign the sovereignty into the hands of Cromwell, whom he regarded as Moses and Joshua in one. It was said that Cromwell ' could not well do less than make that gentleman a Lord who had made him a Prince.' There is a portrait of Rous at Eton in his robes as Speaker.

---

[1] Selden, who had a seat in the Assembly, says : ' There must be some laymen in the Synod to overlook the clergy, lest they spoil the civil work, just as, when the good woman puts a cat into the milkhouse to kill a mouse, she sends her maid to look after the cat, lest the cat should eat up the cream.' Whitelocke and Oliver St. John were of the number.

Bramston says (*Autobiography*), 'The Speaker, Old Rous, and the rest juggling togeather by an instrument delivered up the gouernment to Crumwell.' 'Thoroughly engaged in the guilt of the times,' is Clarendon's summary verdict. Rous's rude translation of 'the Psalmes of David into English Meeter' was substituted by the House of Commons, Nov. 4, 1645, for the exquisite Psalter of Cranmer, and, with the *Paraphrases* and Barton's version, was long the sole spiritual hymnody of the presbyterians, who still use it. The Long Parliament had been petitioned to help the minister against the people 'who doe interrupt him when he readeth the Psalmes, by taking every other verse out of his mouth, with a hackering confused noise.' His *Works* were printed in 1657, with an engraving 'by the curious hand of Will. Faithorne' from the Pembroke picture. This folio is called 'Treatises and Meditations dedicated to the Saints and to the Excellent throughout the three Nations.' It includes the *Art of Happiness* (1619), *The Diseases of the Times* (1622), *Oyl of Scorpions* (1623), *Testis Veritatis* (1626), *Catholike Charity* (1641, complaining of Roman intolerance), *The Great Oracle*, *The Mystical Marriage* (1653), &c. Besides the *Works*, are his parliamentary speeches, *Mella Patrum*, the patristic writings of the first three centuries, (1650), and *Interiora regni Dei* (printed after the Restoration, in 1665). Hearne also mentions '*The lawfullness of obeying ye Present Government*—1649, 4to—The Author *Fr. Rouse*, Provost (*sed contra jus fasque*) of *Eaton* Coll., Who was Author likewise of *The Bounds and Bonds of Publick Obedience*. Lond. 1649, 4to.' (*Collections*, O. H. S., i. 78.)

The following extract from a parliamentary speech may be given as a specimen of Rous's style :—

'I desire it may be considered how the sea of Rome doth eat into our religion and fret into the very banks and walls of it, the laws and statutes of this realm. I desire we may consider the increase of Arminianism, an error that makes the grace of God lackey after the will of man. I desire we may look into the belly and bowels of this Trojan horse, to see if there be not men in it ready to open the gates to Romish tyranny, for an Arminian is the spawn of a Papist. And if the warmth of favour comes upon him, you shall see him turn into one of those frogs that rose out of the bottomless pit. These men having kindled a fire in our neighbouring country, are now endeavouring to set this kingdom in a flame.' (Neal, *History of the Puritans.*) It was this speech, and one of Pym's, which determined the Commons to reply by their *Vow* to the Declaration prefixed by King Charles and Laud to the Articles. In the *Heavenly University* (1638), Rous allows the New Man to employ pagan learning, as a Gibeonite, to cleave wood and draw water for his service in the Sanctuary. Only, 'Whatsoever time thou bestow'st in Study be sure to set apart some time wherein to *study the Holy Ghost*; who, sitting in his Chair of Grace, teacheth his Scholars inwardly to see those Divine and Heavenly Truths which may advance thee in the way to Heavenly Glory.' The book is pious and quakerish rather than Calvinistic—troubled consciences exceedingly quake and tremble at the thunders of Sinai, so that the world asks, Why do ye skip as lambs and tremble as little lambs? Illustrations from the ' holy fathers' and 'divine Soliloquies of Blessed Thomas à Kempis' are appended to each chapter. He quotes the apostrophe of ' an Ancient Scholar in this University ' to his spirit, taught in the philosophy of eternity, ' Be not thow Exalted above the Sons of Art and Reason ; do not thou despise their Academical Learning; do not thou mock at their Corner-Cap, Hood and Tippet ; let them enjoy their *Degrees.*' For these qualities and its doctrine—suspected as popish—of the Inward Light, without denial of 'the more Unerrable Lights of God's Church,' the *Academia Caelestis* was reprinted in 1702 by a high churchman [1].

It is not mentioned in the *Athenae* that Rous was chairman of the Committee of Lords and Commons appointed May 1, 1647, to supervise and direct the Oxford Visitors. The Committee sometimes sate at the Painted Chamber, Westminster, sometimes in Rous's lodging, whither Fell, Morley, and others were cited to appear. Rous was for extreme measures against all academians who denied the authority of Parliament, but Selden and Whitelocke were more afraid of illegal action. In January, 165$\frac{9}{0}$, Rous and the Visitors had high differences, the London Committee insisting on filling places with men whom the Oxford Ministers deemed scandalous and unfit.

In 1659 Rous, together with Lambert and Montagu, urged upon the Protector the foundation of a college at Durham with the buildings and revenues of the Cathedral. It was intended that it should be erected into a University. Oliver dying, however, the old Universities made strong representation to Richard Cromwell against the multiplying of small degree-conferring bodies, and the project dropped. The Little Parliament, over which Rous presided, had proposed 'that all Lands belonging to the Universities and Colleges in those Universities might be sold, and the Monies that should arise thereby be disposed for the publick Service.'

By his will, dated March 8, 165$\frac{7}{8}$, proved Feb. 10, 165$\frac{8}{9}$, Rous devised an estate of £40 *per an.* out of the tythes of Bookham Magna, Surrey, to maintain two students, and also £20 *per an.* for a third, issuing out of a pension paid for certain tenements in the manor of Mutton, Cornwall, during the lives of two Bigfords, and after their decease from a tenement at Cowkbury, Devon ; the scholars to be of low fortunes, viz. under £10 *per an.*, of a fit age for learning, and of his own posterity or of the stock of Robert, Richard (both were at .

---

[1] *The Sufficiency of the Spirit's teaching without humane Learning,* by How a cobbler, and Kiffen an anabaptist minister (1683), is a specimen of the anti-academic writings of the seventeenth century.

Broadgates), and Arthur, his brethren, or of the descent from his sisters Nichols or Upton (married (2) to John Wilshere), or, failing such, then to be elected of the two upper forms of Eton school. They were to study divinity, and to give some public specimen of their proficiency therein before becoming bachelors in arts, and not to enjoy the benefaction above seven years. (Chalmers incorrectly describes the benefaction as for the support of three Fellows. He says that Rous bequeathed other property to pious uses.) All other conditions were to be settled by his executor, Anthony Rous[1], and his nephew, Master Ambrose Upton, prebend of Christ Church. But this was not done, and the conditions of election remained uncertain till 1757, when an indenture tripartite was made, under the provisions of which the scholars were thereafter appointed. In 1857 the three Exhibitions were consolidated as *one Scholarship*, worth now £60 yearly. In 1852 there were two exhibitioners enjoying each £29 2s. 6d. for seven years.

The Cookbury rent-charge was shifted in 1864 to Killatree Farm at Pyworthy, Devon. Ambrose Upton (of Lupton, Devon) and his brother Thomas were fellows of All Souls. Ambrose's son Francis Upton (1656–1711), a physician, was at Pembroke. Several members of the family sate for Dartmouth or for the county. Rous's other sister married, I think, John Nicholls, of St. Kew, Cornwall (entered Broadgates in 1584). Antony Nicoll (entered Pembroke 1694) was M.P. for Tregony, 1708–10.

In examining claims of kindred the College has acknowledged the issue of Rous as legitimate. He was not the kind of man whom one would expect to make a runaway love-match, but I learn from private records that he did this in his youth. The marriage was disputed when he was dead, and his considerable fortune was left in Chancery to accumulate[2]. His kinsman, Francis, a young physician of great talents,

---

[1] Grandson, if I mistake not, of Francis Rous's eldest brother Ambrose, of Halton, whose sons, William (M.P. for Truro 1625) and George Rous (of the Middle Temple), entered Broadgates together, Feb. 14, 1612. Anthony entered Exeter in 1633. His brother Richard was M.P. for Bossiney (Tintagil) 1661. A sister of Francis Rous married Jacob Northcote, Esq.; their monument is at Newton St. Cyres. The family descended from Sir Ralph Rous, seated at Modbury, Devon, *temp.* Henry III. Rous of Edmerston, a cadet, moved to Halton, in St. Dominick Parish, *temp.* Elizabeth. John, great-uncle of Francis, bought the mansion, which is now a farm-house. The Rous arms are, Or, an eagle displayed preening her wing, azure.

[2] I remember, as a boy, hearing among Devonshire relatives of an enormous accumulation, and of the efforts made in the past to prove the union, alleged to have taken place at Creed's Combe, a real one. Rous's heir at law in 1795 was the Rev. Richard Rous of Clist St. George, 'representing the provost's brother' (d. 1810). His daughter and heiress married an Ellicombe. Speaker Rous's Parliament, during the few weeks of its existence, enacted civil marriage.

and author of a work on Greek antiquities, distinguished himself on the field of battle and in the Commons. Anthony, John, and Robert Rous, all members of Parliament, were, Noble thinks, his sons. Rous Exhibitions have been held, for the most part, by Etonians[1], and, though Rous's will speaks of his posterity, founder's kin was not claimed for some time. The portrait of Rous in the Hall was given by PETER CREED, of Stoke Fleming[2].

Sir JOHN BENNET, afterwards Lord OSSULSTON, besides his assistance in building the College, gave in 1672 certain fee farm rents in six places in Gloucestershire, amounting then (and now) to £17 11s. 8d. Also rents in four-and-twenty places in Derbyshire, amounting to £43 15s. 4d. These were to maintain *two Scholarships* of £10, open to all members of the College who are not of the original foundations nor eligible into them, and *two Fellowships* for Bennet scholars of two years' standing. The Fellowships were septennial, but the holders might be elected for seven years more if they should have been found useful to the Society. In 1802 the Duke of Portland was appealed to as to whether Ossulston Fellows were eligible for presentation to the rectory of St. Aldate's. In 1852 they were still receiving the original stipend (being a rent-charge) of £20 each, and the Scholars £10. This foundation is now merged in the Corporate Fund. We have seen (page 263) that it created some jealousy among the Fellows of the older foundations. Lord Ossulston presented to the College 'a great silver Cup.'

Lord Ossulston was elder brother of the more famous Earl of Arlington. They were great-grandsons of the co-Founder Tesdale's half-sister Elizabeth[3]. He was born at Arlington in 1618, and entered Pembroke

---

[1] He particularly desired to be buried at Eton—'a place which hath my deare affections and prayers that it may be a flourishing nursery of pietie and learning to the end of the world.' Whitelocke (who strangely writes on Oct. 25, 1657, as though Rous were dead) hoped to step into his shoes there, but was made a Lord by Cromwell instead. Allstree, Rous's Restoration successor, was the humorist who placed in the Christ Church strong-box, where the Puritans hoped to find treasure, a halter and a groat.

[2] Entered as kin-exhibitioner Oct. 30, 1723. He was great-great-grandson of Rous's daughter or niece Dorothy, wife of William Bayley, who was chaplain in the Rebellion to the Lord Roberts, and ejected from Stoke Fleming rectory in 1662. An uncle, Dr. JOHN CREED (entered Pembroke 1703), was Canon of Wells. John Henry Newman was related to the Creeds. Lysons does not seem to know of this picture. He says (*Cornwall*, p. 78): 'Thomas Bate Rous, Esq., of Courtyralla in Glamorganshire, the immediate descendant and representative of [Rous of Modbury], has an original portrait of Francis Rous.' Faithorne's print is, he says, from the Eton picture.

[3] Wood (*Gutch*, iii. 260) and Dr. Ingram say that Tesdale was Lord Ossulston's grandfather.

as a gentleman-commoner, April 24, 1635. Student of Gray's Inn, 1636.
In the wars he fought on the royal side, and, when Charles II was
crowned at Westminster, was admitted to the Order of the Bath, and
shortly to the royal intimacy. Mr. A. I. Dasent, in his *Saint James's
Square*, says: 'Among dissolute residents Lord Ossulston lent his house
for a masquerade ball, to which none but debauchees of both sexes were
invited.' He was Captain of the Band of Gentlemen Pensioners. From
1663 to 1679 he represented Wallingford, the home of his forefathers.
On Nov. 24, 1682, he was created Baron Ossulston of Arlington, his
Majesty taking into consideration the constant and faithful services performed to his royal Father, of blessed memory, in the rebellious times,
as also to himself. Ossulston is a hundred of Middlesex. He was one of
eighteen lords who petitioned James II, to the King's grave displeasure, for
a parliament. Ossulston died Feb. 11, 1695[1]. He was twice married.
The busts of his wives with his own, in white marble, ornament his
monument at Arlington. His son Charles, second baron, married in
1695 the daughter and heiress of Lord Grey, Earl of Tankerville, at
whose death those titles expired. Lord Ossulston was then created, in
1714, Earl of Tankerville. The portrait of the first lord in the College
Hall was painted by R. Phillips. It bears the words 'ROB. COOPER
memor Patroni et Coll. Pemb. D.D.' (1721). Dr. Cooper was the first
Ossulston Fellow, 1673; Rector of Arlington, 1681; Archdeacon of Dorset,
1698. Ob. 1733. He gave £100 towards the Chapel. He wrote *Proportions concerning Optick Glasses*, an *Introduction to Geography*, &c.

GEORGE TOWNSEND, of Rowell, in the county of Gloucester, and of
Lincolnshire, Esq., by will dated Dec. 14, 1682, and proved Nov.
29, 1683, devised 'Little Aston Farme in the Parish of Cold Aston in
the said County of Glouc[r]. and the tythes of Corne thereof by me
demised to Charles Trinder Gent. for ninety and nine years at the rent
of fourscore pounds by the year,' to the Master, Fellows, and Scholars,
upon special trust and confidence to pay, imploy, and bestow 'the
first year and half-year's rent thereof after my decease for and towards
the necessary building or repairing of the said Colledge, the next
half-year's rent thereof for and towards the providing of fitting studies
and necessary bedsteads feather-beds and other bedding and furniture
of chambers to be used in succession,' rent free, by *Scholars* to be
placed therein, in number *eight*, chosen out of the chief school in

[1] Lysons (*Middlesex*) points out that his epitaph implies that he died in 1686,
aged seventy. Burke gives that year. Collins gives the date 1685, Edmondson
1689. The Arlington registers prove that he was buried Feb. 15, 1694. His will
was dated Nov. 28, 1694, and proved Feb. 18, 1694. See also Wood's *Life and
Times*, O. H. S., iii. 479 and note. (But the London Coffee letter there cited
gives his age as eighty-nine instead of seventy-seven.) Wood quotes 'Feb. 14, W.,
corps of Lord Ossulston carried from Westminster to Dawley in Middlesex to be
there buried—he died very rich.'

Gloucester by the Mayor, six of the senior Aldermen and the chief Schoolmaster, and out of the schools of Cheltenham ('in which I was a Scholar'), Chipping Campden, and Northlatch, or Northleach [1], by the respective chief Schoolmasters, Ministers, and Bailiffs. These schools, all in Gloucestershire, were each to supply a fitting grammar scholar every fourth year, the exhibition being tenable for eight years. Residence (to begin at the Feast of the Annunciation) was enforced. ' And my desire is that all the said Scholars for their four last years of residence in the said Colledge addict their Studies to Divinity, for whose encouragement therein I will that my Rectory of Stifford and Vicarage of Grayes Thorock in Essex and the Donatives of Uxbridge and Colebrooke so often as any of them shall fall void be conferred on such of the said Scholars as shall be fitting Divines at the nomination of my Son in law William Kenwricke Esquire during his life and after his death [my Grandson] James Silverlocke or his heirs.'

In 1852 there were five residents, receiving £52 each. In 1857 it was ordained that no exhibitioner should enjoy the profits of his place after his seventeenth term (i.e. four years and the term required between B.A. and M.A.); the four juniors were to have rooms. The lack of endowment for post-graduate study of Divinity is now seriously felt; and it is to be regretted that Townsend's provision for this purpose was swept away instead of being modified. In 1881 the Scholarships were fixed at £80 each and rooms. Townsend's portrait in the Hall bears the words: ' 1647, aet. 45. D. d. Johan. Edows, A.M., Georgii Townsend Consang. 1743.' John Edows, of Adderbury, Oxon, took M.A. from New College, 1728.

In 1700 Mrs. ROBINSON, sister of Bishop Hall, gave the College a fee farm rent from Horspath, value £8 8s. 4d., but charged with a payment of £1 14s. to the Rector of St. Aldate's for two sermons, on Holy Thursday and Christmas Day.

Dame ELIZABETH HOLFORD, of the parish of All Hallows, Steyning, in the city of London, widow of Sir William Holford, of Witham, in the county of Leicester, Bart., by will dated Nov. 19, 1717, left £1,000 to accumulate at interest in mortgage on Government securities till £1,300 should be attained. With this sum land was to be

---

[1] There was a Richard, son of Anthony, Townsend, of Cambden, who entered Trinity, as 'pauper,' in 1699, and a Thomas, son of Thomas, Townsend, who entered Queen's, as 'pauper,' from Northleach, in the same year. Robert, son of George, Townsend, who entered Pembroke in 1665 (rector of Wallingford and canon of Sarum), was from Heddington, Wilts.

purchased in Oxfordshire or some place near to the University, and conveyed to the Master and Fellows upon trust to pay £20 *per an.* to each of *two Exhibitioners*, to be chosen out of those of the Scholars who should be sent to the University by the Governors of Sutton's Hospital or Charterhouse, and be in receipt of a pension out of Sutton's Charity. The testatrix died Nov. 3, 1719, and in 1737 the capital sum amounted to the prescribed £1,300. Scholars were from that date elected; and in 1752 an estate at Tiddington, Oxon, was purchased for £2,400, £1,100 being provided by the College, of which £300 was a gift of Dr. SAMUEL BAKER, Canon and Chancellor of York (entered 1687), to be expended as the College might direct, and £200 a gift of Dr. BENJAMIN SLOCOCK (Fellow 1712, Proctor 1720, Chaplain of St. Saviour's, Southwark, 1725 [1]) for the support of a lecturer in Hebrew, or else for the benefit of certain Fellows or Scholars. In 1857 Dame Elizabeth's two Scholarships were consolidated into one, to be called the Holford Scholarship. The Scholar at present receives £60 yearly. Lady Holford left five similar Exhibitions to Christ Church, two to Worcester, and two to Hart Hall.

The Reverend WILLIAM OADES, Rector of Dummer, Hants, by will dated Sept. 21, 1730, bequeathed nearly the whole of his property, real and personal, to the College in trust (1) to pay £10 *per an.* to any descendant of his brother or sister who may fall into poverty, there being not more than one recipient at a time, and (2) to divide the residue into eight parts; to pay six of these parts to the heirs and descendants of his brother or sister, and the remaining two parts, in sums not exceeding £5, in equal proportions, among so many *Servitors and Batellers* of the poorer sort in the College as they shall deem fit. Other minuter regulations were made for the trust. Mr. Oades died in 1731, and his effects realized £2,434 7s. 10d., which was invested in an estate near Basingstoke, the College obtaining a licence in mortmain. In 1852 there were two senior Exhibitions of £25, and two junior of £20. The Commissioners did not vary the provisions of the will in 1857. Six-eighths of the net proceeds are paid to a descendant of the testator, and two-eighths to Scholars in need of assistance. Failing issue of his kin, Mr. Oades gave 'jus haereditatis totius' for various College and Church uses.

EDMUND BOULTER, of Hasely Court, Oxon, and of Harwood, Yorks, Esquire, by will dated March 21, 1736, after making specific bequests to various relatives and to the Mayor and Aldermen of the

---

[1] Dr. Slocock's portrait is in the Hall. He gave £21 to the Chapel.

city of Oxford for the erection of an almshouse, gave to the College a rent-charge of £20 yearly for *one Scholarship*, to be called, in honour of his uncle, Sir John Cutler, *Cutler-Boulter's Scholarship*, for educating (by preference) an ingenious youth of kindred to himself, his wife, or his uncle-in-law, Mr. Michael Walls, and he constituted the Earl of Arran and his daughter, Elizabeth Boulter, executors of his will. Soon after his death, on April 21, 1736, a suit was instituted in Chancery, the Attorney-General *v.* Earl of Arran and others, and the estate was administered in the Court. No applicant for the Scholarship appeared till 1792, when Richard Iremonger was elected. The total sum in the hands of the Court now amounted to £2,499 7s. 1d. three per cent. annuities. In pursuance of an order of the Court the College framed a scheme for the establishment of *a second Scholarship*, and it was confirmed June 30, 1796. The Court continued to administer the fund till 1857, when the University Commissioners ordained that the two Scholarships should be consolidated with the Exhibition founded by Dr. John Ratcliff, so as to maintain two Scholars, to be called the Boulter and Ratcliff Scholars. They now receive £80 each. In 1852 there were two Cutler-Boulter Exhibitioners receiving £36 8s. each for seven years.

In 1749 Sir JOHN PHILIPPS, Bart., of Picton Castle, Pembrokeshire, founded *one Fellowship* and *one Scholarship* for natives of that county, or, in default of such, of any county in South Wales. He also gave the perpetual curacy of West Haroldston with Lambton, in Pembrokeshire, to be accepted under pain of forfeiture by the Fellow of his foundation who might not be Master, nor Bursar, nor Rector of St. Aldate's. The Scholar was to succeed to the Fellowship on a vacancy. In 1852 the Fellow's place was worth £80 yearly, that of the Scholar £40. They are now merged in the Corporate Fund. Sir John was the sixth baronet. He entered the College Aug. 4, 1720; created D.C.L. April 12, 1749; M.P. for Caermarthen 1741-7, for Petersfield 1754-61, for Pembrokeshire 1761-4. He died June 23, 1764. His father was the 'great and good' Sir John Philipps who took part, as a prominent layman, in the foundation of the Society for Promoting Christian Knowledge and other institutions. He was a Commissioner for building the Fifty Churches, and through his aid Whitefield was enabled to take his degree. His son, Sir RICHARD (1738–1823), who entered the College Feb. 3, 1761, was created Baron Milford in 1766. M.P. for Pembrokeshire 1765-70, 1786–1812, for Plympton 1774–9, for Haverfordwest 1784–96. Sir ERASMUS[1] PHILIPPS, portions of whose

Diary are given below, matriculated from Pembroke on the same day as his younger brother, Sir John. The latter was a Privy Councillor.

The Reverend JAMES PHIPPS, M.A., Rector of Elvetham, Hants, formerly Tesdale Scholar, by his will dated Nov. 4, 1763, bequeathed to the College, besides other properties, the manor or lordship of Temple Cowley and Littlemore, Oxon, together with £3,000 in Government securities, for a fund out of which to purchase *four advowsons* of the yearly value of £150 each, for the benefit of the Tesdale Fellows; after which the profits were to be appropriated towards the increase of the stipends of the Tesdale Fellows by £10, and of the Scholars by £5, and towards the payment of £10 to a chaplain to read prayers, in addition to his usual salary; anything remaining over was to be put into the College chest for the purchase of books 'or whatever may be an ornament or benefit to the College.' Mr. Phipps died Dec. 18, 1773, but a life-interest resided in his relict till her death, Oct. 8, 1778. With the bequest were bought the following advowsons: Coln St. Dennis in Gloucestershire, Ringshall in Suffolk, Liddiard Millicent in Wiltshire, and Sibson or Sibstone in Leicestershire. The estate and repair fund, on which the cost of the additions to and repairs of the College buildings is charged, receives the residue after the payment of £10 to the chaplain and £40 to the corporate revenue. In 1846 £3,000 of the Phipps fund was devoted to the erection of the new Hall. The portraits of Mr. Phipps ('T. Bardwell pinxit 1749') and Mrs. Phipps hang in it.

Dr. JOHN RATCLIFF, by will made in 1774, bequeathed to the College £1,000 four per cent. Bank annuities, upon trust to pay £26 yearly to *one Exhibitioner* appointed by the Master, who should be the son of a clergyman in the diocese of Gloucester and intended for Holy Orders, the Exhibition to be holden for seven years, subject to certain conditions as to residence; the residue of the proceeds were to be divided among the lecturers or moderators of the College in such proportions as the Master of the College shall appoint. In 1852 the Exhibition was only worth £18 18s. 8d. Dr. Ratcliff, by the same will, gave

---

[1] Another Erasmus, an uncle, was killed at Bantry Bay. This name came into the family through Elizabeth Dryden (see page 102), wife of the second baronet. Horace Walpole writes (Aug. 11, 1748): 'I am taking great pains to verify a probability of my being descended from Chaucer, whose daughter, the lady Alice, before her espousals with Thomas Montacute, earl of Salisbury . . . was married to a sir John Philips, who I hope to find was of Picton Castle, and had children by her. . . . Thank my stars and my good cousin the present sir J. Philips, I have a sufficient pedigree to work upon; for he drew us up one, by which *Ego et rex meus* are derived hand in hand from Cadwallader, and the English baronetage says from the Emperor Maximus. . . . Yours ever,—CHAUCERIDES.'

£1,000 for the improvement of the College buildings, £100 worth of books, and £100 for any public use the Master should approve. He died in 1775. There no longer being any moderators, the money that would have been paid to them is added to the ' College Bag.' Dr. Ratcliff also left £600 to repair the prebendal house at Gloucester, and bequeathed £400 to Exeter College, of which his father was a Fellow. His Mastership extended from Feb. 23, 1738, to July, 1775.

FRANCIS WIGHTWICK, Esquire, of Wombridge, Berks (where there are several family monuments), by will dated May 20, 1776, left to the College a contingent reversion of his plate, books, pictures, and also of two estates for the sustenance of *four Fellows and three Scholars*, preference being given to persons of the name or kindred of Richard Wightwick, B.D. By the death, March 1, 1843, without male issue, of a nephew, Mr. Francis Wightwick, of Sandgates, Chertsey, this bequest came to the College May 4 of that year. An enlargement by £500 of the licence in mortmain was procured the next year in consequence. The College was confirmed in the possession of its eight advowsons, and empowered to hold others to the amount of £3,000 yearly. The salaries fixed by Francis Wightwick for his Fellows and Scholars being no longer proportionable to the surplus to be distributed among the Fellows and Scholars of the Tesdale and Wightwick foundations, the Duke of Wellington was petitioned to allow a modification of the arrangement ' in a spirit of liberality and equity.' The Fellowships were raised from £40 to £70, the Scholarships to £40. No person ever appeared to claim kin to Richard Wightwick for these [1]. The estates which supported the Francis Wightwick Fellows and Scholars are his lands, &c., at Binfield, now Binfield House (lately occupied by the gallant General Stewart who fell in the Soudan), those at Waltham St. Lawrence, now Beenham's Farm, and a rent charge of £70 issuing out of the manor of Bramley, Yorks. At Waltham stood Wombridge House, a fine manorial building, destroyed early in this century, on the walls of which hung the handsome portrait of HANCOX WIGHTWICK (who died as a young man in 1731), now in the Common Room parlour, and the picture, now in the College Hall, of (I think) SAMUEL WIGHTWICK, executor of the co-Founder's will, great-grandfather of Francis Wightwick, of the date 1652 [2]. A third picture,

---

[1] The first Scholar elected (1845) was HENRY STUART FAGAN, afterwards Head Master of Market Bosworth School, where Johnson was usher, and of Bath Grammar School.

[2] Mr. A. R. BAYLEY, B.A., who has kindly helped me in several particulars, identifies, in his useful *Catalogue of Portraits in the possession of Pembroke College*,

which came into the possession of the College from Wombridge, is a Wightwick or Rudge family group by Phillips, Hogarthian in style. It hung in a small farm-house close to Wombridge House till the memory of the present tenant of Beenham's, and was used by the farmer's children as a target for their bows and arrows. These pictures, the plate, and some legal books, now in the College Library, were heir-looms of Wombridge. The Francis Wightwick foundation is now merged in the Corporate Fund.

Dr. JOHN SMYTH, who succeeded Dr. Sergrove as Master, April 28, 1796, by will dated Oct. 16, 1809, after certain legacies, left the reversion, after the death of three persons, of the residue of his personal estate to his successor or successors in trust to purchase *one or more advowsons* for the benefit of such Fellow or Fellows to whose foundation there should not be any benefice appropriated. Brink-worth, Wilts (where Penn had property), was acquired in 1831 from Lord Holland for £5,600. In 1871 there remained in hand £3,683 14s. 6d. Government stock. About Dr. Smyth there is a story that his real name was Cromwell, but that owing to the odium attaching to the name he changed it. There was considerable mystery about his birth, and he himself was for a long time in ignorance of his own parentage. The truth is however (as appears from papers in the possession of the College) that he bore his mother's name, and that his father was John Revett, Esq., of Kensington, an officer in the Guards. His father's sister, Mary Revett or Rivett, was married to a great-grandson of Oliver Cromwell, Colonel Charles Russell, of Checkers, grandson of Sir John Russell, Bart., by his union with Frances Cromwell. Dr. Smyth was at one time a naval chaplain. In days when the world was larger than it is now, he was distinguished among Heads of Houses by having been a traveller. The late Mr. G. V. Cox records in his *Recollections* (1868) that 'Dr. Smith was said to have exercised so largely what is called the "traveller's privilege" in relating and *embellishing* the stories of his travels as to have gained the sobriquet of " Sinbad the Sailor."' He entered Pembroke from Abingdon Nov. 13, 1761, aged 17; B.A. 1765; M.A. 1769; B.D. and D.D. 1796. Besides the prebendal stall at Gloucester, he held the rectories of St. Aldate's (1789), Coln Rogers (1799), Radford (1801), and Fairford (1804), and was perpetual curate of Eastleach

the third quartering on this picture. The arms are: Quarterly, 1st, az., on a chevron, arg., betw. 3 pheons, or, as many crosses patée, gu. (for *Wightwick*); 2nd, arg., 3 boars' heads, sa., a chief of the last engrailed (for *Jenkes*) ; 3rd, a garb or, betw. 3 bezants (for *Grosvenor*); 4th, as the 1st (for *Wightwick*); see Pedigree.

Turville (1799). Dr Smyth died Oct. 19, 1809. His portrait in the Hall, by H. Howard, R.A., is said to have been painted from Dighton's caricature. It was bought in 1811 ' out of Tesdale and Wightwick funds.'

Mrs. SOPHIA SHEPPARD, widow of the Rev. Thos. Sheppard, D.D. (of Amport, Southants, sometime Fellow of Magdalen), a sister of Dr. Martin Routh, gave, May 7, 1846, £12,000 three per cent. Bank Annuities, for *two Fellows*, to study law or medicine, and not bound to residence. The foundress was to nominate the first two Fellows. Afterwards they were to be elected by the Master, the Vicegerent, and the four senior Fellows present. Marriage, or an estate of £500 a year in land, was to vacate the fellowship. In an address of thanks to Mrs. Sheppard the Master and Fellows say : ' Destined by its Royal Founder to promote the study of law and medicine as well as that of Theology and so to nurture men qualified to serve God in Church and State alike, Pembroke College has owing to the character of its foundations become almost exclusively a seminary for ecclesiastics. Your endowment, conceived in the spirit of wisdom and liberality, promises to restore to it the lustre which it derived in former days from the names of Sir Thomas Browne and Lord Chancellor Harcourt, Sir William Blackstone and Dr. Beddoes.' They ask the favour that her portrait may be placed in the Hall. The reply of the aged lady—she was above eighty years of age—is an admirable specimen of the old high-bred courtly and delicate style of composition. In it she says : ' The first idea of endowing Lay Fellowships and offering them to Pembroke College arose from hearing that a young man must take Holy Orders or lose his Fellowship after a very short period.' Mrs. Sheppard's only nominee was a nephew, Mr. Martin Routh.

The Rev. CHRISTOPHER CLEOBUREY, M.A. (son of the Rev. John Cleoburey, of St. Helen's, Abingdon), Rector of Liddiard Millicent, Wilts, and many years Fellow (1820–56), by will dated Dec. 3, 1855, after certain private bequests, gave in reversion after his wife's death £1,000 three per cent. Bank Annuities towards the purchase, when opportunity should offer, of the Wolsey Almshouse ; £300 for making a niche over the entrance gateway of the College, and placing therein a statue of King James I [1]; and, as a further proof of gratitude to Pembroke College, he gave £4,300 Government Stock, £400 thereof to purchase books for prizes to members of the College who should be placed in the first class ' in Literis Humanioribus ' or ' in Disciplinis Mathematicis et Physicis,' the residue for the founding of *one Scholar-*

---

[1] It has actually been placed in the vacant niche in the Hall tower.

ship, open without restriction to persons of under nineteen years, the election to take place on April 22, the Founder's birthday. The 'Cleoburey Scholar' is to receive in money £100 *per annum* and the remaining dividends of £3,900 in books. Accumulations may be applied to augment these sums to £130 and £30, or to rewarding meritorious but unsuccessful candidates. By a codicil, dated Aug. 10, 1857, the testator gave to the College, in the same reversion, the entire residue of his personal estate, for the renovation or rebuilding of any parts of the College, or in making additions thereto by the acquisition of the Almshouse or otherwise, or else in purchasing and removing the houses on the north side of St. Aldate's Church, and laying the site of them into the churchyard. Mr. Cleoburey died Oct. 29, 1863, and on the death of his wife in 1882 the bequests fell to the College—in all £12,800. £6,000 of this was applied towards the purchase (for £10,000 and the fixtures £1,000) of the Almshouse. The testator 'trusted to the good faith of the Master and Fellows to carry out' his intentions. He had built the glebe-house at Liddiard Millicent[1] chiefly through a 'desire to benefit his beloved College.'

Certain relatives and friends of the Rev. THOMAS FREDERICK HENNEY, M.A., Fellow and Tutor, who died in 1859, to testify to his services and do honour to his memory, subscribed a sum of money to found a Scholarship, to be called the *Henney Scholarship*, subject to such conditions and regulations as the College shall from time to time determine. Its annual value is, at present, £90. The first Henney Scholar (1863) was WILLIAM BALLYMAN HULL, long Chairman of the Norwich School Board. JOHN HARROWER, Professor of Greek at Aberdeen University, and ALBERT EARNSHAW, Fellow of Durham, were later Scholars on this foundation.

Mrs. DOROTHEA WIGHTWICK (third daughter of Richard Fryer, Esq., M.P., of the Wergs, Staffordshire), who married, in 1829, Stubbs Wightwick, Esq., J.P. and D.L., of Great Bloxwich, Staffs., and Capel Court, Cheltenham, gave, May 16, 1889, £5,000 to support at least *two Scholars*. Their stipend has been limited to £90. Preference is to be given to descendants of Mary Morson or of Susanna Thacker, sisters of the foundress, and in the second degree to candidates from Cheltenham Proprietary College. The College was empowered to

---

[1] In the old Manor House the tragical suicide of a love-sick clergyman took place in 1764. There was till recently a 'priest's hole' behind the altar of the chapel. The Clintons, out of whom came the ducal house of Newcastle, occupied the place from 1105 to 1421.

frame bye-laws regulating duration of tenure, condition of celibacy, and the like, and has excluded married persons, persons over twenty-five, and members of the University of more than two terms' standing. A Scholarship is tenable for two years, renewable for two years more, and, in a special case, for a fifth year. Scholars must attend Chapel, unless *extra ecclesiam Anglicanam.*

Two characteristic pastels of Mr. Stubbs Wightwick came to the College at the same time, one by Richard Dighton, of Cheltenham, the other (dated 1833) by Albert Burt, of Southampton.

Contributors to the erection of the various College buildings have been, or will be, mentioned in their place.

NOTE.

IN connexion with the subject of Pembroke Benefactors a conversation which took place in 1778 between Johnson and an old fellow collegian, Oliver Edwards [1], may be recalled here. Boswell describes their meeting in London after fifty years as 'one of the most curious incidents in Johnson's life.' Mr. Edwards, a decent-looking elderly man in grey clothes and a very curly wig, accosted Johnson one day in Butcher-Row with familiar confidence. Johnson remembered him with pleasure and astonishment. However, when Edwards said, 'Ah, sir! we are old men now,' he replied hastily, 'Don't let us discourage one another.' He asked Edwards if he remembered their drinking together at an ale-house [2] near Pembroke-gate, and exchanging Latin verses over their mugs. At this point Edwards made a remark which Burke and Reynolds pronounced an exquisite *trait* of character :—'You are a philosopher, Dr. Johnson. I have tried too in my time to be a philosopher; but, I don't know how, cheerfulness was always breaking in.' Edwards wished he had continued at College, been ordained and retired, 'like Bloxham [3] and several others,' to a comfortable cure. But Johnson held that the life of a parish priest is not easy. His parishioners are a larger family than he is able to maintain. 'I would rather have chancery suits upon my hands than the cure of souls.' They clubbed Pembroke memories, and Edwards mentioned a gentleman who had left his whole fortune to the College [4]. JOHNSON : 'Whether to leave one's whole fortune to a college be right must depend upon circumstances. I would leave the interest of the fortune I bequeathed to a college to my relations or my friends for their

---

[1] Entered June 25, 1729. Johnson had not seen him since 1729. This helps to prove that Johnson was not resident after that year.

[2] There is an old inn just opposite the gateway called 'Leden Hall' and one at the end of Pembroke Street called 'The Horse and Chair.' Probably it was the former.

[3] Matthew Bloxam, matr. March, 26, 1729; from Warwickshire.

[4] The Rev. James Phipps, whose bequest fell to the College in this year.

X 2

lives. It is the same thing to a college, which is a permanent society, whether it gets the money now or twenty years hence.' On another occasion he said: 'Sir, the English Universities are not rich enough. Our fellowships are only sufficient to support a man during his studies to fit him for the world, and accordingly in general they are held no longer than till an opportunity offers of getting away. Now and then, perhaps, there is a fellow who gets old in his college; but this is against his will, unless he be a man very indolent indeed. A hundred a year is reckoned a good fellowship; and that is no more than is necessary to keep a man decently as a scholar. . . . Our Universities are impoverished of learning by the penury of their provisions.'

CHAPTER XXIII.

THE LATER STUART PERIOD.

On the death of Parker, the papalist bishop of Oxford, in 1688, 'one Hall, a Conformist in *London*, who was looked on as half a Presbyterian, yet because he read the Declaration, was made Bishop' (*Burnet*). This was TIMOTHY HALL, son of a wood-turner who owned some houses in the parish of St. Catherine by the Tower, where Timothy was born. He entered Pembroke Dec. 12, 1654, aged 17, and was 'trained up there under a Presbyterian discipline (which caused him ever after to be a Trimmer)[1].' Cheseman was his tutor. B.A. Jan. 15, 1658.

Ejected in 1662 from the parsonages of Norwood and of Southam, Hall thought it better to conform, and became rector of Horsenden, 1668, perpetual curate of Prince's Risborough, 1669–77, vicar of Bledlow, 1674–7, and rector of Allhallows Stayning, 1677. He was curate of Hackney in 1685, and lecturer there in 1688. When James II ordered, in April, 1688, the Declaration of Liberty of Conscience to be read in every church, Hall was one of the handful of London clergy who complied, 'or at least gave half a Crown to another (the Parish Clerk I think) to do it.' His nomination to the vacant see of Oxford, followed by a mandatory letter for his creation to be Doctor of Divinity, caused the deepest resentment. He was consecrated privately at Lambeth, Oct. 7, 1688. When however he arrived 'to take possession of his house at *Cudesden*, the Dean and Canons of *Ch. Ch.* refused to install him, the gentry to meet or congratulate him, the Vicech. and Heads to take notice of him, or any Master or Bachelaur to make application to, or take holy Orders from him.'. At the next Trinity Embertide there were eighty-four to be ordained. '*Timothy* Bishop of *Oxon* was then, as 'tis said, in *Oxon*, lodged at Dr. *Lashers*[2] house in *Pennyfarthing* Street, and deputed [Baptist Levintz], bishop of *Man*, to perform the ceremony in Magdalen Chapel. On Jan. 17, sixteen days before the last day of grace, Bishop Hall took the oath of allegiance to William and Mary.' 'This Mʳ. *Hall*, called by some *Doctor*, by others *Sir, Hall*, died miserably poor at [Homerton in] *Hackney* near *London*,' April 10,

---

[1] *Athenae*, ii. 685.
[2] Joshua Lasher, M.D., St. John's. Buried in St. Aldate's.

1690[1]. He was succeeded in the bishoprick by Dr. Hough. Wood mentions two printed sermons of Hall's, one at the funeral of Robert Huntingdon, the anti-Olivarian parliamentarian, in 1685. Lysons mistakenly calls Hall 'a Roman Catholic.'

ROBERT GROVE, who entered Feb. 22, 165$\frac{9}{1}$, is probably identified in the *Alumni Oxonienses* with Robert Grove, Bishop of Chichester (1634–96), who took part in drawing up the Petition of May, 1688, against James II's Declaration for Liberty of Conscience. The Bishop (who graduated from Cambridge) is better remembered as an elegant scholar. He lies in his cathedral.

WALTER HARTE, the nonjuror—father of Pope's friend, the biographer of Gustavus Adolphus, to whose pupil, Philip Stanhope, the *Chesterfield Letters* were addressed—was a Tesdale fellow of Pembroke from 1674. His father was Edward Harte, innholder of Abingdon. Walter matriculated Dec. 6, 1667, as a scholar (1667–1674), M.A. 1674, incorporated at Cambridge 1676. There is a picture of him, painted by Zelman in 1685, engraved by Hibbart in 1767, and a small head-piece in the *Amaranth.*

Harte was Vicar of St. Mary Magdalen's, Taunton, at the time of the Bloody Assize, and deemed it his duty in that capacity to wait on Judge Jefferies[2] in private and remonstrate with him on his severities against the rebels. Jefferies, who knew a man when he saw him, listened without disrespect to the courageous priest's admonitions, and, very much to his credit, when a prebendal stall at Bristol was vacant a few months after, suggested Harte's name for the preferment. He was also advanced to a canonry of Wells[3]. At the Revolution he refused to take the oaths to William and Mary, and on Feb. 1, 169$\frac{0}{1}$, was deprived of all his preferments, retiring to Chipping Norton and to Kentbury, Bucks. Here this stout old man died, Feb. 10, 173$\frac{7}{8}$, at the age of eighty-five. Queen Anne, at the instigation of Sir Simon Harcourt, of the same college, afterwards Lord Chancellor, had offered M[r]. Harte a bishoprick, but he declined it. The successive occupants, however, of the see of Bath and Wells, Drs. Kidder, Hooper and Wynne, so respected his piety and learning that they contrived he should receive the profits of his stall at Wells till his death. Walter Harte the son records that he was a most laborious student all his life.

Addison's tutor, while his father was a prebendary of Sarum, was a Rev. Mr. Naish. Mr. Macray thinks this is perhaps THOMAS NAISH,

[1] The parish register says, 'The Right Reverend Father in God Timothy late Lord Bishop of Oxford dyed the 9th and was buried the 13th of April, 1690' (*Lysons*).
[2] The College very nearly had Lord Jefferies—a better lawyer than judge—for its Visitor.
[3] Mr. Foster however (*Alumni*) dates these preferments 1684.

who entered Pembroke in 1684 (son of Thomas of New Sarum), afterwards Sub-dean of Salisbury and Master of St. John's Hospital at Wilton [1].

I may here mention, as adherents to the exiled King, FRANCIS WOLFERSTON, a lawyer, 'the stiffest of nonjurors' (entered 1657), and WILLIAM SCLATER, Vicar of Brampford Speke (entered 1659). Also NATHANIEL SACHEVERELL (1687), uncle of the famous High Church champion. Hearne notes under Aug. 31, 1711, 'Dr. (or Mr.) Kymberley, Chaplain to ye Ld Keeper, is made Prebendary of Westminster.' This was JONATHAN KIMBERLEY (1667). He had been chaplain to Charles II and canon of Lichfield. Queen Anne further gave him the Deanery of Lichfield.

The founder of Worcester College, Sir THOMAS COOKES [2], entered Pembroke June 7, 1667, aged 17. His father was Sir William, first baronet, of Northgrove Manor, Feckenham, Worcestershire.

Sir Thomas was born at Bentley Pauncefot, in the parish of Tardebigg. He was a liberal patron of Bromsgrove Grammar School, and also endowed the school at Feckenham. Here in 1699 John Baron, fellow of Balliol, preached a sermon before him in the hope of diverting a great expected bounty to that College. In his will, dated three years before, Sir Thomas gave to the Archbishop of Canterbury, the Bishops of Oxford, Lichfield, and Gloucester, the Vice-Chancellor, and all the Heads of colleges and halls in the University of Oxford, the sum of £10,000 to purchase lands, the profits of which were either to build an ornamental pile of buildings in Oxford, and endow the same with so many scholars' places and fellowships as they should think the revenue would maintain, or to endow such other College or Hall in Oxford with such and so many fellowships and scholars' places as they should think fit, preference being given to persons educated at Bromsgrove or Feckenham. He had originally intended with the £10,000 to build a workhouse in his own county. The hopes and fears of the different rivals in Oxford for Cookes's benefaction are recorded by the Rev. C. H. O. Daniel in Mr. Clark's *Colleges of Oxford*. It fell finally to the defunct Gloucester Hall, within whose buildings a new College was founded, July 29, 1714, two days before Queen Anne's death. The circumstances recall those of the foundation of Pembroke, though in the case of the latter there was unbroken continuity with the past. Sir Thomas Cookes died June 8, 1701.

---

[1] The Rev. E. H. Aston, rector of Codford St. Mary, has lent me a book of MS. sermons, in which Naish has transcribed a conversational account of the proceedings 'against Dr Huff in Magd: Colledge Hall Oxon.' This he may have got hold of through Addison. His MS. Diary was in the Phillipps Collection.

[2] Originally Cooksey; Walter de Kokesay was Sheriff of Worcestershire, 19 Edw. II. I have heard the village people speak of Squire 'Cooksey.' This old and honourable family is nearly extinct.

One of the original Fellows of Worcester was Dr. SAMUEL CRESWICKE, who entered Pembroke, Apr. 6, 1709, D.D. 1727. He was Chaplain to George II (1729), Dean of Bristol (1730), and Dean of Wells (1739). Ob. 1766.

SIMON VISCOUNT HARCOURT, Lord High Chancellor of England, belonged to an impoverished cadet branch of the great French house of Harcourt, descended from that Bernard, of the royal blood of Saxony, whom Rollo estated near Falaise. One of his grandfathers was the valiant Sir Simon Harcourt, the first to die for the King in Ireland; the other was Sir William Waller, the parliamentary general, whose daughter, Anne, was taken in marriage by Sir Philip Harcourt. The latter's elder son, Simon, born at Stanton-Harcourt, was at school with Trevor and Harley, under a clergyman named Birch, at Shilton, near Burford, whence he proceeded to Pembroke March 30, 1677, aged 15. At this College, Campbell says, he 'was strengthened in his faith in the divine right of Kings'—in spite of Bishop Hall. 'At the same time he occupied himself diligently in classical studies, and he acquired a taste for poetry and polite literature which stuck by him through life.' He resided, writes Campbell, three or four years, 'but there is no entry in the Registers of any degree.' Mr. Foster however gives it: 'B.A. Jan. 21, 1678.' So also Wood : 'B. of Arts of Pembr. Coll.' When Queen Anne visited Oxford in 1702, Harcourt, then Solicitor-General, 'for having so strenuously advocated the orthodox doctrines of the High Church, both ecclesiastical and political, now received amidst tremendous applause the honorary degree of Doctor of Laws' (not LL.D. but D.C.L., Aug. 27, 1702). He was then re-admitted of Christ Church, being described as ' nuper Coll: Pembrok : '

Entered of the Inner Temple in 1683 (bencher 1702), he had been elected Recorder of Abingdon in 1690[1], 'and had to act the Judge in the presence of the villagers among whom he gamboled as a boy' (Campbell); Member (1690–1702). In and out of Parliament by his wit, eloquence and legal ability he quickly acquired an ascendency. He delivered powerful speeches against the bill attainting Sir John Fenwick, and even refused to subscribe the Association of the Commons on the discovery of the assassination plot. Harcourt had in 1701 the conduct of the impeachment of Lord Chancellor Somers. On Anne's accession Harcourt was knighted and made Solicitor-General, being recognized as the greatest of the Tory lawyers. The bill for the Union with the Kingdom of Scotland

---

[1] But Wood speaks as though Harcourt was Recorder before this, and was ousted in 1687 by Richard Medlicot. He adds later, 'Harcourt in againe' (*Life and Times*, iii. 264).

was drawn by him, and in such a manner as to prevent parliamentary discussion of the points on which the Commissioners had agreed. In 1703 he prosecuted Defoe for a blasphemous libel, viz. *The Shortest Way with Dissenters.* While the author of *Robinson Crusoe* was in the pillory, the mob drank his health, crowned and pelted him with roses, and cursed Harcourt. Whig writers however allow him to have been untainted by corruption. He was made Attorney-General, Apr. 23, 1707, but resigned on Feb. 12 following, on the formation of a Whig ministry, 'and singular as it may be,' writes Campbell, 'by a voluntary surrender enrolled in court. This act is unprecedented.' The Queen however recalled him in 1710, and made him Lord Keeper. In that year, in spite of growing blindness (for which he was at this time couched), he was the leading counsel on the high-church side at Sacheverell's trial. He had sate for Bossiney in Cornwall 1705–8, for Abingdon again in 1708, but was unseated by a partisan vote of the Commons, a system he had himself encouraged. The Duke of Marlborough also removed him from being steward of Woodstock Manor. He was elected however for Cardigan in 1710, and again in that year for Abingdon. The Queen created him Baron Harcourt, of Stanton-Harcourt, Sept. 3, 1711. As such he negotiated the Treaty of Utrecht. In Swift's *Journal to Stella* he writes under April 7, 1713: 'My Lord Keeper Harcourt was this night made Lord Chancellor.' Noble says unaccountably that he presided in the Lords for nearly a year without a peerage. That has frequently happened, but Harcourt was already a baron. As Chancellor he refused to issue a writ of summons to the Elector of Hanover. The hopes of the Jacobites hung on Anne's life; her sudden death found them unready. The Elector, however, 'Lord Harcourt being as eminent a person as ever adorned the high station he filled, prudently made him one of the Lords Justices till his arrival in England,' Sept. 20, 1714; and, though Harcourt was then made to give up the Great Seal, he turned cat-in-pan sufficiently to be created in 1721 a Viscount and a Lord in Regency, and to have his pension doubled. His friend Swift was disgusted :—

> 'Come, trimming Harcourt, bring your mace,
> And squeeze it in or quit your place.'

In 1717 he procured Lord Oxford's acquittal.

Campbell thinks that Harcourt preserved his consistency, and Noble says that 'he preserved his reputation unsullied till his death.' This occurred July 27, 1727, in Cavendish Square. He had been struck with paralysis while visiting Walpole, with whom he was now intimate. He is buried at Stanton-Harcourt, which his family have owned since the seventeenth century. He acquired the Nunenham-Courtenay estate in 1710.

At Cokethorpe, near Stanton-Harcourt, the Queen paid him a State visit. He had given up his own house to Pope. Harcourt and Gay were Pope's only visitors there, and there they witnessed together the tragical fate of John Hewet and Sarah Drewe. On a pane of glass in Pope's Study is inscribed :—'In the year 1718 Alexander Pope finished here the fifth volume of Homer.'

Harcourt wrote a poetical address to Pope, prefixed to the latter's works. He also erected a cenotaph in Westminster Abbey, with an inscription by Atterbury, to the poet John Philipps. Swift called him 'a great man,' before he joined the Trimmers. In truth Harcourt was the most powerful and skilful orator of his day, but not a great judge. There are two portraits of him at Nunenham by Kneller, one in the hall of the Inner Temple, a fine picture at Abingdon, and one hangs in Pembroke College Hall. These give the impression of an amiable and polished as well as noble-looking man. Lord Harcourt was thrice married, once clandestinely to the daughter of his father's chaplain. The title became extinct in 1830.

THOMAS SOWTHERNE, who entered Pembroke as a servitor Nov. 28, 1679, from Stratford-on-Avon (B.A. 1683), is identified in the *Alumni* with the Royalist soldier-poet whose plays, in the golden pre-Grub-street times, drew down Fortune's affluent horn into his lap. This identification is as old as the dramatist's own lifetime, for he wrote to Dr. R. Rawlinson to say that he never was at Oxford. Gildon also affirms that he was sent from Stratford to 'Pembroke Hall, Oxford,' but it seems beyond doubt that the author of the *Spartan Dame* was born in 1660 at Dublin, and there educated. The two Thomas Sowthernes were thus almost exactly contemporary.

The most notable Pembroke writer of the end of the seventeenth century was ARTHUR COLLIER, the metaphysician, who anticipated Berkeley's Idealism. He succeeded his father, grandfather, and great-grandfather in the Rectory of Steeple Langford, near Wilton, where he was born. Sir Richard Hoare says [1] :—

'On the South side of the altar is a curious monumental effigy of a priest with a book in his hand and the following inscription :

'The effigies of the Rev. M^r. JOSEPH COLLIER, who was instituted Rector of this parish in ye beginning of the last century, *viz.* An'o D'ni 1608, and was burried in 1635.

'He was succeeded by his sone Henry, who, in the time of the rebellion, was sequestered from the parsonage 15 years, and retook possession on ye 18th of Sept. 1660, and dyed in March 1670. Arthur, his youngest son, succeeded him, and dyed in Sept. 1696. He was succeeded by Arthur, his eldest son, and the fourth of this family who was Rector of this parish.

'Margaret, relict of ye last-named Arthur Collier, ordered this inscription to be placed here, and also that over the grave-stone of the said Arthur, on the first of July, 1734, in testimony of her affectionate regard.'

On the south chancel wall is a marble tablet inscribed :—

'In memory of the Rev. M^r. ARTHUR COLLIER, Rector of this parish, who was Born Oct. 18, 1680. He married Margaret, daughter of Nicholas

---

[1] *History of Wiltshire*, Hundred of Branch and Dole, pp. 12-14.

Johnson, Esqre., by whom he left Issue two sons, Arthur and Charles, and two Daughters, Jane and Margaret. He was buried 9 Sept. 1732.'

The shield on it exhibits—Quarterly, 1st and 4th, a cross patty fitchy, for Collier ; 2nd and 3rd, a chevron between two cinque-foils in chief and a flower de luce in base ; impaling five fusils conjoined in fess between three wolves' heads erased. No tinctures are shown. In the floor close by is a plain stone, dated July 1, 1734, where husband and wife lie.

Giles Collier, clothier of Bristol, was patron when Joseph Collier was presented to Langford. The latter's three-quarter effigy, in Hoare's book, occupies a marble triptych covered with skulls, skeletons, and odd bones. There now only remains (on the north side of the altar) the effigy in a mean modern niche. His grandson, ARTHUR COLLIER, father of the philosopher, had been one of eleven children turned out of the parsonage with their mother into the deep snow, after Henry Collier's flight from parliamentarian violence. The parents, reduced to beggary, brought up the children to mean trades, except Arthur, the youngest, who was sent by friends to wear the gown at Winchester and afterwards at Pembroke. He married Anne daughter of Thomas and Joan Currey of Misterton, and died, according to a separate inscription in Langford Church, Dec. 9, 1697. The date of his eminent son's birth is given in the register as Oct. 12, not 18:—'Arthur ye Son of Arthur and Anne Collier was borne October 12, q^r. before five of the clock in Morning, and Baptiz'd Novemb. 4: 1680.'

His uncles Henry and Joseph were transported to Jamaica, and sold as slaves, for their share in Penruddocke's rising against the Cromwellian Government. He himself entered Pembroke July 1697, migrating to Balliol Oct. 22, 1698, and later to Wadham. He did not therefore at once succeed his father at Steeple Langford, as the monument seems to suggest, two other rectors intervening. He was instituted in 1704. The year before, at the age of twenty-three, Collier had completed his ' *Clavis Universalis*, or a New Inquiry after Truth, being a Demonstration of the non-existence or Impossibility of an external World,' but it was not published till 1713. Meanwhile, in 1709, Berkeley's *Theory of Vision* appeared. The Bishop's work is far superior in literary grace, and the *Clavis* was not improved in respect of style by translation into German by Eschenbach in 1756. It did not win its author immediate fame. He corresponded, however, on philosophical subjects with Warburton, Hare, Whiston, and Courayer. In the *Dictionary of National Biography* Collier is described as ' an original and ingenious disputant, sympathizing with the high-church party in which he had been educated, but led by his peculiar turn of mind across the limits of orthodoxy,' inclining to Apollinarian views. In 1719 he wrote letters to the Jacobite *Mist's Journal*, assailing Hoadley's affirmation of the innocence of 'sincere' errors. 'His theological writings are a curious parallel to Berkeley's *Siris*, showing the same tendency to a mystical application of his metaphysics but working out his theories in a more technical and scholastic fashion.' His papers were discovered in this century in a house at Salisbury, and Benson's *Memoir* is based on them. The MS. Commentary on the LXX, however, had been burnt by a housemaid. Collier was always in debt, and had domestic troubles. His brother William, Rector of Baverstock, Wilts, 1713, had shared his tastes, combining horse-racing, however, with metaphysics. Norris the Platonist was a near neighbour at Bemerton Rectory. Collier's daughter, Margaret, accompanied Fielding on his voyage to Lisbon.

The following letter from a father [1] to his son, a fellow-commoner of the College, *temp.* James II, gives a picture of another class of undergraduate. The writer, JOHN COLLINS, of Betterton, Berks, (matriculated March 18, 165⅞; B.A. 1661), was grandson of Elizabeth Dewe, granddaughter of Tesdale's uncle and guardian, Richard.

'Charles—I am sorry to hear you should have soe little discretion to run yourself into such danger as to goe to Abingdon & especially at such a time. I shall say nothing of your behaviour there but advise you to leave off such frolicks : you wrote to me y^t it would be unhandsome for one of your quality not to have money in y^r pockett, I should account myself indiscreet to enter you a gentleman & not to maintain you there accordingly, but let me advise you in this according to the proverb to cut your coat according to y^r cloth, t'is true you are placed in the same rank with gent: but you might know y^t there is a great difference in the estates of Gent: there be some tis probable that you may be in company with that have ten times more estate than I have or ever you will have, & therefore must not think to spend with them & truly I must stretch hard to maintain you in this quality & therefore be as frugall & discreet as you can, & come as seldom amongst them as you can possibly come off with creditt, & by God's blessing you shall not want to maintain you in your equipage with good husbandry & following your study will prevent the spending of money besides the advantage y^t will accrue to you during y^r life, I received a letter from a Gent last week which was of y^r quality & newly come from Oxon in which was scarce a word of ortography but I hope better things of you I have here enclosed sent you my coat of arms wch you may place up in your study & because you may be able to blazon it which many cannott, which seems ridiculous, & because I suppose you have but little skill in it I will do it wch is Vert a Gryphon passant or a chief Ermin. The crest is a Gryphon head erased vert crowned or & because there is to many arms there is a misticall meaning I will likewise declare it to you once for all & I desire you not to forget it. The field vert signifies husbandry the Gryphon in Authors is an emblem of watchfulness, his being passant signifys diligence & industry, the colour or denotes riches the chief ermine sygnifys honour in chief—which put together resolves into this that by diligence & industry in our calling we attain to riches the foundation & way to honour where note the Gryphon is not rampant, as

---

[1] A copy of this letter is lent me, together with the Accompts of a later descendant (*vide infra*), by Sir Robert H. Collins, K.C.B., Comptroller of H.R.H. the Duchess of Albany's Household, who married Miss Mary Wightwick, of the other Founder's kindred.

whereby a man should attain to riches & honour by rapacity and ambition but by honesty & humility all which is aptly expressed in this motto " Per callem collem " such motto belonging to arms not only expressing the mystery of them but alluding to the names of the person who bears them soe one Dr Collins a famous Cambridge man took for his motto " colens Deum et regem " now look into your Roman history & there you shall find a great & noble family of the Collini which took their name a portâ Collinâ & the gate so called which led in collem, soe that as I said before this motto *per callem collem* takes in the mystery of the coat as much as to say *per virtutis callem honoris collem ascendimus*[1] which that you may attain to live virtuously att the beginning y[t] you may gain reputation hereafter or rather that you may pray to God to give you sanctified virtues here which is grace y[t] you may attain everlasting glory is not only the advice but the prayer of

y[r] loving father Jo: Collins

May 7, 1682 (?) Imprimis venerare Deum.'

Among lawyers educated at Pembroke about this time were RICHARD BRYDGES (1693), treasurer of Lincoln's Inn 1740; JOHN MARSH (1700), treasurer of the Middle Temple 1747 ; and POLLEXFEN DRAKE (1711, son of Sir Francis Drake, M.P.), commissioner of appeals in Excise.

Some members of Parliament were Sir JAMES HOUBLON (City of London 1698); JOHN HANBURY (Gloucester 1701, Monmouthshire 1720); WHARTON DUNCH (Appleby 1700, Richmond 1705); Sir RICHARD NEWMAN, Bart. (Milborne Port 1700); his grandfather, RICHARD NEWMAN (entered 1635), High Steward of Westminster, was imprisoned by Cromwell; SAMUEL LOWE (? Aldeburgh 1718); JOHN NEALE (Wycombe 1722, Coventry 1722, 1727, 1737); EMANUEL PIGOT (Cork City 1735–60).

Bishop Hall was succeeded in the Mastership by COLWELL BRICKENDEN or Brickenton, elected Scholar (kin to Tesdale) Aug. 9, 1680, aged 16, matriculated Dec. 10, B.A. 1685, M.A. 1687, B.D. and D.D. June 28, 1710, Rector of Chawton, Hants, 1690, and of Inkepen,

---

[1] The writer, who married Anne Fettiplace of Earl's Court, was entitled to impale the arms of Portugal. Beatrice, daughter of King John the Great (d. 1432), after being wedded to Fitzalan Earl of Arundel and Gilbert Lord Talbot, had to her husband Sir Thomas Fettyplace (Sheriff of Berks and Oxon), of Childrey, an estate in the possession of his descendants now or till lately. The name became extinct in 1806. The son to whom John Collins writes entered Pembroke April 18, 1684, aged eighteen. He was admitted of the Inner Temple 1685 ; J.P. for Berks. His younger brothers, JONATHAN and THOMAS, were Fellows of the College. He was thrice married : (1) to Anne Head of Odcott; (2) to Elizabeth Coghill of Bletchington ; (3) to Anne White of Fryer's Court, co. Berks.

Berks, 1703.   His father was Richard[1] Brickenden, of Inkepen, Esquire.

Hearne (*Collections*, ed. Doble, O.H.S., ii. 344 sq.) records : 'Feb. 15 (Wed.), 17$\frac{0}{1}\frac{7}{8}$.   On Monday Morning last the Corps of the B^p of Bristoll (after it had layn in state several days) was convey'd from his Lodgings at Pembroke Coll. (where he died) to Bromesgrave in Worcestershire, in order to be buried in the Church there, at which Place he was born.   This Morning at eight of the Clock came on the Election for a Master of Pembroke College.   The two Candidates were Mr. Colwell Brickenden and Mr. Will. Hunt, both of them formerly Fellows, but at present Country Divines.   The former took the Degree of Master of Arts in 1687, and the latter in 1696.   Both of them have the Reputation of being honest Men, and endued with true Church of England Principles ; but then there is this Difference between them : Mr. Brickenden has seven Children, Mr. Hunt not above two or three ; Mr. Brickenden is an illiterate Person, Mr. Hunt is a man of Learning ; Mr. Brickenden is a boon Companion, or, as some style it, a Sot, Mr. Hunt is a Man of Sobriety & Discretion, and came recommended by the Letters of the B^p of Bathe and Wells, and divers Men of Figure, Learning, Temperance and Virtue.   In reference to this Election I must here note that Mr. Hunt had infallibly carried it had it not been for the Defection of one Mr. Mouldin, who has had hitherto the Character of a man of Honesty.   This Mr. Mouldin had several times solemnly promis'd to serve Mr. Hunt when

---

[1] But in the *Alumni* 'Colwell.'   I make it out thus :—

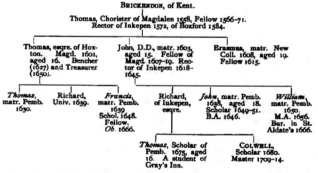

BRICKENDON, of Kent.

Thomas, Chorister of Magdalen 1558, Fellow 1566-71. Rector of Inkepen 1572, of Boxford 1584.

Thomas, esqre. of Hoxton.   Magd. 1601, aged 16.   Bencher (1627) and Treasurer (1650).

John, D.D., matr. 1603, aged 15.   Fellow of Magd. 1607-19.   Rector of Inkepen 1618-1645.

Erasmus, matr. New Coll. 1608, aged 19. Fellow 1615.

Thomas, matr. Pemb. 1630.

Richard, Univ. 1639.

Francis, matr. Pemb. 1639 Schol. 1648. Fellow. *Ob*. 1666.

Richard, of Inkepen, esqre.

John, matr. Pemb. 1638, aged 18. Scholar 1649-51. B.A. 1646.

William, matr. Pemb. 1650. M.A. 1656. Bar. in St. Aldate's 1666.

Thomas, Scholar of Pemb. 1675, aged 16.   A student of Gray's Inn.

COLWELL, Scholar 1680. Master 1709-14.

Thomas, son of Edmund, Brickenden, Fellow of New College (expelled 1648) and Canon of Wells (1674-1700), was also from Berks.

a Vacancy of the Headship of Pembroke Coll. should happen, and 'twas upon this Consideration that the Master of Balliol College (of wch Coll. Mr. Hunt has an ingenious Brother Fellow) made a First Kinsman of his Cook of that College, telling Mr. Mouldin expressly at the same time that 'twas with Intent and expectation that he should appear for Mr. Hunt if he thought fit to stand for Master of Pembroke Coll. Mr. Mouldin gratefully acknowledg'd his Favour, and promis'd upon the Word of an honest Man that he would oblige the Master in his Request to the utmost of his Power, and that Nothing should draw him from giving his Vote for Mr. Hunt. But when the time of Tryal came, whether upon Prospect of the Rectory of St. Aldates in Oxoñ (wch belongs to Pembroke Coll. & wch Dr. Hall enjoy'd for several Years) or for sake of a Wife, or whether it was upon any other secular Interest, 'tis certain that a little before the Election he went over to Mr. Brickenden's party, and there being 13 Electors in all, 7 voted for Mr. Brickenden and 6 for Mr. Hunt [1], who would have had 7 had not Mr. Mouldin most shamefully and scandalously broke his word, and deserted his Friends when 'twas expected he should have done a kindness and have shew'd himself to have a sense of graditude.'

Brickenden's reign is notable for the annexation of a Gloucester canonry to the Mastership by Queen Anne, through the good offices of Lord Chancellor Harcourt. Dr. Brickenden did not live to enjoy the dignity, dying August 23, 1714.

NOTE.

Anno 12 Annae Stat. 2, Cap. 6 (June 8, 1714).

'AND whereas her Majesty has been graciously pleased, by her letters patents under the great seal of *Great Britain*, bearing date at *Westminster* the eleventh day of *November* in the twelfth year of her reign, to incorporate *Collwell Brickenden*, doctor in divinity, the Master of *Pembroke* College in the university of *Oxford* and his successors, masters of the same college, by the name stile and title of master of *Pembroke* College in the university of *Oxford*; and did thereby grant to the said master and his successors, masters of the same college, for their better support and

---

[1] Dr. WILLIAM HUNT, elected Tesdale Scholar Aug. 3, 1685; M.A. 1696; B.D. and D.D. 1718; rector of Chaffcombe 1699; vicar of Chewton Mendip 1706; canon of Wells 1710; archdeacon of Bath 1711; rector of Bath, SS. Peter and Paul, 1712, and of Christian Malford, Wilts, 1730-3. His father was Stephen Hunt of Kingsclere, Hants. Dr. JOHN MOULDEN, an Abingdonian, entered Nov. 12, 1692; B.D. and D.D. 1720; rector of St. Aldate's 1709, and there buried May 28, 1724. He was killed by a fall from his horse.

maintenance, that canonship or prebend in the cathedral church of the holy and undivided *Trinity* of *Gloucester*, which should first happen to be void, and in the gift of her Majesty her heirs and successors from and after the date of the said grant; to have and to hold the said canonship or prebend, to the said *Colwell Brickenden*, master of the said college and his successors, masters of the same college, of her Majesty, her heirs and successors, in pure and perpetual alms, for and during his and their respective continuance in the said mastership; and did thereby likewise unite such canonship or prebend, as aforesaid, to the said corporation for ever [here follows the recital of a similar grant of a Rochester prebend to the provosts of Oriel and a Norwich canonry to the masters of Catherine Hall in Cambridge], Be it therefore enacted by the Queen's most excellent majesty etc., That the said several and respective recited letters patents and all and singular the clauses articles and things therein respectively contained shall be and are hereby ratified and confirmed, and the said several and respective canonships or prebends shall be, from time to time, for ever, held and enjoyed, according to the true intent and meaning of the several and respective letters patents aforesaid.'

CHAPTER XXIV.

GEORGE THE FIRST'S REIGN—JOURNAL OF A GENTLEMAN-COMMONER.

DR. MATTHEW PANTING, the next Master, was elected Sept. 3, 1714. A fortnight earlier he was instituted to the Rectory of St. Ebbe's. He matriculated Nov. 5, 1698, aged 15 (son of Matthew, of Oxford); B.A. 1702; M.A. and Fellow 1705; B.D. and D.D. 1715; Rector of Coln Rogers 1718; died Feb. 12, 173⅞, and was buried in St. Aldate's, where there was formerly an inscription to his memory 'on a pillar facing the lower south door.' Johnson admired him as 'a fine Jacobite fellow.' Panting gave Whitefield the servitor's place which brought him to the College, and though he spoke sternly to him he does not appear to have gone beyond his duty. Hearne styles him 'an honest gent,' and says: 'He had to preach the sermon at S. Mary's on the day on which George Duke and Elector of Brunswick usurped the English throne; but his sermon took no notice, at most very little, of the Duke of Brunswick[1].' This was a few weeks before his election as Master.

Dr. Panting's mastership is notable for the building of the Chapel. His son, Matthew, was Fellow of All Souls. In one of the buttery books is scrawled by the Bible Clerk 'Pretty Miss Pant.' The St. Aldate's registers contain the names of several of his children.

The first *alumnus* of note at the beginning of the Hanoverian period was PHILIP MORANT (1700–1770). This learned antiquary, the second son of Stephen Morant[2] by his wife Mary Filleul, was born at St. Saviour's, Jersey, Oct. 6, 1770.

---

[1] The Terrae Filius of 1721 complains that 'if you were to turn out one Jacobite H—d of a college, another as bad is ready to step in his room.' In 1733, after the rejection of the Excise Bill, town and gown drank the healths of James the Third, Ormonde, and Bolingbroke, round bonfires amid boisterous revelry. Charles Wesley writes in 1734, 'My brother [John] has been much mauled and threatened more for his Jacobite sermon on the 16th of June.' The Government showed considerable forbearance. Still, as the high churchmen had no deaneries or sees to look forward to, it was fair they should have their fling.

[2] The Morant arms (*temp.* Edw. III) are in the east window of Warehorne Church, Kent, viz. gules, on a chevron, arg., three talbots passant sable.

Philip passed from the tuition of the Rev. Thomas Woods at Abingdon School—where is preserved a copy of the *De Oratore,* given to the Library by 'Mr. Mourant, a former scholar'—to Pembroke, Dec. 17, 1717. B.A. June 10, 1721. He resided at the College till his ordination, Sept. 23, 1722.

Bishop Gibson nominated him to the preachership of the Anglican church at Amsterdam, but he did not go there. Instead he was licensed as curate of Great Waltham, Essex, where he remained from 1722 (1724, *Dict. Nat. Biog.*) till 1732, helping the Vicar, Nicholas Tindal, in preparing a new edition of Rapin's *History of England.* Morant greatly impressed Bishop Gibson by his argumentative power and antiquarian learning, and on his recommendation the Regent, Queen Caroline, made him, Aug. 16, 1732, chaplain at Amsterdam. He retained this post till Michaelmas 1734. On April 20, 1733, he was preferred to the rectory of Shellow Bowells, and held it till Nov., 1734. From Jan. 17, 1734, to April, 1738, he was Rector of Broomfield; from Sept. 19, 1735, to 1743, Rector of Chignal Smealey; from March 9, 1738, to 1770, Rector of St. Mary's, Colchester; from Jan. 21, 1743, to Oct. 1745, Rector of Wickham Bishop's; from Sept. 14, 1745, to 1770, Rector of Aldham—all these places are in Essex. He thus was always a dualist, though not a pluralist. The wide knowledge of Essex thus acquired fitted him to be the historian of that county. Morant's great work, the *History and Antiquities of the County of Essex* (2 vols. folio, 1760-8), incorporates his *History of Colchester.* On Nov. 20, 1755, he was elected F.S.A., and on the recommendation of Thomas Astle, Keeper of the Tower Records, husband of Morant's only daughter, he was intrusted by the House of Lords with the preparation for the press of the ancient records of Parliament. He had great skill in palæography, and, as a native of Jersey, he possessed an unusual familiarity with the old Norman-French. The *Rotuli Parliamentorum* between 1278 and 1413 were edited by him. A chill caught in being rowed towards Lambeth, where he lived in order to be near his labours, ended his life, Nov. 25, 1770. He was taken to Aldham to be laid beside his wife (Anne, daughter and heiress of Solomon Stebbing of Great Tey) in the chancel of the now ruined church of Aldham. The slab is still visible. A marble tablet, bearing an inscription written by Astle, was removed to the new church in 1854 :—

PHILIPPO MORANT, A.M. hujus Ecclesiae Rectori: Vir fuit Eximia simplicitate et moribus plane antiquis, bonorum studiosus, omnibus benevolens, eruditione denique multiplici repletus. Gentium origines agrorum limites in hac provincia feliciter investigavit; ad vitas Britannorum insignium illustrandas quam plurimum contulit. His studiis a prima juventute usque ad mortem totum se dedit, nec ostentandi gratia sed quod reipublicae prodesset. Obiit Nov^bris 25° A.D. 1770. Aet. 70. Et ANNAE uxori ejus matronarum decori ex antiquis familiis Stebbing et Creffield oriundae: Obiit Julii 20° A.D. 1767. Aet. 69. Optimis parentibus Tho: et A: Maria Astle posuerunt.

Until 1734 he spelled his name Mourant, and was so matriculated, but afterwards reverted to the earlier and more correct form. Morant published a number of historical and theological writings. The articles in *Biographia Britannica* signed 'C.' (Colchester) are by him, and also the *Life of Stillingfleet.* A number of his letters and collections are in the British Museum among the Stowe MSS. The Marquess of Buckingham acquired the MSS. under Astle's will. Other Morant papers and sermons are at Colchester. Mr. C. F. D. Sperling has written an account of Morant and his works in the *Essex Review* for January 1894. The portrait prefixed is most characteristic of 'mores plane antiqui'—a keen-looking portly man in a wig, with a very large aquiline nose.

Bishop ROBERT DOWNES, who entered July 15, 1721 (B.A. from Merton 1724; D.D. at Trinity, Dublin, 1740), the son of Bishop Henry Downes, became Bishop of Ferns 1744, of Down 1752, and of Raphoe 1753 till his death, June 30, 1763.

JOURNAL OF A GENTLEMAN-COMMONER.

The following excerpts from some portions[1] of the Diary of Mr. (afterwards Sir) ERASMUS PHILIPPS, son of Sir John Philipps, fourth baronet, of Picton Castle, and other seats in Wales, give a not unpleasing picture of a young man of quality of this date:—

1720, Aug^st 1. Went from London wth my Father and Bro. John[2] in Haynes' Grand Alrighman Coach for Oxford, where my brother and self were, the next day, Aug. 2, admitted Fellow Commoners of Pembroke College by Mathew Panting, D.D., the Master of It, and took an oath to obey the Master and observe the statutes of the College, etc. Paid Mr. Hopkins, the College Butler, 1*l.* 2*s.* 6*d.* Entrance money. Din'd the same day wth the Rev^d. M^r. Sam. Horne (Master of Arts, one of the Fellows and Junior Dean of the College) whose pupil I was. Next day din'd wth the Master and his Lady at the Lodgings.

Aug^st 4. . . . Paid the Rev^d. M^r. W^m. Jordan (one of the Fellows of Pembroke and one of the Bursars and Chaplain to ditto[3]) and the Rev^d. M^r. W^m. Blandy[4] (another Fellow and the other Bursar) 10*l.* for my Caution, to remain in their hands till I leave College: paid 'em also 10*s.* for a key of the College Garden.

Sep^t 20. Rode to Portmead (1 mile from Oxford) where M^r. Stapleton's horse run against M^r. Jerningham's and won the 40*l.* plate.

[1] *Notes and Queries*, Second Series, Nov. 10, 1860: 'College Life at Oxford One Hundred and Thirty Years Ago.'
[2] Afterwards Sir John, the benefactor mentioned on page 301.
[3] Afterwards Johnson's tutor.
[4] Compiled *Chronological Tables.*

Sep: 21ˢᵗ. The Galloway Plate, value 15*l.*, was run for by one horse; after which several horses ran for a Hanger, which showed good diversion. At night went to Assembly at the Angel, where the affair was a Flat Crown.

22ⁿᵈ. Walked to Portmead, where Mʳ. Freeman's Horse run against Mʳ. Jerningham's and Mʳ. Garret's Mare, and won the 20*l.* Plate. After this was a Foot race between several Taylors for geese, etc. At night went to the Ball at the Angel. A Guinea Touch.

23ʳᵈ. Several horses run for a Leash of does given by Montague Venables Bertie, Earl of Abingdon. [He gives a list of the company present.]

24. I was made free of the Bodleian Library, and took the usual Oath not to Embezzle the Books, etc.

25. Made a present to the Bodleian Library of a Grammatica Damulica (a Malabar Grammar), a very great Curiosity. . .

ditto. Presented Pembroke College Library wᵗʰ Mʳ. Prior's Works[1] in Folio, neatly bound, wᶜʰ cost me 1*l.* 3*s.* Revᵈ. Mʳ. Thomas Tristram, M.A. and Fellow and Librarian of the College, entered me on this occasion a Benefactor to its Library.

Sept. . . Din'd with Dʳ. Hugh Boulter, the Dean of Christ Church and Bishop of Bristol at his lodgings in College.

Sept. . . In this month I was twice Senior of Pembroke College Hall[2].

Oct. 30. My Father and Bro. Buckley[3], with Cosin Rowland Phillips of Orlandon[4], and Mʳ. Bernewitz came to Oxford from Picton Castle, and next day went for London.

Xmᵉʳ 20. I set out from Oxford for London.

172⅘ Janʸ 5. My sister Katharine died at Picton Castle in the 23ᵈ year of her Age, and was in a few days after Interred in Prendergast Church; the Revᵈ. Mʳ. Jno. Pember, Rector of the Parish, preaching her Funeral Sermon. . . . A neat marble Stone is erected for her,

---

[1] Prior says: 'And Cowley's verse keeps fair Orinda young.' 'Orinda' had married into the Philipps family. On the flyleaf of the Poems the gift is dated 'Decʳⁱˢ. die 7ᵐᵒ. 1721.'

[2] 'Custom for him that comes first into the Hall any day at Dinner or Supper-time, whether Graduate or Undergraduate, to sit Senior all the Time and exercise his Authority in giving others Leave to go down, if desir'd, etc. The same Custom is observ'd in University and Wadham Colleges.' (Pointer.)

[3] Bulkeley Philipps of Abercover. From him descended the Lord Milford of the second creation and the baronet of the second creation, to whom, successively, Richard Lord Milford bequeathed the large Pembrokeshire estates. The will was disputed recently by the present baronet of the first creation.

[4] A third cousin (ob. 1768). From his uncle descends the present head of the family, the Rev. Canon Sir James Erasmus Philipps, twelfth baronet, to whom I am indebted for access to family records.

whereon is some Account of the Deceased. This Funeral was extreamly handsome (the Expense of it amounting to about 600*l.*), and was attended by the Chief Gentry of the Countrey. . . . I was inform'd from a good hand, that upon this Occasion there was a Struggle between Orielton and Colby Coaches about Precedency.

Feb. 27. Died, Cosin Kitty Walpole [1] at the Bath. She was daughter to the R[t] Hon[ble] Robert Walpole, Esq[re].

1721, March 28. Went a Foxhunting with Geo. Henry Lee, Earl of Litchfield, John Leveson Gower, Lord Gower, Marq[s] of Carnarvon, S[r] W[m] Wyndham, Bart., M[r]. Villiers (Brother to Villiers, Earl of Jersey), etc. Din'd at Woodstock.

April 14. Rode with M[r]. Wilder [2] (Fellow and Vicegerent of Pembroke) and M[r] Le Merchant to Newnam, where dined upon Fish at the pleasant place mentioned page 107 [of this diary]. Coming home, a dispute arose between these two Gentlemen, whom with great difficulty I kept from Blows.

July 4. Went up the river a fishing with M[r]. Wilder, M[r]. Eaton, M[r]. Clerk, M[r]. Clayton (Gent. Commoner), M[r]. Sylvester [3], and M[r]. Bois, all Pembrokians, as far as Burnt Isle, whereon we landed, and dressed a leg of Mutton, which afterwards we dispatched in the wherry. The passage to this diminutive Island is wonderfully sweet and pleasant.

13. Went to the Tuns with Tho. Beale, Esq[r] (Gent. Com̃oner), M[r]. Hume, and M[r]. Sylvester, Pembrokians, where Motto'd, Epigrammatiz'd, etc.[4]

[1] Beautiful Katherine Shorter, the unhappy first wife of Sir Robert Walpole, was her mother. Sir John Shorter, Lord Mayor, married Elizabeth Philippa.

[2] Of Tesdale descent. Rector of St. Aldate's and of St. John Baptist's. Ob. 1743.

[3] Tipping Silvester preached a 29th of May sermon before the Corporation of London, 1732 (British Museum *Tracts*).

[4] 'I rise about nine, get to breakfast by ten,
Blow a tune on my flute or perhaps make a pen,
Read a play till eleven or cock my lac'd hat,
Then step to my neighbour's till dinner to chat.

. . . .

From the coffee house then I to tennis away,
And at five I post back to my College to pray.
I sup before eight, and secure from all duns
Undauntedly march to the *Mitre* or *Tuns*;
When in punch or good claret my sorrows I drown,
And toss off a bowl "To the best in the town."
At one in the morning I call what 's to pay,
Then home to my college I stagger away,
Thus I tope all the night as I trifle all day.'

('The Lounger,' *Oxford Sausage*).

There is a burlesque account of the proceedings of the Poetical Club, which met

19. Sent M^r W^m. Wightwick, Demy of Magdalene College, a Copy of Verses on his leaving Pembroke[1].

I laid 20 Guineas to one with M^r. Clerk that I was not married in 3 years; laid the same Bett again with M^r. Beale.

July ... M^r. Solomon Negri (a Native of Damascus) a great Critic in the Arabick Language[2] and perfect Master of the French and Italian Tongues, came to Oxford, to consult and transcribe some Arabick Manuscripts in the Bodleian Library; fell acquainted with this Gent. and with M^r. Hill, an ingenious Friend of his that came down with him; and enjoy'd abundance of Satisfaction in their Conversation.

Aug^st 7. I was Enter'd a Student of Lincoln's Inn.

Dit. Went with Mr Blandy to Abingdon to an Election of a Scholar from the Free School there to Pembroke College; on this occasion there were a good many Oxonians, who were entertain'd with Several Copies of Verses and Declamations. The Election fell upon Mr Bacon, a very Ingenious Youth, son to the Revd Mr Bacon of Reading. Din'd with Mr Philipson the Mayor.

17. Began to learn on the Violin of Mr Wheeler, to whom paid 10s. Entrance.

Dit. Went with Mr Tristram to the Poetical Club (whereof he is a Member) at the Tuns (kept by Mr Broadgate), where met Dr Evans, Fellow of St. John's and Mr J^no Jones, Fellow of Baliol, Members of the Club. Subscribed 5s. to Dr Evans's *Hymen and Juno* (which one merrily call'd Evans's Bubble, it being now South Sea Time). Drank Gallicia Wine, and was entertained with two Fables of the Doctor's Composition, which were indeed Masterly in their kind: But the D^r is allowed to have a peculiar knack, and to excell all Mankind at a Fable.

31. At Mr Tristram's Chambers wth Mr Wanley, the famous Antiquarian, Keeper of the Harleian Library, Mr Bowles, Keeper of the Bodleian Library, and Mr Hunt of Hart Hall, who is Skill'd in Arabick.

Sept. My Father, Brother Buckley, and Mr Bernewitz came from London to Oxford, and lodg'd at Mr Best's near our College.

7. Rid out wth my Father, Mr Jorden, and Bro. John to Shotover

at the Three Tuns, in Amhurst's *Terrae Filius*, No. XXVI. This tavern was opposite All Souls. There is a Three Tuns hostelry in St. Ebbe's Street under the western wall of Pembroke.

[1] Of Ashford. Fellow of Magdalen 1727–44; Proctor 1735.

[2] Gibbon writes: 'Since the days of Pocock and Hyde Oriental learning has always been the pride of Oxford, and I once expressed an inclination to study Arabic.'

Hill, whence had a good view of Co[l] Tyrrell's beautiful Seat. Din'd at Wheatley. Coming back saw Cudsdon, the Bishop of Oxford's Palace, an old House, and D[r] Panting's House [1], both pleasantly seated.

. . Show'd my Father the Colleges and Curiosities of the University.

19. Went with my Father to Newnam by Water, leaving Eafly, Kennington, Littlemore, & Sandford on the Right and Left. This is a most agreeable Passage.

Oct. 9. I was Unanimously Elected a Common Council Man of the Town and County of Haverfordwest.

Nov. 1. A Great Gaudy this day in Pembroke College, when the Master dined in Publick, and M[r] Beale, M[r] Clayton, &c. went round the Fire in the Hall (an ancient Custom the Juniors are obliged to comply with). Lord Ossulstown's Picture was Hung up this day in the Hall. This Lord was a considerable Benefactor to the College, whereof he was a Member.

5. M[r] Francis Peyne, Batch. of Arts, made an Oration in Pembroke Hall Suitable to the Day.

17. Brought an Essay on Pride to D[r]. Panting, who then desired me to declaim Publickly in the Hall on the following Thesis, 'Virtutem amplectimur Ipsam praemia si tollas.'

Xm[br] 18. Set out for London in Bartlett's Stage, paying Passage 10s, & arrived next day.

172½, Feb. 13. Went to the Great Cockmatch in Holy well, fought between Other Windsor Hickman, Earl of Plymouth, & the Town Cocks, which beat his Lordship.

March 7. Baron Price and Justice Dormer at Oxford attended y[e] Nisi Prius, where were only Six Causes. The Usual Counsel, M[r] Holmes the Junior Proctor, and M[r] Hector the Junior Collector, made their Speeches in the Theatre. The Proctor's was a delicate and masterly Peice of Oratory, as indeed was likewise the Speech of M[r] Slocock [2], Junior Proctor, an. 1720, which I forgot to mention. M[r] Henry Church (the Junior Collector, a Pembrokian) came off very handsomely.

1722, March 25. A Gaudy in Pembroke College.

Dit. Hon[ble] M[r] Edward Nevil (Brother to George Nevil Lord Abergavenny) Nobleman of Wadham, gave me D[r] Barn's *Anacreon.*

April 4. Went a Circuiting wth M[r] Collins of our College. This is an Exercise previous to a Master's Degree.

---

[1] Had the Master, then, besides his College and Canonical houses, a country residence?

[2] Dr. Benjamin Slocock, mat. at Pembroke 1708. *Vide supra*, p. 300.

6. Mr Dolben, Mr Colchester, Mr Walker, and Mr Hervey, Gentlemen Commoners of Baliol, Mr St John & Mr Smith, Gent. Coṁoners
of Oriel, wth Mr Unit of Worcester, and my Self, made a Private Ball
at Mr Conyer's for Miss Brigandine (my Partner)¹, Miss Hume, Miss
Brooks's, &c.

May 16. Rode out wth Mr Clayton to Basisley, Mr Lenton's Seat².
Near here met Mr Clayton's three Sisters (all fine bred women; the
youngest, Miss Charlotte, is a beautiful Creature, and has a deal of
L'Esprit), Miss Lenton, a very agreeable Person, and Miss Clerk of
Burford, sitting upon a large Oak, breathing the Evening Fresco.
Walk'd with the Ladies about two hours, and then return'd.

July 3. Gave Mr Horn an Essay on Friendship. In the Evening
went with him, Mr Birch, Mr Hume, Mr Sylvester, & the Wightwicks³
to Godstow by water, taking Musick and Wine with us.

Aug. 7⁴. Went to Portmead, where Lord Tracey's Mare *Whimsey*
(the Swiftest Galloper in England) run against Mr Garrard's *Smock-
faced Molly*, and won the Size Money (a Purse of 40 guineas) with all
the Facility Imaginable. She Gallops indeed at an incredible Rate
and has true mettle to carry it on. Upon this occasion I cou'd not
help thinking of Job's description of the Horse, and particularly of
that expression in It, *He swalloweth the Ground*, which is an Expression
for Prodigious Swiftness in use among the Arabians, Job's Country
men, at this day.

Sept. . . Made a Present to . . Mr Andrew Hughs, Scholar of
Pembroke⁵, of my Key of that College Garden.

Sept. 18. Went to the Races at Bicester. This place is also call'd
Burcester, perhaps, as much as to say, *Birini Castrum*. . . . Camden
remarks y^t Gilbert Bassett built here a monastery in honour of S^t
Edburg; ye memory of the Latter I find is now preserved in a Well
call'd S. Edburg's Well, as also in a Green Foot Path leading to It,
call'd Tadbury Walk, corrupted for the Edbury Way Walk. This

---

¹ An Oxford toast. Was she daughter to the late Master! In the *Oxford
Sausage* are some ' Verses on Miss Brickenden going to Newnham by water.'

> 'The lofty trees of Newnham's pendent wood
> To meet her seem to rush into the flood,
> Peep o'er their fellows' heads to view the fair,
> Whose names upon their wounded barks they bear.'

² Lenthall of Besselsleigh. Descended from Speaker Lenthall.
³ The brothers William and Curteis. The latter became Fellow.
⁴ Even a young man of means appears to have stayed up during the Long
Vacations. His home was in Wales.
⁵ Matr. 1714; Rector of Coln St. Dennis 1727.

day's Sport was fine. 19th. Mr Hawe's Horse won the Galloway
Plate.... Butcher's Company acted Plays here during the Races. I lay
at the Swan.

24. Treated Pembroke College in the Common Room.

Oct 1. Took up my Caution Money (£10) from the Bursar, &
lodg'd it wth Dr Panting, the Master, for the use of Pembroke College.

Mr. Philipps appears to have done many things and thought many
things which the horsey or fashionable undergraduate of the end of
the nineteenth century does not do or think. He was drowned in the
Avon near Bath through a fall from his horse, October 15, 1743, aged
forty-three. He died unmarried, having more than won his boyish
'bett' of two and twenty years before. At the time of his death he
had succeeded to the title. From 1726 he was M.P. for Haverfordwest.

Sir Erasmus wrote on economic subjects, and was also a generous
amateur of the fine arts. Fenton in his *Pembrokeshire* describes his
death as 'a loss to his country. To him as 'emeritissimo Patrono et
Maecenati' J. B. Jackson dedicated his sepia drawing of Titian's
'Legend of the Virgin.' It bears his arms: Arg. a lion rampant sa.,
ducally gorged and chained or. The crest a lion as in the arms. The
dedication begins 'Per Illustri ac Nobili Viro Dno Dno Erasmo
Philipps Barronetto Artium zelantissimo Fautori et de re litteraria
optime merito.' Some lines on his death, penned by Anna Williams,
appeared in her *Miscellany*.

CHAPTER XXV.

JOHNSON.

DURING Panting's Mastership the greatest of the sons of Pembroke, SAMUEL JOHNSON (born September 18, 1709), entered as a commoner and *generosi filius*, October 31, 1728. Michael Johnson's fortunes were then at a low ebb, and it has been asked how it was found possible to send his son to College. Boswell says: ' I have been assured by Dr. Taylor that the scheme never would have taken place, had not a gentleman of Shropshire, one of his schoolfellows, spontaneously undertaken to support him at Oxford, in the character of his companion; though in fact he never received any assistance whatever from that gentleman.' In the previous century young men frequently took their tutor with them to College. Hawkins states that the proposal came from Mr. Andrew Corbett, of Longnor, and was accepted. Croker, however, points out that the young gentleman-commoner matriculated twenty months before Johnson, viz. May 3, 1727. Boswell certainly implies that Johnson went to Pembroke on the strength of the proposed bear-leading *reversed*, but he expressly adds that no assistance was given from that quarter. How then was he supported at College? Croker suggests that he was sent thither by his godfather, Dr. Swynfen, a Lichfield physician, who was himself from Pembroke [1]. Among the contributors to the building carried out at the close of the seventeenth century was his brother (M.P. for Tamworth 1708–10, 1723–26), Mr. Richard Swynfen, of Swynfen. There were several Swynfens at the College. Johnson's humane care of Mrs. Desmoulins may have been induced by gratitude towards her father. On the other hand, Boswell records that he was deeply incensed when a Latin paper, in which he had eloquently described to Dr. Swynfen, in the College vacation of 1729, a violent attack of hypochondria from which he

---

[1] SAMUEL, son of Francis SWYNFEN, of Stafford, gent., matr. March 31, 1696, aged sixteen; B.A. 1699; M.A. (from New Inn Hall) 1703; B.Med. 1706; D.Med. (from Pembroke) 1712; appointed Lecturer of Grammar for the University July 16, 1705 (Hearne, *Collections*, i. 8); died May 10, 1736.

was now for the first time suffering, was shown by the latter to others, and that he was never fully reconciled to him.

The following entry is in the Caution Book :—

'Oct. 31, 1728. Rec^d then of Mr Samuel Johnson, Coffner of Pem. Coll: ye sum of seven Pounds[1] for his Caution, which is to remain in ye Hands of ye Bursars till ye said Mr Johnson shall depart ye said College leaving ye same fully discharg'd.

Recd by me, John Ratcliff Bursar.'

Adams, afterwards Master, was present when the old bookseller, newly arrived by the Lichfield stage, brought his son round to the College.

'On that evening his father, who had anxiously accompanied him, found means to have him introduced to Mr. Jorden, who was to be his tutor. . . . He seemed very full of the merits of his son, and told the company he was a good scholar, and a poet, and wrote Latin verses. His figure and manner appeared strange to them ; but he behaved modestly, and sate silent, till, upon something which occurred in the conversation, he suddenly struck in and quoted Macrobius ; and thus he gave the first impression of that more extensive reading in which he had indulged himself.'

The following lines describe such a scene :—

'When now mature in classic knowledge
The joyful youth is sent to College,
His father comes, a vicar plain
At Oxford bred—in Anna's reign.
And thus, in form of humble suitor,
Bowing, accosts a reverend tutor :
"Sir, I'm a Glo'stershire divine
And this my eldest son of nine ;
My wife's ambition and my own
Was that this child should wear a gown.
I'll warrant that his good behav'our
Will justify your future favour ;
And for his parts, to tell the truth,
My son's a very forward youth ;
Has Horace all by heart—you'd wonder—
And mouths out Homer's Greek like thunder—
If you'd examine and admit him,
A scholarship would nicely fit him,
That he succeeds 'tis ten to one ;
Your vote and interest, sir !—'tis done[2]."'

[1] The usual sum at all Colleges in those days for a commoner.
[2] *Oxford Sausage*, 'The Progress of Discontent,' 1746.

But if the swans of many fond parents are descended from geese, Michael Johnson's ugly duckling was for once to come to something great.

Johnson did not appear before the Vice-Chancellor to be matriculated for nearly seven weeks, a delay unusual and against the University statutes [1]. The following is the entry:—

'1728, Dec. 16. Saml Johnson, 19, Mich. fil. Lichfield Civ. Com. Stafford. gen. fil.'

WILLIAM JORDEN, his tutor (matr. C. C. C. 1702; B.A. from Pembroke 1705; M.A. 1708; B.D. 1728), founder's kin to Wightwick, was of some standing in the College. Under date 1711 is the entry: 'For ye Latine Lecture, £2 0 0. Will. Jorden' (his kinsman, Thomas Jorden, being then praelector Graecus). He became tutor and chaplain in 1720. Johnson, however, declared that Jorden 'scarcely knew a noun from a verb,' and supposed the Ramei had their name from *ramus*, a bough. He told Boswell in 1776: 'He was a very worthy man, but a heavy man, and I did not profit much by his instructions. Indeed I did not attend him much. The first day after I came to college I waited upon him, and then staid away four. On the sixth, Mr. Jorden asked me why I had not attended. I answered I had been sliding in Christ Church meadow. And this I said with as much *nonchalance* as I am now talking to you. I had no notion that I was wrong or irreverent to my tutor.' BOSWELL: 'That, sir, was great fortitude of mind.' JOHNSON: 'No, sir; stark insensibility.' He gave Mrs. Thrale a similar account, namely, that 'meeting Mr. Jorden in the street he offered to pass without saluting him; but the tutor stopped and enquired, not roughly neither, what he had been doing. "Sliding on the ice" was the reply, and so turned away in disdain. He laughed very heartily at the recollection of his own

---

[1] In 1581 Leicester had proposed to the University:—

'' Whereas the old order of Matriculation is that within 6 dayes of every Scholar's comming to Oxford he shall take an oath to observe the statutes of this University etc, and forasmuch as by the negligence and carelessness of many Hedds this hath been and dayly is omitted, insomuch that many Schollers have lived here a long time being never registered in the Universitie booke, nether at any time hearetofore swoorne to the said Universitye, and by this meanes many Papists have hearetofore and may hereafter lurke among you and be brought up by corrupt Tutors . . . That no Scholler be admitted into any College or Haule unless he first before the Vicechancellour subscribe to the Articles of Religion agreed upon, take the Othe of the Queens Majesties Supremacy, sweare to observe the Statutes of the Universitie, if he be of lawfull years to take an Othe, and have his name regestred in the Matriculation Boke.' It was enacted that he should do this not later than the Friday seven-night after his admission, under a fine of 40*s.* for every week to be paid by the Scholar and 20*s.* by the Head.

insolence, and said they endured it from him with a gentleness that, whenever he thought of it, astonished himself.' On one occasion, being fined for non-attendance, he made the rude retort, ' Sir, you have sconced me twopence for a lecture not worth a penny.' Dr. Adams, however, who was two years Johnson's senior, told Boswell that he attended his tutor's lectures and the lectures given in the hall very regularly. If Jorden was not a great clerk, he was something better, and Johnson learned to love and respect him. He said, ' When-ever a young man becomes Jorden's pupil, he becomes his son.' Mrs. Thrale records his saying, ' That creature would defend his pupils to the last ; no young lad under his care should suffer for committing slight irregularities, while he had breath to defend or power to protect them. If I had sons to send to College, Jorden should have been their tutor.' Nevertheless, when his younger schoolfellow, John Taylor, had gained his father's consent to join him at Pembroke, Johnson, though his society ' would have been a great comfort to him, fairly told Taylor that he could not, in conscience, suffer him to enter when he knew he could not have an able tutor.' He got his friend placed under Mr. Bateman, of Christ Church, of whose lectures Johnson had so high an opinion that he used to go across and get them second-hand from Taylor, until, seeing that his ragged shoes, through which his feet were appearing, were noticed by the Christ Church men, he went no more. He was too proud to accept of money, and some one, probably in delicate kindness, having set a pair of new shoes at the door of his chamber, he flung them passionately away. He told Mrs. Thrale, ' The history of my Oxford exploits is all between Taylor and Adams.' Adams was Jorden's cousin.

Boswell writes : ' The fifth of November was at that time kept with great solemnity at Pembroke College, and exercises upon the subject of the day were required. Johnson neglected to perform his. . . . To apologize for his neglect, he gave in a short copy of verses entitled *Somnium*, containing a common thought, "that the muse had come to him in his sleep, and whispered that it did not become him to write on such subjects as politicks ; he should confine himself to humbler themes :" but the versification was truly Virgilian.' Mrs. Thrale says : ' Johnson told me that when he made his first declamation he wrote over but one copy, and that coarsely ; and having given it into the hand of the tutor who stood to receive it as he passed was obliged to begin by chance and continue on how he could, for he had got but little of it by heart ; so fairly trusting to his present powers for imme-diate supply he finished by adding astonishment to the applause of all who knew how little was owing to study.' In Pointer's *Oxoniensis Academia* (1749), among the ' Customs' is mentioned 'custom for the Undergraduates of this College to make Verses on the 5th of November, and to have two Copies of them; one to present the Master, the other to stick up in the Hall, and there to remain till a Speech on this occasion is spoken before Supper (for their Gaudy is at Supper and not Dinner).' There were formerly seven Gaudy-days, one of which was an oyster-feast, but the great Gaudy was on Powder-plot day, because of the connexion with King James. On that occasion 'the Master dined in Publick, and the juniors (by an ancient custom they were obliged to observe) went round the fire in the hall.' Johnson here told Warton: ' In these halls the fireplace was anciently always in the middle of the room till the Whigs removed it on one side.' There was never, however, a side fireplace in this room. Latterly the annual Gaudy-day has been the first Thursday in November, possibly because, while the seniors rejoiced in one quadrangle, the juniors, commemorating the bloody-intended Massacre by Gunpowder, 'went round the fire' in the other.

Boswell goes on: ' Having given such a specimen of his poetical powers he was asked by Mr. Jorden to translate Pope's *Messiah* into Latin verse, as a Christmas exercise. He performed it with uncommon rapidity, and in so masterly a manner that he obtained great applause from it, which ever after kept him high in the estimation of his college, and, indeed, of all the university.' The version was shown by Dr. Arbuthnot's son, then at Christ Church, to Pope, who returned it with the words: ' The writer of this poem will leave it a question for posterity whether his or mine be the original.' Pope, however, was a better judge, and Johnson a better writer, of English than of Latin verse [1].

In the same hall, now the library, Johnson dined daily, and abused the muddy ' coll,' or College ale, as unlikely to inspire Latin poets [2] :—

> 'Carmina vis nostri scribant meliora poetae?
> Ingenium jubeas purior haustus alat.'

' The pleasure he took,' wrote Bishop Percy to Boswell, ' in vexing the tutors and fellows has been often mentioned. But I have heard

---

[1] It was printed in the *Miscellany* of JOHN HUSBANDS, Fellow of Pembroke 1728.
[2] In the ' Panegyrick on Oxford Ale' (*Oxford Sausage*, 1746), the old October is apostrophized, however, thus :—
> ' Balm of my cares, sweet solace of my toils,
> Hail, juice benignant!'
At Exeter, a century before, the first Lord Shaftesbury had resisted an attempt to weaken the College beer.

him say, what ought to be recorded to the honour of the present
venerable master of that college, the reverend WILLIAM ADAMS, D.D.,
who was then very young, and one of the junior fellows, that the mild
but judicious expostulations of this worthy man, whose virtue awed
him and whose learning he revered, made him really ashamed of himself, " though I fear," said he, " I was too proud to own it."

'I have heard from some of his contemporaries that he was
generally seen lounging at the college gate with a circle of young
students round him, whom he was entertaining with wit and keeping
from their studies, if not spiriting them up to rebellion against the
college discipline, which in his maturer years he so much extolled [1].
He would not let these idlers say "prodigious," or otherwise misuse
the English tongue.'

' Even then, sir,' Oliver Edwards told Boswell half a century afterwards, ' he was delicate in language, and we all feared him.'

Dr. Adams told Boswell that Johnson was caressed and loved by all
about him, was a gay and frolicsome fellow, and passed at Pembroke
the happiest part of his life. When Boswell mentioned this to him he
replied, ' Ah, sir, I was mad and violent. It was bitterness which they
mistook for frolick. I was miserably poor, and I thought to fight my
way by my literature and my wit; so I disregarded all power and all
authority.' His lines in the *Vanity of Human Wishes* reflect the lot
which he had tasted :—

> ' When first the college rolls receive his name,
>   The young enthusiast quits his ease for fame ;
>   Through all his veins the fever of renown
>   Spreads from the strong contagion of the gown.
>   O'er Bodley's dome his future labours spread,
>   And Bacon's mansion trembles o'er his head. .
>   .   .   .   .
>   Deign on the passing world to turn thine eyes,
>   And pause awhile from letters to be wise.
>   There mark what ills the scholar's life assail,
>   Toil, envy, want, the garret [patron] and the jail.'

Dr. Birkbeck Hill, whose pious care for the glory of the greatest son
of his College has brought to light everything, probably, that can be
known about Johnson's residence at Pembroke, shows from the batell
books that his weekly bills were not particularly small. They range
from 7*s*. 11*d*. to 12*s*. 6*d*. Carlyle, in the modern picturesque style,
depicts the rough, seamy-faced, rawboned servitor starving in view of

---

[1] Fifty years later he complained that subordination was sadly broken down in
Colleges, as everywhere else.

the empty or locked buttery. Mr. Leslie Stephen also, without the excuse of ignorance, talks about 'servitors and sizars.' Johnson was not a servitor and did not starve. He did not wait, but was waited upon. He was fag-master, not fag. 'It was the practice for a servitor, by order of the Master, to go round to the rooms of the young men and, knocking at the door, to enquire if they were within, and if no answer was returned to report them absent. Johnson could not endure this intrusion, and would frequently be silent when the utterance of a word would have ensured him from censure, and . . . would join with others of the young men in hunting, as they called it, the servitor who was thus diligent in his duty; and this they did with the noise of pots and candlesticks, singing to the tune of " Chevy Chase " the words of that old ballad—

"To drive the deer with hound and horn."'

Johnson's room was over the gateway, at what used to be the top of the tower, but is now the second floor. Dr. Jeune often heard an aged College servant identify it. In 1784, a little before his death, Johnson had a desire to mount once more the narrow winding stair. He was very infirm, and the porter had to push him up. This janitor was alive in 1837, and gave the account to Mr. J. Coke Fowler[1], who matriculated in 1833. Boswell, who also specifies its position, says, 'The enthusiast of learning will ever contemplate it with veneration.' The front window is only a yard or two from the Master's house, and one day Dr. Panting heard Johnson soliloquizing in his strong, emphatic voice : 'Well, I have a mind to see what is done in other places of learning. I'll go and visit the Universities abroad. I'll go to France and Italy. I'll go to Padua—And I'll mind my business. For an Athenian blockhead is the worst of all blockheads.' Dr. Adams told Boswell this. Johnson himself related that one day, as he was turning the key of his chamber, he heard his mother, who was at Lichfield, distinctly call him by name. Perhaps it was here that he began to learn the flageolet. The rooms are internally almost unchanged, though half a century ago (and again in December, 1871) they narrowly escaped destruction. The Rev. N. Howard M'Gachen (matr. 1844) writes :—

'During my residence a fire broke out in the rooms once occupied by Dr. Johnson, and the furniture was hurriedly removed to a place of safety. Among other articles there was a self-acting piano or some such instrument. In the act of removal the button was accidentally touched, which set the music going, and it was melancholy to hear it, in the quad, playing some lively air while the fire was going on above.'

[1] From 1853 a stipendiary magistrate in South Wales.

The staircase balusters must be the same which Johnson clutched in his headlong descents after the flying servitor. Any one who has occupied that narrow stair[1] can imagine the noise of his unwieldy body tumbling down it in hot pursuit.

In those days there was no distinction of senior and junior common-room. For one thing, the Fellows were usually younger than they are now. In one of Johnson's later visits to Oxford, Dr. Adams told him that in some of the Colleges the Fellows had excluded the students from social intercourse with them in the common-room. Johnson approved of this. ' They are in the right, sir : there can be no real conversation, no fair exertion of mind amongst them, if the young men are by.' They walked with Dr. Adams into the Master's garden and into the common-room. JOHNSON (after a rêverie of meditation): ' Aye! here I used to play at draughts with Phil Jones and Fludyer. Jones loved beer, and did not get very forward in the Church. Fludyer turned out a scoundrel, a whig, and said he was ashamed of having been bred at Oxford. He had a living at Putney, and got under the eye of some retainers to the court at that time, and so became a violent whig: but he had been a scoundrel all along to be sure.' BOSWELL: ' Was he a scoundrel, sir, in any other way than that of being a political Scoundrel? Did he cheat at draughts?' JOHNSON: ' Sir, we never played for *money*[2].'

The summer common-room at Pembroke on the town-wall was, till its demolition in 1869, the only one left in Oxford, except that at Merton. Dean Burgon wrote in 1855: ' This agreeable and picturesque apartment was in constant use within the memory of the present Master; but, while I write, it is in a state of considerable decadence. The old chairs are drawn up against the panelled walls; on the small circular tables the stains produced by hot beverages are very plainly to be distinguished : only the guests are wanting, with their pipes and ale—their wigs and buckles—their byegone manners and forgotten topics of discourse.' When Johnson revisited this room with Dr. Adams,

---

[1] Having choice of rooms on first coming to the College, a freshman's religious reverence led the historian to become the occupant of this eyrie. After a term or two I deemed myself unworthy of the spot, and, one of the largest rooms in College falling vacant, moved *in locum spatiosum*.

[2] Fludyer was on the Wightwick foundation, and was of Johnson's standing. ' Nov. 27, 1728. Joh. Fludyer, 16. Joh. fil. Abingdon. Com. Berk. Gen. fil.' His father was Mayor of Abingdon in 1722, and excused from serving in 1757 on account of his ' great age.' Jones was a year senior. ' 1727. Dec. 5. Phil Jones 18. Rich. fil. S^{cti} Petri in Ballivo Civ. Oxon. Gen. fil.' In the buttery book is scrawled : ' O yes, O yes, come forth Phil Jones, and answer to your charge for exceeding the batells,' with other uncomplimentary references.

z

smoking in common-room was being discontinued. A Latin poem, recited in the Theatre on July 8, 1773, at Lord North's Installation, decrying the change of times, speaks of the

> 'Camerae Communis amor, quâ rarus ad alta
> Nunc tubus emittit gratos laquearia fumos[1].'

Boswell says that he cannot find that Johnson formed any close 'intimacies' with his fellow-collegians. He was senior to Shenstone, Blackstone, Graves, Hawkins, and Whitefield, none of whom matriculated before he left. Two of his contemporaries 'got forward in the Church,' FRANCIS POTTER, Prebendary of Bath and Wells, Archdeacon of Taunton and of Wells, and WILLIAM VYSE, Treasurer of Lichfield Cathedral and Archdeacon of Salop.

When Johnson first entered the College Adams told him that he was the best qualified for the University that he had ever known come there. But his reading at Oxford, as all through his life, was desultory and fitful. He gorged half a book and left the rest untasted. In October, 1729, at the beginning of his last term, he made fierce resolutions against sloth : 'Desidiae valedixi ; syrenis istius cantibus surdam posthac aurem obversurus.' Yet he considered method in reading to be mischievous[2].

He told Boswell that what he read solidly at Pembroke was Greek —not the historians, but Homer and Euripides, and a little epigram. He was fondest, however, of metaphysics, but did not go deeply into them. Indeed he was not metaphysical, as his refutation of Berkleyism by dashing his foot against a post evinces. One book he read which deeply impressed his mind. He had been a lax talker, rather than thinker, against religion till he went to Oxford. 'When at Oxford I took up Law's Serious Call to a Holy Life, expecting to find it a dull

---

[1] In the *Oxford Sausage* the ex-fellow who has taken a living regrets the time
> 'When calm around the common room
> I puff'd my daily pipe's perfume !
> Rode for a stomach, and inspected
> At annual bottlings, corks selected,
> And dined untax'd, untroubled, under
> The portrait of our pious Founder.'

[2] He observed many years later: 'Idleness is a disease which must be combated; but I would not advise a rigid adherence to a particular plan of study. I myself have never persisted in any plan for two days together. A man ought to read just as inclination leads him, for what he reads as a task will do him little good. A young man should read five hours in a day and so may acquire a great deal of knowledge.' Dr. Johnson was ignorant that the end of education is to pass examinations. An old gentleman gave him some advice when at College which he often recalled : 'Young man, ply your book diligently now, and acquire a stock of knowledge ; for when years come upon you, you will find poring upon books will be but an irksome task.' Johnson, though not a diligent, was a voracious and feverish reader.

book, as such books generally are, and perhaps to laugh at it. But I found Law quite an overmatch for me; and this was the first occasion of my thinking in earnest about religion.' The non-juror's strangely impressive blending of masculine common sense, literary raciness, and mystical piety was exactly what was likely to lay hold on a mind like Johnson's. He called it 'the finest piece of hortatory theology in any language.' A book which he found in the College Library fascinated him—the Portuguese Jesuit Lobo's *Voyage to Abyssinia.* This, after leaving Oxford, he borrowed, to translate it out of French into English. It subsequently suggested to him the plan of *Rasselas.* He does not appear to have returned the book.

Boswell says: 'Dr. Adams, the worthy and respectable master of Pembroke College, has generally had the reputation of being Johnson's tutor. The fact, however, is, that in 1731 Mr. Jorden quitted the college and his pupils were transferred to Dr. Adams; so that, had Johnson returned, Dr. Adams would have been his tutor. It is to be wished that this connexion had taken place. His equal temper, mild disposition, and politeness of manners might have insensibly softened the harshness of Johnson. . . . Dr. Adams paid Johnson this high compliment. He said to me at Oxford in 1776, "I was his nominal tutor; but he was above my mark." When I repeated it to Johnson his eyes flashed with grateful satisfaction, and he exclaimed, "That was liberal and noble." '

Adams' compliment certainly appears to imply that Johnson was actually under his tuition, and supports the positive assertion of Boswell as to the length of Johnson's residence :—

'The "res angusta domi" prevented him from having the advantage of a complete academical education. The friend to whom he had trusted for support had deceived him. His debts in College, though not great, were increasing; and his scanty remittances from Lichfield could be supplied no longer, his father having fallen into a state of insolvency. Compelled therefore by irresistible necessity, he left the college in autumn, 1731, without a degree, having been a member of it little more than three years.'

We have also Johnson's remark to Boswell that he was at Pembroke with Whitefield, and (smiling) 'knew him before he began to be better than other people.' But this is inexplicable, and proves too much; for Whitefield entered in November, 1732, whereas Johnson had footed it to Bosworth some months before[1].

---

[1] '1732, Julii 16. Bosvortiam pedes petii.' He divided his father's effects the day before. It is difficult to account for the years 1730 and 1731. The *Memoirs*

As, however, Croker and Dr. Hill observe, there is one witness
which is conclusive—the buttery books. These prove that Johnson
batelled in College from Nov. 1, 1728, till Dec. 12, 1729. He
resided continuously during these fourteen months, Dr. Hill being
misled by a slip in Prof. Chandler's transcript from the books when he
says that he was absent for one week in the Long Vacation of 1729.
After Dec. 12, 1729, the name is entered every week (except for some
months in the winter of 1730) till Oct. 1, 1731, but with no charges
against it, save that a few pence are charged on May 15 and Sept. 30,
1730. After March 12, 173⅔, 'Johnson' appears at the *end* of the
commoners, which I think Dr. Hill has not observed. The conclusion
he draws is irresistible, that Johnson ceased to reside in December,
1729. Croker supposes that the hypochondriacal attack of that year
brought his residence to an abrupt termination, but that his name
remained on the books in the hope that his health and his means
would enable him to return. 'If Johnson had remained in College in
1730 there were two scholarships to which he would have been eligible,
and one of which Dr. Hall did not doubt that he would have obtained.'
The whole question, with the evidence from the dates of Johnson's
College friends, has been patiently unravelled in Dr. Hill's *Johnson ;
his Friends and Critics*. The explanation of Adams' remark that he
was but nominally his tutor can only be that Johnson's name was on
the list of his pupils, but that he was not in residence. Croker
unnecessarily affirms, 'Dr. Adams was never in any sense Johnson's
tutor.'

A recent writer[1] observes : 'It is questionable whether Johnson's
connexion with Pembroke is more of a credit or a disgrace to the
College. His abilities and learning were well known; his poverty also
was notorious ; yet no substantial help was afforded him.' On the
other hand it has been thought that the College did help him
pecuniarily. It is certain that the authorities did not reckon too
nicely with him, for his account was allowed to run on for eleven
years :—

say, 'He went to Bosworth immediately after he had left Oxford.' The following
part of a letter in the College library describes him at the age of twenty-five:
'Solihull, ye 30 August, 1735. . . . The feoffees desired some time to make
enquiry of ye caracter of Mr Johnson, who all agree that he is an excellent
Scholar, and upon that account deserves much better than to be Schoolmaster
of Solihull. But then he has the caracter of being a very haughty ill-natured
gent., and that he has such a way of distorting his Face (which though he can't
help) ye gent. think it may affect some young ladds ; for these two reasons he is
not approved on. . . . Henry Greswold.'
[1] The Rev. Frederick Arnold, *Oxford and Cambridge*.

'March 26, 1740. At a convention of the Master and Fellows to settle the accounts of the Caution, it appear'd that the Persons Accounts underwritten stood thus at their leaving the College.

'Caution not Repay'd   Mr Johnson £7. 0. 0.
Battells not discharg'd Mr Johnson £7. 0. 0.'

It is unlikely that the batells exactly balanced the caution. Even if it be the case that pecuniary help was not given, it has to be remembered that College funds are strictly appropriated. Johnson was forward to express bitter resentment when no helping hand was given to the slow rise of worth by poverty depressed. But he had till his death 'love and regard' for the College, and dwells on the 'zeal and gratitude of those that love it.' In later life, when commending a learned Benedictine to the hospitality of the Master and Fellows, he spoke of himself in no mere phrase of civility as having ' had the honour of studying among' them. He thought of bequeathing the house at Lichfield to the College, but was reminded of the claim of some poor relatives [1].

In the early struggling years, while he wrote *famae famique*, Johnson was not likely to revisit his College, from which Jorden and Adams were gone. But when he had won repute and friends he renewed his Oxford days. In, or soon after, 1752 he passed a considerable time at Oxford in the society of Bennet Langton and of Beauclerk, who had the charm, the wit, and the morals of his royal ancestor. ' What a coalition,' said Garrick. ' I shall have my old friend to bail out of the round-house.' In Langton's rooms he wrote an *Idler* in half-an-hour and sent it off unread. In 1754 he lodged for five weeks at Kettel Hall to consult the libraries for his Dictionary, though, Boswell says, he collected nothing for that purpose. Warton says that he had not been to Oxford before. Johnson gave him a third version of the playing truant episode :—

'When Johnson came to Oxford in 1754, the long vacation was beginning, and most people were leaving the place. This was the first time of his being there, after quitting the university. The next morning after his arrival, he wished to see his old college, Pembroke. I went with him. He was highly pleased to find all the college servants which he had left there still remaining, particularly a very old butler [2]; and expressed great satisfaction at being recognized by them, and conversed with them familiarly. He waited on the master, Dr. Radcliffe, who

[1] The dignified-looking old house has been put to various base uses and was lately (1895) in danger of demolition.
[2] Croker, on Dr. Hall's authority, says that this butler was the old servant who was Dr. Ratcliff's residuary legatee. But Dr. Ratcliff did not die till 1775.

received him very coldly. Johnson at least expected, that the master would order a copy of his Dictionary, now near publication; but the master did not choose to talk on the subject, never asked Johnson to dine, nor even to visit him, while he stayed at Oxford. After we had left the lodgings, Johnson said to me, "There lives a man, who lives by the revenues of literature, and will not move a finger to support it[1]. If I come to live at Oxford, I shall take up my abode at Trinity." We then called on the reverend Mr. Meeke, one of the fellows, and of Johnson's standing[2]. Here was a most cordial greeting on both sides. On leaving him Johnson said, "I used to think Meeke had excellent parts, when we were boys together at the college: but, alas!

'Lost in a convent's solitary gloom!'—

I remember, at the classical lecture in the hall, I could not bear Meeke's superiority; and I tried to sit as far from him as I could, that I might not hear him construe." As we were leaving the college, he said, "Here I translated Pope's Messiah. Which do you think is the best line in it?— My own favourite is,

'Vallis aromaticas fundit Saronica nubes.'"

I told him, I thought it a very sonorous hexameter. I did not tell him, it was not in the Virgilian style. He much regretted that his *first* tutor was dead; for whom he seemed to retain the greatest regard. He said, "I once had been a whole morning sliding in Christ-church meadows, and missed his lecture in logick. After dinner he sent for me to his room. I expected a sharp rebuke for my idleness, and went with a beating heart. When we were seated, he told me he had sent for me to drink a glass of wine with him, and to tell me he was *not* angry with me for missing his lecture. This was, in fact, a most severe reprimand. Some more of the boys were then sent for, and we spent a very pleasant afternoon." Besides Mr. Meeke, there was only one other fellow of Pembroke now resident; from both of whom Johnson received the greatest civilities during this visit, and they pressed him very much to have a room in the college.'

It seems that in the Long Vacation at that time there were twenty-five residents out of a *maximum* of little more than fifty.

The next year in the summer he again visited Warton at Kettel Hall. In Johnson's famous audience of George III he told the King that it gave him pleasure to go to Oxford and pleasure to leave. He ever looked on himself as a University writer. But Boswell mentions no further stay in Oxford till 1767. In 1768 he stayed with Chambers, Vinerian Professor, in New Inn Hall, for a long visit. He expatiated to

---

[1] Dr. Ratcliff was a great invalid. Johnson is unjust to him, for he was a considerable benefactor to the College.

[2] JOHN MEEKE, elected Scholar 1726, therefore Johnson's senior. Ob. Sept. 1763. Horace Walpole relates a mistake that he made about Meeke (*Letters*, Oct. 3, 1763). Meeke died in Nell Gwynne's old timbered house near Maidenhead, but was brought to St. Aldate's for burial.

Boswell on the advantages of Oxford for learning. The next year he was at Oxford again. No other visit is recorded till 1773, and after that till 1776, when Dr. Adams, the new Master, took him round Pembroke, as previously narrated. The next year he again went there. Murphy says he stayed at the College in August, 1783. Of the 1784 visit Boswell gives a minute account. The Oxford post-coach took them up at Bolt Court on June 3. Mrs. Beresford, an agreeable American lady, travelling with her daughter, was awed at finding what company she was in, but nearly got into trouble by mentioning that her husband was a member of the American Congress, a remark which Johnson, fortunately, did not overhear. He was very gracious and communicative on the journey. At the inn where they dined he was human enough to be exceedingly dissatisfied with the roast mutton —' as bad as bad can be : ill fed, ill killed, ill kept, and ill drest.' 'He bore the journey very well, and seemed to feel himself elevated as he approached Oxford, that magnificent and venerable seat of learning, orthodoxy, and toryism. Frank [the negro] came in the heavy coach, in readiness to attend him, and we were received with the most polite hospitality at the house of his old friend Dr. Adams, master of Pembroke college. . . He was easy and placid with Dr. Adams, Mrs. and Miss Adams, and Mrs. Kennicott, widow of the learned Hebræan, who was here on a visit.' Boswell had to leave, but returned on the 9th, ' happy to find myself again in the same agreeable circle at Pembroke college, with the comfortable prospect of making some stay.' The late venerable Bishop of Chichester, Dr. RICHARD DURNFORD (who himself entered the College in 1820), remembered his father, the Rev. Richard Durnford, relating that, when a Pembroke freshman, he was invited one evening to the Lodgings by Dr. Adams—who was a friend of his family—Johnson and Boswell being of the party. The latter had quitted the room for a few minutes, and on his return ran eagerly to the Master, placing his hand on his arm, and asked : ' *Has he said anything*[1] ?'

This, however, must have happened at the visit in November. The Biographer gives a number of conversations which took place at the Master's. One of Johnson's remarks was this : ' I would be a papist if I could. I have fear enough, but an obstinate rationality prevents me. I shall never be a papist unless on the near approach of death, of which I have a very great terrour. I wonder that women are not all papists.' He also argued for certain pre-Reformation practices.

---

[1] I was favoured with an account of this reminiscence in a letter from his lordship, dated Dec. 24, 1894. From the Bishop's father Archbishop Howley learned to fish with a worm.

One day in Dr. Adams' coach Boswell took courage to tell Johnson that many who might have been benefited by his conversation had been frightened away by his roughness, and to ask whether he would not have done more good if he had been more gentle. JOHNSON: 'No, sir; I have done more good as I am. Obscenity and impiety have always been repressed in my company.' BOSWELL: 'True, sir; and that is more than can be said of every bishop.' He was full of tenderness, however, in that house. Miss Sarah Adams, an accomplished and bright girl[1], who ventured on the dangerous enterprise of arguing with Johnson, happened to tell him that a little coffee-pot, in which she had made him coffee, was the only thing she could call her own; to which, rolling, no doubt, and blinking, he replied gallantly: 'Don't say so, my dear; I hope you don't reckon my heart as nothing.' Boswell says: 'There was something exceedingly pleasing in our leading a college life, without restraint and with superior elegance, in consequence of our living in the Master's house and having the company of ladies. Mrs. Kennicot related, in his presence, a lively saying of Dr. Johnson to Miss Hannah More, who had expressed a wonder that the poet who had written *Paradise Lost* should write such poor sonnets :—"Milton, madam, was a genius that could cut a colossus from a rock, but could not carve heads upon cherry-stones."' There were, however, some occasions which were not *mollia tempora fandi*, as when Boswell was told not to cant in praise of savages. He does not mention Hannah More's visit, but the following letter to her sister is dated Oxford, June 13, 1784:—

'Who do you think is my principal cicerone in Oxford? Only Dr Johnson! And we do so gallant it about! You cannot imagine with what delight he showed me every part of his own College (Pembroke) nor how rejoiced Henderson looked to make one of the party. Dr Adams had contrived a very pretty piece of gallantry. We spent the day and evening at his house. After dinner Johnson begged to conduct me to see the College; he would let no one show it me but himself. "This was my room: this Shenstone's." Then, after pointing out all the rooms of the poets who had been of his College, "in short," said he, "we were a nest of singing birds. Here we walked, there we played at cricket." He ran over with pleasure the history of the juvenile days he passed there. When we came into the Common room we spied a fine large print of Johnson[2], framed and hung up that very morning, with this

---

[1] She married Benjamin Hyett, Esq., of Painswick House, but died without issue in 1804, aged fifty-eight. Painswick was left to her cousin Francis Adams, who assumed the additional name and arms of Hyett in 1815. Dr. Adams had two brothers and four sisters.

[2] When Johnson saw his portrait by Trotter he said: 'Well, thou art an ugly fellow; but still I believe thou art like the original.'

motto, "And is not Johnson our's, himself a host?" under which stared you in the face, "From Miss More's *Sensibility*." This little incident amused us: but alas! Johnson looked very ill indeed; spiritless and wan. However he made an effort to be cheerful, and I exerted myself to make him so[1].'

A letter from Miss Adams in the College Library, dated June 14, 1784, says :—

'On Wednesday we had here a delightful blue-stocking party; D[r] and M[rs] Kennicott and Miss More, D[r] Johnson, M[r] Henderson, etc., dined here. Poor D[r] Johnson is in very bad health, but he exerted himself as much as he could, and being very fond of Miss More he talked a good deal, and every word he says is worth recording. He took great delight in shewing Miss More every part of Pembroke College, and his own rooms, etc., and told us many things of himself when here.' June 19. 'We dined yesterday for the last time with D[r] Johnson. He went away today.' Johnson himself says : 'I returned last night from Oxford, after a fortnight's abode with D[r] Adams, who treated me as well as I could expect or wish : and he that contents a sick man, a man whom it is impossible to please, has surely done his part well[2].'

At the end of the year, in the dark November days, he was again at the College, where he spent four or five days. He and his old friend had much serious talk together, especially about prayer. Miss Adams writes, Dec. 23, 1784, 'He promised to come again, as he was, he said, nowhere so happy.' But he went back to London to die, not amid terrors, but with Christian tranquillity and hope.

Johnson to all the world is *Doctor* Johnson. Until his forty-fifth year, however, he had no University degree. But Boswell observes that, the Master's degree being desired for the title-page of his *Dictionary*, his friends thought that, if proper exertions were made, the University of Oxford would pay him the compliment. Johnson wrote anxiously to Warton about it : 'I shall be extremely glad to hear from you again to know if the affair proceeds. I have mentioned it to none of my friends, for fear of being laughed at for my disappointment.' Early in 1755 the diploma passed the suffrages of the Heads, on the recommendation of the Chancellor, the Earl of Arran, and on Feb. 20 it was carried in Convocation with no dissentient voice—

'Cum vir doctissimus SAMUEL JOHNSON, e Collegio Pembrochiensi, scriptis suis popularium mores informantibus dudum literato orbi innotuerit ; quin et linguae patriae tum ornandae tum stabiliendae (Lexicon scilicet Anglicanum summo studio, summo a se judicio congestum propediem editurus) etiam nunc utilissimam impendat operam.'

---

[1] *Memoirs*, i. 261.   [2] *Letters to Mrs. Thrale*, vol. ii. p. 372.

Johnson, deeply gratified, wrote a Latin letter of thanks to the Vice-Chancellor. Ten years later Trinity College, Dublin, paid him the unsolicited compliment of creating him *Doctor Utriusque Juris*, and after another ten years his own University conferred on her illustrious son, as rightly acknowledged to be ' in Literarum Republica PRINCEPS jam et PRIMARIUS,' the Doctorate in that one branch of Law which alone, through the jealousy of Henry VIII, she has to bestow. Johnson, though he called himself 'Mr.' to the end, was above the littleness of affecting to undervalue the honour done him by the University. When he 'gallanted it about' with Hannah More he wore his doctor's gown with pride, and was scrupulously academic. Speaking of the Universities, he said that though degenerated they still were homes of learned men and abounded in conveniences and opportunities of study to be found nowhere else. ' There is at least one very powerful incentive to learning—I mean the genius of the place. This is a sort of inspiring deity.' Oxford in particular, as the ' home of impossible loyalties,' drew a passionate affection from him, and those characteristics which made Gibbon [1] revile the place endeared it to Johnson. He had the feeling expressed by Newman in 1833 : ' Oxford, of course, must ever be a sacred city to an Oxonian, and is to me.' Pembroke he loved none the less that it was reputed the most Jacobitical of the colleges.

An object of interest to visitors to the Common Room is Dr. Johnson's tea-pot, a piece of Worcester, with roses, lilies, and sprays in blue on a white ground. It was acquired with a view to presentation to the College by Mr. Alfred Thomas Barton, M.A., now Vicegerent and Senior Tutor, from the writer of the following letter:—

'Sir — Dr Johnson's Tea Pot belonged to my paternal grandmother, Mrs Samuel Parker (maiden name Charlotte Bagnall). She was brought up by Sir Thomas and Lady Aston at their place at Frodsham in Cheshire, where also lived as Vicar the Rev^d — Gastrel, who afterwards lived at New Place, Stratford on Avon, and cut down the celebrated mulberry tree in that garden. Jane Gastrel his wife was a great friend of my grandmother's, and also was very intimate with Dr Johnson. So by that means my Grandmother was thrown very much into the Doctor's society when at Lichfield.

'In this way the Tea Pot and other things came into her possession. In Boswell's *Life of Dr. Johnson*, page 68, vol. 2, pub. 1831, alluding to the Tea Pot, is a note at the foot of the page: "The Revd Mr Parker of

---

[1] 'To the University of Oxford I acknowledge no obligations; and she will as cheerfully renounce me for a son as I am willing to disclaim her for a mother.'

Henley is in Possession of a Tea Pot which belonged to Dʳ Johnson, and which contains about 2 quarts."

'The above was the Revᵈ Samuel Hay Parker, only child of William and Charlotte Parker, and the same who on taking his Degree in 1827 gave Dʳ Johnson's Letters and Papers to the Library of his College (Pembroke) through Dʳ Hall, on 1 June in same year.

'His first Curacy was at Henley in Arden in Warwickshire in 1828. He afterwards went to Stratford on Avon, where he died in 1844. The Tea Pot was given to my Brother, who left it to me (his Eldest Sister).

'Sarah Anne Parker.'

'8 Janʸ 1885. Waterloo, nʳ Liverpool.'

'I suppose no person,' writes the Biographer, 'ever enjoyed with more relish the infusion of that fragrant leaf than Johnson. The quantities which he drank of it at all hours were so great, that his nerves must have been uncommonly strong not to have been extremely relaxed by such an intemperate use of it. He assured me that he never felt the least inconvenience from it.' The only literary controversy he ever deigned to pursue was with Jonas Hanway, a misothé-ist, on this great argument. On one occasion he is recorded to have drunk twenty-two cups at a sitting. It was from this [1] teapot, probably, that blind Mrs. Williams poured for Boswell, who fancied that she put her finger down a little way into the cups to see if they were full. In his first elation at being admitted to such domestic intimacy with Johnson he 'willingly drank cup after cup, as if it had been the Heliconian spring. But as the charm of novelty wore off I grew more fastidious ; and besides I discovered that she was of a peevish temper.' In it, too, was made the tea which, without milk and with cross-buns, formed the sole Good-Friday meal. Johnson did not enjoy drinking tea at Garrick's, for Garrick was of a saving nature and grumbled at lovely Margaret Woffington for making it blood-red. In the same cabinet is a pretty Worcester cider-mug, authenticated as used for gruel by Johnson during his visits to Kettel Hall. It was acquired Oct. 28, 1858.

In the Library is the little deal varnished desk on which the *Dictionary* was written. This, with 'a chair and a half' and five or six Greek'folios, formed the *curta supellex* of Johnson's garret when Dr. Burney was received by him there in 1758. Dr. Adams found him one day busy at the *Dictionary* and was surprised at the smallness of the apparatus used.

'ADAMS: This is a great work, Sir. How are you to get all the Etymologies? JOHNSON : Why, Sir, here is a Shelf with Junius and

---

[1] Burke mentions a silver tea-pot of Johnson's belonging to W. Hoper, Esq.

Skinner and others; and there is a Welsh gentleman who has published a collection of Welsh proverbs who will help me with the Welsh. ADAMS: But, Sir, how can you do it in three years? JOHNSON: Sir, I have no doubt that I can do it in three years. ADAMS: But the French Academy, which consists of forty Members, took forty years to compile their Dictionary. JOHNSON: Sir, thus it is: This is the proportion. Let me see; forty times forty is sixteen hundred. As three to sixteen hundred, so is the proportion of an Englishman to a Frenchman. With so much ease and pleasantry could he talk of that prodigious labour which he had undertaken to execute.' (Boswell.)

Johnson, however, employed six amanuenses, five of them Scotsmen, whom, nevertheless, he treated as a father his sons. Also in the Library is another small deal escritoire which once belonged to Johnson, and afterwards to a person of notoriety, at the sale of whose effects it was acquired. An inscription on it states that it was bought with the other furniture of Edial Hall by a Mr. Elvery, being then known as 'the Doctor's desk.' Mr. Elvery's grandson, Mr. John Styche, of Edial, sold it with his other effects in December, 1880, the purchaser being Mr. T. Page, of Lichfield, who parted with it in the following April to the last possessor.

The superb and characteristic portrait, in perfect condition, which now hangs in the Common Room, is certainly not, as Mr. Napier alleges, a *replica* of the Reynolds in the National Gallery, which was painted for Mrs. Thrale, to take the place of the 'Blinking Sam' picture, in 1778. It was presented to the College in 1850 by Mr. Andrew Spottiswoode in recognition of kindness showed to his son, Mr. William Spottiswoode. The latter informed Mr. Napier in 1883: 'It was painted by Reynolds for a relative of ours, Mr. Strahan[1], and always remained in the house where he lived (10, Little New Street, Shoe Lane) until it was removed to Pembroke College. Johnson and Reynolds were both friends and frequent guests at that house.' Miss Adams told Johnson that he ought to give Pembroke his picture to hang in the hall. 'His answer was that he had no right to be placed among the Founders and Benefactors in the Hall; that the most he could aspire to would be a place in the Lodgings if the Master could find room for his picture there.' There is an inferior picture, ascribed to Reynolds, in the Master's house, given in 1804 by Mr. Panton Plymley, or Corbett (knight of the shire for Salop 1820–30), who entered in 1800, aged 14, and a copy of the picture in Trafalgar Square, lately presented by E. J. Leveson, Esq., now hangs in the Hall. In the Library is a small oval framed pencil sketch. The features are aged

[1] Mr. Andrew Strahan, Mr. Spottiswoode's uncle.

and drawn; the wig is a flowing one. On t is written 'Done by permission of Mr. Samuel Johnson himself for the Rev^d. H. Bright. 1769.' At the bottom 'The Head of Dr. Johnson from a seal of the Rev^d. G. Strahan.' The Library also contains a bust by Bacon, copied from the statue in St. Paul's. The famous Samuel Whitbread wrote, on Dec. 17, 1796, to the Master saying that his father had left directions that it should be presented to the College.

A copy of Johnson's *Political Tracts* in the Library has, in his hand, 'To Sir Joshua Reynolds from the Authour.' Sir Joshua has written his own name on the title-page. Two College exercises, some letters and other papers written by Johnson, and the prized MS. of the *Prayers and Meditations*, are preserved here.

Biographical sketches of Johnson, 'warm from the heart when his friend was scarce buried,' were written by THOMAS TYERS, who, entering Pembroke in 1738, aged thirteen, was afterwards called the Boy Bachelor. Rich, unmarried, inquisitive, talkative, valetudinarian, distinguished among 'the mob of gentlemen who write with ease,' affecting to be ashamed of the imputation of authorship, the intimate of great men in London, and at Ashted 'considered by all the surrounding gentry a man of profound learning who had some little peculiarities in his manners,' Tyers was the typical Eighteenth Century *dilettante.* Yet 'Dr. Johnson loved him.' Tyers, he said, always told him something he did not know before. He was, the *Gentleman's Magazine* says, the 'son of the famous Jonathan Tyers, the original embellisher of Vauxhall Gardens, and a joint-proprietor of that delightful spot. Many of the poetical trifles which were exhibited in these gardens were the production of his pen.' He dedicated a pastoral called *Lucy* to Lord Chesterfield, and one called *Rosalind* to Lord Granville. These were printed for Dodsley. He also wrote *Rhapsodies* on Pope and Addison (1781–3), *Dramatic Conferences* (1782), *Political Conferences*, and many other works. A drawing of Tyers by Taylor has been engraved.

NOTE A.

JOHN TAYLOR, LL.D., OF ASHBURNE.

JOHNSON told Mrs. Thrale: 'The history of my Oxford exploits is all between Taylor and Adams.' He kept up a life-long intimacy with Dr. Taylor, though the Whig interest in Derbyshire had no stronger supporter, and Boswell could perceive nothing congenial in the characters of the two men. Taylor was a litigious Tom Tusher. His private wealth and political connexions surrounded him with fat livings, pluralities, dignities, and power. He affected the hearty broad-shouldered squire with a touch of parson superadded, was diligent on the bench and liberal to charities; yet the farmers of Market Bosworth would throw away their milk rather than pay 'white tythe' to the non-resident rector. His pew at Ashburne, once the chantry of the Holy Cross, was hung with velvet used at George III's Coronation, the perquisite of his Westminster stall; in his mansion, where the chantry-priest had starved, Dr. Taylor was served, like a bishop, by a large grave butler in purple and a white wig. He had hopes of a deanery, and subscribed to the arming of volunteers against the invasion of the Young Chevalier. Johnson said: 'Sir, I love him; but I do not love him more; my regard for him does not increase. As it is. said in the Apocrypha, "his talk is of bullocks." I do not suppose he is very fond of my company. His habits are by no means sufficiently clerical: this he knows that I see; and no man likes to live under the eye of perpetual disapprobation.' He wrote Taylor's most orthodox sermons (*Conciones pro Taylore*). However he said, 'Sir, he has a very strong understanding.' Johnson liked venison, and Reynolds suggested to Boswell that the explanation of his attentions to Taylor was that the latter, as Johnson told him, had made him his heir. This seems unlikely, both from Johnson's character and because Taylor was likely to outlive him. He read the service in the Abbey (unfeelingly, Malone and Steevens said) over Johnson's grave, dying himself early in 1788, aged seventy-seven. Johnson clung wistfully to old intimacies. A little before his death he wrote to Taylor: 'Dear Sir,—What can be the reason that I hear nothing from you? . . . Do not omit giving me the comfort of knowing that after all my losses I have yet a friend left. I want every comfort. My life is very solitary and very cheerless. . . . O! my friend, the approach of death is very dreadful. It is vain to look round and round for that help which cannot be had. Yet we hope and hope, and fancy that he who has lived to-day may live to-morrow. But let us learn to derive our hope only from God. In the meantime let us be kind to one another. I have no friend now living, but you and Mᵣ Hector, that was the friend of my youth. Do not neglect, dear sir, Yours affectionately Sam. Johnson.' This is not the letter of a legacy hunter. Dr. Taylor, who was twice married, left his estates to his shoeblack and page, William Brunt, to spite his relatives whom he overheard, when in a grave illness, discussing the distribution of his property. The boy, the son of a vendor of besoms, swooned at hearing the news. He was in truth descended from Dr. Taylor's grandfather, and took thenceforward the name of a common ancestor, Webster. The gold coin which had been placed round Johnson's neck by Queen Anne, when touched in childhood for the King's Evil, Taylor bequeathed to his patron and friend, the Duke of Devonshire. I am indebted for most of the foregoing note to the Rev. Francis Jourdain, M.A., Vicar of Ashburne and Rural Dean, a loyal member of the College.

NOTE B.

FRESHMEN'S GAUDIES—GOING ROUND THE FIRE (see pp. 327, 334).

THE custom at Merton of singing hymns round the charcoal fire on holy days and vigils from Allhallowmas to the Purification is described by Wood, and also the initiation of freshmen on these occasions. At Exeter, Shaftesbury, while a senior in 1637, had a principal hand in putting down 'that ill custom of tucking freshmen.' These 'freshmen's gawdies' (*vide supra*, p. 280) were the same no doubt at Pembroke, and probably in the Broadgates times were connected with the All Saints' festival. Wood (*Life and Times*, i. 133, 138), says:—

'On the holydayes their nights and eves, at all these fires every night, which began to be made a little after five of the clock, the senior undergraduats would bring into the hall the juniors or freshmen between that time and six of the clock, and there make them sit downe on a forme in the middle of the hall, joyning to the declaiming desk; which done, every one in order was to speake some pretty apothegme, or make a jest or bull, or speake some eloquent nonsense, to make the company laugh. But if any of the freshmen came off dull, or not cleverly, some of the forward or pragmatical seniors would "*tuck*" them, that is, set the nail of their thumb to their chin, just under the lower lipp, and by help of their other fingers under the chin, they would give him a mark, which some times would produce blood.' At Shrove-tide 'the fire being made in the common hall before 5 of the clock at night, the fellowes would go to supper before six, and making an end sooner than at other times, they left the hall to the libertie of the under-graduats, but with an admonition from one of the fellowes that all things should be carried in good order. While they were at supper in the hall, the cook was making the lesser of the brass pots ful of cawdel at the freshmans' charge; which was brought up & set before the fire in the hall. Afterwards, every freshman, according to seniority, was to pluck off his gowne & band, and if possible to make himself look like a scoundrell. This done, they were conducted each after the other to the high table, and then made to stand on a forme placed thereon; from whence they were to speak their speech with an audible voice to the company: which if well done, the person that spoke it was to have a cup of cawdle and no salted drinke; if indifferently, some cawdle and some salted drink; but if dull, nothing was given to him but salted drink or salt put in college beere, with tucks to boot. Afterwards when they were to be admitted into the fraternity, the senior cook was to administer to them an oath over an old shoe, part of which runs thus— "Item tu jurabis quod penniless bench non visitabis &c." the rest is forgotten, and none there are now remembers it. After which spoken with gravity, the Fresh-man kist the shoe, put on his gowne and band and took his place among the seniors. This was the way & custome that had been used in the college, time out of mind, to initiate the freshmen; but between that time & the restoration of K. Ch. 2 it was disused, and now such a thing is absolutely forgotten.' See also *Life and Times*, iv. 60.

CHAPTER XXVI.

WHITEFIELD.

ALMOST contemporary at the College with the great high-church moralist of the fireside and the study was the reviver, or creator, in England of pietistic Calvinism, the most powerful pulpiteer of the last century. GEORGE WHITEFIELD, born in the Bell Inn at Gloucester Dec. 16, 1714, was taught Latin and Greek at the St. Marie de Crypt School, where at the annual visitations his eloquence already attracted attention. His father had died when George was a baby, and his mother was glad of his help in the inn. 'At length I put on my blue apron and snuffers and became professed and common drawer for nigh a year and a half.' One day an old schoolfellow, a Pembroke servitor, visited the 'Bell,' and related that he had not only discharged his College expenses for the term but had received a penny; at which the ale-wife cried out, ' That will do for my son. Will you go to Oxford, George?' 'With all my heart,' he replied. His schoolfellow's friends promised their interest to procure him a servitor's place at Pembroke. 'For a twelvemonth I went on in a round of duties receiving the sacrament monthly, fasting frequently, attending constantly on publick worship, and praying often more than twice a day in private. One of my brothers used to tell me he feared this would not last long, and that I should forget all when I came to Oxford. . . Being now eighteen years old, it was judged proper for me to go to the University. GOD had prepared my way. The friends before applied to recommended me to the master of Pembroke College. Another friend took up ten pounds upon bond, which I have since repaid, to defray the first expense of entering, and the master [Dr. Panting], contrary to all expectations, admitted me servitor immediately.'

Whitefield entered Pembroke a few months after Shenstone. He matriculated Nov. 7, 1732. Shenstone, however, as a gentleman-commoner, occupied a very different social position. In *A Short Account of God's Dealings with the Reverend George Whitefield* we read :—' Soon after my admission to *Pembroke* College I found my having been used to a publick-house was now of service to me. For many of the servitors being sick at my first coming up, by my diligent and ready attendance I ingratiated myself into the gentlemen's favour so far that many chose me to be their servitor.

' This much lessened my expence, and indeed God was so gracious, that with the profits of my place and some little presents made me by my kind tutor, for almost the first three years I did not put all my relations together to above 24*l.* expence. And it has often grieved my soul to see so many young students spending their substance in extravagant living. . . I was quickly sollicited to joyn in their excess of riot with several who lay in the same room [1]. God, in answer to prayers before put up, gave me grace to withstand them. And once in particular, it being cold, my limbs were so benummed by sitting alone in my study, because I would not go out amongst them, that I could scarce sleep all night. But I soon found the benefit of not yielding ; for when they perceived they could not prevail they let me alone as a singular odd fellow.

' All this while I was not fully satisfied of the sin of playing at cards and reading plays till God, upon a fast day, was pleased to convince me.

' Before I went to the University I met with Mr. *Law's* " Serious Call to a Devout Life," but had not then money to purchase it. Soon after my coming up to the University, seeing a small edition of it in a friend's hand, I soon procured it. God worked powerfully upon my soul, as He has since upon many others, by that and his other excellent treatise upon Christian Perfection. I now began to pray and sing psalms thrice every day, besides morning and evening, and to fast every *Friday*, and to receive the Sacrament at a parish church [2] near our College, and at the Castle, where the despised Methodists used to receive once a month.

' The young men so called were then much talked of at *Oxford*. . . For about a twelvemonth my soul longed to be acquainted with some of them, and I was strongly pressed to follow their good example, when I saw them go through a ridiculing crowd to receive the Holy Eucharist at *St. Mary's.* At length, God was pleased to open a door.

[1] The present sitting-rooms were then shared for sleeping, the present bed-room and servants' pantry forming the studies.
[2] Not, I think, St. Aldate's, used till this year as the College Chapel, but probably St. Ebbe's.

It happened that a poor woman in one of the Workhouses had attempted to cut her throat, but was happily prevented. Upon hearing of this, and knowing that both the Mr. *Wesleys* were ready to every good work, I sent a poor aged apple-woman of our College to inform Mr. *Charles Wesley* of it, charging her not to discover who sent her. She went ; but, contrary to my orders, told my name. He having heard of my coming to the Castle and a parish church Sacrament, and having met me frequently walking by myself, followed the woman when she was gone away, and sent an invitation to me by her to come to breakfast with him the next morning. I thankfully embraced the opportunity.'

Charles Wesley lent him books, which convinced him that 'true religion is a union of the soul with God.' 'From time to time Mr. Wesley permitted me to come unto him and instructed me as I was able to bear it. By degrees he introduced me to the rest of his Christian brethren. . . I now began, like them, to live by rule, and to pick up the very fragments of my time that not a moment of it might be lost. Whenever I ate or drank or whatsoever I did I endeavoured to do all to the glory of God. Like them, having no weekly sacrament (although the rubric required it), at our own college, I received every *Sunday* at *Christ Church.* I joined with them in keeping the stations by fasting *Wednesdays* and *Fridays,* and left no means unused which I thought would lead me nearer to *Jesus Christ.*

'Regular retirement, morning and evening, at first I found some difficulty in submitting to; but it soon grew profitable and delightful. As I grew ripe for such exercises I was from time to time engaged to visit the sick and the prisoners and to read to poor people, till I made it a custom, as most of us did, to spend an hour every day in doing works of charity.

'The course of my studies I soon intirely changed. Whereas before I was busied in studying the dry sciences, and books that went no farther than the surface, I now resolved to read only such as entered into the heart of religion.'

He mentions several short fits of illness, in which he is much cheered by the society of his new friends, with whom he spent many sweet and delightful hours. 'Never did persons, I believe, strive more earnestly to enter in at the strait gate. They kept their bodies under even to an extreme. They were dead to the world, and were willing to be accounted as the dung and offscouring of all things, so that they might win *Christ.*'

Some fell away under the displeasure of a tutor or head of a College, or in changing a gown from a lower to a higher degree. As for himself, ' God was pleased to permit Satan to sift me as wheat. . . At my first setting out, in compassion to my weakness, I grew in favour both with God and man, and used to be much lifted up with sensible devotion, especially at the blessed Sacrament. But when religion began to take root in my heart, I was visited with outward and inward trials.

' The first thing I was called to give up for God was what the world calls my fair reputation. I had no sooner received the Sacrament publickly on a weekday at *St. Mary's* but I was set up as a mark for all the polite students that knew me to shoot at. [[1] By this they knew that I was commenced Methodist ; for though there is a Sacrament at the beginning of every term, at which all, especially the seniors, are, by statute, obliged to be present, yet so dreadfully has that once faithful city played the harlot, that very few masters and no undergraduates (but the Methodists) attended upon it.]

' Mr. *Charles Wesley*, whom I must always mention with the greatest *deference* and respect, walked with me (in order to confirm me) from the church even to the college. I confess, to my shame, I would gladly have excused him ; and the next day, going to his room, one of our Fellows passing by, I was ashamed to be seen to knock at his door. But, blessed be God ! this fear of man gradually wore off. . .

' Soon after this I incurred the displeasure of the Master of the College, who frequently chid, and once threatened to expel, me, if I ever visited the poor again. Being surprized by this treatment, and overawed by his authority, I spake unadvisedly with my lips, and said, if it displeased him, I would not. My conscience soon pricked me for this sinful compliance. I immediately repented, and visited the poor the first opportunity. . . My tutor, being a moderate man, did not oppose me much, but thought, I believe, that I went a little too far. He lent me books, gave me money, visited me, and furnished me with a physician when sick. In short he behaved in all respects like a father ; and I trust God will remember him for good in answer to the many prayers I have put up in his behalf.

' I daily underwent some contempt at college. Some hath thrown dirt at me ; others by degrees took away their pay from me ; and two friends that were dear unto me grew shy of and forsook me.'

These trials he found useful. But his inward struggles were to him as the buffetings of the Evil One, who he came to believe had possession of his body. ' When I kneeled down I felt great heavings

---

[1] These words are omitted in the 1756 edition of the Autobiography.

in my body, and have often prayed under the weight of them till the sweat came through me. At this time *Satan* used to terrify me much, and threatened to punish me if I discovered his wiles. It being my duty, as servitor, in my turn to knock at the gentlemen's rooms by ten at night, to see who were in their rooms, I thought the devil would appear to me every stair I went up.'

Then he sets himself to break the chain of sensual appetite. ' Accordingly by degrees I began to leave off eating fruits and such like, and gave the money I usually spent in that way to the poor. Afterwards I always chose the worst sort of food, tho' my place furnished me with variety. I fasted twice a week. My apparel was mean. I thought it unbecoming a penitent to have his hair [1] powdered. I wore woollen gloves, a patched gown and dirty shoes ; and, though I was then convinced that the kingdom of God did not consist in meats and drinks, yet I resolutely persisted in these voluntary acts of self-denial, because I found them great promoters of the spiritual life.'

Besides Law, his favourite books at this time are à Kempis and Castaniza's *Spiritual Combat.* Castaniza says that he who is employed in mortifying his will is as well employed as though he were converting Indians ; a thought which much impressed Whitefield and led him to shut himself up in his study to learn to know and conquer self. Afterwards he considers this was one of the devices of Satan, ploughing with God's heifer. ' His main drift was to lead me into a state of quietism.' Satan suggested to him to leave off all forms and not use his voice in prayer at all.

' The devil also sadly imposed on me in the matter of my college exercises. Whenever I endeavoured to compose my theme, I had no power to write a word. . . *Saturday* being come (which is the day the students give up their compositions) it was suggested to me that I must go down into the hall, and confess I could not make a theme, and so publickly suffer, as if it were for my Master's sake. When the bell rung to call us, I went to open the door to go downstairs, but feeling something give me a violent inward check I entered my study and continued instant in prayer, waiting the event. For this my tutor fined me half-a-crown. The next week *Satan* served me in like manner again ; but now, having got more strength and perceiving no inward check, I went into the hall. My name being called I stood up, and told my tutor I could not make a theme. I think he fined me

[1] But Graves makes him say in later life, that nothing contributed more to the conversion of sinners than a good periwig.

a second time ; but, in imagining that I would not willingly neglect my exercise, he afterwards called me into the common-room, and kindly enquired whether any misfortune had befallen me, or what was the reason I could not make a theme ? I burst into tears and told him it was not out of contempt of authority, but that I could not act otherwise. Then at length he said he believed I could not ; and when he left me told a friend, as he very well might, that he took me to be really mad. This friend, hearing from my tutor what had happened, came to me, urging the command of Scripture to be subject to the higher powers. I answered " Yes, but I had a new revelation. Lord, what is man ? " '

Perhaps if Whitefield had not so cast aside those ' dry sciences,' for the study of which after all he had been sent to Oxford, theme-making would have been less troublesome to him. The College which supported him required theme-making, but in that ' new revelation' and that ' Lord, what is man ? ' comes out the impatience of authority which characterized developed Methodism.

On another occasion we see him silently praying under a tree in Christ Church walk, in imitation of Jesus Christ, ' for near two hours, sometimes lying flat on my face, sometimes kneeling upon my knees, all the while filled with fear and concern lest some of my brethren should be overwhelmed with pride. The night being stormy it gave me awful thoughts of the day of judgment. I continued, I think, till the great bell rung for retirement to the College.

' Soon after this the holy season of *Lent* came on, which our friends keep very strictly, eating no flesh during the six weeks except on *Saturdays* and *Sundays*. I abstained frequently on *Saturdays* also, and ate nothing on the other days (except on *Sunday*) but sage-tea without sugar and coarse bread. I constantly walked out in the cold mornings till part of one of my hands was black. This, with my continued abstinence and inward conflicts, at length so emaciated my body that at Passion-tide, finding I could scarce creep upstairs, I was obliged to inform my kind tutor of my condition, who immediately sent for a physician to me.

' This caused no small triumph among the collegians, who began to cry out, " What is his fasting come to now ? "

' . . As fast as I got strength after my sickness, my tutor, physician, and some others were still urging me to go into the country. . . I wrote letters, beseeching my mother, if she valued my soul, not to lay her commands on me to come down. She was pleased to leave me to my choice.' Whitefield found, however, a temporary retirement necessary for health. This was at the end of his ninth term. He spent three quarters of a year at Gloucester, and then returned to Pembroke. At the end of his fourth year the time came for him to leave. He says, however: 'My friends urged several reasons for my continuing at the University. . . No one was left to take care of the prison affairs. They further urged that GOD blessed my endeavours there as well as at *Gloucester*; that the University was the fountain-head; that every gownsman's name was legion; and that if I should be made instrumental in converting one of *them*, it would be as much as converting a whole parish. At the same time, unknown to me, some of them sent to that great and good man, the late Sir *John Phillips* [1], who was a great encourager of the *Oxford* Methodists; and though he had never seen but only heard of me, yet he sent word he would allow me 30*l.* a year if I would continue at the University. Upon this, finding the care of the prisoners to be no more than under GOD I could undertake with pleasure, and knowing that the University was the best place to prosecute my studies, I resolved, GOD willing, to wait at *Oxford* a blessing on the first fruits of my ministerial labours.' He did not, however, long carry out this intention. Having received the diaconate at Gloucester on June 20, 1736, at the age of twenty-one, and 'driven fifteen mad' out of a vast auditory of his townsmen by his first sermon, he a week later put on his bachelor's gown, the expenses of his ordination and degree being defrayed by five guineas from the good Bishop of Gloucester (Dr. Martin Benson) and Sir John Philipps' allowance. Before finally leaving Oxford he ministered once again to the poor wretches in the Castle. In a passage which he afterwards excised, perhaps as sounding undutiful, he writes: 'Oh the unspeakable benefit of reading to the poor and exercising our talents while students at the University. . . Would the Heads and Tutors of our Universities follow His example, and instead of discouraging their pupils from doing anything of this nature send them to visit the sick and the prisoners, and to pray with and read practical books of religion to the poor, they would find such exercises of more service to *them* and to the *Church* of God than *all* their private and publick *lectures* put together.'

Whitefield, after his seventh voyage to Georgia, died exhausted by

---

[1] Of Picton Castle. *Vide supra*, p. 301; described by his cousin, Horace Walpole, in 1746 as 'a noted Jacobite.' The 'Holy Club,' 'Bible Bigots' or 'Bible Moths' were of distinctly nonjuring proclivities. Whitefield can have had little in common, at bottom, with the Oxford Methodists, except a spirit of unworldliness and mortified devotion.

his labours at Newbury Port in New England, Sept. 30, 1770, aged fifty-five. He usually described himself as ' A.B., late of Pembroke College, Oxford.' Meeting his old tutor at Bristol in 1748 he told him that ' his judgment (as he trusted) was a little more ripened than it was some years ago.'

Whitefield's stature was above the middle height. He was slender, but well proportioned, his features regular, his complexion fair, his eyes small, lively, and of a dark blue colour, but one of them oblique —the result of measles in his childhood. When he began to speak this defect was forgotten—how few sermons could carry conviction against a squint![1] His manner was graceful and natural, his voice unusual both in strength and melody. Graves describes him at home as having an episcopal appearance in a purple night-gown and velvet cap.

NOTE A.

JOHNSON AND WHITEFIELD.

JOHNSON, as we have seen, said he knew Whitefield at Pembroke, though it is not easy to explain this. Though himself, as Boswell remarks, ' in a dignified manner a methodist,' and believing in ' the whole discipline of regulated piety,' as also in the powerful influences on the heart of the Holy Spirit, and though he praised the sincerity of a man who would travel 900 miles in a month and preach twelve times a week, Johnson disparaged the Gospel of Assurance and the Inward Light. He would allow no merit to Whitefield's oratory, which David Hume said was worth travelling a score of miles to hear. ' His popularity, Sir, is chiefly owing to the peculiarity of his manner. He would be followed by crowds were he to wear a nightcap in the pulpit or were he to preach from a tree.' Boswell tells us : ' Of his fellow-collegian, the celebrated Mr. George Whitefield, he said, "Whitefield never drew as much attention as a mountebank does. . . . I never treated his ministry with contempt ; I believe he did good. He had devoted himself to the lower classes of mankind, and among them he was of use. But when familiarity and noise claim the praise due to knowledge, art, and elegance, we must beat down such pretensions."' He placed him in one of the four classes of Egotists. Johnson approved of the expulsion of the six methodist undergraduates from Edmund Hall ; they had come to Oxford, he said, to be taught religion, not to teach it.

---

[1] Graves records : ' He has preached to twenty thousand people at a time . . . they would have plucked out their eyes and have given them to him.' (*Spiritual Quixote*, i. 81.)

NOTE B.

SERVITORS.

WHITEFIELD, Mr. Overton remarks, had 'exchanged the drawer's apron for the degrading badge of a servitor.' 'After two or three years' experience in this scarcely less menial capacity than he had filled at home, he found himself at the age of twenty-two with hardly any intellectual or moral discipline, without having acquired any taste for study, without having had the benefit of associating on anything like terms of equality with men of refinement, suddenly elevated to a degree of notoriety which few have attained.' Again, 'Whitefield's training at Oxford, no less than at Gloucester, was all calculated to foster a habit of servility.' It would appear to follow from this kind of reasoning that there should be no servants, or that one who, like Whitefield, has been born in a menial position should be given no facilities for obtaining a higher education[1]. But for his servitorship he would have ended his days among the pewter pots, serving boors, or become a mere ranting preacher in an obscure conventicle. Had these exhibitions been of more value and attended by no conditions of service, either Whitefield would not have obtained one, or he must have gone from the provincial beer-house to associate as an equal with dandies and gentlemen wits, the victim of worse humiliations than any he could experience in carrying about the alejack in the College hall. The truth is that servitorships and other graduations of rank at the University belong to an older and less sophisticated constitution of society. The mediæval University drew the studious and aspiring of all ranks of life, in vast numbers, into its embracing commonwealth, each student retaining there the social condition which was his at home. There was no more degradation in service inside the University than outside it, nor at one time were menial offices considered to disgrace even youths of noble degree, who often acted as pages. The servitors of a college corresponded to the lay brethren of a monastery. They were not poor gentlemen, but came from the plough and the shop. Such a system was already beginning in the eighteenth century to be 'not convenient.' The Universities were no longer great *pandocheia* nurturing all conditions and sorts of youth. It had come to be not unusual for a servitor—as was the case with Jago, Shenstone's friend—to be, if not gentle-born, at any rate the son of a country curate. Johnson wished the institution abolished. It lasted in ill odour till comparatively recent times, a clear anachronism. Since its abolition none come to College but *generosorum filii*, or those who, from a humbler

---

[1] Graves, speaking of servitors of this College, makes Wildgoose say sensibly : 'I don't see why a man should be ashamed to have appeared in a situation which was agreeable to his circumstances. There is nothing ridiculous in a small fortune or even a low birth. But there is in the discovery that we are too anxious to conceal them, and even give the lye to them by our dress and appearance.' (*Spiritual Quixote,* i. 336.)

condition, will dress, talk, and deport themselves like the public-school men around them. There are still servants attached to the Colleges, but they are not admitted to lecture room or chapel, and they leave Oxford what they were intellectually when they came to it. The conception of equal comradeship among students is an attractive one, and any other is now impossible. But it has necessitated the discommuning of the 'poor clerk' and the loss of a great ideal. Half a century earlier Wesley's father had footed it to Oxford with forty-five shillings in his purse, and been admitted as a servitor of Exeter: during five years' residence he received but a crown from his family. Dr. John Prideaux, Bishop of Worcester, who also had trudged to Oxford, served the spit in Exeter kitchen. He was chosen Fellow, and thence advanced to a mitre. Robinson, Bishop of London and Ambassador to the King of Sweden, went to Brasenose from the furrow. Bishop Jeremy Taylor left the barber's block for a sizar's place at Caius. A poor Pembroke student, John Moore, starting with a small exhibition ascended the throne of St. Augustine and became the first non-royal subject of the Crown. Whitefield himself, when at the end of his College career he found the priesthood within his grasp, boasted: 'For my quality I was a poor mean drawer; but by the distinguishing grace of God am now intended for the ministry. As for my estate I am a servitor.' Pembroke to him had been no harsh stepmother. 'I left,' he writes at parting, 'my sweet retirement at Oxford.'

CHAPTER XXVII.

THE CHAPEL.

For more than a century after its foundation Pembroke had no separate Chapel, but continued to use Docklinton's aisle. The Charles I panelling of the Master's pew is now in Stanton St. John's church. But in 1728, the year of Johnson's matriculation (who attended St. Aldate's for daily prayers, while Whitefield worshipped there for two months only, afterwards attending the new Chapel), the College, encouraged by a benefaction of £210 from Bartholomew Tipping, of Oxford [1], and a legacy of £100 from Dr. Charles Sloper, sometime Fellow (Proctor 1697), Chancellor of Bristol, resolved to build itself a place for worship. Among contributors were the Earl of Arran, then Visitor (£100), the Earl of Pembroke (£50), the Rev. James Phipps (£105), Dr. Panting, the Master (£21 10s.), Archdeacon Robert Cooper (£100), Dr. Samuel Baker, Canon and Chancellor of York (£50), the Rev. John Haines (£50). The College found £375 14s. 4d. Mr. Adams, the manciple, had left in his will £20 for the purpose. This and Dr. Sloper's legacy seems to show that the project had been in the air for some time [2]. Chapels had been built for Hart Hall in 1716 and at Queen's in 1719. The building was not finished till 1732. Mr. Tipping, who is described in *Oxonia Depicta* of the next year as 'inter munificos Benefactores primus,' and whose arms are on the screen, had canvassed all his friends for funds, and the foundation-stone was laid by him. On July 10, 1732, the

---

[1] An earlier BARTHOLOMEW TIPPING entered, with his elder brother JOHN, May 8, 1635. Their father was Bartholomew Tippinge, of Chequers, Stokenchurch, Oxon (ob. 1656), son of Bartholomew, of Woolley Park, Chaddleworth, Berks. The eldest brother of the latter, Sir George, of Whitfield and Draycott, Oxon, was father of 'Eternity Tipping,' and great-grandfather of Sir Thomas, who sate for Oxon and for Wallingford at the close of the century. The mansion house at Chaddleworth was built by Bartholomew, the Pembroke benefactor, in 1690. The last of this line, Mr. Bartholomew Tipping, died there in 1798.

[2] The College 'hath now full power to receive benefactions and neede of helpe for necessaryes for Chappell, Library, Hall ... Thomas Clayton, Maister' (in 1624).

Chapel was consecrated by Dr. John Potter [1], Bishop of Oxford, afterwards Primate. A sermon from Gen. xxviii. 20-22, on religious vows
and dedications, was preached by the Master. Sir Jemmet Raymond
afterwards gave £50 to improve the approaches to the Chapel.

'This edifice,' writes Dr. Ingram, 'is small but elegant; being
ornamented with Ionic pilasters between the windows and surmounted
by a panelled parapet which judiciously conceals the roof. The
interior is very neat.' We need not smile at the adjectives of a bygone
taste. Elegance and judiciousness are good and somewhat rare
qualities, and they are displayed by the early Georgian fane which
was described in recent guide-books as 'a neat Ionic structure.' The
interior is admirably proportioned, an excellent screen divides the
chapel from the ante-chapel, the oak panelling and seating is sufficiently
good, and there is a pleasing marble altarpiece, in which is framed
a graceful copy by Cranke of our Lord's figure in the picture executed
by Rubens for the Petits Carmes—St. Theresa pleading at the feet of
the risen Saviour for the souls in Purgatory [2]. It was given, about
1786, by a Fellow-Commoner, Mr. Joseph Plymley (from 1804
Corbett), afterwards archdeacon of Salop [3]. He presented, in 1824,
the picture of Shenstone. The floor of the Chapel is of black and
white marble squares. On the screen are these arms :—

> East side : A Dove holding in its beak an Olive Branch. In base
> two Serpents embowed. Crest, a Dove treading on a Serpent.
> For Sloper of Woodhay, Berks.
>
> West side : Or, on a bend engrailed, vert, three Pheons of the field.
> Crest, out of a ducal coronet, or, an Antelope's head, vert, attired
> and maned of the first. Motto, *Vive ut Vivas.* For Tipping.

---

[1] Hearne in earlier days had the very poorest opinion of Dr. Potter as a Whiggish
divine. He is 'our sneaking,' 'our spruce,' 'our White Liver'd' Regius Professor.
The inaugural lecture, on May 7, 1708, of 'Y⁰ famous Low-Church Man' was
'a very flat immethodical & poor leaden Discourse.' 'How he can be said to be
a modest Man I cannot see, having declin'd nothing yᵗ has been offer'd him. . . .
It looks rather yᵗ he is an ambitious, conceited, proud Man. But let us not judge.'
There was little merit in Potter's *Clement of Alexandria*, or in his 'riff-raff notes
upon Lycophron.'

[2] 'I could not look on it without emotion'; Mrs. Jameson (*Legends of the
Monastic Orders*, pp. 423, 424).

[3] Ob. 1830; father of PANTON (see above p. 348), of UVEDALE (a judge), and of
JOSEPH (rector of Holgate), all of Pembroke. The last-named presented to the
Library in 1837 the Syriac Scriptures and other books. The Corbets of Longnor,
Salop, were Johnson's friends. They were for generations knights of the shire.
Edward was one of the Parliamentary Visitors. Sir John, second baronet, was
a Rumper and on the commission to try Charles I. Sir Vincent fought for
the King.

The exterior may be compared with the New Buildings in Magdalen Grove, begun Oct. 1733, and with a portion of Queen's which was finished that year. Pembroke College, with the new Chapel, is engraved in Williams' *Oxonia Depicta* of 1733. Dr. Ingram says: 'It is remarkable that in the print of this College by Williams the tower gateway, as finished in 1694, is first seen in the angular situation which the present gateway occupies.' It would seem that Dr. Ingram was not acquainted with Burghers' print.

The Chapel has now been elaborately embellished, but I give three descriptions of it as it was in its simplicity. One from the old *Oxford Pocket Companion*: 'The Chapel is a small but elegant Building; and though seldom visited by Strangers, this Cabinet (for so it may be deservedly called) merits that favour more than some others which rarely escape their notice.' One from Salmon (1749): 'The Chapel is a fine Piece of Architecture (but not large) built of hewn Stone and extremely well furnish'd without and within: The marble Pillars, particularly at the Altar, are exceeding beautiful.' The third is from Rowley Lascelles' *Dialogue after the manner of Castiglione*, 1821:—

Il Cortegiano: This Chapel is a handsome building of the Ionic order. I admire much the altar-piece.

Falkland: It was for the sake of its chapel I ranked this among the classical Colleges; the rest of its buildings are homely and rustic. Four well-proportioned windows, with semi-circular heads, range along that northern front, in which is the handsome doorway. Between each of the former is an entablature and a low blank attic, which nearly conceals the finely arched roof.

Il Cortegiano: I observed over the altar a picture of Our Saviour after the resurrection; it is a painting of considerable merit; a copy by Cranke after that of Reubens in the cathedral at Antwerp.

Falkland: The design and colouring are highly natural.

Edgar: But ought they not to be *supernatural*?

Falkland: Westward of the Chapel is the garden, in which is a pleasant common-room and an agreeable terrace-walk formed on the city wall. . . .

The Lady Gertrude: I like this plain gateway opening beneath a low tower that conducted us into the quadrangle.

Edgar: Have you seen a bird's eye view of this College in Loggan's plates? Its plan and terraced walks really look like an enchanted palace or like the Borromean Isles and gardens in the Lago Maggiore.

Il Cortegiano: You must have been under some enchantment when you thought so; or you saw it perhaps in a dream?

Edgar: No, indeed: or at least if I did, it was a waking one.

A person of truly idealizing imagination!

In 1792 £150 was spent in repairs of the Chapel. In 1824 the ceiling was renewed. Dr. Ingram writes : ' The interior has been very recently repaired and improved.' In 1884 the Master and Fellows resolved to make the building really worthy of its sacred purpose, and invited Mr. Charles Eamer Kempe, M.A., himself a member of the College, to submit plans for a scheme of decoration. The work of Mr. Kempe for the Church in the revival of mediæval decorative art and the rescuing of the crafts ancillary to architecture from the ' ecclesiastical shop' to which an earlier school of architects had relegated them, is now recognized throughout England. Pembroke Chapel has now a most beautiful interior. The ceiling, divided as before into three compartments, is enriched with a variety of plaister mouldings and worked reliefs, bound together with fillets and ribands. In the most western are the College arms, and in the corners four tablets, bearing the titles (from the ancient sequence *De Nomine Jesu*) :— (1) *Receptor Advenis*, (2) *Columna Naufragis*, (3) *Patronus Orphanis*, (4) *Montile Regibus*. The middle compartment has a large shield inscribed with the letters I. N. R. I. In the corners are the words, (1) *Nomen quod est super omne nomen ;* (2) *Sit Nomen Domñi benedictum;* (3) *Redemptor Omnibus ;* (4) *Corona Fortibus*. The eastern division of the ceiling has a long cross with the Sacred Monogram, and in the corners the titles, (1) *Magister Insciis*, (2) *Lucerna Deviis*, (3) *Medela Sauciis*, (4) *Levamen Anxiis*. The whole is very richly coloured and gilded, as is the cornice.

On either side, and on the east wall, standing on brackets, are painted statuettes under curious wooden canopies. On the right of the altar is St. Peter, on the left St. Paul. On the north wall, between the windows, are St. John, Zechariah, Isaiah. On the south wall, St. Luke, Micah, Daniel. Niches remain for Moses and David.

The most remarkable feature of the decoration is the superb glass, richly painted in the Renaissance manner, which might be placed in the same building with the finest Flemish work of the sixteenth and seventeenth centuries [1]. The easternmost window on the north side—the least striking, perhaps, of the eight—represents the Annunciation. An angel above holds a scroll inscribed 'Deus de Deo,' and two cherubic boys exhibit the words 'Benedicta tu es in mulieribus.' The medallions below are of Zacharias and Esaias, the prophets of the evangelical Hope. Facing this window is the Nativity. The legends here are

---

[1] 'The scheme of glass illustrates the Doctrine of the Incarnation : the pictures which show it, the writers who defend it, and the founders and benefactors who may be regarded as teaching it in Oxford.'

'Lumen de Lumine,' 'In terra pax,' 'Hominibus bonae voluntatis.' The second window on the north side represents St. Bernard and St. Anselm, attended by two figures, 'Contemplatio' and 'Theologia.' St. Anselm is writing his *Cur Deus Homo.* Two cherubs carry a scroll on which is written, 'Notum fecit Dominus salutare suum.' Opposite is the Adoration of the Shepherds. Angels bear the words, 'Gloria tibi, Domine, qui natus es de Virgine,' and the boyish forms below exhibit 'Quem vidistis, Pastores, dicite annuntiate nobis, in terris quis apparuit, Natum videmus et choros angelorum collaudantes Dnûm. Alleluia.' In the upper part, with delightful incongruity, is a medallion of Francis Rous, of Barebones fame, in Puritan hat and cloak; at the bottom, 'Ex dono Henrici Elford Luxmoore hujus Collegii nuper Scholaris, Beneficiorum memoris a Francisco Rous sibi et Etonensibus collatorum.' Two shields show the arms of Eton College and of the donor (arg. a chevron between three martlets sable). In the third window on the north St. Cyril of Alexandria and St. Hierome are represented writing, attended by Veritas and Sapientia. The legend above is 'Veniet desideratus omnibus gentibus,' and, below, the University motto, 'Dominus illuminatio mea.' The corresponding window on the south side reminds the spectator that the College is a royal foundation. It represents the Coming of the Wise Kings, mounted on great sumptuously caparisoned German steeds and attended by pages. Two boys uphold the royal arms of England and Scotland. The legends are 'Per Me reges regnant,' 'Beati Pacifici,' and 'Magnificatus est Rex Pacificus super omnes reges universae terrae.' The other two windows, added in 1892 as a memorial to the late Master, are of a slightly different tone. In that on the north side King Charles I kneels, stately and devout, before the altar of the College Chapel—a pardonable anachronism—in his white Coronation robes, with crimson and ermine mantle, and jewels. On the page of the richly bound book before him is inscribed 'In verbo Tuo sperabo.' On the ground lie axe, sceptre, and crown. Two attendant figures, Benefactio and Abnegatio, carry scrolls, on which can be read, 'Erunt reges nutritii tui,' and 'Majorem hac dilectionem nemo habet, ut animam suam ponat quis pro amicis suis.' In the background is St. Aldate's Church. Above, a medallion shows Queen Anne and Gloucester Cathedral. At the sides are the arms of Lord Ossulston (gules, three demi-lions argent), and of Bishop Hall. At the foot is written, 'Mementote in Dnŏ Evan Evans, S.T.P. Qui per xxvii annos huic Collegio benignissime praefuit et obdormivit in Xto ix Kal. Dec. A.S. mdcccxci. In cujus memoriam amici et sodales

gratis animis hanc vitreâ ponendâ curavere.' Facing this is an
extremely rich Founders' Window, in which appear the figures of
King James, the Earl of Pembroke, Tesdale, and Wightwick, the
two last kneeling at faldstools. Four shields exhibit the arms of
Herbert, Tesdale, Wightwick, and the Marquess of Salisbury, the
present Visitor. In a small oval are, on a field gules, three garbs or
—the signature of the artist. In the background of the picture is
the inside of the Old Quadrangle, as modernized. In all the windows
the ironwork has been kept, which is always desirable both for strength
and to break up the coloured surface with black geometrical lines.

The altarpiece was in 1884 raised, and the marbles re-polished and
gilded. The moulded decoration framing it was added. The *mensa*
of the altar itself is a massive slab of marble standing on an arcaded
frame of oak. On the delicately carved alabaster gradine are a lofty
cross and candlesticks. The latter are copies in silver of bronze
candlesticks in the Certosa at Pavia, and the cross (which has a rayed
centre) was designed by Mr. Kempe to match them. They are thus
inscribed: 'Candelabrum hoc in usum altaris Collegii Pembrochiae
d. d. Aluredus T. Barton, A.M., Socius, 1885,' and '. . . Athelstanus
Riley, Art. Mag., 1885.' The cross: 'Hoc signum Redemptionis
nostrae dedit dedicavit D. M. Socius, olim de fundatione B. Caroli
Regis Scholaris, aⁿᵒ 1885.' On the credence, of polished walnut, are
the great silver-gilt alms-dish (1731), the excellent silver-gilt candlesticks (1679), among the oldest in England, which used to stand on
the retable, and a tray with crewets, also silver-gilt, of Spanish rococo
workmanship. This has the inscription: 'Ad calicem Salutis prae-
parandam has phialas collegio Pembrochiae dono dederunt Ath. Riley
in art. mag., H. C. R. Cunnynghame in art. bacc. A. D. 1885,' with the
arms of the College. The alms-dish is inscribed thus: 'Sacrum hoc
Donum contulêre Benjamin et Nicolâus Hyett Filij Caroli Hyett
Armigeri de civitate Gloverniâ et Colleg. Pembrochiani Sup. Ord.
Commensales.' The former was Dr. Adams' son-in-law. The lights
are inscribed thus: 'D.D. Gul. Howard Fil. Natu Secundus Comitis
Carleolensis e Coll. Pemb. Sup. Ord. Com.[1] An. Dom. 1694,' with
the College arms (the rose, wrongly, on a ground *or*) and the arms
of the donor.

The fine Commonwealth flagon and William and Mary chalice and
patens were somewhat clumsy for reverent handling, and were superseded by the crewets above mentioned and by a beautiful chalice and
paten designed by Mr. Kempe. The latter is inscribed 'Venerabili

[1] *Vide supra*, p. 274.

Corpori Jesu,' the former 'Venerabili Sanguini Jesu.' It was the disused chalice that touched the lips of Johnson and of Whitefield.

To the stalls of the Master and Vicegerent were added rich curtains on wrought-iron supports. The marble floor of the sanctuary was taken up and renewed, the woodwork throughout the Chapel cleaned of its foxy oiled appearance, the gas abolished and candles in old-fashioned sconces substituted. A new heating apparatus was also introduced. It is permitted to regret that the two closets (in which the other sex could worship as members of the Invisible Church) were abolished in 1884. They were entered from the ante-chapel.

In 1893 the undergraduates presented a petition to the Master and Fellows expressing their desire for the introduction of some music into the services, and their readiness to assist in this as far as possible. In a paper inviting subscriptions for an organ it was said, ' It is not proposed to have a choral service, for which the building would be inappropriate, and the means at the disposal of the College inadequate, but a simple Service with hymns and chorales in which all members of the congregation may join in unison.' In Mr. Kempe's original drawings an organ (of painted woodwork) was designed, affixed to the west wall of the ante-chapel and reached by a staircase. For this he now substituted a classical design, with uncoloured wood and plain pipes, played from the ground. This is the more effective in appearance amid so much colour. The case is in part made out of Archbishop Sheldon's organ-case, removed from the Theatre. It should be mentioned that the greatest part of the cost was defrayed by the Master.

The window and demi-window of the ante-chapel are still plain. Rich ' carpets of silk' to cover the altar, a new sanctuary carpet, the completion of the decoration on either side of the altar, and possibly some embellishment of the screen and other woodwork, are waiting for further funds. The entire cost of what has been carried out has been more than £4,000.

There have been no regular sermons in Chapel for half a century. But a venerable member of the College [1], who entered in 1824, told

[1] The Rev. ROBERT MORGAN JONES, who died Oct. 21, 1895, aged ninety, for nearly fifty years Vicar of Cromford, Derbyshire, and from 1870 to 1886 Rural Dean of Alfreton, was an interesting link with the past. His grandfather was a Pembrokeshire farmer, to whose house the arms of the French soldiers after their famed descent upon Fishguard Bay were carried. Mr. Jones told me that as a boy he used the ammunition for shooting rabbits, and started on the coach for Oxford wearing a Frenchman's military coat. (The French, 1,400 strong, surrendered to a handful of Yeomanry and some red-cloaked Welshwomen.) He was a Scholar of Pembroke—the examination was merely to construe ' Est in conspectu,' &c. *Vide supra*, p. 289.

me that Charles Wightwick, then Vicegerent, used to preach, in his day, fifteen-minute sermons out of a book. Dr. Jeune preached there on one occasion; but sermons had then been dropped.

The services had not always been said nakedly and plainly. In the sixties a voluntary choir and a harmonium produced some music, and ritualistic innovations began to alarm those in authority[1]. HERBERT AUGUSTUS SALWEY, however, early in 1868 was allowed to introduce a choir of boys on Sunday evenings. Though subsidized by the College it was not of long continuance.

It was the custom until the Mastership of Dr. Evans to bring the Holy Sacrament to the communicants kneeling in their places. With the arrangement of the seats usual in a college chapel, such a practice was painfully inconsistent with reverence. It is very unlikely, however, to have been a puritan survival, and savours rather of monasticism. The custom[2] was only this last year (1896) abolished at St. Mary's, but is retained at Christ Church, once in each month. A mere Calvinistic illegality would scarcely have escaped the vigilance of such a Visitor as Laud; nor, if introduced by Langley, would it have outlived the Restoration. If invented by Bishop Hall could it have survived the migration to the new Chapel under high-church Dr. Panting?

A photograph of the Chapel, as it was, was taken in 1884. It was amid such surroundings that Johnson humbly worshipped on his visits to the College, in his later years, while the Chapel was crowded with sightseers who had flocked thither to gaze at him. Bishop Jeune told Mr. Burgon that aged persons in his time remembered this.

---

[1] See below, in a later chapter, under 'Minutes.'

[2] Referred to, perhaps, as my friend the Rev. ROBERT GEORGE LIVINGSTONE (late Tutor and Vicegerent, formerly curate of St. Mary's, under Burgon) reminds me, in Keble's lines:

> 'Sweet, awful hour! the only sound
> One gentle footstep gliding round.'

Laud, Dec. 19, 1636, put a stop to the Eucharist being *celebrated* in the *body* of the Church of St. Mary's. We find Bishop Juxon complaining that the communicants expected the priest to forsake his place and bring the Sacrament to them. Archdeacon Bostock, in 1640, says: 'They sit still in their seats or pews to have the blessed Body and Blood of our Saviour go up and down to seek them all the church over.' A college chapel, however, resembles the chancel of a church; and the rubrick clearly expects 'those that are minded to receive the holy Communion' to be 'conveniently placed' there, apart from 'the people.' So Cosin, in his *Regni Angliae Religio Catholica* (1652), says, 'The Exhortation ended, those who are about to communicate enter the choir.' The Prayer Book of 1549 ordered non-communicants to depart out of the quire. Bishop Ridley went further, and in 1551 caused 'the vaile to be drawn that no person should see but those that received, and he closed the iron gates of the quire on the north and south side that non might remain in the quire' (Wriothesley's *Chronicle*).

CHAPTER XXVIII.

THE SINGING BIRDS.

WHEN Johnson told Miss More that Pembroke had been in or about his time a nest of singing birds, he included some, perhaps, of but a small pipe. Not theirs the 'enchanting shell,' 'sovereign of the willing soul, parent of sweet and solemn-breathing airs.' Of WILLIAM SHENSTONE, however, Burns said : 'His divine Elegies do honour to our language, our nation, and our species.' In the more measured words of a modern critic, Shenstone 'added some pleasing pastoral and elegiac strains to our national poetry. His highest effort is the *Schoolmistress*, a quaint and ludicrous sketch in the manner of Spenser, vivid as a picture by Teniers or Wilkie. His *Pastoral Ballad* is the finest English poem in that order. No modern poet has approached Shenstone in the simple tenderness and pathos of pastoral song.' There is, of course, some affected Arcadianism in his poetry. He was a Tibullus, playing with verse.

Shenstone, eldest son of ' a plain uneducated country gentleman,' was born at Halesowen [1]. His mother was one of the Worcestershire Penns. The dame who gave him his first schooling is pourtrayed in the *Schoolmistress*. The child so delighted in books that when any of the family went marketing he or she was expected to bring back reading for William, who carried it off to bed and laid it by him. Once, when there was none for him, his mother induced him to sleep by putting under his pillow a piece of wood wrapped up to resemble a book. Leaving Halesowen Grammar School, aged seventeen, Shenstone matriculated on May 25, 1732, from Pembroke: ' a society,' Johnson adds with pardonable partiality, ' which for half a century has [2] been eminent for English poetry and elegant literature. Here it appears he found delight and advantage, for he continued his name there ten

[1] His matriculation entry, however, appears as ' Gul. Shenstone, 17, Tho. fil: Wickstone in com. Leicest. Gen. fil.'

[2] Chalmers, mistaking Johnson, says, 'for half a century *had* been eminent,' which is not correct.

years, though he took no degree. After the first four years he put on
the civilian's gown, but without shewing any intention to engage in the
profession. . . At Oxford he employed himself upon English poetry,
and in 1737 published a small miscellany, without his name.' This
was a sheaf of verses described as '*Poems upon Various Occasions*,
written for the Entertainment of the Author, and printed for the
Amusement of a few Friends, prejudiced in his Favour.' Shenstone
took such pains to suppress this undergraduate attempt that the price
of the duodecimo went up to £15[1]. He gave himself at College to
logic, natural and moral philosophy, and the mathematics, in which he
attained considerable proficiency, and to which he frequently in his '
writings alludes. The author of the *Spiritual Quixote* says :—

'Mr. Shenstone made but few acquaintance in the University. A degree
of bashfulness from his confined education, joined with a consciousness of
his own real abilities, made him not inclined to make advances to
strangers; indeed, though those that knew him highly loved and esteemed
him, yet the singularity of his appearance rather prejudiced some people
against him. . . . According to the unnatural taste which then prevailed,
every school-boy, as soon as he was entered at the University, cut off his
hair, whatever it was ; and, without any regard to his complexion, put on
a wig, black, white, brown, or grizzle, as "lawless fancy" suggested.
This fashion no consideration could at that time have induced Mr. Shenstone to comply with. He wore his hair, however, almost in the graceful
manner which has since generally prevailed ; but, as his person was rather
large for so young a man and his hair coarse, it often exposed him to the
ill-natured remarks of people who had not half his sense; insomuch that his
friends were often in pain for the unfavourable opinion which strangers
sometimes expressed of him, and were under a necessity of vindicating
him, as Horace is *supposed* to have done Virgil, by allowing his foibles
and balancing them with his more valuable good qualities.

'Rideri possit
—At est bonus—at ingenium ingens
Inculto latet hoc sub corpore.'

'Mr. Shenstone had one ingenious and much-valued friend in Oxford,
Mr. Jago, his Schoolfellow, whom he could only visit in private, as he wore
a servitor's gown ; it being then deemed a great disparagement for a
commoner to appear in public with one in that situation ; which, by the
way, would make one wish, with Dr. Johnson, that there were no young
people admitted, in that servile state, in a place of liberal education[2].

[1] See Isaac d'Israeli's *Shenstone Vindicated* (*Curiosities of Literature*, vol. iii.
p. 95). Dodsley says he was accounted a Beau at Oxford.
[2] He asks, 'What good end can it answer in these times when every genteel
profession is so overstocked, to rob our agriculture or our manufactures of so many
useful hands, by encouraging every substantial farmer or mechanical tradesman to
breed his son to the Church ? . . . Mr. Jago, however, who was the son of a clergyman

'Though Mr. Shenstone obtained no academical honours nor took any degree in the University, he did not, like many young coxcombs of more parts perhaps than application, or who, from too large an allowance from wealthy parents, have bid defiance to the established discipline, speak contemptuously of the fruit to which he was too indolent to climb up. On the contrary he was fond of an academical life and greatly approved of its institution ; and, as his fortune was a very sufficient foundation for a genteel profession, he intended to have taken his degrees and to have proceeded in the study of physic.'

His coming into the estate at Leasowes took him away, however, from ' nursing his flame ' by ' list'ning *Cherwell's* osier banks.'

'He prolonged his stay in the country beyond what the business of the college regularly admitted. And having once neglected to return to the University at the *proper* season, he deferred it from time to time, till at length he felt a reluctance to returning at all.'

After a short ' beating about literary coffee-houses ' in town, Shenstone settled down to rural rêverie, as the ' father of landscape gardening[1].' The Leasowes became famous in Shenstone's hands as an elaborated Arcadian toy. Its winding waters, *bijou* lakes, and murmuring cascades spanned by a Chinese bridge, its tiny groves, mæandering walks and miniature prospects, were contrived with taste and skill, attracting numberless visitors. Shenstone delighted to show them round, but was irritated when asked if there were any fish in his streams and pools. He so lived in his demesnes that he neglected his house, and if the rain came in could find no money to patch the roof. Johnson says :—

'In time his expences brought clamours about him, that overpowered the lamb's bleat and the linnet's song ; and his groves were haunted by

in Warwickshire, with a large family, and who could not otherwise have given his son a liberal education, may be thought an instance in favour of this institution.

'But I make no doubt that a respectable clergyman, as Mr. Jago's father was, might, by a very slight application to the head or fellows of almost any College, have procured some scholarship or exhibition for a youth of genius and properly qualified ; which, with a very small additional expence, might have supported him in the University without placing him in so humiliating a situation ; which, in some future period of his life (when perhaps his parts might have raised him to some eminence in the world) might put it in the power of any purse-proud fellow collegian to boast that he had waited on him in the College; though perhaps all the obligation he had lain under to such a patron was the receiving sixpence a week, not as an act of generosity but as a tribute imposed on him by the standing rules of the society.'

[1] Is it not thus? You may either look at a house or from a house. If the former, you make your garden formal and architectural. When architecture and man himself became uninteresting, people looked out of window, and landscape gardening came in. We love Nature because we have lost Art. Had we anything of human interest to gaze at, we should put ' scenery ' back into its proper place as the beautiful frame of Man and his handiwork.

beings very different from fawns and fairies. He spent his estate in adorning it, and his death was probably hastened by his anxieties. He was a lamp that spent its oil in blazing.'

The *delubra deorum* had better have remained cowhouses. Shenstone laments in *The Progress of Taste* :—

> ' But did the Muses haunt his cell,
> Or in his dome did Venus dwell?
> When all the structures shone complete,
> Ah me! 'twas Damon's own confession,
> Came Poverty, and took possession.'

Shenstone died at the Leasowes of a putrid fever on February 11, 1763, and lies in Halesowen Church under a plain stone. He was unmarried, but not heart-whole. Dodsley describes him as a man of much tenderness and generosity, large, clumsy, and heavy-looking, except when his face was lit up by some sprightly sentiment. His hair was grey very early. He seldom wore anything, summer or winter, but a plain blue coat and scarlet waistcoat with a broad gold lace. He is thus painted in the portrait in the College Bursary. There is an urn erected to his memory at Hagley by his friend and neighbour, Lord Lyttelton, and Montesquieu inscribed to him ' in bad English but in pure taste,' amid memorials dedicated to Virgil and Theocritus, a garden seat at Ermenouville, ' the Leasowes of France [1],' as was done by others elsewhere. If he ' incongruously blended the rural swain with the disciple of virtù,' at any rate his were not the counterfeited pastorals of a Fleet Street poet, but transcriptions of real sentiments and places.

Gray (who is said to have borrowed from the *Schoolmistress* the idea of the famous line ' Some mute inglorious Milton here may rest ') had no patience with Shenstone's sentimentalities about nature and the country and simplicity. ' He goes hopping along his own gravel walks, and never deviates from the beaten path for fear of being lost.' He pictures him exchanging endless letters and verses with neighbouring clergymen of a poetical turn. As a writer, however, no one can deny to Shenstone skill and fastidious grace, though he is delicate and tender rather than bracing. ' When forced from dear Hebe ' will always live wedded to Arne's delicious air. Boswell records Johnson's emotion at Henley when recalling the lines :—

> ' Whoe'er has travell'd life's dull round,
> Where'er his stages may have been,
> May sigh to think he still has found
> The warmest welcome at an Inn.'

[1] ' Château gothique, mais orné de bois charmans, dont j'ai pris l'idée en Angleterre.'

Of his *ferme ornée* Wesley in his *Journal* (iv. p. 225) writes :—

'I never was so surprized. I have seen nothing in all England to be compared with it. It is beautiful and elegant all over. There is nothing grand, nothing costly; no temples, so called ; no statues (except two or three which had better have been spared :) but such walks and shades, such hills and dales, such artless cascades, such waving woods with waters intermixed[1], as exceed all imagination. . . . I doubt if it be exceeded by anything in Europe.'

Wesley adds that Shenstone laid out the whole of his patrimony in improving the place, ' living in hopes of great preferment grounded on the promises of many rich and great friends. But nothing was performed, till he died at forty-eight, probably of a broken heart.' Graves was supposed to have glanced at his friend in his novel, *Columella, or, The Distressed Anchoret.*

Graves describes in a lively manner the côteries in the College :—

'Having brought with me the character of a tolerably good Grecian, I was invited to a very sober little party, who amused themselves in the evening with reading Greek and drinking water. Here I continued six months, and we read over Theophrastus, Epictetus, Phalaris's Epistles, and such other Greek authors as are seldom read at school. But I was at length seduced from this mortified symposium to a very different party, a set of jolly, sprightly young fellows, most of them west country lads, who drank ale, smoked tobacco, punned, and sang bacchanalian catches the whole evening. . . . I own with shame that, being then not seventeen, I was so far captivated with the social disposition of these young people (many of whom were ingenious lads and good scholars) that I began to think them the only wise men. Some gentlemen commoners, however, who were my countrymen (amongst whom were the two late successive lords[2] Ch—d—th), who considered the above mentioned as very *low* company (chiefly on account of the liquor they drank[3]) good naturedly

---

[1] ' And having shown them where to stray
　　Threw little pebbles in their way.'
But this is unkind. Rather—
　　　　　　　　' Sweet interchange
　　Of river, valley, mountains, woods, and plains.'

[2] JOHN THYNNE HOWE, second Lord CHEDWORTH, ob. s. p. 1762, and HENRY FREDERICK HOWE, third Lord, ob. unmarried 1781, sons of the Right Hon. John Howe of Wishford Magna, created Baron Chedworth in 1741, for whom on his ennoblement the motto was suggested ' Hoc erat in votis '—in allusion partly to his seat ' Wishfort,' and partly to his votes in Parliament, which helped him to that honour. They entered Pembroke together, from Abingdon, on Nov. 25, 1731, aged seventeen and sixteen, and lie together at Withington, Gloucestershire. Arms : Or, a fess between three wolves' heads couped sable.

[3] The Panegyrist of Oxford Ale in the *Oxford Sausage* denounces such fastidiousness :—
　　' The lewd spendthrift, falsely deem'd polite,
　　While steams around the fragrant Indian bowl,
　　Oft damns the vulgar sons of humble ALE.'

invited me to their party; they treated me with port wine and arrack punch; and now and then, when they had drunk so much as hardly to distinguish wine from water, they would conclude with a bottle or two of claret. They kept late hours, drank their favourite toast on their knees, and in short were what were then called "bucks of the first head." This was deemed good company and high life; but it neither suited my taste, my fortune, or my constitution. There was, besides, a sort of flying squadron of plain, sensible, matter-of-fact men, confined to no club, but associating with each party. They anxiously inquired after the news of the day and the politics of the times. They had come to the University in their way to the Temple, or to get a slight smattering of the sciences before they settled in the country. They were a good sort of young people, and perhaps the most rational of the college, but neither with these was I destined to associate.

'In each of the above-mentioned parties, except the water-drinkers, I had once or twice met Mr. Shenstone and another young man, a Mr. Whistler, of a gentleman's family and born to a genteel estate in Oxfordshire. Neither Mr. Shenstone or Mr. Whistler however seemed quite in their element amidst those sons of Comus, the politer votaries of Bacchus, or with the matter-of-fact society, not from any opinion of superior understanding, but from a difference of tastes and pursuits.

'Our more familiar acquaintance commenced by an invitation from Mr. Shenstone to breakfast at his chambers, which we accepted, and which, according to the sociable disposition of most young people, was protracted to a late hour; during which Mr. Shenstone, I remember, in order to detain us produced Cotton's Virgil Travestie, which he had lately met with. . . . In short, this morning's lounge, which seemed mutually agreeable, was succeeded by frequent repetitions of them, and at length by our meeting likewise, almost every evening, at each other's chambers the whole summer, where we read plays and poetry, Spectators or Tatlers, and other works of easy digestion, and sipped Florence wine. . . .

'We began to be considered a dangerous triumvirate, and as meditating some design of unfriendly import: to which a very trifling incident added "confirmation strong as proof of holy writ."

'As I was a scholar of the house, and had some dry studies prescribed to me, which I thought it necessary to pursue with regularity and strict attention the whole morning, I did not like to be interrupted. Mr. Shenstone one day came into my room, and, as I could not listen to any conversation, he took up a pen and said he would write my character; this (at least what he called such) he wrote impromptu, and left it on my table; which an impertinent fellow, coming in soon after, saw and read without knowing who was the subject of it, and immediately retired unnoticed. And now it was discovered that we three, Mr. Shenstone, Mr. Whistler, and myself, shut up ourselves to write the characters of the whole society; and we were thenceforth, for some time, considered in no very favourable light by the rest of the college.'

ANTHONY WHISTLER, whom Graves here mentions, after being at Eton entered Pembroke on Oct. 21, 1732, from Whitchurch,

Salop, aged seventeen. He is the author of the *Shuttlecock* and several pieces in Dodsley's *Miscellany*. He was, at College, 'a young man of great delicacy of sentiment, but with such a dislike to languages that he is unable to read the classics in the original, yet no one formed a better judgment of them. He wrote, moreover, a great part of a tragedy on the story of Dido.' He is described twenty years later as living in elegant style and evincing a refined taste and softness of manners. Shenstone paid him a visit, but his friend did not like his roughness and fell out with him. Whistler died in early middle age, in 1754. 'The triumvirate which was the greatest happiness and the greatest pride of my life is broken,' Shenstone wrote to Graves. 'Tales animas *oportuit* esse concordes.'

Richard Graves himself was the son of Hearne's friend, the Gloucestershire antiquary (1677–1729).

RICHARD GRAVES, senior, eldest son of Samuel, of Mickleton Manor, entered Pembroke June 3, 1693; B.A. 1699. He married Elizabeth, daughter and co-heiress of Thomas Morgan. Hearne (*Relliquiae*, 2nd ed. iii. 31) commends his modesty, sweetness of temper and kindness to his tenants and to the poor. His large antiquarian and topographical collections passed to his friend James West, who wrote his epitaph at Mickleton. At West's death they were bought by the Earl of Shelburne. His valuable cabinet of Greek and Roman coins was purchased by another friend, Roger Gale, said to be 'Mr. Townsend' in the *Spiritual Quixote*.

RICHARD GRAVES, the younger, is remembered as one of our earlier novelists and as a voluminous writer of prose and verse. He was born at Mickleton Manor, May 4, 1715. When Mr. Smith, the curate, thought him sufficiently seen in Homer and Hesiod, he was sent, aged thirteen, to Roysse's School, and entered Pembroke Nov. 7, 1732, as an Abingdon scholar, the same day as Whitefield. They took B.A. together, June 25, 1736[1]. The same year he was elected Fellow of All Souls.

After studying medicine in London he came back to Oxford, and proceeded M.A. 1740. In that year he was ordained deacon. As soon as he was a priest, Fitzherbert, Johnson's friend, gave Graves the donative of Tissington in Derbyshire, and for three years he was chaplain at Tissington Hall. In 1744 he was curate of Aldworth, near Reading, living in the house of a gentleman farmer named Bartholomew, with whose youngest daughter Lucy, a beautiful but uneducated girl[2] of

---

[1] He was probably for a time under Whitefield's influence. He makes Wildgoose say: 'I remember when I was at Oxford I used to pray seven times a day, and fasted myself to a skeleton. I powdered my wig and went every month to the Sacrament with the *Companion to the Altar* in my pocket.'

[2] Graves had at one period another attachment, namely, to the extraordinarily accomplished Utrecia Smith, to whom he placed a memorial in Mickleton Church. She is celebrated by Shenstone in his *Fourth Elegy*—'Ophelia's Urn.'

sixteen, he fell in love, and married her. He then sent her to London, where she acquired what she lacked. The history of Rivers and Charlotte Woodville in the *Spiritual Quixote* is Graves's own story. On the wall of the chancel at Claverton is a handsome, festooned urn, inscribed: 'Luciae conjugi carissimae Ricardus Graves conjux infelicissimus fecit et sibi, Obiit Cal. Maii. 1777. Aet. 46.' Having forfeited his fellowship and offended his family, Graves was forced to exert his literary talents. By the interest of Sir Edward Harvey he became rector of Claverton (where he enlarged the house), holding the adjoining vicarage of Kilmersdon in plurality from 1763. Lady Chatham also made him her chaplain. His means increasing, he bought Combe Manor, Somerset. For thirty years he took pupils, amongst whom were Malthus, Henry Skrine, a son of Bishop Warburton, and Prince Hoare, the artist. Malthus, who learnt with Graves 'little but Latin and good behaviour,' administered the Holy Sacrament to him on his death-bed. He died Nov. 23, 1804, a link between this century and the Oxford Methodists. There are portraits of Graves by Northcote and Gainsborough. 'In frame he was short and slender, and he was eccentric both in dress and gait; but his features were expressive, and his conversation was marked by a sportive gaiety.' This 'amiable, well-read, and lively old man ... was well known to all the frequenters of Bath, and he might be seen on the verge of ninety walking almost daily to Bath with the briskness of youth.' (*Dict. Nat. Biog.*) He mixed with all shades of society—a whig, but a zealous churchman. Between 1744 and 1763 Shenstone paid him repeated visits at Claverton. He is buried there.

Of his many prose and verse publications, written in a clear, lively style, and very popular in his day, the best known, the *Spiritual Quixote* (1772), is a good-natured and discriminating satire on the Methodist movement. It contains some very free portraiture of Whitefield, and of his mother, the landlady of the *Bell*, to the interior of which we are introduced. 'A late writer,' he says, 'does Mr. Whitfield the honour of being the first author of Methodism; whom he also calls a fellow of Pembroke college in Oxford. But as Mr. Whitfield disclaims all worldly grandeur, and with great humility assures us that (like the blessed Founder of our religion) he was born in an inn, so, like him, (I am persuaded) he will confess "that he came not to be ministered unto, but to minister." For he was really a servitor, and not a fellow, of that learned society.' Graves describes a Pembroke room :—

'When I first went to the University' (he makes Wildgoose relate), 'I lived in a large chamber, hung with green baize; the bed was placed in a sort of recess, separated from the dining-room by two large folding doors, which were thrown open, when I went to bed, to make it more airy. I happened once to wake about midnight, and, it being starlight, saw on the further side of the room a tall figure in white, near six feet

high. It seemed to have a square cap on its shoulders, but was without
a head. . . . I leaped out of bed, when lo! I embraced in my arms a white
surplice, which a scholar of the house, having left in my room after
evening prayers, had hung upon a brass peg, over which I had suspended
my square cap such as they wear in the University.—Yes, yes, your
trenchard caps, I have heard of them, says Tugwell.' Again, 'I knew
a man who, having read at how great a price the earthen lamp of
Epictetus was sold after his death, and flattering himself that the implements of his lucubrations might be valued as curiosities by posterity,
determined to renounce the use of candles (as a modern invention) and
(like that philosopher) to study by a lamp; which to his utter confusion
he happened to overturn, and spilled a considerable quantity of oil upon
an handsome folio which he had borrowed of his tutor.'

The hero in chapel was accustomed to follow the lessons in a Latin
Bible. Before graduating as Bachelor he was created 'senior soph'
by the solemn imposition of Aristotle upon his head, paying a fee of
ten guineas. The following, in which the rustical whims of his friend
Shenstone were very likely in his mind, may be given as a specimen of
Graves' style, which has both humour and good humour:—

'She was a woman of fine understanding, though her judgment
appeared sometimes almost eclipsed by the brilliancy of her imagination.
To amuse herself in her solitary situation, she had formerly indulged the
suggestions of her fancy, and turned my Lord's Park into a poetical
Arcadia: where her Ladyship and a female companion or two lived
almost the whole summer a mere pastoral life; and ranged about, with
their crooks in their hands, like so many Grecian shepherdesses.
Garlands of flowers, or baskets of fruit, were seen suspended on every
beautiful oak, with rustic pipes, rakes, pitch-forks, and other rural
implements, disposed in a picturesque manner, in different parts of
the Park. Nay, the poor Chaplain was forced to leave his bottle and
his pipe, and back-gammon table, with my Lord; and even neglect his
pastoral function assigned him by the Bishop, to attend her Ladyship
and her bleating lambkins; and to sit whole afternoons under a spreading
tree, to entertain them with his flute. For the Steward had actually
bought her Ladyship "a score of sheep at Banbury-fair" (according to
Justice Shallow's expression) for this romantic purpose. The inclemency
of the weather, however, in this Northern climate was by no means
favourable to these lovely Bœotians. Neither did many of the pastoral
functions suit with the delicacy of a modern woman of quality. For her
Ladyship frequently caught the tooth-ach, and was forced to have
recourse to a neighbouring Apothecary (a character seldom introduced
in the ancient Bucolicks); and one of her companions met with a terrible
accident in the discharge of her office: for having seized the leg of
a large bell-weather with her crook, which was fastened to her wrist by a
blue ribband, the rude unclassical brute struggled with such force to
disengage himself, that he pulled down the poor Pastora, dragged her

some yards, and disfigured her face to such a degree, that she could not appear again for six weeks; and this put an end to this extravagant scene in pastoral life. Lady Sherwood was now grown tired of the country. . . . The Physician therefore had an hint given him, to order her Ladyship to Bath for her health,' where Whitefieldism took her fancy. There is a good deal of lively Dutch realism in the pictures of Bath society. 'I take Bath, as a public place,' says Rueful, 'to be a better school for any young fellow than all the Universities and Colleges in the world[1].'

Another contemporary of Shenstone was ROBERT BINNELL, author of some learned notes in Grainger's *Tibullus*. He was of Shifnal, Salop; matriculated Aug. 28, 1732; M.A. 1739.

One of the 'singing-birds' was WILLIAM HAWKINS (1722–1801), poet and divine, entered Pembroke Nov. 12, 1737. He was the eldest son of William Hawkins (1673–1746), serjeant at law, author of the *Treatise of the Pleas of the Crown*, and a descendant of Sir John Hawkyns, the famous Elizabethan sea-captain. His mother was a sister of Soame Jenyns, and through his grandmother he was descended from the co-Founder Tesdale. On March 2, 1741½ (B.A. Feb. 26), he was elected a Tesdale Fellow. Serjeant Hawkins lived in Oxford, and his son dwelt there some years composing poems, plays, and sermons. M.A. 1744. On June 6, 1751, he succeeded Lowth as Poetry Professor, and held the Chair until 1756.

In 1764 he was presented to the Rectory of Little Casterton, Rutland-shire, but removed almost at once to Whitchurch Canonicorum, which he retained till death. Prebendary of Wells, 1767. Bampton Lecturer, 1787. He died in a fit at Oxford, Oct. 13, 1801. In 1758 Hawkins had collected his many productions into three volumes, (1) theological tracts; (2) dramatic and other poems, including *The Thimble* ('an heroi-comical Poem in four Cantos by a Gentleman of Oxford,' in imitation of the *Rape of the Lock*), *Henry and Rosamund*, and the *Siege of Aleppo*; (3) lectures on poetry and Creweian orations. Goldsmith reviewed these productions for the *Critical Review* somewhat severely. Hawkins defended himself, and Goldsmith rejoined. Hawkins translated the first six Aeneids, but was *poeta factus* rather than *natus*. The *Poems on Various Subjects* were issued in 1781. The version of *Cymbeline* acted in 1759 at Drury Lane was said to be 'entirely ruined by his unpoetical additions and

[1] Graves had three sons at Pembroke. To the youngest, CHARLES GRAVES, was written the *Letter from a Father to his Son at the University*, dissuading him from listening to Dr. Priestley's *Address to Young Students*. After giving proofs of the Saviour's Godhead, he tells his son that he has subscribed the Articles ' in obedience to your Father; as, unless you saw manifest and *important* reasons to the contrary it was your duty to do.' He begs him not to turn aside from his studies in the wide field of theological controversy. There were four generations of the family at the College.

injudicious alterations.' He fell foul of Garrick about this and others of his plays. Hawkins was 'an indefatigable printer of sermons.'

It was right that a house which had been noted in earlier ages as a nursery of lawyers should be able to claim the name of the greatest of modern jurists. Sir WILLIAM BLACKSTONE, the posthumous son of a Cheapside silk-mercer, of a good Wiltshire stock, having been nominated by Walpole on the foundation of the Charterhouse, at the age of fifteen was head of the school and thought qualified to proceed to the University. He was entered as a commoner at Pembroke Nov. 30, 1738, with a view, no doubt, to one of the exhibitions of Dame Holford's foundation for Charterhouse scholars. He had already been elected to an exhibition by the governors of the school, to commence from Michaelmas, 1738; but he was permitted to continue his studies there till December 12, the Founder's Day, that he might speak the customary oration, which he did with much credit. At this time also he obtained the Benson gold medal for verses on Milton. So well pleased were the Master and Fellows of Pembroke with their boyish student, that in the following February they unanimously elected him a Holford exhibitioner. At College he worked at his books assiduously, chiefly the classical poets, but gave attention also to logic, mathematics, and other branches of science.

Mathematical knowledge as applied to the Queen and Mistress of the Arts fascinated his versatile genius at this time, and at the age of twenty he compiled a treatise on the Elements of Architecture. In his under-graduate days were written most of the 'originals and translations' which he is said to have afterwards collected in an unpublished volume. A modern biographer observes that nothing has been lost to English literature by Blackstone's seeking in poetry only a relaxation. His poem, however, called *The Lawyer's Farewell to his Muse*, written on his relinquishing lighter studies for that of the law, excites the admiration of Chalmers. Blackstone knew how to appreciate both Shakspeare and Addison, and, as befits a great Judge, never ceased to be a man of letters. He was entered of the Middle Temple, Nov. 20, 1741. In November, 1743, he was elected into the Society of All Souls, and from that date divided his time between Oxford and the Temple. On June 12, 1745, he commenced B.C.L., and on November 28, 1746, was called to the Bar. Not having a fluent or graceful delivery or powerful patrons he made his way slowly there. At Oxford he was more appreciated, his services to All Souls as Bursar and Steward of the Manors being especially great. The completion of the Codrington Library remains as a monument of his financial and architectural ability[1]. In 1749 he was chosen Recorder of

[1] It had been perhaps a sufficient title to the gratitude of posterity to have founded the All Souls cellar, the first at any College. This was done to avoid the necessity of resorting to the tavern.

Wallingford. The next year he commenced D.C.L., his legal acumen being displayed in the great argument upon Founder's Kin, the claims of which were being found by the College of which he was a Fellow embarrassing and less than kind. He was also the reformer of the Clarendon Press. Blackstone's *Lectures on English Law*—a novel subject at Oxford—suggested to Mr. Viner the foundation of a Chair, and he was elected the first Professor. Bentham, a critical hearer, described the man and his lectures as ' cold, precise and wary, exhibiting a frigid pride.' In 1757 he was elected Michel Fellow of Queen's, and here again his financial capacity and fine taste have a lasting memorial in the imposing buildings on the High Street. As Assessor to the Vice-Chancellor's Court he gave some valuable legal opinions affecting the privileges of the University. In 1761 his marriage with Sarah Clitherow having vacated his All Souls fellowship, he was appointed by the Earl of Westmorland Principal of New Inn Hall. In this year he became Member for Hindon, Wilts ; in 1763, having declined the coif, he was made Solicitor General to the Queen. In 1765 he began to republish his Lectures in the form of the famous *Commentaries on the Laws of England*, the first attempt to popularize the mysteries of Law.

The *Commentaries* have had an extraordinary influence and authority even down to the present day, though fiercely attacked by the school of Bentham and Austin. The French mind is eminently precise and legal, but French jurists have cited Blackstone as an authority above all the lawyers of France. He has been accused of 'an oppressive spirit of orderliness.' In 1766 he severed himself from Oxford, resigning his professorship and principalship, and in 1768 was returned as burgess for Westbury. The opinion given by him against Wilkes was said to contradict a passage in the *Commentaries*, and in the next edition the passage was altered. Hence it became a toast at Whig banquets, 'The First Edition of Dr. Blackstone's Commentaries!' In 1770, having refused the post of Solicitor General, he received the patent of Judge of the Common Pleas. His last years were spent in retirement at Wallingford. He died there Feb. 14, 1780, aged fifty-seven, and lies in St. Peter's Church, where a tablet records his fame. A few weeks before his death he began to prepare a body of Statutes for the new college founded at Cambridge by Sir John Downing. Blackstone was a corpulent man, languid and irritable, but averse to party violence, a good friend, a public-spirited neighbour and colleague, above all, an upright and clear-headed judge. His portrait in the Bodleian by Hill was presented in 1785 (see Gutch, ii. 978). At All Souls is his statue by Bacon. Blackstone bore argent, two bars gules, in chief three cocks of the second ; a mullet in fess point for difference. He presented in 1754 a silver beaker to Pembroke College. He describes himself on it as ' Hujusce Collegii per quinquennium Commensalis et dn̄ae Elizabethae Holford e Schola Carthusiana Alumnus.'

CHAPTER XXIX.

TWO ARCHBISHOPS, SOME LAWYERS AND SCHOLARS.

Dr. WILLIAM NEWCOME, Archbishop of Armagh (son of Joseph New-come, Rector of Barton-in-the-Clay, Beds, and Vicar of St. Helen's, Abingdon), is chiefly remembered as a precursor of modern Revision of the translation of the Holy Scriptures. He came of an originally Nonconformist stock [1] in Bunyan's county, but was born at Abingdon, April 10, 1730. He entered Pembroke as an Abingdon scholar Oct. 31, 1745. B.A. 1749; M.A. from Hertford College 1753. There he was vice-principal and a tutor of considerable repute, one of his pupils being Charles James Fox. 'Upon some occasion of innocent sportiveness with his illustrious pupil,' writes Bishop Mant [2], 'he met with an accident which caused the loss of his right arm.' They maintained their friendship to the close of life.

In 1765 Newcome was made B.D. and D.D., and became chaplain to the Earl of Hertford, then Lord Lieutenant of Ireland, by whom he was advanced the following year to the see of Dromore. In 1775 he was translated to Ossory, and in 1777 to Waterford and Lismore. Two years later his merits recommended him for the vacant Primacy, which in *Collectanea Politica* is said to have been 'rescued from a monopolizing breed of jobbers and given to learning and piety.' In one of Lord Charlemont's *Letters* (Jan. 10, 1795) the writer says that the Lord Lieutenant, 'regardless of ministerial influence or convenience, has placed at the head of the Church a prelate not from recommendation but from character, and whose unassuming virtue, conduct, principles and erudition have alone recommended him to that high office. In [this nomination] publick utility has alone been considered. Newcome had no English patron but Charles Fox.' Newcome succeeded at Dromore the Honble. Henry Maxwell, and at Armagh Lord Rokeby, while he was followed in the primatial throne by the Honble. William Stuart. He certainly had no such aristocratic credentials. 'I learn, however,' writes Bishop Mant, 'from a relation of the primate that he had on this occasion another " English patron," for that he was promoted to the primacy by the express appointment of King George III; such at least is the traditional belief of his family.' He had, however, a considerable fortune, and spent large

---

[1] He was grandnephew of Henry Newcome, the Royalist Nonconformist of the Commonwealth.

[2] *History of the Church of Ireland*, i. 734.

sums on his cathedral and palace. The Archbishop's primary Charge enforced on the priesthood the duty of residence, even in parishes where there was no church. He also promoted catechizing, as ordered in the rubrick, and revived the office of rural deans. His *Harmony of the Gospels*, published in 1778, had involved him in controversy with Dr. Priestley respecting the duration of our Lord's ministry. In addition to some similar treatises, he began to take in hand a new translation of the Bible. In 1785 he put out *An Attempt towards an improved Version, a Metrical Arrangement, and an Explanation, of the Twelve Minor Prophets*, followed in 1788 by his *Ezekiel*. Bishop Mant says, 'In two of his publications, however, he has been especially unhappy, if not from their bearing a tinge of unwholesome liberality on matters of very serious import, at least from the precedent they have afforded to men of unsound principles, and from the discontent which they are calculated to produce in the minds of others. His " Historical View of the English Biblical Translations; the expediency of revising by authority our present Translation, and the means of executing such a work," published in 1792, may give good reason to think that his zeal outran his judgement; for that any imaginary and problematical benefit contemplated in a new version of the holy Scriptures for publick use would be more than counterbalanced by the disrepute cast on the old version, and the distrust of its fidelity thus exerted on the popular mind.

'His posthumous publication of an *Attempt towards Revising our English Translation of the Greek Scriptures* is liable to the same exception, and in effect it has been made the occasion and the basis, which he could hardly have anticipated and which it is to be presumed he would have deprecated and deplored, of another work under the title of an "Improved Version of the New Testament, published by a Society for the Promotion of Christian Knowledge" . . . [1808]. The primate's family[1] lamented and condemned the use which had been made of their relative's authority, and others who have no natural connection with him, but who feel for the honour of the Church in which he bore so high a station, will long continue to grieve at the sight of his name placed in such an unholy association.' Chalmers is of the same opinion. The Unitarian editors of the Version alluded to by Bishop Mant, were, he says, defective in scholarship and critical power. Archbishop Newcome himself was as well equipped as any in his day for a work beyond any man's capacity. He died at his house in St. Stephen's Green, Jan. 11, 1800, aged seventy, and was laid in the new Chapel of Trinity College, Dublin. He was not a politician, and was happy to withdraw from state and from public affairs to his literary studies. Yet he was assiduous in his great office, and lived respected by all. Newcome's interleaved Bible in four volumes folio, containing his collations for Revision, is at Lambeth.

Archbishop JOHN MOORE (1731–1805), the typical Church ruler of the easy-going ' common-sense ' era of ' moderation ' at the point

---

[1] His relative, Bishop Stock of Killarney, addressed an indignant expostulation to the editors.

where it met the incoming tide of modern revival, yet with a touch of old-world romance in his career, is one of many examples of the efficiency of the system now superseded in bringing poor men of talent to the front. The son of Thomas Moore, a Gloucestershire grazier (Nichols says a butcher in Gloucester ; but Moore matriculated as 'generosi filius'), he held the Primacy between two aristocrats, Cornwallis and Manners-Sutton. His father sent him to the Cathedral School, whence he removed, with a view to Oxford, to St. Marie de Crypt School. Nichols[1] says, 'On account of the docility of his behaviour and his promising talents, some friends procured him a humble situation at Pembroke College.' But he was not a servitor. He entered March 27, 1744, aged fifteen, as a Townsend scholar. He took M.A. 1751 (in which year he was ordained deacon at Gloucester); B.D. and D.D. 1763. ' While at College he applied himself with great assiduity to his studies and acquired universal respect by the modesty of his demeanour, the regularity of his conduct, and his classical attainments' (Cunningham). Moore resided for nine years.

An accident was the beginning of his fortunes. Dr. Bliss, the Savilian professor, being on a visit to Blenheim Palace, was desired by the second Duke of Marlborough to recommend a governor for the Lords Charles and Robert Spencer. While Bliss was trying to think of some suitable person, young Moore of his College was seen strolling in the park. Without hesitation Bliss pointed him out to the Duke as the man he required. The appointment however was not without humiliation, the Duchess insisting that the handsome but modest young preceptor should have his seat at the second table and not with the family. ' But this mortification did not continue long, as this haughty Dame, when she became a widow, actually courted the very same tutor to receive her hand. Mr. Moore, from a strong principle of honour, declined the advantage of the connexion[2] ; and so sensible was the [third] Duke of the generosity of his conduct that, as the first token of his gratitude, he settled an annuity of 400*l.* upon him, and obtained for him [from the King] very valuable church preferments.' From 1763 to 1771 he was canon of Christ Church ; in 1761 he received one of the golden prebends of Durham, in 1771 was made Dean of Canterbury, and in 1775 Bishop of Bangor. His consecration occasioned 'A Word of Comfort from Bangor to Canterbury on the loss of her Dean' :—

[1] *Literary Anecdotes,* vol. viii. 94 n.

[2] It was while acting as tutor to the young Duke of Buccleuch that Adam Smith in 1765 inspired a great French lady with tender sentiments which he did not reciprocate. Another and perhaps better version of Moore's introduction to the Duke is that Moore passed through the College quadrangle while his tutor, John Hopkins, was conversing there with his Grace's steward. I am indebted to Canon Scott-Robertson, who has in the press a Life of Archbishop Moore, for several corrections of common mis-statements.

'Cease, Canterbury, to deplore
The loss of your accomplished Moore,
    Repining at my gain.
I soon may have most cause to mourn;
To *you* he'll probably return,
    With *me* will scarce remain.'

Which was answered by 'A Voice from Canterbury' :—

'To *me*, you prophesy, our mitred Moore
Revolving years may probably restore,
    And thus in vain attempt my tears to dry.
I scarcely know my Masters but by name,
Triennial visits and the voice of fame,
    For, ah! my Palaces in ruins lie.'

The prediction came true, for in 1783, the metropolitical throne having
been declined by Hurd and Lowth, the King desired them to recommend
the fittest, in their judgement, of their episcopal brethren. Both, without
consulting together, suggested Dr. Moore. 'While occupying the first
station in the Church, Archbishop Moore avoided all other activity but
that of Christian piety and spiritual duty. He scarcely took any part in
political disputes, neither did he adopt any steps to influence the minds
of the dissenters on the one hand, nor to alarm the friends of orthodoxy
on the other.' He was certainly not a great Primate. On the other
hand, he connected himself with the philanthropic movements which
were then beginning to stir, warmly promoted Sunday schools, and
co-operated with Wilberforce in his efforts towards association 'for
promoting reformation of manners,' the improvement of the condition
of the natives of India and the negroes of Barbados, and the revival
of missions to the heathen. When Wilberforce, however, begged the
Archbishop to put himself at the head of the Church Missionary
Society, founded in 1799, Moore 'with provoking caution' replied that
he must be content to watch its proceedings with candour. The most
notable event of Moore's primacy was his consecration in 1787 of an
episcopate for America, in the persons of White and Provoost, three
years after hands had been laid on Seabury by the Scots prelates. This
was not done without difficulty and circumspection. 'We cannot,' wrote
the Primates and their suffragans, 'but be extremely cautious lest we
should be the instruments of establishing an ecclesiastical system which
will be called a branch of the Church of England, but afterwards may
possibly appear to have departed from it essentially either in doctrine or
in discipline.' Moore was an esteemed and amiable prelate, well seen
for learning, but not above his age. He married first a sister of Sir
James Wright, Resident at Venice, and secondly, in 1770, Catherine,
daughter of Sir Robert Eden, sister of Lord Auckland, a celebrated
beauty. One of his sons was Member for Woodstock. He died Jan. 18,
1805, aged seventy-three, and was buried with much solemnity at Lambeth.
Dighton's caricature of this prelate is in the Hope Collection. His portrait
by Romney at Lambeth is a half-length. Another, in profile, is Hamilton's
study for his picture of the nuptials of George IV. According to an idle

tradition, the Primate had a large wen on the side of his face, which made him unwilling to be seen in public. It is not the case that he set the fashion of Archbishops being enthroned in their absence, though this is often asserted. There is a full-face portrait at Canterbury deanery[1].

It has been mentioned that Archbishop Moore promoted the Sunday school system. This movement was brought into general notice by Raikes, a Gloucester bookseller, and by THOMAS STOCK, incumbent of St. John Baptist (1782), Gloucester, and perpetual curate of St. Aldate's in that city. Stock, born at Gloucester 1750, entered Pembroke Oct. 27, 1767. Fellow 1772. He died in 1803 Vicar of Glasbury[2].

At this time there was studying at the College JONATHAN WILLIAMS of Rhayader, author of the *History of the County of Radnor*, and a learned Welsh divine (1754–1821). Among men of affairs I have the names of EDWARD HERBERT (matr. 1722), M.P. for Ludlow 1754–70, of ROBERT WILLIAMS, the banker (matr. 1750), M.P. for Dorchester 1807–12, and of Colonel EDWARD DISBROWE (matr. 1770), M.P. for Windsor 1806–18.

Some eminent lawyers at this time carried on the old traditions of the House. The Vinerian Professorship was held 1777–93 by RICHARD WOODDESON, D.C.L., who entered Pembroke May 29, 1759. Proctor 1776. Moral Philosophy Lecturer 1777. He was also counsel to the University, and a Commissioner of bankrupts. Buried in the Temple Church (bencher 1799) Nov. 5, 1822.—An earlier bencher of the Middle Temple (1750) was ELFRED STAPLE, matriculated 1716.—Sir JOHN KYNASTON POWELL, Bart. (entered 1770; B.A. 1774); took B.C.L. from All Souls 1777; D.C.L. 1814. Knight of the Shire for Salop 1784–1822.—Sir JAMES WATSON, Knight (entered 1777), was Serjeant-at-Law and (Mr. Foster says) made a Judge in 1795. M.P. for Bridport 1790–6.—JAMES SEDGWICK (matriculated 1797, aet. 25) held various high legal appointments.—Three noted civilians recorded in Coote's *Lives* were Henderson's friend, Dr. CHARLES COOTE (matriculated 1778), Dr. MAURICE SWABEY[3], Chancellor of Rochester

[1] Dr. NATHANIEL FORSTER, chaplain to an earlier Archbishop (Herring) and also to Bishop Butler, editor of the *Hebrew Bible* and of *Plato's Dialogues*, entered Pembroke 1732, aet. 14. Fellow of C.C.C.; Prebendary of Bristol; Vicar of Rochdale.

[2] Sunday schools were much patronized by the Evangelical clergy. They cannot be considered a good substitute for the rubrical catechizing in Church—which still continued in many places—and must be regarded as the makeshift of an un-ecclesiastical age. It is certain, however, that, but for Raikes and Stock, millions of children must have grown up in gross ignorance of the Christian faith.

[3] A grandson, the Rev. HENRY SWABEY (Scholar 1844–50), was Rector of St. Aldate's (1850–6) and Secretary of the Christian Knowledge Society (1863–78). He helped to found St. Katharine's Training College, where a window in the Chapel records his memory. He was Stroke of the College Eight.

(matriculated 1778, aet. 25), and Sir JOHN SEWELL (matriculated 1784), Judge of the Vice-Admiralty Court at Malta.—The face of a Lincoln's Inn chaplain, WILLIAM WALKER (matriculated 1771), has been made immortal by the brush of Constable.

I will mention here several Channel Islanders of distinction. DAVID DURELL was born in Jersey 1729, and seems to have been descended from Dean Durell, the controversial divine, who rendered the Common Prayer Book into Latin and French. The family was a prominent one in the island. He entered April 2, 1747. Elected to a Fellowship at Hertford, he succeeded Dr. Sharp as Principal 1757. D.D. 1764; Vice-Chancellor 1765-7. In 1767 he was made Canon of Canterbury. He died in Hertford College Oct. 19, 1775, aged forty-seven, and is buried in St. Peter's in the East. Durell was a skilful Orientalist, and elucidated the Samaritan Arabic version as well as the Hebrew text of the prophetic parts of the Pentateuch. In his *Critical Remarks on the Books of Job, Psalms, Ecclesiastes, and Canticles* (Clarendon Press, 4to, 1772), he earnestly advocated a new translation of the Holy Scriptures. He advanced a considerable sum for building the Oxford Market. While Vice-Chancellor he expelled the Six Methodists of St. Edmund Hall. I should here mention, parenthetically, the thirty-second Principal of Magdalen Hall (1788–1813), HENRY FORD, D.C.L. (matr. Pembroke 1776), who at the age of twenty-seven became Lord Almoner's Professor of Arabic (1780–1813). Canon of Hereford 1790.

Dr. RICHARD VALPY (Valpied) was born Dec. 7, 1754, had five years' schooling at Valognes in Normandy, and then was sent to Southampton Grammar School, aged fifteen. Valpy all but entered the Royal Navy, and never lost his taste for the sea and for the science of war. He entered Pembroke as a Morley Scholar April 1, 1773, aged eighteen (son of Richard, of Jersey, gent.). B.A. 1776; M.A. 1784; B.D. and D.D. 1792; F.S.A. For fifty-five years (1781–1836) he was head-master of Reading Grammar School, which he rescued from nothingness. From 1787 he was Rector of Stradishall, Suffolk. Died March 28, 1836. He was painted by Opie. His son, ABRAHAM JOHN VALPY (entered 1805), attained eminence as author, printer, and publisher, on a vast scale, of classical works. There is a long article devoted to his memory in the *Gentleman's Magazine* of 1855 (i. 204). Ob. 1854. Valpy's successor at Reading was ROBERT APPLETON: matr. 1822; ob. Feb. 5, 1875.

Another successful schoolmaster, JOHN LEMPRIÈRE, born ' in Insula Caesariae,' proceeded from Winchester to Pembroke Jan. 17, 1786;

B.A. 1790 ; M.A. 1792 ; B.D. 1801 ; D.D. 1803. Before graduating he was assistant-master at Reading Grammar School, and the next year is found connected with St. Helen's, Jersey. While quite a young man he published the *Classical Dictionary*. The preface is dated from Pembroke College, November 1788. It opened a new world of imagination to English boyhood, but the articles are somewhat superficial. The *Dictionary*, however, went through many editions down to 1888. In 1791 Lemprière was master at Bolton Grammar School. From 1792 to 1808 or 1809 he was a successful pedagogue at Abingdon School, and was Vicar of St. Helen's 1800–11. At Abingdon he brought out the first volume of his *Herodotus* and a *Universal Biography*. Leaving Abingdon, he became Master of Exeter Free Grammar School. From 1811 he was also Rector of Meeth, Devonshire, and from 1823 Rector of Newton Petrock. Dr. Lemprière died Feb. 1, 1824. The *Classical Dictionary* was translated into Latin, with an attack on the author, at Deventer, in 1794.

The fine Lawrence[1] in the Common Room represents Sir THOMAS LE BRETON (son of Francis Le Breton, Dean of Jersey), who, after entering Jesus College from Winchester (1783), migrated to Pembroke Feb. 23, 1784, and became Fellow (1784–90). In 1786 he won the Latin Verse (' Pictura in Vitro '). After practising at the bar of the Royal Court he became in 1802 Attorney-General of Jersey, in 1826 Lieutenant-Bailli, and on Lord Carteret's decease in 1826 Bailli, having been knighted the year before. He was also President of the Assembly of the States. His eldest son was Attorney-General or Procureur. Sir Thomas was twice married. He was born Sept. 29, 1763, and died in March, 1838. Several members of this family were at Pembroke. WILLIAM CORBET LE BRETON (matriculated 1831, Fellow of Exeter 1837–42) was Dean of Jersey 1850, Rector of St. Helen's 1875.

In 1796 entered from Jersey CLEMENT HUE ; D.Med. 1807. He was many years Physician and Lecturer at St. Bartholomew's and Physician to Christ's Hospital and the Foundling. Late in life Dr. Hue was offered the President's chair of the College of Physicians, but declined it, as he did also the Treasurership of St. Bartholomew's. He died June 23, 1861.

---

[1] Presented to the College in 1882 by Sir Thomas Le Breton's granddaughters, Mrs. Wilson and Mrs. Thorne. The engraving by B. Holl was published in 1830, in Fisher's *National Portrait Gallery*. There are some reminiscences of Le Breton in Pycroft's *Oxford Memories*.

CHAPTER XXX.

MEN OF SCIENCE—MASTERSHIP OF DR. ADAMS.

THE old-world Rosicrucian, a lonely and pale student amid his crucibles and black-letter tomes, was as great a contrast as can be to the busy type of scientific pioneer exemplified by Smithson, Gilbert and Beddoes. First, however, should be mentioned, as belonging to the earlier part of the eighteenth century, NATHANIEL BLISS, born at Bisley Nov. 28, 1700. He matriculated from Pembroke Oct. 10, 1716[1]. Rector of St. Ebbe's 1736. He succeeded Halley as Savilian Professor (1742–64). Fellow of the Royal Society 1742; Astronomer Royal 1762[2]. He died at Greenwich Sept. 2, 1764. There is a portrait of him by Martin and a scarce etching by Caldwell from a drawing of Bliss scratched on a pewter during dinner by George, Lord Parker, afterwards Earl of Macclesfield, whose frequent guest and scientific coadjutor he was. Under it were the words, ' Sure this is Bliss, if bliss on earth there be.'

JAMES LEWIS SMITHSON or MACIE (born in 1753 ; died at Genoa, where he has a monument, 1829) was (as he boasted) natural son of Sir Hugh Smithson, first Duke of Northumberland, and Elizabeth Keate Macie, ' heiress of the Hungerfords of Studley and niece of Charles, the Proud Duke of Somerset.' He matriculated under his mother's name, May 7, 1782; created M.A. 1786. Later he took

---

[1] The father of the discoverer of vaccination, the Rev. STEPHEN JENNER (matr. April 6, 1720), was at the College with Bliss. He was buried Dec. 9, 1754, at Berkeley, where his famous son had been born May 17, 1749. Another son, STEPHEN JENNER, entered Pembroke in that year. He became Bursar and Vice-President of Magdalen. Ob. 1797. For the Jenners see the Rev. THOMAS DUDLEY FOSBROOKE's *Smyth's Lives of the Berkeleys*. That eminent antiquary, editor of the *Berkeley Manuscripts* and author of a *History of Gloucestershire*, was a Scholar from 1785. F.S.A. 1799. Mr. Fosbrooke died Sept. 24, 1857.

[2] FRANCIS DEMAINBRAY, son of George III's Astronomer at Richmond and Chaplain, Stephen Demainbray, was Fellow of the College 1814–27: Bursar 1824. Ob. 1846.

the name of Smithson. He had the reputation at Pembroke of excelling all others in the University in chemical science. While still a Pembroke undergraduate he conducted a geological exploration of the coasts of Scotland. Berzelius declared afterwards that he was one of the most accomplished mineralogists in Europe. Gilbert pronounced him the rival of Wollaston. A carbonate of zinc discovered by him is called Smithsonite. He became Vice-President of the Royal Society and a member of the French Institute. 'He was for some fifty years an object of European interest to men of science' (Wilson). Smithson's craving for posthumous fame, however, was expressed by him in these words: 'The best blood of England flows in my veins : on my father's side I am a Northumberland ; on my mother's I am related to Kings. But it avails me not. My name shall live in the memory of man when the titles of the Northumberlands and Percys are extinct and forgotten.' He accordingly bequeathed the contingent reversion of his property, ultimately £120,000, to the United States Government, to found an institution at Washington 'for the increase and diffusion of knowledge among men.' It came to the United States in 1838, though many voices were raised against the acceptance of a gift chiefly meant to glorify the donor ; and in 1846 was founded the Smithsonian Institute (as he had directed it should be called), including a library, art gallery, and museum, to which were granted the Government collections. The Institute has since become the 'rallying-point for the workers in every department of scientific and educational work.' It has lately presented its publications, in more than 200 volumes, to the Pembroke Library. Besides the picture of Smithson by Johns (1816), there is a curious oil painting of him as an undergraduate, in cap, gown, and bands.

DAVIES GILBERT, who pronounced Smithson's eulogy in the Royal Society, was born March 6, 1767, at St. Erth, Cornwall, where his father, Edward Giddy, was curate. He entered as a gentleman-commoner, as DAVIES GIDDY, April 12, 1785. M.A. 1789 ; D.C.L. 1832.

High Sheriff of Cornwall, 1792. He became President of the Geological Society of Cornwall, and the Linnaean Society owed much to his support. He helped Trevithick and the Hornblowers to improve the steam-engine. But Gilbert's best title to fame is as the discoverer of Sir Humphry Davy. He found the boy one day swinging carelessly on Dr. Borlase's gate in Penzance, was interested in his talk, and invited him to his house at Tredrea, giving him the use of his library. He and Beddoes between them afterwards launched Davy on his scientific career. Giddy, as he was still named, calculated for Telford the chains required for the Menai Bridge. He was elected for Helston in 1804, and sate eight times for Bodmin (1806-32), being one of the most assiduous members the House of Commons has ever known, and remarkable for the short periods which he spent in sleep. He 'took a prominent part in parliamentary investigations connected with the arts and sciences.' By his union with Mary Ann, only daughter of Thomas Gilbert of East-bourne, Giddy acquired extensive estates round that town, and on Dec. 10, 1817, he assumed the name of Gilbert. In 1811 he wrote on the bullion question. In the Corn Law riots of March, 1815, his London house (6, Holles St.) was attacked. In 1820 he was chosen Treasurer of the Royal Society, and in 1827 succeeded Davy as President. He resigned his chair to the Duke of Sussex, Nov. 30, 1830. In that year he selected Brunel's design for Clifton Suspension Bridge. Gilbert's nomination of the eight writers of the *Bridgewater Treatises* under the Earl's will was much criticized. He took much interest in archaeology, and antiquarian and literary subjects. In 1827 he published a *Collection of Christmas Carols,* and about that time two mystery plays in the now extinct Cornish tongue, *Mount Calvary* and *The Creation.* His largest work is *The Parochial History of Cornwall,* four vols. 1838. He died on Christmas Eve, 1839, at Eastbourne, and lies in the Gilbert chapel there. In St. Erth Church is a long biographical inscription. The Royal Society possess Gilbert's portrait by Phillips.

A few months before Gilbert, Dr. RICHARD POWELL entered the College. He was Fellow of the Royal College of Physicians, 1796, and physician to St. Bartholomew's Hospital, 1801-24. He died Aug. 18, 1834. A little earlier, Dr. RICHARD EDWARDS (matr. 1788 ; B.C.L. 1795) was Lecturer in Chemistry at St. Bartholomew's ; F.R.C.P. 1803 ; Censor 1805. Ob. Sept. 12, 1827.

The eruption of restless intellectual energy which marks the volcanic fourth quarter of the century is exemplified in the Bristol physician and writer, THOMAS BEDDOES. 'From Beddoes,' wrote Southey on hearing of his death, 'I hoped for more good to the human race than any other individual.' 'I felt,' wrote Coleridge, 'that more had been taken out of my life by this than by any former event.' Yet Beddoes is remembered less by any scientific achievements of his own than as the fosterer of Davy's genius and the father of the author of *Death's Jest Book.*

The son of a Shropshire farmer (he was born at Shiffnal, April 13 or 15, 1760), he got his schooling at Shiffnal, at Brewood, at Bridgenorth, and in the house of a Staffordshire rector. He entered St. John's Nov. 15, 1775, but migrated to Pembroke in 1776. Though still a boy he mastered French, German, and Italian, and through these languages the best works on chemistry, botany, and mineralogy. While at Pem-broke, however, Beddoes anticipated as one of the greatest pleasures of manhood the power of sitting down uncontrolled and playing whist all day and night. His whist memory was extraordinary. After leaving Oxford, where he had 'taught himself,' he studied medicine in London, and translated Bergman, Scheele, and Spallanzani. In 1783 he moved to Edinburgh. In that intellectual centre he was President of the Royal Medical and Natural Societies, enjoying the friendship of Sir James Mackintosh. In 1786 he returned to Oxford and proceeded M.D. (B.A. 1779; M.A. 1783). Five years later Beddoes was made Chemistry Reader (the Professorship was not founded till 1803), attracting, he says, the largest class assembled in Oxford since the thirteenth century. The great merits of Mayow were recovered by him from the dust of forgetfulness in 1790. He incurred much ridicule, however, by agitating the University over the discovery of an extinct crater at Coniston, the specimens which he exhibited to a special meeting summoned by him turning out to be slags from an old furnace. When the French Revolution broke out, Beddoes' sympathies took fire, and so pronounced were his politics that he found it advisable, in 1792, to resign his Readership. About this time he wrote a curious poem denouncing English aggrandizement in India, and also a popular moral tale, *Isaac Jenkins*, after the manner which his sister-in-law, Maria Edgeworth, made famous. A short residence in France, where he became acquainted with Lavoisier, cured him of some illusions, and the 'infernal club of Jacobins' so disgusted him that he went back to England and settled at Bristol, 'where he began that career of medical and physiological researches, experiments and lectures which made him so generally conspicuous' (Chalmers). Darwin greatly valued him. Beddoes 'had the happy faculty of viewing every subject on its most brilliant side.' 'He had the mind,' wrote the *Edinburgh Medical Journal* after his death, 'of a poet and a painter, and displayed the powers of his imagination in vivid representations of facts. He was a pioneer in the road of discovery.' A controversy between Dr. Beddoes and Prof. Hailstone on the rival merits of the Plutonian and Neptunist hypotheses led them to make a geological tour along the Cornish coast. Davies Gilbert accompanied them and brought young Humphry Davy under their notice. Beddoes had recently established the Pneumatic Institution at Clifton and required an assistant. Gilbert recommended Davy, and with much trouble got his mother and the apothecary to whom he was apprenticed to let him go. Dr. Beddoes treated Davy[1] with the utmost liberality. In 1801, however, the Institute was given up, and he went to London, where he enjoyed a large practice. He died on Christmas Eve, 1808, aged forty-eight, 'at the moment,' says Davy, 'when his mind was purified for noble affections and great works'; 'literally worn out,' Atkinson says, 'by the action and reaction of an inquisitive nature and of restlessness for fame.' 'He was undoubtedly,' writes Dr. Chalmers, 'capable of great things, but too hurried, too sanguine, too unconscious of the lapse of time, and too little aware of the want of opportunity for any one man to accomplish any very numerous ends, either of invention

---

[1] 'Much as Davy needed the bridle, Beddoes required it still more. He was as little fitted for a Mentor as a weathercock for a compass.' Paris's *Life of Davy* (1831).

or reformation.' Nevertheless, in the opinion of Dr. Garnett, Beddoes was 'a remarkable and highly interesting man; an enthusiast and a philanthropist ; vigorous, original and independent.' His house at Clifton was the rendezvous of a brilliant circle—Coleridge (who through Beddoes became sub-editor of the *Morning Chronicle* in 1796), Poole, Southey, the Wedgwoods, Maria Edgeworth, Davy, and others of mark. Sir Humphry tells us that Beddoes was reserved and dry in manner. 'Nothing could be a stronger contrast to his apparent coldness in discussion than his wild and active imagination, which was as poetical as Darwin's. He had talents which would have raised him to the pinnacle of philosophical eminence if they had been applied with discretion.' On his death-bed he wrote me a most affecting letter, regretting his scientific aberrations. I remember one expression : " Like one who has scattered abroad the *avena fatua* of knowledge, from which neither branch nor blossom nor fruit has resulted, I require the Consolations of a friend."' In 1811 was published Stock's *Memoirs of the Life of Thomas Beddoes.* I have seen a portrait of him at Clifton, and his daughter-in-law, Mrs. Cecilia Beddoes, tells me that she has his picture by Birch. There is a list of his many publications in Chalmers.

Smithson, Gilbert, and Beddoes all matriculated under Dr. Adams, whose memory, in requital of his kindness to him, is linked to Johnson's fame. His example as that of a distinguished divine who was 'considerably deep in chemistry' is cited by John James in the *Letters of Radcliffe and James* (ed. Evans, O. H. S., p. 177) in defence of his own addiction to ' this new science.' Dr. WILLIAM ADAMS was of Wightwick descent, and was born at Shrewsbury, Aug. 17, 1706. His father was mayor of Shrewsbury in 1726. His mother's father, Edward Jorden of Prior's Leigh, esq., was high-sheriff of Shropshire in 1720. Adams matriculated young, Aug. 6, 1720. Chosen Fellow in 1727, he succeeded his cousin William Jorden as tutor in 1731. After Easter 1732 he ceased to reside, vacated his Fellowship, and accepted the perpetual curacy of St. Chad's in his native town. His name disappears from the batell books after March 7, 173⅘. In 1747 he was made canon of Lichfield, in 1749 canon of Llandaff; precentor 1750. Rector of Holgate, Salop, 1748; of Bedwas, Monmouthshire, and of Cwm, Flintshire, 1774. In 1755 Mrs. Elizabeth Cressett of Counde, Salop, presented him to that parsonage, which he retained till his death. In 1756 he revisited Oxford to proceed B.D. and D.D., and then went back to Shrewsbury, ' where he discharged the duties of his ministry with exemplary assiduity, patience and affection, and contributed a very active part in the foundation of the Salop infirmary.' On Dr. Ratcliff's decease, July 13, 1775, Dr. Adams, though forty-three years absent from the College, and though he had outlived almost all his contemporaries, was, on July 26, elected Master, 'as a mark of respect,' says Chalmers, 'due to his public character.' He resigned St. Chad's 'to the lasting regret of his hearers,' but was, in 1777, made archdeacon of Llandaff. 'Over the College he presided with universal approbation, and engaged the affections of the students by his courteous demeanour and affability, mixed with the firmness necessary for the preservation of discipline.' He died at his prebendal house at Gloucester, Jan. 13, 1789, and is buried in the Cathedral church, where an inscription (given in Boswell) eulogizes his virtues. It is therein recorded that 'ingenious, learned, eloquent, he ably defended the truth of Christianity.' This refers to Adams' *Essay on Hume's Essay on Miracles*, 8vo. 1752, considered one of the ablest answers to the Scots philosopher. Courtenay in the *Poetical Review*, 1785, speaks of

> 'Candid Adams, by whom David fell,
> Who ancient miracles sustained so well.'

Leland in his *View of Deistical Writers* (1754) makes free use of the treatise of Adams, who had specially examined the evidence for the Jansenist miracles at Paris. Adams told Boswell that he had dined with Hume, who shook hands with him and said, 'You have treated me much better than I deserve,' and that they exchanged visits. Boswell did not approve of these smooth civilities bandied with an aggressive infidel, and Johnson was of the same opinion. Adams has been styled 'a whig and a lowchurchman.' He preached, however, at St. Chad's, Sept. 4, 1769, against Romaine, to whom he had lent his pulpit, and who had argued for the existence of Calvinian doctrine in the XXXIX Articles. Adams' sermon 'On true and false Doctrine' led to a series of pamphlets between the friends of the two divines. Boswell speaks of Adams' 'amiability.' Warburton sent a message by him to Johnson telling him how much he honoured him for the Chesterfield letter. Adams delivered the message, which much gratified Johnson, but had the courage himself to expostulate with him and to defend Lord Chesterfield, telling Johnson, who spoke of the nobleman as 'the proudest man this day existing,' that he exceeded him in pride.

In the College library are preserved the *Prayers and Meditations*, written throughout in Johnson's decided hand. Boswell records:—

'On Friday, June 11th [1784], we talked at breakfast of forms of prayer. JOHNSON: "I know of no good prayers but those in the Book of Common Prayer." DR. ADAMS (in a very earnest manner): "I wish, Sir, you would compose some family prayers." JOHNSON: "I will not compose prayers for you, Sir, because you can do it for yourself. But

I have thought of getting together all the books of prayers which I could, selecting those which should appear to me the best, putting out some, inserting others, adding some prayers of my own, and prefixing a discourse on prayer." We all now gathered about him, and two or three of us at a time joined in pressing him to execute this plan. He seemed to be a little displeased at the manner of our importunity, and in great agitation called out, "Do not talk thus of what is so awful. I know not what time God will allow me in this world. There are many things which I wish to do." Some of us persisted, and Dʳ Adams said, "I never was more serious about anything in my life." JOHNSON: "Let me alone, let me alone: I am overpowered." And then he put his hands before his face, and reclined for some time upon the table.' On Feb. 17, 1785, two months after Johnson's death, Dʳ Adams wrote to Boswell: 'His last visit was, I believe, to my house, which he left after a stay of four or five days. We had much serious talk together, for which I ought to be the better as long as I live. You will remember some discourse which we had in the summer upon the subject of prayer, and the difficulty of this sort of composition. He reminded me of this, and of my having wished him to try his hand, and to give us a specimen of the style and manner that he approved. He added that he was now in a right frame of mind, and as he could not possibly employ his time better he would set in earnest about it. But I find upon enquiry that no papers of this sort were left behind him, except a few short ejaculatory forms suitable to his present situation.' Boswell remarks: 'Dʳ Adams had not then received accurate information on this subject; for it has since appeared that various prayers had been composed by him at different periods, which, intermingled with pious resolutions and some short notes of his life, were entitled by him *Prayers and Meditations*, and have, in pursuance of his earnest requisition, in the hopes of doing good, been published, with a judicious and well-written preface by the reverend Mʳ Strahan, to whom he delivered them.'

Dr. Adams, however, wrote (Oxford, Oct. 22, 1785) to the *Gentleman's Magazine* that he had never seen the book before publication, and had he been consulted would certainly have given his voice against it. Mr. Strahan in his preface says that it was Adams' repeated request which at first suggested to Johnson the design

'to revise these pious effusions and bequeath them, with enlargements, to the use and benefit of others. Infirmities, however, now growing fast upon him, he at length changed this design, and determined to give the Manuscripts, without revision, in charge to me. Accordingly one morning, on my visiting him by desire at an early hour, he put these Papers into my hands, with instructions for committing them to the Press, and with a promise to prepare a sketch of his own life to accompany them. But the performance of this promise also was prevented, partly by the hasty destruction of some private memoirs which he afterwards lamented, and partly by that incurable sickness which soon ended in his dissolution. . . .

That the authenticity of this Work may never be called in question, the original manuscript will be deposited in the Library of Pembroke College in Oxford. Dr Bray's Associates are to receive the profits of the First Edition, by the Author's appointment; and any further advantages that accrue will be distributed among his poor relations.'

The *Prayers and Meditations* seems to me the most pathetic book of the eighteenth century, laying bare as it does the weakness of the strong, the inward agonizing of the Hercules of moralists, the tenderness, the humility, the simplicity, of that most human of despots. It is also a *locus classicus* for prayer for the dead, fasting, and other points of church practice in the time of George III. Adams no doubt felt the sacredness of such a self-pourtrayal, but we are grateful to him for being the unwilling cause of the book being published, as well as the MS. preserved[1].

A Gloucestershire botanist-divine was JOHN LIGHTFOOT (matr. 1753; B.A. 1756; M.A. 1766), Fellow of the Royal and Linnaean Societies. He held various preferments in Hants and Notts, and died Feb. 20, 1788.

Adams was succeeded, Jan. 28, 1789, by a descendant of Richard Tesdale, the co-Founder's guardian, WILLIAM SERGROVE, who entered from St. Paul's School, Nov. 3, 1762, aged 16 (son of Thomas Sergrove of London); B.A. 1766; M.A. 1769; B.D. 1778; D.D. 1789. Rector of St. Aldate's 1774–89; Vicar of Penmark with Llanwit Major and Lliswarney, in the diocese of Llandaff. He died in London, April 16, 1796, aged forty-nine.

Before closing this chapter mention should be made of Sir ARTHUR BROOKE FAULKNER, born in 1779, who, after studying at Dublin and Cambridge, took M.A. and M.D. from Pembroke July 12, 1806. He was Fellow of the Royal College of Physicians, Physician in Ordinary to H. R. H. the Duke of Sussex, and Physician to the Forces. He served with the army in Spain, Holland and Malta. Knighted 1815; died May 23, 1845.

---

[1] Dr. Adams married, Jan. 12, 1742, Sarah, daughter of Thomas Hunt of Boreatton, Salop, esq. Their daughter, Johnson's vivacious young friend, was married in 1788 to Mr. Benjamin Hyett of Painswick House. She died in 1804 without issue, her husband's estates being bequeathed to her father's nephew Francis Adams, who took the name and arms of Hyett in 1815. Mr. Francis Adams Hyett, the present owner of Painswick House, possesses a picture of Dr. Adams by Opie, a copy of which, presented by Mr. FREDERICK BARLOW DE SAUSMAREZ (Scholar 1868–73; H. M. Inspector of Schools 1877), now hangs in the Hall. Mr. Hyett also has a pencil-sketch of Johnson drawn by Miss Adams on one occasion that Johnson visited the College. This was exhibited by Mr. de Sausmarez at the Dinner of past and present members of the College 'Johnson' Society in celebration of its 500th meeting, on June 23, 1896.

CHAPTER XXXI.

JOHN HENDERSON—'A FORGOTTEN GENIUS.'

JOHNSON's room in the tower was occupied half a century after him by the 'Boy-Professor,' an eccentric young man of extraordinary parts and precocity, JOHN HENDERSON, called the Irish Crichton. He was born March 27, 1757, at Ballygarran, of pious and respectable parents, brought to England, and sent to Wesley's school at Kingswood, where he received ' a small school education,' and became himself, at the age of eight, a teacher of Latin. At twelve years we find him teaching Greek and Latin at Trevecca College, then governed by J. W. Fletcher, afterwards Vicar of Madeley. Two years later Mr. Fletcher was forced to leave, and Henderson retired to his father's house near Bristol, where he both studied and gave lessons. At the age of twenty-two he accidentally in a stage-coach met Dean Tucker, who was so astonished by his conversation that he wrote to Henderson's father urging that he should be sent to the University, and with the letter sent a gift of more than £150 to be expended on his education. This kind dignitary said afterwards that ' whenever he was in the company of young Henderson he considered himself as a scholar in the presence of his tutor.' It appears from Hannah More's *Life* [1] that this present was augmented by a subscription. Accordingly on April 6, 1781, John Henderson matriculated at Pembroke. Here his unquenchable thirst for knowledge, vast powers of application, and amazing memory gave him an encyclopædic insight into the various branches of literature and science, his mind retaining and accurately arranging accumulated stores of varied learning. Besides ' the obsolete English writers,' on which he ' discoursed with cool and sententious eloquence,' he was skilled in Persian, Arabic, Hebrew, Greek, Latin, Spanish, Italian and German literature, conversing fluently in all these tongues. Indeed he ' could not only assume the dialect of every nation in Europe, but the accents of particular districts so completely that he might have passed for an inhabitant of either.' To Rosicrucianism, demonology, and midnight research for the philosopher's

[1] Vol. i. p. 194.

stone, which caused it to be whispered in the University that he had communion with ghostly and dark powers, he added scholastic divinity, metaphysics, law, chemistry, mathematics, and a practical acquaintance with medicine. During a fever which raged in Oxford the young student practised gratuitously among the poor, sitting all night with them and selling even his Polyglot Bible to buy drugs. He is said to have saved many lives. Not only were his liberality and humanity without measure or prudence, but his panegyrist ascribes to him 'a general blaze of merit and virtue.' He does not, however, deny that Henderson gave way to at any rate occasional intemperance, or, as a hostile critic in the *Gentleman's Magazine* puts it, 'while he "drank large libations near the well-spring of truth," he dashed them too copiously with another liquor not less intoxicating.' Henderson had from the first been known as a man of whimsical habits. A contemporary [1] at the College writes :—

'I had never seen Mr H. before he entered at Pembroke College, though his fame had previously reached my ears. One morning, while I was occupied in my apartments at this College, I was surprized by the unexpected appearance of the joint-tutors of our society, introducing to me a stranger who from the singularity of his dress and the uncouthness of his aspect (I speak not with any disrespect) attracted my notice in an uncommon degree. His clothes were made in a fashion peculiar to himself; he wore no stock or neckcloth; his buckles were so small as not to exceed the dimensions of an ordinary knee-buckle, at a time when very large buckles were in vogue. Though he was then 24 years of age, he wore his hair like that of a school boy of six. This stranger was no less a person than Mr H., who had that morning been enrolled in our fraternity, and had been recommended to apartments situated exactly under mine [2]. . . . Mr H. passing some hours of that day with me, I was gratified with a rich feast of intellectual entertainment. The extent and variety of his knowledge, the intrinsic politeness of his manners, his inexhaustible fund of humours and anecdote, concurred to instruct, please, and amuse me. From this period I was frequently honored with the society of Mr Henderson.'

After eulogizing Henderson's many endearing virtues, he proceeds :

'His mode of life was singular. He generally retired to rest about day-break and rose in the afternoon; a practice however that was frequently interrupted by the occasional attendance which he was obliged to give at the morning service of the college chapel. He spent a great part of the day in smoking, and, except when in company, he usually read while he smoked.'

---

[1] 'C. C.' (Charles Coote) in the *Gentleman's Magazine*, lix. p. 295, April 3, 1789.
[2] From this, and the allusion on p. 399 to the pump, I gather that Henderson did not occupy Johnson's chamber on first coming to the College.

Agutter tells us that before going to rest Henderson

'used to strip himself naked as low as the waist, and taking his station at a pump near his room would completely sluice his head and the upper part of his body ; after which he would pump over his shirt so as to make it perfectly wet, and, putting it on in that condition, would immediately go to bed. This he jocularly termed "an excellent cold bath." '

On one occasion he ate nothing for five days. To relieve pain he indulged excessively in opium. Shenstone had eschewed the periwig of his day. Henderson objected to powder.

' He would never suffer his head to be strewed with *white dust* (to use his own expression), dashed with pomatum, or distorted by the curling irons. Though under two and thirty years of age at his death, he walked, when he appeared in publick, with a most apparent caution and solemnity, as if he had been enfeebled by the co-operation of age and disease.'

His friend, Hannah More, whom he helped Johnson to lionize round the College, deplored his unprofitable way of life. ' One righteous week,' he told her, ' would restore me.' But he could not go seven long days without his drug. In a letter of entreating sympathy she yet struggled to save him. The non-fulfilment of the hopes formed for him was ' one of the heaviest disappointments met with in life.' The writer of an article called ' A Forgotten Genius ' in the *Speaker* of June 1, 1895, thinks that there are in the following words a hint of what might have been :—' If you had not estranged yourself from the society of our family, you would have found a friendship that neglect has not been able to destroy. Of Patty you *know* this to be true. Of myself I feel that it is so.' Patty was a younger Miss More. Wesley, in his *Journal*, remarks that ' with as great talents as most men in England, he had lived two and thirty years and done just nothing.' It should be said, however, that, while he was at Oxford, a number of writings which he had left in his father's house at Hanham, in an unlocked trunk, were used by a maid to light fires with. His conversation was wonderfully sprightly as well as learned, and he had a gift of good-natured mimicry, due to the acuteness of his memory and the extended modulation of his voice, which is said to have been fairly astonishing. A German fellow-student, coming into a room where Henderson was taking him off, was downright frightened, and avowed he had thought he heard himself speaking at a distance. Johnson, in his old age, conversed with the erudite undergraduate as an equal, and was not displeased to find him a tory and high churchman. Boswell records, in 1784 :—

'On Saturday, June 12, there drank tea with us at Dr Adams, Mr John Henderson, student of Pembroke College, celebrated for his wonderful acquirements in alchymy, judicial astrology, and other abstruse and curious learning.' Again, 'Mr Henderson, with whom I sauntered in the venerable walks of Merton College, and found him a very learned and pious man, supped with us. Dr Johnson surprised him not a little by acknowledging, with a look of horrour, that he was much oppressed by the fear of death. The amiable Dr Adams suggested that God was infinitely good. JOHNSON : "That He is infinitely good, as far as the perfection of His nature will allow, I certainly believe; but it is necessary for good upon the whole that individuals should be punished. . . . I am afraid I may be one of those who shall be damned." DR. ADAMS : "What do you mean by damned ?" JOHNSON (passionately and loudly) : "Sent to hell, sir, and punished everlastingly.". . . MRS. ADAMS :. "You seem, sir, to forget the merits of our Redeemer." JOHNSON : "Madam, I do not forget the merits of my Redeemer ; but my Redeemer has said that he will set some on his right hand and some on his left." He was in gloomy agitation, and said, " I'll have no more on't." '

Henderson himself wrote on the awful subject of the state of the lost. Johnson used to talk with the young man for hours together in Latin, either classical and elegant, or at times colloquial ; and one evening they amused the listeners by a polysyllabic dialogue, like the sesquipedalian talk of giants, in which, whenever legitimate terms ran short, they coined some new Gargantuan vocable, fit to be recorded by the lexicographer of Titans. Heads of Houses indeed were often seen in Henderson's room. He remained at Pembroke for five years, taking B.A. February 27, 1786, soon after which he left Oxford, withdrew himself from social intercourse, and gave free rein to the mystical bent of his mind, devoting his great powers chiefly to the doctrines of Behmen and the theories of Lavater, and to the subject of commerce with the dead. There is a letter from Priestley in the *Gentleman's Magazine* (vol. ix. p. 287), April 18, 1789, enclosing two letters from Henderson, dated ten years before. Priestley says :—

'When I lived at Calne, and presently after the publication of my *Disquisitions relating to Matter and Spirit*, I received an anonymous letter from Bristol about some intercourse with spirits ; and hearing that Miss Hannah More had said that the letter probably came from Mr Henderson, I wrote to him about it ; and as the letter was carried by a friend who was going to Oxford, I told Mr Henderson that, if he could call up any spirit, my friend was willing to be disposed of as he should think proper for the purpose. In what manner I expressed myself I do not now recollect; but it is evident that Mr. Henderson did not consider me as very credulous on the subject.'

He was not, it appears, the author of the anonymous letter. But in answering Priestley's communication he described his intellectual and spiritual struggles. These had ended by rescuing him from infidelity, but left him the victim of many crude opinions and disbeliefs. While still in early manhood John Henderson passed into the mysterious spirit-world. During a visit to the College he fell ill, and after severe sufferings, endured with gentle constancy, died on All Souls' Day, 1788. The body was taken from Oxford by William Agutter, of Magdalen, who had preached Johnson's funeral sermon before the University, and buried in St. George's, Kingswood, but exhumed a few days later by Henderson's father. He was afterwards re-interred in St. George's beside the mother, lost in boyhood, whose name he never mentioned without a tear, and on whose grave he would sometimes lie all night in supplication. Mr. Agutter's '*Sermon occasioned by the death of the celebrated Mr. J. Henderson, B.A., of Pembroke College, Oxford*, preached at St. George's, Kingswood, Nov. 13, and at Temple Church, Bristol, Nov. 30, 1788,' on the text 'Moses was learned in all the wisdom of the Egyptians,' is a striking, though enthusiastic, estimate of this remarkable Georgian mystic and student, 'the most dutiful of children, the faithful friend, the engaging companion, the sincere Christian.' The resemblance to the son of Amram, not only as regards learning but in respect of a serene 'meekness' of character, is much insisted on. He 'possessed a sovereign command over himself and through the whole of his life was never known to be angry,' nor was his simplicity conscious of the admiration which his extraordinary attainments excited. Seven years after his untimely death, his pupil Joseph Cottle [1] published a

---

[1] Cottle, the poet-publisher of the Augustan age of Bristol, the befriender of Coleridge, was the 'English bard' lampooned by Byron as 'Boeotian Cottle, rich Bristowa's boast.' His brother was Amos. 'O Amos Cottle! Phoebus! what a name.' Two of the Cottles were at Pembroke. Joseph published the first volumes of Wordsworth, Coleridge, and Southey. The writer in the *Speaker*, alluded to above, remembers on Cottle's walls the portrait of a young man of brilliant, lively eyes, following and penetrating the observer. This picture of Henderson is now, he says, the property of Pembroke College. It was, however, forgotten and put out of sight till a year ago, when Mr. GEORGE WOOD, Tutor and Bursar, helped by an accident, identified it. It has been cleaned, and now hangs in the Common Room. It is by William Palmer, and represents Henderson, aged twenty-five, but very boyish in appearance, looking up from a volume of Scotus. The picture was painted for Hannah More, who bequeathed it to Cottle. Before he died, in June 1853, he desired that it should be presented to the College.

Monody to John Henderson and a Sketch of his Character,' which
Lamb pronounced 'immensely good.' From this fine and feeling
poem I extract the following :—

> ''Twas his the times of elder fame to view
> And all that GREECE or ROME e'er writ or knew;
> Now on bold pinion float mid Plato's blaze,
> Now patient tread the SCHOOLMAN'S thorny maze.
> In thrice ten years his soul had run the round
> Of human knowledge, simple or profound;
> Alike could shape the log, or glance his eye
> To where with Suns the Zodiac belts the sky:
> E'en as the Lark, that groundling builds its nest,
> Now bends the stalk beneath its speckled breast,
> Now pierces clouds, and with a startling trill
> Salutes the day-star glittering o'er the hill!
> Not souls from him lay ambush'd; he could trace
> The mute, unlying language of the face [1].
>
> .   .   .   .
>
> So vast a mind did I dare venture near?
> O yes! for perfect Love excluded Fear.
> Tho' like an eagle he could stand sublime
> On summits which no toil might hope to climb,
> And tho' whene'er he spake the sage was mute,
> As maiden list'ning to her lover's lute,
> Yet did kind Heaven one WORTHIER gift impart,
> The priceless Treasure of a LOWLY HEART.
> O hear, thou proud one! thou whose soul assumes
> Or Wisdom's robe, or Wit's aye-dancing plumes;
> Tho' Learning's alpine height before him shone,
> He on the footstool fix'd a nobler throne.
> E'en children doated on his accent mild,
> And sported careless round their fellow child.
> Ye sons of calumny! go, hide your head!
> Away, ye VAMPIRES! that devour the dead!
> Who fain would force the long-clos'd wound to bleed,
> And hunt through Paradise to find a weed.
> When droop'd his frame beneath its restless lord,
> And cut its sheath the keenly-temper'd sword,
> What if an artificial aid he sought,
> Worn out with prodigality of thought?
> What if, his frail car driven with heedless force,
> He fir'd the wheels in his too rapid course?
> 'Tis true, the midnight bowl he lov'd to share,
> Yet never cloud it rais'd, it shot no glare;

[1] Alluding to his studies in Physiognomy as a science—'making his eye the
inmate of each bosom.'

But only made with stimulation kind
The body wakeful to the unsleeping mind; 》
But only (till unmechaniz'd by death)
Kept the pipe vocal to the player's breath.

. . . .

In mem'ry let those holy hours be kept,
When by his couch of pain I watch'd and wept ;
And heard his lips with faultering tone disclaim
The cymbal-tinkling praise of human fame.
The simplest truths, that else had quickly fled,
Are oracles, heard from a sick friend's bed :
How deeply then *his* precepts must I prize,
(Lov'd by the good and echo'd by the wise)
Who, while he writh'd beneath disease's rod
Still spake of Faith, of Mercy, and of GOD.
O hither come, all ye! whose smoky lamps
Burn dim and foul mid doubt's unwholesome damps ;
O hither come! from me, the mourner, hear
What smiles a dying Christian's lips can wear,
When some kind Angel soothes the lab'ring breath,
And lifts th' emancipating wand of Death.
Then only not the friend of all mankind
When to thyself a foe. Farewell, GREAT MIND !'

One biographer tells us that ' his very infancy denoted something extraordinary and great. He was born, as it were, a thinking being, and was never known to cry or express any infantine peevishness. The questions he asked as soon as he was able to speak astonished all who heard him.' Cottle, speaking of the presages of greatness which Henderson showed from the first, says hyperbolically that

' His infant scan
Pierc'd through the frames of Nature and of Man.'

Till he came to College he had no means of mental improvement but books. But his intellect governed all he read.

' The ideas he had been so rapidly accumulating were not in his mind a tangled forest or huge chaos, but were organized into systems and laid out into fertile gardens. It was this quality which made him so superior a disputant ; for as his mind had investigated the various systems and hypotheses of men, so had his almost intuitive discrimination stript them of their deceptive appendages and separated fallacy from truth, marshalling their arguments so as to elucidate or detect each other. Yet he never interrupted the most tedious or confused opponent ; tho' from his pithy questions he made it evident that from the first he had anticipated the train and consequences of their reasonings. . . . His conversation was such as might have been expected from a man whose fancy was so creative, whose knowledge so omnifarious, and whose recollection so unbounded. He combined scholastic accuracy with unaffected ease; condensed and pointed, yet rich and perspicuous. Were it possible for his numerous friends by any energy of reminiscence to collect his discourse, JOHN HENDERSON would be distinguished as a voluminous author, who yet preserved a Spartan frugality of words.

'In all companies he led the conversation: yet, though he was perpetually encircled by admirers, his steady mind decreased not its charms by a supercilious self-opinion of them. . . . In no instance was his superiority oppressive. Calm, attentive and chearful, he confuted more gracefully than others compliment. The tone of dogmatism and the smile of contempt were equally unknown to him. Sometimes indeed he raised himself stronger and more lofty in his eloquence, then, chiefly, when, fearful for his weaker brethren, he opposed the arrogance of the illiterate Deist or the worse jargon of sensual and cold-blooded Atheism. He crowded his sails and bore down upon them with salutary violence.

'. . . His honor was the anxious Delicacy of a Christian who regarded his soul as a sacred Pledge that must some time be redelivered to the Almighty Lender; his benevolence a circle in which SELF indeed might be the center, but ALL THAT LIVES was the circumference.—This tribute of respect to thy name and virtues, my beloved HENDERSON, is paid by one who was once proud to call thee TUTOR, who once enjoyed thy friendship, and who will do honor to thy memory till his spirit rests with thine.'

When this friend lamented to him that he was leaving to mankind no benefit of his vast and varied acquirements, Henderson finely replied, 'More men become writers from ignorance than from knowledge. Let us think slowly and write late.' But 'DEATH called him to graduate in a sphere more favourable to the range of his soaring and comprehensive mind' than that University 'of which for some years he was the pride and ornament.'

As an example of his self-command and tranquil sweetness of dis - position, the following is given:—

'A student of a neighbouring College, proud of his logical acquirements, was solicitous of a private disputation with the renowned HENDERSON. . . . Having chosen his subject, they conversed for some time with equal candor and moderation; but Henderson's Antagonist, perceiving his confutation inevitable (forgetting the character of a gentleman), threw a full glass of wine *in his Face*. HENDERSON without altering his features or changing his position, gently wiped his face and then coolly replied, "This, sir, is a *digression*: now for the Argument." It is hardly necessary to add, the insult was resented by the Company's turning the aggressor out of the room.'

Henderson's unequalled renown among his Oxford contemporaries has left but faint memories to the present generation, though

Dr. Kennicott, the famous Hebraist, said of him, 'The greatest men I ever knew were mere children compared with Henderson,' and Edmund Burke, then Member for Bristol, entreated him to study for the legal or the ecclesiastical profession, believing that he must certainly attain the very highest eminence in either.

In the Hope Collection there is a curious picture of Henderson (there called ' Reverend '), surrounded by zodiacal emblems, by Bagwell.

NOTE.

DREAM OF HENDERSON'S DEATH AT OXFORD.

N. J. A. writes in *Notes and Queries*, 1854, x. 26, 27:—

'I have collected these particulars of his last illness, which I took down nineteen years ago from the lips of a highly respectable inhabitant of Bristol. John Henderson had a relation named Mary Macy, who lived on Redcliff Hill . . . she had the gift of second sight. One night she dreamed that John Henderson was gone to Oxford, and that he died there. In the course of the next day John Henderson called to take leave of her, saying he was going to Oxford, to study something concerning which he could not obtain information in Bristol. Mary Macy said to him : "John, you will die there." He said, "I know it."

'Some time afterwards Mary Macy waked her husband, saying, "Remember, John Henderson died at two this morning, and it is now three." Philip Macy made light of it, but she told him, in a dream she was transported to Oxford, where in reality she had never been. She there entered a room and saw J. H. in bed, the landlady supporting his head, and the landlord and others surrounding him [1]. Looking at him she saw others give him medicine, after which J. H. saw her and said, "Oh, Mrs. Macy, I am going to die. I am glad your are come, for I want to tell you that my father is going to be very ill, and you must go and see him." He then proceeded to describe a room in his father's house and a bureau in it, "in which is a box containing some pills ; give him so many of them and he will recover." Her impression of the room was most vivid ; she even described the appearance of the houses on the opposite side of the street. The only object she seems not to have seen was a clergyman who was in attendance on J. H. Henderson's father, going to the funeral, took Philip Macy with him, and on the way to Oxford Philip told him particulars of his son's death, which they found to be strictly true, as related by Mary Macy. Mary Macy forgot then about the pills, but sometime after she was sent for by John Henderson's father, who was ill ; remembered her dream, found the bureau and the pills . . . and he was cured.'

[1] Another account is that he died in College.

CHAPTER XXXII.

AN OLD DAY BOOK.

A DAY-BOOK of accounts, kept, between 1768 and 1804, by a Tesdale Scholar and Fellow, has come into my hands. JOHN COLLINS, of Betterton, Berks, son of the Charles Collins mentioned on page 316, was chosen Scholar August 5, 1767, aged thirteen or fourteen, and came up on May 2, 1768.

He brings with him from home £5 5s. 9d., and his first purchases consist of necessaries, such as wine-glasses, an extinguisher, two tea-pots, a green table-cloth, and so forth. His books, bought from time to time, show what a boy-student's library of that date was like. I give them as they come :—

	£	s.	d.
Treatise on Short Hand	0	2	6
Sallust, Juvenal	0	4	6
Livy	0	4	0
Cicero's Orations	0	2	6
Ainsworth's Dictionary	0	10	6
Holyday's Juvenal	0	6	0
Ward's Mathematicks	0	5	6
Shenstone's Works. 2 Vol:	0	5	0
Shakespear's Plays. 9 Volumes	0	18	0
Beauties of English Poesie. 2 Vol:	0	5	4
Saunderson's, Duncan's & Watts's Logick	0	9	6
Prior's Poems	0	7	0
Tully de Officiis	0	5	6
Xenophon's Memorabilia	0	6	6
Echard's Roman History	0	5	0
Kennett's Antiquities	0	3	0
Observations on the Classicks	0	3	6
Rowe's Sallust	0	3	0
Thompson's Seasons	0	3	0
Guardian, 2 Volumes	0	4	6

	£	s.	d.
Binding and Gilding of Books, etc.	0	9	6
Do.	0	10	4½
For Deale Shelves in my Study	0	9	8
History of England	0	6	6
Rollin's Belles Lettres	0	13	0
Poemata Italorum	0	3	0
Sampson's Horsemanship	0	1	0
Terence	0	2	0
Martial	0	2	0
Cornelius nepos	0	1	6
Trapp's Prælectiones poeticæ. 3 Volumes . . .	0	3	0
Phalaris's Epistles	0	2	6
Whitby's Ethices	0	2	6
Langbin's Ditto	0	1	6
Simpson's Euclid	0	6	6
Bartholine's natural Philosophy	0	1	0
Waller's Works	0	2	0
Cornelius Nepos in English	0	1	0
Hurd's Commentary on yᵉ Ars poetica	0	1	0
A Small Terence	0	1	0
Compasses etc.	0	6	6
Milton's paradise lost & regain'd	0	7	6
Rutherfort's System of Philosophy. 2 Vols. 4ᵗᵒ . .	1	4	0
Dodsley's Collection of Poems	1	4	0
Book of Plays	0	1	0

This is the last entry before his Bachelor's degree, May 30, 1771. Six days later he was elected Fellow, and on that day there is entered:

		£	s.	d.
	Hiring of Joseph Andrews	0	0	6
June 19th.	Spectators	0	16	0
July 5th.	Hiring of Peregrine Pickle . . .	0	1	0

A year afterwards :—

	£	s.	d.
Tristram Shandy	0	2	6

Then no more literary entries till he takes his Master's degree, after which the book purchases of the Fellow, from 1780 ordained, become few and rare :—

	£	s.	d.
Farringdon Hill, a Poem by Pye of D.	0	2	6
An Heroick Epistle to Lord Craven	0	1	0

These were of local Berkshire interest.

Pamphlet in answer to Dʳ Cooper's Fast Sermon by		£	s.	d.
Mʳ Shrove		0	1	0
Mother Goose		0	1	0
Ogden's Sermons		0	5	0
Do.		0	9	0

	£	s.	d.
Carr's Sermons	0	10	0
Akenside's Poems	0	6	6
Subscription to John du Pre's [1] Sermons . . .	0	6	0
Subscription to Mr Jones's Sermons of Bampton . .	0	5	0
Bartleiana Pharmacopeia	0	4	6
Abstract of Game Laws	0	1	0
Joe Miller's Jests	0	1	6
Hawkins's Book agt Catholics	0	4	6
Scripture Lexicon	0	3	6
Bible at Newbury	0	7	6
Paley's Companion in visiting ye Sick	0	2	6
Pd Miss Delamotte Subscription to Mr Beresford's Virgil	1	1	0

These are all the purchases for twenty years.

The following disbursements and receipts, from 1768 onwards, may seem to be worth putting down here, though not all relating to Oxford. I have selected the entries which seem most representative.

	£	s.	d.
Phaeton mobile	0	1	0
Papering of my Study	1	3	6
Painting of my Room	0	9	0
Listing my Doors and windows	0	3	6
A Pound of Sugar	0	0	10
¼ Pound of Tea	0	3	0
Shoe Buckles	0	4	0
Sea Lion	0	1	0
Paid Hearne for a Cap	0	6	0
Paper a Quire	0	1	0
Paid Haines for two pair of Breeches . . .	1	4	9
Half a Pound of Cocoa	0	0	6
A Pack of Cards	0	1	8
Answering under Batchelor	0	2	6
A Pair of Shoes	0	7	0
Gave a Polish Nobleman [He was not yet seventeen] .	0	1	0
A Punt	0	0	6
Supper at ye Mitre	0	1	9
For a Letter to Abingdon	0	0	1
A Pound of Candles	0	0	8
Up the Water	0	1	8
A Bottle of Rum and 3 of Port Wine . . .	0	9	0
Dinner, Horses, etc., Fairford	0	13	0
Horse from Franks's	0	2	6
Fruit	0	0	3
Barber	0	1	0
Knockup	0	0	3

[1] Dr. JOHN DU PRÉ, entered Pembroke 1780, aet. 13; Fellow of Exeter 1773-83.

	£	s.	d.
Liceat for ye Schools	0	3	0
A Testamur	0	1	0
A Pair of Gloves	0	3	6
Do.	0	2	0
Whey [a frequent entry]	0	0	3
An ounce of Green Tea	0	1	0
Copy-Book	0	0	6
May 30, 1771. Batchelor's Degree	4	7	2
Coffee House	0	1	4
Dozen of Wine	0	19	6
June 5, 1771. Writing Name in ye Vice-Chancellor's Books	0	1	0
June 12, 1771. Registring my Name	0	5	0
Do. Plate-Money [1]	3	3	0
Do. Common-Room Fee	1	1	0
Horse Home [to Betterton]	0	5	0
Horstler and Turnpikes	0	1	0
A Pound of Jar Raisins	0	1	0
Down the Water etc.	0	6	6
Ferry	0	0	1
Ticket for ye Theatre	0	5	0
Changing a Guinea	0	0	3
Painting Room etc.	0	7	0
Feb. 30 [sic] 1772. Paid at being presented to determine	0	16	8
March 3, 1772. Paid Thirds [2] for Pigot's Room	14	6	0
Dinner at ye Angel	0	3	6
Lecture upon Heads [3]	0	2	6
Going into Court	0	0	6
March 10, 1772. Fees in the Schools	0	4	0
March 11, 1772. Liceat	0	1	0
Subscription for a Clergyman's Daughter	0	5	0
Dean and Aristotle for presenting etc.	0	12	6
March 26, 1772. Liceat fees in the Schools etc.	0	5	0
Tea at Abingdon	0	1	0
Beer etc., Hunting	0	1	0
Fortnum for a Pair of Barragon Breeches	0	14	0
Tennis	0	7	0
A Bag Fox	0	1	0
A Pair of Fustian Breeches	0	9	0
May 7, 1773. Paid Roberts for not being at Prayers	0	1	0
Dinner etc. at Cumner	0	5	0

[1] See p. 274.
[2] The in-coming tenant paid the out-goer two-thirds of the original cost of the furniture. So in Wilding's Accompt Book (*Collectanea*, I, O. H. S., ed. Fletcher, 255, 264), in 1687, 'Reced of my Chum for thirds, oo. 05. oo,' when he was leaving. The year before, 'To Colenet for thirds, oo. 05. oo.'
[3] A burlesque lecture by Charles Lee Lewes.

	£	s.	d.
June, 1773. Austings in yᵉ Schools¹	0	5	0
Theatre	1	0	0
2 Bottles of Perry	0	1	6
Shrub Punch	0	1	0
Billiards	0	2	0
Gave a broken Tradesman	0	1	0
Dinner, Supper, etc. at yᵉ Abingdon Visitation	0	12	6
For Fishing Tackle	0	0	6
½ a Guinea under Weight	0	2	6
A silk Handkerchief	0	4	6
¼ of a Pound of british Herb Tobacco	0	1	3
Play at Abingdon & Supper at Powell's with Stock	0	6	0
A Razor	0	5	0
Musick Room	0	3	0
2 Wall Lectures	0	1	0
A Bag Fox with yᵉ Duke of Grafton's Hounds	0	1	0
Feb. 26, 1774. A Key of yᵉ Common Room Garden	0	1	6
Hares found sitting with yᵉ Duke of Marlbro' Hounds	0	2	0
Breakfast at Ladds's Blue Boar	0	1	0
March 2, 1774. Liceat for Declamations in the Schools	0	7	0
2 Declamations in the Schools	0	2	0
Chaise & Play at Abingdon with Hawkins	0	9	0
March 1774. Liceat for Examination	0	4	6
Testamur	0	1	0
Quodlibets²	0	0	6
Woodstock Gloves	0	3	6
April 14, 1774. Fees for Master's Degree, 3 terms, & every other Dispensation	6	3	0
Fees in College, Master £2 10s. Dean 15s. Bursʳ 3s. 6d. Napkin 2s. 6d.	3	11	0
Sieur Rea's Slight of Hand	0	1	0
Tom Kilburn for carrying my Gown for Degree	0	1	0
Turnpikes and eating at yᵉ Dog-House with Hawkins	0	2	0
Oranges at Woodstock	0	1	0
Fee to Sherwood for Master's Degree	0	5	0
Coquus, his Fee for Master's Degree	0	2	6
Dinner at Wheatley with Hawkins, Willᵐˢ & Gapper	0	5	0
Dinner etc. at Hincksey with Hawkins, Lewis, Ponten	0	3	0
Jones yᵉ Barber for cutting my Hair	0	2	0

[1] The bachelor was obliged ' in Quodlibet, sic dicunt, disputationibus semel et iterum sui periculum facere; tandem in circulis Augustinianis, quos nominant, aliquot horarum disputationes pomeridianas ad D. Mariae iterum & tertio habere.' Fitzherbert's *Descriptio* (*Elisab. Oxford*, O. H.S., p. 18). They had their name from the disputations of the Austinian Friars. ' Austens' were neglected a century before; see Wood, *Life and Times*, ii. 428, 430. ' Doing Austins' was abolished in 1800.

[2] These were to be performed in the Chancel of St. Mary's. See *Collectanea*, I, ed. Fletcher, O. H. S., p. 265.

	£	s.	d.
Tea at Medley [1] with Lewis, Williams, Phillips & Hawkins	o	3	o
A Pint of Wine at y⁰ Coffee House	o	1	o
Tennis with Hayward	o	3	6
Billiards paid for Roberts	o	3	o
Nov. 11, 1774. A Sheet of Stamp Paper for Bursars Bond	o	2	6
Dinner, Supper, etc. at Witney with Hawkins & Jones	o	2	o
Gave a Girl in Bridewell	o	2	o
Wine & Fruit in y⁰ Common Room . . .	o	5	6
Coffee House Supper with Corbet, Kynaston, etc. .	o	2	o
Coffee House Cards etc. with Luxmoore Lewis & Blagrove	o	3	o
Lost at Whist at y⁰ Star with Bertie, Curtis etc. . .	o	6	o
Waiter at Tom's Coffee House a Xystmas Box . .	o	o	6
Accidents tho' not *Kynastonian*	o	1	o
Breakfast at Coffee House after Yeatman's Examination	o	1	o
Sermon case	o	1	6
Ticket etc. Oratorio Messiah Musick Room (March 20, 1777)	o	5	o
A Man from Charles Town South Carolina . . .	o	1	o
A Hat of Parsons	1	1	o
A Pair of Black Silk Stockings of Underhill . .	o	13	6
House Boat up y⁰ water	o	1	o
Cucumbers from Paradise Garden	o	1	o
Oxford Musick	1	o	o
Oxford Races	1	o	o
Aylesbury Races	1	o	o
Dinner etc. at Lambourne entrance Day . . .	o	8	6
Subscription to y⁰ Plate	1	1	o
Dinner, Supper, etc. at Lady Craven's Play Newbury .	1	1	o
Shoeing Stella	o	2	o
Shooting at Besslesleigh	o	10	6
A Piece of Velvet for Breeches	3	3	o
A Pair of Spurs, bought of Moore	o	7	o
Subscription to y⁰ Society for y⁰ Propagation of Gospel	o	10	6
Abingdon Races	o	8	o

[1] As in George Wither's ditty (1620) :—

> 'In summer time to Medley
> My love and I would goe,
> The boatemen there stood ready,
> My love and I to rowe:
>
> For creame there would we call,
> For cakes, for pruines too,
> But now alas sh'as left me;
> Falero, lero, loo.'

When Fair Rosamund solaced herself at Medley with the nuns of Godstow it was a place of great resort from Oxford.

	£	s.	d.
Harry Mullinder for riding my black Horse . . .	o	1	o
Expences at Fairford with Pick^s & Hawkins Snipe Shooting	1	13	o
P^d for a Waistcoat for Hawkins won of me at Cards .	o	13	6
Briefs at Peasmore	o	1	o
Shepherd for finding my Hat	o	1	o
May 13, 1780. Entering Name for Orders . . .	o	1	o
May 21, 1780. Ordination Fees	o	14	6
To ye Fire at Drayton	o	10	6
P^d John Goodwin a Bill for Wine common Room .	1	10	6
Ticket for Ball	o	5	o
Journey in a one Horse Chaise with Servt to & from Northampton & extra Expences	5	o	o
Gathering at ye Death of a Fox	o	2	o
A Box of pectoral Lozenges	o	2	6
Intelligence of a Buck in the Coppice . . .	o	1	o
Boot Garters	o	1	6
Lost at Picquet with Swinnerton	o	1	o
Gave a Man for taking a Nest of Weasels . .	o	1	o
Lost at All Fours with Taylor	o	1	o
Carr: Portmanteau to Oxford Musick Week . .	o	o	6
Ball Ticket & Negus Oxford Races	o	5	6
Raffle for Finder's Guns	1	1	o
P^d Bullock Forfeits for Non-attendance at the Reading Club, & taking Name out of it . . .	1	10	6
Night-Cap & Combs	o	5	o
Cricket to July	2	18	6
Newbury Assembly Expences	1	4	o
Lost at Cards at Ld Hintons	o	2	o
Rec^d of Ld Hinton for my bay Horse . . .	57	15	o
Certificate for shooting	2	3	o
Flooring the Hall	9	10	6
Oratorio at Oxford (Feby 1785) [1] . . .	o	11	o
Sadler's Balloon & Theatre Musick . . .	o	13	o
Half a Lottery Ticket with Hawkins . . .	7	10	o
Bought a blue Coat of Jim Hawkins . . .	o	8	6
G. Woodward's Certificate of taking Degree . .	o	3	6
Badger King's Heath	o	1	o
Stephen's Man for Catching Hawks . . .	o	1	o
Coursing at Park	o	2	6
Horse Tax April (1788)	1	o	o
Catechists at Peasmore [his curacy] . . .	o	13	o

[1] A vocal and instrumental concert was given every Monday evening, except in September and Holy Week, at the Holywell Musick Room. The *Messiah* was performed in Lent, some other oratorio in Act term, and in Easter and Michaelmas terms a piece of choral secular music. The best singers, such as Mara and Catalani, took part.

	£	s.	d.
Presentation, Institution, etc. & Expences to Town & in Herts	25	7	0
May 11th 1789. Pd 2 Paymt of first Fruits	6	2	8
Tenths	2	12	8
Rec'd at Cheshunt 10sr for Colonel Craig's Vault Bands	0	6	0
Recd Surplice Fees from April 88 to ye End of May 89	33	11	6
Paid Mr Boutflower Curate a yr & Qr	62	10	0
Subscription for Clergymen's widows	1	1	0
Dinner and Horse Alfred's Head	0	5	0
Bed and Expences Star Oxford	0	9	0
Lockinge Feast	0	3	0
Letter	0	0	6
Clerical Charity	1	1	0
Recd for a Wedding	1	1	0
Ursula Brett a Qr of Oats	0	19	0
Pd Stone for Gown & Cassock	17	3	0
Lost at 3 Card Loo at Brewhouse	2	2	0
Rec'd of Mr Penny Remr of Tithes & offerings including 5gs for Mr Jephson's vault	39	16	6
Gave Penny for collecting	5	5	0
Pd for Duty 4 Sundays Septr & October	7	5	6
Pd Moiety of first Fruits	6	3	0
Pd of Gunpowder	0	2	6
Debentur from ye Exchequer	0	11	0
For preaching a Sermon	0	10	0
Gave a swedish Captn	0	5	0
Hertford Assembly	1	7	0
Hatfield House Ball	0	6	0
Recd for 2 Grave Rails £1 1s. 0d. & £2 2s. 0d. Present from Mr Vincent Xtening	3	3	0
Mansfield for ½ a Load of Hay & Straw	2	2	0
Pd Allan & Smyth for 6 Dozen Port & 2 Sherry	11	13	0
Recd at Oxford Thirds of my Room	8	17	6
Mrs Elderton's Funeral	2	2	0
Recd of Penny 3 Months Fees & for Scarf	7	9	0
Books for Confirmation	0	9	6
Visitation Procurations Synodals etc. for 2 yrs.	2	8	0
Subscription to Sunday School [1]	1	1	0
Rackstraw's Museum	0	3	6
Breaking ye bay Filley	1	11	6
Fish at Hatfield sent by Ld Salisbury's Servt	0	1	0
Spalding Farrier's Bill for firing Black Horse	1	3	6
Recd from ye Exchequer Modus	53	12	0
Search at Lambeth	0	10	6
Play Drury Lane Siege of Belgrade	0	6	0
Recd for a licence	1	13	0

[1] The date is 1790.

	£	s.	d.
Present to yᵉ Parish officers for first Licence . .	0	5	0
Subscription at Club & Whist	1	4	6
To Sunday School Purse towards Deficiency . .	0	11	6
Recᵗ as Surrogate for an Administration . . .	0	10	6
Miss Tysson's Wedding	5	5	0
Sunday School Boys Dinner	0	2	6
March 13, 1792. Sixteenth of Lottery Ticket . .	2	9	0
Recᵈ of Mʳ Penny Part of Easter offerings . . .	5	5	0
Sold my bay horse Jack to Mʳ Moore for . . .	14	0	0
Lewis for Graves & Hairpowder	0	6	5
Ticket for yᵉ Messiah, Coach hire & Expences in Town	2	0	0
Feast	1	8	0
Westminster Quitrent	15	2	4
Dinners at Piazza with Ferrers Coach & Plays . .	1	12	6
Horse at Tattersall's	0	15	0
Keep of 2 Spaniels	3	7	6
Raffle at Mʳ Delamare's for a Gown	0	5	0
By Rent of Vicarage House at Cheshunt 2 yʳˢ to Decʳ 1798	40	0	0
Easter offerings	88	12	6
Recᵈ of Mʳ Ives Half a yʳˢ Rent for Common Lands .	50	0	0
Recᵈ part of Easter offerings for yᵉ yʳ 1804 . . .	70	0	0
By Six Installments of assess'd Taxes to Febʸ 99 . .	21	14	0
L. Tax & Property Tax for yᵉ yʳ 1803	30	15	8

Mr. Collins's scholarship was worth £15 and his fellowship £20 annually. Besides this £20 he divided with the other Fellows moneys such as rents and fines, thus—'Teddington dividend to Michˢ. £2 16s. 2d. Tenbury to Lady Day £2 5s. 5d. Dunster and Beef Hall to Michˢ., 1774, £0 11s. 8d.' 'May 14. 1779: Recᵈ of Du Pré [1] Bursar for Timber on Coll. Estates 10l. 6s. od.' His 'Battles' for 1774-5 come to—

St. Thomas's Quarter	4	15	6
Lady Day	3	10	0
Midsummer	3	16	6
Michaelmas	3	0	0

In 1775, though but twenty-two, he is Junior Bursar and receives in that office for the year £37 14s. In 1776, £31 2s. 8d. After his election as Fellow he occupied better rooms, paying and receiving 'thirds' for the furniture; thus :—

Thirds of Pigot's Room	14	6	4
Recᵈ of Mʳ Parker Thirds for my Garret . . .	4	4	0

[1] MICHAEL DU PRÉ, matr. 1780, aet. 13; Fellow of Exeter, 1792-1818; Rector of St. John's, Jersey; chaplain of a foot regiment. See *Gentleman's Magazine*, ii. 571.

As a Scholar his batells had been in 1767–8 :—

	£	s.	d.		£	s.	d.		£	s.	d.
St. Thomas	. 2	8	0	In 1769	5	3	0	In 1770	5	15	6
Lady Day	. 2	7	6	„	. 4	11	6	„	. 8	1	6
Midsummer	. 4	3	6	„	. 6	18	0	„	. 5	6	6
Mich⁵ .	. 4	12	6	„	. 3	19	0	„	. 4	15	0

There are also every year ' Deductions,' both as Scholar and Fellow, varying between £1 10s. and £4 4s. These are the same as Decrements. He pays no room rent. . His personal expenses as an undergraduate came to about £5 a month while in residence. But the periods of residence seem short and broken. In some loose jottings Mr. Collins calculates the sum he received from his father, during the eight years of his residence at Pembroke, at £190, of which £130 was pocket money [1].

---

[1] A finely executed miniature of Mr. Collins has been shown me by his daughter-in-law, Mrs. John Collins, of Lockinge, whose son, Sir Robert H. Collins, K.C.B., put the above book into my hands.

CHAPTER XXXIII.

ROMANTIC AND TRACTARIAN MOVEMENTS.

Two of the poet Coleridge's brothers—EDWARD and GEORGE
COLERIDGE—were at Pembroke. The former matriculated Dec. 17,
1776, aged fifteen (B.A. 1780), the latter April 27, 1780, aged sixteen.
Edward became vicar of Buckerell, Devon. George, after holding
a mastership at Hackney, succeeded his father [1] at Ottery St. Mary,
and as chaplain, priest, and master of King Henry VIII's Free
Grammar School. Samuel Taylor Coleridge speaks of him as ' my
earliest friend.'

After their father's death, ' He is father, brother, and everything to me.'
Very tender were the relations between them. In 1794, as Private Silas
Comberbacke, the younger wrote letter after letter to the elder, pouring
forth a passion of repentance. One ends, ' My brother, my brother, pray
for me, comfort me, my brother!' In another he writes,' Your letters are
a comfort to me in the comfortless hour—they are manna in the wilderness. . . . Shall I confess to you my weakness, my more than brother?
I am afraid to meet you. When I call to mind the toil and wearisomeness
of your avocations, and think how you sacrifice your amusements and your
health, when I recollect your habitual and self-forgetting economy, how
generously severe, my soul sickens at its own guilt. . . . Yet you, my
brother, would comfort me, not reproach me.' On the reconciliation of
the prodigal with his family in 1796, George received him with joy and
tenderness at Ottery, but when at a later date Samuel proposed to be
separated from his wife, the long-suffering elder brother sorrowfully shut
his doors to him, and this proved a lasting rupture between the poet and
the old home. The Poems of 1797 were dedicated to George Coleridge.
He died Jan. 12, 1828.

CHARLES KINGSLEY, father of a more famous Charles, spent his

---

[1] The Rev. John Coleridge was likened by his son Samuel to Parson Adams.
By way of simplifying grammar for boys he proposed to call the ablative
quale-quare-quiddative case. This divine loved to quote the Old Testament in
Hebrew, which he commended to the attention of his flock as ' the immediate
language of the Holy Ghost.' This exposed his successor, himself a learned man,
to popular depreciation.

Oxford days at Pembroke and Brasenose (matriculated Dec. 12, 1800).
In the *Life* of his son he is described as 'a man of cultivation and
refinement, a good linguist, an artist, a keen sportsman, a natural
historian.'

He was educated at Harrow and Oxford, and brought up with good
expectations as a country gentleman, but having been early in life left an
orphan, and his fortune squandered for him during his minority, he soon
spent what was left, and at the age of thirty found himself almost penniless and obliged for the first time to think of a profession. He decided
on holy orders, 'sold his hunters and land, and with a young wife went
a second time to college, entering his name at Trinity Hall, Cambridge.'
From him Charles Kingsley 'inherited his love of art, his sporting tastes,
his fighting-blood—the men of his family having been soldiers for
generations.' He became Rector of Barnack, but in 1830 moved to
Clovelly. 'The people sprang to touch the more readily under the
influence of a man who, physically their equal, feared no danger and
could steer a boat, hoist and lower a sail, " shoot " a herring net, and haul
a seine, as one of themselves . . . When the herring fleet put out to sea,
the Rector, accompanied by his wife and boys, would start off down street
for the Quay to give a short parting service, at which " men who worked "
and " women who wept " would join in singing out of the old Prayer Book
version the 121st Psalm.' In 1836 he became Rector of St. Luke's,
Chelsea. One who knew him at Barnack speaks of him as 'a type of the
old English clergyman, where the country gentleman forms the basis of
the character which the minister of the Gospel completes [1].'

The revolutionary school of poets has next to Shelley no better
exponent than Thomas Lovell Beddoes (1803–1849), the most

---

[1] The following is the Epitaph placed by his son on his gravestone:—
'Here lies
All that was mortal
of
Charles Kingsley,
Formerly of Battramley House, in the New Forest, Hants,
And lately of St. Luke's, Chelsea.
Endowed by God with many noble gifts of mind and body
He preserved through all vicissitudes of fortune
A loving heart and stainless honour;
And having won in all his various cures
The respect and affection of his people,
And ruled the Parish of Chelsea well and wisely
For more than twenty years,
He died peacefully in the fear of God and in the faith of Christ
On the 29th of February, 1860,
Aged 78 years,
With many friends and not an enemy on earth,
Leaving to his children as a precious heritage
The example of a Gentleman and a Christian.'

E e

notable writer of the time of 'exhaustion and mediocrity' between
Shelley's death and the matchless music of Tennyson. Tennyson
rated *Death's Jest Book* very highly, and Browning declared 'If I were
ever Professor of Poetry, my first lecture at the University should be
on Beddoes, a forgotten Oxford poet.' On the other hand Beddoes
writes from Oxford: 'Mr. Milman (our poetry professor) has made
me quite unfashionable here, by denouncing me as one of a
" villainous school." ' At that time, however, he had only published,
as a freshman, his *Improvisatore*, a crude pamphlet of which he
speedily became so ashamed that he suppressed every copy he could
procure.

Thomas Lovell Beddoes had for father the chaotic genius Dr. Beddoes,
already described, and for mother Maria Edgeworth's sister Anna,
a talented lady to whose 'healthy, noble, kind influence' Davy bears
grateful testimony. From his uncle Lovell Edgeworth he obtained his
second name. He was born at Clifton, July 20, 1803. His father, dying
when he was five years old, left him to the guardianship of Davies Gilbert,
P.R.S. From Bath Grammar School he went, aged fourteen, to the
Charterhouse, where he 'distinguished himself by his mischievous deeds
of daring, by the originality of his behaviour, and by his love of the old
Elizabeth dramatists, whom he early began to imitate.' He was not
seventeen when he was entered at his father's and his guardian's college,
May 1, 1820. 'At Oxford he was eccentric and rebellious, priding himself on his democratic sentiments.' All that Beddoes has left that is worth
keeping was produced, written, or begun in the next few years. In 1822
he published a schoolboy drama, the *Bride's Tragedy*, the unusual
promise of which attracted attention in the reviews. Barry Cornwall in
particular welcomed the new poet with enthusiasm, and became his friend.
He describes him at the age of twenty-one as 'innocently gay, with
a gibe always on his tongue, a mischievous eye, and locks curling like the
hyacinth[1].' His college days indeed were the happiest part of his life.
While an undergraduate he busied himself with several dramas, such as
the *Last Man* and *Love's Arrow Poisoned*. In 1824 he was summoned
to Florence to his mother's death-bed, and stayed in Italy some time,
becoming acquainted there with Landor and Mrs. Shelley. Mr. Gosse
says that Beddoes was 'the first perhaps to appreciate the magnitude of
Shelley's merit, as he was certainly the earliest to imitate his lyrical work.'
It is to his enthusiasm for this master that the production, in 1824, under
the guarantee of himself and several others, of Shelley's *Posthumous
Poems* is due. Meanwhile, his reading for his degree was interrupted.
He writes to Kelsall, afterwards his biographer, from a retreat which he
had hidden from his family, that he has before him 'the very hardest
reading' for an examination for which he is absolutely unfit. He describes

---

[1] His sister-in-law, Mrs. Cecilia Beddoes, tells me that she does not know of
any portrait of him.

himself as living in a deserted state and sinking into deep despondency.
In May, 1825, he was at Pembroke, and wrote inviting Procter :—

> ' Come, shake London from thy skirts away.
> So come. Forget not it is England's May.
> For Oxford ho! by moonlight or by sun.
> Our horses are not hours, but rather run
> Foot by foot faster than the second-sand,
> While the old sun-team, like a plough, doth stand
> Stuck in thick heaven. Here thou at morn shalt see
> Spring's dryad-wakening whisper call the tree
> And move it to green answers; and beneath
> Each side the river which the fishes breathe
> Daisies and grass, whose tops were never stirred,
> Nor dews made tremulous, but by foot of bird.'

He took B.A. May 25, 1825. Writing on June 8 from the College to
Kelsall, he announces the projection of the most famous of his writings :
' Oxford is the most indolent place on earth. I have fairly done nothing
in the world but read a play or two of Schiller, Aeschylus, and Euripides ...
I am thinking of a very Gothic-styled tragedy for which I have a jewel of
a name—*Death's Jest Book*. Of course, no one will ever read it.' About
this time, too, he wrote *Torrismond* and the *Second Brother*. But his
unpopularity at Oxford, as a red radical, made him give up the idea of
publishing a volume of lyrics called *Outidana*. He now resolved to forsake
literature and give his whole attention to medicine. In July, 1825, Beddoes
went to Göttingen, where he studied for four years. He liked the free and
easy life and methods of study. ' There is an appetite for learning, a spirit
of diligence, and withal a good-natured fellow-feeling wholly unparalleled
in our old apoplectic and paralytic Almae Matres.' He adds, ' I find
literary wishes fading pretty fast ... I will frankly confess to you that I
have lost much if not all of my ambition to become poetically distinguished.'
Certainly German metaphysics and politics dried up the creative faculty
in Beddoes as in Coleridge. He returned to Oxford to take M.A. April 16,
1828. In 1829 he went to study medicine at Würtzburg and was made
M.D. by that University, but before actually receiving the diploma had
to fly from Bavaria, where he was in ill odour with the government. He
had afterwards to leave Strassburg for a like cause. Zürich was the home
of his activities, as physiologist and politician, till the counter revolution by
the peasants in September, 1839, and defeat of the Liberal cause. He saw
his friend the minister Hegetschweiber murdered before his eyes. In
March, 1840, he had himself to fly secretly. His wanderings were for
some years obscure, but he wrote much German verse at this time. In
1846 he came back to England, rough and eccentric in habit. It is said
that he arrived at the residence of a relative riding a donkey. The
Procters tried to befriend Beddoes, but found him almost insane. A bravado
about setting Drury Lane on fire with a bank note was due to a less
respectable cause than craziness. His existence, he wrote, was mono-
tonous, dull, and obscure. Settling next year in Frankfürt, his disgust

with life was coloured a darker hue by blood poisoning got in performing a surgical operation. His republican friends had deserted him, and he became more and more a recluse, allowed his beard to grow, and 'looked like Shakspeare.' His appearance hitherto, however, is said to have strikingly resembled that of Keats. It is known now that his mysterious accident in May, 1848, leading to the amputation of his leg, was an attempt to take his own life. He showed much fortitude under physical suffering, but recovery was slow, and in the night of January 25, 1849, he destroyed himself with the deadly poison called kurara. He was found with a mocking pencil-scrawl pinned to his breast, beginning with the words ' I am food for what I am good for—worms,' and ending ' I ought to have been among other things a good poet.' Twenty years before he had written some lines for his cousin Miss Zoë King (to whom Landor, Kenyon, Eagles and others penned sonnets, and who cherished with romantic loyalty his fame), in which he speaks of what ' might have been,' but now he must pass away

> ' Into forgetfulness, into the cold
> Of the open, homeless world without a hope.'

The story of this brief, troubled, and undisciplined career is an infinitely sad one. Kelsall, in 1872, left a number of his friend's letters to Browning, who for a long time refused to open the box. At last he invited Mr. Gosse, by whom the *Letters* have since been edited, to help him examine them. When the key was produced Browning said in great agitation, ' I am sure we shall come upon some dreadful secret. I cannot bear to lift the lid.' At the very top were letters relating to the hitherto unrevealed suicide at Basle, which Kelsall desired should be made known to the world after a due delay. Mr. Swinburne describes the *Letters* as ' brilliant,' and considers that Beddoes' ' noble instinct for poetry' is better shown in them than in his verse. The *Poems* were published by Kelsall in 1851. Mr. Gosse says that Beddoes ' belongs to the tribe of scholar-poets.' He has no sustained inspiration, but is ' a poetical artist of consummate ability. Of all the myriad poets and poeticals who have tried to recover the lost magic of the tragic blank verse of the Elizabethans, Beddoes has come nearest to success. If it were less indifferent to human interests of every ordinary kind, the beauty of his dramatic verse would not fail to fascinate. To see how strong it is, how picturesque, how admirably fashioned, we have only to compare it with what others have done in the same style, with the tragic verse, e.g. of Barry Cornwall, of Talfourd, of Home. But Beddoes is what he himself calls a "creeper into worm-holes " . . . He dedicates himself to the service of Death, not with a brooding sense of the strange terror of mortality, but from a love of the picturesque pageantry of it . . . As a lyrist he appears on the whole to rank higher than as a dramatist. Several of his songs, artificial as they are, must always live.' Beddoes lies in the hospital cemetery at Basle.

There were with us till the last few months two venerable men who were at Pembroke with Beddoes, the Rev. EDWARD HAWKINS (Scholar

1818–25), canon-residentiary of Llandaff, and RICHARD ROGERS COXWELL-ROGERS, Esq., J.P., D.L., High Sheriff of Gloucestershire in 1857. He matriculated Feb. 21, 1822. Both his grandfathers were at Pembroke in the days of George the Second.

It is in one sense a true paradox to say that the revolutionary and mediævalist movements were hatched from the same egg. In another sense it is quite untrue; for Tractarianism was but an impassioned assertion of old-fashioned, well-established Church principles. Rather earlier than the Hackney School, but himself born at Hackney, the friend of W. Stevens and H. H. Norris and brother-in-law of Archdeacon Watson, Dr. THOMAS SIKES, vicar and patron of Guilsborough, Northants, carried on the Caroline traditions, and prepared a circle of minds for the Revival of 1833. Dr. Liddon in his *Life of Pusey* (i. 257, 258) thus refers to him :—

'Side by side with Evangelicalism there were also convictions which had been handed down across the dreary interval of the eighteenth century, and which here and there found expression in the lives of holy men, who taught Latitudinarians and Methodists how the great men of the Caroline age in the Church of England had believed, and lived, and died. Such men as Jones of Nayland and Dr. Sikes of Guilsborough, and, at a somewhat later period, Mr. Norris of Hackney, and Mr. Joshua Watson, were of this company. The first two were theologians, inheriting and contemplating truths on which the Non-jurors had laid stress, and living in communion of thought and sympathy with the ancient Church. . .

'Dr. T. Sikes was especially regarded by Pusey as a [1] precursor of the Oxford movement. He had graduated at Pembroke College, Oxford, in 1788; but his earlier University life had been passed at St. Edmund Hall, which was already at that date a home of Evangelicalism. Its earnest but defective teaching made a deep, though not a wholly satisfying impression on the thoughtful undergraduate; and, when he turned from the lectures which he heard in the Hall to the weight and learning of a really great divine like Thorndike, his religious future was determined. He lived a life of retirement in his little country parish in Northamptonshire; but men, young and old, came to him for the sake of his thoughtful and stimulating conversation, to which vigour of intellect, extensive reading, a disciplined sense of humour, and a piety of an ancient rather than a modern type, contributed the chief features. One of his conversations, which took place so late as in 1833, and was at the time reported to Pusey, was often referred to by him as having a sort of prophetical value.'

Dr. Pusey spoke of it thus in a 'Letter to His Grace the Archbishop of Canterbury,' 1842 (pp. 27-29):—

'It may also be a relief to your Grace to know—it has come as a great

[1] In Canon Perry's opinion '*the* precursor' (*English Church History*, iii. 160).

relief to my own mind, since of late I have known it—that this confusion in which we now are, was not unforeseen. I mean not that it may not have been aggravated by any want of wisdom in myself or others; still it was anticipated as the necessary consequence of the restoration of the doctrines which we have been employed to restore, before any of us were thought of as likely to be the instruments, or we ourselves had begun to look forward to the work, which has since been laid upon us. It will doubtless be refreshing to your Grace to see the words of one, whom in his inferior office, and as a Divine, you must have valued; how with the oracular prescience given to aged piety, when, as about to pass from this world, it receives, from time to time, a Divine insight into the things of that into which it is entering, he delineated in outline strangely faithful the very form and order of things which were to be after his departure, but of which there were yet no signs.

'We may well be reconciled to troubles which were thus marked out to us beforehand, as what we must necessarily pass through. And while we are thus content to bear them, and to be stigmatized as the causers of them and the "troublers of Israel," they who are set over us may perhaps be the rather encouraged to bear their share cheerfully, and not be grieved at us, as if we alone by our errors caused what, independently of us, it was foreseen would be. He, to whom the conversation was addressed, tells me, " I well remember the very countenance, gesture, attitude and tone of good Mr. Sikes, and give you, as near as may be, what he said.

' " I seem to think I can tell you something which you who are young may probably live to see, but which I, who shall soon be called away off the stage, shall not. Wherever I go all about the country, I see amongst the clergy a number of very amiable and estimable men, many of them much in earnest, and wishing to do good. But I have observed one universal want in their teaching: the uniform suppression of one great truth. There is no account given anywhere, so far as I see, of the one Holy Catholic Church. I think that the causes of this suppression have been mainly two. The Church has been kept out of sight, partly in consequence of the civil establishment of the branch of it which is in this country, and partly out of false charity to Dissent.

' " Now this great truth is an article of the Creed; and if so, to teach the rest of the Creed to its exclusion must be to destroy 'the analogy or proportion of the faith,' τὴν ἀναλογίαν τῆς πίστεως.

' " This cannot be done, without the most serious consequences. The doctrine is of the last importance, and the principles it involves of immense power; and some day, not far distant, it will judicially have its reprisals. And whereas the other articles of the Creed seem now to have thrown it into the shade, it will seem, when it is brought forward, to swallow up the rest. We now hear not a breath about the Church; by and bye, those who live to see it will hear of nothing else; and just in proportion perhaps to its present suppression, will be its future development. Our confusion now-a-days is chiefly owing to the want of it; and there will be yet more confusion attending its revival. The effects of it I even dread to contemplate, especially if it come suddenly. And woe betide those, whoever they are, who shall, in the course of Providence, have to bring it forward. It ought especially of all others to be matter of catechetical teaching and training. The doctrine of the Church Catholic and the privileges of Church membership cannot be explained from pulpits; and those who will have to explain it will hardly know where they, are, or which way they are to turn themselves. They will be endlessly misunderstood and misinterpreted. There will be one great outcry of Popery from one end of the country to the other. It will be thrust upon minds unprepared, and on an uncatechized Church. Some will take it up and admire it as a beautiful picture; others will be frightened and run away and reject it; and all will want a guidance which one hardly knows where they shall find. How the doctrine may be first thrown forward we know not; but the powers of the world may any day turn their backs upon us, and this will probably lead to those effects I have described." [1]

Others of his conversations, extracted from Mr. Norris's *Diary*, are given in Churton's *Memoir of Joshua Watson*, p. 30 (second edition). Dr. Liddon considers that Mr. Gladstone (*Gleanings of Past Years*, vii. pp. 216–218) does less than justice to Dr. Sikes' standpoint. He died Dec. 14, 1834. Watson, writing to Norris a description of his death, speaks of 'the sweet counsel which we three took together at the commencement of our career' at Guilsborough. Sikes used to reproach Watson 'for not having so ardent a love for music as he himself had, urging that it would be the employment of heaven.' He was 'to the poor of his parish an unwearied benefactor.' He left a small estate to augment the poor vicarage where he had laboured.

In the autobiographical memoir prefixed to Mrs. Mozley's edition of Dr. Newman's *Letters* we are told that in the last half year of his school life at Ealing 'he fell under the influence of an excellent man, the Rev. WALTER MAYERS, of Pembroke College, Oxford, one of the classical masters, from whom he received deep religious impressions, at the time Calvinistic in character, which were to him the beginning of a new life.' It was an open question till the last moment whether Newman was to go to Oxford or Cambridge. Had the choice been for Cambridge, what a difference, humanly speaking, to the future of the Church of England! It may be surmised that Newman's attachment to Mr. Mayers had some share in influencing him for Oxford. It was by his advice, seven years later, that Newman entered into holy orders [1], and subsequently became curate of St. Clement's.

---

[1] 'Newman held almost fiercely that secular education could be so conducted as to become a pastoral cure. . . . He recollected that, in the Laudian statutes for Oxford, a tutor was not a mere academical policeman or constable, but a moral

There is a remarkable letter to him from Newman, while an undergraduate, written under strong religious indignation against the
revelries and profanities which had grown up round the Trinity
College Gaudy. He tells Mr. Mayers that he is intimate with very
few. 'An habitual negligence of the awfulness of the Holy Communion is introduced. How can we prosper?' He also writes to
this kind counsellor about his examination hopes and fears. We find
Mr. Mayers dining with him at Oriel. Newman's first sermon (June 23,
1824) was preached at Over-Worton, Oxon, which cure Mr. Mayers
served. We are told, ' One day, after working with his private pupils
till the evening, he sat down to his article [on Cicero for the
Encyclopaedia Metropolitana] till four o'clock next morning, and then
walked over from Oxford to Worton, a distance of eighteen miles, in
order to appear punctually at the breakfast table of a friend, the Rev.
Walter Mayers, who on quitting home had committed his pupils in his
parsonage to his charge.' On April 1, 1828, Newman writes to his
mother, 'I have a sermon to prepare for Worton to-morrow.' This,
it is stated, was his friend's funeral sermon [1]. Mr. Mayers matriculated
Dec. 8, 1808; Scholar 1812-16; Steward of Junior Common Room;
B.A. 1812; M.A. 1815.

Ten years before the Tract movement began, ROBERT STEPHEN
HAWKER, the eccentric high church poet, usually known as Hawker
of Morwenstowe, said to be the first clergyman who revived the
Edwardian vestments, entered the College. He was born at Stoke
Damerel, Dec. 3, 1804, the son of Mr. Jacob Stephen Hawker,
a medical man, practising at Plymouth, who was afterwards ordained,
and for thirty years Curate and Vicar of Stratton in Cornwall.
Robert was brought up by his grandfather, the famous Dr. Hawker,
incumbent of King Charles the Martyr, Plymouth, and author of
Morning and Evening Portions. Some of his strange pranks are
related by Mr. Baring Gould in his *Life of R. S. Hawker.* Having
been articled to a west-country attorney, he persuaded an aunt to send

and religious guardian of the youths committed to him. If a tutor was this, he
might allowably, or rather fittingly, have received holy orders; but if the view
of Hawkins was the true one, then he, Newman, felt he was taking part in a heart-
less system of law and form, in which the good and promising were sacrificed to
the worthless and uninteresting.' *Autobiographical Memoir.*

[1] But Mr. Mayers died Feb. 22. He was brother-in-law of Miss Maria R.
Giberne, who is described in the *Reminiscences of Oriel,* and who was an intimate
and valued correspondent of Dr. Newman till her death in the convent of the Order
of Visitation at Autun in 1885. Newman's sister Mary died on Jan. 5, 1828,
and on the fiftieth anniversary of the death this lady recalls to him the minute and
delicate details of those early days of sacred intimacy.

him to school at Cheltenham and afterwards to Pembroke, where he matriculated April 28, 1823. His father, however, was still a poor curate, and in the Long Vacation of 1824 told him that he could no longer keep him at college. Mr. Baring Gould relates the sequel : ' There lived at Whitstone four Misses I'ans, daughters of Colonel I'ans. They had been left with an annuity of £200 a-piece, as well as lands and a handsome place. . . Directly that R. H. learnt his father's decision, without waiting to put on his hat, he ran from Stratton to Bude, arrived hot and blown at Efford, and proposed to Miss Charlotte I'ans to be his wife. The lady was then aged forty-one, one year older than his mother. She was his god-mother and had taught him his letters.' Such a union, by-the-by, was uncanonical. ' Miss I'ans accepted him and they were married in November, when he was twenty. . . On Hawker's return to Oxford with his wife after the Christmas Vacation (and he took her there riding behind him on a pillion) he was obliged, on account of being married, to migrate from Pembroke to Magdalen Hall.'

Jeune visited him in Cornwall the next year, and joined in some of Hawker's mad pleasantries. (It was about this time that he astonished the people of Bude by personating during several moonlight nights a mermaid with comb, glass, and wig of seaweed, chanting among the rocks and waves.) He took B.A. in 1828, and was ordained in 1829. Coming up in 1836 for M.A. he observed Jeune, as Dean, trying to pilot to the Vice-Chancellor's chair a very corpulent gentleman-commoner, whose unwieldy form got hitched more than once in the crowd. Hawker said in a deep whisper : ' Why, your peg's surely mazed, maister.' Spasms of uncontrollable laughter choked Jeune's utterance of the ' Praesento ad vos.' In 1827, Hawker won the *Pompeii* Newdigate. His volumes of religious verse afterwards gave him a foremost place among the poets of the Church Revival. But it is his extraordinary personality which has most characterized the memory of the Cornish vicar. A very remarkable portrait is prefixed to Mr. Baring Gould's *Memoir*. Hawker died August 10, 1875—in what communion was afterwards a matter of dispute and recrimination. Everything the man did was, perhaps purposely, *bizarre* and unaccountable, down to the last. The celebrated ' Trelawney ' ballad, or *Song of the Western Men*, which even Macaulay and Scott mistook for an antique, owed its publication to Davies Gilbert. Mr. Alfred Nutt styles Hawker's unfinished *Quest of the Sangraal* ' a magnificent fragment.' A recent critic says, ' It is austerely great and beautiful, a thing of burning imagination and vehemence, steeped in the atmosphere of old dreams and early mysteries, profoundly and passionately musical, yet distinct and firm throughout.'

During the Tractarian warfare Dr. JOHN STEDMAN (matriculated 1806) published a Latin letter from Erasmus to Gregory XVI (not unlike Dr. Dickinson's *Pastoral Epistle from His Holiness the Pope,* 1836), entitled *Erasmi Roterodami ad Gregorium Dec. Sext. Pont. Epistola Singularis.* Oxonii, Baxter, 1841. His father, THOMAS STED-MAN (entered the College 1768), succeeded Dr. Adams at St. Chad's, Shrewsbury.

The memorable formula 'Nobis procuratoribus non placet' was not used during the Tractarian movement for the first time in 1844. In 1836 the Rev. EDMUND GOODENOUGH BAYLY [1], Fellow of Pembroke, Proctor with the Rev. Henry Reynolds, of Jesus College, used the words on the occasion of the proceedings against Hampden. The following account is taken from the *Life of Dean Stanley* (i. 158) :—

'The agitation grew every week, and on March 11th the "Heads," by a majority of one, consented to submit to Convocation a statute which deprived the new Regius Professor of two of the functions attached to his office, viz. of his place on the board for the nomination of Select Preachers, and also on that of taking cognizance of heretical preaching at Oxford, on the ground that "in consequence of his public writings the University had no confidence in the present Professor." The day fixed for the Convocation was March 22nd. Dr. Hampden's inaugural lecture was delivered on March 17th, and was followed by a second pamphlet from Dr. Pusey—"Dr. Hampden's Past and Present Statements compared."

'When the decisive day arrived the Sheldonian Theatre was crowded with an excited throng of graduates and undergraduates. But the two Proctors brought the proceedings to an abrupt close by exercising their right of veto, and the assembly broke up amidst shouts, groans, and shrieks from galleries and area, such as no deliberative assembly probably ever heard.'

In a number of the *Oxford Chronicle* of 1840 the following appears :—

'During the past week two more victims to the treacherous dealing of University Professors and Tutors have openly seceded from the Establishment and joined the Communion of Rome ; their names are Mr. Peter Renoux, a Bible Clerk of Pembroke College, and Mr. Douglas, B.A., a Gentleman-Commoner of Christ Church. Both parties, we understand, are now with Dr. Wiseman at Oscott. . . . Mr. Renoux is the reputed author of a tract on *The Holy Eucharist,* at first attributed to Mr. Williams, and which, as we have reason to believe, was published with the knowledge and sanction of Mr. Keble.'

Sir PETER LE PAGE RENOUF, the distinguished Oriental scholar here spoken of, entered March 12, 1840 (son of Joseph Renouf, of Guernsey) as Bible Clerk ; a few months later he became Oades Exhibitioner. He resigned in 1842. In 1855 he became Professor of Ancient

---

[1] Mr. Bayly died Oct. 3, 1886, aged eighty-two. The Tutors' Protest against the Gorham Judgment was signed in 1850 by both the Pembroke Tutors.

History and Eastern Languages in the Roman Catholic University of Ireland. From 1864 to 1886 he was one of H.M. Inspectors of Schools. In 1885 Mr. Renouf was made Keeper of Egyptian and Assyrian Antiquities at the British Museum. He was knighted last year (1896) at the Birthday.

A leader on the Evangelical side in the middle of the century was CHARLES EDWARD OAKLEY, who came up from Rugby as an Exhibitioner Feb. 20, 1851; afterwards of Wadham and Magdalen. He took a brilliant first-class in Law and History, in which School he was in 1859–60 an Examiner; Johnson Theological Scholar 1855; B.C.L. and M.A. 1857. Mr. Oakley went to the Crimea as Chaplain to the Forces. Afterwards he was Rector of Wickwar, 1856, and of St. Paul's, Covent Garden, 1863. He declined the bishoprick of Melbourne. He died Sept. 15, 1865, aged thirty-four. Lady Georgina Moreton was his wife.

I may here glance at the names of some scholar-divines of the closing Georgian time. JOHN VINICOMBE, B.D., whose fine portrait by Opie was bequeathed to the College by Sir Rose Price, was Ossulston Fellow from 1783 to 1803, and Tutor. He was for several years in the West Indies with Mr., afterwards Sir Rose, Price, a fellow Cornishman. Mr. Vinicombe died, somewhat mysteriously, in College Feb. 29, 1808. He bequeathed £50 to buy books for the Library.—THOMAS HANCOCK, Scholar 1812–17, was Head Master of Caermarthen Grammar School, dying April 6, 1824, aged thirty-seven.—Dr. CHARLES KEVERN WILLIAMS, Scholar 1820–6, Fellow 1826–30, D.D. 1844, was Head Master of Lewes Grammar School 1829.—Dr. CHARLES PENNY (matriculated 1827, D.D. 1850) was Head Master of Crewkerne Grammar School 1838–75; Rector of Chaffcombe 1848–75.—ALFRED WALLIS STREET, Scholar 1838–43 (he entered Magdalen Hall March 30, 1833, aged twenty-four), was Professor at Bishop's College, Calcutta, 1839–51.—Dr. GEORGE RICHARDS (matriculated April 27, 1837; D.D. 1858) was Senior Tutor Chaplain and Warneford Professor of Classics in Queen's College, Birmingham, 1846–55; Rector of Marlingford 1880.—JAMES WHITE (matriculated 1823), an historical and miscellaneous writer, was Vicar of Loxley, and died March 26, 1862.

An eminent Queen's Counsel, GEORGE MORLEY DOWDESWELL, entered in 1825. Bencher of the Inner Temple 1867; Treasurer 1883; Recorder of Newbury 1854.—JOHN GERVAS HUTCHINSON BOURNE (matriculated 1821; Fellow of Magdalen 1828) became Chief Justice of Newfoundland. Ob. 1845.

CHAPTER XXXIV.

BICENTENARY—MODERN BUILDING AND REBUILDING— THE WOLSEY ALMSHOUSE—THE BACK LODGINGS.

DR. SERGROVE, we have seen, died April 16, 1796, and in his room was chosen, on April 28, JOHN SMYTH, for whom see among the Benefactors (p. 304). The long Mastership of his successor, Dr. GEORGE WILLIAM HALL, lasted from Nov. 2, 1809, to Dec. 10, 1843—'an ancient Whig, who gradually softened down into a moderate but consistent Conservative[1].' A window in the north aisle of Gloucester Cathedral and a tablet in the south cloister (where he is buried) record his memory. His father was Mr. John Hall, of Chelsea, historical engraver to George III. Like Dr. Sergrove he was educated at St. Paul's School, and then temporarily at Abingdon. He entered as a Wightwick Scholar Nov. 4, 1788. Fellow and Tutor 1795; D.D. 1809; Select Preacher 1810. Rector of Taynton, Gloucestershire, 1810. Vice-Chancellor 1820-24. Some that remember him describe Dr. Hall as a little mild man with kindly face, not a striking scholar or character, but, it seems, keenly interested in books and antiquities. One who was at the College in George IV's days tells me he never preached, lectured, or dined. He had however a vigorous Vicegerent in CHARLES WIGHTWICK. The same old Pembrochian writes concerning 'Ruler Wightwick':— 'The *crack of his whip* as he crossed the quad, on reaching his rooms (in the S. E. corner), from the country at the beginning of each term was the *mot d'ordre* for the term, and all eyes were centred on him as autocrat of the whole College. The Master and other fellows and tutors in his presence were mutes, and his word was law, as far as regarded all the doings and discipline of the undergraduates, before, during, and I believe after my time. To me he was a special patron and a helper in books, inasmuch as he gave me breakfast and private help twice a week at his rooms without any charge and from pure good will.' He was Proctor in 1812; Senior Bursar from 1826. He died Rector of Brinkworth, Wilts. The handsome portrait in the

[1] Gloucester local press.

Common Room by Sir Martin Shee has been engraved by Cousins.
Dr. Hall's second lieutenant, WILLIAM BEACH THOMAS (classical Tutor,
1826–30, and Dean; Public Examiner, 1827–28), was a fine scholar,
a conscientious and courteous don. Mr. Thomas became canon of
St. David's in 1859. He died July 21, 1876, aged seventy-seven.
His brother FRANCIS (Fellow 1831–43) was denounced by the *Times*
for a magisterial decision. Archdeacon GEORGE HOUGH, senior
Colonial Chaplain at the Cape, was Fellow 1812–3. He died Aug. 1,
1867. A well-remembered kin-Fellow [1] of this time (afterwards
Bursar), was JOHN SHEFFIELD Cox (Fellow 1820–60), described by
one who knew him in the fifties as a good instance of the old style
Senior Fellow—cracked and eccentric, exhibiting a mixture of shrewd-
ness with some absurdity; a fisherman of course. At one time
a hardworking curate of Spitalfields, he died Rector of Sibston.
Many absurd anecdotes of him are remembered there. RICHARD
FRENCH LAURENCE (Fellow 1821–3) was Bodley's Sub-Librarian
(1822) and afterwards Treasurer of Cashel. Ob. Sept. 29, 1882.

Dr. Hall married a Miss Kennedy, aunt of the famous scholar. His
elder son, GEORGE CHARLES HALL (Scholar 1830–1), was Select
Preacher 1845–6; another, WILLIAM DAVID HALL (matriculated 1834),
became a Fellow of New College.

Early in 1824 it was resolved that, 'the 29th June ensuing being the
two-hundredth anniversary of the day on which the Letters Patent of
King James the First were dated, constituting Broadgates Hall
a College by the name of Pembroke College, the same be observed as
a grand Gaudy or day of rejoicing.' Three years before, the Hall had
been somewhat enlarged and beautified from the designs of Mr. Harris.
At the eastern end part of the passage communicating with the Back
Lodgings was taken in; to the west the room was lengthened by four
feet, and the oriel, with painted glass by Egginton, thrown out. The old
window had in it the arms of the University only. At the same time the
position of the side windows was altered [2], the roof of the transverse

---

[1] He was descended from Elizabeth Dewe, granddaughter of Richard Tesdale.
Her great-grandson, Mr. Cox's great-grandfather, married Catherine Sophia,
daughter of John Duke of Buckingham, and it was at Althorp that Mr. Cox was
baptized (Jan. 7, 1799). Dr. Sergrove the Master was Elizabeth Dewe's great-
great-grandson.

[2] 'July 27, 1620. Thomas James, Doctor in Divinitye Justice of Peace undertaketh to glasse one of the windowes of the Hall at his owne charges.

'(*Note.*) The greatest windowe in the new Hall is glassed at his charge.

'August 7, 1620. Lionell Day, Bachelour in Divinity Rector of Whichford in
the County of Warwicke, undertaketh to build a whole windowe in the new Hall,
stone work, iron, glasse, &c.' (From Principal Clayton's *Contributors' Book*.)

portion of the hall raised, and the ornamental cornice with its
armorials added. Warmth was obtained by a hot-air dispenser placed
in the old buttery. A handsome high table and side-board were given
by the Master; the Gothic chairs used in the present Hall were given
chiefly by the Vicegerent and Fellows. Among the other contributors
were Dr. Maurice Swabey, the eminent civilian, Sir John Sewell,
Davies Gilbert, Dr. Valpy, and Dean Durand of Guernsey. The total
expense to the end of 1824 was £1,839 8s. 3d., in which is included
the making a new passage from the quadrangle to the Back Lodgings.
The College itself contributed £450.

The following account of the Bicentenary celebration is from the
Oxford Herald of July 3, 1824:—

'On Wednesday last, the day of the public Commemoration of Benefactors to the University, the Master and Fellows of Pembroke College
celebrated the commencement of the third century from the endowment
of the College by a sumptuous entertainment in the hall, to which such of
the present and former Members of the College were invited as, from their
local situation, could be expected to attend. At half-past five the company
sat down to dinner, all the tables being filled. After the toast " To the
pious Memory of the first Founders of Pembroke College," an appropriate
Latin Oration was delivered by Mr. Edmund Goodenough Bayly, the
Senior Founder's-kin Scholar on the Tesdale Foundation [1]. The evening
was spent in the greatest hilarity, amid the pleasing recollection of past
intimacies, and with lively and reiterated demonstrations of that reciprocal
esteem and attachment which, in a well regulated society, will ever exist
between the governors and the governed.'

On the same morning, Dr. Hall being then Vice-Chancellor, he,
'accompanied by the Heads of Houses, the young Nobility of the
University, &c., proceeded in their dress robes from Pembroke College
to the Theatre' for the Encaenia. His vice-cancellariate had been
uneventful. On being admitted to office in 1820 he spoke of himself
as 'primus qui fasces in Collegium suum introduxerat.' There is
a drawing of Dr. Hall by W. Wright in the Hope collection, dated
Sept. 1824.

After the erection of the Chapel the College buildings had undergone no further change till the early days of the Gothic movement.
Any reaction from the prevailing utilitarian meanness of the closing
Georgian era would have been respectable, and this movement was at
first an enthusiasm, the handmaid of a revival of Faith. Yet it effaced
a thousand artistic charms, to give us a machine-like imitation by
inferior workmen of an inimitable past. We do things better now,

[1] Entered 1820. *Vide supra*, p. 426.

but in an eclectic spirit, sticking angels or fiends here and coats of arms there, without believing much either in the supernatural or in chivalry.

I make these remarks because, so far as I am aware, the Pembroke new frontage was the earliest specimen, on any scale, of revived mediæval building in Oxford, where however the tradition of the Pointed style had never quite died out[1]. The doctrinal revival of 1833 *followed* the architectural renaissance, both of course being parts of the same movement of mind. Restoration, more or less on the lines of the old design, had begun at Magdalen as early as 1822. The Perpendicular oriel of the present Pembroke Library, as stated above, was thrown out in 1821[2]. In 1825 however Balliol was building in the classical style. The Gothic front of Pembroke dates from 1829. Within a year or two St. Mary Hall, All Souls, and Exeter were being transformed in that taste.

The description of the work in Carlos's Skelton, 1843, will not be generally accepted. 'The entire front of the College has been recently new faced in the Gothic style, of which it is a poor example.' However ill-advised the disguising of a good old building behind a mask of modern fifteenth-century masonry, the design has both grace and proportion. The result however is that a visitor casually examining the College buildings would find nothing except the Grecian chapel to suggest to him that Pembroke College had any existence before the time of William IV. There are worse looking Colleges in Oxford, but there is none so entirely divested of any marks of antiquity. About the unhappy transformation of St. Aldate's Church—pictorially and historically a unit with Pembroke—a word has already been spoken.

In Lewis's Topographical Dictionary the Old Quadrangle is described as ' the work of different periods, but regularly built. The interior has been newly faced with Bath stone, and altered from the Palladian to the later English style. The northern front and Master's lodging were also originally Palladian, and have been appropriately decorated after a design of Mr. Daniel Evans of Oxford. The oriel over the gateway is constructed on the model of the remains of one in John of Gaunt's palace at Lincoln.' More alteration was made on the exterior than the inside of the quadrangle. The outside dormers were

---

[1] See *Gentleman's Magazine*, LX. (1790), pt. ii. p. 789.
[2] The striking Almanack top of 1824 represents the building from this side. I know of no picture of its earlier appearance, except Storer's cuts of 1821. One gives 'Summaster's' and a bit of the Hall; but the Hall is almost hidden by a shrub. The other (in Chalmers) shows an oblong west window.

... ... third storey, and the fenestration altered to
... ... a small window, two large ones being together
... ... row. All the windows were given hood-
... gate-tower, transformed to match the rest of
... storey, and crowned by an elegant parapet
... design of which was suggested by Mr.
... ows. A prominent and handsome pinnacled
... ured heads of founders and worthies, now
... another shallower oriel answered to it
... noticed that at the eastern corner is carved
... Majesty, with her new crown and sceptre,
in Skelton's print, however (1831), and in
... work is shown as finished, but the east end
... design. The Almanack top of 1838 gives the
... ... is. The explanation is that, in the hope of
... ... W ... y Almshouse, demolishing it, and then building a
... ... towards Christ Church, the College left the eastern
end in a plain and unfinished state. But when this hope was
abandoned, the eastern end was completed by the same architect,
Mr. Evans. This was resolved upon on the first anniversary of the
Queen's Accession. In Ollier's *Views of Oxford* (1843) there is
a large plate by Delamotte showing the completed frontage and
part of St. Aldate's, viz. Docklinton's aisle and the chamber over it.
Carl Rundt, painter to the King of Prussia, has a plate of the front,
looking east, in *Views of the Most Picturesque Colleges*, Part I. But
in his drawing it lacks a parapet.

In the interior of the quadrangle an embattled parapet now ran over
the second row of windows, just showing the roof, and the dormers
in their old positions. The ground-floor and first-floor windows
were re-arranged, but united as before with stringcourses. The large
dormers were Gothicized and crowned with parapets. The drawing
here presented, which I take from N. Whittock's *Microcosm of Oxford*,
gives a view of the interior of the quadrangle in 1829, just before the
alterations. A vignette in Napier's *Boswell*, by C. Stanfield, R.A.,
shows it during the alterations. Mackenzie shows it in 1836. The
roof has been newly covered (in 1870) with excellent green Stonesfield
slates, but the inferior stone with which the building was faced, and the
introduction, everywhere but in the attics, of sashes and large panes
have sadly robbed it of its character, much as sightless eyeballs make
a face expressionless. The old masonry can be seen outside the east
end from the Almshouse. Over Brewers Street, the irregular back of the

NORTH-WEST INTERIOR ANGLE OF THE OLD QUADRANGLE BEFORE THE ALTERATIONS OF WILLIAM THE FOURTH'S REIGN, SHOWING THE DIFFERENCE IN STYLE BETWEEN THE EARLIEST AND LATEST PORTIONS OF THE QUADRANGLE, THE ENTRANCE TO THE ANCIENT REFECTORY OF BROADGATES HALL (NOW THE LIBRARY), AND OVER IT THE LIBRARY BUILT IN 1709. THE UPPER OF THE TWO TOWER WINDOWS WAS JOHNSON'S CHAMBER

College on the top of the twelfth century wall remains nearly un-changed. But that is all. Within the last ten years creepers have been allowed to grow over the face of the quadrangle.

The beginning of the next Mastership was marked by a more im-portant change in the appearance of the College, through the erection of a new range of buildings on the site of the Back Lodgings—*molem, magalia quondam*—followed three years later by the building of a fine Dining Hall at right angles to the new rooms [1]. No such enlargement of any College had taken place for at least half-a-century. The growth of the Society under Dr. JEUNE made extension necessary ; and, much as we may regret the disappearance of the time-honoured buildings and of the old-fashioned gardens between them and the city wall, the plan for a large inner court was certainly effective. Quad-rangle it cannot in strictness be called, since the Chapel is the only building on the south side. To have built along this site would have necessitated the re-edifying of the town-wall from its foundations. With the irregular range of older buildings on the east, the 'New Quad-rangle,' especially when the creepers, luxuriant as only Oxford creepers are, clothe the walls with their autumn hues, is very pleasing, though a passer-by, glancing in through the College gateway, might hardly suspect the existence of this spacious place, with its spreading lawn and diversified buildings. The sets of Rooms, for Fellows and Under-graduates, with Bursary and Senior Common-room, were finished in 1846, the plans having been finally approved on Nov. 14, 1844. They had been prepared by Mr. Charles Hayward, of Exeter, nephew and pupil of Sir Charles Barry. On Feb. 12, 1845, the tender of Mr. Daniel Evans and Mr. Symm for £5,286 14*s.* was accepted. The funds available were 'the residue of the money left by Dr. Radcliffe for repairing the College,' £1,366 14*s.* borrowed from Dr. Smyth's Trust, £400 offered by the Master, Dr. Jeune, on condition that the Fellows of the Ossulston Foundation should be entitled to rooms rent-free like the other Fellows—this was agreed to 'for ever'; the rest was raised by subscription. The massive carved furniture in the Common Room was given by the tutorial staff.

The energy of Dr. Jeune and the public spirit of the small and poorly-endowed College over which he presided are shown by the resolution come to in October, 1846, to take in hand the erection of

---

[1] What the exterior of the Old Quadrangle facing west had looked like before it was remodelled may be seen from Storer's drawing in Chalmers. In 1843 it had been proposed to build new chambers for the reception of the new Fellows and Scholars on Mr. Francis Wightwick's foundation, his bequest being allowed to accumulate for the purpose.

a new Hall and offices and the renovation of the east end of the ' New Court ' and the west side of the Master's House, the plans being prepared by Mr. Hayward. The Hall was contracted for in March, 1847, by Mr. Matthew Awdrey, of London, for about £5,000[1]. Towards this outlay it was determined to use £3,000 belonging to the Phipps legacy as well as all other moneys in the funds over which the College had control, £3,000, however, being retained in the funds to accumulate at compound interest as a sinking fund for the replacement of the moneys sold out and of the caution money in the hands of the College, which also was used. Simultaneously with this expenditure £1,000 was advanced to the Master, then about to enter on the duties of Vice-Chancellor[2], for the enlargement and improvement of the Master's House, to be repaid by the Master for the time being in thirty annual instalments of £54 5s. 9d. each, the interest being calculated at 3½ *per centum*. By April, 1858, however, it appeared that £1,473 3s. 11d. had been expended, of which the College advanced another £300, £173 3s. 11d. being reckoned for new fixtures and tenants' repairs. The 'increase and restoration' of the Lodgings had been principally the addition of another storey. The plans were drawn by Messrs. Fuljames and Waller.

In this year the advowson of St. Aldate's was sold to the Simeon Trustees for £1,040 6s. 3d. Consols, and it was proposed that the proceeds should become the nucleus of a fund for building a new Chapel. Fortunately another use was found for the money. In 1820 the advowson of Codford St. Peter, Wilts, had been purchased from Mrs. Sophia Kellow for £3000, for the benefit of Wightwick Fellows[3].

A glance at one of Dr. Ingram's pretty woodcuts will show what the back of the Master's House looked like before Dr. Jeune's alterations. The chief change is in the position of the windows. Three of the original gables still remain. The character of the buildings erected on the north side of the New Court is of a plainer Gothic than the earlier work of 1829, the chief adornment being the oriel windows on either side of the Fellows' staircase. The new Hall is a really excellent example of revived mediævalism. The dark hammer-beamed roof, though only the main timbers are of oak, is very striking. It has a prettily designed louvre[4]. There is the usual large oriel on

[1] Mr. Hayward, Dr. Jeune observed, was the only architect in his experience whose estimates were not exceeded by the expenditure.

[2] H. R. H. the Prince of Wales was matriculated here by Dr. Jeune, Oct. 17, 1859.

[3] From money, the Master thinks, given specifically for this purpose, as they did not share in the Phipps benefaction.

[4] ' Before the louvre was begun,' Mr. Orger recalls, 'the space for it was covered with boards. One night, after midnight, the College was aroused by hearing the

the dais, a minstrels' gallery, and a great baronial fireplace. The oak panelling is not remarkable, and the armorial glass in the windows is fortunately fading into gradual disappearance. A strange contempt for Church Latin is shown in more than one incredible barbarism carelessly inscribed on the glass[1]. As in the ancient refectories, there are two doors, at the opposite end to the high table, faced, as you go out, by the buttery hatch. The kitchen and its 'necessary suburbs,' without which (says Fuller) all is marred, were built in 1869 under the direction of Mr. Buckeridge. The kitchen had been the present servants' hall, and before 1847 was in the south-west corner of the Old Quadrangle. The tower of the Hall is used as a muniment room.

The present passage 'between quads' was widened in 1845. Before that a communication went through the present janitor's bedroom into the Master's backyard, to the Back Lodgings. A path led from this corner to the Chapel door. The view of the New Hall and Quadrangle is the subject of the Almanack top of 1858. It shows a doorway, abolished in 1869, on the basement, close to the steps.

In 1879, the ornamental open-work parapet of the Gateway Tower and the twisted chimneys of the College front being greatly decayed, though scarcely half a century old, and damaged by a storm, Messrs. Bodley and Garner designed the present plainer parapet, gurgoyles, and chimneys, and the niche in the face of the tower, containing, for want of something less commonplace, a shield carved with the College arms. The tower was very slightly raised. The gateway armories and the one in the other quadrangle have lately been painted at the charges of the two tutors.

THE WOLSEY ALMSHOUSE.

In 1888 a very important addition was laid to the College by the purchase from Christ Church of the Wolsey Hospital, once, Wood maintains, a seminary dependance of St. Frideswyde's, but after the decay of learning a habitation for the Priory servants and retainers. One James Proctor occupied it at the time of the Dissolution. When 'the great child of honour, Cardinal Wolsey[2],' made the Priory into

well-known voice of J. H. H. M^cS—— singing at its full pitch his (and our) favourite song 'The Port Admiral.' He and another man (I think it was his great friend R. P. B——) had taken advantage of the ladders which the workmen had left, first reaching to the parapet of the Hall and then up the roof to the place of the louvre. They carried a bowl of punch, and placed it on the boards, each sitting astride of the roof opposite each other, while they pledged each other, by turns and sang.'

[1] Such as 'Deaconus,' for Deacon, and for Dean; 'Episc. Amarch.' for the Primate of All Ireland, &c. *Horresco referens.* These things can only be told in a footnote, where they may be unobserved.

[2] Shakespeare, *Henry VIII*, Act iv. Scene 2.

a College, he 'turned also these tenements into an Hospitall (" πτωχοδοχεῖον insigne ") to receive and have releife from it. But his designes failing before compassed, and falling into the King's hands, this with his college was left imperfect both in its buildings (as it now remaineth) and its revenews. But afterwards King Henry VIII, taking upon him to perfect the college in some sort in its endowment setled here also the number of 24 almesmen and each to have 6£ per annum; which continueth soe to this day[1].' So Dr. Ingram speaks of the Almshouse as remaining till 1834 'in an unfinished state,' 'having the appearance of ruins.' In his pictures, however, and in Skelton's (1819), the south portion is actually ruinous, not merely incomplete, and it was so, no doubt, in Wood's time also. Skelton considered the building to have the appearance of having been erected ' in the early part of the fifteenth century.' Possibly Wolsey found a tumbledown edifice (James Proctor cannot have needed the entire accommodation), and merely re-constructed the northern part of it. On the back of a deed belonging to Magdalen the almshouse is spoken of as ' de novo constructa[2].' In the archives of St. Aldate's Church, in the twenty-sixth of Henry VIII, mention is made of ' a quit rent going out of a tenement or garden ground next ye South gate taken downe by ye sd Cardinall, 6d.' ' Brewer's tenement ' on the New College ground (the east part of the College Old Quadrangle) was pulled down before the twentieth year of Henry[3]. The fine open timber roof in the interior of the Almshouse is said to have been brought by Wolsey from Oseney Abbey[4]. Skelton says: ' It is manifest from the present appearance of the ruins that these buildings once occupied a much larger space than is now covered by them; but the exact extent it would be perhaps difficult to determine.' This I fail to understand, as the limits are clearly defined.

Wood is mistaken in saying that Henry VIII settled here his almsmen. In consequence of the King's death no lodging was built or provided for them. Indeed, though the building called, from the use to which Wolsey put it, ' le Almshouse ' has at various times been

[1] Wood, *City*, i. 193.

[2] The deed relates to a tenement ' close to the churchyard, viz. in the corner as one goes from the church to the hall called le Bollehall,' and is endorsed ' Copia evidentiae pro domo Collegii [Magd.] prope Broadgates nunc infra domum eleemosynariam de novo constructam.' Wood MS. D. 2, fol. 165; see pp. 56, 57. Wood adds, 'Xt Ch. Almshouse q. whether this Bollehall did not stand where Ch. Ch. Almshouse did stand.' But he writes in the margin, ' procul dubio haec dorsura est falsa.'   [3] Wood MS. D. 2, foll. 67, 284.

[4] The joiner's account for taking down the Oseney roofs is given by Wood, *City*, ii. 227.

appropriated to this purpose, no lodging has ever been provided for eight out of the four-and-twenty. And for a considerable period the place, or parcel of it, was tenanted as a yard for the store and sale of timber. ' The said Dean and prebendarys must forether Covenante to find there '—i.e. ' in the said cathedrall chorche,' not necessarily in the Almshouse—' for ever twenty-four pore Mene suche as shal be from tyme to tyme be appointed by the King's Majestie his heires and successores or such as he or they shall assigne for the same purpos, givinge yearlie unto every of them £6 0 0.' The bedesmen, subject to the royal approval, have from the first been nominated by the Dean, and have usually been old soldiers or sometimes sailors. The deed of dotation is dated Dec. 11, 1546. In the statute ' de ecclesiâ frequentandâ' it is provided that ' the whole number of students, servants, and almsmen shall be present at the sermons on Sundays and Holidays.' All are to receive the Holy Sacrament, and ' before they shall resort thereto the Almsmen, Scholars and Servants shall repair to the Catechism to be instructed.' The Eleemosynarii are to frequent the church and pray for the King. Also ' that they be no Railers or Wailers of any, especially their superiors. That they live peaceably, quietly, and cleanly in their chambers.'

In Mr. G. V. Cox's *Recollections* (1868), the writer says that ' forty or fifty years ago' Christ Church resolved to pull the Almshouse down, and gave the few remaining occupants notice to quit. But one, a fine old Scotsman named Carrick, refused to go, reminding the Chapter that he held his place by the same tenure and from the same source as themselves. The Chapter gave way, and the Wolsey Hospital was preserved. Mr. Cox observes that Pembroke College, until it was new fronted, was not very distinguishable from it.

A very favourite project at the time Mr. Cox speaks of, with a view to improve the appearance both of Oxford and of Pembroke, was the removal of the old Hospital. The *Crypt or Receptacle for Things Past*, vol. i. part 2, p. 204 (1829), says: ' Another grand improvement we are happy to learn is again talked of, the demolition of a few ruinous almshouses between Christ-church and Pembroke, by which the latter College may be new fronted, and the intermediate space laid down in grass. The fine façade of Christ-church could then be seen to some advantage, while at present it is nearly lost; and as these almshouses are the property of the crown and of no value to any one, we are not without hopes that this will be effected [1].'

[1] Dr. Tatham's *Oxonia Explicata et Ornata* (1773) had suggested the demolition of the houses in the churchyard and the widening of the lane in front of Pembroke, in order to give a better view of Christ Church.

On Feb. 16, 1832, it was resolved by the Pembroke Society to write as follows to Christ Church :—

'Should the consent of the Crown be obtained for the removal of the Alms Houses and the rebuilding them elsewhere (not at the expence of Pembroke College), the Master and Fellows would engage to furnish a plot of ground in the parish of Cowley for that purpose. The Alms-houses being removed, the College proposes to take down and rebuild, on their own ground, the Eastern end of their College in a style corresponding with the work on the North side lately completed. The area in front (having no wish to build thereon, and desirous that no one else might be permitted to build) they would enclose with a wall and iron railing, and plant the interior with shrubs.

'On the subject of the houses between the Alms Houses and Penny-farthing Street they have nothing to offer, desirable as it is that they should also be removed ; but they consider that this object is in progress.'

This plan would have given the College for the first time a frontage to a principal street. Until 1844 no carriage could drive up to the College from that side.

In 1834, 'with a view to the great improvements projected in this part of the city,' the Dean and Chapter of Christ Church—the nego-tiation with Pembroke having fallen through—restored the Almshouse from the very creditable designs of Mr. Underwood, who refaced much of the structure, added the battlements and the large gables, and put the building back on the north so as no longer to project in front of the College. The walk before the College was relaid, and railings took the place of the churchyard wall. The cost of widening the street [1] 'to lay open the new front of Pembroke College,' and of buying the fee simple of the four houses standing against the east end of the church, was £2,500, raised by subscription, the University giving £200, the Commissioners under the Oxford Mileways Acts £600, Sir Robert Inglis £100, T. B. Estcourt, Esq., £100, Davies Gilbert, Esq., President of the Royal Society, £100, and Lord Grenville, the Chancellor, Visitor of the College, £50.

In 1868 the Dean and Chapter petitioned Chancery for a re-constitution of King Henry VIII's trust. The old building, they said, required constant repairing. The accommodation being limited, there was only room for single men. As at that time the number of almsmen had fallen from twenty-four to nine it might be supposed that in so large a building, covering 1,266 superficial yards, there

---

[1] Wood says, after speaking of the church (*City*, i. 194): 'Hamel here and then the hall. Hamel hath been bigger before the Hospitall was partly built upon it.' Which, however, Mr. Clark refers to the strip of land between the Almshouse and the College, running north and south.

would be no lack of accommodation. However, it was thought that the veterans would be more happy and contented among their own friends, and it was proposed to send them to their homes, their yearly shot being increased from £6 to £16. By which doubtless necessary reform one more picturesque element was subtracted from our drab urban civilization [1].

The Wolsey Hospital next became the residence of the Treasurer of Christ Church, the Rev. R. Godfrey Faussett, and in 1877 it underwent some slight external and considerable internal modification.

Although the idea of making an eastern front to Pembroke College had been given up, the hope that a building so important and so of a piece with the College would some day become part and parcel of it was still entertained. In 1857, as already mentioned (p. 305), the Reverend Christopher Cleoburey left a large sum to the College with this object. After several fruitless communications at intervals had passed between the two bodies, Christ Church finally, in 1888, offered to sell the freehold. And thus 'Segrym's Mansions' at last were added to our House. The purchase, though prudent in view of the dignity and possibly the amenity of the College, was somewhat heroic. Should the Society ever require to extend its borders, there will be no necessity to build; but at present it cannot itself use this handsome and roomy building. It is now employed for a private residence [2], and has even been thought of for an episcopal palace.

In Turner's water-colour of Tom Tower in the National Gallery (No. 805) the Almshouse, as it was before 1834, is seen projecting in the foreground of the picture. Mackenzie's print (1835) shows it as altered. There are views of the Almshouse in Ingram and (exterior and interior) in Skelton (1819).

THE BACK LODGINGS.

Until 1844 there were standing on the south side of Beef Lane, where the New Buildings are now, two old detached gabled buildings, commonly called the Back Lodgings. Three cuts in Ingram show the back and front of them, under the name of 'Ancient Halls.' I have also before me some coloured sketches made by an artistic undergraduate before and during

---

[1] It was about this time (in 1869) that the pensioners in Greenwich Hospital were allowed to take money in lieu of their board and lodging, and go where they liked.

[2] The late Prof. G. J. Romanes came to reside there in 1890, and there his death took place a few years later.

their demolition. These chambers are delineated, in whole or in part, in the bold line engravings of Vertue (1744), Williams (1733), Burghers (1700) and Loggan (1675). The less lofty and more western of the two was a double building, shaped like the letter L, the two parts having no connexion and being entered by separate doors. In Vertue's drawing, however, which alone gives the whole College, there is no hint of any edifice at right angles to Beef Hall Lane, and in Ingram the projection of this part is not well marked. The more eastern set of chambers was modernized on the south side, apparently about a century ago. In the unpublished collection of drawings made by J. C. Nattes in 1804, now in the Bodleian, there is a very striking and picturesque sketch of these tenements from the side of the lane. The windows have stone mullions, labels, and the upper ones transoms. Those on the ground floor have heavy wooden 'shuts.'

The Rev. HENRY ROBINSON WADMORE, who has kindly sent me his water-colour drawings referred to above, writes about the character of these buildings :—

'They were late Tudor—almost Jacobean ... My rooms were in the westernmost part. The buildings were very dilapidated, and the ground floor and top floor were not used. When my old rooms were being pulled down and the paper hung on canvas removed, the wall was seen to be frescoed with panels marked out with lake and the centre green—a rough imitation of marble. On removing the fire-place the original stone fire-place was found, very broad and certainly Tudor. It must have been used for wood burning.' Several correspondents who had rooms in this building write that the ceilings were very low, and that on entering you went down a step—a sign of the outside ground having risen. The present Master tells me that these Back Lodgings had every appearance of very considerable antiquity. They have not the Elizabethan look of the front of the Master's House, as seen in Loggan, with its wooden casements and projecting upper storey. That was rebuilt in 1596. The rooms in the easternmost building were considered the best in College [1].

Are the Back Lodgings to be identified then with the mediæval halls for students of which an account has been given above (pp. 40–49)? These were Mine or Minote Hall on the ground belonging to St. John's Hospital (Magdalen), just west of the present Master's House ; the double hall of St. Michael and St. James on the All Souls land next it ; Beef Hall on ground belonging to the University ; Wylde's Entry on Magdalen land at the end of Beef Hall Lane ; and south of that Wolstan or Dunstan Hall, belonging to the University. The last three were in St. Ebbe's parish, the others in St. Aldate's. The parish boundary, by the last Ordnance Survey, is a line drawn from the west end of the Chapel to the Common-room servants' room. Some crosses, however, to be seen in Brewers Street, let into the wall, are about fifteen feet west of the end of the Chapel [2].

[1] One who lived in the western building within a decade of Waterloo writes : 'My room had a large square window with iron bars, very convenient for introducing late Suppers from Inns and cookshops.' He speaks of roast hare, flanked by bowls of ' bishop ' and ' archbishop.'

[2] Sir J. Peshall mentions a ' cross within Pembroke College ' as the bound.

The identifications are very puzzling. But it seems certain that a part of the buildings shown by Loggan in 1675 and pulled down in 1844 was Beef Hall. In the Tanner MSS. 338, fol. 59, under a 'Viewe of the howsing and lands of y⁰ Universitie of Oxon lying within the limite of Oxford taken and made in March Anno Dni 1636',' is entered : ' St. Ebbe's parish—Beofe hall and the two gardens belonging to it. The tenement is upon repairing and likely to be done verie well.' Two years earlier, next the All Souls land was ' a hall belonging to y⁰ universitie' (Wood, MS. D. 2). Thenceforward the name is of common occurrence in leases and accounts till 1863, as ' all that house or tenement commonly called Beef Hall.'

As regards Minote, we know that after 1575 it was rented for students' chambers by principal Summaster¹, and was known as Summaster's Lodgings, a name which, Wood tells us, it bore a hundred years later : ' now Summaster's Lodgings.' This is borne out by the College accounts. — In 1657, ' slatting Somersett building 2l 6s. 10d.'; 1654, 'Sir Spurway's chamber in Somerset's buildings'; and so in 1651. This then must have been the more eastern of the two blocks of rooms destroyed in 1844. Beef Hall we have seen was, in 1636, old enough to need thorough reparation. It may be assumed that the other building, if it needed re-slating in 1657, was older than the foundation of the College, which, however straitened in means, was not likely to erect anything so homely and unacademic as these Back Lodgings. Between the two buildings Burghers shows a walled-up door upon the street. This is a clear indication of a pre-collegiate date.

The only drawing extant of the buildings in Broadgates times is the map of Ralph Agas—practically reproduced by Speed (1605) and Hollar (1643)—referred to above on page 37. There was doubtless much reconstruction in Elizabeth's reign.

Asking what traditions existed early in this century as to the identity of these two blocks, which were connected by a wall some fifteen or eighteen feet long, we find Dr. Ingram, in 1837, writing: 'Adjoining to [the Master's] Lodgings westward was formerly a tenement belonging to Magdalen college, called Mine, Mignot or Minote hall, and afterwards Summaster's Lodgings ... Another tenement ... was divided into Durham or St. Michael's hall and St. James's hall, situated between Minote hall on the east and Beef hall on the west. These buildings still remain as we pass into the fellows' garden, and are partly inhabited by students.' It is not quite clear which buildings Dr. Ingram means as still remaining ; but at any rate his words include the hall of St. Michael and St. James. Storer's *Oxford Visitor* (1822) has a cut of the eastern building, and

The St. Ebbe's procession went ' over the Wall into the Master of *Pembroke's* Garden close to the Chapel ; from thence through Mr. *Shirley's*, a Tanner, in Beef Lane.'

¹ But a paper in the College muniments quotes a lease in the Magdalen Ledger, F. 264, of a garden-ground in St. Aldate's parish, demised to William Broade, anno Eliz. 18 (1576), for twenty years, and charged later upon Pembroke. The Magdalen bailiffs and bursars, however, seem to have been confused about their two properties along Beef Hall Lane.

identifies the other with St. Michael's Hall. Skelton (1818) calls them
Summaster's, formerly Minote, and Beef. In Wade's *Walks in Oxford*
(1816), we read, ' Part of one of these [detached edifices] which is on our
right hand as we go into the Fellows' garden was formerly called Durham
Hall, east of which was Mignott or Mine Hall, now as well as the
former occupied as chambers.' The entrance to the Fellows' garden was
opposite the door of the eastern part of the double building. In Fletcher's
copy of Gutch's *Wood* (1810), the name 'Beef Hall' is placed under
a sketch of the *easternmost* building, which shows how confused the
traditions were. In this sketch a bracket under the roof is clearly of
Charles l's time, or perhaps of 1657, when Summaster's was 'slatted.'

To turn back to the statements of Wood, who was an observant boy
in Oxford during the Great Rebellion. He says: ' On the ground of
St. Michael's . . . is now the comeners house of easement for this college.'
(This the old engravings show on the space connecting the two buildings.)
' On the other ' (i.e. seemingly, on the ground of St. James) ' chambers
for the students thereof.' I take it, however, that, west of 'Summaster's,'
Wood's identifications are partly guesses, for even the situation of Beef
Hall was not certain. ' Beef Hall seems to be the house where Collyer
now lives in Beef hall lane, so it is where the white porch is ' (MS. D. 2,
fol. 224).

Turning to leases : In 1634 the Warden and Fellows of the College of
the souls of all faithful people deceased let to Pembroke College their
tenement and garden with the appurtenances thereof, ' the which sometymes was two messuages scituate and beeinge in the parish of St Aldate
in Oxon aforesayd betweene the ground whereon in times past hath been
an Hall belongeinge to the Hospitall of St John's without the east gate on
the east parte and a Hall belongeinge to the Universitie of Oxon on the
west parte, which also is extended from the common streete to the towne
wall, for a terme of forty years.' This need not mean that Minote was
no longer standing, but only that it was not in 1634 an independent hall ;
but if so, one would gather that Beef *was* existing as an academic hostel.
It was, however, just before this date ' not inhabited by anie scholars.'
The two messuages on the All Souls land had become one tenement. In
1629 it is described as ' a tenement in ancient times divided into two,' in
1622 as ' a garden of All Souls,' in 1612 as ' a parcel of ground sometimes
[i.e. formerly] called Michaell Hall.' As late as 1845 it is ' the parcel of
ground commonly called Michael Hall ' lying on the east of ' that house
or tenement commonly called Beef Hall.' In a lease of 1637, however,
the Magdalen land (Wylde's Entry), University land, and All Souls land
appear to be united under the general name ' Beef Hall,' and from 1655
a series of leases speak of a building on this ground consisting of ' two low
rooms, two chambers, and two cocklofts.' The 1637 lease does not
mention this, but in it the College reserves and lets separately ' a cockloft and two chambers, one upper and one lower,' for the reception of
scholars.

Summaster's or Minote—in the Latin edition of Wood (1678) as in the
English (1665) described as lying ' on the west side of Cambey's Lodgings '—
must be the easternmost detached building of the Back Lodgings. The

little piece of ground separating this from the other block of rooms cannot have sufficed for the double hall rented from All Souls, but was probably, as Wood states, the site of St. Michael's. The eastern portion of the double building to the west may then have represented the other part of the All Souls property. This leaves the tenement at right angles to it to represent Beef Hall, unless, conceivably, a building still further west and used as stabling for the Master, were Beef Hall, or the remains of it. It seems impossible to regard the double building as the double hall of SS. Michael and James, because of the parish boundary. I do not feel sure that that double building was not entirely in St. Ebbe's parish. In that case it was Beef Hall; but then the two saints will have no more accommodation than the two Judges of Assize in the Vice-Chancellor's chair in St. Mary's! The objection to regarding the transverse part as Beef is that the latter has then no front to the lane named from it and is reduced to a cockloft and an upper and a lower chamber. Wylde's Entry was in Wood's time 'a void piece of ground,' 'a garden ground.'

Beef Hall.—In 1626, two years after the foundation of Pembroke, this was a private house. But on Apr. 1, 5° Caroli I (1629), the College, with a view to future needs, acquired the lease for £120 (*vide supra*, p. 214). In 1637, under the name of 'Beef Hall,' the College let everything west of the Magdalen land (Minote) for 20*s.* rent and £20 fine, to John Peacock of Chorley in the parish of Cumnor, except the Master's stable, and a cockloft and upper and lower chamber, let for 1*d.* to Mr. John Darby, M.A., for the reception of scholars of Pembroke. These rooms Mr. Darby assigned, in 1639, to William Turner the College coquus. In 1655 the premises formerly rented by Darby and Peacock are found tenanted by George Pryce, the College butler, and, in consideration of the surrender to the College of the lease made in Peacock's favour, were let to Pryce for 20*s.*[1] The premises are described as 'all situate lying and being in the parishes of St. Ebbe's and St. Aldate's alias St. Tolls or one of them.' There stood on them a tenement consisting of two low rooms, two chambers, and two cocklofts, and they comprised also one little parcel of ground, 39 feet long and 12 broad, 'whereupon certain chambers were heretofore built which were consumed lately by ffire[2], on the west of the said tenement'; a garden ground 50 feet long and 40 broad (adjoining a parcel of ground on which stables were heretofore standing), 'now walled in'; and a parcel of ground on the south of the said

---

[1] Pryce paid 3*s.* hearth-money in 1665. The College paid 53*s.*—as much as 'Winchester' (New) College. (*Oxford City Documents*, ed. Rogers, O. H. S., pp. 79, 81.)

[2] This phrase, 'consumed lately by fire,' is found in all leases down to 1719. It might be surmised that the mediæval halls along Beef Lane were consumed in the great conflagration of 1644. On Sunday afternoon, October 6, there 'happened a dreadful fire in Oxford; such an one for the shortness of time wherein it burned that all ages before could hardly parallel.' Beginning in the north of the city 'it flew over the gardens and backyards to Penny-farthing street, all which, except the east end, it burnt. From thence to Beef Hall Lane, which lane also, except the east end, it consumed. From thence to Slaying Lane.' (*City*, ii. 473.) There are houses, however, in the western part of Pembroke Street which must be older than 1644, and it seems that only the further end of Beef Lane suffered.

tenement and parcel of ground and the said stables 42 feet long and 21 broad. The tenant was to pay 20s. yearly in the great hall of the College. The lease was renewed in 1671 at a rent of £1 6s. 8d., and in 1679 for nineteen years more. In 1696 the premises were let to John Price of the University of Oxon, gent., the lease being renewed in 1707 and 1712, at the same rent. In 1707 they were 'now in the tenure of Roger Hornblower, Jane Underwood, widow, and William Hathaway.' In 1719 they were let to William Culley, brewer, at the same rent, and in 1726, being 'now or late in the tenure of the Master and John Hopkins, their assignes or under-tenants,' they were leased to the said Hopkins for £1 6s. 8d., he being the College butler. He surrendered his twenty-one years' lease for £100 in 1730, at which time some ground on the left hand was in the occupation of Robert Wilkins, carpenter, together with the shop or workhouse adjoining. Of the premises rented by Hopkins, part was tenanted by the Master of the College. From this time probably Beef Hall came to be used by the College entirely for academical purposes. In 1749 the rents for 'Dunster and Beef' amounted to £14, Hopkins paying 10s. The old quit rent of 10s. 10d. for 'Beef Hall' (i.e. Beef seven shillings and a groat, and Dunstan—'the tenements forming the Common Room garden'—3s. 6d.) was raised to £5 5s. when the University renewed the lease in 1845. In the accounts of 1654 the 7s. 4d. is entered as 'a quit-rent for beefe hall to Magdalene colledg. rec'd by Daniell Hogg.' 'Magdalene' must be a mistake.

A remarkable man had his chamber in Beef Hall at the time George Pryce rented it, the great scholar and philologist FRANCIS JUNIUS (1589–1677). François Du Jon, son of the Flemish divine of that name, came to England first in 1620 to prosecute his Anglo-Saxon researches, and paid frequent visits to the libraries of Oxford, which he loved with more than the devotion of a son. Wood records under date October 1676: 'This month Mr Junius came to live in Oxford with his intention to lay his bones here and give his MSS. to the library. He came for the sake of Dr Marshall and took his chamber against Lync. Coll. for a time; and soon after in Mr Price his house in Beef-hall Lane, purposely to disgest some notes for the press . . . Mr Junius tarried here till Aug. 1677 and then went to Windsore with an intent to returne to live in Oxon and die there; but was overtaken with a feaver. He left the University a hundred Saxon, Frank, Gothic and Teutonic MSS. and also his Gothic Saxon and Latin types [1].' The 'obscure house in St. Ebbe's parish' (Chalmers), where he last lived, is identified by the College leases. Junius is buried in St. George's Chapel.

I know not whether Robert Minote who gave his name to Minote Hall was a progenitor of Lawrence Minot (floruit c. 1340), whose *Halidon Hill* and other poems celebrated the martial achievements of Edward III, and whom Dr. Craik describes as the first English versifier who deserves the name of poet.

[1] *Life and Times,* ii. 358.

CHAPTER XXXV.

REFORM.

THE earlier Founders believed that any lad of average parts who was willing to study might be made into a student. They supplied him with bare necessaries and hedged him round with scholastic discipline. There was no reason therefore why their bounty should not be annexed to certain schools, localities, or families. The idea of vocation, or of competition, scarcely entered their minds. 'The local stimulus of rewards confined to special birthplaces,' the present Archbishop of Canterbury said in 1851, 'did much then to encourage learning; but we have now outgrown the need, and only feel the fetter. The change of manners too has deprived us of the check which once restrained idle men from undertaking what was then a laborious life.' The mutation of times was causing the College, even in Dr. Hall's mastership, to chafe at the restrictions of its close foundations. A number of entries in the Minutes prove that the governing body were jealous for the honour of learning. In one year, 1836, two Fellows (Channel Island and Tesdale) and two Abingdon Scholars were rejected as not *sufficientes doctrinâ*, and the College, acting on a decree of Archbishop Laud, filled their places from elsewhere. In the latter case, the College invited Mr. Valpy, of Reading School, to send two of his youths to Abingdon to be elected there if deemed competent by the electors. The Abingdon authorities refused to allow the election to take place till the Visitation, six months later. The College then informed them that the election would be held in the walls of the College, and invited their attendance. They protested and refused to come. The Reading candidates were examined at the College, but rejected for insufficiency. An arrangement with Abingdon was finally brought about by the Duke of Wellington, who received 'the thanks of the Master and Fellows for his Grace's determination of the matter, and for his paternal care of the interests of the

College.' The Duke had dismissed appeals from the rejected Fellows. In 1841 Gloucester candidates were rejected. In 1843 the College refused to re-elect a Bennet Fellow who had been non-resident ever since his election, in that he could not be said to have been 'very useful in the society.' In 1846 an undergraduate Fellow was suspended. In 1849, complaint being made of Scholars from the Crypt School at Gloucester being plucked wholesale, the College prayed the Visitor to sanction the extension of the Townsend Scholarships to any school in that county, or, should no competent candidate appear, that they should be thrown open. 'The four Schools have long been, and are still, in a state of decay, sometimes having no scholars at all. . . . It has been commonly the practice of the electors to nominate young men educated elsewhere.' The Duke sanctioned a by-law to that effect.

After the theological movement, the political events of 1848 had brought about a Liberal reaction. It cannot be said that the un-reformed Oxford of 1830–50 was destitute of striking personalities and powerful intellectual forces acting on the outside world. The 'decay of eccentricity' in reformed Oxford has been a subject of complaint, and eccentricity is but character run wild. We are as though a steam-roller had passed over us. Still the Laudian con-stitution of things was doomed. 'The *sine quâ non* with me,' Mr. Gladstone wrote to Pusey, April 1, 1835, 'would be that the Universities should not be vexed by the interposition of Parliament.' The Duke of Wellington, addressing the Peers, July 9, 1838, said, 'I entreat your Lordships to let them work out these reforms as they think fit.' On April 23, 1850, however, Mr. Heywood, M.P. for North Lancashire, in an aggressive speech of the 'monkish rookeries' type, moved an humble Address for a Commission of 'Inquiry into the state of the Universities of Oxford, Cambridge, and Dublin.' Lord John Russell said he was prepared to advise her Majesty to accede to the prayer as regards Oxford and Cambridge. In September, the Commission being appointed, its composition was keenly resented as entirely of a party character[1]. Dr. JEUNE, Master of Pembroke, was one of the Seven, and undoubtedly their leading spirit. He was

[1] 'Considering the weight and rank of the University as an institution, the weight of its associations, its ancient honours, its lofty names, its largeness, its solidity, its great religious and historical position in the country, it was hardly an act of common respect to select a board which was to sit in critical and judicial attitude upon it exclusively from one school of religious speculation, of recent growth and no considerable numbers.' (*Quarterly Review*, June, 1853.)

indeed absent from not a single meeting. On May 21, 1851, the University petitioned the Crown to revoke the Commission as 'unconstitutional and illegal,' and the large majority of the Colleges refused to furnish the Commissioners with information. Pembroke, naturally, was one of the few that responded. Nowhere was modification of the Statutes more needed. The Vicegerent, the Rev. THOMAS FREDERICK. HENNEY, as well as the Master, was a strong Liberal. Stanley told the Rev. EDWARD REDMAN ORGER, my informant (Fellow of St. Augustine's, Canterbury, 1855, Sub-Warden 1866–80), that he heard Henney say, 'Well, if they come to Pembroke, I shall say, Wal/k in, gentlemen, wal/k in. You cannot by any possibility make things worse than they are[1]!' The Commissioners reported in May, 1852. Nothing need be said here respecting the reform of the University. Their proposals for Pembroke were mainly these:— Fellows not to be obliged to take Holy Orders or to proceed to the superior degrees; the number to be reduced to ten, with a larger income; Fellowships to be thrown open and equalized[2]. The Scholars to remain the same in number, to receive the third of a Fellow's stipend, and all Scholarships to be thrown entirely open, except five, reserved for Roysse's School. The Master to receive a fixed stipend. Oaths to observe the Statutes to be unlawful. The obligation to enforce attendance at chapel twice a day to be relaxed. The intra-mural exercises and lectures, reading the Vulgate at meals, corporal punishment, and other obsolete regulations, to be removed from the Statutes. Fellowships and Scholarships not to be voided by £40 or £10 property. Mrs. Sheppard's provision for a Medicine and a Law Fellow to remain unaltered. The obligation of celibacy to be retained for all Fellows. The Commissioners observe as regards Abingdon :—

'The School does not possess such resources as to render it possible that it should at any time produce a large or continuous supply of persons qualified to do credit to the School or the College. We are of opinion that five out of the sixteen Scholarships should henceforth be offered for competition to the boys educated at that School. The number of boys elected to Scholarships which it has sent during the thirty years which elapsed between 1820 and 1850 has not exceeded twenty-two. An election

[1] 'Quisquis es, armatus qui nostra ad flumina tendis, . . .
Umbrarum hic locus est, Somni Noctisque soporae.'
Virg. *Aen.* vi. 388, 390.
[2] Archbishop Whately remarked on the *federal* constitution of Pembroke, some foundations being inferior to others. It was doubted if the Philipps Fellow had a vote for the election of Master.

once a year will therefore afford more regular encouragement than has yet been afforded to the School, and, as we shall propose that the Scholarships shall be increased in value, the School will be placed in a much better position than it has ever yet occupied.'

On June 3, 1853, the College, consulted by the Earl of Derby, the Visitor, resolved unanimously, ' that, in the opinion of this Meeting, the College has no power under any existing law to repeal or alter any of its Statutes without or with the consent of the Visitor.' It was resolved further that ' It is desirable that numerous alterations should be made in the Statutes of the College.' Impediments to its efficiency were indicated, such as those pointed out by the Commission. It was further resolved that ' It is desirable that all graduates of the University should be eligible to the office of Master of the College ;' that Fellows' stipends should not be more than £250 nor less than £200, and that only eight Fellows could receive £200 at present; that the Scholars, not fewer than sixteen, should receive a quarter of a Fellow's stipend, and chambers ; that the Master should receive a stipend equal to four Fellowships; that a quarter of the net revenues of the College be set aside for a Domus fund ; all Fellowships and Scholarships to be freed from restrictions (with no reservation in favour of Abingdon). It was also resolved ' that it is desirable that the College should receive power from the legislature to carry out the changes herein proposed, under the control of its Visitor,' and ' that the College should be empowered to regulate its internal administration by by-laws, which could be freely made or repealed.'

These resolutions were sent to Lord John Russell and to the Earl of Derby. The former acknowledged them as ' interesting and encouraging.' The latter was glad to find the College concurring with him in the opinion that the interference of Parliament should be permissive only, not effecting alterations by its own authority. He deprecates the sweeping away of trusts solemnly committed to the College by founders, whose bounty it had accepted *accompanied by conditions* which could not honourably be now set aside. The Visitor was however prepared to co-operate in opening Fellowships, 'as far as can be done consistently with the maintenance of good faith.' He notes that nothing is said as to the part the Fellows are to take in future in the tuition of the College : an important question in view of a general re-adjustment of incomes. As to the Scholarships, he cannot concur in severing the connexion between a College and certain Schools; but the requirement of sufficiency should be adhered to. Lord Derby ends : ' I earnestly desire to promote by all legitimate means the advancement of the College with which I have the honour of being more peculiarly connected.'

The Master and Fellows were unwilling to wait for the chances of a measure affecting the whole University. They boldly asked for a *privilegium*. The Earl of Derby had discouraged the idea. Legislation must be of a general character applicable to all the Colleges. On June 15, 1853, Lord John Russell wrote a letter marked ' Private ' to Dr. Jeune, in which he said :—

'With reference to your letter of the 10th inst., I have now to state that I do not think I could bring the question before the Government without further proceedings on the part of the College. I send you in confidence a letter from Mr. Gladstone in the matter. It seems to me also that the business of the session is too much advanced to allow of the introduction of so important a subject. When the College has fully decided on its course, your official communication ought to be directed to Lord Palmerston, as Secretary of State for the Home Department.'

The enclosure, which I have Mr. Gladstone's permission to insert here, was as follows :—

'*Private.*   Downing Street, June 13, 1853.

' My dear Lord John,

'I return the communication from Pembroke College, Oxford, and I think many advantages would attend the passing of a permissive act during the present session.

'The question however is now not a very simple one, and it occurs to me that if Parliament is to grant such an Act to a single College, or on the strength of plans or intentions of reform promulgated by a single college, there ought to be in these plans to make the process a safe and easy one some approach to completeness.

'The disposal of Fellowships by examination subject to considerations of character seems to be an unobjectionable project, but two important questions arise upon it.

'1. Shall election by merit be guarded in any manner by appeal ?

'2. Shall the Fellowships acquired by merit be subject to any other conditions of avoidance than marriage and non-ordination ?

'I do not remember that the principle of appeal from the Master and Fellows has been much discussed. In the present state of things it cannot be said to be urgently required, yet in the long run a self-elected body wants in some form or other a check of this kind. If a mild form of it could be devised it would, I think, be very desirable ; and perhaps the mildest (at least it is the mildest which occurs to me) would be to make the Visitor's consent necessary to a valid election.

'As regards the second point you have adverted to it in the House of Commons, and I confess it seems to me highly requisite if these endowments are to be made effective that Fellowships not connected with residence for the purposes of study or tuition should become void after

G g

a certain number of years. I imagine that if the College were willing to accept this principle, it would facilitate the passing of a permissive bill through Parliament.

'I remain, very sincerely yours,

'The Lord John Russell.' 'W. E. GLADSTONE.

The following was from Mr. Gladstone to Dr. Jeune:—

'My dear Sir, 'Downing Street, June 27th, 1853.

'I was much pleased to find from your letter that my opinions respecting the terminability of Fellowships—of little enough weight as being mine—were supported by your authority. Our Fellowships cannot, I think, be safe until they are wholly purged of the character of being sinecures; and of this they cannot get effectually rid without some such provision as you desire.

'I postponed answering your letter that I might speak to Lord John Russell about an enabling bill; but I fear that from the length to which the session has run and the pressure of other business we can hardly hope for it; for I cannot but hope that your College would have set such an excellent example, and in such a case much depends on the "prærogativa tribus." One College doing the thing well will be of far more use to Oxford than lame and half-hearted attempts from half a dozen.

'I remain, dear Dr. Jeune,

'Most faithfully your's,

'Rev^d. the Master of Pembroke.' 'W. E. GLADSTONE.

Jeune somewhat distrusted Mr. Gladstone's latent toryism. Had he not spoken against the Address for the Commission? 'He is still to my mind "Pusey in a blue coat."'

The movement for University Reform, as was perhaps inevitable, had taken a complexion of political party. Although the Government had postponed the main religious question, partly on the ground that privileges extended to Dissenters and Unitarians must also be extended to Romanists [1], the Commission was suspected by Churchmen as part of a general attack on ecclesiastical institutions, and of an endeavour to secularize education. There was also what Keble called a 'hard priggishness,' a want of reverent sympathy and of historic imagination, in the able men who had set their hands to the work, which was characteristic of the Reform era. People who might have agreed on a temperate and constructive modification of ancient institutions, to suit them to altered times, were made to feel that their

[1] The *Edinburgh Review* (July, 1852) urged patience on the Dissenters on that ground. 'A fatal blow would be dealt to the peace and studies of the University if the Roman Catholics were allowed to break in upon the inmost life of an institution in which almost every building and every endowment would supply unfailing materials for irritation and contest.'

ideals were fundamentally irreconcilable with the ideals of those who talked of national foundations having been converted by a dominant party into haunts of cloistered bigotry[1]. At Pembroke there were only two lay Fellows out of thirteen. Now that the clerisy was no longer the only learned profession, and that the original idea of a College as a home of study and prayer for poor scholars living according to religious rule had become obsolete, little resistance would have been made to the introduction into a College of a much larger lay (not necessarily the same thing as secular) element, security being taken for religious supervision, tuition, and devotion. But when the Commissioners hinted (*Report*, p. 163) that under a reformed system we should have escaped the Tractarian Movement, and that 'it is important that the zeal of the instructors of the ministers of the English Church in its chief seminary should be tempered by the calmer judgment of lay-colleagues,' they were felt to be speaking with the Laodicean voice of Walpole and Hoadley. Again, the Commissioners argued very forcibly that founders' intentions had already been set aside in important particulars. Two-thirds of the Fellows (e. g.) were non-resident. (At Pembroke the non-resident ones paid Archbishop Laud's 3*s.* a week fine.) But the crude statement that 'the services of the Church of England have, in obedience to the law, been substituted everywhere for those of the Roman Catholic Church[2]' was, in the form in which they reiterated it, not likely to conciliate opponents who had been urgently teaching the continuity of the *Ecclesia Anglicana.* The argument, by the by, did not touch Pembroke, a post-Reformation foundation[3]. That founder's kin should not be claimed after a certain lapse of time, that scholarships leading necessarily to fellowships offered, under modern circumstances,

---

[1] The new enthusiasm of reform had to encounter the new reactionary idealizing of the past. The middle classes and the middle ages—things most diverse—came into authority together. There seemed nothing in common between men who regarded the Colleges as 'relics of a mischievous mediævalism, inconsistent with the healthy temper and wider views of modern European life,' and conservatives who declared, 'It is a blessed thing for the country that there should be some one place fenced around with chapels and with cloisters, where some few men may live and die removed from all this giddiness and din, to preserve even the name of truth and the memory of the past' (*Quarterly Review*, 1838). Yet all ideals are reconcilable, and a practical and moderate scheme might have been agreed on.

[2] 'The service *in this Church of England* these many years hath been read in Latin.' *Book of Common Prayer.*

[3] As early as 1709 the Whigs proposed the repeal of statutes obliging Fellows to Holy Orders 'upon the Supposition of their being established in the times of ignorance and Superstition.' In 1782 this idea was revived. Fellows were to be allowed to marry; their incomes to be reduced. The surplus was to go to pay off the National Debt.

a premium to idleness, that the close confinement of foundations to certain schools or counties was disadvantageous to a College and liable now (when a man born in Yorkshire is not necessarily a Yorkshireman) to all kinds of abuses, were contentions that needed little proof. Still there was a human interest, a family bond, in such connexions. The localities, too, more or less neutralized each other.

The Colleges did not move. The *Edinburgh Review* of January, 1854, said:—

'The Government has announced that it will only wait a short time to see whether the Universities are themselves disposed to introduce the required changes. . . . The attempts made to open any fellowships have as yet been very faint. Pembroke College in Oxford, indeed, of which one of the Commissioners is Master, and which is most miserably depressed by close fellowships, has tried to move. But if Pembroke has Dr. Jeune for its Master, it has Lord Derby for its Visitor; and there seems little doubt, from what he is reported to have announced, that Lord Derby will use his influence against the movement for opening the fellowships.'

Six months later the College petitioned the House of Commons :—

'The humble Petition of the Master, Fellows, and Scholars of Pembroke College, in the University of Oxford, Sheweth—

'That Pembroke College was founded in the year 1624 by King James the First at the costs and charges of Thomas Tesdale and Richard Wightwick for the study of Theology, Civil and Canon Law, Medicine, Languages and other good arts.

'That the Statutes passed for the Government of the College by Commissioners appointed by the Crown limited the choice of the Fellows and Scholars of the College on the original foundations partly to persons of the kindred of Thomas Tesdale, with a preference to those educated in Abingdon School, and to persons of the name or kindred of Richard Wightwick, wherever educated ; and partly to youths educated in Abingdon School, without reference to their parentage.

'That experience has shewn that neither from particular localities or families, nor from schools with small endowments situated in poor places, and not possessing the means of local extension, can be expected a supply of Scholars likely to do credit to the College or to advance the main objects for which Colleges were founded.

'That on Fellows of Colleges devolve chiefly in our time the education of the students of the University, and that to the efficiency of Collegiate instruction a fair proportion of students of talent and attainments is as indispensable as a succession of Fellows of superior merit ; but that such students can scarcely be secured without open Scholarships of adequate value.

'That the Statutes specially require, and the Country expects, that young men not on the foundation shall be educated in Pembroke College ;

that the number of such students has greatly increased there of late years; that they amount at present to an average of twenty; and that the College has recently erected, at great cost, a new Hall and apartments for such students.

' That two engrafted foundations very scantily endowed, but comparatively open, principally enable the College to discharge its educational functions.

' That if richer Colleges, where the restrictions on the election to Fellowships and Scholarships are.only local, shall be enabled, by the wisdom of Parliament, to open their foundations, and to attract to themselves the ablest men as Fellows and Scholars, it is only just that a poor College from which the same educational duties are required shall be relieved of all its shackles, for otherwise every improvement in other Societies will place it in a situation positively and relatively worse, till at last it must lose public confidence and see itself deserted.

' That such must inevitably be the case with Pembroke College if, other Colleges being set at liberty, it is to continue limited in its choice of Fellows and Scholars to the few boys educated in an obscure school, to the kindred of Founders, and to confined localities ; if it is not permitted to avail itself of the talents and energies of all the Fellows by extending to them all equal privileges and emoluments ; if it cannot by reducing the number of its Fellowships render them sufficiently valuable to attract to itself a fair share of superior men ; and if it is precluded from making provision for the election of its Fellows and Scholars according to personal merit and fitness.

' That it cannot reasonably be hoped that any of these beneficial objects can be attained in case the improvements which may be desired by the College shall be liable to the veto of two-thirds of a body external to the College, and looking naturally to the advantage of individuals and the small school in its patronage rather than to the interests of the College or the great University of which the College forms a part, or the promotion of religion, learning, and science generally, the great ends for which Colleges and Universities are founded and endowed.

' That no improvements deserving of consideration can be effected in Pembroke College without touching in a greater or less degree those of its foundations which are connected with Abingdon School.

' Your petitioners therefore earnestly intreat your Honourable House not to place them under the controul of a small municipal corporation, but to release them from all such foreign intervention in the election of Fellows and Scholars as they are now subject to, and to enable them generally, by the removal of restrictions, to discharge their high duties with efficiency and honour.

' And your petitioners will ever pray. Done in Pembroke College the 21st day of June, 1854, in witness whereof we have hereunto affixed our common seal.

L. S.

'FRANCIS JEUNE, D.C.L.,
Master.'

On Aug. 7, 1854, new Commissioners, of whom Dr. Jeune was not one, were appointed to frame *Ordinances* for the Colleges.

The Master and Fellows thereupon drew up a new Code of Statutes in Latin, and on Nov. 22, at a Convention specially called, it 'was ordained, decreed, ruled and resolved' (under 17 & 18 Victoriae, c. 81), that these be the Statutes of Pembroke College, subject to the sanction of the Commissioners. The chief points dealt with are :—

(1) Times and hours of Divine Service.

(2) No one to defend any error 'bonis moribus aut Christianae veritati repugnantem.'

(3) The Master to be in Holy Orders so long as the canonry shall be annexed to his office.

(4) A 'sponsio sollennis' to be substituted for all oaths.

(5) The Master's Salary to be commuted. (In 1863 it was fixed at four Fellowships, free of all charges.)

(6) Fellowships to be open. Fellows to be 'coelibes, bonae famae, doctrina et ingenio spectabiles, Ecclesiae Anglicanae fidem amplectentes.'

(7) The number of Fellows, viz. twenty, or more.

(8) Fellows not obliged to proceed to B.D.

(9) A benefice of £300 or income of £500 to vacate.

(10) 'Si quis Sociorum Ecclesiae Anglicanae renunciaverit, officio suo seu loco in Collegio statim cedat.'

(11) Fellows to be chosen for excellence not only in Latin and Greek or Moral Philosophy, but in Mathematics, Physical Science, and other good arts.

(12) Fellows to receive £200 yearly.

(13) Scholars, their number and endowments, viz. £50 and rooms.

(14) Founder's kin abolished. Six Tesdale and two Wightwick Scholarships to be reserved for Abingdon School, three Rous Exhibitions for Eton and two Holfords for Charterhouse; otherwise all to be open.

(15) The status of unincorporated 'Exhibitionarii' and Scholars. Bible Clerks to rank as Scholars, and to be nominated by the Master for four years.

(16) Of the *Famuli*.

(17) The prescribed exercises and disciplinary rules to be altered.

(18) Duties and powers of the Vicegerent.

These Statutes the Commissioners were disposed to accept, but thought they went too far in some respects. Communications passed between them and the College for nearly a year.

Memorandum by Dr. Jeune, Oct. 12, 1859 :—'At the end of September the Oxford Commissioners informed the Master that they had altered their views respecting the distribution of the funds of the King Charles Foundation and requested him to call a Meeting of the College to consider the question afresh. The Master did so, but, as might have been expected, failed to collect a sufficient number of Fellows. In consequence, on the day preceding the beginning of Michaelmas term, the Commissioners, three in number, at the London Inn at Exeter, at half an hour before midnight, refused to affix their seal to the Statutes of which they had approved and which had been altered in some important points against the sense of the College in order to satisfy the Commissioners. The College has thus lost the credit of effecting its own reforms [1].

'FRANCIS JEUNE, D.C.L., Master.'

The Commissioners next drafted an Ordinance in English. The following is taken from the College Minutes :—

Convention holden Nov. 5, 1856.

A 'Revised draft of an Ordinance for Pembroke College' transmitted to the Master by direction of the Oxford University Commissioners having been taken into consideration, It was resolved unanimously,

1. That this Convention, while it is not prepared to reject the ordinance as a whole, entertains strong objections to several of its provisions, and thinks it necessary, in order to justify the present authorities of the College in the eyes of their successors, to record some of its views on the subject generally ; that is to say,

2. That this Convention regards the restrictions imposed on elections to the foundation of King Charles the First as injurious to the College as a place of learning and education, and as unjust to other localities which are to share their privileges with the Channel Islands without reciprocity.

3. That this Convention regrets that the principles which have been applied to Scholarships and Exhibitions generally, viz. tenure during five years and fixity of emolument, have not been applied to the Exhibitions of Mr. Townsend.

4. That this Convention disapproves of the provision by which compulsory residence is imposed on Fellows, because it appears wrong to lay down as the rule what is intended to be the exception, because the rule may be vexatiously enforced, because the proper way to secure the services of fellows is to offer an adequate remuneration, because

---

[1] Dr. Fowler (*History of Corpus Christi College*, O. H. S., p. 324) says that all the Colleges except Exeter, Lincoln, and Corpus left it to the Commissioners to draw up Ordinances for them.

compulsory services are not likely to be valuable, and because compulsory residence without employment may lead to evil.

5. That this Convention regrets that the Commissioners should have substituted for the complete and harmonious code drawn up by the College and long approved by the Commissioners an ordinance which, being in a language different from that of the Statutes of the College, amending only by implication, and leaving much untouched, cannot, or cannot without great difficulty, be fused with the Statutes into one uniform and consistent whole.

6. That this Convention doubts the legality of the provision which goes to deprive the College of the profits of King Charles' foundation pending a vacancy.

7. That this Convention regrets that the College should have been deprived of the honour of effecting its own reforms.

An Act of this year, 1856, gave power to sever from any Headship any benefice with cure of souls. This would not include a canonry.

The final Ordinances of the Commissioners for the government of Pembroke College are dated Feb. 19, 1857. The chief points were these :—

The Mastership: no preference to present or former Fellows or to members of Balliol or University Colleges. The incapacity of the Master provided for. Stipend commuted.

King Charles Fellowship converted into Scholarships, the Channel Island connexion being retained.

All other Fellowship foundations, and Scholarships founded by Tesdale, Richard Wightwick, Sir J. Bennet, and Sir J. Philipps, to be consolidated.

Fellowships to be ten in number and equalized, and freed from restrictions. Candidates, except Professors, Principals, and persons of eminence, to be examined. Amount of property to vacate a Fellowship raised. Fellows not obliged to Holy Orders; but if there be eight Fellows, four to be in Orders; if from nine to eleven, five; if from twelve to fifteen, six.

Professors and Principals, if Fellows, to be allowed to marry, if permitted by a two-thirds vote.

Scholarships to be of not less than £50 value (inclusive of all allowances) and rooms; except those of King Charles and Bishop Morley.

Honorary Fellows may be elected.

The Master to have a double vote and casting vote.

Of the incorporated Scholars, five at least to be from Abingdon

School, but with no preference to Founders' kin or otherwise. The others to be elected without any restriction, after examination, and maintained out of the Common Fund. A separate Ordinance was made, May 28, 1857, respecting the Townsend Scholars, who were still to be elected from the Schools named by the Founder. The changes made in respect of the other foundations have been mentioned in the chapter on Benefactors (XXII).

The Master and Fellows to make a declaration of fidelity and obedience to the Statutes instead of an oath. Scholars to be admonished by the Master to obey the Statutes.

New powers given to make regulations for the daily performance of Divine Service. Repeal of scholastic, disciplinary, and sumptuary rules.

The Visitor; lawful to visit at least every ten years. Appeals to him. Statement of revenues, &c., to be laid before him every tenth year.

These ordinances did not altogether put an end to disagreements between the College and some of the favoured schools, and as late as 1877 the Marquess of Salisbury, as Visitor, was appealed to to settle a controversy of this kind.

In the session of 1877, Mr. Goschen having moved to sever the canonry of Rochester from the Provostship of Oriel, Mr. W. K. Wait, M.P. for Gloucester, wrote to Dr. Evans, the Master, offering to move a similar clause for Pembroke. The College declined on account of its inability ' out of its extremely limited revenues to make adequate compensation to the Master.'

This occurred during the discussion of what turned out to be a sweeping measure of reform. The College had the year previously addressed the Marquess of Salisbury, their Visitor, upon the new Universities bill. Among other suggestions they wished the Commissioners to be empowered to provide retiring pensions; that preferential rights in elections should be commuted instead of abolished; and deprecated power being given to the University to legislate for the Colleges. On Nov. 5, 1874, the Master had replied to the questions submitted to the College through the Vice-Chancellor that no part of its revenues was available for University purposes.

In December, 1878, the draft of New Statutes, in English, was considered by the College. They were finally approved by the Queen in Council, May 3, 1882. A few principal points will be here noted. They provide for the appointment of a Vice-Master in case of the Master's incapacity. Fellowships are to be of two classes,

Tutorial and Ordinary, the latter tenable for six years following a year of probation, the former for successive periods of ten years. In 1851 the Pembroke tutors had urged that Fellowships should be terminable. The College may elect to an Ordinary Fellowship, without public notice or examination, any professor or person of noted attainments who shall undertake, if required, to perform some definite literary, scientific or educational work in the College or the University, or under the direction of either. If there be no Fellow in Holy Orders of the Church of England residing and giving religious instruction, the Master and Fellows must, at the next vacancy, elect one; and they may, if they think fit, at any time elect to an Ordinary or Tutorial Fellowship a person in Holy Orders or willing to be admitted to Holy Orders, who appears to them eminently qualified to give religious instruction; but there may not be more than two Fellows at a time who have been elected under this clause. Tutorial Fellows must be unmarried, and not be more than five in number. Examination for Fellowships shall be such as to render them accessible from time to time to excellence in every branch of knowledge for the time being recognized in the Schools of the University. But the Sheppard foundation remains unaltered. The College may elect any distinguished person to an Honorary Fellowship. As regards Scholarships, four of at least £75 yearly value, are reserved for persons educated for two years past at Abingdon School, to be nominated by the Master and the Master and two Senior Governors of Christ's Hospital at Abingdon, and elected after examination by the Master and Fellows, if in their judgement of sufficient merit. The connexion with the Channel Islands, with Eton, with Charterhouse, and with the Gloucestershire Schools, is retained, the College always having power, if no 'sufficient' candidate appear, to throw open the Scholarship *pro hâc vice.* Founder's kin is wholly abolished[1]. Four 'Foundation Scholarships' and two 'Boulter and Radcliffe' and two 'Oades and Stafford' Scholarships shall be open always to general competition, but no person shall be eligible as an Oades and Stafford Scholar who is not in need of assistance. These eight and the four Abingdon Scholarships are charged upon the corporate revenues. Scholarships are held for two years, with power to the College to renew for two years more, and, for special reasons, for a fifth year. The Henney Scholarship is unaffected. The Visitor is to be, as from the beginning, the Chancellor of the University.

[1] The Dorothea Wightwick Scholarship, founded since 1878, carries certain preferences based on kindred to the foundress.

As regards clerical fellowships, celibacy, and local connexions, these Statutes, compared with those made for most other Colleges, were conservative [1]. In Oxford generally the full effect of the changes made in respect to the Church and marriage of Fellows is not yet seen, and in the former case the effects have been obscured by the accident of an ecclesiastical revival, now already (in Oxford, at any rate) on the ebb. Religious influences and ordinary discipline are both left in a somewhat precarious position, dependent less on statute than on the good feeling and good sense of the various governing bodies. But at Pembroke the difficulties consequent on the latest legislation have been, and will no doubt continue to be, less felt than elsewhere. It is not a barrack of undergraduates officered by a stranded tutor and an adventitious hired chaplain.

The old Statutes regarded the College as a self-contained institution. By way of reaction, in 1851, it was thought by some that tutors lecturing to school-forms might be dispensed with altogether. Mansel makes Jeune say in *Phrontisterion* :—

> ' " Tutor," benighted wretch! didst thou say " Tutor ?"
> Who talks of Tutors now? The coin's not current.
> Professors, man, Professors are the thing [2].'

Probably more has resulted educationally from the voluntary system of inter-collegiate lectures than from professorial enlargement. Another aim of reformers was ' the great extension of the University to classes hitherto excluded.' The revival of Non-Collegiate Students, ' camerâ degentes,' has disappointed sanguine hopes. They gravitate to the Colleges. The opening of College endowments to merit, it might have been foreseen, must operate to the disendowment of those who cannot afford the expensive preliminaries of becoming merito- rious [3]. The truth is the two reforms conflicted with one another.

---

[1] Events had moved far since 1852. The *Edinburgh Review* remarked in July of that year: ' It is very important that there should be a close connexion between the Universities and the National Church; but an infusion of the lay element—*and it could never be a large one*—at Oxford would work incalculable good.'

[2] ' We step out of our studies with hearts dilated with the magnificent outlines of the Temple of Knowledge in which we dream that we minister, and we find ourselves not in an academical auditory but among the lower forms of a grammar school.' *Mark Pattison.*

[3] It has been often remarked that the effect of reform was to make a present of academic endowments to the upper middle class. An instance however on the other side is that of the late Professor Chandler, who, without those expensive preliminaries, gained, by Jeune's discernment, an Ossulston Scholarship, the essence of which was openness. He was elected in 1853 to a Francis Wightwick Fellow-

'We do not need poor men,' said the Pembroke tutors in 1851, 'but able men.' 'We think it a serious evil for a man to be educated beyond his intellect, or raised to a station which neither his taste nor his abilities will enable him to adorn.' A real effort, however, has been made to assist frugal undergraduates in the College to be economical and to check the extravagant. Some particulars as to expenses at Pembroke half a century ago will be found on pages 32–34, and 377, of the Commissioners' Report. At the same time the College has a reputation for a comfortable and refined commissariat.

Mr. JOHN CORDY-JEAFFRESON (matr. 1848), in his *Annals of Oxford* (vol. ii. p. 303), says:—

'It would, I am of opinion, be impossible to name a period when the collegiate system was more efficiently carried out than it was during my term of pupilage. And whilst I venture to give this deliberate testimony respecting the general state of the University, I may remark that the college in which my days were chiefly spent was fortunate in having rulers who exerted themselves strenuously and successfully to make it a model of academic discipline. Its tutors were men of great natural abilities and large attainments ; and, whilst all of them displayed abundant zeal and conscientiousness in the performance of their duties, one of them habitually exceeded the obligation of his office in discharging the teacher's functions. . . . The general government of the house was no less exemplary than the action of its tutorial staff[1].

'To raise his comparatively small and slightly endowed house to pre-eminence over greater and wealthier colleges was beyond Francis Jeune's power, but he effected wonders for the society of which he was for several years the chief ruler. He gave it honourable status in the Class-lists, procured the enlargement of its buildings, reformed its economy for the benefit of students of narrow means, and was no less judicious than indefatigable in his endeavours to inspire its members with manliness of purpose and contempt of frivolity. A

ship, to mark the appreciation by the College of his attainments and conduct. On the other hand the instance cannot be quoted on behalf of the barbarous test of competitive examination, for this great Aristotelian, on coming to Pembroke, barely knew the Greek alphabet.

[1] Less favourable, it is fair to add, are the recollections of Canon Dixon, the ecclesiastical historian (matr. 1852), who writes : 'the College had a sort of reputation as a working College. I am not willing to say much, but I did not find it in a good state. The Master did nothing in tuition except a Sunday Lecture in Greek Testament. There was very little discipline, no social intercourse between the fellows and the undergraduates, and Collections were merely a nominal ceremony.'

finer Master of a college than the late Bishop of Peterborough never lived. A vigilant and firm disciplinarian, he was prompt in correcting the excesses of his undergraduates, exhibiting no leniency to those of them whose misconduct was all the more likely to prejudice the discipline of the house because they were young men of superior birth, affluence, or personal style. But, though properly stern to insolent offenders, he overflowed with compassionate considerateness and Christian concern for collegiate "black sheep" to whom a sentence of expulsion would have involved life-long degradation. To wean scape-graces of this unattractive sort from their vicious propensities, to restore them to physical and moral health, and to send them into the world unscarred in fame, he deemed no care excessive, no condescension derogatory to his dignity. . . . Nor was he less abounding in sympathy for students who had no need of his forbearance and tenderness. That his college should achieve the main purpose of its institution by swelling the ranks of the intelligent, cultivated, and zealous clergy, he was especially desirous; but none of his men—or "boys," as he used to speak of them in his loud, hearty, shouting voice—ever started off from college on manhood's journey, by some track seldom chosen by University graduates, without words of pleasant encouragement and serviceable counsel from the shrewd and unconventional Master.'

In Mr. Augustus Hare's *Story of My Life* (vol. ii. pp. 5, 6) there is an account of the last election at Pembroke under the old Statutes. He says:—

'GEORGE SHEFFIELD[1] and I were inseparable out of doors, though I often wondered at his caring so much to be with me, as he was a capital rider, shot, oarsman—in fact, everything which I was not . . . It was about this time that the Bill was before Parliament for destroying the privileges of Founder's kin. While it was in progress we discovered that George was distinctly "Founder's kin" to Thomas Teesdale, the founder of Pembroke; and, half because our ideas were conservative, half because we delighted in an adventure of any kind, we determined to take advantage of the privilege. Dr. Jeune, afterwards Bishop of Peterborough, was Master of Pembroke then, and was perfectly furious at our audacity, which was generally laughed at at the time, and treated as the mere whim of two foolish schoolboys; but we would not be daunted, and went on our own way. Day after day I studied with George the subjects of his examination, goading him on. Day after day I walked down with him to the place of examination, doing my best to screw up his courage to

---

[1] Fourth son of Sir Robert Sheffield, of Normanby, Bart. He was first at University, and then Scholar of Pembroke from 1856 to 1861. On leaving he entered the Diplomatic Service.

meet the inquisitors. We went against the Heads of Houses with the enthusiasm of martyrs in a much greater cause, and we were victorious. George Sheffield was forcibly elected to a Founder's-kin Scholarship at Pembroke, and was the last so elected. Dr. Jeune was grievously annoyed, but, with the generosity which was always characteristic of him, he at once accorded us his friendship and remained my most warm and honoured friend till his death about ten years afterwards. He was remarkable at Oxford for dogmatically repealing the law which obliged Undergraduates to receive the Sacrament on certain days in the year. "In future," he announced in chapel, "no member of this college will be compelled to eat and drink his own damnation."'

Fellow-commoners were discouraged after Jeune's accession to office. The last was THOMAS COLLINGS BRÉHAUT, who matriculated March 6, 1845, aged twenty-six. He gave the College a twenty-four hours' scare once by not coming back from the river, and being supposed drowned. Mr. Evan Evans manned a boat to search for him, but the gentleman-commoner had been assisting a lady and her husband in some plight. Mr. Bréhaut was Chaplain to the Gaol at Guernsey from 1858.

CHAPTER XXXVI.

MASTERSHIP OF DOCTOR JEUNE.

DR. FRANCIS JEUNE, the eldest son of Francis Jeune, was born in the parish of St. Brelade, Jersey, May 22, 1806. His family, which had settled in the island in Elizabeth's reign, was honourable but unpretentious. He was educated at St. Servan's College at Rennes. Many years after, in 1862, on the occasion of the International Exhibition, Dr. Jeune preached in French in Westminster Abbey. He matriculated from Pembroke Oct. 21, 1822, and the same year was elected to a Morley Scholarship. An old dignitary told me he remembered Jeune, in the critical days just before the Schools, sitting in the sun at ten o'clock outside his room, which was next the old Buttery Hatch [1], reading the newspaper. The race is not always to the slow, and the hare generally wakes in time to canter in. But Jeune, to the consternation of all, broke down utterly in *vivâ voce* in the *Ethics*. He wrote, however, to Dornford and told him he knew his Aristotle, was set an exceptionally stiff paper, and came out in the First Class. B.A. 1827; M.A. 1830; B.C.L. and D.C.L. 1834; Ossulston Fellow 1830–7; Tutor 1828–32; Public Examiner 1834.

On his return from Canada in 1834 [2] he was appointed head-master of King Edward's School, Birmingham, which he resuscitated and remodelled. In 1838 he became dean of Jersey and rector of St. Helier's, on the recommendation of Lord John Russell. From 1844 to 1864 he held the rectory of Taynton, Gloucestershire, a church of Cromwellian date. In 1844 Jeune had returned to Pembroke as Master. The election, held on Dec. 22, 1843, was determined in his favour by the casting vote of the Vicegerent, Mr. Henney. The supporters of the Rev. CHARLES FREDERICK PARKER, rector of Rings-hall, protested on the ground, (1) that an Ossulston Fellow was not

---

[1] Overhead lived little ——, now deceased, whose rooms and curly ringlets caused him to be known as the 'Buttery Cupid.'

[2] *Vide supra*, page 289, n. 2.

eligible : (2) that a Philipps Fellow (Mr. Evan Evans, afterwards Master) was not qualified to vote; (3) that Mr. Henney, not being 'one of the senior Fellows,' was not legally Vicegerent. The seal, however, was attached to the paper, but the Vice-Chancellor refused to admit Dr. Jeune. After five days, Henney and two other Fellows met, together with Dr. Bliss, the University Registrar, and Jeune, having taken the oaths of allegiance and supremacy, was admitted by Mr. Henney to the place of Master, and subscribed the oath required by the College statutes. The matter going before the Duke of Wellington, as Visitor, his Grace, in a letter dated Jan. 29, 1844, decided, on an *ex parte* statement of Mr. Parker's supporters, that neither Ossulston nor Philipps Fellows could elect, or be elected, to the Mastership. The practical result of this decision was, of course, that Dr. Jeune's election was null and void, and that Mr. Parker had been elected Master. There was, however, now no Vicegerent to present him, as required by the Statutes, to the Visitor. On Feb. 5 Dr. Jeune sent to the Visitor an answer to the statement of Mr. Parker's supporters, who in turn forwarded a rejoinder. The College remained for a considerable time without a governor. At last the Duke laid the matter before the eminent counsel, Sir William Webb Follett, who advised him that the summary methods of a court-martial were unsuitable to disputes of this nature, that the appointment of Vicegerent, even if originally informal, had been long acquiesced in, and that the other objections to Dr. Jeune's election were invalid. The Duke accordingly gave a final decision to that effect, on April 13, 1844, and, with soldierly candour, directed that both it and the earlier contradictory decision should be entered in the College archives, to serve as a warning to himself and to others his successors not to determine questions too hastily and without having weighed the evidence of all the parties interested. There was consternation in Hebdomadal[1] circles when the new Head took his seat. Dr. Routh, condescending to pun, spoke of the 'forward young man of Pembroke.' Jeune devoted himself to urging on the Government the appointment of a reforming commission, on which, as we have seen, when constituted, he sate, and himself drafted the greater part of its Report. 'To him are to be largely ascribed the Examination Statutes which established the Schools of Natural Science and of Law and Modern History, and, though the original idea of a middle class local examination was suggested by Dr. Temple [now Lord Primate], it was mainly worked

---

[1] For an extraordinary misprint here see the *Dictionary of National Biography.*

out under his auspices and by his zeal and energy. He was probably the ablest man of business in his day at Oxford.' Mr. Gladstone once said that he had known two clergymen who, in his opinion, if their professional duties had allowed it, were quite capable of discharging the functions of a Chancellor of the Exchequer. The two were Dr. Hannah of Brighton and Dr. Jeune. Sitting with him on the first Hebdomadal Council, Jeune discovered that Pusey also had great business talents. Pusey, on the other hand, found that ' Jeune is not the sort of man some of our friends have thought him ; he is a person of clear and strong, if somewhat narrow, faith, and brings an acute and powerful mind to the support of positive truth.' Jeune's somewhat hard and unimaginative Liberalism, however, had placed him in resolute antagonism to the *Via Media* and high church movement. Preaching in St. Mary's on St. Luke's Day, 1846, he attacked Pusey's sermon on Absolution of eight months before, and accused him of Romanism, taking up himself the untenable ground that the solemn formula in the Visitation of the Sick refers to the removal of Church censures only. Pusey replied the following Advent with his sermon *The Entire Absolution of the Penitent.* It is curious to read in a letter from Newman to the Rev. R. H. Froude, of Nov. 7, 1833, ' Mr. Jeune of Pembroke joins heartily: he has been converted by Jeremy Taylor on Episcopacy.' Jeune was Vice-Chancellor 1858–62. In January, 1864, Lord Palmerston [1] suggested his name for the deanery of Lincoln, and a few months later, on June 27, he was consecrated Bishop of Peterborough. He died at Whitby, of heart disease, after a brief episcopate (whose dragoon-like vigour had contrasted with the mild rule of Bishop Davys), Aug. 21, 1868, and was buried in his cathedral church. Magee succeeded him.

During the twenty years of his Mastership, Dr. Jeune lifted a small and poor College into a leading position. Whereas in 1843 there were only two matriculations, in the year after he became Master there were twenty-eight, a number exceeded only at five Colleges. In 1848 only three Colleges had a larger entry. As a reformer he went on his way like a Roman road, equally regardless of obstacles and of scenery. The Rev. E. R. Orger, above quoted, writes :—

[1] The Rev. Compton Reade writes : 'I was at the Gaudy when Jeune was congratulated on having the nomination to the see of Gloucester. He looked glum and held his tongue. Next day it transpired that, with his usual incaution, he had *told* that Palmerston had made him the offer. The news reached the *Times* and was announced. But Pam had not asked the Queen, and as she saw the *Times*, Her Majesty refused.' Jeune's ambitions proceeded from a consciousness of his ability to be useful.

'In carrying out his plans he disregarded, it was said, the letter of statutes when it stood in his way, as well as the personal feelings of those who suffered from his measures. I was often reminded of this in meeting ——, who always spoke with great bitterness of the way in which he had been ousted of his scholarship. He had one of the few open ones, and there seemed no prospect of his giving it up. He was within his rights, he maintained; but he was somehow compelled to resign. The Master used to acknowledge that he had an indifference to the opinion of others when he felt he was right. He showed himself above rules and restraints in other ways. Dr. Stanley was Canon of Canterbury when I went there in 1855. He told me that the members of the first University Commission were often surprised and annoyed by finding that what had been discussed at their meetings had become known and was matter of common talk. The matter used to be traced to Dr. Jeune; and, when he was remonstrated with, he took a bold line and said: "I did it on purpose, to intimidate them." In reference to the opponents of University Reform, he once spoke to me of Dr. Hawkins, the Provost of Oriel, as "their clever man."' It was perhaps a bolder feat to send about his business Le Grand, the magnificent French cook of the College. Mr. Orger continues: 'In reference to the undergraduates his influence and teaching were very stimulating. In my time the only lecture we had with him was a Hall lecture on Sundays and Saints' Days. He lectured on one of the Epistles of the New Testament. His manner was altogether original; he said very startling things, and this, combined with the rapidity with which he spoke and his foreign intonation, making it difficult to follow him, gave his lectures an exciting effect. Many of the men were shocked by some of his sayings and by what was called his irreverence. I fought many battles on his side.

'He used to distinguish some of the men by the freedom with which he spoke to them. This took place particularly at Collections. He would ask unusual questions, and then take a man aside for a talk, in which he would speak in the most interesting way, and with a want of reserve which was flattering.

'He used to point out to us marks to aim at in after life. Mitchinson told me that he found him once reading a book on Botany, and said to him: "You take an interest in that? Resolve to succeed Daubeny." The highest point he directed me to was not above the rank of *Archdeacon*. He practised no disguise as to his own ambition. It was amusing to see his excitement when a vacancy occurred among the Bishops.

'He belonged at bottom to the Evangelical school, but added a freedom of thought which was unusual in it. He had no sympathy with the "Oxford Movement." He used to speak very freely of Dr. Pusey. He spoke to my father about his "impudence" in the way in which he alluded to his suspension in the first sermon which he preached after it had expired. And he said to me once : " Pusey labours under an *ignoratio elenchi*. He never proves his point, but something like it." In parting with St. Aldate's by sale to the Simeon Trustees, he was influenced partly by dislike of the ringing of the bell at seven o'clock, his dinner hour, and by theological preference. The Bishop of Oxford (Wilberforce) told me that the Master had " done him." He was prepared to have the living purchased, but it was managed in the other way. I believe, however, that the Trustees appointed an admirable man.

'I think on the whole that the Master was not popular. We were afraid of him, but proud of him at the same time.'

The Rev. PHILIP HEDGELAND, Prebendary of Exeter (matr. 1846), writes :—'I remember Hatch (who in such a subject was surely an expert) saying of Jeune in 1858, " He is the *broadest* man I ever knew." Jeune almost went out of his way to affect cynicism. Rolleston told me that, when he saw Jeune after getting his " first," the Master's congratulations were summed up with, " Remember, as long as you succeed I am your friend." He did not really mean this, as I can prove by another story. For some domestic reasons I asked leave to go out of residence for a term. He was reluctant, and I have now his letter in which he says, " If pecuniary matters have anything to do with your wish to remain in the country, I think I can undertake to remove the difficulty." '

In the same way the Rev. WILLIAM DE QUETTEVILLE (Fellow 1851–62) writes:—'I cannot say how much I owe to Jeune's unceasing kindness to me from the time I matriculated. He was a man who was not well known by many ; but he was firm in his friendships, and had the kindest of hearts beneath a somewhat stern exterior. Wherever he went he left his mark. . . . I have heard that the clergy in the diocese of Peterborough were learning to appreciate him.'

Of similar tenour are the words of the late SAMUEL FLOOD JONES [1], Precentor of Westminster (1869), Priest in Ordinary to the Queen (1869), Vicar of St. Botolph, Aldersgate (1876), President of Sion College, ob. 1895—who matriculated in 1848 :—' Jeune used to call

---

[1] Precentor Flood Jones lies in the south cloister of the Abbey, where the feet of the 'children of the choir' pass daily over his head. He devoted his life and high talent to the elevation and reverent rendering of the musical services. In all the great national ceremonials of which the Abbey is the scene his fine presence and melodious voice were for many years prominent.

us to a lecture in Hall on Sundays, which prevented men going to University sermon or churches. Some, by protest or favour, were allowed absence; but those who attended were sometimes a little startled at a *flippancy* in the Master's dealing with sacred subjects. I learnt much from him however, and I treasure his memory as one of my kindest friends. He was rough sometimes at first—as when he asked a youth whom I took to him for matriculation "if he had any brains or was quite a fool." Yet there was that thorough frankness and good nature in him, and that readiness to condescend even to the weak, that while I was at Pembroke, and ever after when I saw him, I found him one of the truest and most real of men.'

Dr. Jeune's lectures on the Epistles to the Corinthians took the place of a Saturday lecture read by his predecessor, Dr. Hall, which one who entered in 1841, the Rev. WILLIAM LANGLEY POPE, D.D., told me had been given up just before his time. Jeune's lecture was from noon to one on Sundays. The Rev. GEORGE GAINSFORD, the respected Vicar of Holy Saviour, Hitchin, who entered in 1848, writes :—' It was given in the Hall, and the Bible clerks had to prick the names. It was a point with many men, who were not in the habit of attending University sermons, always to go when Dr. Pusey preached. Dr. Pusey, as is well known, was very lengthy, whereby men attending his sermons did not get back to Pembroke until past 12 o'clock, too late for the Master's lecture. Then, when they were called to account, they had the satisfaction of saying that they were hearing Dr. Pusey's University sermon, which they considered was a "good score" off the Master. I considered his lectures very profitable, and above all very original, and I had pleasure in attending them, though I never had any kind of sympathy with Dr. Jeune's " broad-low " views.'

HENRY, afterwards Professor, CHANDLER on one occasion asked to be excused the lecture, as he wished to leave the College at twenty minutes before one. The Master, however, met his petition with a peremptory and inexorable refusal. As Chandler had never made such a request before, had always carefully prepared his book, and was known to be perhaps the hardest reader in College, he was deeply mortified and hurt. On Sunday the Master was evidently on the look-out for him, for he called him up and desired him to translate a passage, which he did. He then retired to his place, and the lecture proceeded as usual. Suddenly, at twenty minutes to one, the Master drew out his watch, looked at it, and then, to the surprise of every one, said he did not propose to continue the lecture any longer that morning. Jeune thus maintained his consistency, and Chandler kept his appointment. The Master always felt a prophetic interest in Chandler's career and a deep pride in his success. One day, when he was in for the Schools, Jeune saw him in the quadrangle leaning against some railings which then guarded the north-west corner of the grass plot. How had he done? 'Not well, I fear,' Chandler said. ' I feel dreadfully nervous about the result.' ' Nervous, nervous ! ' replied Jeune, in his quick, blunt way. ' You should not be nervous. Do you know what nervousness is? Nervousness is only vanity[1].' He did not himself know the feeling. The Rev. GEORGE WILSON KEIGHTLEY, Rector of Great Stamford (matr. 1844), speaks of Jeune's insensibility to music. His duties as Master lay lightly on him. The Rev. EDWARD BARTRUM, D.D., Head-master of St. Edward's School, Berkhamsted (matr. 1852), says :—

'Asked to state the duties of the Head of a College, he replied that these were to write a few letters, and to see a few young gentlemen in the morning. What then are the duties of a Dean of a Cathedral? "All the duties," was his answer, "of the Head of a College except writing a few letters and seeing a few young gentlemen in the morning." I well remember his saying to me that no man begins life till he is fifty. I think he was about fifty at that time, and was expecting that promotion to a higher post which came in due course. One of our men who had certainly over-read himself told the Master, in the presence of a number of under-graduates, that he (Dr. Jeune) hoped and wished to be, but never would be, a Bishop. . . . He was regarded as a man of unusual ambition, and it was a common saying in Oxford that when a new Bishop was made, his name would begin with a J ; he would be a Jeune, a Jacobson, a Jackson, or a fourth whose name I cannot recall.'

Dr. Jeune's last sermon before the University, I am credibly informed, was on the text ' If they have called the Master of the House,' &c. (St. Matt. x. 25). Old Pembroke men, and any who remember the famous Pembroke triumvirate, will appreciate the audacity of the allusion. His handsome, strong, French-looking face, once compared to Fechter's, is depicted in the portrait by Tweedie which hangs in the Hall.

'Bishop Jeune's Memorial Prize' of £40 may be competed for by such licensed curates of the diocese of Peterborough or in the Island of Jersey, and such graduates of Pembroke College, as have not been in Holy Orders more than ten years. The subject is appointed by trustees, and the dissertations must be 'in harmony with the late Bishop's published statements,' which are to be especially gathered from his Charge and Sermons[2].

[1] Prof. Chandler repeated these anecdotes to the late Vicegerent, the Rev. R. G. Livingstone, now Rector of Brinkworth, from whom I had them.

[2] Published by Messrs. Seeley & Co. The subject for 1891 was, ' The

Through his relationship to Dr. Jeune the College has the honour of numbering among its members the accomplished Cambridge scholar and divine, Dr. EDWIN HAMILTON GIFFORD, Senior Classic and Senior Medallist (1843), who incorporated as D.D., Dec. 5, 1889. Dr. Gifford was from 1848 to 1862 not the least eminent of the Head-masters of Birmingham School. In 1884 he succeeded Bishop Claughton as Archdeacon of London and Canon of St. Paul's. Select Preacher 1879. The Venerable JOHN SINCLAIR[1], who entered the College a few months after the battle of Waterloo, and was Vicar of Kensington from 1842 till his death on May 22, 1875, had been Archdeacon before Claughton.

Jeune's essentially modern and unvisionary mind can have had scant sympathy with the Wardour Street antiquarianisms of pre-Raphaelite dreamers. But some of his King Edward's School pupils were leaders of that somewhat self-conscious movement; and, as Pembroke received many undergraduates, in Jeune's suite, from Birmingham, a good deal of poetic and mediævalist socialism came to birth within the College walls. Dr. GEORGE BIRKBECK HILL[2] (matr. March 1, 1855; D.C.L. 1871) writes :—

' In the north-eastern corner of the Old Quadrangle, on the ground-floor left, my old friend C. J. Faulkner[3] (afterwards Fellow of University) had his rooms. He was one of a small society which I was invited to join just after he had gone into lodgings in Pembroke Street, but which had existed for at least two years before my entrance. We met almost every night and had eager talks. Most of the men were from Birmingham—from King Edward's Grammar School—though Faulkner was from the Edgbaston Proprietary School of that town. The Pembroke men who formed this society were, besides myself and Faulkner, Canon Dixon, the Church historian, Dr. Hatch, and William Fulford[4], a minor poet of considerable merit. The outsiders were William Morris, author of *The Earthly Paradise*, Burne-Jones the artist, Cormell Price, late Head-master of Westward Hoe School, Maintenance of the Protestant Simplicity of the Public Worship of the Church of England.'

[1] He was son of Sir John Sinclair, Bart., P.C. (1755-1835), who was M.P. for Caithness, Lostwithiel, and Petersfield, and President of the Scottish Board of Agriculture.

[2] An excellent crayon portrait of this eminent *alumnus* now hangs in the Common Room parlour. Dr. Hill is an Honorary Fellow of Pembroke.

[3] CHARLES JOSEPH FAULKNER, matriculated from Pembroke 1851; Scholar 1853; Fellow of University 1856; Mathematical Tutor; most whist-loving of he sad socialist race, and affectionately remembered as ' Citizen Faulkner.'

[4] The Rev. WILLIAM FULFORD, matriculated Dec. 7, 1850. Sir Edward Burne-Jones and Mr. Morris were of Exeter; Mr. Price was a Brasenose man.

and Macdonald of Corpus, whose sisters are married to Sir Edward Burne-Jones and Sir Edward Poynter. Dixon, Hatch, Fulford, Burne-Jones, and Macdonald were all, I believe, exhibitioners from King Edward's School. When I belonged to the society, we generally met in either Fulford's, Faulkner's, or Hatch's lodgings in Pembroke Street. Hatch had the ground-floor rooms in the old house on the eastern side of the passage from Pembroke Street. Sometimes we met in my rooms, one of the attics in the New Quadrangle. I remember at one of these meetings it was resolved to establish the *Oxford and Cambridge Magazine*, which lasted about a year, Fulford being the editor. Rossetti contributed to it the *Blessed Damozel*, and Burne-Jones and Morris often wrote for it. In few rooms, I fancy, has there been more of that eager talk which Tennyson describes in the *In Memoriam* than in Faulkner's room in the outer quad and in Hatch's rooms in the old house in Pembroke Street. . . . Moore [1] did not belong to our set.'

One of the first Birmingham boys to follow Jeune to Pembroke had been JOHN WILLIAM CALDICOTT (Exhibitioner 1846; Scholar of Jesus College 1850; Tutor there 1854–60; Public Examiner 1859–60; D.D. 1874), who was Head-master of Bristol School 1860–83. He was known at Pembroke for original opinions of a pronounced high-church character, which he afterwards exchanged for extreme radical and latitudinarian views. Rector of Shipston-on-Stour 1883.

RICHARD WATSON DIXON (matr. June 3, 1852), one of the pre-Raphaelite band above mentioned, who gained the Arnold Essay in 1858 and the Sacred Poem in 1863, published in 1861 *Christ's Company and other Poems*, which was followed by other poetical works. He is better known as the learned author of the *History of the Church of England*. He became Hon. Canon of Carlisle in 1874, Vicar of Warkworth in 1883. In 1885 he was invited to stand for the Poetry Professor's chair, but withdrew before the election.—EDWIN HATCH, a leader of a different theological school, was born of Nonconformist parents at Derby, Sept. 4, 1835. He entered Pembroke as an Exhibitioner Nov. 10, 1853. While an undergraduate he contributed largely to magazines and reviews. He took B.A. 1857 (Ellerton Essay 1858), entered the ministry of the Church of England, and worked zealously in an East London parish. In 1859 Hatch was appointed Professor of Classics in Trinity College, Toronto, and in 1862 Rector of the High School of Quebec. Returning to Oxford in 1867, he took M.A.

---

[1] Dr. EDWARD MOORE, Principal of St. Edmund Hall, the learned editor of Dante. *Vide supra*, p. 240.

and became Vice-Principal of St. Mary Hall, until 1885. (A pre-decessor of his in that office, WILLIAM HAYWARD COX (matr. Pembroke 1821), Fellow of Queen's 1828, Prebendary of Hereford 1854, Rector of Carfax 1849–58, was still living. He is the 'Αλέκτρωρ of the twelve candidates for the Oriel Fellowship in 1826[1].) Hatch's influence in academic affairs was considerable. He was the first editor of the official *University Gazette* (1870), and brought out the *Student's Handbook*. In 1884 he became Secretary to the Board of Faculties. The name of Hatch will always live through his labours on the Septuagint. ' No Englishman of the present generation,' says Prof. Sanday, 'had given greater promise of becoming a distinguished theologian.' But his mind was tinged with a profound dislike of ecclesiasticism. The Bampton Lectures of 1881 on *The Organization of the Early Christian Churches*, while keenly resented by Anglicans, were welcomed in Scotland and Germany. Edinburgh made Hatch a Doctor of Divinity, and Harnack translated the Bamptons into German. In 1887 Hatch published *The Growth of Church Institutions*. His Hibbert Lectures of 1888 on *Greek Influence on Christianity* were published after his death by Dr. Fairbairn. A volume of devotional poems called *Towards Fields of Light* exhibits the deeper side of Hatch's richly stored mind. He died in the prime of intellectual vigour on Nov. 10, 1889. From 1882 to 1884 he was Grinfield Lecturer on the LXX ; from 1884 Reader in Ecclesiastical History. Select Preacher 1886. In 1883 he was presented to Purleigh, Essex.

An earlier Bampton Lecturer was THOMAS WINTLE, B.D., Scholar, Fellow, and Tutor of the College (matr. 1753, aet. 15). His virtues and attainments are highly extolled in the *Gentleman's Magazine* (1814, ii. 192).—EDWARD GARBETT, the Bampton Lecturer of 1867, was at Pembroke before his election to a Brasenose Scholarship (1837). He is remembered as an eloquent preacher and leader of the declining orthodox low-church party. He was Boyle Lecturer 1860–1863.

Two years after Mr. Garbett's course, the Bampton Lectures were delivered by ROBERT PAYNE-SMITH, ' one of the very few great Syriac scholars' (according to the *Times*) 'that exist in Europe.' Born at Chipping Camden, he entered Pembroke, aged seventeen, as a Towns-end Scholar (1837–50). By Dr. Jeune's advice he turned his attention early to Oriental studies. In 1840 he gained the Boden Scholarship for Sanskrit, and in 1843 the Pusey and Ellerton for Hebrew. He

[1] See *Reminiscences of Oxford* (Frederick Oakeley), ed. L. M. Quiller Couch, O. H. S., pp. 323, 345.

was ordained priest in 1844, but accepted a mastership in the High School at Edinburgh, which he left to become Head-master of Kensington Grammar School (1853–57). But the interest of Oriental studies took him back to Oxford, and he was appointed Sub-Librarian in the Bodleian. Though a textuary rather than a great divine, he was made in 1865 Regius Professor of Divinity and Canon of Christ Church, and in 1871, on Dr. Alford's death, Mr. Gladstone recommended him for the deanery of Canterbury. By this time earlier Tractarian influences on his mind had been checked, and in 1873 he made a tour in America in support of the propaganda of the Evangelical Alliance. His membership of the committee appointed by Convocation for the Revision of the New Testament translation resulted from his fame as an orientalist. The great work of his life, the *Syriac Dictionary* issued by the Clarendon Press, was almost finished at his death, which took place March 31, 1895, at the deanery. It may be noted that a former Dean of Canterbury, Archbishop Moore, had also come to the College from Gloucestershire as a Townsend Scholar, and occupied a stall at Christ Church.—Slightly senior at Pembroke to Payne-Smith was CHARLES ADOLPHUS ROW (Scholar 1834–8), whose Bampton Lectures of 1877 went through six editions. His numerous works on Christian evidences have had a large sale on both sides of the Atlantic, and Mr. Row was created D.D. by the University of the South in 1888. He was Head-master of Mansfield Grammar School from 1848 to 1861, and in 1874 was appointed to the prebendal stall of Harleston in St. Paul's Cathedral. He died Nov. 24, 1896.—The elucidation of Holy Scripture in the light of Oriental learning, a tradition in Oxford since the days of Laud, has been fostered by the zeal of HENRY (HALL) HOUGHTON, born in Dublin Dec. 10, 1823, Scholar 1841–5. Though disabled by ill health from active clerical labour, it was the desire of his life to promote the accurate study of the sacred Writings, and in conjunction with an uncle, the Rev. John Hall, Canon of Bristol, he founded in 1868, 1870, and 1871 the Hall and Hall-Houghton Prizes, two for Greek Testament, two for Septuagint, and one for the Syriac Versions, all five to be awarded annually. His uncle dying in 1871, Mr. Houghton succeeded to the estate of Melmerby, Cumberland, and changed his name to Hall-Houghton. He gave the Church Missionary Society £4,500 in all for the promotion of the systematic study of Holy Scripture by the natives of North India, West Africa, North-West America, and New Zealand. He died at Melmerby Hall, Sept. 4, 1887.—The Boden Sanskrit Scholarship was awarded in the first year of its foundation (1833) to WILLIAM

ALLDER STRANGE, afterwards Head-master of Abingdon School
(1839–68); Abingdon Scholar of Pembroke 1829–37; D.D. 1847;
Vicar of Bishop Middleham from 1868 till his death, April 17, 1874.
His successor at Abingdon was EDMUND TRISTRAM HORATIO HARPER,
who entered the College as a Townsend Scholar in 1841.

In the unwritten story of devoted pastoral toil, some names, serving
here for example only, are not soon forgotten.   Such was JAMES
OCTAVIUS RYDER (matr. 1845), who labouring among a fever-stricken
people at Welwyn, Herts, took the infection and died, April 24, 1870.
Mr. Orger writes :—

'Ryder's case was remarkable. He got a first-class chiefly, it was said,
owing to the examiners' admiration of the brilliant way in which he did his
Pindar, an uncommon book to take up.   He brought a knowledge of it
to Oxford with him from Birmingham School, where he was under Prince
Lee.   Henney had examined him there—which led to his coming to
Pembroke [as Bible clerk]—and constantly referred any question of
scholarship to him in Lecture.   He seemed to take no great pains, and
was supposed to be going in for a Pass.   A remonstrance of mine,
I believe, determined him to change his mind.   He began to read hard,
though late, and his success at last surprised us.   He determined to stand
at All Souls.   There was a great audacity about it.   He told me the All
Souls men said they had never rejected a First Class man, and he would
test it.   He called upon Sneyd, the Warden, and was kindly received.
His name was in his favour, but not much else.   He was short, and his
manner was not good.   The Warden was very anxious that he should be
able to establish his relationship to the noble family of that name, which
he said he was unable to do, and also lent him a copy of the *Stemmata
Chicheliana*, to see if he could not make out that he was Founder's kin.
The fight over him was long and fierce, and the election was delayed
much beyond the usual time.   But it ended in his favour. . . . Ryder
became ultimately the intimate friend of the Warden, aristocrat as he
was, who left him his property.'

The work among the miners of the well-known Vicar of Rugeley,
RICHARD MACGREGOR GRIER (matr. 1853), has left a permanent impress
in the Midlands.   He was made a prebendary of Lichfield in 1876.
He moved in 1888 from Rugeley to Hednesford, where he died almost
suddenly, Aug. 27, 1894.   Prebendary Grier was an eager advocate
of the political claims of the artisan class, and was thought to be
designed for a bishoprick by the Liberal Government.   But he had
a great power of awakening loyalty and devotion in all ranks[1].—At
Ladybrand in South Africa a church has been erected, and in the

---

[1] Fifteen very feeling *Sonnets* to his memory, as that of 'Spiritual Father,
Teacher, Guide, and Friend,' from the pen of Beatrice Ethel Charles, were
published at Walsall in 1895.

cathedral of Bloemfontein a stall for the support of an itinerant canon has been endowed, to record the memory of JAMES DOUGLAS, of Modderpoort (matr. 1861), son of Henry Douglas, Canon of Durham. He was Missionary Superior of St. Augustine's, Ladybrand, from 1875. 'Few men in this State,' said the *Friend of the Free State* after his death from overwork in August, 1894, 'have been more universally beloved and respected. . . . An eloquent and forcible preacher, he worked incessantly, travelling in all directions and in all ways, preaching, visiting, giving counsel and doing kind actions everywhere and to all sorts of people.' The Bishop of Bloemfontein speaks of 'the special devotion with which Father Douglas gave himself to the work of seeking for the spiritual well-being of our scattered and isolated people.'—Among living workers Pembroke men will recall the name of ALBERT BARFF (matr. 1848), Prebendary of St. Paul's, sometime Chaplain of Cuddesdon under King and Liddon, afterwards Vicar of North Moreton, Master of St. Paul's Cathedral Choir School, and Vicar of St. Giles's, Cripplegate. At College he stroked the Eight, and was President of the Boat Club.—An earlier prebendary of St. Paul's was CHARLES MACKENZIE, Scholar 1825–33, Head-master of St. Olave's Grammar School 1832–55, Vicar of St. Helen's, Bishopsgate, 1836–46, Rector of St. Benet, Gracechurch, &c., 1846–66, Principal of Westbourne College 1855–64, founder of the City of London College, Prebendary of St. Paul's 1852, Rector of Allhallows, Lombard Street, 1866 till his death April 11, 1888.—The canonry of St. Paul's vacated by the death of Dr. Liddon was filled by the appointment of WILLIAM CHARLES EDMUND NEWBOLT, Scholar 1863–8, Vicar of Dymock 1870–7, and of Malvern Link 1877–87. From 1887–90 he held the responsible post of Principal of Ely Theological College [1].—Other well-known London clergymen are SAMUEL JOHN STONE (matr. 1858), Vicar of St. Paul's, Haggerston, 1874, author of *Lyra Fidelium*, of *The Knight of Intercession*, and of such familiar hymns as *The Church's One Foundation*, and *Weary of Earth*—his hymn, *Lord of our Soul's Salvation*, was, by the Queen's command, sung at the Thanksgiving for the recovery of the Prince of Wales—and JOHN WILLIAM HORSLEY (matr. 1863), the devoted and humour-gifted Chaplain of Clerkenwell Prison and Vicar of Holy Trinity, Woolwich, and latterly of St. Peter's, Walworth.—And, speaking of laughter in grimy riverside parishes, would any history of

---

[1] Canon Newbolt's father, the Rev. William Robert Newbolt, was a Student of Christ Church. His grandfather, Sir John Henry Newbolt, Knt., was Chief Justice of Madras.

Pembroke be complete without mention of the 'twinkling eye and merry face' of JOHN OXENHAM—usually called 'Johnny'—BENT (matr. 1851), incumbent of St. John the Evangelist, Woolwich, since 1868—the wit of the College in the early fifties, at whose quaint answers and questions the whole Lecture would explode [1]? Of about the same date were THOMAS HOG GIRTIN, a strange humourist, afterwards the special correspondent of the *Standard* at Naples, where he was honoured by a public funeral; JAMES MERRICK GUEST, from 1862 Head-master of Handsworth Bridge Trust School; CHARLES HILL WALLACE, F.R.G.S., Vicar of Holy Trinity, Clifton, from 1867, and Hon. Canon; HENRY RUDGE HAYWARD, Scholar 1849–58, Fellow 1858–64, Archdeacon of Cirencester since 1883, sometime steward of the Junior Common Room; Bishop M——, 'that wonderful *multum in parvo*, taking a part in almost everything intellectual, and able, then as now, to dispense almost entirely with tired nature's sweet restorer. On the night previous to his *vivâ voce* in Classical Greats it was said that he read until seven, slept until nine, then rose, breakfasted, went to the Schools, and was as cool as a cucumber under an hour's cross-questioning.'—And here I may recall the names of EDWARD GREATOREX (Scholar 1841), Precentor of Durham 1862–72; of GEORGE KNOWLING (matr. 1845), Vicar of Wellington 1865, Prebendary and Canon of Wells 1872; of JAMES TANNER (First, Math. Mod. 1852), who was Head-master of King Edward's School, Chelmsford, from 1867 to 1877, when he retired to the rectory of Chipping Ongar; of WILLIAM ROBINS SMITH (First, Mod. 1852), Principal of Bath Proprietary College 1860–74, Rector of Monnington-on-Wye 1874; of THEODORE CRANE DUPUIS (matr. 1850), Vicar of Burnham 1867, Prebendary of Wells 1879—he was son of a former Fellow, CHARLES SANDERS SKELTON DUPUIS [2] (matr. 1814); of Dr. HENRY MOWLD ROBINSON, born in Greece, matriculated 1857, D.D. 1877, Head-master of Archbishop Harnett's School, Chigwell, 1868, Warden of Chardstock 1876, Head-master of Bishop Cotton's School at Simla 1885; and of JOSIAH

---

[1] As a Scholar it was his duty to read the lessons in Chapel. When the genealogical tables occurred, a contemporary says, '"Johnny" took his fences in a manner which made even the Master smile a saturnine smile.' With John Oxenham Bent must be linked his elder brother ROBERT PAUL BENT (matr. 1846). Applying personally to the Ecclesiastical Commissioners for a grant in augmentation of the meagre cure of Jacobstowe, Devon, he was asked: 'You are the incumbent, sir?' 'That, gentlemen, rests with you,' was the reply. 'At present I am the Bent without the income.'

[2] Grandson of Dr. Dupuis, 'organist and composer' to George III, who was buried in Westminster Abbey church July 24, 1796.

SANDERS TEULON, who entered the same year, but was shortly elected to a scholarship at Lincoln. Principal of Chichester Theological College 1886, Canon residentiary of Chichester 1888.

In 1853 TOM HOOD the younger[1] came to the College.—The year before, COMPTON READE, nephew of the novelist and himself not unknown as novelist and poet, entered. Rector of Kenchester 1887; Lecturer at Curzon Chapel 1886.—Towards the end of Jeune's Mastership JAMES HAMILTON WYLIE was elected Scholar (1863–8); H. M. Inspector of Schools 1873; author of the *History of the Reign of Henry the Fourth.*— REGINALD FITZHUGH BIGG-WITHER, afterwards Warden of St. Thomas's Diocesan Home, Basingstoke, and Rector of Worting, an authority on matters connected with Oriental Christianity, entered in 1860.—ROBERT MAIN, Fellow of Queens', Cambridge, incorporated Oct. 6, 1860. He was first Assistant at the Greenwich Observatory 1845–60; Radcliffe's Observer 1860–78. Ob. May 9, 1878.—The well-known black and white artist, SYDNEY PRIOR HALL, was a Scholar from 1862 to 1865. He was attached to the suite of the Prince of Wales in the royal progresses through India. Mr. Hall is a Knight of the Order of the Saviour of Greece. In his earliest line, however, that of caricature, he contributed to the gaiety of Colleges. His contemporaries remember him as 'the Pembroke Shakespeare,' a name given him because of a supposed likeness to the bard.—A regretted name in a kindred branch of journalism is that of ARTHUR LOCKER, for twenty-one years (1870–91) editor of the *Graphic,* who was taken from us on June 23, 1893. Born at Greenwich Hospital[2], July 2, 1828, he entered the College from Charterhouse in 1847. The varied experience of travel on many continents added to his equipment as a novelist, as a writer of *vers de société* (in which line, however, he has been excelled by his brother, Mr. Locker-Lampson), and as a literary reviewer. He was on the staff

---

[1] Editor of *Tom Hood's Annual*; hero of the *Parental Ode*—
　　'Thou idol of thy parents! Drat the child!
　　　There goes the ink.'

[2] Mr. Locker came of a distinguished race of seamen. His father, Captain Edward Hawke Locker, F.R.S., a friend of Southey and Scott, was Commissioner of Greenwich Hospital, which owes to him its collection of naval pictures. He carried dispatches to Wellington and had a remarkable interview with Buonaparte at Elba. The grandfather, Captain William Locker, son of an accomplished literary friend of Dr. Johnson, accompanied Hawke to execute the arrest of Admiral Byng. When in command of the *Lowestoft* he had Nelson under him for a time as lieutenant. He died in 1800 as Lieutenant-Governor of Greenwich Hospital. William IV stopped before his portrait to remark, 'There's the best man I ever knew.' Captain Locker had reproved the royal admiral for swearing.

of the *Times* from 1865 to 1870. ' Many young writers,' the *Daily Graphic* said in announcing his death, ' owe their first step in the world of letters to him.'—CHARLES FITZWILLIAM CADIZ, Puisne Judge at Natal 1876, entered the College in 1849; and HENRY BOLD KNOWLYS, an Indian Judge, entered in 1855. I am confining these brief notices to men (not mentioned elsewhere) who matriculated under Jeune, but I may after these names mention that of Sir WILLIAM JOHN ANDERSON, Chief Justice of British Honduras from 1890, who came up in 1865.

I am indebted to C. Moberly Bell, Esq., Manager of the *Times*, for the following note on a distinguished Pembrochian :—

' Sir JOHN SCOTT came to Egypt in 1873 on the ground of ill-health, and without any intention of practising there; but, becoming known and extremely popular, he was asked to plead before the British Consular Court in Alexandria, and very soon had by far the largest practice there. General Staunton, who was then Her Majesty's Representative, consulted him in reference to the establishment of the International Courts, and in 1875, much to his surprise, offered him the post of British Judge at the Court of Appeal. He accepted it, and in the second year became Vice-President. In 1882 he was made a Judge of the High Court in Bombay, but in 1890, at the request of Sir Evelyn Baring (now Lord Cromer), he was lent to the Egyptian Government, and a year later was appointed Judicial Adviser to the Khedive, and resigned his position on the High Court. Thus he has done very excellent work, creating the whole judicial administration of the country from Alexandria to Dongola. In February, 1894, he was created a K.C.M.G.'

The College has supplied, if I mistake not, during this century, eleven rulers to the home and colonial Church. These were (besides Bishop Jeune) :—DANIEL GATEWARD DAVIS, who came from St. Kitt's to the College in 1808, and was steward of Junior Common Room; Bishop of Antigua 1842-57.—JOHN JACKSON, sent by Valpy to Pembroke in 1829; steward of Junior Common Room. He was in the First Class with Liddell, Scott, Lowe, and Canning. Ellerton Prize 1834; Scholar of Pembroke 1835-8; Head-Master of Islington School 1836. In North London he won a position as a preacher, and at Stoke Newington were delivered the successful sermons on *The Sinfulness of Little Sins*. First incumbent of St. James', Muswell Hill, 1842; Select Preacher 1845, 1850, 1862, and 1866; Chaplain to the Queen 1847; Boyle Lecturer 1853; D.D. 1853; Vicar of St. James's, Piccadilly, and Canon of Bristol 1853; Bishop of Lincoln on the recommendation of Lord Aberdeen 1853-68. As such he welded together the counties of Lincoln and Nottingham. When in 1868 Tait was translated from London, Mr. Disraeli recommended Bishop Jackson for that great see. His episcopate was marked by anxieties arising out of the Ritual question, by the establishment of a Diocesan Conference, by the creation of the new diocese of St. Alban's, by the rearrangement of the boundaries of Rochester and Winchester, and by the creation of a suffragan bishoprick for East London. He died suddenly on the festival of the Epiphany, 1885, and is buried at Fulham. Bishop Jackson was reserved in character, but fatherly and sympathetic. His portrait was painted by Mr. George Richmond. Mr. Pycroft, who was one of his countless pupils, speaks admiringly in *Oxford Memories* of Jackson's excelling qualities as a private tutor at Oxford. 'I heard that his head was in a whirl, and that the vacation came just in time to save him. He said, "My head is giving way: the truth is I have done too much."'—Closely connected with Jackson throughout his career was HENRY MACKENZIE, who after leaving Charterhouse engaged for a time in commercial pursuits, but at the age of twenty-two entered the College Oct. 11, 1830. Steward of Junior Common Room 1831; Perpetual Curate of St. James's, Bermondsey, 1840. His friend Maurice procured his removal to Great Yarmouth in 1844; but four years later Bishop Blomfield recalled him to London, as Vicar of St. Martin's-in-the-Fields. In 1855 he retired to a country cure. Bishop Jackson then made his old College friend his Examining Chaplain, and appointed him to the Lincoln stall once held by George Herbert. Subdean and Canon residentiary 1864; Archdeacon of Notts 1866. In 1870 the long-dormant office of Bishop Suffragan was revived in Mackenzie's person by Bishop Wordsworth. There was at first some not un-natural dislike in Nottinghamshire to being under the charge of a 'curate-bishop,' but this was removed by his dignity and tact. Infirmity and age led to his retirement in 1878, in which year he died. He is buried at Collingham.—The patriarch of modern prelates, a true Selbornian and a scholar *maxime Etonensis*, RICHARD DURNFORD, has already been mentioned. His vigorous life of nearly ninety-three years closed only in October, 1895. After leaving Pembroke for a Magdalen demyship, he was president of the newly-born United Debating Society in 1823 and 1825; president of the Union 1826. Of the Cricket Club, the members of which used to ride on horseback to the old Bullingdon Club ground, he was a prominent member. Fellow of Magdalen 1827–36; Rector of Middleton 1835–70; Archdeacon of Manchester 1867–70; Canon 1868–70; Bishop

of Chichester 1870–95. Durnford contributed to Praed's *Etonian*
and to *Musae Etonenses.*—OCTAVIUS HADFIELD (matr. 1832) zealously
administered the see of Wellington from 1870 to 1893 ; Primate of New
Zealand 1889–93 [1].—JAMES WILLIAM WILLIAMS was the revered Bishop
of Quebec from 1863 to 1892. He entered Feb. 23, 1848, aged twenty-
two. At Pembroke he was a great recluse, one of his few friends being
Henry Chandler. Bishop Williams, Bishop Mitchinson, Flood Jones,
and Arthur Locker were nearly contemporary on the same staircase in
the ' New Quad,' presided over by the old scout Virtue, so called on the
principle on which the Eumenides received their name.—To be boyishly
energetic in the West Indian climate could have been possible only to
Dr. JOHN MITCHINSON (Scholar 1851–55 ; Fellow 1855–81 ; president
of the Union Society 1857 ; D.C.L. 1864 ; Select Preacher 1872–3).
He was Head-master of the King's School, Canterbury, 1859–73, and
in 1873 was consecrated for the see of Barbados and the Windward Islands, acting also from 1879 as coadjutor to the Bishop of
Antigua. Retiring in 1881 Bishop Mitchinson accepted the College
living of Sibston. His lordship has been coadjutor to the Bishop of
Peterborough since 1881. Archdeacon of Leicester 1886 ; Select
Preacher 1872–3 and 1892–3; Ramsden Preacher at Cambridge 1883;
Honorary Fellow of the College 1884.—Other Bishops of missionary
sees are: Dr. WILLIAM THOMAS THORNHILL WEBBER (matr. 1856), Vicar
of St. John the Evangelist, Holborn, 1867–85 ; Member of the London
School Board 1882–5; Bishop of Brisbane 1885.—Dr. WILLIAM
MARLBOROUGH CARTER, Scholar 1870. He rowed in the Eight
1870–73, and at Henley in 1872 ; steward of Junior Common Room
1873. After several years' labour in large parishes, Mr. Carter was
placed (1880) in charge of the Etonian Hackney Mission, over which he
presided for ten years. On Michaelmas Day, 1891, he was consecrated
Bishop, Zululand being assigned as his see.—Dr. HENRY EVINGTON
entered the College in the same year as Bishop Carter, aged
twenty-two. He was ordained from Islington in 1874, and worked
as a missionary at Osaka for twenty years. Secretary for the Japan
Mission 1885–8, and Examining Chaplain to Bishop Bickersteth
of Central Japan 1887–94. On March 4, 1894, Mr. Evington was
consecrated for the bishoprick of Kiushiu, South Japan.

Of Dr. Jeune's lieutenants the good-humoured personality and
large figure of THOMAS FREDERICK HENNEY, mentioned on an earlier
page, will long be remembered. Scholar 1829–41 ; Fellow 1841–60;

---

[1] The Bishop's brother, GEORGE HORATIO HADFIELD, was Fellow 1837–44.

Tutor and Junior Dean 1848. Ob. July 13, 1860. 'An excellent lecturer,' writes one of his pupils; 'but I do not think it occurred to him to exercise any influence on us outside the lecture-room.' A polished scholar of the Shrewsbury pattern, he was in the famous First Class in which his contemporary at the College, Jackson, figured. Nineteen years later Henney was one of the first batch of Moderators. Even in his favourite pursuit of fishing he threw the fly and built the stately iambic line simultaneously. Indeed, a thorough wetting while thus preoccupied led to his death. Owing to his sensitiveness to undergraduate false quantities, he kept on his table a bottle of smelling salts, to which from time to time he had recourse. But, morbidly shy, the crudest guesses on the part of the lectured would draw nothing from him but 'Precisely, precisely, precisely.' Bishop Jackson appointed him Prebendary of Lincoln and Examining Chaplain. Henney's bent was, like Jeune's, in a non-antiquarian direction, and, being questioned on returning from his first visit to Lincoln what he thought of the minster, he said, 'I walked round it, but I did not go inside. I thought I should have many opportunities of doing that.' He had been a student of Lincoln's Inn before ordination.—Even less ecclesiastically-minded was that amiable, genially grandiose don, THOMAS DOUGLAS PAGE, Scholar 1855–61, Fellow 1861–72, Bursar 1862, Dean 1864, Proctor 1872, who died Rector of Sibston Sept. 26, 1880. He was outlived by a predecessor in the bursarship, HAVILLAND DE SAUSMAREZ, a Cambridge wrangler, who held a King Charles Fellowship from 1836 to 1851; Bursar 1846; Rector of St. Peter's, Northampton, 1850–73; died April 17, 1882. Mr. de Sausmarez was of a retiring disposition, and was not much known to the undergraduates.— WILLIAM GAY, a Rugbeian, afterwards (1869) Vicar of Burley-on-the-Hill, was elected Fellow (1845–54) at the same time as the brothers EDWARD THOMAS WILLIAM POLEHAMPTON (1845–60), Rector and Vicar of Hartfield 1859, and HENRY STEDMAN POLEHAMPTON, killed at Lucknow—of whom I shall have more to say. Three other brothers were at the College, of whom THOMAS STEDMAN POLE-HAMPTON (Wightwick kin Scholar 1846–57, Fellow 1857–63), became Vicar of Ellel, Lancashire (1864–69), and of St. Bartholomew-the-Less, &c., London (1869–78); Chaplain at Oporto 1878–85.— HENRY STUART FAGAN (Fellow 1850–52) was a very able man, of somewhat explosive Home Rule opinions. He was Head-master successively of Bosworth and of Bath Grammar Schools; Rector of Charlcombe, Bath, 1859–70; Vicar of St. Just-in-Penwith, 1870–72; Rector

of Great Cressingham 1882, in which year he died. His eminent
contemporary as undergraduate and Fellow, GEORGE ROLLESTON, died
also comparatively young, June 16, 1881. He matriculated Dec. 8,
1846, aged seventeen; Scholar 1850–51; Fellow 1851–62; Honorary
Fellow 1862–81; M.D. 1857; Fellow of Merton 1872–81; Fellow
of the Royal and Linnæan Societies; Lee's Reader in Anatomy;
Linacre Professor of Physiology 1860–81. After his death, in 1883,
there was founded to do honour to his memory a University Prize,
consisting of two years' income of about £1,200, for research in
Morphology, Physiology, Pathology, or Anthropology, open to such
members of the Universities of Oxford and Cambridge as have not
exceeded ten years from their matriculation. Professor Rolleston's
striking features are preserved in the crayon drawing presented to
the College by Professor Goldwin Smith, who wrote the Latin lines
underneath.—Dr. CHARLES THOMAS COOTE was Fellow from 1846 to
1851; Radcliffe's Travelling Fellow 1849–59.—EDWARD WILLIAM
HAWKINS, Fellow 1860–70, Senior Dean 1865, became Rector of
Ringshall in 1870.—THOMAS CHARLES LITCHFIELD LAYTON, Fellow
1854–6, was Rector of St. Aldate's 1856–9.—Among living Fellows of
the mid-century whom I have not yet mentioned, the Rev. JOHN ORMOND
(Scholar 1846–56, Fellow 1856–57) has been good enough to furnish
me with several reminiscences of old days. The names of other
Fellows of that time are to be found in Mr. Foster's *Oxford Men and
their Colleges.*

CHAPTER XXXVII.

COLLEGE CUSTOMS, LIFE, CLUBS AND SOCIETIES.

CASTING eyes of retrospect over the Victorian era, we look back to social customs different in many respects from that extreme polish of culture at which we have now arrived. In the memory of living persons dinner was still at four o'clock, undergraduates (in academical costume) promenaded in the High Street, dressed themselves for dinner, and used the skilled offices of the College *tonsor*. Rude digestion was not unknown, and Fellows drank beer, at any rate in their rooms [1]. Smoking was viewed by the elegant with some dislike. It was a favourite undergraduate joke, when the daily tankard of Henney, then dean, was carried up to his rooms over the gateway, to follow it on some pretext, as soon as the dean had had time to light his segar, taken from a large assortment of favourite brands, and to remain, while Henney tried to conceal what he was smoking behind his back, till it might be supposed extinguished. Dr. Birkbeck Hill tells me :—

'I knew an old Somersetshire parson, WILLIAM WILKINS GALE, who entered Pembroke soon after the Peace of 1815 [2]. He had learnt to smoke before entering. A day or two after he came into residence, some men of the College found him smoking in his room. They warned him that he would be "cut" if he continued the practice. He would not give it up, however, and before he left smoking had become pretty common. He must have been a powerful man in his prime, for he had a large frame. As we were walking up St. Aldate's he stopped in front of the Town Hall, and said that just there he had fought and thrashed a "bargee," a noted bruiser of the town. In later life he was a zealous teetotaller. When he was my guest at one of the undergraduates' tables in Hall, an aged scout —Old Harry he was always called—came bustling up to him bearing a

---

[1] In the earlier part of the present Master's time, strong beer was drunk in the old Common Room. The windows of the room had no curtains, and the polished oak floor was uncarpeted till Edwin Parker gave a large rug in 1839. Uncushioned Windsor chairs stood around.

[2] The Rev. W. W. Gale matriculated June 1, 1818, aged sixteen; died Jan. 2, 1872.

great silver tankard, known as the "Overman[1]," which would hold half
a gallon, and crying out, "I say, Mr. Gale, do you remember drinking
off this tankard at a draught?" My friend modestly disclaimed the feat,
which indeed the hardest drinker could not have performed. He owned,
however, to having drained a quart—a sconce—without taking breath, and
so, according to the well-known unwritten law, had made the sconcer pay
for it.'

The cosy system of messes, each ordering its own dinner, in lieu
of the old unappetizing commons, was started by Robert Paul Bent,
already mentioned, about 1848. It was not an economical system, and
has lately been modified. Just before 1848, B——, remembered as a
London dignitary, by self-denial had kept his batells for the year down
to £60. It was one day proclaimed in College: 'B—— is going to
have a friend to breakfast, and has ordered an egg!' But he was
generally respected. There was a good deal of idealism and 'high
seriousness' among young men fifty years since. Mr. Orger speaks
of one who entered the College at the end of Dr. Hall's Mastership,
HENRY BASKERVILLE WALTON, a first-class man, afterwards Fellow,
Tutor and Dean of Merton, and Vicar of St. Cross, Holywell, from
1851 till his death on Oct. 5, 1871. He says: 'Among the greatest
advantages received from his friendship was his introducing to my
notice Whytehead's *College Life*. It opened my eyes to the theory of
it, and to the meaning of many things which surround one in the
University.' Mr. Walton edited with Mr. Medd *Edward VI's First
Prayer Book.* He was brother-in-law of WILLIAM ROBERT BROWELL
(matr. 1824), a former Tutor of Pembroke.

The manciple's slate, used in the old Hall, now the Library, hangs
there now. It is still his duty to make the round of the tables and
note who are dining, for to dine is a part of College rule. The Rev.
John Polehampton says:—

'All I can remember about old Haskins, the Manciple, is his lanky
figure and proportionately lanky MS. book, and his assuring us on one
occasion, "Pickles, sir! Why, pickles is out of season." Also I recall
myself persuading his simplicity (or his good-nature) that my pet King
Charlie[2] was a cat, and so escaping tax! He used to march in about
the middle of dinner and go from table to table, and call each man's name;
to which each answered "Bread" or "Beer," or both; for there was
always a strong spirit of *badinage* afloat. He, on receipt of a reply, or
even no reply, made a mark against each man's name. We never attached

---

[1] Presented by GEORGE OVERMAN, Counsellor-at-law; matr. 1728.
[2] The rule against dogs was not very strictly enforced. Something had to be
done, however, when John Polehampton's smuggled spaniel walked into Hall, and
begged of Henney at the head of the high table.

the slightest importance to the custom, and neither knew, nor cared to know, what it all meant! I should say it lost itself *en route* to the new Hall. I have no remembrance of it there.'

One custom which survived translation to the new Hall is referred to by the Rev. Frederick Arnold [1] thus:—

'There is a curious old custom at Merton which corresponds with one at Pembroke. When dinner is over, the senior Fellow strikes the table three times with a trencher. The sound brings up the butler, who then enters on his book what each Fellow has received from the buttery. Then the grace cup is handed round, and the trenchers being struck once more the Bible clerk says grace.'

The present Vicegerent, my friend Mr. ALFRED THOMAS BARTON, tells me:—' It was always the custom when Grace was said regularly after meat to rap one trencher on another twice. This lasted for almost six or seven years after I came here in 1865. They were two of the old wooden trenchers always used in the Hall until the new Hall was built, and remembered by Prof. Chandler as used in his undergraduate days for the bread and cheese after dinner. I never saw more than these two, and what became of them I never knew. Probably as individual *objects* they may have been neither old nor interesting; but as the last relics of a vanished usage they really were.'

Leave being often given to the lower tables to withdraw before the high table had finished dinner, Camden's composition, popularly supposed to contain an allusion to ' Senatus Populusque Romanus,' but which Johnson told Boswell, towards the end of his life, that he could still repeat, came to be but seldom heard. A grace before meat was therefore introduced in the year 1887. It has points of resemblance to those in use at Corpus Christi, at Christ Church, and at Worcester. The two graces are as follows:—

GRACE BEFORE MEAT.

Pro hoc cibo, quem ad alimonium corporis nostri sanctificatum es largitus, nos Tibi, Pater omnipotens, reverenter gratias agimus; simul obsecrantes ut cibum angelorum, panem verum coelestem, Dei Verbum aeternum Jesum Christum Dominum nostrum nobis impertiare, ut Eo mens nostra pascatur, et per carnem et sanguinem Ejus alamur, foveamur, corroboremur. *Amen.*

---

[1] *Oxford and Cambridge.* A somewhat similar way of giving the signal for Grace continues, I believe, at Brasenose.

AFTER MEAT.

Gratias Tibi agimus, Deus misericors, pro acceptis a Tua bonitate alimentis; enixe comprecantes ut serenissimam nostram Reginam[1] Victoriam, totam regiam familiam, populumque Tuum universum tuta in pace semper custodias. *Amen.* .

The Junior Common Room celebrated its centenary by a Dinner in Hall on June 19, 1894. Though certainly adding to the expenses of some undergraduates, and for a long time confined practically to the wealthier among them, such an institution has given reasonable facilities for sociability and hospitality, across the walnuts and the wine, without the necessity for extravagant outlay. This is the oldest wine-club in Oxford—the Corpus one dates from 1797. Its earlier accounts, beginning in 1794, were rescued recently from a bookstall.

Few members of the College have a recollection going further back than Mr. JOHN EUSTACE GRUBBE, of Southwold, Suffolk, J.P., who was born in the Waterloo year, and matriculated Nov. 22, 1832. Speaking of the Back Lodgings and a masquerade there one summer evening, he writes:—

'I recollect being a member of a certain Secret Club, called by its members, to whom alone its existence was known in those days, the "Orontofoozle Club." The late Master was a member, as were also Jackson (the future Bishop), I think Mackenzie[2], Newton[3], Substance Evans[4], Giffard[5], and Shute[6], and others whose names I do not remember.

'The Club had only an active existence during Collections. Then a meeting was held in a room in the Back Lodgings on the ground floor, and, I think, in the centre of the three blocks of buildings, at the luncheon time, and lasted during the hour allowed for that purpose. A hot luncheon

---

[1] In Jan. 164⅚ the Master of one College 'called for the Grace they said publickly in Hall, and, being taken down, he dashed out the King and the Queen's name, and commanded that henceforth no memory should be made of them.' Gutch, ii. 614.

[2] Bishop HENRY MACKENZIE, matr. 1830. *Vide supra*, p. 479.

[3] FRANCIS WHEAT NEWTON, matr. 1831; of Barton Grange, Somerset; High Sheriff 1861.

[4] The Rev. ARTHUR EVANS, matr. 1830; Rector of Bremilham, Wilts, 1840; and of Somerford Parva 1847; ob. April 11, 1893. Mr. Evans married a sister of the Rev. HENRY WIGHTWICK, Scholar 1827–39; Fellow 1839–42; Rector of Codford St. Peter 1841–84; ob. June 28, 1884.

[5] EDWARD GIFFARD, matr. 1831; son of Sir Ambrose Hardinge Giffard, Bart., of Ceylon. Mr. Giffard died in 1867.

[6] The Rev. HARDWICKE SHUTE, matr. 1832; Vicar of Milton, Oxon, 1848–66; ob. May 11, 1884.

(chops and steaks) was provided, and, I think, beer. Nothing else was allowed. Shutters were closely shut, curtains drawn, and the room lighted with candles. Every member had a name given him at his entrance selected from the Old Testament, and having the same initial letter as his own name. A system of fines was established, consisting of a penny, or halfpenny, for every breach of the Club rules. I cannot, of course, recollect all the rules, as they were numerous, the object being to trap one another into a breach, and so extort a fine and provoke merriment. The following formed part of the code :—1. Calling a member by any but his right name. 2. Quoting Latin or Greek, or making use of any but English words. It was also a fundamental rule not to divulge the existence of the Club, or do or say anything which might lead to its discovery. I do not know what the penalty was. A fine would have been of little use, and expulsion worse still. I remember one member was introduced because he had somehow found out something about the Club, and it was thought advisable to shut his mouth by electing him. It was really a jolly way of breaking the monotony of a very dull business.

' I should say that the *professed* object of the Club was to put a stop to the copper coinage of the Realm—not, I believe, very legal—by absorbing all the pieces ! I need not say that the object was never effected ; but I remember, some years after I had left College, the late Master, then a fellow, upon one of my visits to Oxford, produced a large brown-holland bag brim full of halfpence and pence, and consulted me as to what he should do with its contents. The Club had come to an end. He was treasurer at its close. And no arrangement had been come to as to what was to be done with its assets. I think we determined to give it to the Junior Common Room or the Boat Club.'

Very different has been the grave and serious existence of the ' Johnson,' the College literary society, to whose hebdomadal papers and discussions many can look back not only with edification but with delight. Never since has one cared to track the Origin of Evil, with the metaphysical ardour peculiar to youth, back to its primal fount. Those universal subjects which we determined with the mingled cynicism and generosity, the teachableness and infallibility, of twenty-one, are now a matter of resigned indifference to us. But many friendships were then cemented for life. And was ever tea and coffee better— or stronger? I speak of my own generation only, in recalling the keen, legal mind of W. J. T——, the psychical researches of F. P——, most *naïf* of spiritualists and vegetarians, the Attic salt of St. G. S—— (our senior and mentor), C. A. C——, the mirth-loving champion of everything heterodox, that tender-hearted *malleus schismaticorum*, D. P. H——, *fortemque Gyan fortemque Cloanthum.* The unbroken career of the ' Johnson'—the other day it celebrated its five-hundredth meeting, at which Mr. Austin Dobson's appropriate verses were splendidly declaimed, through the author's modesty, by Canon Ainger, Master of the Temple—was indeed nearly terminated on one occasion by the great constitutional question about the introduction of anchovy toast. For we discussed the least and the greatest topics with equal zest and earnestness. And as, when others were asking ' What is Truth ? '; Charles Lamb's enquiry was rather 'What are trumps?' so it was not unusual to end evenings so philosophical with the 'clean hearth and the rigour of the game.'

The Debating Society, unlike the ' Johnson,' has no proper name. It was originated about 1864[1]. Mr. Horsley writes: 'We started a Debating Society that gave us good practice. Sydney Hall, Wylie, Newbolt, Kershaw, Hull, Overton, and I were frequent speakers; but sometimes it languished, and Hull (now at St. Peter's, Norwich) and I now and then tossed up to see which side of the question we should take.' At a later date the Society was the object of various practical jokes. It is remembered how, the Boat Club being short of funds, a number of boating men, whose nominal subscription to the Debating Society made them legally members of it, went up one night in a body and boldly voted the transference of the accumulated moneys of this intellectual association to athletic purposes.

The Pembroke Musical Society has long had the prerogative of leading off the Commemoration Week with its summer concert.

The annual Pembroke Dinner in London was begun in 1887, through the patriotic energy of HUGH COLIN ROBERT CUNNYNGHAME (*vide supra* p. 367) and my dear friend, side by side with whom I entered College life, HERBERT WILSON GREENE, recently Vice-President of Magdalen College, but to everything Pembrochian still devoted. His cousin, WILLIAM CONYNGHAM GREENE, C.B. (Scholar 1873–5), has been chosen to succeed Sir Jacobus de Wet as the Queen's Agent in the South African Republic. Both are Harrovians.

The moral and religious ebb and flow of the age have been reflected in the undergraduate world more, perhaps, than among their seniors. The least likely men would be caught with new ideas. ' H——,' writes Mr. Horsley, ' was one of a band of high churchmen we had there ; and I remember upbraiding him for going to Hall on Friday, and his answering, "Ah, my dear fellow, I've a Catholic mind, but a Protestant stomach." '

Fifteen years after this there was again strong ecclesiastical feeling in more than one direction. Pembroke supplied a First-Classman as

[1] I am told, however, by Dr. Birkbeck Hill (matr. 1855) that there was a Debating Society in his time. He remembers defending Tennyson in a full room. Mr. Livingstone recalls its existence in 1856. Bishop Mitchinson writes that he learned there how to think on his legs in 1852.

co-founder to the Church Army, and earnest preachers to the Martyrs' Memorial, while simultaneously compline was devoutly said in scouts' pantries fitted up as oratories, pictures and busts of Laud and King Charles [1] adorned many a sage-papered room, oak-apples decked every breast on the twenty-ninth of May, and high church religious feeling showed its reality in more enduring and self-denying ways. Nor must the revival at this time of hippocras and roast swan, and of the real commoner's gown, *talaris* and of four ample breadths, be forgotten. That revival and much of the æsthetic and ecclesiastical movement is associated with the influence of an Etonian whose indomitable and good-tempered courage has since gained him the nickname of the 'School-Board Athanasius.' Neither, in speaking of religious influence, can I forbear to think of two friends, the gentle Bampton Lecturer for this year (1897), whose brilliant academic career is closing for the present with his resignation of the principal Librarianship of the Pusey House, and L. S. M——('Cato Major'), whose Lambeth and Farnham ancestry fitted him to exercise an almost archiepiscopal supervision of our morals; and many more who have since entered the service of Church or State.

At Oxford in the seventies the school of moral and social fervour, which embodied the reaction of the new and emotional against the old and philosophical Liberalism, was attracting to itself many intense and able young men, lacking something perhaps, in some instances, of the Shakesperian and *Elia-tic* spirit. With this movement Pembroke had a passing connexion in the person of ARNOLD TOYNBEE, who showed himself only in the walls of the College, and then was rapt to a higher sphere.

Sir Alfred Milner, now Governor of the Cape, in his memoir of a loved and admired friend, says: 'When little more than eighteen he went away by himself, and spent nearly a year alone at a quiet seaside retreat, reading and thinking, his whole mind possessed, even thus early, with a passionate interest in religion and metaphysics and in the philosophy of history. A year or two later, having, by his father's will, a small sum of money at his command, he resolved to devote it fearlessly to the completion of his education, and, after much pondering over the how and the where, finally turned to Oxford.' Toynbee entered Pembroke as a commoner Feb. 5, 1873. The Master of Balliol (Mr. Jowett), however, 'had taken note of Toynbee almost from the moment of his arrival in Oxford, and had been at considerable pains to get him transferred from Pembroke to Balliol—not without a severe brush with the authorities of the latter [? former] college.' In a letter with which he has favoured me, Sir Alfred writes: 'Toynbee competed for the Brackenbury (History) Scholarship at Balliol in the autumn of 1873. He was beaten by another friend of mine,

[1] Connected, it may be, with the King Charles foundation is a lingering tradition that Pembroke men (and members also of Jesus College and Exeter) have the right to wear a silver tassel. Or was it only Fellows on that foundation ?

Mr. P. Lyttelton Gell, but his papers made a very great impression on the examiners, and Jowett seized the occasion to offer him rooms at Balliol. To this the then Master of Pembroke, Dr. Evans, I think, not unnaturally objected, and it ended in Toynbee's severing his connexion with Pembroke *and the University* for some six months, and re-entering (I fancy this was a fresh matriculation) as an undergraduate at Balliol in the autumn of 1874.' The Pembroke Convention Book records that Mr. Toynbee had, with the Master's consent, stood for a scholarship at Balliol, and been honourably mentioned; but that he had then, without the privity of the Master or the Tutors, made a private arrangement, direct or indirect, with the Master of Balliol to migrate thither as a commoner. Finding the matter arranged without their consent, the College had vetoed it, where-upon Mr. Toynbee applied to become unattached; but the College unanimously refused the request on the ground of ' the obvious facility of the Unattached system for effecting prohibited migrations *indirectly*,' and of the desirability of 'discouraging migrations from College to College.' Toynbee appealed unsuccessfully to the Visitor. The *Spectator* (Dec. 1, 1894) says: ' Dr. Jowett managed to draw him away from Pembroke to Balliol.' It must be added that, unless it be assumed that a small College is bound to discern the future prophets and reformers among its freshmen and hand them over on demand to any bigger institution more desirous or more worthy to be *nutrix leonum*, it is impossible to see why the authorities of Pembroke should have gone out of their way to make an exception in this instance. However, Toynbee's translation was the beginning of an unusually striking career. Though he took only a pass degree (1878), through the discernment of Jowett he was at once appointed to be lecturer in political economy and tutor of Balliol. Without ceasing to be a thinker he plunged into the thick of economical and social politics, and was quickly recognized as a leader in the battle against *laisser-faire*, and in the enthusiastic counter-revolution which aimed at undoing the results of the enthusiasms of an earlier generation of reformers. Toynbee was an idealist rather than a visionary, and might, if he had lived, have achieved something memorable, which only idealists can do. But his bodily powers were unequal to his strenuous spirit; his health broke down, and he died in the spring of 1883, aged thirty. ' Toynbee Hall' in East London preserves his fame in the way with which he would have been best pleased.

Two portraits in the possession of the College record the attachment of members of Pembroke to the late and the present Master. The portrait of Dr. Evans was painted in 1883 by Mr. Ouless, R.A.; that of Dr. Price in 1896 by Mr. Marmaduke Flower. Dr. EVAN EVANS matriculated from Jesus College, June 22, 1831, but migrated to Pembroke, of which he was a Fellow 1843–64, Tutor, Dean, and Vicegerent. On March 8, 1864, he succeeded Dr. Jeune as Master; D.D. 1878; Vice-Chancellor 1878–82. With the exception of his Vice-cancellariate, wrote the *Times* after his death, ' Dr. Evans took little part in the business of the University, but devoted himself entirely to College duties and interests. He was of a hearty, active, genial disposition, possessed of strong common-sense, generous to a fault, a staunch friend, but with a magnanimity which raised him both in and out of office above the littleness of partizanship. He was of a manly character and vigorous physique; in his day an enthusiastic cricketer, he never lost his interest in the game. Even in his old age he was an ardent fives-player, and, in short, he appreciated all manly sports.' Mr. Ouless's vigorous painting hardly does justice, perhaps, to the venerable and kindly look, the *mitis sapientia*, of the late Master. Dr. Evans died at the College, Nov. 23, 1891, aged seventy-seven. The appointment of a successor fell to the Visitor, the Marquess of Salisbury. It cannot be necessary here to dwell on the distinguished career, and the weighty services to the University, and not least to the University Press, of the present eminent holder of the office, Dr. BARTHOLOMEW PRICE [1].

THE BOAT CLUB.

The Club was formed in the Michaelmas term of 1841, chiefly through the efforts of Mr. MARTIN JOSEPH ROUTH (Fellow 1846 till his death in 1874), nephew of the famous President of Magdalen.

1842. Starting twelfth the boat made six bumps in the seven nights. The head boat (Oriel) being unable to row at Henley requested Pembroke to take its place. Owing to the absence of some of the crew this could not be done. The late Dean of Canterbury, ROBERT PAYNE SMITH, rowed in this crew.

1843. Silver oars and rudder purchased for College Pairs.

1845. HENRY LEWIS [2] rowed No. 4 in the Oxford Boat.

1846. JOHN and HENRY STEDMAN POLEHAMPTON (nicknamed ' Ben ') distinguished themselves in the Henley pairs, and in the next year also. The eight was a 'queer boat of Noulton's with steerer (HENRY SWABEY [3]) in the middle.' Mr. HENRY POLEHAMPTON rowed bow at Putney for the University. The present flag was adopted.

1847. The Eight (3rd) was ' universally acknowledged to be the best on the River.' The Torpid went to second place. This year (or the year

---

[1] University Mathematical Scholar 1842; Sedleian Professor of Natural Philosophy 1853; Member of the Hebdomadal Council 1856; Curator of the University Chest; Curator of the Bodleian Library; Perpetual Delegate of the Press; Delegate of the University Museum; F.R.S.; F.R.Astr.S.; Honorary Fellow of Queen's College 1868; served as a Royal Commissioner for enquiring into the Property and Income of the Universities of Oxford and Cambridge, 1872; Fellow of Winchester College 1873; Visitor of Greenwich Observatory. Dr. Price is in his 240th term of continuous residence, without interruption, counting (as this College has always hitherto counted) four terms to the year. He matriculated March 16, 1837.

[2] Vicar of Stowmarket 1861; ob. 1876.   [3] *Vide supra*, p. 386.

before) Messrs. EDWARD [1] and HENRY POLEHAMPTON and FREDERICK KOE swam in one and a half hours from Iffley to Oxford. (See *Sporting Magazine.*) Scratch Fours instituted.

1849. 'Dissension and lukewarmness throughout the Club.' Six of the crew had left, and the Eight went down to eleventh place.

1850. Christ Church [2], in gratitude for the loan of a boat at a critical juncture during the races, presented a handsome Cup for Fours.

1852. A Pembroke Eight rowed over at Henley for the Ladies' Plate. WILLIAM OLIVER MEADE-KING [3] stroked the winning University Four, and rowed No. 7 in the victorious Eight at Putney.

1853. Mr. MEADE-KING stroked the winning University Eight at Henley, and No. 3 in a Four which gained the Stewards' Challenge Cup. The Pembroke Eight and Four at Henley were beaten.

1854. Messrs. MEADE-KING, THOMAS AYLESBURY HOOPER [4], and GEORGE LILLY MELLISH [5] rowed stroke, 5, and 7 in the Eight which beat Cambridge at Putney by five lengths. A Pembroke Four won the Stewards' Cup at Henley.

1855. Three of the crew falling ill, the boat was withdrawn from the College races.

1856. RICHARD NEWMAN TOWNSEND rowed No. 5 in the Oxford Eight at Putney.

1857. A year to be marked with a white stone. The Torpid went second; the Eight went up seven places (to fifth); a Four, after one of the hardest and most splendid contests ever witnessed, won the Visitors' Challenge Cup at Henley from the Lady Margaret crew, representing Cambridge; the Pembroke Eight rowed a magnificent race for the Ladies' Plate; the Four beat the London and Henley crews and carried off the Wyfold Challenge Cup; Messrs. JOHN ARKELL [6] and POWNOLL WILLIAM PHIPPS [7] won the Silver Oars in the O.U.B.C. Pairs; Mr. ARKELL occupied the third thwart in the University Eight which beat Cambridge at Putney by ten lengths. He also stroked a scratch Oxford Eight, with Mr. PHIPPS rowing 7 and CHARLES PAINE PAULI [8] 3, which on the Eton water beat the best Eton Eight ever turned out; and at the close of this glorious year Pembroke won the University Fours, accomplishing the distance in eight minutes and almost 'Cherwellizing' Balliol and other good boats matched against it. Mr. ARKELL soon after was elected President of the University Boat Club. He had stroked the O. U. B. C. Eight defeated at Henley.

[1] *Vide supra,* p. 481.

[2] A nickname given by Christ Church men early in this century to Pembroke was 'St. Opposite's.' The Rev. Prebendary Barff, the Pembroke captain in that year, is my authority for the above account of the origin of the Christ Church Cup Fours. It is also the traditional account.

[3] Rector of Cooling, Kent; ob. 1882.

[4] Captain and Hon. Major, Somerset Militia.

[5] Resident Magistrate, Canterbury, New Zealand; ob. 1881.

[6] Rev. John Arkell, M.A., now Rector of St. Ebbe's. The crafts in which the Pembroke crews rowed this year were specially built by Mat Taylor of Newcastle.

[7] Rector of Chalfont St. Giles 1886.　　　[8] Of the Inner Temple 1867.

1858. The Torpid became Head of the River. Mr. ARKELL again rowed at Putney. His sudden absence from the races at Henley caused the loss of the Visitors' and Wyfold Cups. RONALD HENRY CHEATLE rowed No. 2 in the winning Trial Eight, and WILLIAM RICHARD PORTAL steered the other boat.

1859. Mr. PORTAL again was coxswain in one of the Trial Eights, and Mr. ARKELL stroked the winning Oxford Eight at Putney, and also the Oxford Pair which won the Silver Goblets at Henley.

1860. The Rev. HENRY MOWLD ROBINSON, D.D. (*vide supra*, p. 476) presented a very handsome Cup for Fours.

1861. PHILIP EDWARD POPPE rowed No. 2 in the winning Trial Eight.

1862. At Tewkesbury Regatta Messrs. POPPE and FREDERICK ORMISTON LYUS won the Town Plate for Pair Oars, and a crew composed of six Pembroke and two University men beat the Tewkesbury Eight by ten lengths over a short course. A Barge was purchased.

1864. GILBERT GEORGE COVENTRY[1] rowed in the winning Trial Eight, and THOMAS WOOD[3] in the other. The former was steered by WALTER RALEIGH CARR[3].

1865. Mr. COVENTRY rowed No. 4 and Mr. WOOD No. 6 in the University Eight which beat Cambridge by four lengths.

1866. LEWIS ADDIN KERSHAW[4] stroked the losing Trial Eight.

1867. The Eight went down six places.

1868. The Eight recovered five places, and was entered at Henley for the Thames Challenge Cup and the Ladies' Plate, winning the former. HERBERT AUGUSTUS SALWEY (*vide supra* p. 369) presented a pair of silver sculls to be competed for.

1869. JOSEPH WILLIAM BAXENDALE rowed No. 3 in the winning Trial Eight.

1871. ROBERT LESLEY[5] stroked the University Eight at Putney, and was elected President of the O. U. B. C., which office he held for three years. Mr. LESLEY proved one of the finest strokes ever produced at Oxford. At Henley the Eight won the Ladies' Plate in brilliant style, but Pembroke was defeated for the Visitors' Challenge Cup. RICHARD STOVIN MITCHISON[6] rowed No. 4 in the losing Trial Eight.

1872. Mr. LESLEY rowed No. 7, and Mr. MITCHISON No. 6, in the University Eight.

The Red Rose, starting fourth, went to the Head of the River. To commemorate this happy event, Mr. RICHARD LAURENCE PEMBERTON (High Sheriff of Durham 1861), formerly a most zealous member of the Club, presented a valuable silver ewer to the College, with the names of the crew inscribed. The Eight were defeated for the Ladies' Plate at Henley, but a Pembroke Four won the Visitors' Challenge Cup by one

[1] Rector of Woolstone, Glouc., grandson of the seventh Earl of Coventry.
[3] Rector of Grimoldby, Linc., 1872.
[3] Vicar of St. John in Bedwardine, Worcester, 1881.
[4] Of the Inner Temple 1872. *Vide supra*, p. 488.
[5] J.P. for North Riding; Captain Yorkshire Artillery Militia.
[6] Rector of Barby, near Rugby, 1880.

of the finest races ever witnessed. EDWARD HENRY BAYLY rowed No. 3 in the winning Trial Eight.

1873. Mr. R. S. MITCHISON rowed No. 5 in the University Eight. Sliding-seats were used for the first time. HENRY McDOUGALL COURTNEY rowed bow in the winning Trial Eight. The College Eight lost a place.

1874. The Eight went Head of the River, but finished third. ARTHUR MOORE MITCHISON[1] and Mr. COURTNEY rowed No. 4 and No. 7 in the winning and losing Trial Eights respectively.

1875. Pembroke was represented in the University Eight by Mr. COURTNEY and Mr. A. M. MITCHISON. JAMES COLAM SALTER[2] rowed in the Trial Eights.

1876. Messrs. COURTNEY and MITCHISON again rowed at Putney. JOHN WILLIAM WATNEY BOOTH[3] rowed No. 5 in the winning Trial Eight.

1877. The Torpid, starting third, went Head of the River, almost 'Cherwellizing' the other boats. The Eight, considered to be quite the fastest boat on the river, went up one place to second, and, but for the illness of one of the crew, would no doubt have ended Head like the Torpid. ' Qui color est puniceae flore prior rosae?' Messrs. BOOTH and HERBERT BURROWS SOUTHWELL[4] rowed in the losing and winning Trial Eights respectively. GEORGE MURTON steered the winning boat.

1878. The Torpid remained Head of the River. Mr. SOUTHWELL rowed No. 3 in the magnificent University Eight which beat Cambridge by twelve lengths. He rowed this year in the losing Trial Eight.

1879. Mr. SOUTHWELL rowed No. 4 in the Oxford boat. He also stroked one of the Trial Eights, but in the end the frost prevented any race. The Torpid remained Head.

1880. Mr. SOUTHWELL again rowed No. 4 in the University Eight. The Torpid and Eight went down five places each.

1881. The Eight went down five more places.

1882. The Eight went up five places.

1886. The Torpid for the first time entered the Second Division. FREDERICK WYKEHAM CHANCELLOR steered the winning Trial Eight.

1888. ARTHUR VILLIERS BLAKEMORE rowed No. 2 in the winning Trial Eight.

1889. ARTHUR KERSHAW ELWORTHY and GEORGE MERVYN LAW-SON presented to the Club a pair of Silver Goblets to be competed for in coxswainless canvas pairs.

1891. The Eight made five bumps in four nights, and nearly made seven. Pembroke put on an Eight at Henley for the Ladies' Plate and Thames Cup, but it was unsuccessful. The College also reappeared in the University Fours. NEVILL KENDAL stroked, and ARTHUR BELL MORLAND steered, the winning Trial Eight.

---

[1] Of the Inner Temple 1879. The Mitchison brothers were both Eton oars. Of an earlier date was another aquatic Etonian, NAUNTON LEMUEL SHULDHAM (matr. 1850, Fellow of Magdalen College 1865-7), afterwards tutor to H.R.H. Prince Leopold and Vicar of Scawby. Ob. 1874.

[2] Mathematical Master at Cheltenham.

[3] Vicar of South Darley, Derbyshire, 1882.

[4] Denyer and Johnson Scholar. Now Principal of Lichfield Theological College.

HENRY STEDMAN POLEHAMPTON, mentioned above as a 'blue' and an energetic captain, has been called 'the hero chaplain of Lucknow.' He entered the College, like others of his family, with a Wightwick kin-scholarship, bringing with him from Eton a rowing and cricketing reputation. The Polehamptons had a passion for rescuing the capsized, and he was awarded in 1845 the Humane Society's medal *ob civem servatum* for saving a drowning man in Iffley Lasher, two days after the melancholy fate of Messrs. Gaisford and Phillimore at Sandford. Fellow 1845–56. After ordination he was presented by the College to St. Aldate's, but, finding that the benefice would void his fellowship, he accepted the assistant-curacy of St. Chad's, Shrewsbury. His assiduity during the cholera visitation of 1849 endeared him to his flock. In 1855, being offered a Bengal chaplaincy, he married Miss Emily Alnatt. Bringing his bride to Oxford to take farewell of the familiar scenes, he writes home of the University scratch Fours, in which he had 'a last pull for auld lang syne,' two other 'blues' rowing in the same boat, and won a pint pewter, which he took to India to remind him of College days. Less than two years later he found an Indian grave, at Lawrence's feet, by the banks of the Gumti. The first mutterings of the awful impending storm were beginning when Polehampton went out, his station being Lucknow. His diary and letters (studded with affectionate reminiscences of School and College) give a graphic picture of the outbreak of the Mutiny and of its horror. On the ninth day of the Siege, during which he was occupied in ministering to the wounded and the cholera and small-pox patients, in cheering the combatants, consoling the bereaved, encouraging the tender women and children, and other corporal and spiritual works of mercy, he was shot through the body. He believed himself to be recovering, and two days before his death was performing his sacred function for his fellow-sufferers in hospital, but on the twelfth day from that on which he received his wound he died, July 20, 1857—not less constant in death, though finding a less cruel end, than a fellow-chaplain, who, falling wounded, was dragged into church and there crucified, being nailed to his own pulpit, which was then set on fire. Mr. Polehampton's young widow was twice struck by a bullet, but not seriously. An officer lying wounded in the same hospital tells us that, while he was dying, his cheerfulness and composure were the support and comfort of all the sick and dying round him. His last words were 'Peace, now and for ever.' Brigadier Inglis, in his despatch to the Government, mentions 'the honoured names of

Birch, of Polehampton, of Barbor, and of Gall,' who had been ' the tender and solicitous nurses of the wounded and the dying.' In reply, the Governor-General in Council ' cannot forgo the pleasure of doing justice' to these four names. His lordship also says: ' The Governor-General in Council has read with great satisfaction the testimony borne by Brigadier Inglis to the sedulous attention given to the spiritual comforts of his comrades by the Rev. Mr. Polehampton and the Rev. Mr. Harris. The first, unhappily, has not survived his labours.' This Mr. Harris rowed in the Brasenose boat which bumped the Pembroke Eight in which Polehampton rowed. A simple Memoir of their brother was published in 1885 by the Rev. Edward and the Rev. Thomas S. Polehampton, Fellows of the College, aided by Dr. Rolleston.

In the great story of Missionary labour, the name of HENRY DE WINT BURRUP, who rowed bow in the Eight in 1850, has an honoured place. He accompanied Bishop Mackenzie to Capetown in 1860, and shared his perils and toils. Livingstone ascribed the fever which ended the Bishop's life to the incautiousness induced by Burrup's ' wonderful feat' of the ascent of the Shirè river without mishap. The last moments of Mackenzie were soothed by this devoted comrade, who himself dug the Bishop's grave under a large tree, and there laid his remains. A fortnight later, on February 23, 1862, Burrup himself sank and died. He lies buried near Magomero.

With Polehampton and Burrup may be named RICHARD NEWMAN TOWNSEND, mentioned above as a ' blue' in 1856, who died of typhus in the performance of his duty as a surgeon-major, Cork City Artillery, in March, 1877. The *Medical Press*, after describing the labours of this good physician, said: ' Every shop in Queenstown put up a sign of mourning, and all the ships in the harbour had their flag half-mast high. His funeral was attended by upwards of two thousand people of all classes.'

The foregoing record illustrates the way in which a small College passes through periods of glory and of depression. From 1829 to 1883 fourteen Pembroke men obtained the rowing Blue. Only five Colleges show a larger number. Three of the fourteen were Presidents of the O. U. B. C.; three rowed stroke for the University; nine entered into Holy Orders.

The Cricket and other athletic records in my possession are but fragmentary. The names of four Blues are of note among cricketers— Sir JOHN SCOTT[1], K.C.M.G., now Judicial Adviser to H.H. the Khedive

[1] *Vide supra*, p. 478.

(Steward of Junior Common Room 1862), WILLIAM HARRY PATTERSON (matr. 1878), his brother JOHN IRVIN PATTERSON (B.A. 1882), and EDWARD THORNHILL BECKETT SIMPSON (matr. 1886). In recent years EDWARD FOORD-KELCEY, ARTHUR EDWARD NEWTON, and CHARLES LUSHINGTON HICKLEY have upheld the honour of the College in the cricket field.

In the Inter-University Sports HENRY WILLIAM RUSSELL DOMVILE won the Weight-putting for Oxford in 1871 and in 1872. In 1885 EDGAR ROGERS HOLLAND was victorious in the One Mile race, and in 1891 PERCY ROBERT LLOYD[1] in the Quarter-Mile. JOHN LASCELLES in 1868, LEWIS STROUD in 1888, and GEORGE ARTHUR HEGINBOTTOM in 1890 won the University Challenge Cue. Mr. STROUD is a well-known bicycling champion. ARTHUR GLYNDWR FOULKES has won several Challenge Cups with the rifle; CHARLES JOHN WINSER and JOHN WILLIAM WARD have also represented the skill of the University Rifle Corps.

The Union Society has had for President—RICHARD DURNFORD, afterwards Bishop of Chichester; DRUMMOND PERCY CHASE, now Principal of St. Mary Hall (1842); JOHN MITCHINSON (1857), afterwards Bishop of Barbados; and ARTHUR SLOMAN (1875), now Head-master of Birkenhead School. The following have acted as Librarian—JOHN COKE FOWLER (1837), JOHN MITCHINSON (1856-7); EDWARD MOORE, now Principal of St. Edmund Hall (1858-9). As Secretary—HENRY MOWLD ROBINSON (1859); HENRY CHARLES WRIGHT (1875); FRANCIS SCOTT WEBSTER (1880).

Pembroke was one of the earliest Colleges to institute College Sports or 'Grinds,' viz. in 1856.

As this sheet passes through the press, the death is announced of a regarded Lincoln prebendary, JAMES MICHAELMAS BARRETT, thirty years Vicar of St. Peter's in Eastgate, a philologist and Hebraist. At Pembroke, which he entered in 1847, he was noted as an athlete, both on the river (winning the Pairs) and on the running-path. He died March 29, 1897.

[1] Son of Mr. Edward Lloyd, the founder and proprietor of *Lloyd's Weekly* and of the *Daily Chronicle*.

CHAPTER XXXVIII.

MINUTES.

THE Minutes of Conventions begin in 1772. I put down here some of the more noticeable entries not recorded elsewhere.

1772. Caution fixed as follows:—Gentlemen Commoners £24, Commoners £12, Scholars £10, Battlers £6, Servitors £4.

'Ordered that for the future every Person who shall without Leave absent Himself from the Sacrament shall contribute to the Relief of the Poor in the following Proportion: each Gentleman Commoner Five Shillings; Commoners, Scholars and Batchelors of Arts two shillings and sixpence; Servitors one shilling. Which sums are to be put on their names in the Buttery Book, and be allow'd at the end of each Quarter to the Bursar for charitable Purposes—Clergymen of all Ranks who serve churches are excused.'

Sir John Peshall, the antiquarian editor of Anthony à Wood, claimed Founder's kin to Tesdale for his son, but the pedigree put in was disallowed.

A Hebrew Lecturer was appointed, and a senior and a junior Moderator.

'Ordered in Convention that every Fellow upon his admission deposit three guineas for Plate-money and every Scholar fifteen shillings.'

1774. 'Agreed that for the future one Gaudy only (at which every member of the College shall stand to 2s.) should be substituted in the room of the seven which it has been hitherto the custom of the College to observe in the course of the year, and that the day on which such Gaudy is to be kept shall be the 29th day of June[1].'

1776. The word 'scout' appears in the Minutes.

1777. The College roof and parapet wall were repaired.

1789. Gentlemen-Commoners' Plate Money to be £10.

£100 was advanced to the Bodleian Library, to bear no interest.

---

[1] The day of the Incorporation of the College in 1624. But the present Gaudy is on the first Thursday in November. See p. 334.

It was repaid in 1791. The French Revolution was strewing Europe with the wreck of precious libraries, and a unique opportunity presented itself for the purchase of books. Three other Colleges lent sums (Gutch, ii. 949).

1790, Feb. 22. Twenty guineas were unanimously voted 'towards raising a monument in Westminster Abbey to the Memory of the late Dr. Samuel Johnson.' This was erected finally in St. Paul's, the epitaph being written by Dr. Parr, the 'Whig Johnson.' The colossal figure by Bacon cost 1,100 guineas, easily raised by the exertions of the Literary Club.

1792, Nov. 3. £20 voted 'for relieving the French refugee clergy[1].'

Nov. 20. £147 18s. 7d. voted for repairs of the Chapel.

1794, June 3. Forty guineas voted 'from the College Bag, as a subscription towards raising Troops for the internal defence of the kingdom.'

1795. A fee of 10s. to be required for the use of the Library of every Commoner and Scholar, and 20s. of every Gentleman Commoner at the time of admission. (*Vide infra*, p. 502, under the year 1883).

1796. Caution in future to be, Commoners £15, Scholars £12, Independent Masters and others £4.

1797, June 10. Agreed 'to pave from Christ Church before the College, and likewise the whole of Beef Lane, according to Survey,' the College to advance the money to the Commissioners.

1798, Feb. 13. 'Whereas in the present state of publick affairs many corporate Bodies have offered voluntary contributions for the assistance of Government, we, the Master, Fellows and Scholars of Pembroke College have ordered that the Sum of one Hundred Pounds be paid into the Bank as the voluntary Contribution of the College towards raising the Supplies granted by an Act of the present Session of Parliament entitled "An Act for granting to his Majesty an Aid and Contribution for the Prosecution of the war."'

1799. 'In future, without having any Retrospect, the third[2] of College Rooms shall never in any Case exceed the Sum of £25.'

1802. His Grace the Duke of Portland, as Visitor, was appealed

[1] Two thousand copies of the Vulgate New Testament were printed at the Clarendon Press in 1796, at the charges of the University, 'in usum Cleri Gallicani in Anglia exulantis.' 'The University has sent its copies to the venerable Bishop of St. Pol de Leon for distribution, accompanied by a letter, analogous to the generous sentiments which dictate this honourable mark of esteem for the French clergy, who are fully sensible of the value of the gift.' *Gent. Mag.* vol. lxvi. p. 961. In 1792 the University had sent nearly £1200 for the support of the refugee priests.

[2] See p. 413.

to as to whether the Ossulston Fellows were eligible for presentation to the Rectory of St. Aldate's.

'In consideration of the Difficulty and Loss which Mrs. White the Pastry Woman [1] to the College found in Collecting the Sums due to Her from the different members of the College for milk and Cream, &c., resolved that in future those articles should be entered on the College Books at the end of the Quarter, the Bursars receiving the accustomed Poundage.'

1804. The Duke of Portland decided in favour of Guernsey, as against Jersey, presenting for the King Charles I fellowship.

1806. £100 voted to augment the St. Aldate's living.

1808. A sub-librarian appointed, viz. one of the Oades Exhibitioners.

£460 spent on College repairs.

'Keeping a Week' defined as the *victus et cubile* of four days out of seven.

1813. Three guineas contributed 'towards the Collation of the LXX, now preparing for the Rev. Mr. Parsons.'

1814. The offices of Obsonator, or Manciple, and Cook severed.

Tuition fees to be increased, viz. Gentlemen Commoners to twenty-six guineas, Scholars and Commoners to thirteen guineas.

1815. Caution money to be increased, viz. Gentlemen Commoners to £40, Scholars and Commoners to £30, Servitors to £8.

Plate money to be increased, viz. Fellows to five guineas, Scholars to three guineas.

1816. Twenty guineas voted for completing the rebuilding of St. Ebbe's Church.

1817. Fifteen guineas subscribed 'in aid of the labouring poor this winter.'

1818. Fifty guineas voted towards the subscription for promoting the enlargement and building of churches and chapels.

Fifty guineas subscribed to Valpy's Delphin edition of the Classics.

No Scholar to be admitted Fellow who has been refused a testamur —(this rule was enforced in 1821 and in 1838)—unless subsequently he obtain a first class or be placed in the upper part of the second class.

1820. An appeal to Lord Grenville respecting 'the Grace of this House' is recorded.

---

[1] No pastry was supplied from the College kitchen. Well-known pastry women of this date were 'Mother Smith' and 'Tippety Ward,' whose street-cries were an Oxford feature.

1825. Twenty guineas voted towards the repair of St. Clement's Church.

1826. Twenty guineas towards building an English Episcopal Church at Amsterdam.

1839. ' Mr. Roberts[1], fellow on the Wightwick foundation, having notified to the Master that he has become possessed of some freehold property, his fellowship was declared vacant, and Mr. Henry Wightwick, senior scholar, elected in his room.'

(A little while before, a Tesdale Fellow's marriage in the East Indies had been notified.)

1841. ' Mrs. Elizabeth Whitelock having died, the Master appointed her Daughter Sarah Whitelock to succeed her in the Office of Pastry Woman, &c.[2] to the College.'

1845. Commissariat system revised.

Resolved ' that the payment for trenchers shall cease.' Also ' fork-money.' (A number of charges formerly specified are now included under ' College Expenses.' The actual kitchen and buttery charges are below cost price.)

1858. Feb. 24. Among other regulations respecting the common worship of the College is this :—

' The extent to which they shall attend Divine Service is left to the conscience of the Senior Members. Undergraduates will be required to attend eight times at least in each week, of which two shall be on Sunday, and four at the Morning Service. Graduates shall, if on the foundation, wear surplices and hoods on Sundays, Festivals, and their eves ; undergraduate Scholars to appear in their ordinary academical dress.'

(There is no record of the last clause of this rule being rescinded. Yet undergraduates on the foundation wear surplices on all Sundays, holydays, and vigils.)

1865. Dues, fees, and room rents revised.

Bible Clerks, ' their special duties having ceased,' were converted into Exhibitioners.

(They said grace in Hall, and pricked the names of the men in chapel, sitting one on each side on a little projecting bracket. Reading the Vulgate aloud during meals had been discontinued.)

---

[1] SAMUEL WALLIS ROBERTS, B.D., matr. 1806, aet. 14, son of BRYAN ROBERTS, D.C.L., of Antony, Cornwall (matr. 1771).

[2] Several kinds of pudding and tart, described on a list, were brought in on trays and distributed by her from the buttery. She must be distinguished from the 'dessert-woman,' Mrs. Sykes. This purveyor of a primitive form of dessert used to go with her basket containing fruit, candied peel, &c., to the Senior, and then to the Junior, Common Room ; after which she took her station in the gateway awaiting a summons to any of the men's rooms.

1866. Mar. 16. Resolved ' That the Choral Service in chapel be continued for the present on the voluntary principle.

' That the Master be requested to order the discontinuance of those practices in the mode of conducting the choral Service which seem to him objectionable, and that no changes be hereafter introduced without the consent of the Master and the acting Dean.'

1868. Mar. 4. £20 voted as an annual contribution towards the support of the Chapel Choir.

1868. The College took the Buttery and Kitchen into its own hands.

1872. Mar. 18. The Master was authorized to sign and send to the Most Honourable the Visitor a memorial praying his Lordship to take such steps as in his wisdom·he should think best in order to save the rights of the Master and the interests of the College from the operation of the Dean and Canons Resignation Bill.

1873. A shortened form of Morning Prayer authorized.

The College contributed half the cost of putting a railing instead of a wall to St. Aldate's churchyard, the corner next the College gate to be rounded.

1875. Resolved to keep a set of rooms for the use of the College servants.

1877. Resolved that £30 a year be paid for the purchase of books for the Library.

' The Master having laid before the Meeting a requisition signed by twenty-nine undergraduates and Bachelors of the College, asking for more frequent opportunities of receiving the Holy Communion, the request was acceded to.'

(There was instituted a weekly Celebration, in accordance with the rubrick relating to Colleges.)

Combination with Merton College for Scholarship examinations was instituted.

1882. Contribution towards the proposed drainage of the Thames Valley between Oxford and Sandford.

1883. An Undergraduate's Library established.

(*Vide* p. 499. In 1852 undergraduates had the use of the College library, paying an entrance fee of one guinea, and a guinea annual subscription. When I came up, in 1875, this had been discontinued.)

The first Honorary Fellows were elected, viz. the Right Rev. and Right Hon. Dr. JOHN JACKSON, Lord Bishop of London, and the Right Rev. Dr. JOHN MITCHINSON, sometime Lord Bishop of Barbados and the Windward Islands.

APPENDIX A.

UNIVERSITY OFFICES.

THE following members of Broadgates and of Pembroke have filled various high offices and chairs in the University :—

Chancellor.

1397–1400. PHILIP REPYNGDON, Cardinal.

Vice-Chancellor or Commissary.

1467. THOMAS WALTON, LL.D., Principal 1458.
? 1557 and 1562–4. THOMAS WHITE, D.C.L., Principal. Warden of New College.
1765–68. DAVID DURELL, D.D., Principal of Hertford.
1820–24. GEORGE WILLIAM HALL, D.D., Master.
1858–62. FRANCIS JEUNE, D.C.L., Master.
1878–82. EVAN EVANS, D.D., Master.

Burgess.

1660–61. SIR THOMAS CLAYTON, M.D., Fellow ; Reg. Prof. Medicine 1647 ; Warden of Merton 1661.

Assessor in the Chancellor's Court.

1753–60. SIR WILLIAM BLACKSTONE, D.C.L., Scholar ; Fellow of All Souls ; Principal of New Inn Hall 1761 ; Judge in the Court of Common Pleas.

Regius Professor of Divinity.

1865–71. ROBERT PAYNE SMITH, D.D., Scholar; Canon of Christ Church ; Dean of Canterbury.

Regius Professor of Civil Law.

1546–53. JOHN STORY, D.C.L., Principal of Broadgates 1537.
1611–20. JOHN BUDDEN, D.C.L., Principal of New Inn Hall 1609; Principal of Broadgates 1619.

Regius Professor of Medicine.

1612–47. THOMAS CLAYTON, M.D., Principal and Master.
1647–65. SIR THOMAS CLAYTON, M.D., Burgess.
1729–30. WILLIAM BEAUVOIR, M.D., Fellow.

Margaret Professor of Divinity
1676–91.   JOHN HALL, D.D., Master; Bishop of Bristol.

Savilian Professor of Geometry.
1742–65.   NATHANIEL BLISS, M.A., Astronomer Royal.

Sedleian Professor of Natural Philosophy.
1853.   BARTHOLOMEW PRICE, D.D., F.R.S., Master.

Camden Professor of Ancient History.
1622–47.   DEGORY WHEARE, M.A., Fellow of Exeter; Principal of
Gloucester Hall 1626.

Professor of Poetry.
1751–56.   WILLIAM HAWKINS, M.A., Fellow; Bampton Lecturer
1787.

Lord Almoner's Professor of Arabic.
1780–1813.   HENRY FORD, D.C.L., Principal of Magdalen Hall.

Vinerian Professor of Common Law.
1758–62.   SIR WILLIAM BLACKSTONE, D.C.L.

Waynflete Professor of Moral and Metaphysical Philosophy.
1867–1889.   HENRY WILLIAM CHANDLER, M.A., Fellow.

Linacre Professor of Human and Comparative Anatomy.
1860–81.   GEORGE ROLLESTON, M.D., Fellow; Fellow of Merton.

Reader in Ecclesiastical History.
1884–90.   EDWIN HATCH, M.A., Grinfield Lecturer 1880-84; Bampton Lecturer 1880.

Grinfield Lecturer on the LXX.
1880–84.   EDWIN HATCH, M.A.

Radcliffe's Observer.
1860.   ROBERT MAIN, M.A., F.R.S., F.R.A.S.

Bampton Lecturer.
1787.   WILLIAM HAWKINS, M.A.
1794.   THOMAS WINTLE, B.D.
1867.   EDWARD GARBETT, M.A.
1869.   ROBERT PAYNE SMITH, D.D.
1877.   CHARLES ADOLPHUS ROW, M.A.
1880.   EDWIN HATCH, M.A.
1897.   ROBERT LAWRENCE OTTLEY, M.A., Scholar; Senior Student
of Christ Church; Fellow and Dean of Magdalen; Principal Librarian of
the Pusey House.

Reader in Chemistry.
1788–92.   THOMAS BEDDOES, M.D.

Lecturer of Grammar to the University.
1705.   SAMUEL SWYNFEN.

UNIVERSITY PRIZES.

The following University prizes have been won by members of Pembroke :—

Craven Fellow.

1888. HENRY ARNOLD TUBBS, Scholar.

Craven Scholar.

1858. HERBERT CRAVEN.

1879. ROBERT LAWRENCE OTTLEY, King Charles I Scholar; Sen. Student of Ch. Ch.; Tutor of Keble; Fellow and Divinity Dean of Mag-dalen; Principal Librarian of the Pusey House.

Radcliffe's Travelling Fellow.

1822. GEORGE HALL, Scholar, M.A., M.B., M.D. 1823; F.R.C.P. 1830. See *Gentleman's Magazine*, 1845, ii. 320.

1832. CHARLES DAVID BADHAM. Incorporated from Emmanuel College, Cambridge, 1829. Afterwards a leading physician. His brother Charles ('Badham of Wadham'), Professor of Sydney University, was 'pronounced to be the greatest scholar of his day.' Their father, Dr. CHARLES BADHAM, Regius Professor of Physic in Glasgow University, entered Pembroke May 8, 1806; ob. Nov. 10, 1845.

1849. CHARLES THOMAS COOTE, Fellow.

1867. WILLIAM HENRY CORFIELD, Fellow.

1875. CHARLES WILLIAM MANSELL MOULLIN, Fellow; Hunterian Professor, Royal College of Surgeons, 1892.

1886. HERBERT PENNELL HAWKINS, Scholar.

1893. WALTER RAMSDEN, Fellow.

Vinerian Scholar.

1859. FREDERICK PHIPPS ONSLOW.

1886. JAMES STUART SEATON, Scholar.

Dean Ireland's Scholar.

1841. JAMES PEERS TWEED, Scholar; Fellow of Exeter.

(1877 and 1888, *proxime accessit* ROBERT LAWRENCE OTTLEY.)

Boden Scholar.

1833. WILLIAM ALLDER STRANGE, Scholar.

1840. ROBERT PAYNE SMITH, Scholar; Reg. Prof. of Divinity; Dean of Canterbury.

Mathematical Scholar.

1842. BARTHOLOMEW PRICE, Scholar; Fellow; Master.

1847. HENRY STUART FAGAN, Scholar; Fellow.

1853. CHARLES JOSEPH FAULKNER, Scholar; Fellow and Mathematical Tutor of University.

1856. CHARLES JOSEPH FAULKNER.

(1858. *Proxime accessit* EDWARD MOORE, Principal of St. Edmund Hall.)

1868. CHRISTOPHER HENRY EDMUND HEATH, Scholar.

1874. CHARLES LEUDESDORF, Fellow; Senior Proctor.

Pusey and Ellerton Scholar.

1843. ROBERT PAYNE SMITH; Scholar.
1874. JAMES ALEXANDER PATERSON; Scholar.

Johnson Scholar.

1855. CHARLES EDWARD OAKLEY; Exhibitioner.

Denyer and Johnson Scholar.

1881. HERBERT BURROWS SOUTHWELL.

Hertford Scholar.

1876. ROBERT LAWRENCE OTTLEY, Scholar.

Taylor Scholar.

1866. DUNCAN HERBERT HASTINGS WILSON.

Burdett-Coutts Scholar.

1866. WILLIAM HENRY CORFIELD, Fellow.
1875. WILLIAM BRUCE CLARKE.
1883. FREDERICK WILLIAM ANDREWES, Fellow.
1895. WILLIAM BYASS PROWSE, B.A.

Derby Scholar.

1879. ROBERT LAWRENCE OTTLEY, Scholar.

Chinese Scholar.

1885. JAMES HENRY SEDGWICK.

Latin Verse.

1786. THOMAS LE BRETON, Fellow. (*Pictura in Vitro.*)
1872. ANDREW GOLDIE WOOD, Scholar. (*Puella Aurelianensis.*)
1876. ROBERT LAWRENCE OTTLEY, Scholar. (*Orbis Palaeozoicus.*)
1895. LENNOX JAMES MORISON, Scholar. (*Naufragus Ulixes inter Phaeacas.*)

English Essay.

1873. ANDREW GOLDIE WOOD, Scholar. (*The Effects of continued War upon a Nation.*)

Latin Essay.

1872. GEORGE EDWARD JEANS, Scholar; Fellow of Hertford. (*Num in Republica feminarum jura et virorum exaequari debeant.*)
1874. REGINALD MERRICK FOWLER, Scholar; H.M. Inspector of Schools. (*De Coloniis apud Romanos militaribus.*)

Sir Roger Newdigate's Prize.

1827. ROBERT STEPHEN HAWKER, Magdalen Hall. (*Pompeii.*)
1897. JOSEPH EDWIN BARTON, Scholar. (*Gibraltar.*)

Ellerton Theological Essay.

1834. JOHN JACKSON, Scholar; Hon. Fellow; Bishop of Lincoln; Bishop of London. (*The Sanctifying Influence of the Holy Spirit.*)

1850. JAMES OCTAVIUS RYDER, Fellow of All Souls. (*The Fitness of the Times in which the Promises of a Messiah were severally given.*)
1858. EDWIN HATCH. (*The Lawfulness of War.*)
1874. ANDREW GOLDIE WOOD, Scholar. (*The Effect of Christianity in Ameliorating the Condition of Women.*)

English Poem on a Sacred Subject.

1863. RICHARD WATSON DIXON, M.A. (*St. John at Patmos.*)

Arnold Historical Essay.

1858. RICHARD WATSON DIXON. (*The Close of the Tenth Century of the Christian Era.*)
1889. HENRY ARNOLD TUBBS, Scholar. (*The Place of Phoenicia in the History of Civilization and Art.*)

Gaisford Prize for Greek Prose.

1871. GEORGE EDWARD JEANS, Scholar. (*Iceland.*)

Hall-Houghton Prize.
(a) *Greek Testament* (*Junior*).

1879. ALBERT BONUS [1].
1881. AUGUSTUS ROBERT BUCKLAND [2], Scholar.
1894. FREDERIC SUMPTER GUY WARMAN.

(b) *Septuagint* (*Junior*).

1873. ANDREW GOLDIE WOOD, Scholar [3].

(c) *Syriac.*

1876. JAMES ALEXANDER PATERSON, Scholar.

Liddon Theological Student.

1893. LAURENCE ARTHUR PHILLIPS, Fellow.

PRELATES.

The following thirty-one sees have been severally occupied by twenty-five members of Broadgates Hall or Pembroke College :—

Canterbury: JOHN MOORE, 1783–1805.
York: THOMAS YONGE, 1560–68.
Armagh : WILLIAM NEWCOME, 1795–1800.
London : EDMUND BONNER [4], 1539–48, 1553–59.

[1] The Rev. A. Bonus has lately published *Collatio Codicis Lewisiani Rescripti.*
[2] Preacher at the Foundling Hospital; editor of the *Record* newspaper.
[3] This versatile and accomplished young student (besides the four distinctions mentioned above he took 2nd class in Jurisprudence) was known before his early death in Barbados, on July 10, 1874, as a poet of promise through a volume entitled *The Isles of the Blest.*
[4] The Rev. Andrew Clark acquaints me that he has come across an old tradition about Bonner in a letter of John Aubrey's. Of the passage, which will appear in Mr. Clark's forthcoming edition of Aubrey's *Lives*, the following is the substance :—
The usher at Blandford St. Mary's, Dorset, where Aubrey was at school, was

London: JOHN JACKSON, 1869–85.
Bristol: JOHN HALL, 1691–1709.
Chichester: ROBERT GROVE, 1691–96.
  „   RICHARD DURNFORD, 1870–95.
Hereford: EDMUND BONNER (Elect), 1538.
Lincoln: PHILIP REPYNGDON, Cardinal, 1405–20.
  „   JOHN JACKSON, 1853–69.
Nottingham (Suffragan): HENRY MACKENZIE, 1870–7.
Norwich: RICHARD CORBET, 1632–5.
Oxford: RICHARD CORBET, 1629–32.
  „   TIMOTHY HALL, 1688–90.
Peterborough: FRANCIS JEUNE, 1864–8. [Coadjutor, JOHN MITCHIN-
  SON, 1881–].
Salisbury: JOHN JEWELL, 1560–71.
Sodor and Man: JOHN PHILLIPS, 1605–33.
St. Asaph: GEORGE GRIFFITH, 1660–6.
Bangor: JOHN MOORE, 1775–83.
St. David's: THOMAS YONGE, 1559–60.
Llandaff: WILLIAM BLETHYN, 1575–90.
Down: ROBERT DOWNES, 1752–3.
Dromore: WILLIAM NEWCOME, 1766–75.
Ferns: ROBERT DOWNES, 1744–52.
Ossory: WILLIAM NEWCOME, 1775–9.
Raphoe: ROBERT DOWNES, 1753–63.
Waterford and Lismore: WILLIAM NEWCOME, 1779–95.
Antigua: DANIEL GATEWARD DAVIS, 1842–57.
Barbados and the Windward Islands: JOHN MITCHINSON, 1873–81.
Brisbane: WILLIAM THOMAS THORNHILL WEBBER, 1885– .
Kiushiu (South Japan): HENRY EVINGTON, 1894– .
Quebec: JAMES WILLIAM WILLIAMS, 1863–92.
Wellington: OCTAVIUS HADFIELD, 1870–93.
Zululand: WILLIAM MARLBOROUGH CARTER, 1891– .

The following Prelates conferred benefits on the College:—GEORGE
ABBOT (London, Canterbury); WILLIAM LAUD (St. David's, London,
Canterbury), and GEORGE MORLEY (Worcester, Winchester).

THOMAS BEKYNTON (Bath and Wells) was Principal of an old Hall
on the site of the College, and 'divers Irish bishops' are said to have
studied in Beef Hall.

THOMAS STEPHENS (matric. at Pembroke March 31, 1637; B.A. June 30, 1640).
Stephens in later years met Aubrey and told him various traditions about Cardinal
Wolsey, &c. Among other stories, he said that Edmund Bonner had entered
Broadgates Hall as a scullion, afterwards became a servitor, 'and so by his
industry raysed to what he was.' When a bishop, 'in acknowledgement whence
he had his rise, he gave to the kitchin there a great brasse-pott, called Bonner's
pott, which was taken away in the parliament time.' This was told in 1674.
Aubrey, who remembered having seen the pot, 'the biggest, perhaps, in Oxford,'
wrote about it to Wood at once, who notes on the letter 'false,' having probably
made enquiry at Pembroke and found no remembrance there of the tradition.

APPENDIX B.

BURIALS IN ST. ALDATE'S.

THE following names are taken from Anthony Wood's transcript, MS. 5 D., pp. 60–64, 66, and 69, of the St. Aldate's register of burials :—

1552. July 3. WILL DARBYSHIRE prebendary of Poules from Broadgates.

1602. July 24. THO. HAYES, cõmoner of Broadgates. [Matr. Ap. 16.]

1603. Apr. 27. ELLIS PIPON of Brodgates. [Elias, Eliace, from Jersey, matr. 1601.]

1603. Ap. 3. NATHANIELL . . . a poore scholar.

1605. July 25. JOH. WILLOUGHBY, Mʳ of A. of Brodgates.

1606. Feb. 12. JONAS HAYES of Brodgates. [Matr. 1606.]

1611. May 29. WILL. ATKINS B. of A. and Butler of Broadgates. [Matr. Jesus College, 1604.]

1612. July 27. THO. WILLYS of Brodgates.

1612. Aug. 30. ARTH. STROUDE of Brodgates. [*Vide infra*, p. 510.]

1613. Jun. 30. THO. TYNCOMBE of Brodgates, Gent. [Matr. 1610.]

161⅜. Feb. 1. GEORGE SUÑASTER principall of Brodgates.

1620. June 5. Mʳ. THO. SELBYE of Brodgates. [Matr. 1608, M.A. 1615.]

1620. June 24. Dʳ . . . BUDDEN, principall of Brodgates.

1620. July 9. HAMNET HYDE of Brodgates. [Matr. at Magd. Hall 1616, second son of Robert of West Hatch, Wilts. He was first cousin, if I am not mistaken, to the Chancellor, Lord Clarendon, who also was of Magdalen Hall. B.A. from Broadgates (as 'Hamlet'), Feb. 24, 16$\frac{19}{20}$.]

1620. Nov. 20. JOH. WARDE of Broadgates.

1621. Dec. 29. . . . PHIPP, M. of A. of Brodgates. [Christopher; *vide supra*, p. 131.]

162½. Feb. 13. HEN. GROWNDEN of Brodgates.

162¾. March 22. PET. STRONG, a Batler of Broadgates (in yᵉ church). [Matr. 1621.]

162⅛. March 5. NATH. BADCOCK, M.A. of Pem. coll. [Matr. 1621.]

1629. Mʳ NICH. CRUSE, M. of A. of Pemb. coll. [Matr. 1623.]

1629. Mʳ THO. MARROW, M.A. Pemb. coll. [Matr. Lincoln Coll. 1623. Son of Sir Edward Marrow of Berkswell, Warw.]

1630.   Dec. 28.   Mᵣ STEPH. DAGNALL, M. of A. of Pĕb. coll.   [Matr. 1623.]

1638.   . . . . DAN. GARDNER, schol. of Pemb. coll.   [Matr. May 25.]

1643.   Dec. 26.   Mᵣ . . . L ?   Dᵣ Clayton's son in Law.

164⅔.   Jan. 13.   Mᵣˢ . . . CLAYTON yᵉ dau. of Dᵣ Clayton.

1644.   July 6.   Mᵣ GILES BOURNE of Pembr. coll.   [Matr. 1635, from Worc. ; a kinsman, I think, of Bishop Gilbert Bourne.]

1647.   July 13.   THO. CLAYTON Mᵣ of Pembr. coll.

1650.   Oct. 29.   Dᵣ Claytons daughter.

165⅘.   March 16.   Mᵣ . . . CLIFFORD of Pembr. coll.

1653.   Aug. 27.   Mᵣ . . . CLIFFORD of Pemb. coll.

1659.   May 29.   RICH. DRUET a schol. of Pemb.   [Matr. as servitor 1658.]

1660.   . . . . Mᵣ EDW. SOUTHWORTH, B.A. Pemb. coll.   [Matr. 1654, *vide supra*, p. 280.]

1661.   Ap. 9.   Mᵣ JOHN HUNTBATCH, M. of A. of Pemb. coll.

1662.   Aug. 26.   Mᵣ EDW. OWEN of Pemb. coll.   [Matr. 1661.]

166⅝.   Jan. 15.   Mᵣ WILL BRICKENDINE of Pemb. coll.   [*Vide supra*, p. 318.]

1667.   Oct. 6.   Mᵣ JOH. BOWLES, Rector of S. Aldates parish.   [*Vide supra*, p. 228.]

1668.   Dec. 6.   Mᵣ PHILIP MARINELL Mᵣ of A. of Pĕb. coll.   [Matr. 1653. Fellow 1660. *Vide supra*, p. 254.]

1670.   July 24.   Mᵣ PHILIP KEKEWICH comoner of Pĕb. coll.   [Matr. 1668 ; of the Cornish family.]

1672.   May 26.   SAM. HALFORD, comoner of Pemb. coll.   [Matr. 1669.]

1675.   March 26.   Mᵣ URBAN EYRE comon of Pembr. coll.

1675.   Oct. 9.   Mᵣ JOH. SAUSMERS, Fellow of Pembrok. coll.   [Matr. Trin. coll. 1669, aged 14. Son of Dean Sausmarez, canon of Windsor.]

1676   Apr. 16.   Mᵣ RICH. DEWE. A. bac. of Pĕb. coll.   [Tesdale kin Scholar 1672.]

Compared with modern times, when a death in College is so rare an occurrence, this mortality is noticeable.

On the south wall of the nave are two brasses. One is the memorial of ARTHUR STRODE, whom I have mentioned above on page 141. He matriculated Oct. 30, 1607, aged eighteen.

' In obitum optimae spei juvenis Arturi Strode Devoniensis nuperrime in medio templo Londinens. legum studiosi in aula Late-Portens. vitam consummavit 25 Augusti anno Salutis 1612 aetatis suae 23

'Epitaphium
'Non jacet ut reliqui Arthurus prae marmore clarus,
    Quamquam prae reliquis hunc meruisse canam.
Illos defunctos sua nobilitare sepulchra ;
    Attamen ille suum nobilitat tumulum.'

He is represented kneeling before an altar. The arms are, Arg. a chevron between three conies courant, sa.; crest, on a mount, a savin tree, vert, fructed, gu. ; Motto, *Hyeme viresco.* The other brass represents a kneeling figure in bachelor's gown and hood. NICHOLAS ROOPE matriculated Feb. 6, 160⅘, aged eighteen. B.A. Nov. 4, 1610.

'In mortem imaturâ maturi tamen animo juvenis Nicholai Roope Devon. gen. ex aula Late P. in art. bacc. Qui an. agens 27 cum vera Dei invocat. quietiss. obdormivit aⁿᵒ mdcxiii April. die 1°.

> 'Lata locus mihi Porta necis sic Porta valeto
> Lata ; per angustam non placet ire viam.
> Intravi angustam (si fas sit dicere) portam.
> Porta vale (fas sit dicere) lata vale !
> Inveni Portum latum dum lata per orbem
> Nec via nec firmum porta dedere locum.'

The arms are, Argent, a lion rampant per fess gules and vert, between seven pheons azure [1]. Sir John Peshall speaks of these two brasses as being in the chancel, as were also several monuments which have now disappeared. One was :—

'Gulielmus Francklyn de Charlton in Agro [Southton.] nuper Coll. Pembrochiae Alumnus dignissimus et munificentissimus Benefactor, [Filius] Natu Minor Revᵈˡ et doctissimi Viri Thomae Francklyn, A.M. et Coll. Jesu Socii, ad Ecclesiam de Charlton a Celsissimo et Nobilissimo Henrico duce de Beaufort advocatus. Quinque fuere Filii hujus Academiae com. ut primum Orbi literato illuxere pro dolor ! extincti. Obiit Nov. 24° 1718.' Arms, Argent, a bend sable, bearing three Dolphins argent.

WILLIAM FRANCKLYN matriculated Nov. 14, 1710, aged eighteen. He is only mentioned in the *Book of Benefactors* as having bequeathed £10 for a silver cup, and £10 to buy books. Another monument recorded the early death of JOSEPH CANNENS, who matriculated Dec. 14, 1722, aged seventeen.

'Josephus Thomae Cannens Gen. Fil. de Vico Roply in Agro Hant. oriundus, Coll. Pemb. nuper Commensalis. Obiit 1729.'

THOMAS MILLER, from Over Whitakers, matriculated May 4, 1716.

'Thomas, Filius unicus Thomae Miller, Gen. de Whiteacre Super in Agro Warw. Coll. Pemb. nuper Commensalis. Obiit 1718. Aet. 20.'

On the floor of the chancel were these inscriptions a hundred years ago :—

'JOHANNES MARCHANT. Coll. Pembrochiae Commensalis, Apr. 5,

---

[1] Mr. Arthur R. Bayley, who has helped me to decipher these brasses, gives the arms thus. Sir J. Peshall speaks of 'three Pheons, impaling a Spread-eagle.'

1722.' [Son of Henry of Hasleton, Gloc. Matr. June 5, 1714, aged 19 ; B.A. 1718.]

'ROBERTUS SPARKE [Parkes, *Peshall*] A.M. Coll. Pembrochiae Socius, Nov. 2, 1743.'

'JOHANNES MEEK, A.M. Coll. Pembrochiae Socius, Sept. 27, 1763.' [*Vide supra*, p. 342.]

'JOHANNES WILDER, A.M. hujus Parochiae Rector, Sept. 3, 1743.' [Rather Sept. 30, 1742. *Vide supra*, p. 325.]

'JOHANNES MOULDEN, S.T.P. hujus Parochiae quondam Pastor. Obiit 5 Cal. Jun. 1724.' [*Vide supra*, p. 318.]

On a pillar in the middle aisle :—

'MATTHAEUS PANTING, S.T.P. Coll. Pembrochiae Magister. Obiit Feb. 12, 1738. Aet. 55. Vidua Maria Thomae Thornton de Brockhall in Agro Northon. Filia Pietatis ergo H.M. Maerens posuit.' Arms, two Bars in fess, Ermine, on a cant. or, a Milrind, Sable, per Baron, impaling per Femme argent on a Bend gules three Estoils, or, for Thornton.

'Mr W. COLLIER, dyed Nov. 9, 1692.' Arms—Arg. a Chevron Sable, between three Bats, Sable. [*Vide supra*, p. 232.]

Dr. Bloxam (*Register of Magdalen College*, vol. vi, p. 241) mentions that inside the altar rails of St. Aldate's was a slab inscribed 'ROBERTUS ROGERS, S.T.B., Coll. B.M. Magdalenae Socius, obiit April 20, 1761 . . . Variolarum tabe corruptus morti occubuit.' He entered Pembroke, March 24, 173⅜, aged 15 ; demy of Magdalen a year later; fellow, 1744 ; bursar, 1751 ; Vice-president, 1760 ; rector of Yarnton, Feb. 20, 174⅘, on the presentation of Dorothy Dashwood. Living at Iffley, his vote was disallowed in the election of 1754. Rector of Swaby, Lincolnshire, Feb. 1761.

Among the entries given by Peshall are :—

Baptisms.

1623. Nov. 9. SUSANNA Daughter of Dr Clayton, Principal of Broadgates.

1645. Dec. 25. { BRIDGET
1652. Sept. 2. { JANE } Daughters of Dr Clayton.

1722. Jan. 25. SARAH Daughter of MATT. PANTING, D.D. (See p. 321.)

Burials.

1652. Dec. 16. ABIGAIL Daughter of Dr LANGLEY of *Pembroke* College.

1754. The Rev. Mr ROGER BRENT, Fellow of *Pembroke Coll.* and Rector of *St. Aldats.*

There are nineteenth-century memorials of the following Pembrochians :—

Rev. SAMUEL PITT STOCKFORD, matr. 1785, aged 16; B.D. 1808. Fellow and Vicegerent; Rector of St. Aldate's 1802, and of Coln St. Dennis 1809. Ob. 1809.

DAVID LONGVIL MELVIL, youngest son of Robert Melvil, His Britannic Majesty's consul at Amsterdam. He entered Dec. 5, 1827, and died Dec. 1830, aged 22. In Mr. Foster's *Alumni* he is confused with Canon David Melville of Worcester, who happily is still living.

In Peshall's time the chancel was divided off by a 'gallery' (a rood loft?). 'On the south side of the Church is Ducklington's Isle, and on the south side of the Chancel West's Isle or Sepulchre. A Gallery is erected over the West End, above which is the Spire, containing five Bells.'

There is no stone to mark the grave of an unhappy suicide. Wood records (*Life and Times*, iii, 4):—

168¾. 'Feb. 3, F., RICHARD SOUCH, B.A., of Pemb. Coll., lately chorister of C. C. C., son of Richard Souch, junior, millener, was found hanged in his chamber at Pemb. Coll. early in the morning. 'Tis said he hung himself on Wednesday night.' Buried in S. Toll's ch-y. His gr. mother burnt in her bed[1] . . . squint-ey'd.'

In the 1778 *Life of Wood* this is curiously mis-read, 'touch'd in her head.'

[1] See *Life and Times*, ii. 423. The fire 'broke out in a back lower room in John [corrected to Richard] Souche's house a milliner and he and his wife laying over that roome were wak'd and choaked with the smoke. He ran downe to quench the fire: she fell in a soune and there layd, and the fire burnt her. It took hold of Burroughs' house; and the dragoons being very vigilant to quench it, had 5*li* given to them as a reward (by the University, quaere). It was vainly reported that the papists had a hand in it.' This was in Allhallows parish, Nov. 27, 1678.

APPENDIX C.

I am indebted to Mr. George Wood, M.A., Fellow, Tutor, and Bursar of Pembroke, for the following

Note on the College Plate[1].

Although the College cannot boast of such unique specimens as are possessed by a few of the Oxford and Cambridge houses, it has no reason to be dissatisfied with its collection of plate. The Civil War played havock with its silver treasures, and the College still possesses a letter from Charles I, referring to its previous sacrifices, and appealing for further contributions of plate. All was cheerfully surrendered by the College.

From the time of the Commonwealth to the Victorian era no period is unrepresented, unless we except that of James II, which does not seem to have supplied any plate that can be accurately identified.

Naturally, the reign of George III is that to which most pieces belong. The Victorian era comes second in the number of items; but most of these are of the useful kind. The valuable silver of the time of George II is well represented, and many of these pieces are of great merit and interest.

Perhaps the most striking of all is the Altar plate. The beautiful pieces now in use are of recent gift. A fine cross and two candlesticks of exquisite Renaissance design[2], together with a silver-gilt Chalice and Paten, all made in 1884 and 1885, and two silver-gilt cruets and stand of old Spanish workmanship, recently presented to the College, have somewhat thrown into the shade the grand old Communion service of earlier times. A splendid flagon of 1656, a Chalice and Paten of 1696, a Credence-Paten of the same date, two silver-gilt candlesticks of 1679[3], an Alms-plate of 1706, and a silver-gilt Salver of 1731 still remain as survivals of many generations of Oxford students.

Hardly less interesting is the small collection of plate bequeathed by Francis Wightwick, Esq., of Wombridge, Berks, in 1776, which was handed over to the College in May, 1843. The earliest piece is a Salver of 1689. Next comes a Grace-cup of the fourth year of Queen Anne. But all are of great beauty, and admirably illustrate the home life of a country gentleman of the last century.

---

[1] In 1761 the duty paid by this College on plate was five guineas.—D. M.

[2] The bronze original of these lights is one of the series by Annibale Fontana.—D. M.

[3] I give this date in deference to the judgment of a dealer in old plate. I had previously attributed them to the year 1693.—G. W.

The oldest Tankard is of the period of the Commonwealth, and bears the Hall-mark of the year 1658–9. Four fine Tankards belong to the reign of Charles II. But in three cases the lids are nearly a century later. The addition has been skilfully made, and the same course has been adopted in a Tankard of the time of William III.

There are twenty-two 'tuns,' or small goblets without handles, holding somewhat less than half a pint, of which two are real 'tumblers.' These last are the oldest of all; but they bear no date, and unfortunately the Hall-mark is now quite illegible.

For artistic excellence, perhaps the palm must be given to 'a Grace Cup of 1705; to a Soup Tureen of 1737; to three bread-baskets made in 1754, 1774, and 1783; to some sauce-boats of the reign of George II; to two small salvers which bear the Hall-mark 1763, though the border work is perhaps much older; and to a number of pierced salt-cellars, with Hall-marks dated 1675, 1773, and 1775. Still, much of the more recent plate can challenge comparison with that of earlier years. Six Decanter Stands of 1808 deserve to be ranked with the best period of English silversmiths' work; and the new Altar plate is in striking contrast with most modern specimens of ecclesiastical art.

It would seem odd now to make presents of a silver wine-funnel, an Argyll, a pap-warmer, a silver skewer, marrow spoons, snuffers and tray; but these gifts of olden days are still carefully preserved, and a use is found even for some of the least promising of the assortment.

The custom of presenting plate to the College still survives. The Claret Jug given by the Rev. Christopher Cleoburey in 1856, the Pemberton Ewer presented in 1872 to commemorate the success of the Eight which was head of the river, the Tankard with six pegs, and bearing the 'Britannia' mark, given by Mr. Athelstan Riley in 1881, the Oxeye given by the present Vice-Chancellor in 1882 [1], the Altar plate already referred to, and, lastly, a silver-mounted Canette [2] of the Elizabethan age, presented on March 4, 1897, by the Vicegerent, show that the same feelings exist as were shared by men like Sir William Blackstone, Lord Ossulston, and Lord Harcourt, whose names are among many others inscribed on College plate that has its frequent uses, and reminds old and young alike of the virtues of the past.   G. W.

---

[1] Presented by Dr. Magrath in memory of a younger brother, CHARLES FREDERICK MAGRATH, Bishop Morley Scholar 1858–63; died in India 1881.

[2] It is of German pottery, bearing the figure of Jeanne d'Arc, and the date 1590. The beautiful silver mounting is obviously of contemporary workmanship. It is stamped in five places with the mark of the Norwich Assay Office, but has no date mark.—G. W.

APPENDIX D.

A FORM OF PRAYER TO BE USED AT EVENSONG ON THE DAY OF THE COMMEMORATION OF THE FOUNDERS AND BENEFACTORS OF PEMBROKE COLLEGE[1].

PROPER PSALMS.
CXLV, CXLVI, CXLVII.

THE FIRST LESSON.
ECCLESIASTICUS XLIV.

THE SECOND LESSON.
HEBREWS XI. verse 13.

To be said at the end of the Suffrages after the Creed.

Priest. The Just shall be had in everlasting remembrance.
People. And they shall fear no evil report.
Priest. The Souls of the Righteous are in the Hands of God.
People. And no torment shall touch them.

THE COLLECT.

To be said before the Prayer of S. Chrysostom.

O Eternal God, the Life and the Resurrection of all them that believe in Thee, always to be praised as well for the Dead as for those that are alive; We give Thee most hearty Thanks for our Founders, Thomas Tesdale and Richard Wightwick, and all other our Benefactors, by whose munificence we are here brought up to Godliness and the Studies of good Learning : beseeching Thee that we, well using all these Thy Blessings to the Praise and Honour of Thy Holy Name, may at length be brought to the Immortal Glory of the Resurrection; through Jesus Christ our Lord. *Amen.*

---

[1] This form was first used in 1893. But the earlier Statutes (*vide supra,* p. 185) provide for a Commemoration of founders and benefactors. Some Latin *Preces Privatae in usum Alumnorum Collegii Pembrochiae,* making memorial of the principal of these, were compiled in 1884 by one of the Fellows, and used, I believe, by some.

APPENDIX E.

PRINCIPALS OF BROADGATES HALL.

THE following list is based on the one given by Anthony Wood in his *City of Oxford*, i. 603–5. He calls it himself an 'imperfect catalogue' (Gutch, iii. 615), and I have added a few names from other sources, which are indicated in square brackets. The lists in the *Honours Register* and in *Oxford Men and their Colleges* are defective and in some points inaccurate, but I am indebted to Mr. Foster for the dates of degrees and preferments.

BARON, JOHANNES[1]. 1414. Of Merton. [Wood MS. D. 2, p. 472; *vide supra*, p. 30].

WYTHAM, NICHOLAUS. 1425 [*ibidem*].

LYCHFIELD, JOHANNES.

WYTHAM, GULIELMUS. 1436–7 (see Anstey's *Munimenta*, p. 228), LL.D., Prebendary of Southwell, Lincoln, and St. Paul's. (Mr. Foster enumerates eight prebends held by him.) Dean of the Peculiars (1448). Rector of St. Mary le Bow 1454, and of St. Michael Cornhill 1454–72. Archdeacon of Stow (1454), and of Leicester (1458). Dean of Bath and Wells 1469. Obiit July 16, 1472. Mentioned in the University Register (ed. Boase, O. H. S.), i. 286.

LYSTER (or LASTER). 1438 [Tanner MSS. 338].

ATKYNSON, JOHANNES. 1443.

HALLE, ROBERTUS. 1443. Jur. Can. D. Principal of Beef Hall 1451[2], and of ' Adulstane juxta Beef-Halle,' 1458 [Anstey, pp. 620, 675].

SELBY, GULIELMUS. 1443. Proctor 1438. B.A. from New College.

HALLE, ROBERTUS, again. 1444. ' Doctor of Decrees; he was a benefactor to the University' (Wood).

TONGE (or TANGE), THOMAS [Tanner MSS. Henry]. 1445. Prebendary of Southwell. Resigned 1454.

LAWE, GULIELMUS. 1447, March 28. Jur. Can. Bac.

HABERFORTHE (or ABERFORD), ROBERTUS. 1447. Jur. Can. Bac.

LYSTER (or LITTESTER, or LASTER) again. 1450. D.C.L.

SPRIGGE, GULIELMUS. 145⅔, Jan. 16. D.C.L. [Anstey, pp. lxxii, 618].

---

[1] Perhaps Richard Baron, Fellow of Merton 1405, Proctor 1409.

[2] Wood (*City*, i. 590) makes him the third of the Principals of Beef Hall. But in Peshall's Additions to Wood mention is made (p. 18) of the brass, in the chancel of St. Ebbe's, of Richard Emlay, LL.B., Rector of that Church and Principal of Beef Hall, who deceased March 27, 1335. The brass was lost.

TOPPECLEFE, ROBERTUS. 1452–3. Jur. Can. Bac.

WALTON, THOMAS. 1458. In 1462, being then Principal of Broadgates, he exposed caution for the great civil law school in St. Edward's parish in the name of Master John Strettun (Anstey, p. 687). Vice-Chancellor or Commissary 1467.

HIGDEN, BRIANUS. 1505–8. Dean of York.

SCOBYL, —— 1508. [Foster].

MASON, ROBERTUS [Tanner MSS.]

NOBLE, JOHANNES. 1511. [Foster. But à Wood says that he was admitted 'upon the resignation of Dr. B. Hygdon, 9 Mar. 1507' (i.e. 150$\frac{6}{7}$)]. Jur. Can. Bac. Ob. 1522. Monument in St. Aldate's.

PUREFOY (or PURPHRAY), ANTONIUS. B.C.L. 1525. Ob. 152$\frac{6}{7}$.

ARCHER (or ARCH), RICARDUS. Succeeded Purefoy 152$\frac{6}{7}$. D.C.L.

DOCKETT (or DUKYTT), GULIELMUS. 1527. B.C.L. Resigned 1528. 'He was sometime manciple of this place' (Wood).

JOHNSON, THOMAS. 1528, July 11. B.C.L. (see Register, ed. Boase). Resigned 1530.

YARDELEY, GULIELMUS. 1530, Nov. 10. Bac. utriusque juris. Deceased the next month.

SACHEVERELL, ROBERTUS. 1530, Dec. 27. Jur. Can. Bac. Resigned 1532.

WYMMESLEY (or WEMSLEY), GEORGIUS [Ricardus, Tanner MSS.]. 1532, July 26. LL.B. Resigned 1535.

BOOTH (or BOTHE, or BOWTHE), GULIELMUS [Johannes, Tanner MSS.]. 1535, Dec. 4 (Feast of St. Osmund). LL.B. Dispensed Feb. 5, 152$\frac{6}{7}$, because he is going to study overseas. Resigned 1537.

STORY, JOHANNES. 1537, July 29. D.C.L. Hanged at Tyburn 1571. Beatified by the Church of Rome. Resigned 1539.

JEFFREY (or GEFFRE), GULIELMUS. 1539, Oct. 11. Sometime Principal of St. Edward's Hall. LL.D. Advocate of Doctors' Commons 1541. Chancellor of Sarum 1553–8. Resigned principality 1541. Obiit 1558.

WILLIAMS, JOHANNES. 1541, July 24. D.C.L. (after eight years' study and two years' practice) 1543 ; Prebendary of Gloucester 1546 ; Advocate of Doctors' Commons 1550 ; Archdeacon 1554 ; Bishop's Chancellor 1554 ; Preb. of Hereford 1554. Ob. Dec. 1558. Resigned 1542.

YONGE, THOMAS. 1542, Oct. 4. D.C.L. Bishop of St. David's and Archbishop of York. Resigned 1545.

PARRY (or APHARRY), JOHANNES. 1545, May 31. M.A. of Caen, incorporated Oct. 19, 1541. LL.D. Chancellor of Llandaff ; Archdeacon of Northampton 1548. Ob. 1549. Buried in the chancel of Castor church. See Lansdowne MSS. 980, f. 746, and 982, f. 192.

WESTON, ROBERTUS. 1546. D.C.L. Lord Chancellor of Ireland, &c.

AMYSSE (or HEMYS), ROBERTUS. 'Substitutus' 1548. Secular priest and chaplain. M.A. 1530.

WHITE, Dr. [Tanner MSS.]. Probably Thomas White, B.C.L. 1541, D.C.L. 1553. Fellow of New College 1532–53 ; Warden 1553–73 ; Vice-Chancellor 1557 and 1562–4 ; Canon of Winton and of Sarum, Archdeacon of Berks, &c. Ob. 1588. See Foster's *Alumni.*

RANDOLPH (or RANDALL), THOMAS. On Nov. 21, 1549, Jentilis Grenfild, William Tyndall, and Thomas Johnson, on behalf of the other 'scholares' of Broadgates Hall, appeared before the Vice-Chancellor to intimate that they had elected Thomas Randolphe, M.A., to be their Principal in place of Robert Weston, resigned. (*Reg. Univ.*, ed. Clark, O. H. S., ii. 284). He was 'of great imployments as embassador to several princes.' D.C.L.

On June 20, 1550, however, Thomas Darbishire, afterwards Principal, with ten other scholars, brought a statement of their complaints against their Principal, 'Mr. Thomas Randoll.' It was not till Oct. 14, 1553, that, in the presence of a notary public, Mr. Thomas Darbisher was able to bring to the pro-Vice-Chancellor Randolph's resignation. Mr. Richard Bradborne and two others attended at the same time to announce that the scholars of the hall had unanimously elected Mr. Thomas Stempe, LL.D. Mary had come to the throne on July 6.

STEMPE, THOMAS. 1553. LL.D. Winchester fellow of New College, 1539–54. Advocate of Doctors' Commons 1554. Canon of Lincoln 1555. Warden of Winchester College, Rector of Ashington, of Over Wallop, and of Cheselbourne. Obiit Feb. 9, $158\frac{8}{9}$, 'famous (if we may give credit to his epitaph) for his knowledge of the civil and canon laws, of theology and music' (Coote, *Lives of the Civilians*).

GERVAYS, JACOBUS. End of 1555. He was then proctor and fellow of Merton. By leave of Congregation, having studied philosophy for six years, he changed his faculty to Law, Feb. 15, $155\frac{5}{6}$. D.C.L. Warden of Merton after Reynolds 1559. But popish sympathies led to his resignation there.

DARBISHYER (or DARBISHER), THOMAS. 1556. D.C.L. 1555. Archdeacon of Essex. He was Bonner's nephew, and a noted lawyer and Jesuit.

GREENE ——. 1564. No longer Principal in 1566. [Wood MS. D. 2.]

PERCY (PEERSEI), RICARDUS [Tanner MSS.], son of Walter Percehay of Walton-on-Humber. Student of Christ Church 1552; B.C.L. $156\frac{4}{5}$; D.C.L. $157\frac{8}{9}$; for twenty years commissary to the Archbishop of York; rector of Settrington, Yorks, 1591–8. Buried there Nov. 14, 1598. See Foster's *Alumni*.

GRENVILLE (or GREENFIELD), GEORGIUS. Before 1572. Supplicated for D.C.L. 1573. On Feb. 8, $157\frac{3}{4}$, the Vice-Chancellor allowed Mr. George Greaneveyll, Principal of the hall commonly called 'the Broadgates,' to be absent from his hall for six weeks, his place being supplied by a sufficient deputy. On May 27, 1575, Robert Moyle, gent., waited on the Vice-Chancellor with Mr. George Granvile's resignation. William Norwood testified that he had summoned the scholars to elect a successor. They then in presence of the Vice-Chancellor elected a young man,

SOMMESTER, GEORGIUS, 1575. B.C.L. May 2, 1573. (Somerstare.) Clerk of the Market 1600. He retained the principality for an abnormally long period till his death at the end of 1618.

BUDDEN, JOHANNES. $161\frac{8}{9}$, Feb. 1. Principal of New Inn. Regius

Professor of Civil Law.   William Herbert, Earl of Pembroke, then
Chancellor, writing from Whitehall, Jan. 27, stated that he had promised
to confer the first principalships that fell vacant on the two professors of
Law and Physic.   He therefore ordered the election of Dr. Budden in
place of Mr. Summester, deceased.   The scholars accordingly elected him.
Election, since Leicester's time, was no longer free.

On June 14, 1620, in consequence of Budden's death, the University
received an intimation from the Chancellor, writing on June 12, that he
fulfilled the second part of his promise by nominating in his room the
Regius Professor of Physic, Doctor Clayton (*Reg. Univ.*, ed. Clark,
O. H. S., vol. ii. part i. pp. 290, 291).

CLAYTON, THOMAS.   1620.   Last Principal of Broadgates Hall and first
Master of Pembroke College.   Ob. 1647.

MASTERS OF PEMBROKE COLLEGE.

1624. CLAYTON, THOMAS.
1647. WIGHTWICK, HENRICUS.
[1647. LANGLEY, HENRICUS.]
1660. WIGHTWICK, HENRICUS (restored).
1664. HALL, JOHANNES.
1709. BRICKENDEN, COLWELLUS.
1714. PANTING, MATTHAEUS.
1738. RATCLIFF, JOHANNES.
1775. ADAMS, GULIELMUS.
1789. SERGROVE, GULIELMUS.
1796. SMYTH, JOHANNES.
1809. HALL, GEORGIUS GULIELMUS.
1843. JEUNE, FRANCISCUS.
1864. EVANS, EVANUS.
1892. PRICE, BARTHOLOMAEUS.

INDEX

THE END.

OXFORD : HORACE HART
PRINTER TO THE UNIVERSITY

Rev^{da} in Chri
Domino JO
EPISCOPO
Collegii Pembr
et Jn
MDC.G

SHED, A.D. 1700.
NO TOWER WINDOW

Oxford Historical Society.

PUBLICATIONS.

1884.

1. **Register of the University of Oxford.** Vol. I. (1449–63; 1505–71), edited by the Rev. C. W. Boase, M.A., pp. xxviii + 364. (Price to the public, without discount, and prepaid, 16s.)

2. **Remarks and Collections of Thomas Hearne.** Vol. I. (4 July 1705—19 March 1707), edited by C. E. Doble, M.A., pp. viii + 404. (16s.)

1884-85.

3. **The Early History of Oxford (727-1100), preceded by a sketch of the Mythical Origin of the City and University.** By James Parker, M.A. With 3 illustrations, pp. xxxii + 420. (20s.)

1885.

4. **Memorials of Merton College, with biographical notices of the Wardens and Fellows.** By the Hon. Geo. C. Brodrick, Warden of Merton College. With one illustration, pp. xx + 416. (16s., to members of Merton 12s.)

5. **Collectanea, 1st series,** edited by C. R. L. Fletcher, M.A. (Contents:—a. Letters relating to Oxford in the XIVth Century, edited by H. H. Henson; b. Catalogue of the Library of Oriel College in the XIVth Century, edited by C. L. Shadwell; c. Daily ledger of John Dorne, bookseller in Oxford, 1520, edited by F. Madan; d. All Souls College versus Lady Jane Stafford, 1587, edited by C. R. L. Fletcher; e. Account Book of James Wilding, Undergraduate of Merton College, 1682–88, edited by E. G. Duff; f. Dr. Wallis's Letter against Maidwell, 1700, edited by T. W. Jackson.) With two illustrations, pp. viii + 358. (16s.)

1886.

6. **Magdalen College and King James II, 1686-88.** A series of documents collected and edited by the Rev. J. R. Bloxam, D.D., with additions, pp. lii + 292. (16s., to members of Magdalen 12s.)

7. **Hearne's Collections** [as No. 2 above]. Vol. II. (20 Mar. 1707—22 May 1710), pp. viii + 480. (16s.)

8. **Elizabethan Oxford.** Reprints of rare tracts. Edited by the Rev. C. Plummer, M.A. (Contents:—a. Nicolai Fierberti Oxoniensis Academiæ descriptio, 1602; b. Leonard Hutton on the Antiquities of Oxford; c. Queen Elizabeth at Oxford, 1566 [pieces by J. Bereblock, Thomas Nele, Nich. Robinson, and Rich. Stephens, with appendices]; d. Queen Elizabeth at Oxford, 1592, by Philip Stringer; e. Apollinis et Musarum Eidyllia per Joannem Sandford, 1592), pp. xxxii + 316. (10s.)

PUBLICATIONS (*continued*).

1887.

9. **Letters of Richard Radcliffe and John James, of Queen's College, Oxford, 1749-88** : edited by MARGARET EVANS, with a pedigree, pp. xxxvi + 306. (15*s.*, to members of Queen's 10*s. 6d.*)

10. **Register of the University of Oxford, Vol. II (1571-1622), Part 1. Introductions.** Edited by the Rev. ANDREW CLARK, M.A., pp. xxxii + 468. (18*s.*)

1887-8.

11. **Do. Part 2. Matriculations and Subscriptions.** Edited by the Rev. ANDREW CLARK, M.A., pp. xvi + 424. (18*s.*)

1888.

12. **Do. Part 3. Degrees.** Edited by the Rev. ANDREW CLARK, M.A., pp. viii + 448. (17*s.*)

13. **Hearne's Collections** [as No. 2 above]. Vol. III. (25 May, 1710—14 December, 1712), pp. iv + 518. (16*s.*)

1889.

14. **Register of the University of Oxford, Vol. II, Part 4. Index.** Edited by the Rev. ANDREW CLARK, M.A., pp. viii + 468. (17*s.*)

15. **Wood's History of the City of Oxford.** *New Edition.* By the Rev. ANDREW CLARK, M.A. Vol. I. The City and Suburbs. With three Maps and several Diagrams, pp. xii + 660. (25*s.*, to citizens of Oxford 20*s.*; the two Maps of old Oxford separately, not folded, 1*s. 6d.*, to citizens 1*s.*)

1890.

16. **Collectanea, 2nd series,** edited by Professor MONTAGU BURROWS. (Contents:—*a.* The Oxford Market, by O. Ogle; *b.* The University of Oxford in the Twelfth Century, by T. E. Holland; *c.* The Friars Preachers of the University, edited by H. Rashdall; *d.* Notes on the Jews in Oxford, by A. Neubauer; *e.* Linacre's Catalogue of Grocyn's Books, followed by a Memoir of Grocyn, by the Editor; *f.* Table-Talk and Papers of Bishop Hough, 1703-1743, edited by W. D. Macray; *g.* Extracts from the 'Gentleman's Magazine' relating to Oxford, 1731-1800, by F. J. Haverfield. Appendix: Corrections and Additions to Collectanea, Vol. I. (Day-book of John Dorne, Bookseller at Oxford, A.D. 1520, by F. Madan, including 'A Half-century of Notes' on Dorne, by Henry Bradshaw.) With one diagram, pp. xii + 518. (16*s.*)

17. **Wood's History of the City of Oxford** [as No. 15 above]. Vol. II. Churches and Religious Houses. With Map and Diagram, pp. xii + 550. (20*s.*, to citizens of Oxford 16*s.*; Map of Oxford in 1440, separately, not folded, 9*d.*, to citizens 6*d.*)

1890-91.

18. **Oxford City Documents**, financial and judicial, 1268–1665. Selected and edited by J. E. THOROLD ROGERS, late Drummond Professor of Political Economy in the University of Oxford. pp. viii + 440 (+ 2 loose leaves for vols. 6 and 16). (*12s.*)

1891.

19. **The Life and Times of Anthony Wood, antiquary, of Oxford, 1632-1695, described by Himself.** Collected from his Diaries and other Papers, by the Rev. ANDREW CLARK, M.A. Vol. I. 1632–1663. With seven illustrations. pp. xvi + 520. (*20s.*)

20. **The Grey Friars in Oxford.** Part I, A History of the Convent; Part II, Biographical Notices of the Friars, together with Appendices of original documents. By ANDREW G. LITTLE, M.A., pp. xvi + 372. (*16s.*)

1892.

21. **The Life and Times of Anthony Wood** [as No. 19]. Vol. II. 1664–1681. With ten illustrations. pp. xxviii + 576. (*20s.*)

22. **Reminiscences of Oxford, by Oxford men, 1559-1850.** Selected and edited by LILIAN M. QUILLER COUCH, pp. xvi + 430. (*17s.*, to members of the University 10s. 6d.*)

1892-93.

23. **Index to Wills proved and Administrations granted in the Court of the Archdeacon of Berks, 1508-1652.** Edited by W. P. W. PHILLIMORE, M.A. (Issued in conjunction with the British Record Society.) pp. viii + 200. (*10s.*)

1893.

24. **Three Oxfordshire Parishes. A History of Kidlington, Yarnton and Begbroke.** By Mrs. BRYAN STAPLETON. With a coloured map and 2 sheet-pedigrees, pp. xx + 400. (*17s.*, to residents in the three villages 10s.*)

25. **The History of Corpus Christi College, with Lists of its Members.** By THOMAS FOWLER, D.D., President of the College. With three illustrations. pp. xvi + 482. (*20s.*, to members of Corpus 12s. 6d.*)

1894.

26. **The Life and Times of Anthony Wood** [as No. 19]. Vol. III. 168½–1695. With three illustrations. pp. xxxii + 548. (*21s.*)

27. **The Register of Exeter College, Oxford**, with a history of the College, and illustrations. By the Rev. C. W. BOASE, M.A. Third edition, enlarged. pp. [8] + clxxxiv + 400. (*Presented to the Society by the author :* 15s., to members of the College 10s.*)

PUBLICATIONS (*continued*).

28. **The Cartulary of the Monastery of St. Frideswide at Oxford.** Edited by the Rev. S. R. WIGRAM, M.A. With illustrations. Vol. I. General and City Charters. pp. xx + 504 + six pages (loose) of corrections to vol. 24. (21*s.*)

1895.

29. **The Early Oxford Press, a bibliography of printing and publishing at Oxford, '1468'-1640.** With notes, appendixes, and illustrations. By FALCONER MADAN, M.A. pp. xii + 366. (Separate copies can be obtained only from the Clarendon Press, price 18*s.* The Society can only supply it in sets.)

30. **The Life and Times of Anthony Wood** [as No. 19]. Vol. IV: Addenda. With illustrations. pp. xii + 322. (24*s.*)

1896.

31. **The Cartulary of the Monastery of St. Frideswide at Oxford.** Edited by the Rev. S. R. WIGRAM, M.A. With illustrations. Vol. II. The Chantry and Country Parish Charters. pp. xii + 488 + eight pages of additions and corrections (loose) to vol. 25. (21*s.*)

32. **Collectanea, 3rd series,** edited by Professor MONTAGU BURROWS. With illustrations. pp. xii + 450. (21*s.*)

1897.

33. **A History of Pembroke College.** By the Rev. D. MACLEANE. With illustrations. pp. xvi + 544. (21*s.*)

Forthcoming Publications.

The 5th (and last) vol. of CLARK's edition of *Wood's Life and Times,* the 3rd (and last) vol. of the same Editor's *Wood's History of the City of Oxford,* the 4th vol. of *Hearne's Diaries,* edited by C. E. DOBLE and D. W. RANNIE, the *Letter-book of the University from* 1422–1503, edited by the Rev. H. ANSTEY (in two volumes). a reproduction of the unique copy of Agas's map of Elizabethan Oxford, and other volumes are in active preparation.

A full description of the Society's work and objects can be obtained by application to any of the Committee residing at Oxford (P. LYTTELTON GELL, Esq.. Headington Hill; FALCONER MADAN, Esq. (*Hon. Treasurer*), 90 Banbury Road; the Rev. the PROVOST OF QUEEN'S COLLEGE (Dr. MAGRATH); the REGIUS PROFESSOR OF MODERN HISTORY, Oriel (F. YORK POWELL, Esq.); and C. L. SHADWELL, Esq., Frewin Hall, Oxford). The annual subscription is one guinea, and the published volumes as a set can be obtained by new members at one-fourth the published price (i.e. 10*s.* 6*d.* a year). Life Composition for new members is twelve guineas: after five years of subscription it is ten guineas; after ten years, eight; after fifteen, six; after twenty, four. The Society counts compositions among its liabilities (in case it ceased its work), at the rate of one guinea a year from the date of effecting them.

June, 1897.